5TH
EDITION

SECRETARIAL PROCEDURES AND ADMINISTRATION

FORMERLY EFFECTIVE SECRETARIAL PRACTICES

■ **J MARSHALL HANNA**
Professor of Business Education
The Ohio State University

■ **ESTELLE L. POPHAM**
Professor of Business Education
Hunter College

■ **ESTHER KIHN BEAMER**
Secretary Experienced in Advertising,
Architectural, Editorial Research,
Personnel, and Public Accounting Offices

K71

Published by
SOUTH-WESTERN PUBLISHING COMPANY

■ Cincinnati   ■ Chicago
■ Burlingame, Calif.   ■ Dallas
■ New Rochelle, N. Y.   ■ Brighton, England

Preface

This book was written for *you*—and the thousands of other young women who aspire to reach professional status as a secretary. Professional secretarial status is a realistic and attainable goal *provided* you have the training and essential personality qualities. This book will contribute to the development of both of these essentials.

The top-level secretary performs a dual role—operational and managerial. To fulfill her operational role, the secretary must be knowledgeable about many functions and procedures, and at the same time demonstrate a high level of competency in certain secretarial duties. This book will acquaint you with a wide range of office activities. It will also provide you with training in some phases of secretarial activity so that you can attain a high degree of competency.

In her management role, the secretary serves as executive assistant to top management. As such, she is part of the management team. The secretary, therefore, needs management training. *Secretarial Procedures and Administration* (formerly *Effective Secretarial Practices*) has been written to achieve this management orientation. You will find that many of your assignments in this course have a management setting. In this respect, this book differs substantially from other secretarial textbooks.

Secretarial Procedures and Administration is for both the beginning and the experienced secretary. Basic skill in typewriting and in shorthand is assumed; other skills are presented as if they are new ones. Yet the most experienced secretary will find techniques that will improve her efficiency. The authors have taken the viewpoint, however, that learning of techniques is of little value unless this learning is accompanied by the development of a secretarial personality—the ability to work with people. Consequently, the questions and case problems provide rich opportunities for discussion of human relations in business.

The 28 chapters are organized into nine parts. Part 1 analyzes the secretarial profession and identifies the personal qualities needed for success in it. Parts 2 and 3 discuss how the secretary uses her typewriting and shorthand skills in the work situation and how she carries out such related activities as copying and duplicating, processing the mail,

iv

and composing written communications. How to use postal and shipping services, as well as telephone and telegraph facilities, is presented in Part 4. The next four parts cover a wide variety of specialized secretarial duties—filing; planning travel and arranging for meetings and conferences; collecting business information, processing data and preparing reports; and handling financial and legal responsibilities. Part 9 gives new emphasis to fulfilling the supervisory or administrative role. This part examines, also, the wide variety of employment opportunities available to the college-trained secretary, application techniques, and essentials for achievement of professional status.

Suggested readings are listed at the end of each chapter. These readings were carefully selected to conserve your time. You will find that they enrich the chapters and are a valuable learning supplement.

The Reference Guide at the end of the book will help you improve that indispensable tool of the secretarial trade—familiarity with accepted English usage. The guide identifies accepted practices for abbreviating, capitalizing, writing numbers, spelling plurals and possessives, punctuating, and using words effectively. In addition, this section contains a correspondence guide and a brief postal guide.

Each chapter includes a series of discussion questions, problems, and related work assignments. The discussion questions were designed to stimulate an exchange of ideas. To answer many of these questions, you will need to draw on the text, your supplementary readings, and your own experiences. Some questions were designed to measure the maturity of your judgment. The problems and work assignments will provide you with realistic practice in typical secretarial activities.

The case problems at the end of each part simulate office situations. Many are adaptations of problems that have arisen in business offices.

The related work assignments require special forms and stationery. Some work assignments are given in the text, with forms and stationery provided in the workbook. Others, such as the In-Basket projects, are given only in the workbook. The workbook has been developed to save time and to provide additional practice materials.

Secretarial Procedures and Administration is both a textbook and a reference book. It will serve you not only while you are in training, but also when you are employed in a secretarial position.

The authors wish you success. They hope that you will enjoy using these materials in the achievement of your professional goal.

J Marshall Hanna ▪ **Estelle L. Popham** ▪ **Esther Kihn Beamer**

v

Contents

PART 6—Assistance with Travel and Conferences

PART 7—Collecting, Processing, and Presenting Business Data

PART 8—Financial and Legal Facets of Secretarial Work

PART 9—Your Professional Future

PART 10—Reference Guide

— *Ewing Galloway*

As a creative, efficient, and personable office administrator, today's top-level secretary finds herself right in the mainstream of excitement—where the action is.

The Secretarial Profession

A candid look at employment patterns of women precedes an analysis of the secretarial field as a career choice— its advantages and disadvantages, its requirements and responsibilities, its opportunities for supervisory and administrative roles appropriate to the career objectives of the college-trained young woman. This section is planned to set the stage for developing the kinds of operational and managerial competencies the top-level secretary needs in order to develop in her professional role.

Ch.

1   The Role of a Professional
        Secretary

2   The Secretary's Work Day

3   The Secretary as Office Hostess

Ch. 1

The Role of a Professional Secretary

Trends in the labor market are startling. Until the 1950's a girl might expect to work a few years, then marry and retire forever from the labor scene. The largest group of working women was in the 20–30 age group.

But the picture has changed. True, a girl still works until she marries and begins to rear a family. But she marries and has her family early, dropping out of the labor market until the children are in school. Suddenly she realizes that she has 40 or more years of life before her and, more often than not, returns to work. In fact, by 1975 nearly half of all women between 35 and 65 will probably be either working or looking for work.[1] The age group 25–34 will supply the smallest proportion of women workers; the largest number will be 45 to 54 years old.

In other words, the work-life expectancy for single women will be 40 years; for childless married women, 30 years; and for married women with children, only a year or two less. Even in the 1960's the "typical" woman worker was married and 41 years old.

These cold facts suggest that the student should include preparation for an interesting work life, along with the other facets that will fulfill her aspirations for a fruitful life.

Yet every June, young college women graduates who imagine that the world is their oyster haunt employment offices until they are rudely awakened to the need for marketable skills and for business and economic understandings. In countless workshops and seminars older college women are counseled that ability to balance the family budget and drive the neighborhood children to school and dancing class does not make them attractive to personnel interviewers, and that they, too, must bring business competencies with them when they ask for work.

Dr. Ford, former president of the National Federation of Business and Professional Women, says:

> Younger women are failing to take advantage of the new opportunities in business and the professions. Very few college girls today are aware of the problems encountered by the untrained middle-aged woman seeking to reenter the labor force. These same college girls cannot imagine that they may have these same problems—problems created by limited education or experience—twenty years from now.

[1] *Occupational Outlook Handbook*, 1963–64, p. 14.

We must not wait until a woman reaches 35 and has raised her children to tell her what the future holds for her. We must open her eyes to this future NOW, while she is young, and while she can still take full advantage of and realize the value of an education and the selection of an area in which she might make a future contribution.

Traditionally, young men select a goal and carefully plot their education and career experience to reach that goal. We must encourage our young women to do the same. Even though many of these young women will marry, raise a family, or temporarily leave the labor force . . . it is essential that they consider the additional contribution that they will be able to make to society once their family is grown and they have more leisure time. We must help them to see the need of a lifetime plan, a plan for realistic preparation, and the need of education as a continuing, lifelong process.[2]

One field that may well appeal to college women is the secretarial area. It provides a challenging job immediately after graduation and opportunity for the especially able to work up to a supervisory or an administrative-assistant position. The secretary who stops work to rear a family finds that the field may be reentered in later years with relatively little retraining.

This chapter presents an overview of secretarial work and of qualities important to effective fulfillment of the secretarial role. The chapter also assesses future employment opportunities for secretaries.

A Secretary Defined

The job classification *secretary* is probably the most misunderstood term in the entire clerical field. Almost anybody who works in an office may refer to herself as "secretary," or almost any employer may speak of "my secretary" in describing his clerk. In both cases, the term is used for prestige—prestige to the employee for working at such a high level and to the employer for rating an employee of such importance as a secretary.

RECENTLY, the National Secretaries Association adopted its own definition of a secretary: "An assistant to an executive, possessing mastery of office skills and ability to assume responsibility without direct supervision, who displays initiative, exercises judgment, and makes decisions within the scope of her authority."

---

[2]Dorothy Ford, "Where Do We Go from Here?" *National Business Woman* (Convention Issue, 1965), p. 10.

▪ Level of Performance

The correct meaning of the term *secretary* indicates that real secretarial work requires high-level performance. According to *The Dictionary of Occupational Titles,* a secretary is one who carries out the following activities:

 Performs general office work in relieving executives and other company officials of minor executive and clerical duties;

Takes dictation using shorthand or a stenotype machine;

Transcribes dictation or the recorded information reproduced on a transcribing machine;

Makes appointments for the executive and reminds him of them;

Interviews people coming into the office, directing to other workers those who do not warrant seeing the executive;

Answers and makes telephone calls;

Handles personal and important mail, writing routine correspondence on her own initiative;

May supervise other clerical workers;

May keep personnel records.

A good secretary is an expert in public relations, a staff assistant, and the boss's office memory. She is responsible for much of the detail work of the office and is expected to carry out her duties with a minimum of supervision and direction. She represents the company and her employer attractively to the public and displays good human relations in working with all employees in the organization.

A secretary learns how to gain the goodwill and cooperation of her co-workers and the respect of the other executives. She identifies her daily business associates as being on a level above her, on her same level, or on the level subordinate to her. She applies the best principles of human relations at each level. (Examination of problem-personality situations in offices shows that same-level relationships are the most difficult for a secretary to maintain amicably and productively.) She is accurate, highly efficient, and creative, judging when to use initiative and when to consult the employer about his wishes in handling a job. She is flexible in adjusting to changing situations, and she can recognize and meet a deadline. She keeps her boss informed about developments that will affect the efficiency of the office, but she makes certain that she does not bother him with petty problems that she herself can handle with a little thought or research.

▪ The Three Areas of Secretarial Work

A secretary works very much on her own, with little or no supervision. True, she does receive instructions occasionally; but after receiving an assignment, she is depended upon to complete it competently. Having a wide area of freedom is very pleasing to one's ego and is one of the real satisfactions of being a secretary.

Secretarial work can be divided into three general areas: (1) assigned tasks; (2) routine, flow-of-work duties; and (3) original, creative work.

Assigned Tasks. Included among assigned tasks may be such varied items as transcribing a letter, drafting and sending a telegram, making a bank deposit, finding out the flights that leave Sunday night for Washington, making a dental appointment, or getting technical material from the library. In completing these assignments, the secretary may have to change her plan of work to fit the emergencies of the moment.

> ALTHOUGH secretaries are referred to as "she" throughout this book, there are men secretaries too —many of them—who are sometimes favored over women, especially in the transportation field, in the oil and rubber industries, and in firms manufacturing heavy machinery and equipment.
>
> The secretarial desk for a man is an excellent training post for an executive position in his company. The men secretaries have their own professional association, Male Secretaries of America. *For information, write C. J. Helmer, Jr., Director, 14 St. Clair Avenue, Binghamton, New York 13903.*

Routine, Flow-of-Work Duties. In the area of *routine,* the secretary performs duties such as the following without instruction or supervision: opening the mail, filing, replenishing supplies, preparing periodic reports, collecting time-saving reference materials. The secretary exercises her own judgment in performing these tasks as time permits or as a deadline requires.

The executive expects his secretary to be sure that the correlated, executive-secretary work flow is continuous. An annoying delay occurs if he asks for a letter from the files and she has to rummage for it among a stack of correspondence that should have been filed as part of the day's routines. He will consider her efficient if, to save time, she prepares a neatly typed, alphabetic list of frequently called telephone numbers.

The secretary may clip and mark an article that might help her employer.

Original, Creative Work. The secretary uses her own initiative in finding original, creative ways to assist the executive. She anticipates his request for certain work and completes it before he asks for it. She notices that having certain information for instant reference would save his time and make it possible for him to work with greater effectiveness; then she compiles that information. If she discovers that certain comparative figures would help him in making a decision, she ferrets them out and sets them up in compact form. If she comes across an article pertinent to his problems in a magazine that he ordinarily does not read, she clips the article, mounts it on 8½″ by 11″ paper for easy filing, underlines important points, and adds marginal comments, including source and date of the article.

There is no limit to the original and creative work that a secretary can do to help the executive. It is this kind of work that he particularly appreciates and that she finds most gratifying. The more efficiently she handles the work in the other two areas, the more time she has for this kind of secretarial service which makes her role truly that of an executive secretary or administrative assistant.

A study of top-level secretaries shows that they do perform many management functions. When asked to list for several days the "critical" duties that make a difference between *their* jobs and routine ones, the secretaries listed, among many others, the following:

> Pointed out to employer that there was a $3,000 error on a complaint in the company's favor.

> Made out 18-month requisition for envelopes for entire district. (Have been able to save $8,000 annually by supervising stationery and office equipment quantity buying.)

> Reviewed with personnel officer proposed personnel Kardex system prepared by me and approved by director for the section chief's office. Went over draft of instructions regarding the use of the system with him for his recommendations.

> New problems with rising expenses show need for best-trained clerical help. Will consider a training program recommendation.

> Worked on content and layout of company employee manual. Charged with complete responsibility.

> Wrote an editorial on "tardiness" for employer to publish in company paper and made some suggestions for possible news stories for editor.

> Made an analysis of last month's income and expenses as compared with previous months of this year.

> Gathered data on wage-hour law and other labor laws as applicable to a particular labor problem in the plant. When the information required was obtained, it was given to the general superintendent.

> Checked Mr. G's office to see that everything was in readiness for the meeting at ten o'clock. Took in the minute books in case some question should come up—also sent in file on proxies and those to be signed at the meeting, etc.

> Discussed next management message to appear in house organ with editor so that he could prepare a preliminary draft for president's signature.[3]

Why Be a Secretary?

The college woman may choose a secretarial career because it plunks her right into the mainstream of excitement—gets her where the action is. Secretaries to famous people not infrequently become the most important biographers of a historical personality. President Kennedy's secretary did.[4]

Or she may use secretarial work to take her to far-off lands. Letitia Baldridge, too, wrote a book about her experiences as secretary to

[3]Bonnie Lockwood, *A Study of the Character and Duties of the Certified Professional Secretary* (Doctoral dissertation, University of Pittsburgh, 1954).

[4]Evelyn Lincoln, *My Twelve Years with John F. Kennedy* (New York: David McKay Co., Inc., 1965).

Clare Boothe Luce when Mrs. Luce was the United States representative to Italy.[5] Says Miss Baldridge, "I had promised myself I would work
in Europe, and I answered ads and placed ads. I haunted Government
agencies, told everybody I knew French, knew the Continent, had a
college degree and three quarters of a Swiss one. . . . THEY said, "Can
you type and take shorthand?"[6]

Recently secretaries from Britain have invaded the United States,
using their competencies to secure jobs in different cities as they live and
work among Americans—surely a better way to savor life in another
country than on the organized tour. And in many instances nationwide
employment agencies have located the next job for them as they followed
their itineraries. Now American secretaries have turned the tables.
They are getting jobs in London, in Liverpool, in Manchester, as they
gain experience in living abroad. Secretarial jobs with the United
States government overseas, of course, offer outstanding opportunities
for travel. Such jobs are discussed in detail in Chapter 27.

College graduates may also use their stenographic skills as their
entering wedge into some hard-to-crash field such as advertising or
personnel. A recent study of women in executive and managerial positions in Omaha, Nebraska, shows that the most definite pattern for the
promotion of women to positions of leadership includes initial placements involving the secretarial skills.[7] Very often, though, a girl is
pleasantly surprised to find that secretarial work can be more challenging, responsible, and satisfying than a job with a more exciting title.

A top-level secretarial job is an important end objective in itself.
As one secretary to the president of a steel company in Pittsburgh said,
"I think that secretarial work is something to be promoted *into*, not out
of. Although I have been secretary to the president for several years
and have grown in it, I haven't begun to realize the potentials of the job
I have."[8]

■ Responsibility Levels of Secretarial Positions

There are different levels of responsibility in secretarial positions.
At the top level is the secretary to the top executive. He needs a secretary of competence and pleasing personality to assist him with his

---

[5]Letitia Baldridge, *Roman Candle* (Boston: Houghton Mifflin Co., 1956).

[6]Anne Carter Zimmer, College and Careers feature, *Mademoiselle* (May, 1958), p. 124.

[7]Leta F. Holley, *Women in Executive and Managerial Positions in Omaha, Nebraska*
(Doctoral dissertation, University of Colorado, Boulder, 1960).

[8]Lockwood, *op. cit.*

widespread responsibilities.   Such a secretary often has assistants to handle the routine stenographic and clerical work.   When she knows the executive's work thoroughly, has proved her competence, and can, as his *alter ego*, make decisions for him, she is often advanced to the position and salary of administrative assistant.   Secretaries to the presidents or managing heads of large organizations hold positions at this level— although not all are given such a title.

At the next level are secretaries to executives responsible for departmental management. Such an executive works in a narrower and more concentrated field, such as that of research director or sales manager.   The secretary might supervise other office workers in the department. She has the opportunity to learn one branch of business thoroughly.   She may be advanced to be head of a department because of her competence, personality, and knowledge of the company. Her responsibility then is the output of the department and the supervision of the staff.

> "TODAY'S average secretary would not soil her fingers on a mimeograph machine. She doesn't have to. She is busy waging high-level diplomacy on the telephone, meeting clients, juggling the boss's schedule, arranging his trips, his business conferences, and, not rarely, his dinner parties. Her duties have, in a word, contracted and expanded, and both in the direction of greater responsibility, status, and power. . . . At her best, she is, in fact, no longer a secretary; she is an administrative assistant, with her own office, wall-to-wall on the floor, and an income well upward of $7,500 a year."— *Martha Weinman Lear, "The Amanuensis—Evolution and Revolution of the Secretary," New York Times Magazine (October 15, 1961), p. 28. **And that was several years ago!***

According to the system adopted by the Administrative Management Society, secretaries are classified into two categories:

SECRETARY A

Performs the complete secretarial job for a high-level executive or a person responsible for a major functional or geographic operation. Does work of a confidential nature and relieves principal of designated administrative details. Requires initiative, judgment, knowledge of company practices, policy, and organization.

SECRETARY B

Performs secretarial duties for a member of middle management. General requirements are the same as for Secretary A (listed above), but limited to the area of responsibility of the principal.

The secretary described first on this page is obviously *Secretary A*. The secretary described last might be either *Secretary A* or *Secretary B*.

■ Limiting Factors in Secretarial Careers

To be completely fair, this discussion should point up the limiting factors of secretarial work. One of them is intimated in the preceding paragraph. The secretarial title follows the boss's title, not the worker's ability. She is sometimes rated a *Secretary B* rather than a *Secretary A* because of the status of her superior, not because of her ability.

Another limiting factor is the difference in concept of the word *secretary* that different organizations and different bosses can have. An ambitious worker may find herself working for somebody who does not know how to or want to use her abilities to capacity. There are many ways in which she can change the secretarial image, but sometimes the only way to get ahead is to find another job where the employer's image more nearly conforms to the secretary's own.

A final limiting factor is the necessity for the secretary to submerge herself in her employer's problems. As one secretary said candidly, "If I ever quit, it will be because I'm tired of thinking other people's thoughts and want to work on my own." This is the theme that turns up over and over again among college-trained secretaries. "Self-immolation" one girl described it, although she still maintained that she liked her job. According to a *Mademoiselle* analysis, "The better a girl knows her boss's thoughts, actions, and vocabulary so that she can think, act, and write for him with the minimum of direction, the better secretary she is. When more and more people are searching for bigger and better ways to express themselves, this is not the best of news, for 'getting the work out—and not what you get out of it—counts.' "[9]

■ The Job Market

Secretaries are in demand everywhere. A cursory glimpse through the help-wanted section of your local newspaper will confirm this statement. Even though there are some 200,000 secretaries, positions are available in all cities—an important factor to one who prefers a certain location or to one who plans to augment the family income.

A comprehensive study[10] in 1965 of the New York secretary and her job indicates that more than half of the executives queried felt that secretarial job standards have been raised during the past five years. They agreed that the secretarial job now requires more basic intelligence, more formal education, more initiative, and better appearance, in that

[9] Zimmer, *op. cit.*, p. 146.
[10] "A Good Secretary Is Hard to Find," *New York Times* (July 24, 1965), p. 29, col. 3.

order. Even more of the executives said that good secretaries are in shorter supply than five years ago.

It is not expected that automation will change to any appreciable extent the need for secretaries, nor will it influence substantially the number of positions. In fact, the Bureau of Labor Statistics found that in the period from 1950–60, at the same time that the number of stenographic jobs decreased 36 percent, the number of secretarial positions increased 80 percent.[11] One implication of these data is that secretaries cannot use stenographic positions as their training ground any longer, but must bring a higher degree of ability to the position than was formerly the case—a college education, in other words.

■ Secretarial Salaries

Secretarial salaries are among the highest paid for office work. In fact, only one category, *Accounting Clerk, Senior Bookkeeper*, had a higher national median salary than *Secretary A* in the 1967–68 survey of office salaries conducted by the Administrative Management Society.[12] In the East, *Secretaries A* received the highest office salaries paid.

The survey shows that, in general, *Secretaries A* receive about 15 percent more than *Secretaries B*, over 20 percent more than *Stenographers A*, and about 40 percent more than *Stenographers B*.

Comparative salary figures for various sections of the country will enable readers to evaluate employment opportunities in their own locations. These figures reflect recent growth-of-industry figures.

	Total	Eastern	East Central	West Central	Southern	Western
AVERAGE WEEKLY OFFICE SALARIES IN THE U.S.						
1967–68 Administrative Management Society's 21st Annual Survey						
Sec. A	116	119	117	111	110	123
Actg. Clerk A	112	111	115	108	109	119
Tab. Mach. Op.	103	100	106	100	99	114
Sec. B	101	102	103	95	96	109
Steno. A	96	94	98	90	93	104
Steno. B	83	81	86	81	80	92

[11]U.S. Department of Labor, Bureau of Labor Statistics, *National and Economic Manpower Policy* (July, 1965).
[12]*Office Salaries Directory for United States and Canada* (Willow Grove, Pa.: Administrative Management Society, 1967), p. 8.

Can You Become a Successful Secretary?

During this course you can acquire competency in performing most of the duties common to secretarial work. But do you have the temperament for this field, or can you develop the attractive easy-to-work-with personality requisite to secretarial success? Let's consider these two requirements, so that you can focus on developing them at the same time that you are acquiring know-how in secretarial techniques.

▪ Temperament

Each of us has inner drives and innate abilities that determine our personal satisfactions and frustrations. Working as a secretary can be very satisfying for the person who has the temperament for it.

Career Personality. Answer as truthfully as you can the two sets of questions listed below.

Group A	Group B
1. Do you picture yourself as a dynamic, forceful person?	1. Do you think of yourself as a member of a group, not as a leader?
2. Is receiving credit and praise for your efforts and ideas important to you?	2. Do you think you would enjoy wielding influence on matters of import from behind the scenes, as secretaries often do?
3. Do you want to be outstandingly successful in your own right in the business world?	3. Are you good at self-subordination— working for another person's success, thinking according to another person's thought pattern?
4. Are you competitive for recognition? For success?	4. Is it agreeable to you if someone else takes or gets credit for your efforts and ideas?
5. Do you like to plan and manage things in their entirety?	5. Can you be agreeable about having to change plans in the midst of them?
6. Are you bent on bringing others around to your way of thinking?	6. Would you prefer sharing responsibilities, rather than carrying them alone?
7. Do you want to boss others?	7. Can you work under pressure?

If you have mostly "yeses" in Group B, then you should fit happily into a secretarial role. If you have a predominance of "yeses" in Group A, you seem to prefer a career with directive and managerial responsibilities. However, you can use a secretarial job to get *initial* business training in the field of your interest or talent, although it may take self-discipline to submerge your assertive traits.

A secretarial job may provide training in a special field of interest.

Interest in Detail. Is one of your innate qualities that of being detail-minded, detail-capable? Or are you in an ivory tower of thoughts and ideas, of broad generalities, of grand intentions, so that the lowly details are left to shift for themselves? A secretary must have the ability to live with details and nurture them to completion, even though this part of her responsibility might hold little excitement for her.

Even carrying through a simple request such as *"Get Mr. Bender for me, please"* can develop into a series of details. It should be a simple, one-detail kind of task—that of placing just one call. But suppose, as Detail 1, the secretary calls and finds that Mr. Bender will not be in until after lunch. Here is what follows: Detail 2, she must make a note to call him back then. Detail 3, she must inform the executive now that he can't reach Mr. Bender until the afternoon. Detail 4, the executive is now talking on another call so she must make a note to tell him when he is free. Detail 5, she must give the information to the executive the moment he is free. Detail 6, she must call Mr. Bender after lunch.

Details are the very reason for a secretary's existence. Unless you can break each task down into its individual details and carry each one through, you should avoid a secretarial career. You will not be happy, nor will the executive by whom you are employed!

▪ Interest in Words

Do you have an innate interest in words? This question is included at the urgent plea of a top insurance executive who has had excellent secretaries, but for their lack of interest in and knowledge of words. To determine whether you have this interest in words, answer the following questions:

Do you look up the meanings of unusual words?
Do you notice and try out their pronunciations?
Do you read the etymology information?
Do you search out and locate the precise words when writing?
Do you turn to a dictionary or book of synonyms to find distinctions between words of seemingly identical meanings?

If you cannot answer "yes" to these questions, you have not yet acquired "word-interest." Try to develop a sincere and personal interest in your vocabularies. They will be a decided asset to you as a secretary.

Since the secretary helps the executive primarily with communication and since communication *is* words, she must be interested in words. Therefore, if you are to be a competent secretary, you must be above average in *listening vocabulary, reading vocabulary, spelling ability,* and *"guess-ability" as to words dictated.* You cannot be successful if your vocabulary is limited or your spelling is of the hit-or-miss variety.

▪ Personality Requirements and Development

Success on nearly every job requires desirable personality traits. Secretarial work is no exception. For top performance as a secretary, you must discharge your special functions with accuracy, good judgment, follow-through, resourcefulness, and initiative. In your human relations you must show consideration, tact, discretion, loyalty, and objectivity.

Secretarial Checklist. A recent article in a management magazine contains a checklist to assist executives in choosing and evaluating their personal secretaries. They were told to "use it to hire a new secretary, to evaluate your present secretary, or if your present secretary is deficient in any area, give her the checklist to remind her of her responsibilities to you and the company."[13]

[13]"How Good Is Your Personal Secretary?" *Business Management* (October, 1965), pp. 46–47.

RATE YOUR SECRETARY WITH THIS CHECKLIST

1. Does your secretary know the full range of your responsibilities and activities in your organization? Does she understand your personal goals and ambitions, and how they fit in with corporate objectives?

2. Can you leave your office for as much as three or four weeks, confident that your business and personal affairs will be conducted responsibly and expeditiously in your absence?

3. Does she help you organize your time, coordinate your appointments and schedules, meet your deadlines—all without nagging and pestering you? Is she, herself, a well-organized person?

4. Does she initiate, handle and follow through on projects without your having to remind her about them?

5. Is she courteous, helpful, respectful and solicitous of your business associates, visitors, clients and customers? Do they speak of her favorably?

6. Is she imaginative? Creative? Does she present original ideas for your consideration? Does she suggest new ways to improve your work? Her work? Does she suggest new systems or procedures?

7. Is she resourceful? Does she show initiative in getting past a problem without running to you with her troubles?

8. Does she move paper efficiently? Can she tactfully pry loose papers and projects that have remained on your desk too long—and that other executives are waiting for? Does she shake loose data other executives are holding and that you are waiting for?

9. Are her basic secretarial skills (such as filing, stenography and telephone manner) beyond reproach?

10. Is she calm in a crisis? Gracious when tension mounts? When the pressure is on and you lose your temper or self-composure, does she shrug it off and continue to function as well as before?

11. Do you have her absolute loyalty and confidence? Can you trust her with confidential information, both personal and business?

12. Does she read widely and knowledgeably, bringing to your attention published items pertinent to your business or personal affairs?

13. Is she a valuable source of corporate information, obtaining facts that would be difficult, awkward or impossible for you to obtain on your own?

14. Does she have a personal self-improvement program? Does she attend classes and lectures, or participate in programs that are management oriented? Does she try to learn more about your particular company, your particular job, your customers or your industry?

15. Is she articulate? Does she express herself well in summarizing information for you, both verbally and in writing? Does she give instructions clearly and precisely? Does she know how you feel about certain policies or practices, and does she communicate this to others as well as you do?

16. Does she work every day until her job is done, regardless of the hour? Does she willingly work nights or weekends when it is necessary?

17. Is she a manager in the sense that she can farm out her work to others when necessary? That is, can she delegate, supervise and take responsibility for work not completed by herself? Can she train or help train other members of your staff?

18. Can she handle routine matters and projects for you on a day-to-day basis without your intervention?

19. Does she keep track of vital dates for you, dates celebrated by your boss, family and customers (anniversaries, birthdays, religious holidays, vacations and such)?

20. Can she do basic research for you—gather information for a report, for example, or even write a rough first draft?

Obviously, the secretary envisioned in the foregoing checklist is a high-level employee. In fact, the author (a secretary to a top executive herself) says: "Few secretaries, of course, could possibly be rated highly on all criteria. Those who do would more properly be labeled office angels. But the implication is clear. The role of today's executive secretary is surely that of a knowledgeable, efficient, and effective office administrator—one who manages people, paper, and pushbuttons with equal facility."

■ Bridging the Gap Between College and Business

Naturally, you cannot yet measure up to the standards by which top executives rate their secretaries. Nor are desirable traits suddenly acquired when you step into an office; rather, they are developed over a long period of time. The honest uncovering of your weaknesses is the important beginning step. The rating chart on this page can serve as a guide. On each point, rate yourself *excellent, so-so*, or *need improvement*.

Next, set up a specific program for improvement, pinpointed to your low ratings. Concentrate on one or two traits at a time until the behavior seems to be instinctively yours. Then work on two or three more traits until they are habitual. Repeat the process until you have that attractive pleasant-to-work-with personality that will score high on this chart or eventually on the Business Management checklist.

A SELF CHECK ON YOUR SECRETARIAL PERSONALITY

Performance Components	*Human Relations Components*
Accuracy How good am I at finding and correcting errors?	**Consideration** Do I often do kind things without being asked?
Good Judgment Are my decisions usually thoughtful rather than impulsive?	**Tact** Do I avoid ruffling the feelings of others?
Follow Through Do I usually see a job through—implied as well as specific assignments?	**Discretion** Do I refrain from divulging business and personal information?
Resourcefulness Do I usually try various possibilities until I solve a problem?	**Loyalty** Do I stand by my family and my friends through thick and thin?
Initiative Do I often initiate action in my group?	**Objectivity** Can I look at personal situations impersonally?

Suggested Readings ━━━━━━━━━━━━

▪ Books and Manuals

Anderson, Ruth I. *Secretarial Careers* in *Careers for Tomorrow* Series. New York: Henry Z. Walck, Inc., 1961, 106 pp.

Becker, Esther R. *How to Be an Effective Executive Secretary.* New York: Harper and Row Publishers, 1962, 211 pp.

Becker, Esther R., and Peggy N. Rollason. *The High-Paid Secretary.* Englewood Cliffs: Prentice-Hall, Inc., 1967, 233 pp.

King, Alice Gore. *Career Opportunities for Women in Business.* New York: E. P. Dutton and Co., Inc., 1963, 212 pp.

MacGibbon, Elizabeth Gregg. *Fitting Yourself for Business,* 4th ed. New York: Gregg Publishing Division, McGraw-Hill Book Company, Inc., 1961, 403 pp.

Mayo, Lucy Graves. *You Can Be an Executive Secretary.* New York: The Macmillan Company, 1965, 278 pp.

Newton, Roy, and Helen H. Green. *How to Improve Your Personality,* 3d ed. New York: Gregg Publishing Division, McGraw-Hill Book Company, Inc., 1963, 219 pp.

Popham, Estelle L., and Roberta Farrelly. *Opportunities in Office Occupations,* 2d ed. New York: Vocational Guidance Manuals, 1964, 110 pp.

The following periodicals and subscription services provide current, timely information of help to the secretarial student and to the secretary in the office.

▪ Secretarial Subject Matter

Better Secretaries Series. A monthly 48-page bulletin on the development of secretarial skills, available by subscription from Prentice-Hall, Inc., Englewood Cliffs, New Jersey 07632.

From Nine to Five. Twice-monthly pamphlets on specialized topics, available by subscription from Dartnell Corporation, 4660 Ravenswood Avenue, Chicago, Illinois 60640.

P. S.—A Professional Service for Private Secretaries. A twice-monthly bulletin on personal relationships, office procedures, and techniques for the secretary. Bureau of Business Practice, a division of Prentice-Hall, Inc., New London, Connecticut 06320.

The Secretary. The official monthly publication of the National Secretaries Association (International), 1103 Grand Avenue, Kansas City, Missouri 64106, containing association news and interesting features.

Today's Secretary. A monthly magazine (except for July and August) containing timely and informative articles for all levels of secretaries. Gregg Publishing Division, McGraw-Hill Book Company, Inc., 330 West 42d Street, New York, New York 10036.

▪ Fashion, Beauty, Health, and Careers

Glamour. A monthly magazine available at newsstands or by subscription from Condé Nast Publications, Inc., 420 Lexington Avenue, New York, New York 10017.

Mademoiselle. A monthly magazine available at newsstands or by subscription from Condé Nast Publications.

35 Fact Sheets on Careers, such as *Advertising* and *Publishing*, available from Condé Nast Publications.

▪ Office Management, Procedures, and Supplies

Administrative Management. The official monthly publication of the Administrative Management Society of Willow Grove, Pennsylvania, available by subscription from Geyer-McAllister Publications, 212 Fifth Avenue, New York, New York 10010.

Modern Office Procedures. A monthly magazine available from the Industrial Publishing Corporation, 812 Huron Road, Cleveland, Ohio 44115.

The Office. A monthly magazine available by subscription from Office Publications, Inc., 72 Southfield Avenue, Stamford, Connecticut 06904.

Systems and Procedures Journal. A magazine published every two months by the Systems and Procedures Association, available by subscription from 7890 Brookside Drive, Cleveland, Ohio 44138.

Questions for Discussion

1. In what ways did your study of this chapter change your concept of secretarial work?

2. Do you now consider secretarial work a worthy career objective, or do you intend to use it as a stepping-stone? If so, to what? What are some of the advantages of a secretarial career? the limitations?

3. What factors motivate women to work after marriage and rearing a family? Should you make initial preparation for such a later career as an undergraduate? Why?

4. How does the possibility of returning to the labor force affect the present educational plan of the thoughtful student?

5. Do you feel that we can appropriately refer to the secretarial *profession?* Why or why not?

6. If you were in a supervisory or administrative position, what problems of training or retraining or readjustment would you be involved with in regard to the older women returning to work?

7. Why is behavioral science receiving more attention in business today than ever before?

8. Name one or more secretarial or supervisory activities that would require:
   (a) A high level of skill training
   (b) Good economic or basic business understanding
   (c) Superior supervisory ability
   (d) Administrative ability
   (e) A high degree of ability in human relations
   (f) Initiative

9. Why must today's secretary be superior to the secretary of former years?

10. Give an example of when it is NOT permissible to abbreviate each of the following. Then consult the Reference Guide to verify your answers.
    (a) The name of a state or territory
    (b) Parts of the street address
    (c) Publications parts such as column, chapter, and page
    (d) A portion of a company's name
    (e) Dimensions and weights
    (f) The words *Honorable* and *Reverend* when used in connection with a name

11. Select the correct verb or pronoun from the parentheses in the following sentences so that there is number agreement between related words. Then consult the Reference Guide to correct your work. Compose an example similar to any question you missed.
    (a) Your pair of scissors (is, are) being sharpened; my scissors (needs, need) it, too.
    (b) The number of applicants (seems, seem) large; a number (has, have) asked for interviews.
    (c) (This, These) data (constitutes, constitute) a comprehensive collection of all the facts and figures available now.
    (d) Assignments, and not the examination, (determines, determine) your final grade.
    (e) Not only the letter but also the carbons (is, are) messy.
    (f) The professor, together with the students, (plans, plan) to go through the main post office.
    (g) No book or articles (touches, touch) on this subject.

Problems

■ 1. Rate yourself according to the chart on page 16. What personality deficiency needs your first efforts for improvement?

■ 2. Have your voice recorded in the Speech Department and ask for criticism. What realistic improvement plan could help you develop your voice as a more effective tool of communication?

■ 3. On a designated day, dress appropriately but not expensively for the position of a top-level secretary. Divide into groups with not more than eight members to a group. Type a comment about the personal appearance of each other member of your group. These comments will be collected by the instructor for distribution to members of the class as a basis for improvement. Prove that you can be objective both in giving and in accepting the criticisms.

On the basis of criticisms, readings, and observation, prepare a chart listing the colors best for you, hair styles becoming to your face, lines best suited to you, and most effective makeup shades.

■ **4.** What the secretary or administrative assistant says to others in the office is important in determining whether her office relationships will be satisfactory or not. For each of the following situations write what you consider to be an appropriate comment or action:

(a) You have an important airmail, special-delivery letter that needs to be taken to the post office immediately. You ask the office boy to run the errand.

(b) A stenographer who is under your supervision frequently forgets to return or to pay for stamps that she secures from you. What would you say to her the next time she asks for stamps?

(c) You are preparing for your employer an important, detailed report that must be completed tomorrow. Part of the data for the report must be compiled by the secretary to your employer's partner. She has promised to have the data ready today. When you check with her about it, she informs you that she will not be able to complete the work until tomorrow.

(d) A stenographer completes an unusually difficult assignment in very good form ahead of schedule and submits it to you for your criticism.

(e) You overhear one of your associates relating a story that is very uncomplimentary to your employer. You know that the story is absolutely false.

(f) You observe that a new calculating machine operator who is under your supervision wastes considerable time making personal telephone calls and writing personal letters.

(g) Another secretary in your office asks you: (a) "Is your employer going to Europe this summer?" (You have already typed his itinerary.) (b) "Who is going to be general manager when Mr. X retires next year?" (You attended the meeting in which the decision was made.)

(h) During dictation, your employer criticizes one of his superiors and asks you if you agree with the criticism.

(i) Your employer brings you flowers for your desk from his garden at home.

(j) An insurance agent who is attempting to sell your employer a life insurance policy gives you a box of candy.

(k) Your employer unjustly criticizes you in the presence of another employee.

(l) Two weeks ago your employer agreed that you might be away from the office for two days next week to attend the wedding of one of your best friends in a neighboring city. From his dictation you learn that he is now planning a business trip for the same time.

(m) Your employer gets or takes credit for an idea you contributed on a rush job you completed under extremely difficult circumstances.

(n) Your employer, who had a very high regard for the assistant who preceded you, has the habit of saying, "Miss X always did it this way."

(o) You have just been promoted to the position of secretary to the executive vice-president, who passed over several girls who have been with the organization longer than you have.

■ **5.** Throughout this course collect material that you can use for a secretarial handbook when you are employed as a secretary. Set up a file for organizing these materials in folders indexed according to the major divisions of this textbook. Such material could include:

Class notes and returned assignments of future-reference value

Digests or summaries of reference readings

A continuing bibliography of secretarial and business reference books

Clippings about personality traits and successful secretarial techniques

Business letters received (for form and current styles of letter parts)

Diagrams, charts, graphs, typed tables, etc. (for form and subject matter)

Printed business forms used for various purposes

Literature about office machines and supplies

Current information about telephone, telegraph, postal and shipping, travel, and other office services and procedures

Communication tips

Office systems

New developments in office organization and management

Ideas on human relations and developments in business psychology

■ **6.** From a recent Administrative Management Society survey, newspaper advertisements, Bureau of Labor Statistics, or interviews with employment agencies, look for information on salaries for secretaries, including the administrative secretary. Compare, if possible, salary levels in various sections of the country.

Related Work Assignments 1-4

1. Analyzing Important Secretarial Qualities. With two or three other students in the class, build a rating chart of those traits and abilities which are of most importance to a secretary. Then use the chart to rate yourself.

2. Evaluating Your Secretarial Qualities. Compare the rating chart you helped develop in assignment No. 1 with that shown on page 1 of the Workbook to determine what important traits and abilities were omitted from your chart.

Rate yourself according to the chart provided in the Workbook. You may wish to discuss with a friend or the class ways to improve areas in which you rated yourself weak.

3. Comparison of the Rankings of 13 Secretarial Abilities by the Secretary and Her Employer. Referring to the chart on Workbook page 3, answer these questions:

(a) How do you account for the wide difference in the secretary's and her boss's assessment of her competence in supervision and in making administrative decisions?

(b) Is there any area in which the boss gave unexpectedly high ratings?

(c) Why do you think secretaries felt they have little difficulty with handling correspondence on their own initiative and yet their supervisors ranked this ability third among the areas that need improvement?

(d) What overall conclusion could you draw from a study of this chart?

4. Analyzing Secretarial Duties. The instructions and supplies you will need to complete this assignment are provided in the Workbook.

Ch.

2   The Secretary's Work Day

This chapter discusses office environment and how the professional secretary can blend into the picture in terms of appearance, voice, and behavior. It also focuses on the organization of work for top efficiency. It describes techniques that will enable you to "plan your work and then work your plan." Thus it describes attributes essential for the top-level secretary.

You in the Office Environment

As a secretary, you have a dual responsibility for the impressions you create in the office. One is to yourself, for you are judged by your personal appearance, behavior, and attitude; the other is to the office girls with whom you work, for they tend to pattern their behavior, as well as their appearance, after that of the top-level secretary. She sets the standards for careful grooming, acceptable dress, and approved behavior. Her appearance and actions—both good and bad—are observed, analyzed, and copied.

As a college student, you try hard to conform to standards of dress and hair styling that will win acceptance of your peers. Soon you will be trying just as hard to conform to standards of business appearance that will be acceptable to your new associates. Appearance *is* job related, and it is especially so for the secretary, who constantly represents her company to the public.

■ Maintaining Good Posture

The first requisite of attractive appearance is good posture—a carriage that says that you are proud of yourself, that you *are* somebody. Stand and sit "tall"; never slump. Avoid sitting with crossed legs, especially if skirts are short and slim styled. When standing, keep the rib cage pulled in and the derriere "tucked" under. Enter a room with a smooth motion, with head balanced and chin parallel to the floor.

Appearance is job related, especially for the secretary, who sets standards for careful grooming and approved behavior.

—*IBM Corporation*

■ Dressing the Part

The two appearance factors, *being well-groomed* and *dressing appropriately*, are important in the office because they do affect your self-confidence (and, thus, your competence) and the impression that you make on others. They are measures of your pride and judgment. They tell much about you: whether you are lazy and penurious (it takes effort and money to be clean and neat); whether you know what is appropriate in dress for both the occasion and your physical type; and whether you have that lifelong essential—good taste.

Good grooming and appropriate dress are not achieved by wishful thinking. They require homework. Appropriate dress requires pre-planning what you will wear the next day or during the week, and selecting suitable, harmonizing coordinates and accessories. Good grooming requires efficient scheduling of grooming activities and having each garment pressed, clean, and ready to wear. If you are in need of slimming down, you may have to add to your homework the necessary body-trimming exercises or calorie planning.

23

Grooming. You must be well-groomed throughout the day—spotlessly clean and altogether neat. This requirement applies to every detail of your appearance. It means going to work each day fresh from a shower, wearing clothes that are spotless and free from rips.

That clean, neat appearance is a *cost* of working. You are expected to have your washable clothes laundered after each wearing, your other clothes frequently pressed and cleaned; to keep the heels of your shoes trim; to have your hair shampooed, set, cut before it obviously needs it; to keep your nails manicured, and so on. Some of these you can do yourself; the others cost money—money which you are obligated by your very position to spend.

Every business person must guard against being offensive to office associates because of perspiration, body odor, or halitosis. Nervousness, hot weather, overheated offices, prolonged typing, all may cause excessive perspiration. The daily use of a nonperspirant or deodorant as a preventive measure is necessary. There is no excuse for either body odor or halitosis today. A daily bath with one of the excellent soaps to guard against perspiration odor and the use of mints for halitosis are both effective.

You will surely use makeup, but with restraint. Overuse or noticeable use of makeup is acceptable only for those who work in the fields of glamour, cosmetics, or fashion. Keep to the natural color of your hair unless you can afford the money and the time to keep the coloring constant and inconspicuous. You will find that mature secretaries, however, occasionally use color effectively to hide greying hair. The conservative executive in the higher echelons does not like his young secretary to change her hair color at the whim of fashion.

Choosing an Appropriate Wardrobe. Although women's clothes are increasingly casual, office dress is still relatively conservative. Most offices are air-conditioned, so there is no summer license for letting down standards by appearing without stockings or with extremely low-cut necklines. The top-level secretary is expected and obligated to maintain "the tenth-floor look" correlative to her salary and status. Her wardrobe reflects good taste and judgment and at the same time can express her individuality.

Your employer and your colleagues will not remember *what* you wore, but they will definitely have an impression of whether you looked right or wrong. With careful planning you may win the employer accolade, as many secretaries have, "I don't know how she manages on her salary. I *know* what it costs for my wife to look that way."

Dressing with chic takes thought, careful coordination, a clear understanding of your most becoming colors, and disciplined avoidance of impulse buying of "fad" fashions. The business wardrobe should consist of:

> A classic, full-length top coat that will carry you not only through the day but also into the evening
>
> A harmonizing all-occasion, not-too-heavy suit, possibly with a matching jacket
>
> A two-piece suit that may be worn either as a two-piece dress or with blouses in complementary colors
>
> A basic dress or two that can be dressed up or down with accessories, depending on whether it is to be worn on an after-hours date (quiet shade, though not necessarily black if that color is unbecoming)
>
> High- or medium-heeled shoes without ornate decoration
>
> Gloves in harmonizing shades
>
> A becoming hat—although it is conceded that hats are worn less and less

A careful buyer reads the labels, constantly searching for wrinkle-free, drip-dry, or other easy-to-care-for fabrics.

A secretary rarely, if ever, wears a slipover sweater to the office; nor does she, for obvious reasons, wear extremely tight skirts. Flats, loafers, and sneakers are, of course, taboo. If necessary, a well-dressed woman remembers the *foundation* of it all.

▪ Voice

College students usually take a speech course—but not very seriously! Yet the personnel officer in charge of work assignments for twenty college students on an internship program between the junior

> Her voice was ever soft,
> Gentle, and low, an excellent thing in woman.
> *Shakespeare*—KING LEAR

and senior years reported that the one universal complaint of the executives with whom they worked was, of all things, SPEECH.

▪ Behavior

Don't try to impress. It is wise, especially during your first days on a new job, to refrain from trying to impress others. Do not try, in one quick swoop, to create an impression of extreme confidence and competence. For some reason, the Old Guard interprets this as cockiness and waits with pleasure to see you get your comeuppance. With your office associates, start with the attitude that you have much to learn and

—*Standard Oil of New Jersey*

A secretary makes every minute
count. She is punctual in all things.

that you hope they will help you learn because you lack experience. Ask questions. Listen. Do not talk about yourself, especially about anything that sounds boastful.

With the executive, ask questions and *listen!* Do not try to be Miss Personality Plus. Let your personality begin to flower slowly—say, after a week or so.

There are many facets to business etiquette—so many, in fact, that books have been written about them. All, however, are based on courtesy and propriety. When in doubt, ask yourself these questions: Is it considerate? Is it appropriate? When both answers are "yes," you can safely proceed. If one or the other is "no," please refrain. Remember the adage, "When in doubt, DON'T."

The way to make business introductions is given on page 49. If you have other how-to-do-it questions, refer to a current guide, such as the chapter, "Manners and Etiquette in Business," in Emily Post's *Etiquette.* For help on other phases of social etiquette, turn to Emily Post or Amy Vanderbilt. Both advise you well.

■ The Secretary's Attitude Toward Time

A secretary makes every minute count. When she works, she works effectively. When she relaxes, she forgets about work and enjoys her free time. She is punctual in all things: in reporting for work, in having material ready for the executive, in submitting periodic reports, in relaying messages, and so on. A lackadaisical attitude about time can be a source of irritation in executive-secretary relationships. It can also directly affect other office workers in their attitudes toward time; as in other office-behavior situations, the secretary sets the standard.

Breaks or Rest Periods. During both the morning and the afternoon, you will be expected to take 10- or 15-minute breaks. No matter how busy you are, try to take your breaks, even if they are past their usual time. Breaks are given because the relaxation is beneficial. The time "wasted" is gained in revived energy and alertness. It is not "cricket," however, to stay beyond the allotted period. Also, make sure that your telephone will be answered by someone else while you are away from your desk.

Secretarial Working Hours. The secretary often works on a peculiar time schedule. The executive expects her to work late to complete something for him or to take care of banking or other errands on her lunch hour. Thus, the secretary finds her coming-and-going schedule different from that of other office workers. The only thing she can do is to keep track of her time and give a full week's work, scheduling her hours to the executive's convenience. If any of the other office workers comment, she can only be confident in her own mind that she has been fair to the company. She is not beholden, however, to account to them for her elastic schedule.

Her vacations, too, may be more irregular than those of others; for the secretary must defer to her employer's schedule, remaining on the job when his work load is heaviest.

Smoking. Smoking in an office consumes time—often time for which you are paid to be working. You will always be given the privilege of smoking in the girls' lounge during breaks and usually after office hours at your desk. Whether you may smoke at your desk during office hours depends on the policy of the office. Many offices prohibit it. If smoking at desks is permitted, the secretary does not abuse the privilege. She does not smoke in the presence of callers or when she is taking dictation. She exercises careful judgment as to when and from whom she accepts a cigarette.

Working Smarter—Not Harder[1]

This section stresses the importance of work planning. It is devoted to the secretary with a grain of indolence in her makeup, for it is concerned with doing things smarter—with reducing effort, yet getting better results.

---

[1] This slogan is adapted from the National Association of Educational Secretaries, which uses it in publications and workshops.

—General Electric Company, Nela Park

Good organization must be flexible. Try a simple time analysis for a week, noting on the left side of a notebook your plan for the day and on the right side recording times for activities actually carried out. Evaluate the flexibility of your plans.

▪ Saving Time

Work measurement is common in office administration. Secretarial work is less frequently subjected to analysis than work involving more repetitive operations (those of the machine transcriber in a pool, for instance). But you will probably be asked at intervals to do a job analysis of your duties and the time spent in various categories of jobs, on a daily, monthly, and annual basis. If you wonder where your time goes, why not make a simple analysis for a week just to help you improve your work planning?

On the left side of a loose-leaf notebook list the things that should be done each day, numbering them in the order of their importance. As you complete each item, note on the right side of the notebook the activities with which the day was actually spent and the proportion of time given to each item. Study of this time record will show what activities are taking too much time.

Maybe your analysis will indicate too much socializing. Maybe it will show that you spent expensive time doing something that someone else could have done for you—searching for files that could have been requested from the file clerk, going after something that could have

28

been sent to you, delivering in person a message that could better have been telephoned, waiting for the executive to finish his telephone conversations so that he could resume dictation, going to the supply closet for stationery that should have been put in your desk that morning.

Some timesaving practices can be undertaken by you. Others may require the cooperation of your employer or the purchase of new equipment. But you benefit the most, because you thus become time conscious and aware of the importance of work organization.

▪ Working Efficiently

To work efficiently is to work with a minimum of motion, effort, time, and fatigue. It is seeing where motion, effort, time, fatigue, or any combination of them can be reduced, and proceeding accordingly. Efficiency can be applied to every manual office operation—even such tasks as arranging and using desk supplies, opening letters, sealing letters, erasing typewritten matter, and having reference materials at hand.

Efficiency, like personality, is largely self-acquired. To develop awareness and techniques of efficiency, consider it to be a kind of game in which you compete with yourself—a question-and-answer game. You will find it is expertly played by lazy people who get much satisfaction out of reducing fatigue and saving motion, effort, and time.

▪ Working Your Plan

The secretary must not only plan her work; she must also work her plan. Work does not come to her in an even flow. There are periods when the executive must turn out important work in a limited time, and so then must the secretary. Careful planning, though, can reduce (but not completely eliminate) the peak loads if you anticipate periodic jams and distribute part of the work of the rush period to the slack days.

Periodic Peak Loads. A study of the flow of work over your desk for a month will indicate the pattern of fluctuation. For instance, Mondays traditionally bring heavier mail and subsequently heavier dictation, so other Monday plans should be light. A dentist's secretary who usually bills patients the first of the month could spread the preparation of the bills throughout the month in some organized pattern. In your office, summer may bring slack periods ideal for transferring files, typing new card records, bringing address files up to date, and duplicating copies of frequently requested materials.

To help meet the demands of periodic peak loads, make whatever preliminary preparations you can. Address envelopes, fill out parts of forms, prepare enclosures, and purchase or requisition all supplies that will be needed.

Real Emergencies. Even with the best of planning, unavoidable emergencies will occur. An unexpected illness or tragedy may deplete the office force below a functional level. Your employer may be faced with a herculean job and insufficient time in which to perform it. Decide which jobs are crisis items, which you should do yourself, which you can assign to someone else, and which should be deferred for a day. Work calmly and steadily. If necessary, suggest employing temporary help. Accept the possibility of occasional overtime.

Your Plan Versus Your Employer's Plan. You may spend the last few minutes before leaving for the day in planning the next day's activities (a commendable practice), only to discover the following morning that your plan does not dovetail with your employer's. Maybe at the end of the day you have not completed anything you planned. Just remember that your employer's plan always has precedence. He would not be in his present position if he were not a good planner himself, and HE IS THE BOSS. Yet a plan not followed is better than no plan at all.

▪ Memory Aids

A good memory is basic to efficiency. You need a good memory to plan the work for the day and to carry out assignments with the judgment that comes from remembered experience. Try to remember what you *see* on paper and what you *hear*. *Look intently* at the papers that pass through your hands; *listen to everything* everyone says (perhaps not obviously, but listen anyway) and try to remember each detail. A dependable memory is one of the real assists a secretary can give to the executive.

Secretarial Desk Manual. Every secretary should compile and keep up to date a loose-leaf desk manual covering each duty and procedure of her work. Again and again in this textbook you will come across a recommendation to put such information or routines into your desk manual. The last part of this book explains the contents and organization of such a manual. You should, however, begin now to collect in a loose-leaf book all general information and procedures that will be helpful to you as a secretary.

In an emergency, the executive may expect the secretary to work late to complete a rush assignment for him.

The Tickler. The tickler is an efficient memory aid. This strangely named business device was derived from the accounting term *tick*, meaning to *check off*. A tickler is an accumulating record, by days, of items of work to be done on future days and then ticked off when they have been accomplished. Items still in the file beyond the tickler date thus provide an effective warning signal if checked systematically.

The daily calendar can be used as a tickler for the recording of items to be done on specific dates; however, since calendar-page space is limited, a separate tickler is usually set up and maintained. The most flexible kind of tickler is a file box with guide cards for each month and one or two or three sets of date guides from 1 to 31. The guide for the current month is placed in the front of the file. A set of day guides is placed behind the guide for the current month and perhaps the next one or two months. An item of future concern is written up on an individual card, and the card is dropped behind the guide for the proper month and for the proper date. If the item is to be followed up several months later, it is dropped behind the month guide; it is filed according to date when that month comes to the front.

Since an item is often forwarded and reforwarded, the follow-up date is written in pencil so that it can be erased and changed. In fact, since this is but a memorandum type of record, the entire item is usually written in pencil. Annual items, such as due dates of taxes, insurance premiums, and wedding anniversaries, are refiled for next year's reminders as soon as ticked off.

Maintaining a tickler is in the routine area of secretarial work; it is too commonplace for the executive to request, organize, or supervise. But if you should fail to remind him of a tickler-type item, he will become *very* provoked—the extent of the *very* depending upon the embarrassment it causes him and the dollars and cents it costs. The moral is: USE the tickler device as a memory aid in these ways:

1. **To record future-date work**
2. **To remind of work to be done**
3. **To tick off missions accomplished**

To be of dependable help to the executive, you must persistently check a tickler for pending activities.

The secretary has made out an item for the tickler to remind her an express shipment should reach her before the end of a week. Notice that memorandum records are written in abbreviated form.

Follow-up date 11-17

Item Moore exp shipment

Refer to ls

Signed _____ Date 11-1

The secretary can organize her work more efficiently by keeping desk reference files, such as those listing names, addresses, telephone numbers, and affiliation of important clients.

Pending File. The pending file is also a memory aid. It is a file folder in which the secretary temporarily holds mail concerning matters that are pending. It is kept in her desk, in the executive's desk, or in some other place near at hand. If the secretary's desk has a deep file drawer, the pending file can be kept conveniently there. It is not too satisfactory to keep the folder flat, because the folder and its contents often become dog-eared. Unless extra copies are made of incoming and outgoing letters, the pending folder isolates correspondence that should be available in the regular file. The secretary often forgets to check through the pending file, and it grows fat with letters that should have been released to the regular files long ago; however, it is often used because the correspondence on in-process matters is so conveniently at hand.

Desk Reference Files. The secretary can organize her work more efficiently by keeping desk reference files, such as those listing names of important clients, telephone numbers frequently called, addresses of regular correspondents, items that must be followed through before they are placed in the central files, stock identifications and descriptions, and work in process. These desk reference files save much time that would otherwise be lost in hunting for frequently needed facts. The organization of each secretarial desk differs because of the executive's position and type of business. The desk reference files you set up will be those you need most, planned only after you are on the job.

▪ Outside Assistance

If the situation warrants, it is good judgment for the secretary to obtain assistance. When there is not sufficient time to complete a sizable office job, the secretary often asks for additional workers. She tries to obtain help within her own office through the office manager, the typing pool supervisor, or from other secretaries, who often help each other in rush situations. If those avenues fail, she may obtain the executive's permission to telephone her request to an agency that supplies experienced temporary help. Among such agencies are Manpower, Inc., and Kelly Services, Inc.

When the work requires professional skills or abilities beyond those of the secretary or when the job is of such size that it can be done more quickly and at less expense outside, the secretary often turns to a special-service agency—after obtaining the executive's permission, of course. She might find it wise to use agencies that prepare multiple copies of original letters and mail them, that obtain hotel and travel reservations, that take full recordings of meetings and prepare transcripts, that handle all or any of the operations of a duplicating job, that furnish and maintain mailing lists, or that provide competent help for other jobs of a specialized or technical nature.

Upon completion of major work or service, the secretary writes in her desk manual a memorandum in which she identifies the agency or the individuals used, makes a record of the total cost, and inserts a brief evaluation for future guidance.

▪ Supervision of Subordinates

You may have a full-time assistant or two to help you, or you may obtain temporary help from time to time. Supervise the person as you would like to be supervised. Practice the principles of happy human relations. Here are just a few basic principles to remember and follow:

Explain the work to be done, until the person understands it.

Explain the reasons for the work; knowing why makes it more enjoyable.

Check the accuracy of the work; have poor work repeated, but be gracious about it.

See that new work is ready and waiting; don't waste time.

Don't criticize results; instead help her improve her methods.

Realize that the worker is trying to do her best; be tolerant.

Give credit and praise when due.

To instill good work habits, you must set the example, for subordinates imitate their supervisor, whether her habits are good or bad. If you are neat in appearance, they will dress neatly too. If you are prompt and appreciate the value of time, they will be more punctual and work more steadily. If you are enthusiastic and interested in the work they are doing, they will be enthusiastic and interested. If your working materials are well organized and neat, theirs will tend to be also.

> **The Supervisor's Prayer**
>
> Please, when I am wrong, make me willing to change; when I am right, make me easy to live with. So strengthen me that the power of my example will far exceed the authority of my rank.
>
> —*Pauline H. Peters*

Suggested Readings

Becker, Esther. *How to Be an Effective Executive Secretary.* New York: Harper and Brothers, 1962, 211 pp.

Doris, Lillian, and Besse May Miller. *Complete Secretary's Handbook.* Englewood Cliffs: Prentice-Hall, Inc., 1960, pp. 19–23 (follow-up and tickler systems).

Engel, Pauline. *Executive Secretary's Handbook.* Englewood Cliffs: Prentice-Hall, Inc., 1965, 206 pp.

How to Plan Your Office Space. National Stationery and Office Equipment Association. 740 Investment Building, Washington, D.C.

Mayo, Lucy Graves. *You Can Be an Executive Secretary.* New York: The Macmillan Company, 1965, 278 pp.

Neuner, John J. W., and B. Lewis Keeling. *Administrative Office Management,* 5th ed. Cincinnati: South-Western Publishing Company, 1966, pp. 167–236 (color, light, noise, office planning); pp. 523–554 (supervising).

155 Office Shortcuts and Time Savers for the Secretary. West Nyack, New York: Parker Publishing Company, Inc., 1964, 90 pp.

Plan Your Work—A Handbook on How to Work Smarter, Not Harder. 1201 Sixteenth Street, N.W., Washington D.C.: National Association of Educational Secretaries.

Powers, John Robert. *How to Have Model Beauty, Poise, and Personality.* Englewood Cliffs: Prentice-Hall, Inc., 1960, pp. 59–84 (posture); pp. 187–215 (dressing to suit your figure, face, and personality); pp. 228–239 (voice and speech); pp. 260–276 (tips on good grooming).

Whitcomb, Helen, and Rosalind Lang. *Charm—The Career Girl's Guide to Business and Personal Success.* New York: Gregg Division of McGraw-Hill Book Company, Inc., 1964, 480 pp.

Questions for Discussion

1. Why plan your work if your employer frequently disrupts the plan?

2. Your employer frequently calls you for rush dictation late in the afternoon so that you must work overtime. With proper reorganization of his work, much of this necessity for overtime work could be avoided. How could you suggest that he change his habits so that both of you could be more efficient and the overtime could be reduced?

3. In what ways can you reduce periodic peak loads? real emergencies?

4. What is the weakness in using a pending file? How can this danger be averted?

5. Why do you suppose so many executives criticize the speech of college secretarial interns?

6. What would you do first if you were trying to type a telegram which was urgent and the telephone rang, your employer buzzed for you, his superior walked into your office, and your subordinate reported that she had finished her assigned work?

7. The executive often must convert securities to obtain the cash to pay his enormously high quarterly income taxes. What kind of item would you put in the tickler? Under what dates?

8. You discover that the water cooler is leaking and that the floor is covered with water. What, if anything, would you do?

9. Capitalize the following sentences. Then refer to the Reference Guide to correct your answers.
   (a) I wonder: is secretarial work as interesting as it sounds?
   (b) The answer is, sell it, even at a loss!
   (c) What other possibilities are there? to start over? to give up? to repeat each experiment?

10. Show how you would type the number *twenty-five* in the blanks in the following sentences. Then refer to the Reference Guide to correct your answers.
    (a) I believe she is about _____ years old.
    (b) Our new address is 6125 _____ Street.
    (c) The premise is based on a _____ year old book.
    (d) _____ replies were received.

Problems

▪ 1. In many of the problems and related work assignments in this book, you will be working as secretary to Mr. Robert L. Simpson of Continental Products, 320 Euclid Avenue, Des Moines, Iowa 50107, performing a variety of duties that you might expect to do in the office of an executive of a large company. Mr. Simpson's letters cover a wide variety of situations, as he is the general manager of a company with widely diversified products. He is also very active in civic affairs and expects his secretary to handle many details relative to his personal affairs. You will use the stationery and forms that you would expect to find in the offices of Continental Products.

As secretary to Mr. Simpson, you will be expected to decide upon the order in which you will perform the many duties incident to your work. Prepare a form containing the following columnar headings:

To Do At Once	To Do Soon	To Do When Time Permits

List on the form the following duties in the columns under which the duties would normally fall. Consider as duties "To Do Soon" those which would be done sometime during the day after the "At Once" items were taken care of. (List each duty by number instead of writing it out.)

(1) Transcribe a telegram.

(2) Address notices of a meeting to be held a month from today.

(3) Prepare a manuscript for mailing to a trade magazine.

(4) Write up the minutes of a board meeting held yesterday.

(5) Transcribe a letter telling an applicant that there is no vacancy.

(6) Transfer material to the dead files.

(7) Clean out your own desk.

(8) Make a routine bank deposit.

(9) Deliver pay checks to members of your department.

(10) Type a new organization chart for the department.

(11) Locate and file the telephone numbers of all the members of the Kiwanis Club, of which Mr. Simpson is secretary.

(12) Transcribe a recorded telephone message.

(13) Send a form letter to a group of customers regarding a special price offered them on an overstocked item.

(14) Remind Mr. Simpson of an important appointment.

(15) Prepare Mr. Simpson's income tax payment and transmittal record for the quarter ending tomorrow.

(16) Make a hotel reservation for a trip which begins tomorrow.

(17) Prepare an inventory of office furniture for insurance records.

(18) Type the lease for a property that Mr. Simpson has just rented to a man whose occupancy begins in two weeks.

(19) File all the materials transcribed today.

(20) Confirm a speaking date for Mr. Simpson for a meeting to be held two months from today.

(21) Renew the subscriptions to all the office magazines.

(22) Pay the insurance that is due within a week.

(23) Type an annual report to be presented tomorrow.

(24) Duplicate the agenda for a sales meeting to be held three days hence.

(25) Pick up tickets for Mr. Simpson's trip next week.

(26) Correct the page proof for the revised edition of the office manual.

(27) Post payroll items to the personnel cards of the employees in your department.

(28) Clip an item about an honor conferred on Mr. Simpson and paste it in his scrapbook.

(29) **Read an article about the development of a new process by your company.**

(30) **Complete an evaluation of the work of your assistant for her personnel record.**

(31) **Transcribe the dictation of answers to a questionnaire from a graduate student writing a thesis about office procedures.**

(32) **Telephone a client that Mr. Simpson will not be able to see him tomorrow morning.**

(33) **From the monthly telephone bill, charge the long distance calls to the proper departments.**

(34) **Develop a list of short forms for words occurring frequently in your dictation.**

■ **2.** The following items are on your desk on March 2 to be marked for the tickler file. Type the columnar headings shown here and insert the identifying letter of each item under its appropriate time heading.

3–7 Days	2–3 Weeks	Other (Explain)

(a) Notes for an article solicited for the September *Journal of Accountancy*. The deadline for the article is April 1.

(b) A note about setting up a conference with a bank official about a short-term loan to meet the April 1 payroll.

(c) A letter accepting an invitation to speak at a meeting of School of Business seniors on May 8.

(d) The program of the annual convention of the International Controllers Institute to be held on April 6 in Brussells. Mr. Simpson has told you that he plans to attend.

(e) A notice of a meeting on March 8 of the Administrative Committee of which Mr. Simpson is a member.

Related Work Assignments 5-7

5. **Selection of Employee Evaluation Forms**

6. **Job Breakdown Sheets**

The instructions and the supplies necessary for the completion of Related Work Assignments 5 and 6 are provided in the Workbook.

7. **Your Fundamentals.** This is the first in a series of workbook assignments reviewing English usage, grammar, and punctuation. Correct the sentences and then make further corrections where needed by referring to the Reference **Guide** in this textbook.

The Secretary as Office Hostess

Unlike many routine office workers, the secretary will never be replaced by a machine. Why? Because it is she who humanizes the office. She is a public relations representative of her company and of her employer, paid to create a favorable image of both to all visitors and to her co-workers. And in no other aspect of her work is the public-relations responsibility so heavy or challenging as in her work as office hostess. The more responsibility in this direction that she is able to accept, the more valuable she becomes as an administrative assistant.

It is the secretary who must create a pleasant, relaxed office atmosphere that influences callers to react favorably to the executive's point of view and that enables him to work at top efficiency. From the time she welcomes the caller to the time she speeds him on his way, she is the official office hostess, serving as a buffer between the visitor and her employer, interpreting the policy of the company and of her employer, and soothing ruffled feelings (even if there is no justification for them). When the visitor walks away, he should feel, "That's a good company (or a good executive) to deal with. I'll come back here."

Such public relations skill is worth thousands of dollars in goodwill. Some of it is innate, but much of it can be developed on the job. In this chapter two aspects of the work of the secretary-receptionist are discussed: the secretary as an office hostess and techniques for handling the executive's appointments.

The Secretary as Hostess

Think of your own reactions to secretaries you have encountered—the nurse-receptionist in the doctor's office or the secretary in the dean's office. Haven't they been a contributing factor to your reaction to the person you wished to see? Did the effective secretary seem to want to be helpful? Didn't she set the stage for a later successful encounter with her employer? She may have been a sparkling, enthusiastic person or she may have been somewhat dignified. It made no difference as long as she communicated with you in a natural, unaffected manner compatible with her true personality.

—*Los Angeles Department of Water and Power*

Methods of receiving callers vary according to the nature and size of the organization. A company receptionist may screen callers before they are directed to the secretarial office.

■ Office Organization for Receiving Callers

Methods of receiving callers vary among companies. In large organizations all visitors go to a reception desk where a trained receptionist screens callers and directs them to the person who handles the phase of work in which they are interested. The company receptionist tells the secretary that the caller is in the outer office, and then the secretary takes over her responsibilities as office hostess.

In smaller companies the caller may first be received by the switchboard operator. In the very small office the secretary is the caller's initial contact with the company. Thus she has a greater responsibility both in determining the use of executive time and in influencing the reaction of the visitor toward her organization. She tends also to handle the problems of many callers herself as they relate to her realm of responsibility.

The Executive's Preferences. As a new secretary, you will want to find out how the executive wants you to handle callers. You should ask your predecessor, if possible; or you may ask general questions about preferences. You will also learn through experience, if you develop sensitivity to the reactions of others.

Discover answers to questions about executive preferences:

Does the executive want to see everyone who calls? (Many executives make a fetish of their "open-door policy.")

Does he prefer to see callers in a certain category (such as salesmen) at specified times only?

You can get direct answers to these two questions; however, any answers will sometimes be modified.

Do not ask these questions directly. You will soon sense the answer.

Certain persons can always enter the executive's office without first obtaining your permission: top executives, to whom your employer is responsible, and their secretaries; coexecutives, with whom he frequently confers, and their secretaries; and his immediate staff. Special-privilege callers come in with confidence. They know they will be welcome, and usually they introduce themselves to the new secretary.

Which of his personal friends and relatives are likely to call, and which should be sent in without announcement?

Who else should be admitted without appointments?

How should callers be announced? When should you try to help terminate visits? What callers does your employer prefer to avoid?

Watch your employer's reactions to your ways of handling these problems. Sense how he responds to your methods.

Welcoming the Caller. When a caller comes to your desk, give him your immediate and undivided attention. To finish typing the line, to file the last three letters, or to continue chatting with another employee while he stands waiting is unjustifiable rudeness.

You must learn who the unscheduled caller is and what he wants. Smile naturally and greet him with a friendly, "Good morning. May I help you?" If he does not give you his name or business card, you will then have to ask, "May I have your name, please?" or "Who should I say is calling?" You must then get his business affiliation, which usually will explain the purpose of his visit, or your question will cause him to tell you the reason for his call. This is one of the most difficult problems that confronts the receptionist, especially one new in a position; and it requires tact and patience.

The courteous office hostess gives the visitor her immediate and undivided attention.

—Harold M. Lambert

The caller on legitimate business is accustomed to making office calls and will approach the secretary, identify himself, state the purpose of his visit, and ask to see the executive. But occasionally it may be necessary for the secretary to ask, "What did you wish to see Mr. Allen about?" or to say, "I am Mr. Allen's secretary. Perhaps I can help you."

The caller may want to see the executive about a matter that is not within the scope of his duties. It will save the visitor's time, and that of your employer, if you learn the nature of the visit and refer the visitor to the proper person. Nothing is more annoying than to wait half an hour to see somebody only to find that he is the wrong person. The secretary should effect the transfer immediately and skillfully. She might say, "I'm sorry, Mr. Lawrence, but Mr. Alexander handles that for Mr. Allen. If you wish, I'll be glad to see if he can talk with you about it now; or if he can't see you today, I'll make an appointment." Or she might say, "I wonder if you would see Mr. Lane in the Advertising

If the visitor wishes to see the executive about something out of his scope of duties, the considerate office hostess may arrange a meeting with the right person.

Department about that. He is more familiar with our handling of that matter than Mr. Allen is and so can be of more help to you. I'll be glad to see if he is free."

If the caller agrees to see Mr. Lane, the secretary can telephone Mr. Lane or his secretary and explain the situation. She can then say, "Mr. Lane can see you now, Mr. Lawrence. Will you please go to the twelfth floor and tell the receptionist that Mr. Lane is expecting you." In case Mr. Lane cannot see the caller, the secretary might say, "I'm sorry that Mr. Lane can't see you this morning; however, he can see you tomorrow at eleven if that is convenient for you."

In most cases the helpfulness of the secretary in arranging the appointment will more than offset the inconvenience to the caller of having to go to still another office to be served.

If you have the visitor's name and reason for wanting to see your employer and if you have satisfied yourself that the caller's business falls within the employer's province, write the name and purpose of the visit on a slip of paper and take it in to the executive. He will decide whether he wishes to see the visitor. The written memorandum also helps the executive remember to use the caller's name in conversation.

The secretary will be on the lookout for a person with a scheduled appointment. She will be able to greet him by name, possibly saying, "Good morning, Mr. Lawrence. How are you? Mr. Allen is expecting you. You may go right in."

Remembering Names and Faces. One extremely valuable secretarial technique is a natural and easy grace in using a person's name when addressing him. If your caller does not give you his business card, write his name and the reason for his call on your daily calendar during the conversation. To remember names requires:

1. *Attention to the name as it is spoken.* Listen carefully when the name is pronounced. If in doubt, ask the person how to pronounce it or how to spell it. Writing the name phonetically in shorthand or in longhand will prevent mispronunciation. Although hearing one's name is pleasant, having it mispronounced is very annoying.

2. *A forceful effort to remember it.* You can train yourself to remember a person's name by: repeating it when you first learn it; using it when addressing the person; recording it, perhaps in a reference notebook or card file; and associating the person's name and face with his business.

Remembering faces is another attribute of the superior secretary. Several devices may be used to develop this skill. The secretary may keep a card file of frequent callers. Or she may file a business card as it is given to her, associating the name on the card with the face of the

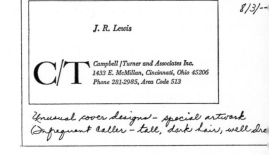

As an efficient memory aid for her receptionist role, the secretary prepares a card for each caller—recording name, affiliation, purpose, date of visit, subsequent visits, etc. If the caller gives her his business card, she may make notations directly on the card and file it. (The illustration at the right shows a business card affixed to a 5" x 3" file card.)

caller. To recognize her employer's colleagues, she should watch carefully for their pictures in company publications, newspapers, or magazines. While reporting a committee meeting, the secretary might draw a seating chart and list some outstanding feature for unknown members so that she could ask for their names later or fill in the names as she hears them mentioned.

Several companies whose success depends upon effective public relations have developed techniques for improving internal relations by helping personnel recognize members of the organization. One, an advertising agency, publishes in its company induction manual an organization chart with the picture and the title of each executive beside his name.

Keeping a Record of Callers. It is very helpful to have a record of callers—their names, dates of calls, business affiliations, reasons for calls, and other pertinent information. Often the secretary finds this record useful in tracking down urgently needed facts, for it gives names and dates and narrows down the search.

In some offices a printed form is used for registering callers. The caller may be asked to write the information about himself on the form, or the secretary may secure the information from him, writing the data on a pad as she talks with the visitor. Later she can transfer the information to the register. If the caller presents his business card, the secretary need only ask the name of the person he wishes to see and the purpose of his call.

Daily registers are used in professional offices, such as those of lawyers or public accountants, because such men usually prepare periodic time reports as a basis of computing costs of services rendered to clients. The register serves as a check list for each period to make sure that the time spent with each client, as recorded, is also entered and charged for on the proper time reports.

REGISTER OF CALLERS   _Monday – May 16, 19--_

TIME	NAME AND AFFILIATON	PERSON ASKED FOR	PERSON SEEN	PURPOSE OF CALL
9:30	H. Arnold – Acove Lighting Fixt. Co.	B. S.	✓	Salesman
10:30	L. Crowe – Standard Plumbing	Q. J.	✓	"
11:45	C. apple – Contr. on Merrill Bldg. for lunch appt.	B. S.		Discuss Progress
1:40	L. Rehula – Flexwood Consultant	B. S.	Q. J.	Hammer Job
3:50	Messenger from Flexwood	—	✓	Brought Samples

This ruled register of callers enables the secretary easily to keep a daily record of helpful information about callers, including purpose of the call.

Some offices maintain an alphabetic card file of callers; on these cards all visits are recorded as they occur. A card is filed by a caller's name and is cross-referenced to show his affiliation. Doctors use the card system as a basis for billing patients and as a record of each patient's medical data. Purchasing agents use it to help them remember the correct names of products and salesmen.

Where the flow of visitors is small, the secretary usually keeps her own personal record of callers conveniently and permanently on her daily calendar.

Deciding Who May Enter. Experienced secretaries, sometimes inclined to become too protective of the executive's time, may turn away too many callers. A cartoon showing the president's door overhung with cobwebs while the secretary explains, "Oh, nobody ever sees Mr. Jones," dramatizes this secretarial attitude, which antagonizes almost everybody. A good rule to follow is: *When in doubt, find out from the executive if he wants to see the visitor.*

If your desk is placed inside the executive's office, callers are inclined to go directly to him, the screening having been done at the receptionist's desk in the outer office. But if your desk is just outside his office, you will probably be responsible for determining who may enter.

Although selected co-workers may enter without your permission, they usually ask courteously if it is convenient for them to go into the executive's office.

The executive's friends and family may have the privilege of going into his office at any time; but if he is busy at the moment, the secretary should ask them to wait, saying that he is busy. She need not go into detail, such as "He is in conference with the general manager," or "He is talking with the vice-president." A statement that he will be free in a few minutes or will return shortly is ample explanation. Learn to know these callers and always try to call them by name. Be friendly with them, but not too cordial, because they are a part of the executive's social and home life and you may appear presumptuous if your manner is too personal.

Clients and customers are always accorded cordial and gracious treatment by the secretary. Salesmen of materials and services related to her employer's work are treated with courtesy and listened to attentively. They may provide technical help in ironing out company problems, and the secretary should tell the executive immediately when such a salesman calls.

If the secretary has reason to believe that her company would have no use for the salesman's product, she may say, "Mr. Ward, I don't believe we would be able to use your product, but let me check with Mr. Allen to see if he wants to talk with you," or "We are using another product, and I am not sure that Mr. Allen has time to see you today, but I will ask him. Just a moment, please." She may also find it appropriate to direct him to another office.

Never, never judge a caller's importance by his appearance. Some outstanding people in the artistic, professional, and industrial world are far from prepossessing in appearance. On one occasion the secretary to a college president decided that an early-morning, very ordinary-looking caller was quite unimportant. Therefore, she did not trouble to tell the president that the man was waiting, because the president was busy at the time. Finally the man grew impatient and left. Later she learned, to her chagrin—and to the great disappointment of the college —that the caller was a very wealthy alumnus who wished to give the school a tremendous sum of money. He never came back.

The Difficult Caller. Being courteous to certain visitors may require considerable discipline and restraint. Some of them are gruff; some are condescending; some are self-important or aggressive; some, even rude. To be gracious to these persons requires strong will power.

The caller who resorts to obvious flattery to get information from the secretary is very obnoxious and usually thick skinned. About the only courteous recourse is to let him know that you intend to remain gracious but will not be bludgeoned. Above everything, the secretary should not answer, except in generalities, the business questions of inquisitive callers. An answer such as, "I really don't know; perhaps Mr. Allen can tell you," will ordinarily stop such questions.

The nuisance caller, such as a peddler, resorts to all sorts of dodges to get past the secretary's desk. It is here the secretary needs to exercise tact and firmness. Be wary of a person who, without giving his name, says, "I'm a personal friend; he knows me," or "I want to see him on a personal matter." The caller with important business has everything to gain by giving his name and the reason for his call. You can explain that you are not permitted to admit callers unannounced. If he still refuses to tell you his name and purpose, ask him to sign his name on a card or to write a short note to the executive. You can enclose either of these in an envelope and take it in to the executive, who can then decide whether to admit him.

A good office hostess welcomes the visitor immediately. She is attentive to his comfort and may engage in brief casual conversation.

Pleasant Waiting. A good office hostess tries to make the visitor as comfortable as possible while he is waiting. She asks him to sit down. She sees that current magazines and an ash tray are close by; she invites him to take off his overcoat, or topcoat, if he has not done so. If she likes and is not too busy, she may talk with the caller casually about general and impersonal things; but good judgment will tell her never to discuss office business.

Admitting the Caller. After an exceptionally long wait, the secretary may remind the executive that the caller is still waiting and then report to the caller that it will be only a few more minutes. The secretary should, of course, cross the room to deliver any message to a waiting visitor privately.

Sometimes the executive walks out to greet the caller. Should there be two callers waiting, indicate who is first. If you escort the caller into the private office while other visitors remain near your desk, or may enter the office, unobtrusively cover the work on your desk or put it into a folder.

For his first call, the secretary may accompany the visitor into her employer's office and present the caller to the executive, stating the purpose of the visit.

If this is the visitor's first call, the secretary may take him into her employer's office, leading the way. In most offices she would knock before entering if the door is closed. She would then introduce the caller and leave unobtrusively, closing the door behind her.

In some cases, although she would wish to show the caller into the executive's office, she may have to say: "I am sorry, Mr. Lawrence, but I am tied up with a long distance call. Will you please go in now."

Introductions. The secretary presents the caller to the executive. Since the caller has heard the executive's name, the secretary may omit it when making the introduction. It is courteous, however, to address the executive as you introduce the caller.

√ **This is Mr. Lawrence of Allied Corporation.**

√ **Mr. Allen, this is Mr. Lawrence, who has an appointment with you.**

√ **This is Mr. Lawrence.**

  NEVER SAY: **Mr. Allen, meet Mr. Lawrence.**

49

Business position rather than sex or age is usually the determining factor as to who should be introduced to whom. The secretary presents customers or clients to her employer as indicated on page 49. In an office the social rule is reversed, and an executive presents his secretary to a man with, "Mr Lawrence, I should like you to know my secretary, Miss Baer." The secretary usually does not rise unless she is being introduced to an older or notable person such as a chief of state or a clergyman. Neither does she shake hands when she is introduced unless the other person offers his hand first. She acknowledges an introduction merely by saying "How do you do, Mr. Lawrence," being sure to address the caller by name.

▪ Interruptions

If it is necessary to give a message to the executive when he is in conference, type it on a slip of paper and take it in to him, usually without knocking if this is less likely to disturb or interrupt the conference proceedings.

When there is a telephone call for the visitor, ask if you can take the message. If so, type it along with your name, the date, and time of receipt. If the one calling insists on speaking to the visitor, go into the conference room and say something like this: "Mr. Lawrence, Mr. Rowett is on the telephone and wants to speak to you. Would you like to take the call here (*indicating which telephone he is to use*), or would you prefer using the telephone in my office?" She then finds other business away from the phone to afford the visitor privacy.

Some callers stay and stay and stay. Usually the executive rises when he wishes to terminate a conference, but occasionally a caller will not take the hint. The secretary may help the situation by taking to the executive's desk a note which he can pretend contains a request for him to go elsewhere, or by apologetically announcing to him that it is time for him to leave for his next engagement. She should not say where, even though it is a legitimate reminder. She might even telephone from a desk out of range and ask if he wants to be interrupted so that he can send the person away. Often his mere answering of the telephone affords a sufficient break in the conversation to make the caller realize he has stayed too long.

A way to reduce overlong visits is to say before the caller goes into the executive's office, "Mr. Allen has another appointment in ten minutes, but he will be glad to see you in the meantime."

Handling the Executive's Appointments

Before the secretary can effectively handle the executive's appointments, she should familiarize herself with his connections—the committees on which he is working, the clubs to which he belongs, the speaking engagements he has planned, and the projects in which he is interested. For instance, the president of a large corporation might be a board member of a college or a number of other organizations, a member of several civic clubs or enterprises, president of a professional organization, or author of a book. If the secretary is acquainted with all these activities, she is better prepared to schedule his appointments.

The executive's personality will also affect his appointment schedule. Is he "all business," maintaining a schedule strictly as planned; or is he a warm, outgoing individual, inclined to chat with people? The latter type of executive will often upset a carefully planned appointment schedule.

▪ Scheduling Appointments

Appointments are scheduled in different ways:

1. **The secretary schedules recurring appointments at which the executive's presence is necessary (i.e., regularly scheduled conferences of boards or corporation committees) on his calendar at the beginning of the year and throughout the year as new commitments are made.**
2. **The executive or secretary may schedule an appointment over the telephone.**
3. **Either the executive or the secretary may schedule an appointment by mail.**
4. **The executive may ask the secretary to schedule an additional conference with someone who is then in his office.**
5. **The secretary may schedule a definite appointment with a caller who just dropped in and found the executive out of the office.**

The secretary is depended upon to furnish complete information when scheduling appointments. Even though the executive merely says, "Make it 3:30 Wednesday," she would specify the actual date and the place on the calendar. It is also wise to give a reminder to the person making the appointment. Unless she has the telephone number of the person making the appointment, the secretary exercises wise precaution by recording the number on her desk calendar so that she can cancel the appointment if necessary.

Oct 19 –	Nov 19 –		Dec 19 –
S M T W T F S	S M T W T F S		S M T W T F S
1 2 3 4 5 6 7	1 2 3 4		1 2
8 9 10 11 12 13 14	5 6 7 8 9 10 11		3 4 5 6 7 8 9
15 16 17 18 19 20 21	12 13 14 15 16 17 18	*1*	10 11 12 13 14 15 16
22 23 24 25 26 27 28	19 20 21 22 23 24 25	*wednesday*	17 18 19 20 21 22 23
29 30 31	26 27 28 29 30		24 25 26 27 28 29 30 31

8:30 a.m.		2:30 p.m.
9:00	*Mr. Peterson*	3:00
9:30		3:30
10:00	*Mr. R.J. Cooper*	4:00
10:30	*Pension Plan*	4:30
11:00	*Conference*	5:00
11:30	*Dentist*	5:30
12:00 p.m.		6:00
12:30	*Mr. Rahbar*	6:30
1:00	*Alms Hotel*	7:00
1:30		7:30
2:00		8:00

IMPORTANT REMINDERS

Call K J S re contract
Call Calhoun re UA Drive 741-3177
Transfer Files
Adv. Talk on P.M.

BIRTHDAYS

TODAY	MEMOS	TO COME
Mrs. Simpson	*RJS NY Tickets in safe* *pick up lamps*	*Galley proof from Atlantic Press*

—Adapted from Memindex Co.

At the beginning of each day the secretary cross-checks the executive's calendar with her own, making them conform by putting pertinent items from her calendar page into his and vice versa. With his complete schedule on her desk, she can remind him when his time is running short and she can take care of preappointment preparations.

Either the appointment book or the calendar pad is used to keep a record of the appointments scheduled. Here the secretary turns journalist and concerns herself with the four "W's" of scheduling appointments, as follows:

√ **WHO**   the person is—his name and affiliation.

√ **WHAT**   he wants—an interview for a position, an opportunity to sell his product, or a business discussion of some sort. Indicate what materials will be needed for the appointment.

√ **WHEN**   he wants an appointment, and how much time he needs.

√ **WHERE**   the appointment is to be held away from the executive's office. Be sure to include the address and room number.

PLANS, SCHEDULES, APPOINTMENTS, ETC.

Sunday Oct. 29	Thursday Nov. 2
	Prelim. Budget Conference
Monday Oct. 30	Friday Nov. 3
Sales Conference	*Prepare talk for Monday Planning Meeting with LL*
Tuesday Oct. 31	Saturday Nov. 4
Sales Conference	*Father's Day at Columbia*
Wednesday Nov. 1	Future--Keep in Sight
Sales Conference	*Final Budget Due Nov. 8 Talk at Com. + Industry Nov. 7*

—*Adapted from Memindex Co.*

A glance at the executive schedule for several days in advance allows both secretary and executive to coordinate and to balance activities to better advantage. With this procedure the secretary can more often avoid an awkward scheduling of appointments.

The Employer's Preferences. In selecting the date and hour for an appointment, the secretary considers the personal preferences of the executive. She may try to:

1. Schedule few, if any, appointments on Monday mornings, because the weekend accumulation of mail requires attention.

2. Allow ample time in the appointment schedule to take care of the mail.

3. Avoid late-afternoon appointments so that work of the day can be completed.

4. Because of the last-minute rush of work, avoid appointments just prior to a trip.

5. Leave free the first day after the executive's absence of several days because of the accumulation of work.

6. Suggest two alternate times for the appointment, rather than asking, "When would you like to see Mr. Lawrence?"

When the secretary grants an appointment, she explains that it is subject to the approval of the executive and may have to be changed. She enters the appointment on her own calendar, as well as on her employer's calendar. Unless the secretary has been given carte blanche in scheduling appointments, she later explains the appointment and asks the executive to approve it.

In arranging appointments, the secretary has an opportunity to exercise good judgment. A young man from Wisconsin planned to visit an Ohio city to apply for an engineering position. He wrote that he would come to the office of the prospective employer the following Saturday morning. The executive was in West Virginia at the time the letter was received, but he was expected to return to his office on the Saturday morning in question. The secretary was concerned over the long trip the applicant would be making at his own expense. She knew her employer expected to be in a nearby Wisconsin city the following Monday and felt the interview might be held there, so she telegraphed her employer to ask his opinion. He wired back to arrange for the appointment at his hotel any time after seven o'clock on Monday night. Thus, the applicant saved a great deal of expense and time, and the employer had his Saturday morning free.

Avoiding Unkept Appointments. Nothing destroys good relations faster than an appointment not kept. Preventing conflicting appointments is one of a secretary's most difficult problems. Sometimes the executive forgets to tell his secretary about appointments made outside the office. Three suggestions from experienced secretaries may prove helpful:

1. **Each morning, try setting aside time to review the executive's calendar with him when you put it on his desk. He may at this point remember an appointment that he forgot to write down.**
2. **Provide the executive with an appointment book that he can carry with him. You may ask to see this book until he becomes accustomed to giving it to you for checking.**
3. **Before the executive leaves, remind him of any unusual appointments such as a very early morning appointment or a night meeting.**

If the executive is delayed in keeping an appointment, the secretary should (if possible) notify the next caller by telephone that he should come at a suggested later time. A secretary is most helpful when she can locate the executive for an appointment he may have overlooked.

If the executive is delayed in meeting an appointment, the secretary should telephone the individual to arrange a later appointment time. The call should be made as soon as possible to minimize the resulting inconvenience.

If the executive finds himself involved in an emergency such that he must ask a replacement to keep an appointment for him, the secretary should explain the situation and apologize for the substitution prior to the appointment.

Saying "No" Tactfully. Obviously appointments should be refused as tactfully as possible. Refusals should be prefaced by a sincere "I'm very sorry, but . . ." and a logical reason given, such as, "Mr. Allen is out of town," remembering to use your employer's name rather than the impersonal "he." This is a plausible reason and much kinder to the ear than the blunt, "Mr. Allen won't see you." Other tactful refusals would be that the executive is in conference, that he must attend a meeting on that day, that he has a heavy schedule for the next two weeks, or that he is getting ready to leave town. If a caller seems very much disappointed over a refusal, you might offer to talk with the caller yourself and relay a message to the executive or take some other appropriate, helpful action.

ⁿ The Actual Appointment

From the record on her own desk calendar the secretary knows when she should be on the lookout for a person coming to keep an appointment. When he arrives, she tells the executive the person is waiting and she talks with him casually if there is a delay. If he is late, it is entirely proper for the secretary to telephone to see if he is on the way.

More than one person is often involved in an appointment or meeting. If possible, the secretary arranges the executive's office before the meeting and sees that there are enough chairs, comfortably arranged; she also provides pencils, note pads, and ash trays.

When the first conferee arrives, a problem is posed: Shall the secretary tell the executive of his arrival, or wait until the entire group has assembled? There is no hard-and-fast rule; the answer depends on the visitor's status, the executive's activity, and the executive's preference. If the visitor is very important, the secretary may not only inform her employer of his arrival, but telephone the other conferees to come now. Otherwise, she may greet the visitor, make him comfortable, and let him wait until the whole group is assembled before disturbing the executive. A gracious secretary will instinctively introduce the conferees as they assemble.

If there is any correspondence or material that will be helpful in the conference, the secretary should have submitted it before the meeting, so that the executive will be familiar with the matter.

If she is within earshot during the conference, she should get additional material as it is needed, often on her own initiative. If the executive is going out to a conference, she should anticipate the papers he will need and have them in his brief case. One public official, who has many conferences in his office and attends many others, appreciates his secretary's clever routine. Before he leaves for a luncheon appointment, she types on a slip of paper the address of his luncheon engagement and his program for the afternoon. This she tucks in his hat band. When he leaves for lunch, he scans it and places it in his coat pocket for further use if needed.

■ Scheduling Appointments by Letter

Appointments with persons out of the city are usually arranged by letter. A request for an appointment is promptly answered in full. A typical letter granting an appointment follows.

Dear Mr. Graham:

Mr. Allen will be pleased to interview you on
Friday, April 30, at 11 a.m. If you cannot
arrange to be here at that time, please let me
know. I will schedule another appointment for
you.

Very truly yours,

When a request for an appointment must be refused, the letter
contains a tactfully phrased explanation. Note the following example:

Mr. Allen is very sorry that he cannot arrange to
see you as requested in your letter of March 12.
He is preparing to leave the city and has very
heavy demands upon his time. Thank you for your
interest.

▪ Canceling Appointments

When appointments are canceled, the secretary usually writes the
out-of-town callers concerned and telephones the local callers. In the
latter case, the executive often asks the secretary to write a letter confirming the cancelation to prevent an embarrassing situation in case
the caller does not receive a telephone message. If possible, a new
appointment should be scheduled immediately to take the place of the
canceled one. The following is a typical letter of cancellation:

Mr. Allen is disappointed that he cannot keep
his appointment with you at 3 p.m. on July 19.
He has been called out of town unexpectedly.

I will let you know as soon as Mr. Allen returns
so that another appointment can be arranged.

Suggested Readings

Doris, Lillian, and Besse May Miller. *Complete Secretary's Handbook.*
Englewood Cliffs: Prentice-Hall, Inc., 1960, pp. 24–32.

Engel, Pauline. *Executive Secretary's Handbook.* Englewood Cliffs: Prentice-
Hall, Inc., 1965, pp. 57–77.

Mayo, Lucy Graves. "The Secretary Meets Callers Impressively," *Communications Handbook for Secretaries.* New York: McGraw-Hill Book Company, Inc., 1958, Chap. 23, pp. 312–319.

Wood, Merle, and Margaret A. McKenna. *The Receptionist.* New York:
Gregg Division of McGraw-Hill Book Company, Inc., 1966, 273 pp.

Questions for Discussion

1. How would you learn the executive's preferences regarding your hostess practices?

2. Describe the use of a card file for frequent callers, the register of visitors, and the appointment schedule. Which of these three office tools would you regard as most important, and why? Do most offices need all three of these kinds of records? Explain your answer.

3. If your employer makes appointments without telling you and they conflict with those that you have scheduled, what should you do?

4. In what ways do you think that reception work in the office of each of the following types of businessmen would differ from each other:

   (a) **A professional man, such as a doctor or a lawyer**
   (b) **A bank executive**
   (c) **The president of a company manufacturing heavy machinery**
   (d) **An elected government official**

5. Insert the proper words in the blanks. Then refer to the Reference Guide to correct your answers.

   (a) **Work it out _____ you can. (any way or anyway)**
   (b) **Let us have your comments _____. (any way or anyway)**
   (c) **_____ of you can do that. (any one or anyone)**
   (d) **_____ can do that. (any one or anyone)**

Problems

1. What would you do in each of the following situations? When the solution calls for a conversation or a note, indicate exactly what you would say.

(a) **A visitor who wishes to see your employer refuses to give you his name or any information about the purpose of the call.**

(b) **A prospective purchaser of a large order calls when your employer has just gone into a two-hour conference with top executives.**

(c) **An old friend stops on his way to the airport, but your employer is making a call at a business office not far away.**

(d) **A frequent caller and good business friend comes to the office and claims that he has an appointment for a particular time, but you have no record of such an appointment. Another appointment is scheduled for that time.**

(e) **A caller who failed to keep his last two appointments telephones for a third one.**

(f) **Your employer has given instructions that you are to discourage callers whose business relates to his personal affairs. A representative of an investment company in which your employer owns stock asks to see him. The last time he was in the office, he took over an hour of your employer's time.**

(g) An important out-of-town client arrives at the office at twelve o'clock to keep a luncheon appointment with your employer. At 11:30 the president of the company called an emergency meeting of all top executives with instructions that it is to be a closed meeting and that they are not to be disturbed. The meeting will probably last well into the afternoon. You could not reach the out-of-town client by phone.

(h) A salesman of office equipment who is waiting to see your employer continually interrupts your work with personal remarks about your appearance and possible after-office-hours pursuits.

(i) Your employer had an appointment to attend the organization meeting of a committee planning an in-service course for members of the Executives' Club. The president of your company called an emergency meeting on budget at the time of the scheduled appointment. Your employer asks you to get his assistant to represent him at the committee meeting.

Related Work Assignments 8-9

8. Scheduling Appointments on a Secretary's Desk Calendar. Make a secretary's calendar appointment page for July 23, similar to the one that is shown on page 52 if the Workbook is not available. The appointments and activities listed below were scheduled in advance for that day. Write up all of the items on the page in a brief but clear form. Your employer is Robert L. Simpson.

(1) Mr. Simpson made a luncheon appointment at the Erie Hotel with L. W. Rasmussen for 12:30.

(2) A letter from S. T. White, of San Francisco, requested a 10 a.m. appointment, which was granted by return mail.

(3) RLS must appoint a committee by the 25th to handle an outing for the Advertisers' Club.

(4) You made a half-hour barber appointment for 11 a.m. for RLS.

(5) Office conference, which Mr. Simpson must attend, is called for 3:15 p.m.

(6) Mr. T. K. Kraus telephoned for an appointment and accepted your suggestion to come in for a 20-minute appointment at 2 p.m.

(7) Mr. White wrote that he is unable to keep the scheduled appointment.

(8) Mr. Thornton, sales manager, requested that RLS come to his office at 9 a.m. for a conference.

(9) Mr. Simpson asked you to verify a 2 p.m. appointment that he believes he made with T. T. Hale. Inasmuch as you have scheduled another appointment at 2 p.m., you called Mr. Hale and arranged for him to come at 10 a.m.

(10) Mr. Simpson asked you to cancel any afternoon appointments that are scheduled to take place before 2:30 p.m. You called Mr. Kraus and arranged for him to come in at 10:30 a.m.

(11) You are to buy a gift for your co-worker, Maria Steffens, for a shower to be held the night of the 23d.

(12) You are to make a dental appointment for yourself.

9. Handling Appointment Records. The instructions and supplies necessary for the completion of this assignment are provided in the Workbook.

Case Problems

1—1 √ conformity

At the end of her college course, Louise Maddox was an honor student, and her secretarial skills were outstanding. She was sent by the Secretarial Department for a job interview for a choice position. Afterward, the interviewer telephoned the chairman of the college department, Doctor Brumage, whom he knew well, to say that they were offering the job to Louise although he was dubious about employing anyone with such an extreme hair style. He asked Doctor Brumage to discuss this job-related factor with the applicant although he, too, had mentioned it during the interview.

When Louise returned to the college, she told Doctor Brumage about the offer and said rather noncommittally that she did not know whether she would accept. During the conversation the hair-styling problem was raised. Louise said, "Yes, he did say that I would have to find another hair style. But I don't know whether I want to work there—or in any other office—if it means that I will have to change my personality."

What is your reaction to Louise's attitude?

1—2 √ error responsibility

Mrs. Dorothy Willis, editor of *Fashion Magazine*, replaces an associate editor by moving a staff writer, Bess Ames, into the position. At home she roughs out a press release about the change. She is not sure of Bess's real first name, so she writes in the draft, ". . . has appointed Mrs.————— Ames to the position of Associate Editor in charge of special features. Mrs. Ames. . . ."

Mrs. Willis asks another associate editor to read the release before it is typed and to make any suggestions for change. The associate editor suggests one addition and pencils the word *Elizabeth* in the blank space. Mrs. Willis makes the recommended change in copy and gives the release to her secretary Nancy Vorse for duplication and release to 100 publications.

The press releases are sent up from Office Services and laid on the window sill until Miss Vorse can mail them. Mrs. Willis is dictating to Miss Vorse when the temperamental Mrs. Ames comes into the office. While waiting, Mrs. Ames picks up a release, reads it, and exclaims, "Dorothy, this thing can't go out. My name isn't Elizabeth; that's the name of my husband's first wife. My name is Evelyn, and it seems to me that you ought to know that much about me after twelve years."

Mrs. Willis looks at the release and says, "Bess, I am terribly sorry for this stupid mistake. Of course it must be done over. Miss Vorse, will you please put an ASP [as soon as possible] on it and rush it to Office Services. It must be out by this evening. And next time I hope that I can depend on you to check the accuracy of simple material. After all, you have been typing it every month on the magazine masthead."

Since two superiors made the mistake, is Miss Vorse responsible for the inaccuracy of the release?

1—3 √ the secretary's loyalties

Helen Timme was secretary to the sales manager of the Tex Corporation, Mr. Alan King, whom she admired greatly. One day the secretary to Mr. Stephen Caruthers, the president of the company, telephoned to say that Mr. Caruthers was reviewing a report on expense accounts and would like Mr. King to explain the unusually high entertainment charges in the southwest district, especially those of Ken Winston. She asked that Mr. King check over Ken Winston's expenses and send the president an explanatory statement justifying these expenditures by the end of the month.

Miss Timme placed the usual report of the telephone call on Mr. King's desk. He returned and, while Miss Timme was in his office, glanced at the message, crumpled it up, and muttered, "SC is going to be plenty willing to pay Ken Winston's expenses when we surprise him with that Birkman order he is working on. I'll just hold off on this for a few days. The order ought to come through this week."

Two weeks later when the president's secretary met Miss Timme in the elevator she said, "Helen, I am really surprised at you for slipping up on such a little thing as relaying a telephone message. Mr. Caruthers had to call Mr. King direct this morning to ask for those expense-account comments. Mr. King was really burned up with you for not giving him the message."

Miss Timme mentally counted to ten slowly and replied, "Oh, I am sorry. If Mr. King hasn't prepared the material yet, I'll work on it myself this afternoon." Then she went to Mr. King's office and said, "Mr. King, do you want me to look up those expense-account figures you forgot to give to Mr. Caruthers last week? His secretary just bawled me out for not giving you the message. You surely put me on the spot. I just want you to know that I don't appreciate the way you handled this."

Evaluate Miss Timme's behavior toward both the president's secretary and Mr. King. Was it appropriate for the president's secretary to criticize her?

—*IBM Corporation*

The secretary combines typing speed and accuracy, problem arrangement ability, and understanding of equipment and supplies to produce high-quality output.

Secretarial Typewriting and Duplicating

The basic machine of the secretary, and of the office, is the typewriter. The secretary has typing competency which includes a high degree of typing speed and accuracy, facility in using special features that have been built into the typewriter, and understanding of supplies which will help to produce impeccable results. As she combines these abilities with wise judgment in the choice and use of copying and duplicating processes, the professional secretary may save not only money but also time which she might use in creative, responsible ways for the benefit of the company.

Ch.

4 Typewriting Equipment and Supplies

5 The Secretary—Master Typist

6 Copying and Duplicating Processes

Ch. 4

Typewriting Equipment and Supplies

Until the day comes—if indeed it ever does—that finished copy can be automatically produced directly from voice dictation, the typewriter will continue to be the main working tool of the office and of the secretary.

The executive naturally assumes that his secretary is the master of her machine. He expects superior work. The quality of typewritten work, however, is influenced not only by the skill and knowledge of the operator, but also by the typewriter, the typewriter ribbon, the paper, and the carbon paper. Superior copy can be produced only when the tools and materials are correlated to the typing job, and the secretary is the matchmaker.

This chapter discusses special features of the typewriter and typewriting supplies as well as considerations involved in purchasing and requisitioning them. All of these factors are of particular concern to the supervisory or administrative secretary. She will often have responsibilities for evaluating the quality of typed materials turned out. In addition, she will frequently be involved with selecting or recommending typing equipment and supplies to purchase. She might even be the one who carries out the purchase of such items.

Typewriters

Although most typewriters are designed primarily for correspondence and general office work, a typewriter can be equipped for such special purposes as billing, preparing copy for bulletin boards, preparing name tags for conventions, and typing statistical material.[1] The movie and television industries, to prepare copy for prompting equipment, use a typewriter that produces letters that are one-half inch high and one inch in width. Thus, there are general typewriters and special-purpose typewriters.

---

[1] If a machine is to be used extensively for typing financial and statistical reports, it should be equipped with decimal tabulation. A fifth row of keys is provided. These keys are tabulator keys which permit the typist to move to the exact place in a column of figures for alignment of numbers.

—*International Business Machines Corporation*

The revolutionary IBM Selectric typewriter eliminates the need for regular type-bars and a movable carriage. The input-output typewriter shown above, designed for use with data processing systems and measurement recording devices, prints out decoded information at speeds up to 15½ characters a second.

▪ Typewriter Variables

Most secretaries prefer the electric typewriter because they can turn out superior work with less effort. Electric typewriters are available in a wide variety of type styles, line spacing, ribbon mechanisms, cylinder lengths, keyboards, and other special features.

IBM Selectric. The IBM Selectric introduced a basic change in typewriter design by eliminating the type bars and the movable carriage. On its own carriage, a spherical element the size of a golf ball moves from left to right across the paper. The alphabet and special symbols are raised on the surface of the sphere. When a key is struck, the element positions the letter or symbol for impression. There is no jamming of keys and less vibration and noise.

One of the distinctive features of the Selectric is that it permits the use of a wide variety of type styles and special symbols. A number of type elements can be purchased, each having a different *type style* and different symbols. To change type styles, the operator removes the element and replaces it with another containing the desired type style. The changeover can be accomplished in a few seconds.

Proportional-Spacing Typewriters. The ordinary typewriter uses a uniform space for each letter of the alphabet. Printing, however, uses proportional spacing; that is, some letters are wider and use two or three times the space of other letters, as shown by the illustration at the right. Typewriters that provide proportional spacing are usually referred to as *executive* models. They produce copy that resembles printing in appearance.

Proportional	·	iiiii
Spacing	·	ooooo
Type	·	wwwww
Style	·	mmmmm
	·	
	·	
Standard	·	iiiii
Spacing	·	ooooo
Type	·	wwwww
Style	·	mmmmm

E X P A N D E D with one
standard space between
letters

E X P A N D E D with
a proportional space two units
wide between letters

E X P A N D E D with
a proportional space three units
wide between letters

—IBM Corporation

Type Sizes and Styles. In addition to the standard 10 (pica) and 12 (elite) characters to an inch, type may also be obtained in sizes of 6, 8, 9, 11, 14, or 16 characters to an inch.[2] For specialized work, type sizes and styles are available in wide variety. For example, one typeface is designed for filling in insurance policies; another, for billing work. There is also a typeface that optical scanning equipment can read.

Several type styles referred to as executive typefaces provide a distinctive and formal appearance. Styles also vary from a schoolbook face resembling printer's type to an informal script that gives correspondence a personal touch. Lightface, boldface, and italics are other choices. A face consisting of all capitals is also available.

When the secretary is searching for a distinctive style in alphabet type or in numbers, fractions, special characters, or symbols, she has a large variety of typefaces from which to choose. Some acquaintance with the equipment available will help her to carry out supervisory responsibilities and to make her own work both distinctive and appropriate.

---

[2]The number of characters per inch is frequently referred to as type "pitch," such as **10 typing pitch** or **12 typing pitch.**

TYPE STYLES

For General Correspondence

Patrician's clean, precise appearance and unique octagonal styling
are a sure combination for consistently attractive correspondence.

--12 characters per inch

Royal Farnsworth, a recently developed type style for executive correspondence will produce a prestige appearance.

--11 characters per inch

Graphic Pica gives a letter-sharp look to business correspondence. It lends an air of formality.

--10 characters per inch

*EXECUTIVE'S UNIQUE AND DISTINCTIVE TYPE FACE ATTRACTS
IMMEDIATE ATTENTION TO CORRESPONDENCE.*

-- 9 characters per inch

For Special Purposes

SMALL DOUBLE GOTHIC HAS 16 CHARACTERS TO THE HORIZONTAL INCH. THIS SURPRISINGLY LEGIBLE
TYPE IS IDEAL FOR PREPARING RULED FORM REPORTS WHERE TYPING SPACE IS SEVERELY LIMITED.

--16 characters per inch

*Small Spencerian's beautiful script style gives your correspondence
a personal and easy-to-read appearance.*

--12 characters per inch

This type has a distinctive upper and lower case formation
that lends itself to Optical Scanning.

--10 characters per inch

Butterick has a very bold face which resembles printer's type.

-- 8 characters per inch

Line Spacing. Although most typewriters provide the standard six vertical lines to the inch, the line spacing can vary from one line per inch (video type) to eight or more, depending upon the type size, style, and purpose. Type styles that use 3, 3.6, 4, 4.5, 5.8, 6, or 8 lines to the vertical inch can be obtained.

Although single, double, and triple spacing are standard on most typewriters, machines with settings for line spacings of 1, 1½, 2, 2½, and 3 lines give greater flexibility in adjusting the spacing of the typewriter to the line spacing on printed forms.

A FORM DESIGNER drew a form carefully according to the standard six lines to the vertical inch. Ten thousand copies were printed. The using department bounced all 10,000 copies back to the designer with the notation: "Vertical spacing not in agreement with our typewriter." *WHO GOOFED?*

—*International Business Machines Corporation*

Among the interchangeable elements for the IBM Selectric is the Universal Symbol element, which provides for more than 88 symbol characters including mathematical, legal, chemical, language accent, and Greek character symbols.

Special Keyboards. Special-purpose keyboards can be obtained. These keyboards include symbols and characters common to a type of work. For example, there are keyboards for each of the following uses: billing, legal, chemical, engineering, mathematical, library, and each of several foreign languages. When ordering a typewriter, you may specify the keyboard desired.

Special-Character Keys. The number of special characters and symbols available on the typewriter can be supplemented by use of interchangeable type heads or devices. A wide selection of special characters and symbols for practically any language, profession, or business can be obtained. Some typewriters have keys on which the type heads are easily removed and changed. On all machines, changeable characters or symbols can be used. The secretary can, within seconds, select the character or symbol she needs and insert or snap it into place for use, as shown with the Remington type head and the TYPIT guide below.

—*Remington Rand*   —*George T. Petsche Advertising*

Half-Space Key. The half-space key or bar moves the carriage only one-half space. It is used for central placement of extra-letter corrections (for example, a four-letter word can be typed exactly centered in the space used by a three-letter word), for expanded headings, and for even distribution of space in "justified" lines.

—Smith Corona, Division of Smith-Corona Marchant, Inc.

Cylinder (Platen) Length. Cylinder lengths vary from 11 to 27 inches. The 13-inch cylinder is most commonly used. Some machines have interchangeable carriages whereby the standard carriage can be removed and an extra-long unit set in its place for a special project such as a chart, graph, table, or special display.

Cylinder Resiliency. Rubber cylinders range from very soft to extra hard. A soft cylinder can be used for ordinary work involving four or five carbons. When more carbons are needed, the cylinder must be harder. Many typewriters have removable and interchangeable cylinders that can be exchanged easily and rapidly.

Fabric- and Film-Ribbon Mechanisms. A typewriter can have either a fabric- or a film-ribbon mechanism, or both, although usually only special-purpose typewriters include the film-ribbon mechanism.

Special Attachments. A number of special attachments can adapt the machine for special uses. Palm tabulators, card holders, label holders, multiple-form holders and aligners, and additional repeat controls are a few of them.

▪ Typewriter-Keyboard Machines

The typewriter keyboard is used on a number of special-purpose office machines. For example, some accounting machines have both an alphabetic and a numeric keyboard. The alphabetic keyboard is nearly identical with that of a typewriter. Other office machines that have typewriter-like keyboards are the card punch, teletype, Computyper, automatic typewriter, and the input writer on the computer console. These machines are discussed in later chapters of this book.

All of these machines have an operational keyboard that conforms closely to that of a standard typewriter. Thus a typist can operate them with a minimum of additional instruction and training.

▪ Selecting Typewriter Ribbons

Fabric ribbons are used on typewriters that have the standard twin-spool mechanism. Film-base and carbon-paper ribbons are used only on machines that have the required special oversize-spool mechanism. Most electrics can use both the film or carbon-paper ribbon and the regular fabric ribbon, and some have an arrangement where a flick of a switch will make the transition.

There is no standardization of spools among typewriter manufacturers; ribbons are wound on some fifty different kinds of spools! To get the proper kind of spool, therefore, you must request a ribbon for the specific make and model of your typewriter.

Thinness. The sharpness of your typewritten work will depend upon the thinness of the ribbon you use—the thinner the ribbon, the sharper the imprint. Also, the thinner the ribbon, the more yardage there is on a spool, which means longer use, which in turn means less frequent ribbon change. Ribbons range from cotton (the thickest), to silk, to nylon, to carbon paper, to coated Mylar or polyethylene film (the thinnest).

	TYPEWRITER RIBBON CHART
Film Ribbon *Mylar or Polyethylene*	—Highest quality ribbon available. Produces sharp, print-like image. Used for prestige correspondence. Excellent for photocopy work. Thinnest and strongest of all film ribbon. Break free. Lint free. Life usually limited to one use.
Carbon-Paper Ribbon	—Produces good image. Used extensively for correspondence and photocopy work. Breaks easily. Lint free. Life limited to one use.
Fabric Ribbon *Silk or Nylon*	—Finest quality fabric ribbon. Produces clear, sharp image that compares favorably with film and carbon-paper ribbons. Lint free. Extra long life. Obtainable in light, medium, and heavy inking.
Cotton	—Available in a variety of grades. Less expensive and shorter life than silk or nylon. Used primarily for routine correspondence, production typing, and for filling in forms. Deposits lint on keys. Obtainable in light, medium, medium heavy, and heavy inking.

Fabric Ribbons. Of the fabric ribbons, nylon ones wear the longest, then silk, then cotton. They are all available in any of several colors or bicolors and in varying degrees of ink concentration.

Film-Base and Carbon Ribbons. The carbon-paper and film-base ribbons are a continuous narrow strip of carbon paper or coated Mylar, acetate, or polyethylene film. They are generally preferred by secretaries for quality work because they print very sharply and do not fill the letters. They are the cleanest ribbons to handle. Also, copy erases easily.

Selection of Stationery Supplies

Most supplies with which a secretary works are available in a wide range of quality. Many factors, particularly the use and quality, must be considered in the selection of supplies.

■ Bond Paper

Bond paper is so called because originally it was used for printing bonds, which had to have long-lasting qualities. It can be made from all-cotton fiber (sometimes called *rag*), from all-sulfite (a wood pulp), or from any proportion of the two. High-cotton-fiber bond bespeaks quality and prestige, and it ages without deterioration or chemical breakdown. It has a good, crisp crackle. It is hard to the pencil touch and is difficult to tear. High-sulfite bond is limper, softer to the pencil touch, and easier to tear.

There are excellent all-sulfite papers in crepelike, ripple, or pebble finishes that many companies use exclusively. Letterhead paper is usually made of 25 percent, or more, cotton-fiber bond. Forms for business records which need last only two or three years are made of all-sulfite or high-sulfite bond.

Watermarks. Hold a letterhead up to the light. See the design or words? That is the *watermark*. It can be the name or trademark of the company using the paper or the brand name of the paper. Since only better bonds are watermarked, the mark is a hallmark of quality.

There is a right side and a top edge to the plain watermarked sheets. Always have the watermark read across the sheet in the same direction as the typing. Put watermarked sheets in your stationery drawer in such a manner that they will be in the right position automatically when they are inserted into the typewriter.

Substance. The weight of paper is described by a substance number. The number is based on the weight of a ream consisting of 500 sheets of 17- by 22-inch paper. If the ream weighs 20 pounds, the paper is said to be of substance 20, or 20-pound weight. Two thousand sheets of 8½- by 11-inch paper can be cut from one ream. Paper is produced in a wide range of weights.

Regular letterheads and envelopes are usually of substance 16, 20, or 24. Airmail stationery is of substance 9 or 13. Other weights, however, are available.

Erasability. You can erase typing from some bond papers with exceeding ease. This feature is usually indicated in the brand name of the paper, such as *Ezerase*. Both ribbon and carbon typing barely rest on the surface of paper of this kind. You can quickly and neatly remove the typing with a pencil eraser while the error is fresh, but you can also easily smear or smudge the surrounding typing. The most difficult papers on which to make neat erasures and corrections are the inexpensive all-sulfite ones, such as those you used in your typing course. A neat erasure can be made without too much difficulty on a 16-pound high-cotton-fiber bond.

▪ Second Sheets

The thin sheets used for file copies of letters and for multicopy typing are described as *onionskin, manifold,* or simply *second sheets.* They are of light-weight paper of substances 7 to 13, in smooth, glazed, or cockle (rippled) finish. A stack of these sheets can be difficult to control because they tend to slither and slide—mostly onto the floor. To avoid frustration, select a finish that has low "slipperiness." Sheets with cockle finish slip less than others and give the appearance of being of better quality, but they create more bulk in the files than do smooth-finish ones.

Copy sheets are used in many offices. They are second sheets with the word COPY printed on them and are used for copies of matter that should be so identified. When specially marked sheets are not supplied, the word COPY should be typed conspicuously on plain second sheets. It should be centered and letterspaced in all capital letters about 1⅓ inches from the top of the sheet.

▪ Letterheads

Letterheads vary widely and depend upon individual taste and the nature of the company's business. Most large companies have a standard company letterhead designed for use by lower and middle management personnel. These letterheads are produced by offset and are standardized to include the company's name, address, telephone number, (including area code) and name and title of the individual. The letterhead sometimes contains information about the company's products or displays the company trademark. All letterheads may be ordered with matching envelopes and blank sheets for the two-page letter.

Top executives usually have "prestige" letterheads that differ from the standard company letterhead in style, printing process, weight of paper, and cotton-fiber content. The cotton-fiber content usually ranges from 50 to 100 percent, and some executives use what is called "101 percent rag," meaning 100 percent cotton fiber of unusually fine quality.

The letterhead of a top executive usually shows only the company name, address (no phone number), and the executive's name and title. In addition, the executive may have a personal letterhead which he uses mainly for outside work with foundations and charity organizations. His personal letterhead may show only his name and address or his name only. In general, as an individual's position becomes elevated in the company, his letterhead becomes more simplified, presenting an appearance of dignity befitting the position.

▪ Carbon Paper

Conventional typewriter carbon paper is thin, dark-colored tissue, coated on one side with carbon. It is available in a great variety of sizes, colors, weights, finishes, and qualities. It is available in special-purpose packs as well as in single sheets.

Topcoated Carbon Paper. Heat and humidity cause carbon paper to curl so that it is frustrating to handle. Most carbon paper now is coated on the uncarboned, or top side, with a metallic, plastic, or varnish finish that makes the sheet curl-free or curl-resistant. The top coating reduces wrinkling; wrinkling "trees" or "veins" the copy. High-quality topcoated carbon paper not only is smudge free but also produces a neater copy and permits more extensive use than does low-quality carbon. Uncoated carbon paper looks worn after a few uses, and a sheet of carbon paper is usually destroyed on the basis of looks—not by scrutiny of the carbon typing it does.

LETTERHEADS AND ENVELOPES

Letterheads

Standard Company: Usually of 16# or 20# bond, 25% cotton-fiber (rag) content

Top Executives: Usually of 24# bond, 100% cotton-fiber content

Envelopes to Match Letterheads

Large: No. 9 (3 7/8" by 8 7/8")   Same weight and fiber content
No. 10 (4 1/8" by 9 1/2")   as letterhead

Small: No. 6 1/4 (3 1/2" by 6")
No. 6 3/4 (3 5/8" by 6 1/2")   For one-page messages

Letterheads (Executive or Professional Sizes[1]): Usually 20# or 24# bond, 50% or more cotton-fiber content

Plain Sheets to Match Letterheads: Same weight, cotton-fiber content, and size as letterhead. Always use plain sheet of matching paper for second page of two-page letter. NEVER use a letterhead for the second page or subsequent ones.

Airmail Envelopes to Match Letterheads: Executive or business size, usually of 9# or 13#. If no airmail envelope is available, use a regular one and fold and attach an airmail sticker over each short edge (because mail sorters cubby-hole sorted mail with the short edges out—and they can see that it is to go airmail if the sticker is over the end). If an airmail sticker is not available, type *AIRMAIL* below the stamp and conspicuously border or underline the word, preferably in red.

Interoffice Letterheads: Business size[2] or smaller; usually of sulfite

Interoffice Envelopes: Oversize, strong, perforated, reusable envelopes with many ruled lines for names of successive addressees

Oversize Envelopes: Strong, white, manila or brown-paper envelopes in which letters and reports can be mailed flat; 9" by 12", or 10" by 13"; gummed flaps, with or without metal clasps

---

[1]*Executive- or professional-size letterheads:* 7¼" by 10½"
[2]*Business-size letterheads:* 8½" by 11"

OTHER PAPER SUPPLIES

Carbon Copy Paper: Thin sheets, usually 8# to 13#, in various sizes, colors, and finishes. Frequently called *second sheets*.

Copy Sheets: Sheets imprinted with the word C O P Y

Carbon Set: A ready-assembled one-use sheet of carbon paper attached to a plain or copy sheet (available for multiple copies also)

Carbonless Paper: Major types—

   (1) A blue or purple sheet with a white wax coating. The force of the typewriter key pushes the white wax aside. The dark color that shows through gives the effect of carbon paper. The sheet mars and scars easily in handling and folding.

   (2) Ink-impregnated paper, sometimes called NCR (*No Carbon Required*, manufactured by the National Cash Register Company). The force of the typewriter key releases the ink and reproduces the letter or character.

Carbon Paper: For description and use, see pages 73 and 76–78.

Duplicator Paper: Business[1] and legal[2] sizes, white and colors, various substances; often called by the process the paper is made for, such as mimeograph paper, offset paper. *Duplicating* paper usually refers to paper designed for use with the direct-process duplicator.

Forms: Usually in pads to prevent waste. Multicopy forms may be continuous, accordion-folded, and perforated. After the "chain" is inserted in the typewriter to type the first set, the rest feed through automatically. Accordion-folded forms often have spot-carbon coating on the back of each copy exactly where the typing is to appear on the copy underneath, to eliminate handling interleaved carbon.

Labels, Return Address: Small slips of paper showing company's return address. Are usually gummed on the back.

Legal Paper: Top-quality legal-size[2] bond; plain or with ruled margins

Manila Sheets: Thin sheets for typing rough drafts or carbons, legal size or business size

Plain Sheets: Paper 8 1/2″ by 11″, usually 13# to 16#, most often used for reports and for general typing. May or may not be of easy-to-erase bond.

Writing Pads:

Ruled Paper: Legal size or business size, usually yellow

Scratch: Assorted sizes. Usually sold by the pound.

---

[1]*Business-size:* 8½″ by 11″
[2]*Legal Size:* 8½″ by 13″ and 8½″ by 14″

Plastic-Base Carbon Paper. Although identified as carbon paper, technically plastic-base carbon sheets are described more accurately as copying film because they employ ink, not carbon; and they consist of film, not paper. A plastic-base sheet (Mylar or polyethylene film) serves as a microscopically thin plastic sponge that forms a coating of tiny, interconnecting cells, each containing liquid ink. The force of the typewriter key squeezes the sponge so that the ink is released on the typing paper. As soon as the type bar lifts, the ink flows back into the unused area, thus re-inking the sheet, which may be used repeatedly. The ink dries immediately; therefore, the copy is smudge free. Plastic-base carbon paper is curl free, easily handled, and difficult to tear. It never trees, comes in one weight and finish only, and makes from 1 to 10 copies in one writing. It has a 50- to 60-time usage.

Carbon Paper Finish. Different finishes or coatings are used for carbon paper, from soft that writes like a soft black pencil, to hard that writes like a hard gray pencil. The finish to be used depends upon such factors as electric or manual typewriter, size of type face, hardness of cylinder, and "blackness" of copy desired.

A lightweight carbon paper with a hard finish produces the sharpest impressions. Plastic-base carbon paper is being used increasingly by secretaries for top-quality work.

GUIDE TO SELECTION OF CARBON PAPER FINISH

Soft Finish — USE IF—typewriter has a soft cylinder.
—typist has a light typing touch.
—copies are grayer than desired when using other finishes.

DO NOT USE IF—typewriter has elite or smaller type face.

Hard Finish — USE IF—typewriter has a hard cylinder.
—typist has a heavy touch.
—typewriter has elite or smaller type face.
—gray copy is desired.

Medium Finish — USE—for all typing situations not covered above.

Guide to Using Carbon Papers. The following guides have been provided for easy reference. These guides must be adjusted to compensate for such variables as hardness of cylinder, touch (if manual), pressure adjustment (if electric), and desired uniformity of copies. As you gain experience, you will be able to predict and adjust for the effect of each of these factors.

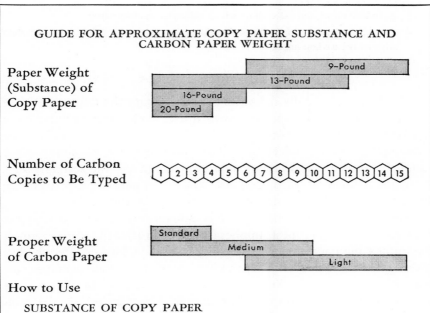

GUIDE FOR APPROXIMATE COPY PAPER SUBSTANCE AND CARBON PAPER WEIGHT

Paper Weight (Substance) of Copy Paper

9–Pound
13–Pound
16–Pound
20–Pound

Number of Carbon Copies to Be Typed

1 2 3 4 5 6 7 8 9 10 11 12 13 14 15

Proper Weight of Carbon Paper

Standard
Medium
Light

How to Use

SUBSTANCE OF COPY PAPER

Find number of carbon copies to be typed.
Look directly above to determine substance of paper to use.
When more than one shaded bar, use any one of the substances indicated.

WEIGHT OF CARBON PAPER

Find number of carbon copies to be typed.
Look directly below to determine weight of carbon paper to use.
When more than one shaded bar, use the heaviest weight indicated, for it will give the longest wear.

EXAMPLE: To type 11 carbon copies use 9# or 13# paper and light-weight carbon.
To type five carbon copies use 13# or 16# paper and medium-weight carbon.

Special-Feature Carbon Papers. Many carbon papers have special features that contribute to efficient and convenient usage. Features include:

1. Extended bottom-edge carbon paper that is one-half inch longer than the typing paper
2. Extended bottom-edge carbon paper with small cutoffs at the top-left and bottom-right corners
3. Extended clean, uncoated, bottom- or side-edge carbon paper
4. A numbered guide to the lines remaining, printed on a clean, extended right edge of the carbon paper

Procuring Supplies

The executive usually delegates to the secretary the responsibility of procuring office supplies proper for their use. Unless the executive has a special need or high cost factors are involved, the secretary uses her own judgment in making selections. The procedures for obtaining office supplies differ for the secretary in a large office and the secretary in a small office; however, each one must "know" supplies in order to choose those that best fill particular executive and secretarial needs.

The secretary in the small office is a direct buyer. The secretary in the large office may request supplies from a central stock, or may request the purchasing department to buy a specific item for her after she has investigated those available. If she has supervisory responsibilities, she may select and purchase for a department or company. In this case, she must make use of the sources of product information to learn the comparative factors and to find dependable sources. Then she must follow businesslike purchasing procedures.

▪ Quality of Supplies

Some businesses feel it is important to use only the highest quality stationery and office supplies; others feel medium quality is appropriate to their situation. Every office uses a pride factor and an economic factor to determine the level of quality it follows. You will not find this quality level precisely stated or written out for you, nor is it a question you can tactfully ask. You will have to deduce it by observation of the present supplies and by cost records.

A SUGGESTION. To reinforce paper to go into a loose-leaf notebook, attach a strip of tape along the back edge of the paper where the holes will be. Punch holes through both tape and paper.

▪ Local Sources of Supply

Local office-supply stores cannot carry all varieties of all brands of all office supplies. Each store carries one or two brands of an item (perhaps not your favorite) in the varieties most commonly sold (none of which may exactly fill your need). Therefore, your selection is limited and often you cannot buy as discriminatingly as you would like.

Salesmen. Representatives of local office-supply agencies may call on you with samples or catalogs and prices. They, too, limit themselves in brands and varieties, so choice is again restricted. The secretary orders over the telephone from the salesman or from his office. Since you cannot possibly know everything about all supplies, it is helpful to have a dependable salesman of whom you can ask advice. When you are in the market for an item, tell him your exact needs. He is trained to help you make a wise selection.

Brand-Name Supplies. Sometimes you want a *specific variety of a specific brand.* If the variety is not sold locally, you can order it from the manufacturer, or you can ask your local office-supply store to order it for you.

Some pieces of equipment, you may decide, produce better results if you use the supplies that are sold by the manufacturer, such as A. B. Dick ink for the Mimeograph, or Gestetner correction fluid for Gestetner stencils. If no local source is listed in the telephone book, order such supplies from the manufacturer.

▪ Collecting Information

Collect specific information about each kind of office supply you use. Suppliers furnish helpful literature. Descriptive, informative folders are often furnished by salesmen or are given away at exhibits of office equipment and supplies. Collect and file such information by subject. It will help you be a better buyer.

▪ Choosing Supplies

Choose supplies that are in the quality range of your office. There is no economy in cheap supplies. Unknown brands may contain inferior materials or may be off-size and, consequently, may be more expensive in the long run than the better grades. *Usually you get just about what you pay for.* A carbon paper of good quality gives many more writings.

Low-priced duplicating inks of poor quality oils and pigments make fewer copies than high-grade inks. The ingredients in cheap inks often separate when the machine stands idle, and the oil seeps through the mechanism.

There is no reason for shifting from one brand of supply to another as long as the one in use is satisfactory and fair in price. On the other hand, supplies are constantly being changed; a product may now be made of entirely different materials and hence greatly improved since the last time you examined or tested it.

When contemplating a change in brand, get samples of competing products and test them all under the same circumstances. Study the findings of published governmental and technical tests. Compare net prices and quality. Analyze the extra service or added efficiency claimed; if the price is higher, try to determine whether the difference is justified in your office.

■ Overbuying

Some office supplies deteriorate when they are held in stock too long; for example, carbon paper dries and hardens, typewriter ribbons dry out, some paper becomes yellow, liquids evaporate, and erasers harden. New products that come out may be preferable to those you have stocked. It is better, then, to err on the side of underbuying than of overbuying. Repeat orders can always be placed shortly before supplies are needed.

You may want to overbuy because of quantity prices. An item that costs 50 cents a unit in small quantities usually costs appreciably less when bought in larger quantities; consequently, it may seem to be economical to order in large amounts. The monetary saving is not always the prime consideration, however. If overbuying results, the economy is dissipated: witness the secretary who bought a dozen quart bottles of ink to get a lower unit price, when her office used one quart of ink a year. Imagine what could happen to ink that is stored ten years!

Some suppliers of duplicating paper have arrangements whereby a year's supply may be purchased at one time; thus you obtain the price advantage of bulk purchase. The paper is delivered in specific lots at designated intervals through the year. Such a plan provides a price advantage without the necessity of storing paper before it is actually needed.

Jerome Builders, Inc.

929 Purdue Avenue   Rockford, Illinois **61101**

564-3796

PURCHASE REQUISITION

DATE	August 10, 19--
PURCHASE REQUISITION NUMBER	2240
DATE WANTED	August 25, 19--
DEPARTMENT	Sales
ATTENTION OF	L. Cox, Stock Clerk
REQUISITIONED BY	A. Riley, Secretary
APPROVED BY	R. Baer, Manager

S
U
G
G
E
S
T
E
D

V
E
N
D
O
R

• Office Supply Company
• Blair Building
• 7039 S. Main Street
• Chicago, Illinois 60606

TO THE PURCHASING AGENT: Please order the items listed below:

QUANTITY	DESCRIPTION	CATALOG NUMBER	PRICE	TOTAL
1 M	Gem Clips			
2	Metal Desk Trays, Letter-size, #17			
1 doz.	Star Transparent Tape, #2			
2 gross	Superb Pencils, Grade F			
1 gross	Superb Pencils, #3			

Note that in this purchase requisition for office supplies, the secretary requisitioned the supplies by both brand name and an identifying description. The other columns are for the convenience of the purchasing agent in filling out the purchase order for these supplies.

■ Requisitions and Invoices

In a large company, most of the supplies are kept in stock and are obtained by submitting a supplies requisition. Items not carried in stock must be requested by submitting a purchase requisition to the purchasing department. This form should provide as detailed a description of the item needed as the secretary can provide, as indicated above.

If the secretary or supervisor has the authority to purchase supplies, she has added responsibilities. She must make a careful record of each item purchased or ordered, check out the delivery of the items, and verify the accuracy of the items and extensions of the invoice or bill that accompanies or follows delivery.

When an item is invoiced (included and charged on an invoice) but is omitted, substituted, or defective, the secretary annotates that fact on the invoice and requests an adjustment.

> REVISING supply purchasing and control procedures has reduced one company's per year employee cost of stationery supplies over 25 percent.
> —*Administrative Management*

81

■ Supply Storage

If you wish to determine how neat and orderly a secretary really is, examine her supply storage cabinet. Certainly a storage cabinet that presents an array of boxes, packages, and articles in complete disorder is no recommendation for her efficiency.

The well-arranged storage cabinet has several characteristics. Like materials are placed together. Materials used most frequently are placed to the front at the most convenient level for reaching. Small items are placed at eye level; bulk supplies and reserve stock are placed on the lower shelves. Shelf depths should be adjustable to fit the items and conserve space.

All packages are identified in oversize lettering made with a felt-nub marking pen, or by a sample of the contents affixed to the front. Unpadded stationery items are kept in flip-up, open-end boxes. (There are no carelessly torn-open, paper-wrapped packages.) Loose supplies, such as paper clips, are kept separately in marked open boxes. A list of all supplies by shelves is often posted on the inside of the door.

Suggested Readings

"Coping with Carbons," *Today's Secretary*. (New York: Gregg Division of McGraw-Hill Book Company, Inc., 1965), Vol. 68, No. 2 (October, 1965), pp. 36, 75.

"Film and Fabric Ribbons for All Office Machines," *Administrative Management*. (New York: Geyer-McAllister Publications, 1965), Vol. XXVI, No. 2 (December, 1965), pp. 34–39.

"Paper for Your Correspondence," *Administrative Management*. (New York: Geyer-McAllister Publications, 1967), Vol. XXVIII, No. 6 (June, 1967), pp. 70–77.

"Selecting and Buying Executive Letterheads," *Administrative Management*. (New York: Geyer-McAllister Publications, 1965), Vol. XXVI, No. 8 (August, 1965), pp. 36–40.

"Special Abilities of Today's Typewriters," *Administrative Management*. (New York: Geyer-McAllister Publications, 1965), Vol. XXVI, No. 6 (June, 1965), pp. 64–72.

Questions for Discussion

1. As secretary to the president of a large corporation, what special features would you prefer to have on your typewriter? As secretary to a news commentator? As secretary to the head of the research division of a chemical company? As secretary to the head of the accounting department?

2. A government study reported that an electric typewriter is justified when typing time averages four hours or more a day, when the work requires a substantial number of carbons, or when copy is being produced for photo offset. This study led one office manager to conclude: "A secretary who has access to a typing pool for her boss's correspondence and who types only occasionally would let an electric sit idle most of the day. The lower priced manual will serve her purpose as well." Do you agree with this conclusion? State your reasons.

3. One of the sales arguments presented for the proportional-spacing typewriter is that it facilitates justifying (making even) the right margin. Some people object to the appearance of a letter that has the right margin justified. They say the letter looks too "symmetrical," is not personal, and carries the initial impression of being a form letter. Express your opinion. Under what circumstances would you recommend the purchase of one or more such typewriters?

4. Refer to the guide on page 77. What substance paper and what carbon-paper weight would you select if you were making (a) 8 carbons, (b) 13 carbons, (c) 3 carbons, (d) 5 carbons?

5. Your text refers to "prestige" letterheads. In what ways may a so-called "prestige" letter differ in appearance from other correspondence?

6. You note that a carbon copy produced by your assistant lacks sharpness and is gray in appearance. Upon further checking you find that the carbon you examined was the fifth copy. What are some of the factors you would consider in your effort to improve the quality of the carbons she produces? What procedure would you recommend in your effort to help her improve the quality of her carbon copies?

7. You are aware that your assistant is in the habit of taking office stationery, stamps, and other materials for her own personal correspondence and needs. What is your responsibility, and how would you handle the situation?

8. Suppose that the individual described in Question 7 is another secretary over whom you have no authoritative jurisdiction. Is your responsibility the same? What would you do?

9. Revise the following sentences. Then refer to the Reference Guide to correct your answers.

(a) It is the consensus of opinion that the buildings are both alike—they have greatly depreciated in value.

(b) The sum total of my experience leads me to believe they are both alike.

(c) It is unnecessary for me to repeat again that we would like to have your payment during the month of October.

If the executive frequently dictated these redundant terms, would you point out their redundancy? If so, how?

Problems

■ **1.** Every secretary must know how to change both film and fabric typewriter ribbons in an efficient manner. An office supervisor might need to demonstrate these tasks. Practice these operations so that you can give an expert demonstration before the class.

■ **2.** Select one type of office supply for special study. The following suggestions are made, but another type may be used.

(a) Typewriter ribbons
(b) Paper for letterheads
(c) Carbon paper and carbonless paper
(d) Type cleaners
(e) Correction products
(f) Interchangeable typewriter symbols

Become a semi-authority on the chosen item—its use, cost, quality, advantages, disadvantages. Give a class demonstration or compile a written report for Mr. Simpson.

■ **3.** Some companies and institutions require detailed specifications to accompany all requests for the purchase of equipment. In the case of a typewriter, for example, the specifications would cover such items as carriage length, cylinder hardness, line spacing, keyboard, special keys, type face, special features and attachments.

Assume you are to be employed as secretary in one of the following departments of your college: mathematics, chemistry, library, engineering, law (select the one with which you are most familiar). You are asked to submit an order, with accompanying specifications, for a typewriter. Compile and present the specifications for the typewriter and prepare an accompanying report of the procedures you used to determine the special features needed.

Related Work Assignments 10-13

10. Ordering Supplies. An examination of your supply cabinet indicates that a number of supplies should be ordered. Prepare purchase requisitions for the following supplies. Use what you learned in this chapter to give all needed details.

> *Requisition No. 101:* **2,000 business-size letterheads for general correspondence**
> **1,000 matching plain sheets**
> **1,000 No. 10 envelopes**
> **2,000 executive-size letterheads (best quality)**
> **1,000 envelopes to match**
>
> *Requisition No. 102:* **2 film ribbons for your own TYPEX Executive typewriter**
> **2 REGAL manual typewriter ribbons, best quality, for your assistant whose typewriter is equipped with elite type and a hard cylinder**
> **50 carbon sets, letter size**
> **20 packs of carbon paper (100 sheets to the pack)**

11. Listing Outstanding Features of Electric Typewriters.

12. Evaluating Note-O-Gram Form.

13. Your Fundamentals.

} The instructions and supplies necessary for the completion of Related Work Assignments 11, 12, and 13 are provided in the Workbook.

The Secretary—Master Typist

How expensive are the business letters you will produce as a secretary? The Dartnell Corporation reports that the average cost of a business letter is over $2.49 and that the cost is increasing each year. Indeed this is no small amount.

Each partly completed letter that finds its way into the waste basket because of an uncorrectible error represents real dollars and cents. Each letter which is marred by a smudge, an obvious erasure, dirty or faint type, or poor page placement fails to look like the $2.49 cost package it represents.

The cost figure explains why top-level secretaries search constantly for ways to increase not only their own output but also the efficiency of those whom they supervise. The first prerequisite for efficiency is "know-how." This chapter presents some of the know-how that practicing secretaries and supervisors use in their continuous drive to produce in the most efficient manner high-quality work that represents their organization as effectively as possible. Practice the techniques new to you so that you may add them to the skills you bring to your work.

You and Your Typewriter

You will quickly become accustomed to "your" typewriter in the office if you will, first, *explore and learn its capabilities;* and, second, *give it the care it requires.* Remember the old adage: The poor workman quarrels with his tools.

■ Instruction Booklets

Every typewriter has a helpful, reassuring booklet of instructions on its use. The booklet accompanies the machine on delivery but often disappears before the machine does. If your predecessor has not left the instruction booklet for you, request one from the manufacturer. It will save you time and give you confident know-how. There is nothing worse than fighting a strange, militant typewriter that has hidden resources.

Learn the capacities of your typewriter. It may have features that you are not aware of, such as aids to accurate repositioning of typing, scales to determine center positions, fractional spacing devices, and tabulating timesavers. The special features of your typewriter are illustrated and explained in the instruction booklet.

▪ Typewriter Care

Even though a typewriter is sturdy and almost self-sufficient, it does require a modicum of attention from you. Read the machine-care section of your instruction booklet. Follow it faithfully or follow the recommendations on page 87.

Handling Carbon Paper

The typing techniques given here may seem commonplace, but the procedures will be those used by master typists. They will help you to produce quality typing and to save motions, time, and material.

▪ Carbon Sheets

You will find the following practices in using carbon sheets to be papersavers and timesavers:

1. Keep your desk supply of carbon sheets flat, carbon side down to prevent curling, away from heat or dampness, and inside a folder or box.

2. Reverse carbon sheets end for end each time you use them, because the carbon quickly wears off where the date line and other letter-part positions fall.

3. Discard a sheet at once if it becomes wrinkled or treed. It will never be usable.

4. Do not discard a sheet just because it looks worn or because the shine is off the carbon side. Check instead the clarity of the last copy typed. Discard the carbon sheet only when the copy is faint.

5. Use extended bottom-edge carbon paper with cutoff corners for the most efficient removal and reuse. If the carbon sheets are square cornered, lay them carbon side down and cut off one-inch triangles from the top-left and bottom-right corners. This space provides room to hold the set of typed sheets and to remove the set of carbons intact in one quick, clean pull. See the illustrations on page 89.

6. Use carbon sheets with cutoff corners as a visible check of the proper insertion of the carbon pack. When the carbon pack is in typing position, you can see through the top page if the cutoff corners are at the top left. If they are at the right, the carbon pack has been inserted carbon side up (which happens occasionally to the best of secretaries).

FOR A LONGER LASTING, MORE RESPONSIVE TYPEWRITER:

1. **Prevent Dust from Accumulating.** Dust and erasure grit cripple and prematurely age a typewriter.
   (a) NEVER erase over the type basket. Instead move the carriage to one side; then erase.
   (b) ALWAYS cover the typewriter when you leave for the day, to prevent the dust stirred up by the cleaning force from settling into the typewriter. Clean the cover with a damp cloth.

2. **Dust the Typewriter Daily.**
   (a) Use an inexpensive, long-handled, watercolor paint brush to dust the hard-to-reach parts.
   (b) Brush toward you, away from the mechanism.
   (c) Dust under the machine, because air currents carry particles up into the mechanism.

3. **Clean the Keys Whenever a Single One Is Filled Up.** Clean the keys gently; avoid pushing them out of alignment. Do not use a pin or a liquid cleaner. Clean the keys in one of these ways:
   (a) Roll a type-cleaning sheet (paper with a chemically treated fiber surface that picks up dirt from type face) into typing position; set the ribbon for stencil and strike each letter several times until the imprint is clean and sharp. This is the cleanest method.
   (b) Use a plastic type cleaner. Press the plastic firmly against the type and pull it away. Repeat the process until keys are clean. Knead and fold the plastic for reuse.
   (c) With a stiff, dry, short-bristled brush, use a light tapping motion —not a gouging motion. Clean the brush by rubbing it on scratch paper frequently.

4. **Protect the Cylinder (Platen).** Keep the cylinder clean. If ink and dust collect on it, it becomes shiny and loses its grip.
   (a) Use a cloth lightly moistened with alcohol to clean the cylinder.
   (b) If the cylinder is removable, lift it out and dust the trough.
   (c) Never lift a typewriter by the cylinder knobs.

5. **Lubricate Sparingly.** Too much oil is harmful. Lubricate only the carriage rail, and oil that only lightly. Keep oil away from rubber parts.

6. **Protect the Paper-Feed Rolls.** To prevent flat spots from developing, release the paper-feed rolls whenever the machine is not in use.

7. **Arrange for Periodic Servicing.** Check the service guarantee. Arrange with a local agency to check, oil, and service your typewriter periodically to keep it in top condition. Service contracts may prove to be economical, also.

▪ Carbon Packs

The number of carbon copies being prepared in the office has been decreasing. This has occurred because of the wide distribution and improvements in copying machines. The making of corrections on multiple carbons is a slow and costly process. Consequently, if a number of copies of a letter, report, or transcript are needed, it may be less expensive to type only the original and reproduce the copies with the copying machine. To assume, however, that the secretary will not need to be skilled in handling carbon paper is unwarranted. The copying machine has not eliminated the carbon copy; in large offices it has merely tended to reduce the number of carbon copies to be prepared.

> TIME SAVER. Suppose you are typing an envelope and want the address on a card for your address file. You can type the address on the envelope and on the file card at the same time. Simply put the card, with a square of carbon paper backed up to it, inside the envelope before addressing the envelope.

Making Up a Carbon Pack. Two common methods used in making up and inserting a carbon pack are the *desk method* and the *machine method.*

Desk Method. Using the following procedure, build the carbon pack on the desk and insert it directly into the typewriter, using a leader to keep the pack straight.

1. **Place a sheet of paper for a carbon copy on the desk; on top of that sheet, place a sheet of carbon paper, *glossy side down.* Add one set (a second sheet and a carbon) for each extra copy desired. Place a letterhead or a plain sheet of heavier paper on top of the pack for the original copy.**

2. **Turn the pack around so the glossy sides of the carbon sheets face you.**

3. **To keep the sheets straight when feeding, use a *leader*—place the pack in the fold of an envelope or in the fold of a narrow folded piece of paper.**

4. **Straighten the pack by tapping the sheets gently on the desk.**

5. **Insert the leadered pack with a quick turn of the cylinder, roll it up, and remove the leader.**

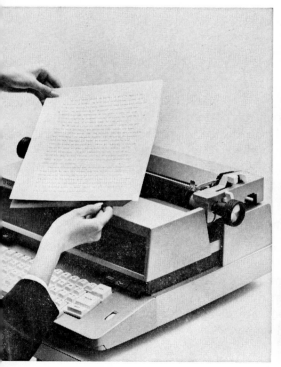

—Royal Typewriter Company, Inc.

Use of an envelope or a folded slip of paper as a leader helps the master typist insert a carbon pack into the typewriter rapidly and evenly. Correct positioning of the cutoff triangles in opposite corners of the carbon pack permits easy removal of the carbons from the pack.

Machine Method. Using the following procedure, build the carbon pack right in the machine.

1. **Arrange the required number and kinds of sheets for insertion into the typewriter.**

2. **Insert the sheets, turning the cylinder until they are gripped slightly by the feed rolls; then bring all but the last sheet forward over the cylinder.**

3. **Place the carbon sheets between the sheets of paper with the carbonized surface (glossy side) toward you. Flip each sheet back as you add each carbon.**

4. **Roll the pack into typing position.**

5. **When the typing is completed, roll the pack nearly to the bottom of the sheets. Operate the paper-release lever and remove the copy sheets by pulling them out with left hand. The paper fingers will automatically hold the carbon sheets in the machine to be removed with the right hand.**

Bottom-Line Slippage. To control bottom-line slippage, roll the pack back to about midpage. Drop a sheet of paper from the back between the original and the first carbon. Roll the pack forward. As you type near the bottom, the extra sheet will hold the pack securely in place. Steady the top sheet with the left forefinger if necessary.

Corrections

Typewriter corrections that defy detection are hallmarks of the master typist. They are an absolute necessity to quality typing. In fact, if any correction is evident in an otherwise excellent piece of typing, the typescript drops from quality level. The three techniques of making nonevident corrections are complete, contained erasures; perfect positioning; and matched typing.

▪ Complete, Contained Erasures

A neat erasure results from the skillful use of erasing tools. The erasing tools are easily obtained, but erasing skill must be acquired.

Erasures. You will use two kinds of erasers—a pencil or other soft eraser to remove surface ink that might smear and an abrasive eraser to remove imbedded ink. Try various brands and shapes of erasers until you find those that you can use most effectively on your office stationery. Keep the erasers clean by rubbing them on an emery board kept at the typewriter for that purpose. Attach the eraser to the typewriter to assure its always being available and have a second one handy, as you would a pen or pencil.

Erasing Shields. Erasing shields are basic to neat and complete erasures. A fastidious typist develops the habit of having shields quickly available and of using them automatically whenever erasures are to be made. Erasing shields are of two kinds for two different purposes:

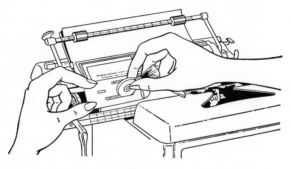

An Erasing-Area Shield. A flat metal or plastic shield with letter-height open spaces is used in or out of the typewriter to confine the erasing. It permits erasing to the extreme edge of an error, yet protects adjacent letters. Lightened or fuzzy letters around an imperceptible correction are telltale and not acceptable in quality typing, for they call attention to the erased area.

A Thick, Pressure-Proof Shield. A shield of metal, rubber, or card stock is used to protect the carbon copies under the page being erased. The shield is placed immediately under the erasing area and on *top* of the carbon. A curved metal shield that hugs the cylinder gives best protection and is easiest to find among papers on the desk. Second best device is a 2- by 6-inch piece of rubber that can be cut from a discarded innertube. It, too, conforms to the cylinder and is easy to find. Some typists use a 5- by 3-inch card as a shield. A card, however, often gets lost among the correspondence because of its whiteness unless it is carefully and consistently placed in a special section of the typist's well-planned working area.

NEVER use a set of paper slips behind the carbons as erasing shields. They are timewasters!

Cover-Ups. White cover-ups that blend into the paper are often applied over an erasure or error. *To fade-out an erasure,* rub a whitening agent into the paper before typing the correction. You can use a piece of chalk, a Ditto correction pencil, an aspirin, or a commercially made touch-up stick. To *cover up an error,* paint over it with a white correction fluid that has been made to match the exact whiteness of the paper. Or put a chalk-coated strip of paper, coated side down, over the error and retype the *error* so that some of the chalk transfers and covers it. Then go back and type in the correction. A special type of correction paper is available for use on carbon copies and with carbon ribbons. Cover-ups are usually more conspicuous than complete, whitened erasures.

Erasing on Ribbon and Carbon Copies. There are many brief but important steps in making a complete and neat erasure:

1. Erase the original first, then the carbon copies. This sequence could save time should you find that the original cannot be erased satisfactorily.
2. Hold the margin release down and move the carriage to one side to avoid erasing over the type basket.
3. Turn the copy forward so that the erasure can be made completely. If the error is near the bottom of the page, roll the paper backward to prevent the carbon pack from slipping.
4. Rub a punctuation mark to be erased from a ribbon copy with your thumbnail on the back of the sheet. The mark, imbedded in the paper, erases more completely if pressed outward.
5. Clean the surfaces of the erasers on an emery board.
6. For each copy to be erased, insert a *pressure-proof* shield under the error and on top of the carbon sheet underneath.
7. For each copy to be erased, position the *erasing-area* shield over the error so as to protect adjacent typing. It may take several positionings to complete the erasure.
8. First use plastic type cleaner, if available, to remove as much of the surface ink or carbon as possible. Press the plastic cleaner down on the error and lift off. Place the plastic on the end of a toothpick or orange stick if necessary. Plastic cleaner is also good for removing a smudge from carbon copies. If plastic type cleaner is not available, use a pencil or soft eraser.
9. Then use an abrasive eraser with light strokes in *one* direction only. Use a "digging-lift" stroke in place of a "scrubbing" action.
10. If necessary, smooth down roughened areas with the thumbnail. Also rub the back of the sheet where the correction was made to smooth the surface and press out any depressions.
11. If ink dye remains in the paper and will not erase, try to fade it out by rubbing with a whitening agent.

■ Perfect Positioning for Corrections

It is easy to reposition the carriage for an immediate correction unless the error occurs at the very bottom of the page. In that case, do not try to correct it at once, for the sheets almost always slip out of line during erasing and repositioning. Instead, finish typing the page, remove it from the typewriter, and then make the correction on each copy separately.

Timesavers in General Positioning. *Line repositioning* can be done much more quickly if you know exactly where your typing line is in relation to the aligning scale. To acquire speed in realigning, look intently as you type a line of words and notice the exact distance *at the typing point* between the bottom of the typed line and the aligning scale. It is the barest fraction of an inch, but memorizing it visually helps you realign more quickly and accurately.

You can find the approximate *letter position* more quickly by keeping the paper guide set at one spot and using it squarely each time you insert sheets into the typewriter. On a reinserted sheet move the carriage to the first letter of the correction. The typing point will be in almost exact position.

A short cut in making the same correction on separate pages is to insert all copies into the typewriter at once, without the carbon paper. After correcting the top sheet, operate the paper release and remove the corrected sheet. The second sheet will then be in approximate position for its correction.

■ Tests for Exact Positioning

To position a reinserted page for a correction, use the paper-release lever to move the page sideways and the variable line spacer to roll it up or down. Test the exactness of position by the following procedure:

> Cover the page of typing with a thin second sheet that you can see through. Roll the two sheets into the typewriter to the correction line. Test for exactness by typing over a letter near the erased error. If the page is not in perfect alignment, adjust the sheets and type over another letter. When the copy is in exact position, roll the sheets forward a couple of inches. Fold back the thin covering sheet, crease it all the way across, and tear it off. Roll the page back into line position, set the carriage at typing point, and type in the correction. This method wastes paper but assures exact positioning of corrections and is the cleanest way of correcting reinserted carbon copies.

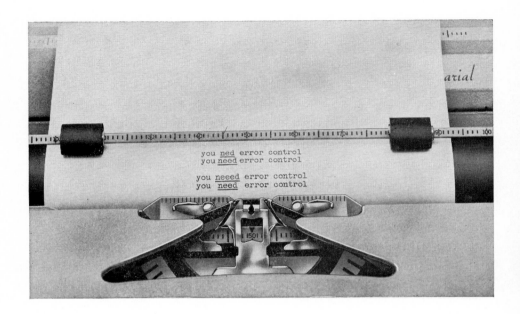

■ Fractional-Space Positioning for Correcting

Corrections that require one letter more or one letter less than the error are inconspicuous if they are centered in the space available, as shown above.

Squeezing and Spreading. To insert a word containing one letter more than the error, proceed as follows after the erasure has been made:

1. Move the carriage pointer to the space preceding the position of the first letter in the word.
2. Depress and hold down the half-space bar or key, type the first letter of the correction, and release the bar or key.
3. Repeat the process for each letter of the correction.

This procedure will leave one-half space before and after the corrected word.

To insert a word containing one letter less than the error:

1. Move the carriage pointer to the space occupied (before erasure) by the first letter of the error.
2. Depress and hold down the half-space bar or key, strike the first letter of the correction, and release the bar or key.
3. Repeat the process for each letter of the correction.

This procedure will leave one and one-half spaces before and after the corrected word.

COST OF CORRECTING ERRORS IN TYPING*

ERASURE COSTS	Predetermined Time Study Occurrence Including 16.66% Personal and Fatigue Factor	Total Sec. with 4 Errors per Original	Total Labor Cost Based on 4 Errors per Original*	Total Labor Cost Associated with Copies only**
Original Only	7.6995 sec.	30.7980	$.02086	
Orig. and 1 Carbon	16.0990 sec.	64.3960	$.04363	$.02277
Orig. and 2 Carbons	25.1985 sec.	100.7940	$.06829	$.04743
Orig. and 3 Carbons	34.2980 sec.	137.1920	$.09296	$.07210
STRIKEOVER COSTS			Labor Cost Associated with Strikeover per Original*	
Manual Typewriter	.8959 sec.	——	$.000607	
Electric Typewriter	.5249 sec.	——	$.000355	

*Based on estimated average labor cost of $2.44 per hour of $.0006776 per second.

**Computed by subtracting labor cost of original only from total labor charge of original with carbon since costs of original will be constant.

—*Administrative Management*

*Cost figures compiled by the Travelers Insurance Company

Inserting a Space or Hyphen. To insert a space or a hyphen between two words, erase the two letters which must be separated. Retype the first letter one-half space to the left of its original position. Retype the second letter by fractional forward spacing. Center a hyphen in the space available by using the backspace key.

```
askyou
ask you
```

```
stilllife
still-life
```

Inserting a Thin Letter in a Word. In some cases you can insert an *l*, an *i*, or a *t* within a typed word by fractional spacing. Experiment with your typewriter to determine in what instances you can use this method of correcting.

```
alignment
insertion
letter
```

```
Time must be of the
         to
essence/permit inter-
linear corrections.
```

```
Time must be of the
         to
essence/permit inter-
```

Making an Insertion Between Lines. When time is of the essence, you may have to make a neat insertion between lines. Use the underline and diagonal keys to indicate the insertion. Find the midpoint between the lines for the line of typing. In single-spaced copy type the correction to the right of the diagonal; in double-spaced copy center the correction over the upper end of the diagonal.

■ Correcting a Topbound Typescript

Typed pages that are bound at
the top can be corrected without
unbinding. Feed a blank sheet of
paper into the machine in the
usual way until the paper shows
about a two-inch top margin.
Insert the bottom of the sheet to be
corrected between the top edge of
the paper and the cylinder. Roll
the cylinder back to the line to be
corrected, position the carriage for
the correction, and type it.

■ Matched Typing

You will have no problem matching the typing of the correction to
the typing on a ribbon copy when using an electric typewriter. On a
manual machine, however, type the correction lightly first. Go over it if
necessary to match the ribbon typing. Do not use deliberate, forceful
strokes; use light, pecking strokes repeatedly until the match is perfect.

Carbon Copies. To make a carboned correction on a reinserted page
of carbon typing, staple together several slips of paper and a piece of
carbon paper, carbon side out. (A convenient size is 1″ x 2½″.) After
positioning the carriage for the first letter of the correction, put the
pad behind the ribbon with the carbon side against the paper. Type in
the correction lightly on a manual machine; retype it if necessary to
match the carbon typing on the page. On an electric machine, make up
several pads of varying thicknesses for the successive carbon copies
and use the one which best matches the copy you are correcting. It may
also help to lighten the key pressure while the correction is typed in.

Strikeover Corrections. A certain few strikeovers are likely to be
imperceptible in the specific type style on your typewriter. Experiment
and learn those that match and blend into the typing. They may include
d over *c* or *o; h* over *n; o* over *c; E* over *F;* and *, ; :* or *?* over *.*

Typing Specialties

Typing specialties that expedite, that control, and that add eye
appeal—in short, those that earn praise—are described in this section.

▪ Multipage Typing

A typing job of many pages, and often of many copies, must be organized in advance and controlled while in process so that it can be carried through to consistent completion. To accomplish this task, formulate the regulations and set them down on paper for both your own reference and the guidance of those who assist you.

The Job Guide Sheet. Set up a job guide sheet covering every point of form and typing instruction that may be needed for a long typing job. Try to answer in advance every question that will likely be raised. Include the items below and all others that might apply to the specific job.

Number of copies to be typed

Kind and size of paper to be used

Weight and finish of carbon paper to be used

Page layout:

> **Paper-guide scale number**
> **Left margin—number on typewriter scale**
> **Right margin—number on typewriter scale**
> **Top margin—number on line-guide scale (discussion below)**
> **Bottom margin—number on line-guide scale (discussion below)**
> **Single- or double-spaced typing**
> **Paragraph indention—number of spaces**
> **Tabulation indention—number of spaces**
> **Tabulation identification—I, A, (1), (a), etc.**
> **Tabulation spacing—single- or double-spaced**
> **Headings—examples and placement**
> **Subheadings—examples and placement**

Handling of typed pages awaiting assembly

Instructions for proofreading

Instructions for collating (see discussion on page 98)

Instructions for binding

Distribution of copies

Disposal of original-draft pages

Top and Bottom Margin Guides. To maintain even top and bottom margins, use carbon paper with the line spaces printed on an extended white edge; or make a numbered line guide as follows:

> **Type line numbers in a column down the extreme right edge of a thin second sheet. Set the paper-bail rolls immediately to the left of the typing column so that you can type to the very bottom of the sheet.**

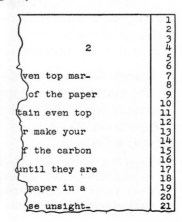

To use a line guide, insert it behind the top sheet of the carbon pack with the line numbers showing along the right edge. If you want a uniform top margin of one inch, turn the paper into the machine until the top edge just catches under the paper bail; with the paper in this position, begin typing.

Treatment of Typed Pages. Keep the original and the carbon copies of each page together in the same order in which they are typed until they are ready to be proofread and corrected. Never leave the carbon paper in a set of typed pages, because pressure exerted on the pack will cause unsightly offset marks on each copy. Do not fasten each set of pages together with a paper clip because the clip leaves crimp marks. Place the bottom copy on top of the set to protect the choice ribbon copy underneath. Also, since the bottom copy is used for proofreading and marking corrections, it will be ready without further handling of the set of pages.

Collating. After the sets of pages have been proofread and corrected, they are ready to be collated. Lay out the copies of the last page across the desk so that hand motions in collating are clockwise. Then lay on the copies of the next-to-last page, original on original, first carbon on first carbon, and so on. When all pages are laid out, check and correct each set for proper page sequence before binding.

■ Display Typing

Very often a secretary must design a typing layout for reproduction. It may be a notice, an invitation, a program, or the like. The finished piece requires that the units of copy, the decorations, and the white space be in pleasing arrangement and that the headings stand out. To achieve this effect, the secretary types blocks of copy and headings in various line lengths, spacing, and styles. She then experiments with their placement on a dummy layout.

Sample Blocks of Copy. To find the most pleasing size and shape for the blocks of copy, type one paragraph or short unit of copy in different spacings and line lengths to obtain a set of samples with which to experiment on the dummy layout. Variations in sizes and shapes are possible by using:

Single-line spacing or double-line spacing
Different line lengths: full width, three-fourths width, etc.
Copy typed in columnar arrangement
Copy or columns typed with even right margins

(MARGINS AT CENTER FOLD)

(PAGE 3)

Please bring along:

a pencil, a pen, a note-
book, and a 9 x 12 enve-
lope. The other needed
items will be supplied
to you at the workshop.

(PAGE 2)

to a winter workshop

arranged for all those
who want to be better
secretaries (and that ob-
viously includes you)!

by the portland nsat

workshop committee, who--
remembering the success
of last year's enriching
sessions--will attempt to
earn your kudos again.

(PAGE 4)

(PAGE 1)

Please call in your
reservation by Monday,
November 8,
to Mrs. Sandy De Lisle,
MAin 1-6879;
or mail the enclosed card.

****
****
*****

YOU'RE
INVITED

This dummy is being used to lay out an invitation that will be stencil-duplicated on one side of 8½″ by 11″ paper and French-folded: first across, and then up and down with the final fold to the left. The broken lines show the fold lines; the solid margin lines, the limit of the typing area. The copy in the upper half of the layout must be upside down so that it will be in reading position when the sheet is folded. (Screened areas indicate the copy that has been affixed in position for a pleasing balance of typed matter to white space.)

Justified Typing with Even Right Margins. Even-right-margin or *justified* typing is illustrated below. To justify copy on a machine with standard spacing:

1. Set the margins for the exact column width desired and type each line of copy in double-spaced form the full column width, filling in each unused space at the end with a diagonal.

2. Pencil in a check mark to indicate where you will insert each extra space within the line. Try not to use an extra space after the first word in a line or to isolate a short word with an extra space on each side.

3. Retype the copy, inserting the extra spaces.

First Copy to Determine Extra Spaces

```
First, set up the column width;///

then type each line of copy the///

full width of the column filling//

in each unused space at the end///

with a diagonal.
```

Final Copy with Even Right Margin

```
First, set  up  the  column  width;
then type  each line  of copy  the
full width  of the column  filling
in each  unused space  at the  end
with a diagonal.
```

Sample Headings. To make sample headings with which to experiment, take the longest heading and type it in different styles by:

1. Using upper and/or lower case
2. Using different spacings between letters; using conventional spacing
3. Varying the styles of underlining: continuous or broken underlining; single or double underlines; use of the underline, the hyphen, or the period key
4. Framing the headings: use of periods, small o's, or asterisks; use of underlines with diagonals; use of hyphens and apostrophes

Decorative Typing. Distinctively typed words, designs, and patterns may be used occasionally as "eye catchers" on the cover page of a notice, announcement of a meeting, or an item to be posted on the office bulletin board. The illustrations at the right are a few that can be done by straight typing and spacing. Such decorative typing is rarely used in business work; it requires more time than the results justify and frequently it is out of place on a business document. It may be used effectively, however, on special announcements where there is need to gain the interest of a number of readers.

The secretary who is a master typist can provide or suggest decorative typing to give attractive display to special feature material.

—Ewing Galloway

■ High-Speed Envelope and Card Routines

You will occasionally have small typing production jobs to do or supervise, such as addressing a hundred or so envelopes or making up a 5 by 3 card index. You should master the following high-speed routines used in specialized typing assignments.

Back-Feeding Envelopes. When you have a number of envelopes to address, you can save time by back-feeding them. Feed the first envelope until only about one-half inch of the bottom of the envelope is free. Then place the top of the second envelope between the platen and the bottom of the first envelope. As you turn the platen to remove the first envelope, feed the third envelope into the type-writer in the same way you fed the second.

Stack the plain envelopes at the left of the typewriter, flaps down and bottom edges of the envelopes toward you. When the envelope in typewriting position has been addressed, turn the platen to remove the envelope; at the same time pick up the next envelope and feed it into the cylinder. Remove the addressed envelope. Stack the addressed envelopes face down at the right of your machine.

Front-Feeding Envelopes. To front-feed envelopes, roll a just-addressed envelope *back* until about one inch of the top edge is free. Have a stack of envelopes at the side of the typewriter in face-up position. Take one and drop it face up between the cylinder and the top edge of the addressed envelope. Roll the cylinder back until the blank envelope is in typing position, then address it. The addressed envelopes stack themselves in sequence against the paper table for occasional removal.

Front-Feeding Small Cards. To front-feed small cards, make a pleat a half inch or less deep straight across the middle of a sheet of paper to form a pocket. The depth of the pleat controls how far down you can type on the cards. Paste or tape the pleat down at the sides to hold it in place. Roll the pleated sheet into the typewriter and align the fold of the pleat with the alignment

scale. Place the first card into the pleat and position it for typing. Draw a line on the paper along the left edge of the card to serve as a continuing guide for consistent margins.

Government Postal Cards. Government postal cards can be purchased in sheets, 4 cards wide and 10 cards long. They can be cut into strips and addressed.

▪ Fill-Ins

The term *fill-in* refers to the insertion of some typed material in a space provided on duplicated or printed letters, bulletins, or business papers. The fill-in may be an address, a salutation, a word, phrase, or figures. On interoffice correspondence no attempt is made to disguise fill-ins, but on outgoing mail fill-ins should match the body of the message. The procedure is as follows:

1. **Use a ribbon that matches the body of the message in darkness of color.**
2. **Set the carriage in position to insert the fill-in. Test the position by typing over a period or comma in the text.**
3. **When the position has been determined, set the paper guide and margins for use in succeeding fill-ins.**
4. **Salutations and addresses are placed more accurately if the lines are typed from bottom to top, unless a pinpoint placement dot from the master shows where to begin the first line.**

▪ Typing in the Red

Red typing is used to indicate losses or decreases on financial statements or to give emphasis to part of the text. The red part of a black and red ribbon, or red carbon paper, or both may be used. The black part of the copy is typed first, leaving blank spaces where the red copy is to be inserted. Type about three inches of the text at a time, leaving space for the red parts to be filled in. Turn the paper forward slightly and place a small piece of red carbon in the proper location behind each black carbon. Roll the pages back into position. If the ribbon is all black, place a small piece of red carbon under the card holder of the typewriter and type in the red figures or words. Then remove all of the red slips.

Suggested Readings

Administrative Management Executives Buying Guide. New York: Geyer-McAllister Publications, published annually.

"Carbonless Paper Simplifies Forms Production and Control," *Administrative Management.* (New York: Geyer-McAllister Publications, 1967).

"Copying with Carbons," *Today's Secretary.* (New York: Gregg Publishing Division, McGraw-Hill Book Company, Inc., 1965), Vol. 68, No. 2 (October, 1965), pp. 36, 75.

McCracken, Lucy. "Goof Proof," *Today's Secretary.* (New York: Gregg Publishing Division, McGraw-Hill Book Company, Inc., 1965), Vol. 68, No. 3 (November, 1965), pp. 42–43, 75.

Questions for Discussion

1. Why would the average cost of a business letter be $2.40 or more?

2. Suppose the executive had three penned-in corrections on the first page of a letter and two on the second—changes that he decided upon before putting on his signature. The time is 4:45 p.m., and he plans to leave promptly at 5 p.m. What would you do?

3. Assume you have typed for your branch offices six copies of a five-page, double-spaced report on dictating equipment. Before assembling the copies, you discover that SoundScriber contains a second capital *S*. The name occurs once or twice on each page. What would you do?

4. Many business firms place their typewriters under service contract with the manufacturer. These contracts provide repair and maintenance service for a specified monthly or annual charge. What services do these contracts usually provide? What does the customer pay for the service? What are the advantages to the secretary of the service contract? (Information may be obtained from local typewriter sales offices or typewriter manufacturers, or from the individual in charge of typewriters for your department in college.)

5. Some office managers claim that it is too expensive to erase and correct typewriting errors. They observe a policy that erasures are not to be made on carbon copies, but on the originals of important letters only. What is your opinion of such a practice?

6. The executive asks you to write and mail letters inviting to lunch his fifteen friends who comprise the No-Agenda Club, which meets on invitation merely for "good conversation." Discuss whether or not you would take time to design and add a bit of cleverness to the invitation by way of a typed motif.

7. Fill in the correct word in each of the following sentences. Then refer to the Reference Guide to correct your answers.

   (a) The letter is (already, all ready) prepared for mailing.
   (b) You will have to choose (among, between) the months of June, July, and August for your vacation.
   (c) The work was distributed (among, between) Helen and Ruth.
   (d) The change of policy has a positive (affect, effect) on office morale.
   (e) It is not possible to (affect, effect) a reconciliation.
   (f) Your attitude will (affect, effect) your promotional opportunities.

Problems

■ **1.** This problem provides practice in making corrections on pages in the typewriter and on pages reinserted into the typewriter—both for originals and carbon copies. With 8½- by 11-inch paper make up a carbon pack of one original and two carbon copies. Type at the top of the page an exact copy of sentences (a) through (d); triple-space between them. While the pack is still in the typewriter, make necessary corrections on each of the three copies.

Type sentences (e) through (g) on the same page. Remove the sheets from the typewriter and detach the carbons. Then make the necessary corrections on the original and the two carbons on sentences (e) through (g).

(a) How many are coming.
(b) We received your letter of Augst 3 today.
(c) There have been fourty replies so far.
(d) There were both old, and new ones.
(e) Our expenses forthe year have increased.
(f) The folowing is a summary of our sales.
(g) Only 154 shares of stock were ssued.

■ **2.** Practice each of the following typing techniques. Be prepared to demonstrate each of them before the class.

(a) Back-feeding envelopes
(b) Front-feeding envelopes
(c) Front-feeding small cards
(d) Making a correction on a topbound typescript
(e) Using a transparent sheet to position a correction
(f) Correct method of cleaning type
(g) Assembling and inserting carbon pack into typewriter

■ **3.** Copy the paragraph "Decorative Typing" on page 100 on a sheet of inexpensive paper; type the line lengths exactly as shown. Indent the first line five spaces. Mark up the paragraph for retyping with even right margins. Retype it according to your marks. If you have not achieved a perfect right margin, retype it. Strikeovers and erasures are permitted, for this copy is to become the master copy from which a stencil will be cut.

■ **4.** There are many techniques that experienced typists use to increase their efficiency, to improve the appearance of the typed copy, or to perform difficult typing assignments. Prepare a short report entitled "A Typewriting Shortcut." In this report describe a typewriting technique or application that you have learned or read and which is not described in this chapter.

■ **5.** This problem will help you realize the flexibility that is possible in typewritten work. Type the centered heading *Recommendations* in four different ways; type it a fifth time in an original version of your own. (Refer to page 98 and page 99 for ideas.) Indicate your personal preference for use with double-spaced copy on 8½- by 13-inch paper.

■ **6.** Try out four type cleaners—liquid, pliable plastic, cushion sheet, and cleansing tissue. Clean one fourth of the keys with each kind. Write a brief evaluation of each method.

■ **7.** Review Chapter 5 to find and try five or more typing suggestions that you have not tried before.

Related Work Assignments 14-16

14. Filling in Form Letters

15. Preparing a Travel Expense Voucher

16. Proofreading

The instructions and supplies necessary for the completion of Related Work Assignments 14, 15, and 16 are provided in the Workbook.

Ch.

6   Copying and Duplicating Processes

"Make ten billion copies, please." This was the collective request that went out last year to secretaries in the 500,000 offices that had copying machines. The magnitude of this request, which represents only one type of reproduction process, dramatizes the extraordinary growth in information dissemination that is taking place in modern business.

Two factors are contributing to this growth: (1) mechanical refinements that lead to increased speed and simplicity of operating the copying and duplicating machines, (2) continuous improvement of the quality of in-office reproduction so that the office can now assume duplicating responsibilities formerly turned over to outside agencies or to special departments within the business.

The secretary has been the focal center of part of the developments. The objective of each manufacturer is to enable the secretary or her assistant to produce high-quality output with his equipment, thus eliminating the need for specially trained operators.

In reading this chapter you will need to differentiate between copying and duplicating. Although office copying is not too rigidly defined, in general it is a process that uses an exposing device and an image-forming process to create copies of an existing original. An office copying machine normally is used to make from one to ten copies. This limitation, however, is changing because of the introduction of the new copier-duplicators. (See page 112.)

Duplicating, on the other hand, is the use of a device to make copies from a specially prepared stencil or master. Duplicating machines are used to produce from 10 to 10,000 or more copies.

There are many kinds of office copying and duplicating machines. They vary in the types of written and illustrative materials they will produce, in quality and appearance of the finished work, in the number of copies obtainable, in speed of reproduction, in cost per copy, and in simplicity and ease of operation.

A secretary must be knowledgeable in both copying and duplicating procedures. A supervisor or an administrative assistant should, in addition, be able to make recommendations about the kinds of machines and

—Minnesota Mining and Manufacturing Company

The photocopy machine can quickly reproduce extra copies of a drawing or an illustration, as well as typewritten or printed papers.

processes preferable for various purposes, to oversee the reasonable use and care of copying and duplicating equipment and supplies, and to evaluate quality of output.

Copying Processes

Copying machines are used to reproduce quickly and exactly such materials as original letters, typewritten pages, financial reports, artwork, drawings, and pictures. All copying machines have one thing in common; they reduce copying errors. If the original is correct, the copies will also be correct.

Here are some of the ways in which the use of a copying machine can save the secretary's time and increase her efficiency:

Copies of an incoming letter can be made and forwarded to several staff members without the delay necessitated by typing copies or routing the letter from one person to another.

If a sentence or short note can be used to answer a letter, the note can be handwritten or typed on the incoming letter and returned to the sender. The file copy of the original with the answer can be made on the copying machine.

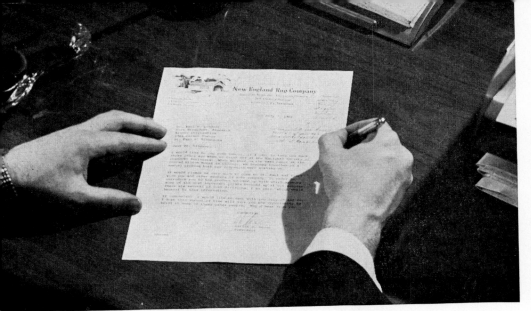

The copying machine is being increasingly used in replying to correspondence. The executive responds in the margins of the incoming letter. Then the original is returned to the sender.

A request for a letter can be accommodated by furnishing a duplicate made on the copying machine, without relinquishing the original letter.

Identical extra copies of accounting papers, statements, statistical reports, tables and statistics from magazines, newspaper clippings, drawings, and illustrations can be made quickly for distribution to departments or individuals.

Copies of incoming orders can be made immediately and routed to the various branches and departments for their use.

File copies can be made of the report itself and of the receipts and other documents that are used to support tax deductions and that are submitted with personal income-tax reports.

Copying processes can be divided into two groups: (1) wet processes and (2) dry processes. In the wet processes liquid or vapor chemicals are used in some phase of the process. In general, a wet process tends to produce sharper copies than does the dry process. The major expansion and use of copying equipment, however, has been in dry copying, especially in electrostatic machines, because the dry process is faster, simpler, and more convenient to use.

■ Wet Processes

The four major wet processes are diffusion transfer, dye transfer, stabilization, and diazo.

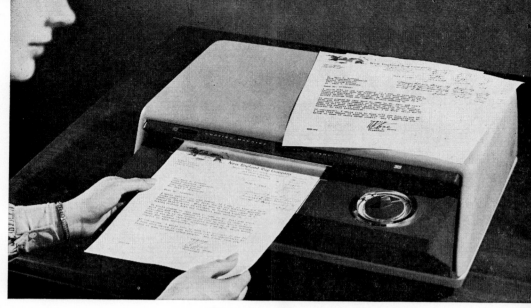

—Minnesota Mining and Manufacturing Company

Photocopies are used for the files and for intraoffice communication. The copier illustrated here uses the thermographic process, which provides a permanent image.

Diffusion Transfer. The diffusion transfer process is also known as the *phototransfer* or the *photocopying* process. It is essentially a modification of the principle of conventional photography.

Microfilming of checks and deposits in banks and of customer sales slips and statements in department stores are applications of this process. Microfilming is not only a copying process but also a method of filing information in an unbelievably small amount of space. Requiring so little storage space, microfilmed records can be kept more readily accessible than can larger records.

Most of the smaller machines do not employ a camera and cannot, therefore, enlarge or reduce copy. In general, the process works as follows: The original is placed in direct contact with a sheet of sensitized paper and exposed to light in a printer. The light passes through the sensitized sheet and reflects back from the unprinted part of the original to the surface of the sensitized sheet, causing these unprinted areas to be made insoluble. Since the printed sections of the original absorb and do not reflect the light, these portions of the sensitized sheet remain soluble. The sensitized sheet (negative) is placed face to face against a sheet of positive paper and inserted into a developing unit where a chemical reaction causes the printed section on the negative to diffuse to the positive sheet where it turns black to form the copy. The two sheets are

passed through a roller to bring them in close contact and remove excess solution. They are then peeled apart. The positive sheet contains a black-on-white image of the original.

Dye Transfer. The dye-transfer process is also known as the *verifax* process or *gelatin transfer* process. The material to be copied is placed face to face with a matrix (a sheet of sensitized paper). Both sheets are placed in a copying unit and exposed to light. The matrix is then placed in a solution where areas not reached by light during the exposure (words and lines on the original copy) are changed into a dark dyelike substance. The matrix is then placed face to face with a sheet of nonsensitized copy paper, and both are passed between squeegee rollers. The dyelike substance on the matrix is transferred to the copy sheet to produce the copy. There is sufficient dye on the matrix to produce approximately five copies. Copies can be reproduced on regular paper of any color or weight and on offset masters. A specially prepared copying paper can be used to keep fading to a minimum.

Stabilization Process. The stabilization process differs from the diffusion and dye-transfer processes in that no negative sheet is involved. A light-sensitized paper, coated with silver halide, is placed in direct contact with the document to be copied; then it is exposed to light. The sensitized paper is then immersed in a developer solution which converts the exposed silver halide to metallic silver in the areas corresponding to the nonimage areas of the document. The paper then goes to a stabilizer bath which makes it relatively insensitive to further light. After leaving the stabilizer bath, the paper is squeezed to remove the excess solution and is air dried.

Diazo Process. The *diazo process* is an improved form of blue-printing that has been adapted for office use. It normally produces black-and-white copies; but other color combinations are possible, since paper of several colors may be used. Special chemically coated paper must be used for copies. The sheet to be copied is placed over the coated sheet, and the two are exposed to ultraviolet light. The reproduction takes place when ammonia vapor comes in contact with the exposed sheet. Since light must pass through the original material, the diazo process cannot copy an original with matter on its underside.

▪ Dry Processes

All dry-copy processes, with the exception of the Telecopier, use the principle of either heat transfer or electrostatic transfer.

Thermographic Process. The thermographic process (used in a machine marketed under the trade name of Thermo-Fax) is also known as the *infrared* or *heat-transfer* process. The process is based on the physical fact that dark substances absorb more heat than light substances. Material to be copied is placed beneath a heat-sensitive copy sheet. Infrared light is then beamed through the sensitized copy onto the original. The dark outlines (words and lines) on the original absorb and hold the heat and turn the sensitized paper dark in the same places.

The copy paper is available in white and other colors. Pencil marks and standard typing and printing are easily copied by this process. Some ball-point and fountain-pen inks and colors will not reproduce.

Transfer Electrostatic Process (Xerox). The electrostatic process is based on the principle that unlike electrical charges attract each other, whereas like charges repel, and upon the property of amorphous selenium which will hold an electrostatic charge in the dark but will allow it to be dissipated by exposure to light. A copying camera throws an image of the document to be copied onto a selenium-coated drum that has been given a positive electrostatic charge. Where the light strikes the drum, the charge is dissipated. The electrostatic charge remains, however, in the image areas. The drum is then treated with a negatively charged powder that adheres to the positively charged lines or letters and thus produces a visible image of the document on the drum, but in reverse. A sheet of ordinary (untreated) paper that has been given a positive electrostatic charge is passed over the drum. The powder image leaves the drum and adheres to the paper where it is permanently affixed by means of heat.

Direct Electrostatic Process (Electrofax). The principle of the direct electrostatic process is basically the same as the transfer electrostatic process. There are two major differences: (1) In the direct method, the electrostatic image is formed directly on the final copy paper and, therefore, does not have to be transferred to it; and (2) a specially coated copy paper designed for the direct process must be used.

Telecopier. Copies may be transmitted any distance over the conventional telephone without special wiring or connections by the use of a telecopier facsimile device. Transmission requires placing the document in a sender, a carbon set in a receiver, telephone headsets in couplers, and then pressing a button. Upon completion the machine stops automatically, and normal telephone conversation can be resumed.

■ **Copier-Duplicators**

In office reproduction, the number of copies to be reproduced can be classified into short runs (up to 10 copies), medium runs (10 to 100 copies), and long runs (over 100 copies). Because of its relatively high per-copy cost and slow speed, the copier has been most economically used for short runs. A duplicating process (stencil, spirit, or offset) has been much faster and more economical for long runs. The medium-run area has represented a grey zone between copying and duplicating. The user has had to weigh the high cost of copying and low cost of duplicating against convenience, simplicity, and urgency.

To fill this gap of the medium run, several manufacturers are now producing combination machines, called copier-duplicators. These machines are designed for both short and medium runs on a graduated price scale. They produce copies at a much faster rate (up to 40 a minute) than the ordinary copier, and the cost for each copy decreases as the length of the run increases. These machines are now capable of competing favorably with duplicators on a cost basis. In addition, copier-duplicators offer speed and convenience in the medium-run range.

There are several types of copier-duplicators. One prominent make is basically a high-speed, high-volume electrostatic copier. The operator merely places the copy in the machine, dials the number of copies desired, and presses a "print" button. The machine automatically produces copies at the rate of 40 a minute. Another make combines a copier with a spirit duplicator. A spirit master is produced by a thermal copier and manually positioned on a drum for running copies. Producing the master and running 100 copies takes less than two minutes.

The 650 electrostatic dry-process copier (left) is teamed with an A. B. Dick offset duplicator (right) in the company's recently introduced high-speed copy-duplicating system. The 650 is capable of master imaging.

A new dry-copy process called adherography is used by another manufacturer. A master is prepared by writing, typing, or printing on a master sheet. A facsimile master can be prepared by using a specially designed copying machine which is based on a photographic process. The operator inserts the master in the duplicator unit, sets a dial for the number of copies desired from 1 to 199, and presses a button. Copies are produced at the rate of 40 a minute on regular paper. As many as 200 copies can be made from one master.

Another copier produces reduced-size copies.

In another system the electrostatic and diazo processes are combined. Although the least expensive of all processes, the diazo method is limited in that it can copy an image that appears on only one side of a translucent original. Under the combined system, the original is copied on the electrostatic machine on a translucent paper. The copies are then made on the diazo unit at a very low cost per copy.

▪ Overcopying

The ease with which copies can be made on the copier has led to the tendency of "overcopying"—that is, making more copies than needed. The urge seems to be almost irresistible, especially on machines that have multiple-copy dials. Overcopying is especially prevalent when the setup is such that anyone in the office can go to the machine and make copies. While each copy costs only a few pennies, the cumulative total adds many dollars to the monthly copying bill.

The secretary will need to exercise good judgment and restraint against what some companies call "overcommunicating." Don't make two copies when one copy, properly routed, will suffice.

▪ Illegal Copying

Because of the ease of making photocopies and the availability of such a machine in the office, there is a temptation to make copies of valuable personal papers and to use or carry the copies in place of the originals. There are rules against, and in some cases penalties for, copying certain papers. Among them are a driver's license, an automobile registration, a passport, a draft card, citizenship papers, naturalization papers, immigration papers, postage stamps, and securities of the United States Government.

Duplicating Processes

The amount of duplicating work performed by the secretary varies widely. In a large office that has a special duplicating department, the secretary may be responsible only for preparing the guide copy and selecting the duplicating process to be used. In smaller offices the secretary may be responsible for the entire duplicating process, including the operation of the duplicator. If duplicating is done by an outside agency (a print shop or office-service business), the secretary may need to handle all arrangements. The secretary, therefore, needs to understand the various duplicating processes in order to select the method best suited to the work to be done.

Stencil, spirit, and offset processes are the ones most commonly used in offices. The stencil process and the spirit process have been widely used because of their simple operation and low initial cost. However, offset duplication for general office use is increasing in popularity because of improvements that have simplified the operating controls of offset duplicator machines.

▪ Stencil (Mimeograph) Process

The *stencil process* is used for the reproduction of all sorts of reports, bulletins, and forms where a large number of copies are needed. Two common stencil processes are mimeograph and Gestetner.

Principle of Stencil Duplication. Stencil duplication involves a stencil and an inked drum. The stencil is a thin tissue coated with a waxy, ink-impervious substance. A typewriter key or a sharp stylus pushes the wax coating aside, exposing the porous fibers. The stencil is placed around an inked drum, and the ink flows through the exposed fibers to the paper.

Up to ten thousand copies can be made from a stencil, depending upon its quality. Stencils can be preserved and reused. Fast-drying emulsion inks make it possible to print on both sides of the paper without slip-sheeting (inserting a blotting paper between sheets). As many as five colors can be reproduced at the same time by the use of a special multicolor ink pad.

The mimeograph process has four important parts—(1) the stencil, (2) the ink, (3) the impression paper, and (4) the mimeograph. It is through the meeting of the stencil, the ink, and the impression paper in the mimeograph that copies are made.

The paper is fed, sheet by sheet, between the cylinder and the impression roller of the mimeograph. As the sheet of paper goes between the cylinder and the roller, the roller lifts up automatically and causes the paper to touch the stencil. At the same time the ink flows from the inside of the cylinder through the openings in the stencil and is deposited on the paper to make the copy.

—A. B. Dick Company

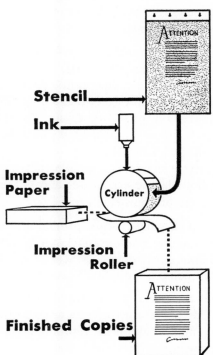

Types of Stencil Duplicators. Stencil duplicators are of two major types: hollow single-drum machines which generally use a fluid or semi-paste ink and twin-cylinder machines that use a paste ink only.

On machines of the single-drum type the stencil is placed on a hollow revolving drum which has a perforated surface covered with an ink pad. The ink is applied to the inner surface of the drum so that it can pass through the perforations to the pad and the openings of the stencil. Thus, ink impressions are made on ink-absorbing paper as the paper is fed through the machine and comes in contact with the stencil.

Near-perfect registration (exact position on page, columns, and lines) can be achieved, making it possible to duplicate fill-ins on printed or duplicated forms.

The twin-cylinder machine uses a silk screen to cover the closed cylinders. The stencil is placed over the screen. The paste ink is fed onto the surface of the cylinders which, in turn, force the ink through the screen and stencil.

Methods of Preparing Stencils. Stencils may be prepared on the typewriter, by hand lettering and drawing with styli, and by several other methods.

The facsimile process, frequently referred to as the electronic method, is widely used for stencil preparation. The process is an adaptation of the principle of the photoelectric cell. Material to be stenciled is placed on one drum of a two-drum machine. An electronic (plastic) stencil is placed on the second drum. The drum rotates slowly; and as it does so, each line is scanned by a photoelectric eye. The eye responds to light reflected from the copy, creating an electrical current. The electrical current activates a needle that moves across the second drum as the photoelectric eye moves across the first. The needle thus records the image on the stencil.

Drawings, forms, printed and typed copy, diagrams, and art work (including photographs) can be transferred to a stencil with relatively high-quality detail. Machines are distributed under the trade names of Mimeofax, Gestefax, Scanomatic, Electro-Rex, and TashaFax.

A special photographic process can be used to prepare stencils. This process permits material to be increased or decreased in size, and it makes excellent reproductions of forms, line drawings, "wash" drawings with variations of shading, and typed material.

Stencils can also be prepared by a die-impressing (embossing) process. First a die of the information to be stencilized is impressed. Then any desired number of stencils may be made from the die. A firm with a price list containing a number of items on which prices fluctuate might prepare a quantity of die-impressed stencils listing the items but leaving the price column blank. Then when a new price list is prepared, only the price of each item needs to be typed into the stencil.

When stencils are used repeatedly to fill in material on a printed form, the form can be printed on the face of a supply of stencils. This procedure assures that when the variable material is typed on the stencil, it will be positioned for perfect registration on the preprinted forms as they run through the machine.

■ Direct Process

The *direct process*, also known as the *liquid, fluid,* or *spirit process,* is widely used for short runs of material to be used primarily for inside-office distribution. "Direct process" comes from the fact that copies are made directly from the master copy as it comes in contact with sheets of paper. Copy to be reproduced is transferred to the *back* of a master sheet. A sheet of direct-process carbon paper is placed behind the master and typing is done on the face of the master. Pressure from the typewriter key transfers a small deposit of dye from the carbon paper to the back of the master. The master is then clamped to the cylinder of the machine so that the carbon-typed side comes in contact with the moistened sheets of paper as they pass through the machine.

An alcoholic fluid (hence, spirit duplicator) is used to dissolve and transfer a minute portion of the dye from the master to the paper. This fluid dampens the blank paper as it is fed into the machine. The chemically moistened paper, under pressure, picks up the impression from the master. Copies dry quickly.

Copies can be produced in blue, green, red, or black; but the best reproductions are obtained in purple. Several colors can be reproduced at the same time. Since the master is made by carbon, it permits tracing. Charts, pictures, and ruled forms can be traced easily and reproduced. Masters can also be printed.

Up to 400 copies can be run from one carefully prepared master. The master may be filed and reused for additional copies when needed. The direct process is an economical, convenient, and rapid method to use in making short runs.

Printed Masters. Skeleton masters can be produced by printing a form with reproducing ink on the back of the master sheet. To use the partially completed master, the typist adds the carbon back, and types in the variable information. For example, if several copies of the sales contract for each installment sale are required, a supply of skeleton contract masters may be printed. The variable facts such as dates, names, addresses, and accounts are then filled in on one of the printed masters and the needed number of copies run off. The correct placement of insertions on a skeleton master can be assured by having the face of the master imprinted to correspond to the copy on the back.

If the copy is to be run on printed forms, accurate registration can be obtained by having the form printed on the face of the master sheet. This procedure will assure correct placement of the duplicated inserts.

Blockouts. Any part of the master may be temporarily blocked out, thus making it possible to produce a number of different forms from the same master. For this reason the direct-process duplicator is widely used in systems work. For example, one master sheet for an order can be drawn up; then by the use of blockout covers, the shipping labels, invoices, work orders, stock-room orders, stock-record cards, back-order sheets, and a number of other forms can be reproduced from the one master. Some machines are equipped with a magnetized metal strip on the drum, permitting the easy placement and removal of a blockout mask. Different forms can be reproduced from the same master by merely inserting and removing this blockout mask.

Azograph. A disadvantage of the direct process is that the printing dye on the master is easily smudged and rubs off. This problem has been eliminated in the *azograph process* by chemical means. However, copies can be produced in blue color only, and the maximum number of copies obtainable from one master is approximately one hundred. Thus, length of run is sacrificed for cleanliness of operation.

▪ Offset Process

The *offset process* is based on the antipathy between grease and water. The outlines on the master hold the greasy printing ink, while the remainder of the surface attracts water and repels the ink. The ink is transferred or offset from the outline to a rubber blanket which, in turn, transfers the copy onto the paper.

This process offers a wide range of possibilities for reproduction, such as printing, pictures, drawings, writing, and typing. All can be put on masters and reproduced. An unlimited number of copies can be run from one master. The masters may be filed and reused. Almost any kind and color of paper can be used. Various colors of ink are usable. Copies can be printed in several colors, but a separate master and a separate run are required for each color. As there is no offset on the back of the sheets, slip-sheeting is not necessary; and copies can be run on both sides of the sheets.

A major development in the offset duplicating field is the production of small, table-top, office-size machines designed to produce high-quality work at low per-copy cost. The objective is to provide a machine that competes with the stencil and spirit duplicators for general office duplication. The operation of these machines has been greatly simplified in order that they may be satisfactorily operated by the secretary and other members of the regular office staff.

Masters. The master may be a paper, plastic, or metal plate. Paper masters are used for short runs and general reproduction work. Plastic plates are used for medium runs; metal masters are used for long runs and for work that is to be of the highest quality.

An offset master may be prepared in a number of ways. The copy may be typed, drawn, traced, or stamped directly onto the master. A photographic process may be used whereby a film negative is made of the original copy through a camera which allows enlargement and reduction. The copy is then transferred from the film to a pre-sensitized plate from which the copies are made.

The newest and most popular method of making masters is to use one of the copying processes. Several of the office copiers (electrostatic, diffusion transfer, or verifax) will transfer copy to paper plates, and some will also transfer to metal plates.

Form-printed and guide-printed masters may also be used. For example, a business may have a business form or other information reproduced in offset ink on a master. Variable and new information may be added to the master by the typewriter, pen, or pencil.

Quality Reproduction. The offset process is capable of producing work of the highest quality. The wide range of paper and variety of colors that can be used make the process especially appropriate where appearance is of major concern, as is the case where materials are going outside the office to customers and to the general public.

This table-top manual embosser, portable and only 11 by 15 inches in size, can emboss any of 72 upper- or lower-case characters at the rate of about 35 three-line plates an hour. A metal address plate is shown below. The plates are kept in trays similar to the one illustrated.

—Pitney-Bowes, Inc.

▪ Addressing Machines

Special equipment is used to address mail for mailing lists used repeatedly, as in advertising campaigns. A machine called a Graphotype embosses the names, addresses, and other information (manually from a keyboard or automatically from punched paper tape or punched cards) on metal plates or plastic cards. The address plates and envelopes are fed into a machine that addresses the envelopes rapidly.

—Addressograph-Multigraph Corporation

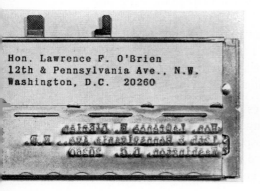

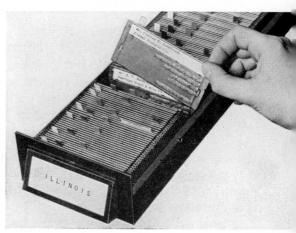

Addressing machine models range from portable, hand-operated models to large high-speed automatic machines that can produce several thousand impressions in an hour.

—Addressograph-Multigraph Corporation

■ Automatic Typewriters

An automatic typewriter produces individually typed letters or copy automatically from a master copy. The master copy is made on either a perforated roll (called a record stencil), or on punched paper tape, edge-punched cards, or magnetic tape as a by-product of typing. After the master stencil, tape, or card is completed, it is fed into the reproducing unit from which it activates the typewriter automatically.

An automatic typewriter can be used as a standard typewriter for regular work and for fill-ins, dates, names, or dictated paragraphs to be inserted in the automatically typewritten letter. The operator usually types the inside address and salutation and then turns on the machine to typewrite the letter automatically. The attachment can be set to stop where a fill-in is to be inserted. A skilled operator can keep four automatic machines in operation, producing form letters that look exactly like individually typed letters, for they are actually typed. Each machine can produce as many as 100 letters of average length a day.

In addition to functioning in the same manner as an automatic typewriter, the Magnetic Tape Selectric Typewriter can be used to retype automatically a letter or lengthy report where a revision is necessary due to errors, insertions, or deletions. If the typist makes an error, she backspaces and strikes over the incorrect character or word. No erasing is necessary. If a word, sentence, or paragraph is to be added or deleted, the tape unit searches the tape until the reference point where the revision is to be made is located. The typist then changes the copy by typing directly over the unwanted information. When all corrections and changes have been recorded on the tape, the letter or report is ready for automatic typing.

The VariTyper enables the typist to use several
type styles and to justify the right margin.

■ Special Machines for Preparing Copy for Duplication

Offices in which a great deal of high quality duplicating work is done frequently are equipped with a VariTyper and/or a Justowriter. Both of these machines make it easy to justify (make even) the right margin. The VariTyper, in addition, permits the use of a variety of type styles and sizes on the same page as with the use of a Linotype machine. For this reason, VariTyping is known as "cold" type.

The VariTyper. The VariTyper (sometimes called a composing machine) differs from the standard typewriter in that the type is removable so that it is possible to use different sets of keys, called fonts, in various styles and sizes. The VariTyper can be adjusted for varying spacing between lines and between letters, thus making it possible to justify the right margin and produce copy that closely resembles printing. It is particularly suitable for condensing statistical material into a small space because one of the very small types can be used. Newspapers, catalogs, and even books are often prepared on the VariTyper.

Justowriter automatic composing machine by Friden, Inc. is a tape-operated copysetting team consisting of a Recorder and a Reproducer. As the copy is typed on the Recorder, shown at the right, a punched tape is prepared.

The Justowriter. With the Justowriter (an electric recorder and reproducer), the copy is typed on the recorder, which punches a paper tape. The reproducer prepares a visible copy for proofreading, then reads the tape and automatically types justified copy at 100 words a minute. The copy may be typed directly on offset plates or on copy paper and transferred to offset plates.

Coded instructions required to justify the right margin are automatically recorded on the tape. The tape is run through the Reproducer, shown at the right, which types the copy and justifies the right margin.

—*Friden, Inc.*

Preparing and Running Stencils

The quality of stencil duplication depends primarily on the quality of the stencil and the care with which it is prepared.

▪ Kinds of Stencils

Stencils are produced by a number of manufacturers, each of whom makes several different grades and kinds. Some grades are designed for short runs, others for long runs. Some are recommended for typing work, others for handwriting and art work. They are available in a variety of colors, the color identifying the type or grade of stencil.

Stencils come in legal, letter, and note size. There are also continuous stencil sheets, for use with tabulating equipment, and stubless stencil sheets which may be filed in the standard filing cabinets. Each brand carries full instructions on the box or inside. To obtain the best results, read and follow the instructions carefully.

Stencils are available for special purposes, such as four-page folder stencils, outline-map stencils, newspaper-column stencils, labeling stencils, and legal-document stencils for use with sheets of perforated gummed labels. There is a stencil designed primar ly for use with the electric typewriter. A stencil is available on which writing and sketching can be done with a watercolor brush and a special solvent ink which dissolves the stencil coating.

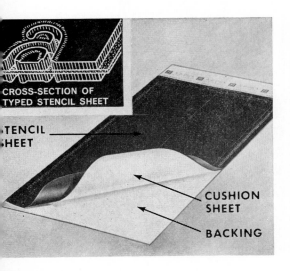

CROSS-SECTION OF
TYPED STENCIL SHEET

STENCIL
SHEET

CUSHION
SHEET

BACKING

▪ Special Sheets

A tissue or coated cushion sheet is usually provided with the stencil. It is to be inserted between the stencil and the backing sheet before the stencil is cut. It cushions the impact of the typewriter keys, serves as a depository for the stencil coating which is removed from the underside of the stencil sheet, and broadens the outlines of each stenciled letter. Color-coated cushion sheets are recommended for use with some stencils to facilitate proofreading.

Plastic Typing Plate. In place of a cushion sheet, a plastic typing plate may be used. The typing plate is inserted between the stencil sheet and the backing sheet (no cushion sheet). It produces a sharp, narrow-line copy.

Transparent Cover Sheets. When a stencil has a transparent (*plio-film*) sheet over the stencil surface, type right onto it and through it. This film sheet eliminates *type fill*—the accumulation of stencil coating in the keys—and reduces the cutting out of such letters as *o, q, d, b, p.* The film also protects the platen and feed rollers from deterioration resulting from the oils in the stencil coating. A transparent plastic ribbon which replaces the inked ribbon can be used instead of the film sheet.

▪ Stocking and Storing Stencils

The coating on some kinds of stencil sheets may deteriorate with age, heat, or humidity. Guard against overstocking. Store unused stencils in a cool, dry place for protection. Weight should be kept off stored stencils; it is best, therefore, to store the boxes on edge rather than flat.

▪ Preparing the Guide Copy

Until you are experienced in typing stencils, you should prepare a guide copy that is accurate in content and layout. Using a paper sheet the size to be used for running off the copies, you should:

1. Mark on the sheet the limitations or boundary lines shown on the stencil.
2. Indicate the positions of all special illustrations or folds so that the typing copy can be adjusted to the right locations; then type the copy to be reproduced.
3. Check the guide copy with the original copy. Many mistakes in duplicating work can be traced to the omission of this step.

▪ Placement of Copy on the Stencil

There are several methods to indicate placement of the copy on the stencil. One is to lay the guide copy on the stencil and jot down the line numbers and spaces for each margin and indention according to the scales printed on the stencil. Another method is to lay the guide copy directly under the stencil sheet and mark the places on the face of the stencil by small dots of correction fluid.

Some duplicating machines permit an adjustment of only about one inch to raise or lower copy on the duplicated sheet. Consequently, it is necessary to place the copy carefully for well-proportioned top and bottom margins.

■ Typing the Stencil

You will be able to produce good stencils if you observe the following recommended procedures:

1. *Clean the type on your typewriter.*

   Typewriter keys must be absolutely clean to get clear, sharp copy. Unless film-topped stencils are used, it is usually necessary to clean the keys after the typing of each stencil. Letters with less surface, like *i, l, c, e,* and *o* (as well as the period), require less pressure and should be watched carefully. It may be necessary to clean them during the course of the stencil typing, especially if the type face is elite in size. A liquid type cleaner should not be allowed to spatter on the stencil sheets, nor should a stiff brush come into contact with the coating.

2. *Prepare the typewriter.*

   Set the ribbon lever to the "off," "white," or "stencil" position. If you fail to do this, the letters will not stencilize completely; only a faint, ragged outline will be reproduced.

   Release card fingers to avoid their hooking into the stencil. Also, move the rolls on the paper bail so that they will not roll on the typed stencil surface.

3. *Follow the instructions.*

   Read the instructions provided by the manufacturer or distributor to determine the correct method of assembling the stencil for insertion into the typewriter.

4. *Type with care.*

   Manual typewriter—Use a firm, slow, sharp, meticulous, letter-by-letter stroking, with a rhythmic, even, staccato touch. Remember to strike the comma, period, quotation marks, and underline key with a lighter touch and to use a slightly heavier-than-normal touch on compact letters such as *m* and *w*.

   Electric typewriter—Experiment to determine the correct pressure. If the pressure is too light, the copy will be uneven; if the pressure is too heavy, the copy will be dense and lack sharpness. To determine the correct pressure, set the indicator at the lowest registration. Move the carriage to the edge of the stencil outside the printing area; while typing a series of periods and commas, gradually raise the pressure to the point where the periods and commas are reproduced clearly and evenly.

5. *Inspect the stencil at the end of each paragraph.*

   See if the typewriter keys are pushing the coating aside properly so that you have clear, even stencilized openings. See if any keys need cleaning or if some are making holes in the stencil. Do not roll the stencil backward any more than is absolutely necessary. There is always a chance that it may wrinkle or tear. When it is necessary to roll it back, hold one corner of the stencil firmly.

—A. B. Dick Company

There are three steps in preparing a stencil for a correction: (1) turn the stencil forward and separate the film from the stencil sheet, (2) burnish, and (3) apply the correction fluid. After the correction fluid has set, type the correction.

Making Corrections on Stencils. The making of corrections on stencils is a painstaking process requiring a light, deft touch. To make a good correction:

1. Turn the stencil forward in the typewriter so that the line is clear of interference. On film-topped stencils, the film must be detached from the stencil heading, as the correction fluid must be applied under the film.

2. When a tissue cushion sheet or typing plate is used, smooth together the edges of the error by rubbing gently with a glass burnisher or the curved end of a paper clip before applying the correction fluid. This procedure prevents the fluid from passing through the stencil and sticking to the cushion or backing sheet. This step is not necessary when a coated cushion sheet is used, as the fluid will not adhere to it.

   Handle correction fluid with care, as it cannot be removed from clothing. Never use it over the writing plate of an illuminated drawing board. When not in use, correction fluid should be kept tightly corked to avoid evaporation.

3. Using a single vertical stroke of the brush, apply a thin coat of correction fluid to the error. The correction fluid should be almost as thin as water for best results. Only a very thin coating of the fluid should be applied over the error— just enough to cover the opening—the less fluid the better, as long as the opening is entirely covered.

4. Let the correction fluid set about half a minute after it has been applied. Test it with the finger for dryness.

5. Type the correction, using a normal or a slightly lighter-than-normal touch. If necessary, make a second light stroke. On an electric typewriter, the pressure adjustment should be lowered slightly.

After final removal from the typewriter, the stencil should be examined for scratches, unnecessary marks, or holes. All of these should be covered with correction fluid. If other blemishes show up after the stencil is on the machine, paint them out with correction fluid.

■ Proofreading the Stencil

Every stencil should be checked paragraph by paragraph while being typed and also read in its entirety after it is taken from the typewriter. Accuracy is paramount in duplicating work.

If the proofreading must be done alone by the secretary, the stencil should be read back phrase by phrase in comparison with the guide copy, if the guide copy has already been checked with the original. The safest method is to have another person read aloud slowly from the guide copy while you check the stencil, holding it up to the light, or from the copy that offsets onto the cushion or backing sheet. Circle each error conspicuously so that it can be located easily for correction.

Patching Stencils. A surprising amount of stencil patching and rearranging is possible. This salvaging work can be done before or after the stencil has been run on the duplicating machine.

The correction or new material to be inserted is typed on an unused section of a spoiled stencil sheet that is still attached to its backing sheet. The piece to be discarded is cut out and the opening neatly trimmed. The new copy is cut with a margin around all sides and placed on the face of the stencil sheet over the opening. Make sure the patch is in proper alignment and that the edges do not cover up any other copy on the stencil sheet. The patch is then anchored with patching cement and sealed all around the edges with correction fluid to prevent leakage at any point.

Replacing Letters. If the centers of the round portions of letters such as "d's," "o's," and "b's" have fallen out of the stencil sheet, it is possible to insert new centers. To do this, type the correct letter at the very bottom of the stencil sheet or on an old stencil. With the point of a pin, pick up the missing part of the letter and lay it carefully in position where it is needed. Apply a mere speck of correction fluid with the point of a straight pin in one or two spots on the edge of the piece inserted. This fluid will hold the inserted letter part in place without spoiling the general contour of the outline.

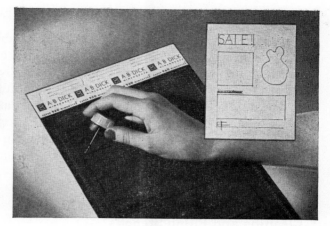

Dots of correction fluid at starting and stopping points of copy areas locate paragraphs, lettering, illustrations, and so forth.

—A. B. Dick Company

■ Guide Points for Salutations and Addresses

When typing a stencil for letters that are to have the inside addresses inserted individually on the typewriter, indicate the beginning position of the address by making a tiny dot on the stencil with a pin at the point where the inside address or salutation should start. This is an efficiency aid to the person who will fill in the addresses. These small dots are almost invisible after the fill-ins are made. They can also be used to indicate folding, cutting, or stapling positions.

■ Handwork on Stencils

The drawing of lines, forms, and illustrations; hand lettering; and other artistic work on stencils require the skillful use of styli, lettering guides, screen plates, and the illuminated drawing board. Best results are obtained when a flexible writing plate is used instead of the cushion sheet under the stencil.

The selection of the correct stylus is very important. In general, the wire-loop stylus should be used for solid-line work and signatures, a wheel stylus for charts, graphs, and ruled forms, ball point for fine detail work, and a lettering guide stylus for lettering. Books and packets can be obtained, providing headings, cartoons, and illustrations designed to be traced on stencils.

■ Running Off the Copies

There are a number of different models and makes of stencil duplicating machines in use in business offices. A detailed instruction booklet accompanies each machine, describing how it should be operated. If you will study this instruction booklet, you will be able to operate your machine satisfactorily. If additional help is needed, call on the company servicing your machine. These companies are always glad to assist users of their machines to obtain the best duplicating results possible.

The stack of duplicated copies should be lifted out of the tray without joggling or straightening and laid aside until the copies are dry. Paper used in stencil duplicating is more absorbent than regular correspondence paper; but, even so, the ink may smear unless the sheets are allowed to dry before they are handled.

■ Cleaning and Filing Stencils

Only those stencils which may be reused are cleaned and filed. Cleaning may be done by placing the stencil between two sheets of newspaper and rubbing the surface of the newspaper to remove the ink from the stencil, using fresh newspaper until all ink is removed. When water-based contact-drying inks are used, wash the stencil with soap in lukewarm water before filing it.

There are special stencil wrappers made of absorbent paper stock for filing stencils that are used with oil-base emulsion (or paste) inks. With these wrappers it is not necessary to clean a stencil before filing it; merely place the stencil in the wrapper, ink side up. The wrapper is then closed, and the entire surface is rubbed with a smooth hard object such as the bottom of an ink bottle or a paper weight. Leave the stencil in the folder from five to sixty minutes; then open the folder, loosen the stencil, and turn it over. Close the folder. A new wrapper should be used each time a stencil is reused. The stencil is left in the wrapper and filed as you would file a regular folder. While there are special file cabinets in which to file used stencils, they can also be filed in empty stencil boxes and stored on edge.

A plan should be followed for identifying stencils for future use. When a stencil wrapper is used, one of the duplicated copies may be attached to the wrapper; or the wrapper itself may be run through the duplicator before the stencil is removed, thus reproducing on the wrapper a copy of the stencil. To avoid excessive handling of stencils, a numbering system is frequently used. The stencil and a duplicated copy are identified with the same number. The copies are then filed in a folder or punched and inserted into a notebook. Thus when a stencil is to be rerun, its number is obtained from the filed copy, and the stencil is located by number.

Direct-Process Masters

The master sheet for the direct-process duplicator is prepared by either typing, writing, or tracing on a master sheet backed by a direct-process carbon. The coated side of the carbon paper is against the back of the master sheet; thus the impressions are made in reverse on the back of the master.

Master sheets are available in sets with the carbon attached and interleaved with tissue which must be removed before use of the master. Long-run, medium-run, and short-run master sets can be obtained. Copies are printed in the color of the carbon paper used with the master. Variety can be obtained very simply by dropping in small pieces of different colored carbon for certain areas on the master. Varying colors in close relationship to each other cause little or no problem on the direct-process master.

Two masters can be prepared at the same time by placing one master sheet with its carbon over another master sheet with its carbon. This makes possible identical copies with one operation and is a time-saver when the length of the run exceeds the number of copies possible from one master.

The carbon paper should be handled with care because it soils the fingers very easily, and the dye is quite hard to remove. Special cleansing cream and soap for removing the dye can be purchased and should certainly be kept easily and quickly available wherever direct-process masters are used. (Creaming the hands before using the carbon makes any carbon stains easier to remove.)

> WHEN A MASTER is to be signed—To keep the master clean while it is on your employer's desk awaiting signature, reinsert the tissue sheet between the carbon and the master. Circle and cut out the space from the tissue where he will sign. Thus when he signs, his signature goes through on the carbon paper beneath.

▪ Preparing Masters

The typewriter keys should be clean and a firm, even stroke used in typing the master. If an electric typewriter is used, it will be necessary to experiment to determine the pressure control that will produce the best copy. An acetate *backing sheet* placed back of the carbon is recommended if the typewriter platen is soft. The paper-bail rolls should be placed so that they do not roll against the master in order that their pressure does not cause smudges to appear on the copies.

▪ Drawing on the Master

Artwork and ruled lines can be traced directly on the master by laying the copy on top of the sheet and tracing over the copy. The impression will be transferred to the back of the sheet by the carbon underneath. A pencil, stylus, or ball-point pen can be used. Halftone effects can be obtained by using a shading plate beneath the carbon copy and rubbing over it. Multicolored drawings can be made by using the different colors of carbon paper.

▪ Making Corrections

Corrections can be made by blocking out the error with a wax blockout pencil as follows:

1. Separate the master sheet from the carbon. (Some secretaries prefer to insert a master set into the typewriter with the bound edges at the bottom so that it is not necessary to detach the carbon in making corrections.) Care must be exercised not to wrinkle the set in placing it in the typewriter.

2. Lay back the master sheet so that the error rests on the flat part of the typewriter, or put a rigid shield underneath it.

3. Scrape the carbon dye from the error with a razor blade or knife or the special stylus with a small blade made for this purpose. Remove remaining carbon with a soft typewriter eraser.

4. Cover the error with a wax block-out pencil. (This step may not be necessary but is an extra precaution and recommended to assure a perfect correction.)

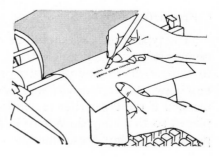

5. Roll the sheet and carbon into approximate position for typing. Slip a small piece of unused carbon paper in back of the error and type the correction. Remove the carbon slip immediately.

Errors may also be corrected by using an adhesive paper correction tape which has the same surface as the master sheet. It comes in single-line and double-line widths. Cut off the length needed and press it on the back of the master over the copy to be corrected. It is not necessary to remove the carbon dye first. Type in the correction. This method is best when there are several letters or more to be corrected.

> A SAFETY HINT! Keep the single-edge razor blade you use for corrections in an empty matchbook, sharp edge inserted where the matches used to be. If you use a double-edge blade, wrap several thicknesses of adhesive tape around the center. Leave the corners free for scraping.

A small area can be permanently blocked out by cutting the area out with a razor blade or by covering it on the carbon side with plastic tape. A self-adhesive correction tape is available in one-, two-, three-, and four-line widths. The tape is put over the word or words to be corrected and the copy retyped. A full line or several lines can be corrected in this manner.

■ Preparing Masters on Copying Machines

Transfer image masters for direct-process duplication can be produced by some office copiers. Production of a master is almost as simple as making a copy from an original. For example, a special reflex-process master is used to produce a master on a thermographic machine. The original and the master unit are combined and passed through the copying machine. The infrared heat causes a transfer of the material to the master sheet, and an exact reproduction of the original is obtained. The master may be immediately placed on the duplicator and run.

■ Reuse of Masters

Masters can be rerun. A master, however, can reproduce in total only a limited number of copies. Additions, changes, or corrections can be made on a master even after it has been run. For example, it is possible to run a dozen copies from a master, to insert additional information on it, and then to run more copies. Instead of removing the carbon paper from the master copy sheet, fold the carbon sheet under the master and leave it attached when placing the master on the machine for the first run. This method keeps the unit set intact and holds the carbon paper in its original position for making the addition and retaining the original alignment.

Offset-Process Master

The preparation of the offset master is no more difficult than the preparation of a direct-process master or a stencil. In some respects it is easier, as the writing is done directly on the face of the master. Guide lines for placement of the copy may be penciled in, the copy is clearly readable for proofreading as it is being typed, and corrections are easily made.

▪ Typing the Offset Master

A special ribbon is required for typing on an offset master. The ribbon, which contains a grease-based ink, may be either a fiber or plastic-base ribbon. The offset ribbon provides black copy and can be used also for general typing work and correspondence. When offset masters are prepared regularly in an office, the offset ribbon can be used for all work, to avoid the inconvenience of changing the ribbon each time a master is to be typed. However, a fiber ribbon should not be reused too many times, or the quality of reproduction will deteriorate. The commonly used plastic-base ribbon produces the sharpest image.

As in all other duplicating processes, the type face should be kept clean and the paper-bail rolls moved so that they ride on the master, but outside the usage area. The typing is done directly on the face of the master. A normal typing stroke is used. If the stroke is too heavy, it will tend to dent the master slightly and cause poor reproductions. Because of its uniform key pressure, the electric typewriter produces excellent offset masters.

Allow a time interval of fifteen minutes to one hour between the typing and running of the master, to permit the image to set.

A nonreproducing pencil may be used to help plan the placement of the copy on the plate. With this pencil, markings can be made directly on the master as guide lines in typing the copy. The pencil marks will not reproduce.

▪ Writing, Drawing, and Tracing

Writing, lettering, drawing, and rulings may be made directly on the offset master. An offset ink, crayon, or pencil that will adhere to the master and leave a film must be used.

An offset carbon paper must be used to trace a form or sketch directly on the master. The carbon paper is placed over the master, carbon side down and the drawing on top of the carbon. The tracing is done with a ball-point pen, hard pencil, or stylus.

Another method of tracing is to use a very thin, translucent tracing paper with a yellow wax coating. The copy to be traced is placed under the master and the tracing paper on top. An illuminated drawing board or scope is used, and the copy is traced with a sharp pencil or stylus. This method eliminates the extra thickness, gives a sharper outline, and protects the original from tracing marks.

A drawing fluid can be brushed on for heavy lettering. Signatures and other data can be put on with a rubber stamp used with an offset ink stamp pad.

▪ Making Corrections

Corrections are made by erasing the error and retyping. A special eraser is produced for this purpose, but any soft (nongritty) eraser may be used. Only a few light erasing strokes are necessary, as the deposit comes off readily. A faint "ghost" image will remain, but it will not reproduce. Clean the eraser by rubbing it on paper after each stroke to prevent ink on the eraser from rubbing into the surface of the master. Avoid touching any other spot as you erase, as it will smudge and the smudge will reproduce. Use a normal touch to type in the correction. A second correction cannot be made in the same spot.

To reinsert a typed master into the typewriter, lay a clean sheet of paper over the master to prevent the typewriter rollers from smudging the typing.

When proofreading, hold the master along the edges to avoid fingerprints on the surface, for they will reproduce.

▪ Cleaning and Storing Masters

A master can be rerun any number of times if it is properly cleaned and filed. To clean a master after a run, use a clean cotton pad moistened with water, and gently clean the surface. Remove any ink or solution left along the edges of the master. The master should then be covered with a thin coating of a preservative (gum solution). After it has dried, it may be placed in a plain, non-oily paper folder and stored in a file drawer. Separate the unused masters by a sheet of paper or a folder, or they may pick up traces of oil or ink from the back of the adjoining master. These spots will reproduce on the finished copy when the master is rerun.

Paper for Copiers and Duplicators

The secretary or supervisor may be assigned the responsibility for buying paper for the office copier and duplicator. The purchasing problem is complicated because several of the office copiers use sensitized papers, and each duplicating process requires its own type of paper.

An important consideration in buying copier paper is to avoid overstocking. Most copier papers have a "shelf life" which should be checked before buying in quantity.

Paper used in duplicating is usually wood sulfite. It comes in a wide variety of colors. The three standard weights for mimeo and duplicating paper are 16, 20, and 24 pounds. Offset paper may carry these same weight identifications or different weights such as 50, 60, or 70 pounds. A 50-pound offset paper weighs slightly less than a 20-pound bond.

Offset paper comes in two general types—coated and uncoated. The coated paper is designed for high-grade work, and offset enamel is the very highest quality. Uncoated paper is used for the majority of in-house work which does not require a high quality reproduction.

Paper for stencil duplicating, unlike that for spirit duplicating, is unglazed and absorbent. Since moisture affects the quality of reproduction and the ease with which the paper is handled by the machine, duplicating paper should be kept wrapped in the moisture-proof covers in which it is received, stored in a dry place, and stacked flat.

Duplicator paper, like other paper, has a top and a bottom side. The best results are obtained by using the paper top side up. The printed label on the package usually indicates the correct printing side.

Commercial Duplication

In every city there are commercial shops that make a specialty of duplicating work. These businesses are usually listed in the Yellow Pages of the telephone directory under such headings as "Letter Service and Addressing" or "Letter Shops." They will prepare the stencil or master, run the copies, address the envelopes, fold and insert the enclosures, and so on. They will do any one phase or the entire job.

If the office does not have adequate duplicating equipment or if time is short, the secretary or supervisor may need to turn to an outside shop. She will then investigate the service offered and the rates charged, place the order, and follow up to see that the work is completed as directed and on time. She should keep a file of information about the shops with which she has worked.

Suggested Readings

"Copying Machine Book—and Xerox Xoom," *Newsweek*. (New York: Newsweek, Inc., 1965), Vol. LXVI, No. 2 (November 8, 1965), pp. 84–88.

Peck, Daniel. "Duplicators: How to Select One," *Administrative Management*. (New York: Geyer-McAllister Publications, 1965), Vol. XXVI, No. 10 (October, 1965), pp. 86–96.

————. "Paper for Copiers and Duplicators," *Administrative Management*. (New York: Geyer-McAllister Publications, 1966), Vol. XXVII, No. 5 (May, 1966), pp. 88–100.

"The Revolution in Office Copying," *Chemical & Engineering News*, Parts I and II. (Washington, D.C.: The American Chemical Society, 1964), (July 13, 1964), pp. 115–129; (July 20, 1964), pp. 85–96. (Also published as a separate report.)

Techniques of Mimeographing. Chicago: A. B. Dick Company, 1966, 26 pp.

Techniques of Offset. Chicago: A. B. Dick Company, 1964, 51 pp.

Questions for Discussion

1. What factors should be considered in selecting (a) a copying machine? (b) a duplicating machine?

2. Indicate which process of copying or duplicating you would recommend for each of the following projects, assuming that all types of copying and duplicating processes are available for use.

   (a) 2,000 copies of a form letter to be sent to sales prospects
   (b) 6 copies of an order to be distributed to department heads with the least possible delay
   (c) 300 copies of a notice to be sent to all salesmen, announcing the annual contest
   (d) 15 copies of a two-page report to be sent to department heads
   (e) 600 copies of a four-page house newspaper that is issued monthly and contains pictures and illustrations
   (f) 55 copies of a one-page announcement showing the route to be followed to reach the annual picnic grounds (The notices are to be placed on bulletin boards throughout the plant.)
   (g) 5 copies of the secretary's minutes of the directors' meeting
   (h) 120 copies of a price list duplicated each week (The list covers 72 standard items arranged in alphabetical order. As the prices fluctuate, a new price list is prepared, duplicated, and distributed weekly to all sales employees.)
   (i) 800 preprinted time cards to be titled each week—one time card for each company employee (The title on the card shows the employee's number, his name, address, social security number, and number of income tax exemptions.)

3. For what purposes would the addressing machine be used in each of the following types of offices or business:

   (a) Publishing company
   (b) Advertising firm
   (c) Payroll department of a large manufacturing company
   (d) Billing and shipping department of a wholesale firm

4. Suppose that you were to mimeograph four pages of building specifications in straight single-spaced copy. After all the stencils were typed, you discovered that you had omitted the second line from the bottom of the first page. What would you do? What would you do if the mistake had occurred in the middle of any page?

5. What are some of the methods by which a duplicated letter can be personalized?

6. What is meant by "overcopying"? Why is it a major problem in the office?

7. A company uses a printed contract for all projects. There are, however, a number of individual insertions that go into each separate contract, such as names, dates, places, amounts. Usually twenty copies are made of each contract for distribution to departments and branch offices. Several contracts are processed each week. Up to this time, fill-ins using carbon paper have been made on the printed contract forms. What suggestions can you make to speed up this work?

8. List criteria you might wish to use as a supervisor to evaluate the appearance of duplicated copies of material.

9. One of your assistants duplicated a report on a stencil machine. Upon examining the copies you note the following:

(a) On part of the copies, one side of the page is lighter than the other side.
(b) The letters are not evenly sharp and are rather broad and heavy.
(c) The center of some of the circular letters such as *o* and *p* and *d* are all ink.

What would you suggest that your assistant do to improve the quality of her duplicating work?

10. Find the words that have been converted in these sentences to unconventional parts of speech; find more suitable words. Then refer to the Reference Guide to evaluate your answers.

(a) They constantly interrupt the program to give a commercial.
(b) People in the know suspect a seasonal upswing.
(c) He gets paid for being an extra each day he is on the set.
(d) Observance of company policy is a must in every office.

Problems

■ 1. Show all your calculations in determining the answers to the following:

(a) If you run a stencil-duplication job on 8½- by 11-inch paper with 1½-inch top and bottom margins, how many lines of single-spaced copy can you place on each stencil?

(b) How many lines of double-spaced copy can you get on 8½- by 14-inch paper with a 2-inch top margin and a 1½-inch bottom margin?

(c) If your paper is 7¼ by 10½ inches and each side margin is 1½ inches, how many spaces are available in each line if your typewriter has pica type? elite?

■ **2.** Be prepared to demonstrate any one of the following:

(a) **Planning the placement of the guide copy on a stencil or offset master**

(b) **Typing the stencil or offset master**

(c) **Correcting errors on a stencil, direct-process master, and offset master**

■ **3.** To help employees you are supervising, prepare an instruction sheet clearly explaining procedures for one of the following activities, illustrating your explanation, if possible:

(a) **Placing the master copy on a direct-process duplicator and running the copies**

(b) **Placing the stencil on a stencil duplicator, running the copies, and removing and preparing the stencil for filing**

(c) **Placing the master on the offset duplicator, running the copies, and removing and preparing the master for filing**

(d) **Using a copying machine**

(e) **Using a heat transfer copier to produce a direct-process master**

(f) **Using a copying machine to produce an offset master**

(g) **Preparing a liquid duplicating master and making five copies**

Related Work Assignments 17-22

17. Duplicating on the Stencil Duplicator.   Mr. Simpson asks you to prepare a stencil and run ten copies of the vertical bar graph shown on page 483.   Underneath the graph you are to type the five suggestions for preparing bar graphs shown on page 484.

(a) **Prepare a guide copy.**

(b) **When you are satisfied with the accuracy and form of the guide copy, plan your stencil placement.**

(c) **Type the stencil and draw lines.**

(d) **Run ten copies. File one copy with the materials that you are collecting for your secretarial handbook.**

18. Duplicating on the Direct-Process Duplicator.   An additional supply of routing slips is needed.   Prepare a master sheet for the direct-process duplicator for the duplicated routing slip shown on page 153.   Plan your work so that you get at least four slips per duplicated page.   Run 10 sheets and cut into separate forms.   File one copy with the materials that you are collecting for your secretarial handbook.

Plan the placement of the copy on the master sheet so that when the duplicated pages are cut, the separate slips will be uniform in size.

19. Duplicating Form Letters
20. Duplicating a Program } The instructions and supplies necessary for the completion of Related Work Assignments 19 and 20 are provided in the Workbook.

21. Your Fundamentals. This is the third in a series of workbook assignments reviewing English usage, grammar, and punctuation. These assignments are based on the Reference Guide in this textbook.

22. Measuring Your Secretarial Information (Parts I and II). The instructions and supplies necessary for the completion of this assignment are provided in the Workbook.

2—1 √ handling customers

Mr. Westerly, Virginia Cramer's employer, is sales manager for a computer manufacturer headquartered in New York. An important West Coast customer, in town for the National Business Equipment show, was a prospective customer for a computer. Mr. Westerly had invited him to be his guest at lunch at the airport before flying in a company plane to a city 200 miles distant to see a computer installation in a company similar to that of the prospect.

Mr. Westerly had to be in Chicago the morning of the appointment but expected to get back by 10:30. At 11 he telephoned from Chicago to say that he had been delayed but would arrive at 12:45. He asked Virginia to take the prospective customer and his assistant to lunch at the airport, where he would join them for dessert.

When Virginia telephoned the hotel, the customer's administrative assistant answered petulantly, "Well, I don't think Mr. Cantor will want to make the trip now. Why should we sit around all day waiting for lunch with a secretary? What could be more important in Chicago than a confirmed appointment in New York?"

If you were Virginia, how would you handle the situation?

2—2 √ secretarial workshop

A brochure addressed to Thelma Turner's employer and announcing a residential workshop for secretaries passes across Thelma's desk. The workshop would require her absence from the job for three work days. Thelma is interested in attending, recognizing it as a part of her professional development. From past experience, however, Thelma feels that her employer would be indifferent to her attending because of the personal inconvenience he would undergo. On the other hand, the company has a policy of upgrading its employees, underwriting the cost of tuition.

What factors should Thelma take into consideration in deciding upon a course of action in regard to attending the workshop?

2—3 √ pre-employment tests

All employees of the Acme Manufacturing Company are hired by the personnel department. Since the company has a factory force comparatively larger than the office staff, the major emphasis in the personnel department has been in recruiting, testing, and obtaining factory employees.

All office services for the company are centralized in one department under the direction of the office manager. A number of clerical typists are employed to perform a wide variety of jobs related to correspondence, filing, forms, duplication, statistical reports, and so forth.

The company has been having difficulty in obtaining qualified typists. Although additional staff have been employed, costly delays are frequently experienced in getting out the office work. Because of pressure, the turnover of typists is high.

When the office manager complains to the personnel department, he is told that all applicants for typing positions take a five-minute straight-copy test and only those typists who are able to type at a rate of 50 net words a minute are considered for employment. The personnel department states that this is a standard higher than that required by most companies.

The office manager believes that an inadequate screening device is being used. The personnel department requests him to submit a list of basic typing skills on which to test future applicants. The office manager in turn delegates this assignment to his secretary.

What items do you think should be tested?

Could the items you suggest be tested? How?

2—4 √ assuming responsibility

Helen Spears is secretary to Mr. Marshall, head of the sales department of the Regal Manufacturing Company. Mary Davenport, a new sales correspondent, is assigned a desk adjacent to Helen. Mary is a very congenial person whom Helen likes very much. Unfortunately, however, Mary starts a conversation with Helen whenever she feels like it. This is very disturbing to Helen, who wishes she could do something about the matter without offending her friend.

The matter comes to a head one morning. Just as Helen is leaving dictation, Mr. Marshall says: "Helen, I wonder if you are aware of the poor example you are setting for the rest of the office staff. I notice that you and Mary are constantly carrying on a conversation. The whole atmosphere of the office seems to be deteriorating, and I am expecting you to do something about it."

Helen is somewhat taken back by Mr. Marshall's reprimand and answers: "Mr. Marshall, I am aware of the situation, but it is all Mary's fault. I have tried to discourage her talking."

Helen is very annoyed at Mr. Marshall; she thinks he should have spoken to Mary and not to her.

What is your analysis of the situation? What action should Helen take?

PART 3

—H. Armstrong Roberts

The secretary is the executive's right-hand assistant in processing mail, producing quality notes and transcription, and carrying out challenging composing assignments.

The Secretary's Communi-
cation Responsibilities

One of the basic ways of doing business is by correspondence. The secretary is the executive's right-hand assistant in handling the voluminous mail that floods his office. She organizes incoming material for efficient handling. She collects pertinent information to support the dictation of replies. She takes and transcribes his dictation so skillfully that sometimes the finished product represents what the executive wishes he had said, rather than what he did say. When she really masters this part of her job, she composes letters and memoranda based on his suggestions.

Ch.

7   **Processing Mail**

8   **Taking and Giving Dictation**

9   **Turning Out Quality Transcription**

10   **Composing Assignments**

Processing Mail

Today's executive could be drowned in the sea of paperwork surrounding him. For instance, almost 150 pieces of mail are addressed to him every day. From the first—and heaviest—mail of the day through the frequent later deliveries, not to mention the intervening telegrams and special-delivery letters, he struggles to keep up with a flood of communications—those he receives and those he must send. His secretary valiantly supports his efforts by *processing* mail as it arrives, following systematic steps that organize the material before it is given to him for action. As she gains in understanding of his job and hers, an efficient secretary gains also in ability to follow up for him an increasing amount of his correspondence as this responsibility is assigned to her. This task is one of the most valuable ones that an administrative assistant can perform.

Steps of processing the executive's incoming mail are described in sequence in this chapter. Processing of outgoing mail is emphasized in later chapters.

The Mailroom Function

Just as soon as the heavy canvas bags are delivered, mail clerks empty them, laying aside the bulky pieces and arranging the envelopes in face-up position for efficient sorting. They place in their proper pigeonholes the envelopes addressed to individuals and departments.

They open the remaining general mail with an automatic opener, remove the contents, and stamp on each piece the date and time of receipt. They staple loose enclosures to their covering letters, and in some instances staple the envelope to the back of its letter.

They hastily scan each letter, decide to whom it should be given, and put it in the proper compartment. Then they deliver both the unopened and opened mail to the proper recipient as quickly as possible.

When the mail arrives, the secretary stops all but the most urgent rush work to process it and get it to the executive. Not just the first mail of the day but each delivery signals the beginning of a familiar cycle.

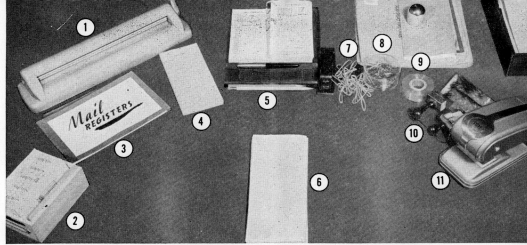

—*Department of Photography, The Ohio State University*

Notice that after the letter opener (1) has been used, it is put to one side. Within easy reach for notations are the tickler file (2), mail registers (3), routing slips (4), and desk appointment calendar (5). The opened envelopes (6) are stacked in front of the secretary; and rubber bands (7), paper clips (8), cellophane tape (9), rubber stamps (10), and the time stamp (11) are handily located.

▪ Needed Supplies

For smooth, coordinated processing of the mail, before you start to open any of it, lay out your supplies. Place each item efficiently in the most convenient position for reach and use:

You will need:

An envelope opener
A stapler, pins, or clips
Pencils
The tickler

You may also need:

A dater or time stamp
A routing stamp or slips
An action stamp or slips
Cellophane tape for mending

▪ First Sorting of Important Mail

The mail may be sorted three times if it is received in considerable volume. On the first sort, pull out only the *important business and personal mail for immediate processing.* Lay aside all envelopes that look as if they might contain letters of importance to the executive. But, you ask, how can you tell from the envelope if the letter will be important? There are two ways:

The Source. The sender's name, address, or the postmark tells you the source or gives you a clue to it. You will soon learn to recognize those business and personal correspondents of high interest to the executive, because you will become familiar with his business activities and certain facets of his personal and family life.

The secretary can greatly aid the executive's follow-up if she uses good judgment in sorting the mail and arranging it for his attention.

Kind of Mail Service Used. An airmail letter, a special-delivery letter, or a certified letter signals "Important." An airmail package takes precedence over a parcel-post package.

After completing the first sorting, stop and process the important mail according to the procedures given on page 150. Do not open the personal letters even though they are not marked as *confidential* or *personal*. Set them aside to give to the executive unopened with the processed mail. Do not be concerned if you find that you have included something that is unimportant. This is preferable to missing something that is important.

▪ Second and Third Sortings

Lay out the mail by kind in a second and a third sorting. Because of their bulkiness, pull out the publications and lay them outside the work area. They can be opened, identified, and scanned sometime later. First, sort the envelope mail into these three groups: business, personal, and advertising.

Business Mail. The bulk of each mail will be business mail—that which relates to the purposes of the office. It, you will quickly learn, has a pattern. Because of its quantity and pattern, sort this group once more into like kinds—envelopes from branch offices, from the home office, from customers or clients, from traveling associates, from suppliers, and so on. Group the first-class window envelopes which usually contain invoices or statements. Put a large X on the back of any incorrectly addressed or odd-looking envelope to remind you to attach it to the letter for the executive's attention.

Personal Mail. Personal mail also has a pattern. If there is enough volume, sort it again according to *the executive's outside activities* and *his financial interests.* Open and process the activities mail from: the societies to which he belongs, the clubs of which he is a member, the organizations which he serves, sources from which he buys items that he collects, and so on. Separate the financial mail into like kinds— such as the bills, the bank letters, investment-house letters, and stock-ownership letters. A new secretary should not open them until the employer gives permission to process them.

Advertising Mail. Advertising mail will be received in envelopes of all sizes, shapes, and colors—for attention value. You can easily spot it, although the advertisers try hard to fool you. The envelopes rarely, if ever, carry first-class postage. They almost always have open ends with sealed flaps. They have precancelled stamps or printed permit numbers and are not postmarked. Open these when you have time, perhaps after the other mail is processed and handed to the executive. Organize the contents of advertising mail (it is always full of floating, loose pieces, it seems) and give them to the executive at your convenience sometime during the day. Do not destroy them. The executive likes to keep up on *direct mail*—as it is called in the advertising profession. He likes to know what is being advertised and how, and sometimes he returns the enclosed postcards.

▪ Opening the Envelopes

Keep the sorted groups intact for convenient handling of the letters later. Open the envelopes along the top edges for the easiest removal of contents. The efficient placement of envelopes and the movements differ according to the kind of opener used. Here is an efficient routine for a right-handed person using scissors or a letter knife:

1. Keep forearm working area free.
2. Place stack of envelopes to the left, flap up, with top edges to the right.
3. Hold envelope with left hand; slip the knife under the flap and with one quick stroke open the edge or cut off a narrow strip along the flap edge with the scissors.
4. Lay the opened envelope down with the left hand, in the left-side area. Keep the cut edges to the right.

The secretary knows that of utmost importance in processing the executive's mail is extreme care not to damage contents of an envelope. The letter opener shown at the left slices a hairline edge from the top of the envelope.

—*Pitney-Bowes, Inc.*

When using a lever-operated letter opener (as illustrated above):

1. **Stack the envelopes with the top edges parallel to the letter opener.**
2. **Insert one envelope, press the lever, and lay the envelope to the left side without changing position of the envelope.**

The letter opener illustrated is hand operated. Mail rooms use electrically driven openers that can open more than one hundred envelopes a minute (or that operate at high rates of speed).

▪ Removing the Contents

To remove the contents, again keep the forearm working area free. Place the stack of opened envelopes to the left, open edges to the right, flap sides up. Pull out the contents with the right hand. With the left, hold the envelope up to the light, glance to see that everything has been removed, and lay it to the far left, still with the same side up. Use both hands to unfold and flatten the letter and attach enclosures. As you open the letter, scan to see if it contains the sender's address; if not, retrieve the envelope and attach it to the letter. Scan also to see if the letter mentions enclosures, and whether those you found agree with the letter. If not, after checking inside the envelope again, underline the reference notation of the enclosure or the mention of the enclosure in the letter and write *"no"* nearby. Attach each marked envelope to its enclosed letter to be given to the executive.

Mend anything torn. Lay the unfolded letters *face down* in a stack to the right to keep them in the same order as the envelopes in case a letter and envelope have to be rematched later.

▪ Dating and Time Stamping

The date of receipt of a piece of mail may be jotted down in pencil in abbreviated form in some convenient place on the face of the letter, such as 4/4/--, not April 4, 19--, in the space between the printed letterhead and the body of the letter. More likely the secretary will use one of the date- or time-stamp devices that are available.

For several reasons it is important to know the date on which each piece of mail is received:

1. It furnishes a record of the date of receipt.
2. It furnishes an impetus to answer the mail promptly. (Each reply should be regarded as a builder of good will, but no reply which is unduly delayed—no matter how courteous or affable it is—will promote good public relations.)
3. A letter may have arrived too late to take care of the matter to which it refers. The date of receipt authenticates that inability.
4. The letter may be undated. The only clue to its date is the date of receipt. (You may find it hard to believe, but undated letters are frequently mailed—even letters typewritten by secretaries.)

▪ Saving the Envelopes

It may be a rule in your office that each envelope be stapled to the back of each piece of mail received. If not, save the envelopes for one day when you need to locate quickly one that you find should be attached to a letter. The envelope may be needed to identify the sender, to determine the sender's address, to investigate the reasons for delayed receipt, to recheck for missing enclosures, to establish legality of time of mailing, and so on. Specifically, these include situations in which:

1. An envelope is incorrectly addressed. When the executive dictates his answer, he may want to mention the correct address for the future guidance of the correspondent, or as explanation of why the letter was not answered more promptly.
2. A letter was missent by the post office and had to be forwarded. This information is needed to explain the reason for a delayed answer.
3. A letter does not contain a return address.

4. The return address in the letter differs from that on the envelope. Sometimes an individual uses business, hotel, or club stationery and does not indicate his return address, even though the answer to his letter should not be sent to him at the address given in the letterhead.

5. The date of the letter differs too much from the date of its receipt. A comparison of the letter date with the postmark date will reveal whether the fault lies with the sender or with the postal service.

6. Neither a handwritten nor a typewritten signature appears in the letter. The name of the sender may appear as a part of the return address on the envelope.

7. A letter specifies an enclosure that was not attached to the letter or found in the envelope.

8. A letter contains a bid, or an offer or acceptance of a contract. The postmark date may be needed as legal evidence.

▪ Reading, Underlining, and Annotating

After the envelopes have been opened and the contents dated, the interesting, secretarial part of handling the mail begins. It involves three steps:

1. Read each letter through once, scanning for important facts. Make necessary calendar notations.

2. Underline those words and phrases that tell the story as you read the letter again. Be thrifty with underlining. Call attention only to the necessary words and phrases.

3. Annotate (write in a margin) any necessary or helpful note to the executive.

Marginal annotations come under two headings:

1. Suggested disposition of routine letters, such as "File," "Ack." (for acknowledge), and "Give to Sales Department." (The secretary anticipates the executive's decision and saves his time, but he may disagree with her suggestion and retain the letter for his own handling.)

2. Special notes, such as "See our last letter attached" (which the secretary will have removed from the files and attached to the annotated letter), or "You verbally promised to make this talk when Mr. B. was in." (Such notes are usually reminders, although some may be of a helpful identifying type—that is, a brief "who's who" of the writer or the company.)

You may be asking, "Shall I, as a new secretary, read, underline, and especially annotate, if my predecessor did not?" The answer is "yes." Act as if it is a part of your understanding of a real secretary's service. If the employer questions the routine, abide by his decision. He is more likely to praise the practice, however, than to question it; if it is intelligently done, it saves him time.

Filing Notations. While processing, add the filing notations on letters that require no replies, to save extra handling. For example, Clyne Crawford's reply to your letter might be filed without further correspondence so the filing notation should be put on the letter during processing. Methods of determining where to file letters and when and how to make filing notations are presented in a later chapter.

Limiting Annotations. Since original letters are sometimes copied on machines and sent outside the organization, an executive may request you to avoid all writing on the face of letters and ask you to add annotations only on the back of them. Usually, however, a colored pencil or ink that will not reproduce can be used. The media and colors that will not appear on copies vary with the different processes of copying, so you may have to determine and obtain the proper ones for your copying machine. On the other hand, many executives want notations copied to achieve compact yet comprehensive records.

The annotations and the date-time stamp indicate that this letter is ready for presentation to the executive.

---------------------------*Reed and Howard, Inc.*

202 Lincoln Avenue   Detroit, Michigan 48230

Telephone 313-381-9024 ---------------------------

November 17, 19--

Mr. William C. Campbell
Carlson Products Corporation
789 South Washington Avenue
Lansing, Michigan 48933

NOV 18 10 29 AM 19

Dear Mr. Campbell:

Thank you very much for your <u>order of November 12.</u> The materials have been <u>shipped by express</u> as you requested. Your invoice is enclosed. Please let us know if you do not receive the shipment within a reasonable length of time.

T-11-21

The <u>question</u> that you raise <u>regarding</u> the use of a card file for your test data is an unusual one, and we hesitate to make a recommendation until we know more about your problem. Our representative, <u>Mr. James E. Cole</u> (who is located at 601 Collins Avenue in Lansing) will be glad to discuss this matter with you in detail. He will <u>call on you in a few days</u> to make an appointment. Feel free to use his services without obligating your company in any way.

Called on you last month

Please substitute the enclosed copy of our latest price list for the copy you now have on file.

Sincerely yours,

James E. Reed

James E. Reed
Sales Manager

mvh

Enclosures: Invoice ✓
Price List

No

▪ Expediting the Executive's Handling of Mail

You can expedite the executive's handling of specific letters by anticipating and preparing for certain procedural steps that he will take. You can be of help to him for the mail services described below.

Letter Requiring Background Information. In many cases a letter cannot be answered unless additional information is at hand. For instance, suppose you are a secretary to a sales manager who receives a letter canceling an order because the customer is tired of waiting for delivery. You would look up and attach all the pertinent information about the order, its date of receipt, its present whereabouts, and the cause of holdup. You may have to judge how much background information you should supply. If the executive will ask you for it anyway, anticipate his request. If it only *might* prove useful, weigh the amount of time required to get it, the amount of time you have to give to it, and the executive's probable attitude.

Letter Referring to Previous Correspondence. When there is need to refer to previous correspondence, get it and attach it to the letter. Write *See attached* in a margin of the letter. When a file is bound, put the letter on the file, and indicate the pertinent correspondence by moving the letters so that the edges extend, or insert paper markers.

Letter Requiring Follow-Up. When a letter refers to mail that will follow, or contains a request that requires additional action besides the routine answer, or when a letter must be answered within a certain time, or if other time factors are involved, follow these steps:

1. Select the earliest date in the future when the action should be accomplished.
2. Write that date on the face of the letter with a key (like *T* for *Tickler,* or *FD* for *Follow-Up Date*) so that the executive and you know that a reminder has been recorded.
3. Make a tickler entry under the selected date.
4. If material is expected in a separate mail, write a note on your calendar page, or send a memo to the mail department describing the mail expected. Indicate such notifications in the margin of the letter. (See also Mail Register, page 155.)

Letter Misaddressed to the Executive. When a letter addressed to the executive actually should have been sent to another, annotate the correct person's name in the top margin and put the letter with the other mail for the employer. He will probably ask you to send it on, but he should see it first because it is addressed to him.

DATE_____

TO _____

Refer to the attached material and

☐ Please note.
☐ Please note and file.
☐ Please note and return to me.
☐ Please mail to _____
☐ Please note and talk with me
    this a.m._____; p.m._____.

☐ Please answer, sending me a copy.
☐ Please write a reply for my signature.
☐ Please handle.
☐ Please have _____ photocopies made
    for _____
☐ Please sign.
☐ Please let me have your comments.
☐ Please RUSH — immediate action desired.
☐ Please make follow-up for _____
    _____

REMARKS:

Signed _____

Please read the attached material and pass
it on to the persons indicated.

Refer to:	Date Received	Date Passed on
Adams		
Ashby		
Caldwell		
Cooper		
Crabbe		
Egnew		
Faulkenberry		
Gerhardt		
Hill		
Jones		
Kaising		
Kerr		
Kumpf		
Pendery		
Pineault		
Pugh		
Rahbar		
Rasmussen		
Robinson		
Roman		
Smith		
Templeman		
Thornton		
Wanous		
Wilson		

Return to:

A secretary devised this check-off slip to save the executive's time in distributing information to and requesting action from his assistants. She provided room for his signature or initials at the bottom because an initialed or signed request is more gracious and personal than a printed name.

One of these duplicated slips is attached to each piece of mail that should be distributed to others. The secretary or executive checks in pencil or ink the names of those to receive it. Since routing slips must conform with changes in personnel, they are often office-duplicated rather than printed.

If you forward material to someone else, be sure to keep a record of the transfer in a looseleaf notebook. Otherwise, you will not be able to follow up properly; or you may lose track of important letters that should be returned to you. For each referred item, indicate:

1. **Date of the letter**
2. **Name of the sender**
3. **Subject**
4. **Name of the person to whom you sent the item**
5. **Action that should be taken, such as** *Reply* **or** *File*
6. **Your follow-up date, if any**

Action Needed by an Associate. Often the executive passes a piece of mail on to one of his assistants for action. He may want it to be acknowledged or to be followed up, or he may want a report on the subject matter. When you can anticipate his actions, use a routing and action slip or stamp similar to those illustrated. Lightly pencil in both the individual's name and the action needed or add the stamp or slip to the letters so that the executive can indicate the routing and instruction.

Mail Needing Routing. Often a piece of mail should be read not only by the executive but by one or more of his assistants or associates. From your knowledge of the office, you will recognize any such piece of mail. To route it to the proper persons, check off the names or initials on a routing form stamped on the piece of mail, or on a routing slip attached to it. Make your checks lightly in pencil so that the executive can change them if he wishes.

Photocopies expedite dissemination of information and in some offices have superseded the old routing-slip routine. An advantage to the secretary is lessened responsibility for follow up. If there is not time to make copies before sending the mail in to the executive, attach a note asking "Copies for BR, RN, and AD?" Write on the original letter for a record the names of those to whom you furnish such copies.

Personal Letter Opened Inadvertently. If you should inadvertently open a personal letter addressed to your employer, stop reading the letter as soon as you discover that it is personal and not business. Refold the letter, replace it in its envelope, and attach a short note to the face of the envelope, "Sorry, opened by mistake—K. A."

Envelope Containing a Bill or Invoice. When an envelope contains a bill or an invoice, if possible verify the prices and the terms with those quoted. Always check the mathematical accuracy of the extensions and the total. Then write "OK" on the face of the bill or the invoice if it is correct, or note any discrepancy.

Envelope Containing a Check or Money Order. Compare the amount of a check or money order enclosed in an envelope with the amount mentioned in the letter of transmittal or the copy of the statement or invoice. If it has been mailed alone, check it with the file copy of the bill to verify the correctness of the amount. Handle the remittance according to the procedure of your office. If it is to be turned over immediately to a cashier, indicate the amount in the margin of the letter or invoice, or prepare a memorandum for the executive, reporting the amount and the date of receipt.

Publications Received. Identify each publication permanently with the executive's name or initials. Scan the table of contents and indicate any item he will probably want to read. If an article is of especial interest, underline the salient points and paper clip all the preceding pages together so that he will turn to it as soon as he opens the publication; or attach a note to the front cover telling him about the article.

| RECEIVED | | FROM | DATED | ADDRESSED TO | | DESCRIPTION | SEP. COV. | REFERRED | | WHERE |
Date	Time	Name/Address		Dept.	Person	Kind of Mail/Enc./Sep.Cov.	RECEIVED	To	Date	FILED
3/14	9:15 am	F. Stevens, N.Y.	3/12	Adv.		Adv. pamphlet - layout	—	Adv.	3/14	Adv.
3/18	9 am	Steel Equipment Co., Chicago	3/11		M.L.A.	Expected catalogs - file cabinets	3/21	Purch.	3/22	Purch.
3/20	1 pm	D. H. Sims, New York	3/19		M.L.A.	ACA Banquet tickets				
3/22	3 pm	L. Cox Lima, Ohio	3/18	Adv.		Book - type faces	4/10	Adv.	4/11	Adv.
3/23	2 pm	A. Ellis, Chicago	3/22		M.L.A.	Special delivery - rush order	—	Sales	3/23	
3/23	9 am	I. R. S. - local	3/21		K. Logan	Quarterly taxes - forms enclosed	—	KL	3/23	
3/26	2 pm	Jones, Inc. - local	3/26	Acctg.		Registered Ch. #345	—	Cashier	3/26	
3/28	9:20 am	R. Keith, Denver	3/26		O. Miller	Insured package	—	Sales	3/28	

▪ Mail Register

It is often desirable for the secretary to keep a *mail register* of important mail for follow-up or tracing purposes. The mail register is used to record special incoming mail (such as registered, certified, special delivery, or insured mail), expected (separate-cover) mail, and mail that is circulated to the executive's associates. For expected bulk mail it may be necessary to give the mail or receiving clerk a memorandum that a package is incoming.

Secretaries say that the mail register is "worth its weight in gold" as a protective record that verifies the receipt and disposition of mail. Only a few minutes are needed to record the entries, since abbreviations are used freely. A ruled form similar to the one illustrated above may be used. The blank space in the "SEP. COV. RECEIVED" column, for example, indicates to the secretary that the executive's banquet tickets have not yet arrived.

▪ Final Arrangement of the Mail

Arrangement of processed and personal mail for presentation to the executive depends on his preferences, his daily schedule, or even his mood. In general, though, the mail is separated into these four groups:

1. **For immediate action**—Possible order of precedence: telegrams, unopened personal letters, pleasant letters, letters containing remittances, important letters, unpleasant letters
2. **To be answered**—Routine letters having no great priority

The secretary processes the mail into several groups and presents as soon as possible the mail requiring immediate action.

3. **To be answered by secretary**—Letters that are usually turned over to you for handling (Don't preempt his right to make this decision.)
4. **To read for information**—Advertisements, publications, routine announcements.

One successful secretary recommends the use of a four-pocket organizer for submitting mail, with each pocket clearly identified as to contents. This organizer keeps the mail confidential, even from those who seem able to read letters upside down. In any case, the mail should be covered if the executive is not at his desk when you present his processed mail.

On a day when the employer has only limited time for the mail, you may wish to submit items from Category 1 only. On a day when he seems to be marking time waiting for the mail, send in only half of it as soon as you have it ready, and take in the rest when it is processed.

▪ Procedure During Executive's Absence

Examine and take some secretarial action on the business mail the executive receives while he is away.

The Executive's Business Mail. In handling his business mail, the executive will expect you to:

1. Set aside those letters that can await his return, but acknowledge their receipt if his answer may be delayed for several days.

2. Give to associates or superiors those letters which must have immediate executive action. Make a photocopy or typewritten copy of each one for the executive's information, noting to whom you gave it, so that he can find out the action taken.

3. Send copies (not originals) of those letters that contain information of interest or importance or that require the executive's personal attention, if they will reach him in time.

4. Answer or take personal action on letters which fall within your province.

5. Prepare a digest of mail and either send it to the executive or hold it for his return, depending on circumstances. (See illustration on this page.)

6. Collect in a mail-received folder: (a) all the original letters awaiting attention; (b) copies of all letters given to others for action; (c) both the originals and answers of letters you have answered. Before giving the file to the executive, sort the letters into logical sequence, with the most important and interesting ones on top.

DIGEST OF INCOMING MAIL

Date	From	Description
4/29	J. B. Moore	Requests material for press release on Project 72 by 5/3.
4/29	Rice Univ.	Invitation to be guest speaker on August 4. No conflict with present schedule.
5/2	Knoxville Office	Asks for raw-material budget approval by May 9.
5/2	Business Week	Request for more information on Project 72 for news release. Referred to JMM.

The Executive's Personal Mail. Do not open the executive's personal mail when he is away unless he expressly asks you to do so. Hold it for him in the mail-received folder. If he is to be away sufficiently long for mail to reach him if it is forwarded, send it to him. It is often easier to retrieve a letter if it is forwarded in a fresh envelope with your business return address than under a corrected forwarding address. Keep in the mail-received folder a running record of all letters mailed to an out-of-town address. Identify each forwarded letter by its postmark date and sender's name or by the postmark city if that is all that is shown.

The Executive's Advertising Mail. Hold the advertising mail in a separate large envelope. Sort and give it to the executive when the press of accumulated work has lessened after his return.

Suggested Readings

Doris, Lillian, and Besse May Miller. *Complete Secretary's Handbook.* Englewood Cliffs: Prentice-Hall, Inc., 1960, pp. 63–70.

Mayo, Lucy Graves. *You Can Be an Executive Secretary.* New York: Macmillan Company, 1965, pp. 51–56.

Neuner, J. J. W., and B. Lewis Keeling. *Administrative Office Management,* 5th ed. Cincinnati: South-Western Publishing Company, 1966, pp. 113–118 (handling incoming mail in large offices from management standpoint); pp. 433–442 (correspondence cost reduction).

Questions for Discussion

1. If you accepted a position as secretary to an executive who did not utilize your services in processing the mail as suggested in this chapter, what would you do?

2. In processing a morning's mail for the president of a corporation, decide what you would do if—
   (a) A letter refers to a letter the executive wrote nine months ago
   (b) A customer's letter complains about the actions of a salesman
   (c) A letter asks that certain material be prepared and sent before the first of the month
   (d) A letter requests a photograph, the responsibility of which is in the public relations department
   (e) A letter contains information of importance to three department heads
   (f) The envelope obviously contains a bill from an engraver who recently supplied personal stationery for the executive
   (g) The letter requests duplicated materials available through your office
   (h) The letter refers to a package being sent as a separate mailing

3. The executive is away on a two-week trip. Decide what you would do with a letter that—
   (a) Asks him to give a talk five months from now
   (b) Requires immediate management action
   (c) Is from his mother, whose handwriting you recognize

4. What steps could you take to obtain the address of a person who inquired for information and prices on your product when the request was typed on a plain sheet of paper with no address given on either the letter or the envelope?

5. If the executive is out of town but expects to return tomorrow, how would you handle each of the following situations?

(a) An airmail, special-delivery letter requesting an estimate on a large quantity of coated paper

(b) A telegram from one of your salesmen sending in a rush order for one of his customers

(c) A letter about a shipment of card stock complaining that one fourth of the blue is two shades lighter than the rest (Samples are enclosed as proof.)

(d) A letter asking the length of time a Mr. Edwards was employed as a salesman by your company and his reason for leaving, and requesting a reference

6. Fill in the correct spelling in the following sentences. Then refer to the Reference Guide to verify or correct your answers.

(a) The executive made a special ——————————— of his secretary. (confidant, confidante)

(b) He is a handsome ———————————. (brunet, brunette)

(c) Alice is a natural ———————————. (blond, blonde)

Problems

■ **1.** Criticize each of the following steps in a secretary's procedure for handling incoming mail. Type your comments for each step.

(a) The secretary arranges all of the mail in a stack and proceeds to open it and to remove the contents of each envelope in sequence.

(b) She flattens out the letters and enclosures and discards the envelopes.

(c) After all the letters have been removed, she checks the letters for stated enclosures. Pertinent enclosures she separates from the letters and sends to those concerned (such as orders for the order department). She discards the advertising.

(d) She then time stamps, reads, underlines, and annotates all letters. She prepares a routing slip for letters requiring the attention of more than one person, and she fastens each routing slip to the proper letter with a paper clip.

(e) She then places the letters, in the order in which they were processed, on the executive desk face up for his immediate attention.

■ **2.** For your assistant or anyone who helps you to process incoming mail or who processes it for your employer during your absence, type the procedure to be followed in processing the incoming mail.

■ **3.** Arrange the model desk in your secretarial practice room for opening and sorting incoming mail. Prepare a list of supplies needed. Have the instructor check the list and your demonstration of letter-opening and sorting techniques.

Related Work Assignment 23

23. Reading, Underlining, and Annotating Letters. This assignment provides practice in the handling of incoming mail. First, type the following letters in good form (or use the letters already typed in original form in the Workbook). Then prepare them for the desk of Mr. Simpson, by reading, underlining, and annotating. Any action you would take that is not covered by the annotations should be stated at the bottom of each letter. The letters were received on March 18 of the current year.

HOLLANDER CORPORATION

Manufacturers of Air Conditioners

1201 Grand Avenue
Des Moines, Iowa 50316

March 16, 19--

Mr. Robert L. Simpson
Continental Products
320 Euclid Avenue
Des Moines, Iowa   50313

Dear Bob

In your talk at the Rotary luncheon yesterday, you referred to a 1963 book that would be helpful to those of us involved in records management--Methods of Information Handling. We are hoping to revise our records retention system this fall, and this book may be just what I am looking for.

I would appreciate your giving me the name of the publisher, the author, and the price. I doubt if I can obtain the book in the local bookstore, so it would also be helpful if you would include the address of the publisher.

Any help you can give me, Bob, will be appreciated. You may know of other books to suggest, for I know you are especially interested in this field. I am enclosing a stamped, addressed envelope for your reply.

Cordially yours

Claude Martin
Claude Martin
Records Manager

cm:ac

Enclosure

EASTMAN AND DURST, INC.

801 East Walnut Street .˙. Des Moines, Iowa 50316

March 17, 19--

Mr. Robert L. Simpson
Continental Products
320 Euclid Avenue
Des Moines, Iowa 50313

Dear Mr. Simpson:

Several times today I tried to reach you by telephone but was unsuccessful. I wanted to let you know that you will be able to buy the 500 shares you want in the newly organized Space Development Mutual Fund. The shares can be obtained at 25½ if you place your subscription by March 19.

It will be necessary to sell either your General Foods (bought at 28) or your Standard Oil of California (bought at 21) to make this change of investments. I suggest that you refer to today's market quotation on both stocks as a basis for your decision.

Then telephone me on March 18, if possible.

Sincerely yours,

David Griggs

David Griggs
Investment Counselor

mvh

THE EMPORIUM • Fourth and Vine Streets • Washington, Iowa 52353

March 17, 19--

Continental Products
320 Euclid Avenue
Des Moines, Iowa 50313

Attention Mr. Robert L. Simpson, General Manager

Gentlemen

We are enclosing our check for $209.25 in payment of your invoice of February 6 for $212.50, less 2% discount.

Will you please advise us if you have sufficient stock on hand to forward us 2,000 units of #68912.

Please note that I have replaced Lawrence Carson as Manager.

Do you have a new catalog? If so, please send one.

Yours very truly

Kirby Edwards

Kirby Edwards, Manager

ep
Enclosure: Check

Ch. 8 Taking and Giving Dictation

Secretarial dictation might include anything from a rather brief dictated instruction to the highly complicated, rapid-fire note taking that a trusted and efficient administrative assistant might do at a high-level technical conference or meeting. Either kind is improved by careful preparation and by well-organized procedures.

The beginning secretary, accustomed to the classroom "I-dare-you-to-get-the-dictation" situation, hesitates to ask questions of the dictator about unfamiliar words or unclear statements. She often dares not make a tactful suggestion even if she thinks that she can improve the end product—the transcript.

Yet for best results, dictation must be a cooperative effort. The secretary complements the dictator by catching omissions, errors, and ambiguities, and by either correcting them herself or calling them to his attention in a helpful way. Each has a role to play. His is the major, decisive one; hers, a supporting but very important one.

Predictation Responsibilities

The secretary should carefully carry out certain predictation tasks that increase her efficiency.

▪ Attention-Today Items

The very first preliminary to dictation is the collection of *attention-today items* that the secretary prepares and gives to the executive early each morning. They include (1) all the items for the day from the tickler, from the secretary's desk calendar, and from the executive's desk calendar, and (2) the unfinished items which have been carried over. Some of the items will require dictating, and some will likely reduce the time the executive can give to dictating. Overdue letters, reports, and shipments or letters and reports that must meet deadlines—all will require dictating attention. The day's appointments, conferences, and meetings—these will affect the time available for dictation.

The secretary will find it helpful to prepare a list of carry-over items or make a note for each. Before the executive begins dictation, she should clip the reminder to the edge of a portfolio or file folder that she places on the executive's desk.

Write up the attention-today items in briefest form. Prepare a list of them in duplicate—one for the executive and one for yourself— so that you will have a copy from which to take unfinished, carry-over items each day. Or prepare a note for each item on a small slip of paper and clip it to the edge of a portfolio or file folder where it will remain in full sight on his desk until he has taken care of it and disposed of the reminder. Try to take the collection of items to his desk as early in the day as possible, but definitely before he begins dictation, whether he dictates to you or uses a machine.

▪ Dictation Supplies

Another predictation responsibility is the daily checking and replenishing of the executive's and your own dictation supplies.

Executive's Supplies. For person-to-person dictation see that the executive has at hand:

> *Sharpened pencils*—An executive often dictates with pencil in hand. He jots down reminders to himself on the letter he is answering; he enters items on his calendar as he commits himself to certain dates; and he may even doodle.

A scratch pad—He often uses scratch pads for auxiliary notes.

Filled stapler, paper clips, pins

Ash tray, matches, cigarettes—Some executives find it relaxing to smoke as they compose during dictation.

Secretary's Supplies. The supplies you take to dictation should be ready and waiting for instant pickup. To avoid clutter at the executive's desk and to save the motions required in handling unneeded supplies, take adequate, but not excessive, supplies.

A notebook—If you have a choice, use a notebook that has:
   a. Green pages ruled in green (easiest on the eyes, especially for transcription)
   b. Spiral binding so that the pages lie flat
   c. Stiff covers so that the book will stand alone for transcription. Take in only one book unless you are near the end of the current one.

A filled pen—Notes written in ink are easier on your eyes at transcription time. Violet ink is reputed to dry quickly and to be the easiest to read under fluorescent lights. A fine-point pen—not a ball-point—is the most satisfactory. It must be a fast, smooth-writing one. Often a secretary buys her own pen for office use, since quality ones are seldom supplied in an office. The objections to using a pen are its running out of ink at crucial moments and the messiness of filling it. These are valid objections and cause some secretaries to use pencils.

Pointed pencils—Choose your favorite kind for holding and for softness or hardness. Some secretaries prefer automatic, thin-lead pencils, of ridged shape that will not roll.

A colored pencil—The executive most often uses red or blue.

Possibly an empty folder or portfolio with pockets on each side—Some secretaries find these of help for organizing materials. They clip notes to the portfolio so that they will remember to discuss the contents with the executive. If the *executive* puts each answered letter in a file folder or portfolio, you are expected to bring it along to each dictation session. Usually, however, he merely hands each letter to you as he finishes with it.

A rubber finger for the left thumb—This is an aid in turning notebook pages.

▪ Answering the Call to Dictation

The executive tries to dictate at approximately the same time every day. Stay at your desk waiting for this call. Do not wander off visiting or handle a matter that takes you out of sight. An *unexpected* dictation call from the executive also could come when you are away from your desk, so leave word with a co-worker or roll a note into your typewriter as to your whereabouts and your time of return. When the executive wants you, he does not like to have to search for you or to wonder when you will return.

Before leaving your desk to take dictation—or for any extended time for that matter—cover, put away, or hide all confidential papers and those of more than general interest—for there are always snoopers. At the time of leaving, ask someone nearby to take care of your telephone calls and visitors.

You may resent being called to dictation when you are engrossed in other work. Some secretaries do, and show it. Whenever a call to dictation comes, do try not to act annoyed at being interrupted. Prepare your desk for leaving, pick up your supplies, and go to the executive's desk with an attitude of willingness and helpfulness.

Person-to-Person Dictation

The secretary's performance during the dictation period affects both the quality of the executive's dictation and the secretary's recording of it.

■ At the Executive's Desk

During actual dictation periods at the executive's desk, the secretary should adopt certain accepted practices. Seemingly unimportant details that often affect the success of the dictation period are the secretary's location, her grooming, and her poise.

The Dictation Chair. In the give and take of dictation, the executive and secretary work together at close range. Your dictation chair will be placed conveniently for him. He may prefer you to sit across from him, beside him, or at the end of the desk. If you have a choice, sit where you have a generous-sized writing area. If he has a tendency to pace the floor while dictating, try not to fence him in.

Grooming. Your grooming at dictation time is under casual but close scrutiny. Your hair, makeup, eyeglasses, hands, neckline—all should be equal to close observation. Personal daintiness is paramount.

Unobtrusiveness. As a thoughtful, considerate secretary, you need to be as unobtrusive as possible during the executive's dictation. He can do his most productive concentrating and effective phrasing when he is able to forget your presence. If you can almost efface yourself during dictation, you are assisting him. This trait requires the ability to take dictation with confidence, to manage your supplies and papers with as few motions as possible, and to refrain from all excess movements.

An executive is always aware of any evidence of a secretary's negative mood or attitude. If you are tense, unsure, critical, lackadaisical, or disinterested, he is uneasy and disconcerted. Unseemly physical actions are especially noticeable—sprawling in the chair, propping up a tired head, constant coughing or clearing the throat, frequent sighing. An oft-repeated nervous mannerism—such as riffling the corners of the notebook or patting and pushing a lock of hair—is as conspicuous as waving a flag. Such moods, attitudes, mannerisms, and actions are anything but unobtrusive.

▪ The Executive's Dictating Speed

Experienced, mature executives usually dictate deliberately. They take the time to express their thoughts carefully and accurately. Younger executives who are still self-conscious about pausing to think in front of their secretaries have a compulsion to dictate faster. They tend to decrease their speed as they lose that self-consciousness. A third type of executive is the naturally fast, fluent dictator. When he interviews secretarial applicants, therefore, he must stress that high shorthand speed is a job requirement. The likelihood is that any executive for whom you work will not dictate too fast for you. He will try instinctively to correlate his dictating speed with your shorthand speed, because his flow of expression is interrupted if he gets too far ahead and has to retreat and repeat.

▪ Enlarging Your Dictation Vocabularies

At this time you have an elementary business vocabulary, but you will acquire two additional vocabularies in each secretarial position— the executive's business vocabulary and his technical vocabulary. You will learn each new word quickly, *if you are attentive*, because:

You will *hear* the new word dictated.
You will *write* the new word in shorthand.
You will *spell* the new word in transcription.
You will *read* the new word when proofreading.

A secretary has to experience only once the embarrassment of using *elegant* for *eloquent*, *dentures* for *indentures*, or *ingenious* for *ingenuous* to learn the meaning, spelling, and pronunciation of each such pair of words that sound somewhat alike in dictation and look somewhat alike in shorthand.

To learn the executive's vocabulary quickly, read file copies of his recent letters and the trade magazines that apply to his field. From them make a list of words new to you. Alongside each one write its shorthand equivalent. Learn the meanings of the words, their spellings, and their pronunciations.

The several secretarial handbooks in the special fields of law, accounting, medicine, real estate, and so on, have word lists which can hasten the enlarging of those vocabularies.

If the executive is a lover of literature and given to quoting from the classics, try to learn his favorites and read them so that you can enjoy his quotations. Keep at hand a copy of Bartlett's *Familiar Quotations* so that you can transcribe them accurately.

▪ Types of Dictation

The dictation given a secretary differs from that taken by a stenographer. Ordinarily the latter takes letters to transcribe, and that is all. A secretary, however, may also receive instructions, reminders, requests, and mail to answer. She may be given first a letter, then an interoffice communication, then a telegram, then a request to go to the bank at lunch hour to get a check cashed, then another letter, then instructions on a tabulation of sales costs, then a request to copy certain paragraphs from a magazine article, and then a memorandum to get an appointment for the employer with the mayor. One of the annoying faults of an inexperienced secretary is her reluctance to take notes of anything except transcription items. She relies on her memory to carry out the instructions, reminders, and requests instead of recording them in black and white—a practice which sooner or later gets her into trouble.

Dictation falls into the two broad categories of communications and instructions.

Communications. The bulk of dictation is in the category of communications. It includes all the dictation to be transcribed—letters, memos, telegrams, outlines, drafts, and so on.

Instructions. During the dictation period, numerous instructions are given to a secretary. *Take down all of these in your notebook:*

Transcribing Instructions. Transcribing instructions are the instructions dictated for transcribing the items listed under communications, above. The executive often gives such an instruction at the end of an item; however, you should place it at the beginning if it:

> Pinpoints the item for rush handling
> Affects the kind of stationery used
> Indicates the number of copies to be typed

Use short abbreviations of your own devising and print them in oversized capitals, such as *RUF* for a rough-draft request, *AM* for an airmail letter that requires airmail stationery, and 5 *CCs* to indicate that six copies must be typed. For fast finding at transcribing time, turn back corners of pages that contain rush items.

Composing Instructions. The executive often delegates the composing of a letter to the secretary. It may be a letter answering one at hand, or a letter to be originated at the secretary's desk. For the former he will usually hand you the letter and say, "Tell him thus and so. . . ." Take such instructions in shorthand verbatim, either in the notebook or on the letter itself. For an originating letter, take down the instructions verbatim in the notebook. It is imperative to have complete, exact instructions for each letter to be composed in order to cover the points the executive requested.

Specific Work Instructions. Specific instructions, such as to cancel one of the executive's appointments, to plan an itinerary, or to write and cash a check, are taken down in shorthand in the notebook. They are conspicuously keyed for easy finding so that they can be handled expediently. One secretary draws a rough box around each work instruction; another writes each one in the right column which she leaves blank for instructions and insertions. Choose your own location and develop your own key signals, but do write all work instructions in the notebook along with the other dictation.

General Work Instructions. Take in shorthand in the notebook all instructions or explanations of office routines and executive preferences in procedure. Transcribe them when there is time and insert them in your desk manual for reference use.

▪ Good Dictation Practices

Each of the dictation practices recommended below is a *good* one because it promotes efficiency in taking shorthand notes; assures efficient, accurate, complete execution of the transcription or instructions; or fosters quiet dictation sessions so that the executive can dictate at his best. See how they are followed in the illustrated notes on page 171.

1. **Write the beginning date of use on the notebook cover—the month, the day, and the year.**
2. **Reserve one place in or on your desk for the notebook. Keep an extra notebook and pencils in the employer's office too, just in case he decides to dictate while you are with him on another job.**

3. Keep a rubber band around transcribed pages to help you find the first blank page on which to write.

4. Keep a filled pen, sharpened pencils, and one colored pencil under the rubber band around the notebook ready for instant use. While transcribing, keep these items together *in one specific place* where they can be quickly reached when a call to dictation comes.

5. Keep a few paper clips around the edges of the notebook cover for possible use during the dictation session.

6. During long periods of dictation, shift from pen to pencil to reduce fatigue.

7. During interruptions, write transcribing instructions in colored pencil and circle implied instructions, such as *attached* or *enclosed*.

8. Date each day's dictation on the first page with the month and year *in the lower right corner in red pencil.* Dictation notes are often the only source of valid reference. If the dictation load is heavy, add a.m. or p.m. to the bottom-of-page notation.

9. If you take dictation from more than one executive, add the dictator's initials to each date or use a different notebook for each dictator.

10. Leave several lines between items of dictation or leave the right column blank to provide room for insertions, changes, and instructions. This is very important! Do not worry about wasted linage. If the executive makes frequent or lengthy changes and insertions, leave six or eight lines or the full right column. If he rarely does this, leave only three or four lines. In other words, adapt to your executive's dictating habits.

11. Should there be no lines available in which to write a transcribing instruction, print it in oversized capitals in abbreviated form diagonally across the beginning of the notes. It will not hinder your reading of the notes underneath.

12. If there is the slightest possibility of inability to transcribe proper names, write them out during dictation.

13. Write uncertain words and unfamiliar terms in longhand if necessary. There is no stigma in the business world if you resort occasionally to longhand. In fact, it is better to be safe with longhand than unsure with shorthand.

14. To remind yourself to clear up an error, a question, an omission, an ambiguity, a redundancy, or the repeated use of words that occurred during dictation, put down some conspicuous signal such as a king-sized X, a question mark, or an upright wavy line.

15. Indicate the end of each item of dictation, *be it a communication or an instruction,* in some conspicuous way, such as with a quick swing line across the column or with a cross. You need a visual aid to assure your transcribing the item completely or your carrying out the instruction.

16. Use pauses and interruptions to read your notes, improve outlines, insert punctuation, and write transcribing instructions in red pencil.

17. Put each letter that the dictator hands you face down on top of the last one to keep the letters in the same order as the dictation.

18. If the executive assigns a number to each letter being answered (so that he does not have to dictate the name and address of the recipient each time), write

only the number in the notebook. At transcription time, pair your numbered notes with the same-numbered letter; and write the name of the addressee in your notebook *above the numbered item* for later identification if necessary.

19. Tape a small calendar on the back cover of your notebook for quick reference during dictation.

20. Add the date of final use to the cover of a filled notebook and keep it for six months or more. If filled notebooks go to a central file, write the executive's name and your name on the cover also.

KEY TO THE PAGE OF DICTATION ➔

① A transcribing instruction is inserted as soon as possible in shorthand, in longhand abbreviations, or in king-sized capitals. Later, it is circled or underlined with a colored pencil for attention value.

② The swing line across the column indicates the end of an item.

③ All instructions for composition are written in full so that they can be followed carefully.

④ The personally devised abbreviation MH is used for Minneapolis Honeywell.

⑤ This instruction signals that a tickler notation must be made.

⑥ A transcribing instruction to make two carbon copies is inserted at the beginning of the item and later circled in color.

⑦ The circled X indicates a question: Should the regional sales manager also get a copy?

⑧ The corner is turned back to help locate quickly the page containing the rush item.

⑨ The right column is left available for work instructions and insertions.

⑩ A work instruction is always identified by a rough box.

⑪ The initials of the executive, JR, are used instead of his whole name.

⑫ The abbreviation *Ins C—3b* identifies the notes as Insert C to be used three pages back.

⑬ Lines are drawn through notes to be deleted.

⑭ *Hospitalization* was written in longhand because there was a mental block on the shorthand form. Rather than leave it out or waste time struggling to write it in shorthand, it was written in longhand.

⑮ Slash lines are used to segregate an insertion from surrounding notes.

⑯ The date of dictation is always written at the *bottom* of the page.

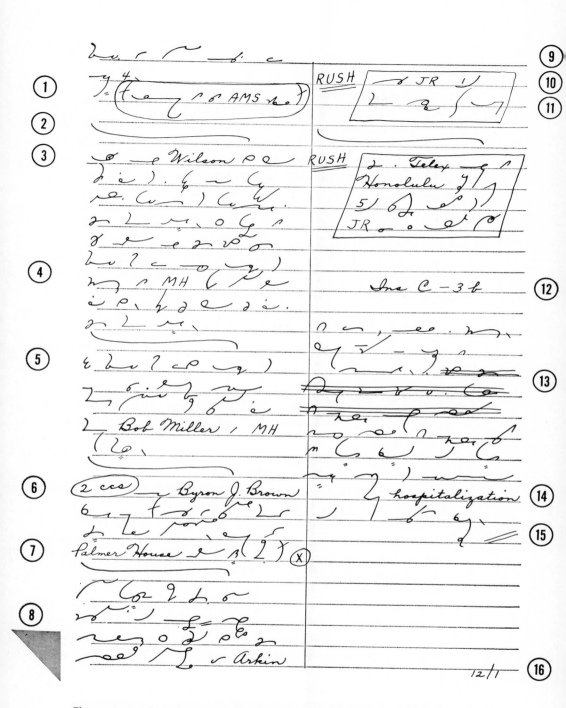

RUSH

Wilson — RUSH

Bob Miller, MH

2 ccs — Byron J. Brown

Palmer House

Arkin

Inc C-3f

hospitalization

12/1

These notes are keyed and signaled for efficient and accurate completion. The practices followed by this secretary are numbered and explained on the opposite page.

171

▪ Changes

You will have to recognize changes of thought during dictation. An executive often starts to dictate a sentence and, after a pause, begins again. Watch carefully to determine whether it is a new thought or a rephrasing of a previous one. An executive who habitually rephrases is a trial and worry to a beginning secretary, but through some sixth sense she learns to recognize which phrases are bona fide. When making a change, some men say, "Cross that out," and then begin to rephrase without mentioning what to cross out. They expect the secretary to know, and she almost always does. When a long change is made far back in the notes, there is seldom enough time to go back, locate the notes to be deleted and cross them out; nor is there likely to be enough room to write in the change. In such a case, treat the change as an insertion, taking down verbatim both the change and the instructions as to what is to be crossed out so that you can go back and make the deletions later. *Do not rely on your memory to handle changes.*

SECRETARIAL ETIQUETTE DURING DICTATION

1. Avoid receiving personal telephone calls at dictation time. Arrange in advance for someone to take any such calls for you. If a call does come through, tell the person immediately that you are busy and will return the call later.

2. Don't look at the executive critically while he is in deep thought. Critical looks disturb his concentration.

3. Refrain from supplying a word when the executive is groping for one unless he asks for your help.

4. Don't interrupt the executive while he is obviously concentrating.

5. When the executive has a brief interruption, such as an associate's coming in to ask a question or a business telephone call, use the time to study and improve your notes. Do not sit there staring or obviously listening.

6. When the executive receives a personal telephone call, leave his office quietly; stay nearby so that you can return as soon as he is finished.

7. When a visitor who comes in undoubtedly will stay a while, take your dictation supplies and accumulated correspondence to your desk and start transcribing.

8. When dictation is resumed after an interruption, read the last several sentences in your notes without being asked, to help the dictator regain the thought.

The executive is about to resume dictation after an interruption. The secretary,
without being asked, is reading back the
last paragraph he dictated to help him
orient his thoughts.

—*Herman Miller Furniture Company*

Interrupting the Dictator. The point has been made that you should be unobtrusive at dictation time—that you should be both vocally and physically quiet. This suggestion implies that you should not interrupt the dictator. There are, however, at least three exceptions when interruptions may be helpful or even necessary.

1. When the executive is so far ahead of you that the thread of dictation is being lost, you must interrupt! Look up inquiringly and repeat the last words that have been taken down. He much prefers that you get complete notes, interrupting if necessary, rather than leave his desk with words and phrases missing or incorrect.

2. When the executive repeats a conspicuous multisyllable word or root word, call it to his attention—if you find he appreciates your help. If the executive said "*elaborate* plans" and then dictated "They have *elaborated* upon this idea," mention impersonally, "We just used *elaborate*." He will then substitute another word, or he may just say, "You fix it up." From then on you would "fix it up" and make the substitution when you go over the notes.

3. When a question comes to your mind about the dictation, insert a clear-up signal at the end of the line. Some men prefer to be interrupted immediately about such a question, others at the end of each item, and still others prefer to wait until all the dictation is completed. The executive will quickly learn your clear-up signal and at a propitious moment will often ask to what it refers.

As a new secretary, do not ask the executive point-blank whether he wants you to interrupt for situations that fall under (2) and (3). He may intensely dislike interruptions during dictation. Be subtle in learning his preferences. Try one method and then another. Watch his reactions and be guided accordingly.

In the midst of a conference, the executive has asked his secretary to come in and record comments on an advertising layout under consideration.

—*H. Armstrong Roberts*

▪ Unusual Dictation

A secretary is often asked to take unusual kinds of dictation, such as those discussed below.

Highly Confidential Dictation. Transcribe highly confidential dictation at a time when there is little likelihood of anyone's being around, most likely during the lunch period or after office hours. Give the original and carbon copies to the executive as soon as possible and destroy the dictated notes. If the carbon paper retains an imprint of the typescript, destroy it also.

Telephone Dictation. In taking telephone dictation, you have the use of only one hand and may have to ask for phrases to be repeated. Since the dictator cannot see how fast you are taking notes, it helps him if you say "*yes*" after you have completed each phrase. To avoid errors, read the entire set of notes back to the dictator.

Occasionally the executive may request you to listen in on a telephone conversation and take notes. This is called *monitoring*. Unless you are unusually speedy, you cannot hope to get every word, but you can take down the main points in the same way one takes lecture notes. When the executive does not tell the person that you are monitoring the call, you cannot ask to have statements repeated. Transcribe such notes at once while they are still fresh in your mind.

Both sides of a telephone call can be recorded on a dictating machine placed near the telephone. Legally, however, the other person must be told. The recording may be kept for reference, or you may be asked to transcribe the entire conversation or abstract the important points.

On-the-Spot Dictation. At times it is necessary to take dictation within a split second, while standing or working at a desk where there is no cleared space. You may even have to take the notes on scratch paper. Practice taking dictation with a notebook on your knee or while

174

The executive, a few minutes before leaving for lunch, dictates a telegram. Notice how the secretary holds her notebook for "stand-up" dictation.

—The Shaw Walker Company

standing using a scratch pad, in order to become accustomed to the awkwardness of such rush work. The idea is to get it done quickly without fuss or commotion. After transcription, date the notes, fold them to less than page size, and staple them to the first blank page in the dictation notebook.

Dictation at the Typewriter. Occasionally the executive may ask you to typewrite something as he dictates it to you. It helps to ask before starting whether it will be long or short, to determine the placement of the item on the page. A retyping, however, is often required, because in the majority of cases the placement is unsatisfactory and insertions or corrections have been necessary.

In taking dictation at the typewriter, concentrate on what is being said to avoid thinking about how fast, slow, confused, or awkward you may appear to the executive. He is probably immersed in the thought of what he is dictating and is not aware of your show of typing skill. Do not stop to erase errors as they are made. It is better to correct the errors or retype the page when the executive has finished dictating and has left your desk.

Printed-Form Dictation. The answers to questions on a printed form are frequently dictated. The executive usually holds the form in his hands; therefore, the information given will seem sketchy and incomplete. If the dictator does not give the identifying numbers or letters of the items, ask him to include them so that you can type the information on the proper lines.

If only one copy is furnished, it may be well to make a photocopy of the completed form for the files. Or it may be advisable to make a

The executive may hold a printed form while he dictates answers to the questions. Since the information he gives will be sketchy, the secretary will find helpful the use of identifying numbers or letters for each item.

carbon copy on a plain sheet and, after it is removed from the typewriter, go back and identify each item by number or letter, together with a brief indication of the information requested. The title and source of the form and the current date should also be added.

▪ Machine Dictation

There is a continuing increase in executive use of dictating machines. An executive frequently gives two types of dictation—machine dictation for the bulk of his work, or for very lengthy items, or while absent from his office and direct dictation for work that may require consultation with you. He will expect you to work out procedures for handling his machine dictation and related papers with the same alertness as for direct dictation, to the end that his typewritten work be of the highest quality.

Secretaries and administrative assistants say that machine dictation during the business day permits them to use the freed time to good advantage on other work. They can often turn over all or part of the transcription to assistants. The feature they especially like, though, is that machine dictation almost completely eliminates overtime dictation periods, except for emergency situations.

Another advantage of machine dictation is that it may be recorded on tape, plastic discs, or plastic belts and mailed conveniently.

The portable dictating machine, about the size of this book, is a boon to the busy executive. He takes it to his home and catches up on

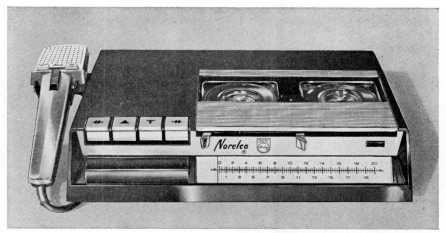

—*Norelco, North American Phillips*

Several kinds of modern dictating machines use tape and provide for backspacing for additions or corrections and for playback. Others use discs or plastic belts.

dictation at night and weekends. He carries it with him when he travels and dictates in automobile or train or while waiting in airports, stations, or his hotel room. He mails such dictation back to the secretary, who sees that it is transcribed promptly and dispatched. It greatly reduces the dictation load that would otherwise accumulate and await his return and permits more timely attention to correspondence and reports.

Dictation equipment is available, too, on many executive flights, on trains, at motels and hotels, and in limousines operating between key cities. The executive may, then, dictate on media for which his office does not possess transcribing equipment. The manufacturer, hoping for a later sales advantage, will provide the necessary transcribing units for such dictation.

If the employer uses his own or his company's equipment, the secretary should see that he is supplied with:

1. *A supply of the discs, belts, or tapes* that his machine requires (Return to this supply the partially used units with the transcribed portions marked off.)

2. *An empty file folder or portfolio* in which to place each piece of related correspondence as he finishes with it

3. *A wax pencil* to date and identify the dictated units

4. *A supply of the printed forms* for listing the material dictated on a unit, for special instructions regarding transcription, or for indicating changes to be incorporated

5. *A supply of the special envelopes required* if the employer encloses the disc, belt, or tape in an envelope as he completes it

—IBM Corporation

The IBM Executary may be used by the executive secretary whose responsibilities include transcribing some material and dictating material for others to transcribe. It features a built-in erase magnet, instant stop-start operation, and playback through microphone or built-in loudspeaker.

▪ Dictation by the Secretary

An executive secretary not only transcribes but also gives dictation. Accustomed to taking dictation, she can develop into an effective dictator with little effort. From personal experience a secretary appreciates the reasons for speaking distinctly, without hurry, and with logical phrasing. If a dictating machine is available, read the instruction booklet. Test how your voice and timing come through. Dictate a practice letter with tricky words and figures; then listen at a later time to see if you can distinguish every word and figure.

A large insurance company asked its transcribers to make a list of desirable dictation manners that were lacking in those from whom they took dictation. Here are a few of their requests:

First, mention the item to be dictated—letter, memo, report, and so on.
Indicate immediately if it is to be a RUSH item.
State the number of copies needed and to whom they are to be sent.
Give instructions about typewritten form—if it is unusual.
Spell out proper names and technical words.
Dictate figures very clearly.
Enunciate precisely.
Be gracious when the transcriber has a question.
Give praise once in a while.
Reject substandard work so that the transcriber keeps up her level of quality.

Suggested Readings

The Art of Modern Dictation. New York: International Business Machines Corporation, 1960, 26 pp.

Aurner, Robert R., and Morris Philip Wolf. *Effective Communication in Business,* 5th ed. Cincinnati: South-Western Publishing Co., 1967, pp. 169–192.

Engel, Pauline. *Executive Secretary's Handbook.* Englewood Cliffs: Prentice-Hall, Inc., 1965, pp. 91–95.

Gregg shorthand textbooks. (The four high school textbooks and the four college textbooks have hints on techniques for handling dictation.) New York: Gregg Division of McGraw-Hill Book Company, Inc.

How Much Do You Know about Business Letter Writing? (40 questions and answers about using dictating machines) New York: Dictaphone Corporation, undated and unpaged.

Mayo, Lucy Graves. *You Can Be an Executive Secretary.* New York: The MacMillan Company, 1965, pp. 56–59.

Neuner, John J. W., and B. Lewis Keeling. *Administrative Office Management,* 5th ed. Cincinnati: South-Western Publishing Company, 1966. pp. 77–78 (dictating equipment).

Questions for Discussion

1. During transcription a secretary finds that she cannot transcribe a portion of an important letter. The dictator is now out of town. What immediate action should she take? What long-range action?

2. Would it be better for the secretary to give her employer a list of attention-today items when she goes in for dictation instead of making a special trip the first thing in the morning?

3. Robert Benchley once confessed, "It makes me nervous to have a young lady sitting there waiting for me to say something so that she can pounce on it and tear it into hieroglyphics." What could his secretary have done to allay his fears of the dictation period?

4. Suppose your employer on a two-week trip used dictating equipment available during a plane flight and sent it to you at the beginning of his journey. When you put the cartridge on your machine, the dictation is so garbled that you cannot transcribe it. What would you do?

5. What would you do if you were called to take dictation—

(a) **At 11:45 and you had a luncheon engagement at 12:10?**

(b) **Just as you were in the midst of giving instructions to an assistant who would have no other work to do unless you finished the explanation?**

(c) **As you were putting the finishing touches on an important report that the executive had instructed you to complete before doing anything else?**

(d) **As you were in the midst of reorganizing your card file?**

6. What would you do if the executive uses many stereotyped phrases of which you do not approve? Makes obvious errors in grammar? Coins words that you do not particularly like? Repeatedly uses a conspicuous word? Mumbles? Dictates obvious punctuation?

7. What would you do if during dictation the executive—

(a) **Hands you a letter of application and tells you to acknowledge it, explaining that there are no openings at present but that the application will be considered if such an opening occurs? He wants you to check the references.**

(b) **Dictates a telegram?**

(c) **Asks you to arrange an appointment for that afternoon with Mr. Webster, the executive vice president?**

(d) **Dictates a long report letter? He asks you to rough it out.**

(e) **Asks you to insert a paragraph near the beginning of a letter?**

(f) **Dictates a word you do not understand?**

8. Give the preferred plural for each of the following words. Then use the Reference Guide to verify or correct your answers.

attorney general	coming in	handful	spoonful
basis	court-martial	higher-up	trade-in
bill of lading	editor in chief	Jones	trade union
Chamber of Commerce	formula	knight-errant	trades union
crisis	good-for-nothing	passer-by	ski

Problems

■ **1.** Twenty letters and the following instructions were given during a dictation period. (a) How would you treat the following items in your notes? (b) What precedence would you give these items?

During the dictation period, the executive said:

(1) "On that Ohio State letter back there, send a copy to Flynn, too."

(2) "Better airmail-special the letter to the Executive Office."

(3) "Remind me Tuesday to order flowers for Mother's birthday."

(4) "See what you can dig up on summer camps or work programs for high school boys Jim's age."

(5) "Make an appointment with the club barber for tomorrow at 9."

(6) "Draft a note of congratulation for me for Dave in the Sales Department. It's wonderful—his being made president of the Sales Executives' Club at 29."

(7) "Call the department store and ask them to pick up that abstract painting I had them send over here on approval."

(8) "My wife wants to go to Florida for spring vacation. Give me a list of flight schedules and rates for leaving on Saturday morning in two weeks and returning the following Saturday in the afternoon."

(9) "Make a rough draft of this and bring it in so I can work on it to send out at 2 today."

(10) "Call Parker Williams in New York for me when we finish here."

Related Work Assignments 24-26

24. Taking Office-Style Dictation. Your instructor will dictate a series of four messages in a style commonly used in offices. Keep your shorthand notes for use in Related Work Assignment 27 of Chapter 9, page 205.

25. Dictation Techniques
26. Special "In-Basket" Project
} The instructions and supplies necessary for completion of Related Work Assignments 25 and 26 are provided in the Workbook.

Ch. 9 Turning Out Quality Transcription

The secretary or administrative assistant has an important role in creating a favorable image of her company and her employer through the visual impressions made by the letters she sends out. Producing and supervising quality transcription that represents her employer, her company, and herself accurately and attractively is one of her most challenging duties—one that requires close concentration and constant exercise of intelligence.

Your Fundamentals

The secretary's tool of the trade is her facility with the English language—her spelling, punctuation, word usage, typewriting style, and use of reference books. She must master the fundamentals so that she can transmit the dictator's ideas flawlessly. She—not necessarily the dictator—is the expert in this area; on her devolves the responsibility for perfection in letter mechanics.

■ Spelling, Punctuation, and the Dictionary

A secretary must know how to spell—everything from common business words through the troublemakers.

Spelling Aids. To master your spelling difficulties, compile and maintain your own list of troublesome words, perhaps using the blank inside-cover pages of this book. If you will persistently write down each misspelling that occurs in your writing and each uncertainty that you have to check in a dictionary, you will have a custom-made list for instant reference.

It may help you also to develop your own mnemonic devices. Many a secretary has clinched correct spellings by word associations or parallelisms that are easy to remember: *calendar* ends with the *a* of *day*; *privilege* has the *leg* that comes from *legal; all right* parallels *all wrong*, and so on.

Punctuation. A secretary must know the rules of punctuation as they apply to formal writing. Some of her work is at that level. A paper that is to appear in print or a report to the board of directors must be punctuated with formal correctness. In routine business writing there is a trend to reduce the amount of punctuation, especially those marks which indicate pauses. Such punctuation is often omitted in the customary places in sentences which are clear in meaning. But whenever you are in doubt, punctuate fully. Comprehensive punctuation rules are given in the Reference Guide (page 713).

The Dictionary. Dictionaries vary—from the very British and formal *Oxford English Dictionary* to *Webster's Third New International Dictionary of the English Language*, which aroused a great furor among scholars of the English language when it appeared in 1961. It contains new words that have crept into the language through usage but have never before been listed. Those willing to accept such words as "finalize" and who see a dictionary as a descriptive record of living language will approve the new *Third*, being guided by the designations *slang*, *substandard*, and *nonstandard* in their choice of a word. Those who look at a dictionary as a source of what the language *ought* to be and who believe that language should be a pure body of words revealed from on high, among which workaday forms are out of place, will choose a more traditional reference.

The *Random House Dictionary of the English Language*, 1966, made the best-seller lists for a reason, for it puts a wealth of authoritative reference materials at the user's fingertips. Other recommended desk dictionaries are *Webster's New Collegiate, American College Dictionary, Webster's New World Dictionary*, and *Funk and Wagnalls' New College Standard Dictionary*. A desk dictionary should be replaced every five years or so with a current edition.

Turning to the dictionary at transcribing time, you want to learn:
1. **The correct spelling of a word—such as *neophyte***
2. **The correct spelling of an inflectional form—such as the past tense of *benefit***
3. **The preferred form of variant spellings—such as *acknowledgment* or *acknowledgement, judgment* or *judgement***
4. **Whether to use one word or two words—such as *high light* or *highlight***
5. **Whether to treat a word as a foreign one and underline it—such as bon voyage and carte blanche**
6. **How to divide a word at the end of a line—*committal*, for example**
7. **Whether to use a hyphen with a suffix or prefix, to join the suffix or prefix to the word or to treat it as a separate word—such as *pre-socratic* and *preview*; *selfsame* and *self-control*; *businesslike* and *droll-like***

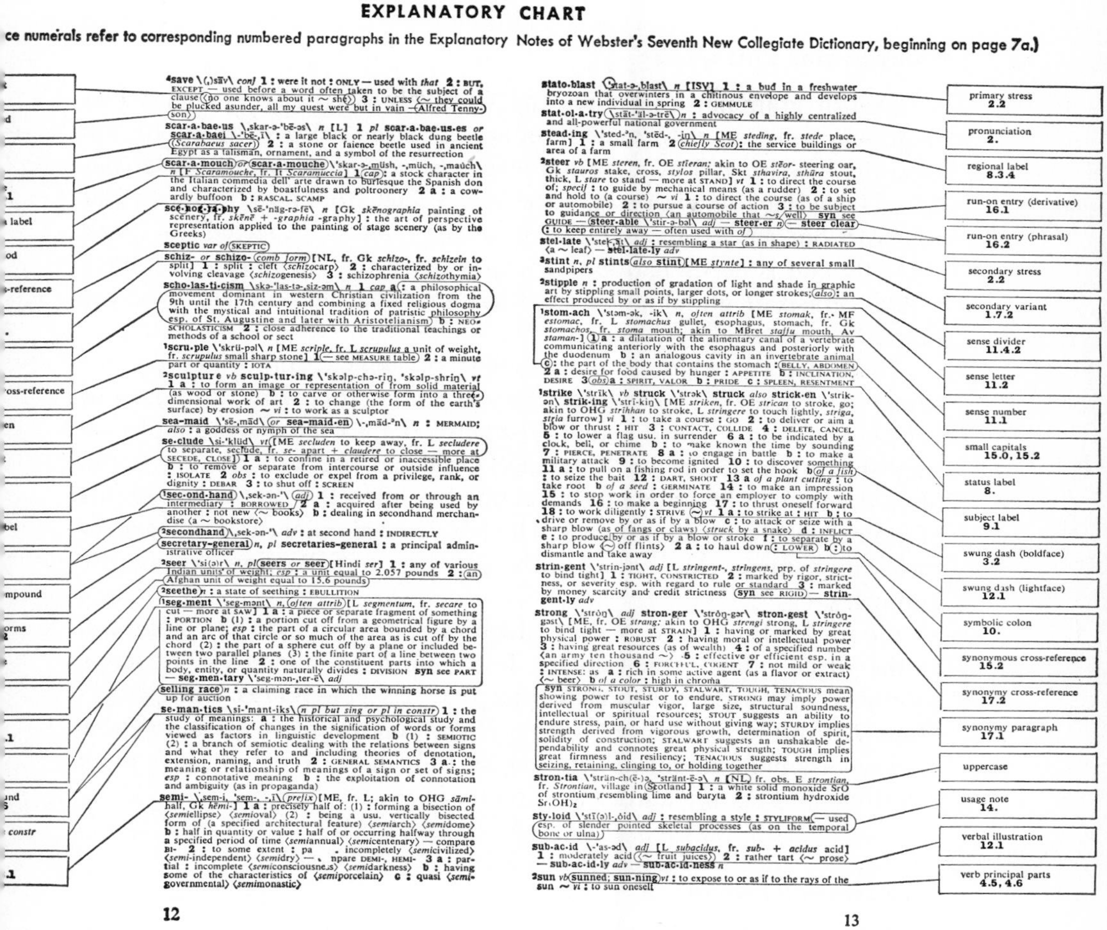

EXPLANATORY CHART

ce numerals refer to corresponding numbered paragraphs in the Explanatory Notes of Webster's Seventh New Collegiate Dictionary, beginning on page **7a.)**

⁴save \(,)sāv\ *conj* **1 :** were it not : ONLY — used with *that* **2 :** BUT, EXCEPT — used before a word often used to be the subject of a clause ⟨go one knows about it ~ she⟩ **3 :** UNLESS ⟨~ they could be plucked asunder, all my past spent but in vain —Alfred Tenny-son⟩

scar·a·bae·us \,skar-ə-'bē-əs\ *n* [L] **1** *pl* scar·a·bae·us·es *or* **scar·a·baei** \-'bē-,ī\ **:** a large black or nearly black dung beetle ⟨*Scarabaeus sacer*⟩ **2 :** a stone or faïence beetle used in ancient Egypt as a talisman, ornament, and a symbol of the resurrection

scar·a·mouch *or* **scar·a·mouche** \'skar-ə-,mü̇sh, -,müch, -,mau̇ch\ *n* [F *Scaramouche*, fr. It *Scaramuccia*] **1** *cap* **:** a stock character in the Italian commedia dell' arte drawn to burlesque the Spanish don and characterized by boastfulness and poltroonery **2 a :** a cow-ardly buffoon **b :** RASCAL, SCAMP

scé·nog·ra·phy \sē-'näg-rə-fē\ *n* [Gk *skēnographia* painting of scenery, fr. *skēnē* + *-graphia* -graphy] **:** the art of perspective representation applied to the painting of stage scenery (as by the Greeks)

sceptic *var of* SKEPTIC

schiz- *or* **schizo-** *comb form* [NL, fr. Gk *schizein*, fr. *schizein* to split] **1 :** split **:** cleft ⟨*schizocarp*⟩ **2 :** characterized by or in-volving cleavage ⟨*schizogenesis*⟩ **3 :** schizophrenia ⟨*schizothymia*⟩

scho·las·ti·cism \skə-'las-tə-,siz-əm\ *n* **1** *cap* **a :** a philosophical movement dominant in western Christian civilization from the 9th until the 17th century and combining a fixed religious dogma with the mystical and intuitional tradition of patristic philosophy esp. of St. Augustine and later with Aristotelianism **b :** NEO-SCHOLASTICISM **2 :** close adherence to the traditional teachings of methods of a school or sect

¹scru·ple \'skrü-pəl\ *n* [ME *scriple*, fr. L *scrupulus*] a unit of weight, fr. *scrupulus* small sharp stone] **1** ⟨— see MEASURE table⟩ **2 :** a minute part or quantity **:** IOTA

²sculpture *vb* **sculp·tur·ing** \'skəlp-chə-riŋ, 'skəlp-shriŋ\ *vt* **1 a :** to form an image or representation of from solid material (as wood or stone) **b :** to carve or fashion form into a three-dimensional work of art **2 :** to change (the form of the earth's surface) by erosion ~ *vi* **1 :** to work as a sculptor

sea·maid \'sē-,mād\ (*or* **sea·maid·en** \-,mād-ⁿn\) *n* **:** MERMAID; *also* **:** a goddess or nymph of the sea

se·clude \si-'klüd\ *vt* [ME *secluden* to keep away, fr. L *secludere* to separate, seclude, fr. *se-* apart + *claudere* to close — more at SECEDE, CLOSE] **1 a :** to confine in a retired or inaccessible place **1 :** to remove or separate from intercourse or outside influence **1 :** ISOLATE **2** *obs* **:** to exclude or expel from a privilege, rank, or dignity **:** DEBAR **3 :** to shut off **:** SCREEN

¹sec·ond-hand \,sek-ən-ⁿ\ (*adj*) **1 :** received from or through an intermediary **:** BORROWED **2 a :** acquired after being used by another **:** not new ⟨~ books⟩ **b :** dealing in secondhand merchan-dise ⟨a ~ bookstore⟩

²secondhand \,sek-ən-ⁿ\ *adv* **1 :** at second hand **:** INDIRECTLY

secretary-general *n*, *pl* secretaries-general **:** a principal admin-istrative officer

²seer \'si(ə)r\ *n*, *pl* **seers** *or* **seer** \'Hindi *ser*⟩ **1 :** any of various Indian units of weight; *esp* **:** a unit equal to 2.057 pounds **2** ⟨an Afghan unit of weight equal to 15.6 pounds⟩

seethe *n* **:** a state of seething **:** EBULLITION

¹seg·ment \'seg-mənt\ *n*, (often *attrib*)[L *segmentum*, fr. *secare* to cut — more at SAW] **1 a :** a separate fragment of something **:** PORTION **b** (1) **:** a portion cut off from a geometrical figure by a line or plane; *esp* **:** the part of a circular area bounded by a chord and an arc of that circle or so much of the area as is cut off by the chord (2) **:** the part of a sphere cut off by a plane or included be-tween two parallel planes (3) **:** the finite part of a line between two points in the line **2** (1) **:** one of the constituent parts into which a body, entity, or quantity naturally divides **:** DIVISION **syn** see PART — **seg·men·tary** \'seg-mən-,ter-ē\ *adj*

selling race *n* **:** a claiming race in which the winning horse is put up for auction

se·man·tics \si-'mant-iks\ *n pl but sing or pl in constr* **1 :** the study of meanings: **a :** the historical and psychological study and the classification of changes in the signification of words or forms viewed as factors in linguistic development **b** (1) **:** SEMIOTIC (2) **:** a branch of semiotic dealing with the relations between signs and what they refer to and including theories of denotation, extension, naming, and truth **2 :** GENERAL SEMANTICS **3 a :** the meaning or relationship of meanings of a sign or set of signs; *esp* **:** connotative meaning **b :** the exploitation of connotation and ambiguity (as in propaganda)

semi- \,sem-i, ,sem-, ,i\ (*prefix*)[ME, fr. L; akin to OHG *sāmi-* half, Gk *hēmi-*] **1 a :** precisely half of: (1) **:** forming a bisection of ⟨*semiellipse*⟩ ⟨*semivowel*⟩ (2) **:** being a usu. vertically bisected form of ⟨a specified architectural feature⟩ ⟨*semiarch*⟩ ⟨*semidome*⟩ **b :** half in quantity or value **:** half of or occurring halfway through a specified period of time ⟨*semiannual*⟩ ⟨*semicentennial*⟩ — compare **BI- 2 :** to some extent ⟨*semicivilized*⟩ — compare **DEMI- 2 :** to some extent ⟨*semicivilized*⟩ — compare **DEMI- 2 :** to some extent ⟨*semicivilized*⟩ a : partly ⟨*semi-independent*⟩ ⟨*semidry*⟩ ~ ⟨*nḡare demi-, mēmi-* **3 a :** par-tial **:** incomplete ⟨*semiconsciousness,s*⟩ ⟨*semidarkness*⟩ **b :** having some of the characteristics of ⟨*semiporcelain*⟩ **c :** quasi ⟨*semi-governmental*⟩ ⟨*semimonastic*⟩

stato-blast \'stat-ə-,blast\ *n* [ISV] **1 :** a bud in a freshwater bryozoan that overwinters in a chitinous envelope and develops into a new individual in spring **2 :** GEMMULE

stat·ol·a·try \stāt-'äl-ə-trē\ *n* **:** advocacy of a highly centralized and all-powerful national government

stead·ing \'sted-ⁿ, 'stēd-, -iŋ\ *n* [ME *steding*, fr. *stede* place, farm] **1 :** a small farm **2** ⟨*chiefly Scot*⟩: the service buildings or area of a farm

³steer *vb* [ME *steren*, fr. OE *stīeran*; akin to OE *stēor*- steering oar, Gk *stauros* stake, cross, *stylos* pillar, Skt *sthavira, sthūra* stout, thick, L *stare* to stand — more at STAND] *vt* **1 :** to direct the course thick, L *stare* to stand — more at STAND] *vt* **1 :** to direct the course of; *specif* **1 :** to guide by mechanical means (as a rudder) **2 :** to set and hold to (a course) ~ *vi* **1 :** to direct the course (as of a ship or automobile) **2 :** to pursue a course of action **3 :** to be subject to guidance or direction (can automobile that ~ well) **syn** see GUIDE — **steer·a·ble** \'stir-ə-bəl\ *adj* — **steer·er** *n*

stel·late \'stel-,āt\ *adj* **:** resembling a star (as in shape) **:** RADIATED — **stel·late·ly** *adv*

²stint *n, pl* **stints** ⟨*also* **stint**⟩[ME *stynte*] **:** any of several small sandpipers

²stipple *n* **:** production of gradation of light and shade in graphic art by stippling small points, tiny dots, or longer strokes; *also* **:** an effect produced by or as if by stippling

¹stom·ach \'stəm-ək, -ik\ *n*, often *attrib* [ME *stomak*, fr. MF *estomac*, fr. L *stomachus* gullet, esophagus, stomach, fr. Gk *stomachos*, fr. *stoma* mouth; akin to MBret *staffu* mouth, Av *staman-*] (1)**a :** a dilatation of the alimentary canal of a vertebrate communicating anteriorly with the esophagus and posteriorly with the duodenum **b :** an analogous cavity in an invertebrate animal **c :** the part of the body that contains the stomach **2** BELLY, ABDOMEN **3** *obs* **a :** desire for food caused by hunger **:** APPETITE **b :** INCLINATION, DESIRE **3** *obs* **a :** SPIRIT, VALOR **b :** PRIDE **c :** SPLEEN, RESENTMENT

¹strike \'strīk\ *vb* **struck** \'strək\ **struck** *also* **strick·en** \'strik-ən\ **strik·ing** \'stri-kiŋ\ [ME *striken*, fr. OE *strican* to stroke, go; akin to OHG *strīhhan* to stroke, L *stringere* to touch lightly, *striga, stria* furrow] *vt* **1 :** to take a course **:** GO **2 :** to deliver or aim a blow or thrust **1** *HIT* **3 :** CONTACT, COLLIDE **4 :** DELETE, CANCEL **5 :** to lower a flag usu. in surrender **6 a :** to be indicated by a clock, bell, or chime **b :** to make known the time by sounding **7 :** PIERCE, PENETRATE **8 a :** to engage in battle **b :** to make a military attack **9 :** to become tainted **10 :** to discover something **11 a :** to pull on a fishing rod in order to set the hook (of a fish) **b :** to seize the bait **12 :** DART, SHOOT **13 a** *of a plant cutting* **:** to take root **b** *of a seed* **:** GERMINATE **14 :** to make an impression **15 :** to stop work in order to force an employer to comply with demands **16 :** to make a beginning **17 :** to thrust oneself forward **18 :** to work diligently **:** STRIVE ~ *vt* **1 a :** to strike at **:** HIT **b :** to drive or remove by or as if by a blow **c :** to attack or seize with a sharp blow (as of fangs or claws) ⟨*struck* by a snake⟩ **d :** INFLICT **e :** to produce (by or as if by a blow or stroke) **f :** to separate by a sharp blow ⟨~ off flints⟩ **2 a :** to haul down (LOWER) **b** ⟨to dismantle and take away⟩

strin·gent \'strin-jənt\ *adj* [L *stringent-, stringens, prp.* of *stringere* to bind tight] **1 :** TIGHT, CONSTRICTED **2 :** marked by rigor, strict-ness, or severity esp. with regard to rule or standard **3 :** marked by money scarcity and credit strictness **syn** see RIGID — **strin·gent·ly** *adv*

strong \'strȯŋ\ *adj* **stron·ger** \'strȯŋ-gər\ **stron·gest** \'strȯŋ-gəst\ [ME, fr. OE *strang*; akin to OHG *strengi* strong, L *stringere* to bind tight — more at STRAIN] **1 :** having or marked by great physical power **:** ROBUST **2 :** having moral or intellectual power **3 :** having great resources (an army of 5000) **4 :** of a specified number (an army ten thousand ~) **5 :** effective or efficient esp. in a specified direction **6 :** FORCEFUL, COGENT **7 :** not mild or weak **:** INTENSE; *as* **a :** rich in some active agent (as a flavor or extract) ⟨~ beer⟩ **b** *of a color* **:** high in chroma

syn STRONG, STOUT, STURDY, STALWART, TOUGH, TENACIOUS mean showing power to resist or to endure. STRONG may imply power derived from muscular vigor, large size, structural soundness, intellectual or spiritual resources; STOUT suggests an ability to endure stress, pain, or hard use without giving way; STURDY implies strength derived from vigorous growth, determination of spirit, solidity of construction; STALWART suggests an unshakable de-pendability and connotes great physical strength; TOUGH implies great firmness and resiliency; TENACIOUS suggests strength in seizing, retaining, clinging to, or holding together

stron·tia \'strän-ch(ē-)ə, 'strän-ē-ə\ *n* [NL, fr. obs. E *strontian*, fr. *Strontian*, village in Scotland] **1 :** a white solid monoxide SrO of strontium resembling lime and baryta **2 :** strontium hydroxide Sr(OH)₂

sty·loid \'stī(ə)l-,ȯid\ *adj* **:** resembling a style **:** STYLIFORM — used (esp. of slender pointed skeletal processes (as on the temporal bone or ulna))

sub·ac·id \'-as-əd\ *adj* [L *subacidus*, fr. *sub-* + *acidus* acid] **1 :** moderately acid ⟨~ fruit juices⟩ **2 :** rather tart ⟨~ prose⟩ — **sub·ac·id·i·ty** \-as-'id-ət-ē\ *n* — **sub·ac·id·i·ness** *n*

²sun ⟨sunned, sun·ning⟩*vt* **:** to expose to or as if to the rays of the sun ~ *vi* **:** to sun oneself

Label	Reference
primary stress	2.2
pronunciation	2.
regional label	8.3.4
run-on entry (derivative)	16.1
run-on entry (phrasal)	16.2
secondary stress	2.2
secondary variant	1.7.2
sense divider	11.4.2
sense letter	11.2
sense number	11.1
small capitals	15.0, 15.2
status label	8.
subject label	9.1
swung dash (boldface)	3.2
swung dash (lightface)	12.1
symbolic colon	10.
synonymous cross-reference	16.2
synonymy cross-reference	17.2
synonymy paragraph	17.1
uppercase	
usage note	14.
verbal illustration	12.1
verb principal parts	4.5, 4.6

12   **13**

—G. and C. Merriam Company

Dictionaries vary greatly. The secretary will find the study of the introductory explanatory notes essential for gaining full benefit of the many kinds of information her particular dictionary provides.

Unfortunately, each of these seven situations is usually indicated in different ways in the entries in different dictionaries. The key to how they are indicated in your dictionary is given in the Explanatory Notes at the front of the dictionary. (Sometimes this section is given a more explicit title, such as "Guide to the Use of the Dictionary.")

When you do locate the explanation, underline it or enclose it in a frame with pencil for easy finding the next time. You thus save con-siderable time on repeat hunts. One secretary hyphenated numerous words, positive that she was right, because she misinterpreted a mark denoting separation of syllables as a hyphen. She had not studied nor checked back to the Explanatory Notes.

▪ Grammar and Usage

English grammar comprises the relatively fixed standards used in communicating at a formal or educated level. Since much of the executive's writing is at a formal level, *the secretary must have a confident knowledge of grammar.* She is expected to know grammatical construction inside out and upside down. She is expected to speak correctly and is depended upon to write correctly. If you do not have a good grasp of grammatical construction, you must obtain it before taking a secretarial position.

There are some points of grammar on which authorities do not agree. As a student and as a secretary, you may follow the authority of your choice—an English textbook, one of the accepted handbooks on English grammar, or the Reference Guide at the end of this book. Should your employer be one who concerns himself with the fine points of grammatical construction and who has decided opinions, always defer to his preference. He, too, has the privilege of following his favorite authority.

Good English usage is that which is appropriate to the situation, to the writer, and to the reader. It has no fixed standards but has a propriety. As a part of this chapter read *Usage—Words and Phrases* (page 727 in the Reference Guide). Were you aware of the differences between grammar and usage and the latitude these differences give to an executive in dictating and to a secretary in transcribing?

▪ Reference Books

A current and comprehensive secretarial handbook will be of frequent and valuable help to you. At the end of this chapter several preferred ones are listed. You will also find it helpful to take this textbook to the office for reference use, since you are familiar with its format and content and will be able to find reference items quickly.

There are also secretarial manuals for special fields: law, medicine, science and technical work, accounting, and so on. These, too, are listed at the end of the chapter for your aid in case your work involves a specialization.

If your office does not supply you with the minimal desk reference books, do buy your own. Find out the titles of the latest books by watching for announcements that come over your employer's desk or appear in the professional magazines in his or your field. You may also go to the library and look in the current year's edition of *Subject Guide to Books in*

The secretary may need to refer to previous correspondence with the company to which she is writing. Notice that the supplies needed for erasing are conveniently placed.

Print. Examine the various books available in several different book-shops. Comparison-shop before you make a selection. You can make sure you are getting the latest editions of the books you select by checking the current *Books in Print*, which lists books by title and author.

Transcription Procedure

To assure efficient transcription, first make certain that all is in readiness: the typewriter keys clean; the ribbon in good condition; the supply of letterheads, envelopes, and carbon paper adequate and carefully arranged for a flow of work without waste motion; reference books within reach; a pencil for use in editing the notes and a colored pencil for identifying or emphasizing instructions at hand; and erasing and correcting supplies nearby. To hold your notebook in an upright position, attach a large button or tie a large knot at each end of a piece of string so that you can set the opened notebook between the buttons or knots.

▪ Order of Transcription

Transcribe the rush and top-priority items in your notes in the order of their immediacy. As a general rule, telegrams should be given attention first. The executive may like to read a telegram before it is sent out, or he may let you be responsible for its accurate transcription. If he

The kind of executive who requests rough drafts so that he can edit and improve them may also appreciate improvements the secretary makes during transcription.

— Underwood Corporation

does not mention his preference, it is safer to have him check the telegram. The first time you might casually ask him (with telegram in hand), "Would you like to read this telegram before it is sent?" and be guided accordingly in the future. Special-delivery and airmail letters should be attended to next, and perhaps taken in immediately for signing and mailing if they are urgent. If time is a factor, give early preference to instructions for subordinates.

If transcription items must be carried over until the next day, have one regular place to store uncompleted work.

▪ Editing and Completing Each Item

Before starting to type an item, read intently through it; then edit and complete it so that it is letter-perfect and ready for smooth, continuous transcription. For a secretary to read and rework her notes is not an indication of incompetence but rather of efficiency. As you read through each item:

Insert punctuation.	Make substitutions for repeated words.
Indicate paragraphs.	Rewrite poor sentences.
Correct errors in grammar.	Verify facts—prices, names, etc.
Correct errors in fact.	Write out difficult spellings.
Eliminate redundancies.	Fill blanks left by executive.
Clarify ambiguities.	Find and insert needed information.

When you feel that a whole paragraph should be changed, type the dictated text on a piece of paper with your revision underneath it. Take it in to the executive and say something like, "I roughed out a paragraph here. I thought you might want to change it because . . . ." Do not try to sell your revision. If he prefers his own, accept it matter-of-factly.

▪ Rough-Draft Transcripts

A *rough draft* is an accurate transcription of notes on inexpensive paper so that editing and polishing can be done. The executive will request a rough draft whenever there is reason for a communication to be carefully written—such as an important letter, a report to a superior, a speech, or a paper to be published. Only one copy is typed unless your employer requests another. Strikeovers and markouts are permitted. In fact, it is inefficient to take final-draft care on a rough draft.

Single-space a rough draft of a letter on letterhead-size paper in exact letter form so that the draft will also serve as a guide to final placement. The margins provide enough room for writing in changes. A rough draft of a report or paper is typed on legal-size substandard paper or on business-size colored sheets because such paper has both attention and reminder value among the other papers on the desk. Since margins of only an inch or so are used on these rough drafts, the drafts are always double- or triple-spaced to provide room for editorial changes to be made.

▪ Secretarial Changes in Dictated Matter

A beginning secretary is concerned about making changes in the executive's dictation. To edit or not to edit depends upon what is to be changed and the executive's attitude about tampering with his communicative endeavors. There are two kinds of changes, however, that must always be made:

1. **Always correct a mistake in fact or grammar. No executive wants a letter to go out with *Monday, July 7*, if it is *Monday, July 8*; nor does he want *the set of illustrations show that*—when it must be *shows that*. Be sure, however, that it is in error before making a change. Avoid the embarrassment of the secretary who changed *criterion is* to *criteria is* because she was not familiar with the singular form and did not check the dictated word in the dictionary.**

2. **Always make a change when a conspicuous word or root word is repeated within the same paragraph. Should the executive dictate *we communicated with him* and then a few sentences later say *as soon as we receive his communication*, change the second clause to *as soon as we hear from him*.**

—*IBM Corporation*

The secretary should move slowly in making changes in the dictated material when she transcribes. She should not transcribe an inaccuracy without calling it to the executive's attention, and she should avoid changes which are merely based on her taste whims.

Choice of words or phraseology is often a matter of personal preference; the secretary should change the words only if she is positive the executive approves. The kind of man who selects each word and phrase with care, or who remembers word for word what he dictates, almost always dislikes to have changes made. The kind of executive who often requests rough drafts or who edits and makes copious changes in transcribed work usually appreciates secretarial improvements. Be guided by the executive's habits. Make minor changes at first. Progress to major changes only if he reacts favorably to the minor ones.

Often this preliminary reading of notes can be done during lulls in dictation when the executive is interrupted for various reasons. If not, a final step will assure following through on the transcription without wasted effort: You should now add instructions to yourself at the pertinent places in the notes regarding such factors as the number of copies, distribution, additions on certain copies, enclosures to be prepared, and under-separate-cover shipments to be arranged. Plan, however, to write the required tickler items later. You can do it more efficiently when handling the carbon copies of the letters transcribed.

Usually the executive will approve if his secretary, after careful thought or investigation, will present an unasked-for rough draft if changes seem important.

Very often a secretary furnishes an unsolicited rough draft because she knows from experience that the executive will make changes that will necessitate a rewrite. To present an unasked-for rough draft and imply that the text could stand editing requires secretarial tact. A plausible, diplomatic explanation is that you made a rough draft for your own guidance in placement or layout but thought the executive might like to scan it before final typing. Or you might say that you made a rough draft because there were one or two places in your notes where you were not sure of his phrasing. Never intimate that you *expect* him to make changes; merely give him a convenient opportunity.

▪ Handling the Notebook Efficiently

You know that for ease in transcribing it is best to have the notebook upright. You will find it efficient to follow these two practices, also: (1) When stopping to twirl a new carbon pack into the typewriter or when interrupted during transcribing, insert a conspicuous signal to yourself (such as that shown on the next page) at the cutoff place in your

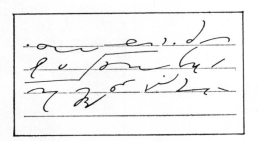

notes. Otherwise, it may be necessary to read through the whole page of notes to find the place again. It is also easy to omit lines of notes when the same word or phrase occurs twice on a page. (2) Since you may not transcribe the items in consecutive order, draw your cancelation line through the item completed as soon as you have completed it. A secretary usually skips or repeats an item only once before she learns that putting in the cancelation line immediately is a protective necessity.

■ **Stationery**

To be able to locate the right letterhead quickly requires that you arrange your desk efficiently. Give some thought to what is the best arrangement for your needs.

Choice of Letterheads. More than likely you will use a variety of letterheads. There will be at least the regular business one, the interoffice one, and the executive's personal letterhead. If the employer serves as an officer or member of the board of an outside organization, he will probably correspond on that letterhead, too.

Waste of Stationery. Letterheads are expensive, and the waste of them is appalling. Office wastebaskets are full of letterheads discarded because of careless work and slovenly corrections. Transcribe carefully and become skillful at correcting. Again, this takes time—but time well spent. One company reduced the cost and waste of hasty transcribing with a huge sign like this.

IT TAKES LESS TIME
TO BE RIGHT
THAN TO REWRITE !

■ **Number and Kinds of Copies**

Some companies require two copies of every letter, one for the individual correspondence file, and another for a bound reading file of all letters mailed each day. In order to save filing space and supplies, other offices have a carbon copy typed on the back of the incoming letter. The majority, however, have one copy made on a second sheet for a correspondence file.

You will be asked to make and furnish certain individuals and departments with carbon copies of every letter you type that relates to subjects of mutual interest. A specific color of stationery is sometimes assigned to each department, and carbon copy sheets of the assigned color must be used for carbon copies. Make a record in your desk manual of persons to whom copies should be sent on each subject so that you can make the correct number and colors of carbons and distribute them properly each time.

■ The Matter of Dating

Date every paper. Use the date of transcription if it differs from that of the dictation. It may be necessary to edit the dictation to make it conform, as "your visit *yesterday*," rather than "your visit *this morning*." On typewritten matter that will not be kept for record, use the abbreviated date form as *8/28/—*.

■ Diacritical Marks

After the transcript has been removed from the typewriter, add any necessary diacritical marks in pencil or ink, whichever is less conspicuous.

■ Letter Placement

If you have difficulty estimating letter length by eye and getting attractive placement on the letterhead, here is a backward approach to setting up placement guides.

Go to the files and remove carbon copies of the executive's letters. Select a short one, a medium one, and a long single-page one. Copy each one on a letterhead in perfect style and attractive placement. Then write each one in shorthand in your notebook. Be guided by a page of your notes taken from dictation to approximate your usual spacing of notes. Remove the pages of notes and attach each set to its own letter. Put them in your desk manual as models for letter style and attractive placement and as shorthand guides with which to measure the length of letters.

■ Letter and Envelope Styles

About one fourth of all large businesses furnish secretaries and stenographers with a correspondence manual, showing the form and style for each letterhead and envelope, forms of address, and so on. If none is supplied, make up your own models from previous correspondence and letter-style authorities. For immediate reference, model letters and envelopes in various styles and punctuation forms are shown on pages 756–759. A comprehensive table on pages 760–761 shows accepted treatments of the various parts of a letter.

■ Proofreading the Transcript

With the typewriter bail serving as a line guide, proofread each page before removing it from the typewriter. Use a ruler to follow the dictated notes. Point with a forefinger to the typewritten material as you look back and forth. Check very carefully the address and any numbers or calculations. Watch for omissions or repetitions that may have occurred because of interruptions. Although there is a temptation to feel that careful editing of the shorthand notes precludes the possibility of errors in grammar or sense,

> I WAS TYPING letters informing customers who were delinquent in making their mortgage payments that, unless the overdue payments were received within a week, their property would be foreclosed. I'm so glad I proofread my work. At the end of one letter I had closed with: "Very truly ours."—*Marcia L. Keller, from April, 1966*, Reader's Digest

proofread mentally as well as visually, for many errors that are passed over in editing the notes stand out clearly in the transcript. As you proofread, jot down on a scrap of paper any enclosures mentioned or any special instructions.

■ Keeping It Confidential

There are always several persons in a large office who are inquisitive as to what is currently happening in the executive offices. Transcripts on the secretaries' desks are often fruitful sources of information: finished letters waiting to be signed, the letter being typed, and carbon copies openly in view. If someone comes to your desk while you are transcribing, roll the letter back into the typewriter, making your action as unobtrusive as possible. Keep the group of transcribed letters covered with a sheet of paper, or in face-down order, or inside a file folder. Carbon copies are just as informative as originals, so treat them with the same respect. Many executives now use an electric wastebasket that shreds paper that might reveal company secrets.

▪ Reference Initials

Reference initials may be treated in a variety of ways:

1. If the executive's name is typed in the closing lines, his initials may be omitted and only the transcriber's initials used.
2. The reference initials may be put on only carbon copies; the letter recipient is not aware that a *blind* carbon copy was sent.
3. Reference initials follow a carefully worked-out pattern whenever others compose letters for the executive's signature.

There are certain situations in which it is poor public relations to indicate that the executive delegated a letter to the secretary or an associate to compose. Reference initials should not blatantly point out the fact that the signer did not dictate the letter, but for record purposes the fact should be evident. Executive Donald Kane and secretary Diane Hartman worked out a reference-initial pattern using the composer's initial first, the transcriber's initial second, and the signer's initial third. Note that in each case reference initials could be taken for those of the transcriber only.

On letters dictated by the executive and transcribed by the secretary for the executive's signature, they used *khk*.

On letters composed by the secretary for the executive's signature, they used *hhk*.

On letters composed by the secretary for her own signature, they used *hhh*.

On letters dictated by Mr. Kane's assistant, M. Dowell, for the executive's signature and transcribed by the secretary, they used *dhk*.

▪ Transcribing Machine Dictation

If you are to learn how to use a transcribing machine, call in the salesman or obtain an instruction manual. Until you acquire confidence and skill, type the dictation in draft form, edit it, and ask the executive to clear up doubts and questions. Set up a table of measures of dictated space to letter length, as a guide for letter placement. Develop your own forget-me-not system for handling insertions and changes.

Return to the executive's desk partially used recordings with the transcribed portions clearly indicated. Otherwise you may repeat an

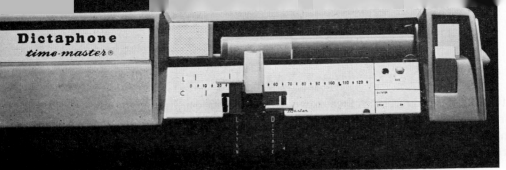

—*Dictaphone Corporation*

The upright lines on the long paper indicator strip show where C's (changes and corrections) follow. The space between the L marks shows the length of the dictated item. The transcriber listens to the C spots first and, if need be, writes notes to herself regarding the changes. She places these notes by the typewriter to guide her as she transcribes.

item. One secretary transcribed a letter on December 15, forgot to mark it off the record, transcribed it again in January with new dictation, mailed it, and received from the correspondent a very puzzled answer that caused much embarrassment to both the secretary and the executive.

The orderly filing of transcribed recordings is difficult. One unit may have on it material dictated on several widely separated dates. Transcribed recordings are not used as reference sources because there is nothing visible to indicate to whom the dictation was addressed or what it was about, and it would take much too long to listen through recordings to locate dictated items.

▪ Enclosures

Whenever an enclosure is mentioned in a letter, there is an implied instruction that you are to obtain the enclosure and attach it to the letter before presenting the letter for signature. If possible, collect all enclosures at the same time. Do not take for use as an enclosure either the file copy of a letter or the original copy of a letter received. Instead, prepare a copy on a copying machine; or typewrite a plain, identified copy.

If an enclosure is small enough not to cover the body of the letter, it is attached to the face. If larger, it is put at the back. To enclose a check or currency, pin or staple it to the face of the letter. To enclose coins, tape them to a card and clip the card to the face of the letter. To enclose stamps, paper clip them to a corner of the letter or enclose them in a small cellophane envelope. Place an envelope to be enclosed so that no fold, or a minimum number of folds, is required. Put page-size enclosures behind a letter and paper clip or staple them to it. Some companies, however, disapprove of fastening page-size enclosures to a letter. They believe the folds are sufficient to hold letter-size sheets together and that folding is made more difficult when the enclosures are fastened to the letter.

194

Should it be necessary to send in a letter for signature without its enclosures, clip a note to it listing the enclosures missing. The note will serve a dual purpose: it will inform the executive that you have not forgotten the items to be enclosed and it will remind you not to mail the letter until the enclosures are at hand.

▪ Under-Separate-Cover Items

Prepare or obtain material to be sent under separate cover and get it ready for mailing. If someone else is responsible, give complete instructions in writing to the person or department, and prepare a typewritten address label. Write a tickler item to check later, to see if the material went out.

You may enclose a letter with a parcel-post package, seal the package, put the parcel-post postage on it, add on the front a notation *First-Class Letter Enclosed*, and add a first-class stamp to the other postage to cover the letter put inside. This procedure saves sending out a great deal of under-separate-cover mail and keeping track of it by tickler items.

▪ Envelopes

The correct forms and placement of envelope-address parts will be found in the Reference Guide on page 759.

Before you remove a letter from the typewriter, drop its envelope between the letter and the platen. When you remove the letter, the envelope will come into position for addressing. Slip the addressed envelope, face up, over the top of the letter and its enclosures. This is the preferred method. Another accepted way is to slip the envelope over the left side of the letter with the flap side up. The envelopes are less likely to slip off in this position and the whole stack of completed letters is more maneuverable; however, it is difficult to check envelope addresses to go with the corresponding letter addresses when the envelopes are in this position.

▪ Identifying Copies

Sometimes a letter has multiple addressees, the letter is sent to several individuals; and all copies are typed in one writing. The names are all listed in the address lines or in the salutation. Treat each copy as an original, individual letter as indicated on page 196.

1. **Put a check mark above or beside the name of the person to whom the copy will be sent.**
2. **Address an envelope for that name; slip the envelope over that copy.**
3. **Send in each checked letter and addressed envelope with the rest of the mail for signing.**

When carbon copies of a letter to a single addressee are to be sent to others for their information, type the names or initials of the carbon-copy recipients following the *cc* reference notation. Such copies are handled the same as multiple-addressee letters except that the sender does not sign each one. The secretary types in the executive's name preceded by (*Signed*) or *S/*.

When *blind copies* of a letter are to be sent, use the reference notation *bc* in the usual position for noting carbon copy distribution. Type the names or initials of the recipients on all copies *except the original letter* and handle them as if they were regular carbon copies. To reduce handling, use a piece of paper to cover the notation position on the original; type the notation before removing the carbon pack from the typewriter.

▪ Submitting Correspondence for Signature

As a last-minute touch before sending in the correspondence, erase any fingermarks or smudges. Carefully read all the correspondence written by assistants and have it corrected before approving it for signing. Take a rush letter in as soon as it is ready and mail it immediately after it has been signed. Submit the rest of the correspondence upon its completion. If there has been a great deal of dictation, it may not be possible to get it all transcribed by mail-signing time. In that case, take in all that is finished. Some men like to sign at noon the mail that is ready and sign the rest just before leaving for the day. Learn and follow the executive's preferences. The correct arrangement of transcribed material is the letter and its envelope, extra carbons, and file copy with its notations.

If the executive is at his desk, present the letters face up. If he is away from his desk, turn the top letter face down to keep it clean and to prevent its being read. An executive sometimes uses a *blotter book* to hold correspondence to be signed. Letters are clipped to the heavy pages in which holes are punched so that the signer can see whether he has signed all correspondence.

Most secretaries arrange to be at the executive's desk when he signs the communications. He often has questions and comments about these items and the work ahead.

■ Nonagreement as to Changes

A frequent point of irritation between an executive and a transcriber is the difference between what the executive thinks he dictated and what has been transcribed. A young worker on her first job almost had the executive tearing his hair over her "That's-what-you-said" habit. On reading a letter to be signed, he would say, "I didn't say this"; and she, bristling, would answer, "Yes, you did! It's in my notes!"

There is only one gracious secretarial way of handling these differences of opinion as to who is at fault. The secretary should take the blame, when she is at fault and when she is not! It really does not make any difference who made the mistake. The important thing is to go about correcting it at once, cheerfully and willingly. If the secretary frowns and is conspicuously resentful at changing a letter, she cannot expect the executive to be pleased with her attitude.

■ Secretarial Signatures

Do develop a good business signature—readable and generous in size. A dainty signature is not fitting for business mail. If you are a man, spell out your first name to indicate that fact. If you are a woman, indicate whether you are *Miss* or *Mrs;* otherwise, correspondents are not sure how to address you and must use the indeterminate form *Ms.* The customary ways for a secretary to sign mail in the executive's absence, or at his request are:

Sign the executive's name in your own handwriting and add your initials. ⟶ Sincerely yours

Robert L. Simpson
L.S.
President

Imitate the executive's signature. ⟶ Sincerely yours

Robert L. Simpson
President

Sign your own name as secretary to the executive. Always type your name below the signature space.

A male secretary should spell out his first name so that the correspondent can address his reply to Mr. _____. ⟶ Very truly yours

Dan Bowman
Dan Bowman
Secretary to Mr. Simpson

For a woman, *Miss* or *Mrs.* may ⟶   Very truly yours
be included or omitted in either the
typewritten or the longhand name.   *Ann Bowman*
If the title *is* included, it is
enclosed in parentheses only when   Miss Ann Bowman
used with the signature. *Miss* is ⟶   Secretary to Mr. Simpson
presumed if no title is given. If   Very truly yours
the name is commonly used by
men, the *Miss* or *Mrs.* is helpful   *(Miss) Ann Bowman*
to the reader, who may need the
information for a reply.   Ann Bowman
      Secretary to Mr. Simpson

■ Readying the Correspondence for Filing

All the correspondence handled at transcription must now be readied for filing. Staple the carbon copy of each reply to the top of the incoming letter it answers. Staple the carbons of letters originating at your desk into sets if the letters are longer than one page. Place pertinent letters in the pending file or make tickler items from the carbon copies, and write each follow-up date on the carbon copy of the letter itself to show that the date has been set and recorded. Add the filing notation before laying the correspondence aside. The matter of designating *where* to file each letter is taken up in Chapters 14 and 15.

Sending the Signed Mail

In some large offices secretaries are relieved of the final work of sending out correspondence. Mail clerks collect the signed letters and the envelopes and fold, insert, seal, and stamp them. In smaller offices the secretary attends to every step of the routine.

■ Folding and Inserting Letters

A letter is ready for mailing when it is signed and all enclosures are assembled. A secretary often folds and inserts the letters while she waits at the executive's desk for him to read and sign the rest of the mail. Every letter should be folded in such a way that it will unfold naturally into reading position. The proper methods are illustrated on page 199.

You can fold and insert a stack of letters very quickly at your own desk by developing a routine based on the steps given on page 200.

Large (Nos. 10, 9, and 7¾)

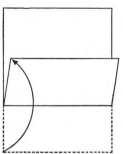 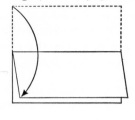 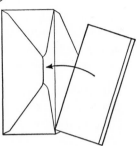

With the letter face up, fold slightly less than one third of the letterhead up toward the top.	Fold down the top of the letterhead to within ½ inch of the bottom fold.	Insert the letter into the envelope with the last crease toward the bottom of the envelope.

Small (Nos. 6¾ and 6¼)

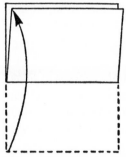   

With letter face up on desk, fold bottom up to ½ inch from top.	Fold right third to left.	Fold left third to ½ inch from last crease.	Insert last-creased edge first.

Window

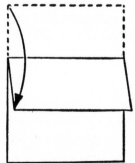 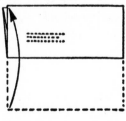 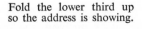 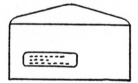

With the sheet face down, top toward you, fold the upper third down.	Fold the lower third up so the address is showing.	Insert the sheet into the envelope with the last crease at the bottom.

Letters are folded in such manner that they can be removed from the envelope and opened easily and quickly in position for reading.

1. Have a cleared space on the desk.
2. Then take a letter from the stack of signed mail; place it before you on the desk and fold it neatly; insert it into the envelope at once.
3. Lay the envelope aside in a stack with the flap up flat (not folded over the envelope) and with the address side on the bottom.

The routine that proves most efficient for you must be worked out. Experiment with some twenty or thirty large and small dummy envelopes and letters until you have developed a routine free of waste motions.

▪ Sealing Envelopes

When all the letters are enclosed, joggle the envelopes into a neat stack. All of the address sides will be down and the flaps will be opened out. Now pick up the stack, grasp the flaps, and bend them back in order to make them flatter. Holding the short edges of the stack of envelopes between the two hands, drop the envelopes off the bottom of the stack one at a time, on to the desk, so that only the gummed part of the flap of each envelope is visible. Then take a moistening tube, and with one swing of the arm start at the bottom and moisten all of the flaps at once. Lay the tube aside on a blotter and start sealing the envelope nearest you by folding over the flap. Continue up the column. As you seal each envelope, pick it up in your left hand and lay it in a stack to the left, flap side up.

In the ceramic wheel type of moistener, a wide wheel passes through a shallow reservoir of water at the bottom. To use this moistener, turn the stack of envelopes over so that the address sides are up. Take the top envelope and, with both hands at the short edges, pull just the gummed part of the flap over the rotating wheel. With the forefingers, fold the moistened flap down over the envelope and lay it aside, address side up.

▪ Stamping

If the sealed envelopes are to be stamped by hand, first remove all those that require special stamping. Lay the rest of them out in columnar form with the address side up, leaving depth enough for the stamps to be pasted. Take a strip of stamps that are joined with the horizontal edges together, moisten a stamp at a time on a nearby sponge or moistener, and affix it to an envelope, working from the top envelope down. For strip stamps that are attached at the vertical edges, as rolled stamps are, lay the envelopes across the desk.

By adopting timesaving routines and by positioning materials for convenient handling, the secretary can increase her efficiency greatly. Notice the location of (1) the stamp box and (2) the postage scale.

Envelopes requiring special stamping should be given individual attention. Those that are sent airmail, special delivery, or to other countries and those that are too heavy for the minimum postage should be handled separately. Write in the stamp position the amount of postage needed. This penciled figure is later covered by the stamps.

Because of the considerable loss incurred from using excess postage and because the recipient has to pay the postage due, every office should have some kind of postal scale. Weigh every piece of mail that may be overweight. "When in doubt, weigh!" Small scales for first-class mail are sensitive to fractions of an ounce. Incidentally, have your scales checked for accuracy periodically.

▪ Routine Mailings

You may be responsible for regular mailings to a specified list—40 branch managers every Thursday, for instance. You can save time by following this routine:

1. Type stencils of the addresses, 10 to the page.
2. Run off 52 copies from each stencil, using gummed-back paper.
3. Cut individual labels from each sheet and affix them to the envelopes.

Envelopes for the year's mailings are ready in three operations.

Secretarial Manuals

The following list of references will assist the secretary in self-development. First is a list of manuals and recommended books on grammar, punctuation, and word usage helpful to any secretary. This general list is followed by aids for three specialized types of secretaries: the tech-sec, the legal secretary, and the medical secretary.

■ General Secretarial Manuals

Doris, Lillian, and Besse May Miller. *Complete Secretary's Handbook*, 7th ed. Englewood Cliffs: Prentice-Hall, Inc., 1960, 582 pp.

Hutchinson, Lois. *Standard Handbook for Secretaries*, 7th ed. New York: McGraw-Hill Book Company, Inc., 1956, 638 pp.

Miller, Besse May (ed.). *Private Secretary's Encyclopedic Dictionary*. Englewood Cliffs: Prentice-Hall, Inc., 1958, 402 pp.

■ Grammar, Punctuation, and Word Usage Aids

A Manual of Style, 11th ed. Chicago: The University of Chicago Press, 1949, 534 pp.

Aurner, Robert R., and Paul S. Burtness. *Effective English for Business*. Cincinnati: South-Western Publishing Co., 1962, 664 pp.

Bernstein, Theodore. *The Careful Writer*. New York: Atheneum Press, 1965, 488 pp.

————. *Watch Your Language*. Great Neck, New York: Channel Press, 1958, 276 pp.

Blumenthal, Joseph C. *English 3200—A Programmed Course in Grammar and Usage*. New York: Harcourt, Brace, and World, Inc., 1962, 535 pp.

Dutch, Robert A. (ed.). *The Original Roget's Thesaurus of English Words and Phrases*. New York: St. Martin's Press, 1965, 1405 pp.

Evans, Bergen, and Cornelia Evans. *A Dictionary of Contemporary American Usage*. New York: Random House, Inc., 1959.

Fowler, Henry W. *Dictionary of Modern English Usage*, revised by E. Gowers. New York: Oxford University Press, 1965, 725 pp.

Gavin, Ruth, and Lillian Hutchinson. *Reference Manual for Stenographers and Typists*. New York: Gregg Division of McGraw-Hill Book Company, Inc., 1968, 192 pp.

Larsen, Leanna A., and Clifford House. *Reference Manual for Office Employees*, 5th ed. Cincinnati: South-Western Publishing Co., 1968, 150 pp.

Mayo, Lucy G. *Communications Handbook for Secretaries*. New York: McGraw-Hill Book Company, Inc., 1959, 568 pp.

Nicholson, Margaret (ed.). *American English Usage*. New York: Oxford University Press, 1957.

Perrin, Porter G. *Writer's Guide and Index to English*. Chicago: Scott, Foresman & Company, 1965, 907 pp.

United States Government Printing Office Style Manual, Rev. ed. Washington: Superintendent of Documents, 1959, 512 pp.

■ Technical Secretarial Aids

Adams, Dorothy, and Margaret Kurtz. *Terminology and Transcription for the Technical Secretary*. New York: Gregg Division of McGraw-Hill Book Company, Inc., 1962, 384 pp.

Adams, Dorothy, and Margaret Kurtz. "The Tec-Sec," monthly column in *Today's Secretary*. New York: Gregg Division of McGraw-Hill Book Company, Inc.

Dunford, Nelson James. *A Handbook for Technical Typists*. Gordon and Breach Science Publishers, 150 Fifth Avenue, New York, New York, 1965, 136 pp.

Laird, Eleanor. *Engineering Secretary's Complete Handbook*. Englewood Cliffs: Prentice-Hall, Inc., 1962, 235 pp.

McLaughlin, Charles. *Space Age Dictionary*. Princeton, New Jersey: Van Nostrand Publishing Company, 1963, 236 pp.

128 World, a magazine for the many technical establishments around Boston. 128 Publishing Company, 66 Walpole Street, Boston, Massachusetts.

Stratford, Alison, and Billie Jean Culpepper. *The Science-Engineering Secretary*. Englewood Cliffs: Prentice-Hall, Inc., 1963, 338 pp.

▪ Medical Secretarial Aids

Agnew, Peter L., and Phillip S. Atkinson. *Medical Office Practice*, a practice set. Cincinnati: South-Western Publishing Co., 1966.

Bredow, Miriam. *Medical Specialties*. New York: Gregg Division of McGraw-Hill Book Company, Inc., 1966, 384 pp.

Miller, Besse May. *Medical Secretary's and Assistant's Handbook*. Englewood Cliffs: Prentice-Hall, Inc., 1960, 236 pp.

Root, Kathleen Berger, and Edward E. Byers. *Medical Terminology and Transcription*. New York: Gregg Division of McGraw-Hill Book Company, Inc., 1967, 412 pp.

Shepro, David, and Edward E. Byers. *Medical Terminology and Transcription: Anatomy and Physiology*. New York: Gregg Division of McGraw-Hill Book Company, Inc., 1968, 384 pp.

▪ Legal Secretarial Aids

Graham, Milton, Norma Curchak, and Herbert Yengel. *Legal Typewriting*, a kit of materials. New York: Gregg Division of McGraw-Hill Book Company, Inc., 1967.

Krogfoss, Robert B. (ed.). *A Manual for the Legal Secretarial Profession*, compiled by members of the National Association of Legal Secretaries. St. Paul: West Publishing Company, 1965, 576 pp.

Leslie, Louis, and Kenneth Coffin. *Handbook for the Legal Secretary*. New York: Gregg Division of McGraw-Hill Book Company, Inc., 1968, 384 pp.

Miller, Besse May. *Legal Secretary's Complete Handbook*. Englewood Cliffs: Prentice-Hall, Inc., 1953, 662 pp.

Sletwold, Evangeline. *Sletwold's Manual of Documents and Forms for the Legal Secretary*. Englewood Cliffs: Prentice-Hall, Inc., 1965, 193 pp.

Suggested Readings

Engel, Pauline. *Executive Secretary's Handbook*. Englewood Cliffs: Prentice-Hall, Inc., 1965, pp. 95–98.

155 Office Shortcuts. West Nyack, New York: Parker Publishing Company, 1964, pp. 15–24.

Questions for Discussion

1. Should a secretary be expected to buy her own reference books?

2. Would any of the three following practices suggested in the chapter be unnecessary time wasters for an experienced, competent secretary?

   (a) Prereading and editing notes before transcribing
   (b) Making a reading file of the day's transcription
   (c) Making rough drafts of items on the chance that they may require rewriting

3. Give your opinion of the following secretarial signature:

   Lee Whitson

   (Mrs.) Lee Whitson
   Secretary to Mr. Wilbur Metcalf

4. An executive, reading the mail before signing it, says, "Something is wrong here. I didn't say this!" The secretary gets her notes, finds the sentence, and says resentfully, "That *is* what you said. I have it down exactly like that." What are your comments?

5. How will the secretary know how many copies of material to transcribe?

6. Do you think that it is fair to the secretary to expect her to take the blame for the executive's errors in dictation?

7. What implied directions would you follow in transcribing:

   (a) A proposed contract for the construction of a new plant
   (b) A personal letter to Henry Wilson
   (c) An acceptance of an invitation to represent a college at the inauguration of a new president
   (d) A reply to a letter of complaint about the service given to a customer by a branch office

8. Type the first lines of letter addresses to James Matthew Robinson, using the:

   (a) Abbreviation of *honorable* before the name
   (b) Words *the honorable* before the name
   (c) Abbreviation of *esquire* following the name
   (d) Roman numeral *II* after the name
   (e) Word *professor* or its abbreviation before the name

   Refer to the Reference Guide to verify or correct your answers.

Problems

■ **1.** For an awareness of today's cost of one first-class letter, compute the cost from these facts:

(a) The executive, who dictates a letter in five minutes and signs it in one minute, earns $500 a week (the work week is 35 hours).

(b) The secretary, who transcribes the letter in 15 minutes, earns $105 a week for a 35-hour week.

(c) The company's printed letterheads cost $10 per thousand.

(d) Their printed envelopes cost $8.50 a thousand.

(e) Second sheets cost $2.50 a thousand.

Do not consider the cost of supplies—such as notebooks, carbon paper, erasers—and the office overhead charged to the executive's department each month.

■ **2.** On the inside cover of your own collegiate dictionary paste a typewritten listing showing exactly:

(a) *How* the following are shown in the dictionary:

Foreign words
Hyphened words
Inflectional forms
Parts of speech
Preferred spellings
Syllabication

(b) *Where* the following can be found in the dictionary:

Abbreviations
Adjective and noun phrases (such as *blind alley*)
Biographical names
Place names

Prepositional phrases (such as *on hand*)
Punctuation
Noun and noun phrases (such as *band wagon*)
Rules of grammar

Having such a reference will save you much time in using a dictionary.

■ **3.** Be prepared to set up and demonstrate: (a) speed sealing of envelopes, using as many types of manual moisteners as possible; (b) speed stamping.

■ **4.** Skill in the use of secretarial publications is part of the necessary equipment of the secretary. Prepare in typewritten form answers to the following questions; then correct your answers, using the reference books designated in the chapter and citing your authority.

(a) What are synonyms for *agent, integrity, mediocrity*?

(b) What is the correct salutation for a clergyman?

(c) What are the approved regular and ZIP Code abbreviations for *Oregon*? *Connecticut*? *Nebraska*?

(d) Is there a space after the first period in writing *Ph.D.*?

(e) How should the following sentence be punctuated?
Did he say Are you going

(f) Should *cooperate* and *reread* be hyphenated?

(g) What is the distinction between *majority* and *plurality*?

Related Work Assignments 27-28

27. Transcribing. Transcribe in the order dictated the four messages for Related Work Assignment 24, page 180. (The necessary forms are provided in the Workbook.) Use an appropriate letter style and make the necessary carbon copies. Type an envelope for each letter. Submit the transcribed material in the sequence in which you transcribe it. For information needed in your transcription, consult the correspondence section of the Reference Guide in this book or other reference books.

28. Transcription-Technique Checklist. The instructions and supplies for the completion of this assignment are provided in the Workbook.

Composing Assignments

During dictation every day you will probably have some letters handed to you with either the oral or written notation, "Tell him . . . ." Your employer may say, "Ask Kansas City why in blazes their request for raw materials isn't in," and expect you to translate this instruction into a courteous request that he will be proud to sign. Or he may be away from the office for a protracted period and you will have to carry on without direct supervision of your letters.

Every day that a letter remains unanswered, the gulf widens between the writer of that letter and the person, or company, to whom it was addressed. No letter, no matter how ingratiating its tone, can build maximum goodwill if the letter is overdue.

EVERYONE appreciates promptness. For that reason . . . we're taking the liberty of an informal reply to your letter. It's the only way we can adhere to our rule of pleasing you by answering each day's correspondence the day of its receipt, for volume sometimes inundates us.

You'll understand, we're sure, for you must face the same problem. In the meantime, if you write again on this subject, be sure to return all correspondence.

Recognizing the necessity for promptness, many companies have a policy of answering every day's correspondence the day it arrives, even if the quality of the reply may suffer. For example, a reply to a request for information addressed to the Administrative Management Society was typed on the incoming letter with the notation at the left clipped to the top of the letter. The recipient appreciated the manner of handling chosen. Notice, too, how this procedure reduces the filing volume.

Whether you compose letters for your employer's signature or write them for your own signature (and each day will bring occasions for both), you will want to become "letter perfect." This chapter discusses, in capsule form, the principles of composing various kinds of business communications in a tone that produces favorable reader reaction and the desired response.

The "How-to" of Composing

Writing ability is nine tenths perspiration and one tenth inspiration. Your employer knows this, so do not worry about the time you must spend in composing a letter; worry about how well the letter represents your employer. If you are unsure of your first draft, read it aloud. A phrase or a word that might antagonize the reader is quickly discernible after an oral reading. When composing a crucial letter, lay your first effort aside for a while; then revise and edit it until it is precise in meaning and diplomatic in tone.

> LETTERS, like people, have personalities which attract or repel.
>
> —*Lord Chesterfield*

Most business letters should be less than a page in length. Remember the famous quotation, "I wrote a long letter because I didn't have time to write a short one." Take time to eliminate unnecessary words, to polish, to "write a short letter."

The best aid to good tone is to visualize the reader as you write. If you know him, visualizing is easy. If you don't, try to picture the kind of person who would hold his position—such as the head of an enterprise, a junior executive, a department head, or a clerical worker. The tone of a letter to a clerk about a routine order could be different from that of a letter to an executive about office systems.

It helps, too, to put yourself in his place. What would be your reader reaction to the facts you are telling him? What would be your reaction to the way you express them? This is writing with the YOU-attitude uppermost in your mind. The techniques of writing for this positive reader response are analyzed in the next pages.

▪ Tone and Reader Response

Tone is the manner of writing that shows a *certain attitude on the part of the writer*. You want the tone of every letter you compose to result in friendly reader response, one of good feeling toward your office. You don't want any letter of yours to create a feeling of annoyance, frustration, confusion, or short-shrift treatment.

Writing in Anger. Never write a letter in anger. To "blow your top" orally is bad enough, but to provide written evidence of lack of composure is a luxury that no business, no person, can afford. Cool off, and then try your hand at composition. (If the employer violates this principle, maybe you can hold up his letter for a few hours. He knows, too, this rule of thumb; and when he calms down, he will follow it and thank you for making him see its importance without your ever uttering a word of criticism.)

The Matter of Style. If you are writing something for your employer to sign, try to make it sound like him, not like yourself. His letters reflect *his* personality, and your goal is to capture his style. Study his dictation and letters in the files; become his *alter ego* in his letter-writing activities, maybe occasionally even surpassing your own skill so that you write what he *wishes* he had said.

If you are writing letters to be signed "Secretary to . . . ," you, too, can develop a style compatible with your business personality—a step beyond the effusive communication of the novice.

■ The Ways of Composing

You can draft a communication in a number of ways. The methods most commonly used are:

1. Compose carefully in longhand. This method is the slowest.
2. Compose in shorthand in the dictation notebook. This method permits you to write as fast as thoughts are formulated, provides opportunity to change and to improve the draft, and furnishes a notebook record. It is the method used by most secretaries who do not have dictating facilities.
3. Compose as you type. This method requires facility of expression and does not allow as easily for changes of mind. It is of help to those who are visual-minded and must see what they write.
4. Compose as you dictate. This method requires the ability to compose orally and takes practice to become skillful.

■ Preparing to Write

The effective writer doesn't just sit down and begin to write. He prepares to write. When you are asked to answer a letter, do these things before you put down one word:

1. *Read* the letter you are to answer, in its entirety. If it is a letter originating at your desk, read through the instructions you are to follow. Know what action you want the reader to take, and *plan* how to make it easy for him to take it.
2. *Decide* on the answers to the questions asked and the information necessary to answer them. *Verify* all data you are going to include. *Collect* information needed before you start writing, so that you can give *complete* information.
3. *Make notes* of what you want to say. Organize the points you want to cover into the best sequence for reader understanding and response. Keep these points in plain sight as you compose.

▪ Sentence Quality

Your writing will improve if you determine to let each sentence express one idea.

One-Thought Sentences. Letter-writing experts place much emphasis on simple, clear, direct writing. Such writing is achieved partly by writing sentences of but one thought. The New York Life Insurance Company, which carries on a continuing program to help its executives and secretaries write better letters, stresses this point in succinct sentences:

> **Put only one idea in each sentence.**
> **Stop at the end of an idea and add a period.**
> **Take a few simple words and arrange them into simple sentences.**
> **Simple sentences are the mainstay of simple writing—a single clause with one subject and one predicate.**

A letter of all one-clause sentences could, however, become monotonous, even though it is easy to follow. It could imply low reader intelligence and limited writing ability. Keep the reader in mind as you write.

Clarity. Clarity is a goal in writing the first draft, but it is usually achieved by rewriting. Rarely is a new secretary so skillful that she can achieve 100-percent clarity on a first try. For this reason alone it is wise for the secretary to draft an important letter and then edit it for clarity.

One-thought sentences make for clarity. Exact, descriptive words help. Rephrasing confusing statements helps. Leaving nothing to be taken for granted helps. Clarity, then, is often the result of a cleaning-up step to make each sentence crystal clear.

Conciseness. A sentence that expresses a thought briefly and clearly is concise, stripped of superfluous words.

Conciseness is a mark of finish and skill. It is important because it is a saver. It saves time—the writer's, the typist's, and the reader's—and it can save paper. To achieve it, state a fact but once. Cut out the superfluous words and phrases in each sentence. Beware, however, of the brusque tone that can be created through *abrupt* conciseness. For instance, "Be here at five," lacks the graciousness of "I'm looking forward to seeing you at five."

In examples that follow, notice where conciseness is an asset and where it is a liability.

Forceful Sentences. To make a forceful impression, writers have found that the active rather than the passive voice is helpful. Passive voice tends to weaken a sentence. When *forcefulness* is not a factor, however, and the writer wants to concentrate on the *you* attitude, passive voice may be used to avoid *we* and *I*. A verbal phrase at the beginning of a sentence may weaken the sentence. Substituting strong verbs enables you to write forceful sentences.

Learning your reaction to our timer will be of great interest to us.	We are interested in your reaction to our timer.
Your letter is being forwarded today to Mr. Crane who is in Memphis this week.	We airmailed your letter today to Mr. Crane in Memphis.

First Sentences. The tone of the letter is almost always set by the very first sentence. It is best then to start with thoughts that reflect the *you* attitude, a genuine interest in the reader. Be gracious and courteous, and use words that are pleasant to the reader, such as those at the right. In the first sentence, establish friendly contact with the reader. The letter-writing situation is similar to a social meeting with a friend. On first meeting him, you do not start by

Thank you, Miss Adams, for telling us . . . you will be glad to know that . . .

You are right. We did . . .

Thank you, Mr. Graves, for asking us . . .

talking about yourself. You talk about him, or of something of interest to him. Note the improved letter openings at the right below, compared to those at the left:

I searched our records both in this department and in Sales to locate the information re- quested in your letter of June 6. I find that	Your request was a real challenge. But I have the information you want. Here it is . . . .
We have your letter of April 10 asking for a copy of our new folder. It was mailed to you.	The folder you requested is on its way. . . .

■ Importance of Words

The choice of words is important in all writing. In business letters words are vitally important because of their effect on the reader. Letter-writing authorities have examined the impact of specific words and kinds of words and make the following recommendations.

Short Conversational Words. The trend in business letters is toward short words that are used in conversation. They usually create a friendly, personal relationship between the writer and the reader; and they help the writer to relax and write just as naturally as he talks.

If a word is long or erudite, chances are you should change it to a shorter, common one. There are readers, however, who are dignified, scholarly, intellectual. You should not write to them in a folksy tone; perhaps it would be in poor taste. Visualize the reader and use the kind of words suitable to him, to his position, or to his probable education.

In the list that follows, look over the commonly used words in business writing, and their short, conversational counterparts. Would you say that the short ones are always preferable to the long ones? That the long ones are always preferable to the short ones?

ameliorate.........improve	endeavor..............try
ascertain..........learn	equitable..............fair
cognizant of.......aware of	initiate................begin
commitment.......pledge, promise	modification...........change
communication.....letter	procure...............get
consummate........complete	remuneration...........pay, salary
determine..........learn	submitted..............sent
disseminate........spread	utilization.............use
effectuate.........bring about	verification...........proof

You, I, and We. The letter reader, being human, is interested most of all in himself. Each *you* and *your* and each word of direct address he reads is pleasant when it is used in a natural, easy way. If, on the other hand, a sentence has been tortuously twisted to bring in the personal tone, the reader becomes annoyed. It is also wise to avoid beginning the letter, and most paragraphs, with *I*—although using *I* as the first word in a paragraph *can* help the writer achieve simple, direct writing in many situations. Unnatural style might result if you rigidly follow the now outdated, never-used rule.

There is a technical point of interest to the secretary in choosing between *I* and *we* in her letters. If a letter is signed THE JONES COMPANY, followed by the writer's signature and title, and *we* is used throughout, the legal responsibility of the writer is reduced. Today the letter writer frequently uses *I, my, we, our, me,* and *us* in correspondence, thus showing his personal interest in the reader, as illustrated at the right.

```
We are pleased that
you wrote us about the
error we made in . . .

You will be pleased to
know that we will be
able to send you . . .
```

Negative Versus Positive Words. In every kind of letter, words of negative connotation are to be avoided. Negative words can cause the reader's hackles to rise; or, as one correspondent put it, they can turn a letter into a brink-of-war communique. Negative words, in their kindest usage, still have an unpleasant tinge. A starting list of negative-reaction words is given here. You can undoubtedly add others (and should!).

alibi	claim	fault
allege	complaint	impossible
biased	defend	reject
blame	evict	so-called
cheap	failure	useless

Words of positive connotation are tone helpers. Use them whenever possible. Compiling your own reference list of positive-reaction words will help you to become alert to using them. Here are a few.

ability	good	please
advantage	gratifying	prominent
benefit	kind	recommend
effective	lasting	responsible
fitting	pleasant	thoughtful

When searching for the right or pertinent word, use a dictionary, thesaurus, or book of synonyms referred to at the end of Chapter 9.

Phrases or Words? The recommendation of business-writing authorities is to reduce wordy and hackneyed phrases to single-word or short equivalents. Oft-repeated phrases like those listed below make a letter commonplace. They imply that the writer is too indolent to find short, apt replacements.

for the purpose of	for
preparatory to	before
in order to	to
make inquiry regarding	ask about
afford an opportunity	allow
for the simple reason that	because
at the present time	now
due to the fact that	because
experience indicated that	we learned
in a position to	can
meets with our approval	we approve
this day and age	today
until such time as	until
reason is because	because
in the course of	during
by means of	by

With but one possible exception, limit your use of such phrases, because they have become trite and tiresome through overuse. The possible exception is in a refusal letter, discussed later in the chapter.

Redundant Expressions. Avoid redundant expressions, those using two or more words when one is sufficient. Their use, unfortunately, indicates that the writer doesn't know any better, or doesn't care. The only way to refrain from using them is to build your own *Watch List*.

baffling and puzzling	reiterate again
invisible to the eye	the only other alternative
new innovation	the consensus of opinion
check into	joined together
matinee performance	small in size
one and the same	true facts

▪ Length of Letter

Write a short letter instead of a long one whenever you can. Try to make a word do the work of a phrase; a phrase, the work of a clause.

The speaker ~~who was~~ *known for his verbosity* attracted only a few listeners. *(Past participial phrase in place of adjective clause)*

~~Anyone who is in Congress~~ (*Any Congressman*) would have studied the problem. *(Noun replacing pronoun modified by adjective clause)*

~~When you read~~ (*In*) the recommendations, you will find a surprising innovation. *(Prepositional phrase replacing a clause)*

Mail early ~~so that you may~~ (*to*) be sure of delivery before Christmas. *(Infinitive replacing a clause)*

He approached his new assignment ~~with a great deal of caution~~ (*cautiously*). *(Adverb replacing an adverbial phrase)*

Special Letters and Publicity

Letters are written for many purposes: to complete records, such as acknowledgments and covering letters; to make simple requests for material or information; to serve as reminders, such as follow-up letters. Because of their simplicity and brevity, these somewhat routine letters are usually the first ones turned over to a new secretary.

Negative letters such as complaints and refusals, letters of business courtesy such as congratulations and sympathy, and formal acceptances and regrets require great skill and knowledge. But they, too, are often given to the secretary or administrative assistant to compose; or she drafts them on her own initiative and gives them to the executive for editing.

▪ Acknowledgments

In general, every letter should be *answered* or *acknowledged* promptly, preferably on the day it is received. In *answering* a letter, one discusses the points raised. In *acknowledging* a letter or material, one merely tells of its receipt and adds any other necessary information. An effective letter of acknowledgment is courteous and complete, and it sounds personal. Read the following examples as if they were addressed to you. Notice how their tone affects your own reader reaction.

This will acknowledge receipt of the package of printed letterheads and bill for it. Payment will follow before the tenth of next month.	Thank you for the prompt delivery of our attractive new letterheads. Our accounting department will issue you a check soon after the first of the month.
We acknowledge receipt of your letter of November 19 and thank you for it.	Thank you for your helpful letter of November 19 about Mr. Smith's credit experience with you.
This is to acknowledge receipt of your request of June 6, which will have Mr. Bender's attention upon his return to the office.	Mr. Bender is out of town, but we expect him back next week. I am sure he will answer your letter of June 6 shortly after his return.

▪ Covering Letters

A universal business practice is to inform the recipient when money or material is sent to him. Such a covering letter tells, with a little dash of personal interest, what is being sent, why, when, and how.

Under separate cover we are sending you a sample case of blotters. When they have served your purpose, will you please return the case, as they are difficult to replace.	Today by Railway Express we sent you a full stock of our blotter samples in a convenient sample case. We are glad to lend these materials to you.
	We hope you will find something that will exactly fit your needs.
	When you are ready to return the case of samples, just use the enclosed address label.

▪ Requests and Inquiries

Every request or inquiry should be phrased courteously and contain complete information. The following example is typical:

```
Will you please send me literature about movable
office partitions.  We plan to remodel our
offices soon and to use movable partitions as a
means of providing greater flexibility in our
office layout.

Since our plans are still in the "idea" stage,
please do not send a representative.  When we
near the point of decision, we shall ask you to
have a representative call.
```

▪ Reminder Letters

Every secretary keeps a tickler of items that have to be completed. Answers awaited, reports due, goods to be received—all are recorded. When an item is overdue, the secretary sends a reminder. She usually writes it without being instructed to do so. She uses tactful phrasing, for no one likes to be reminded of his negligence or lack of promptness. Here is an example:

```
On June 18 we asked you to send us detailed in-
formation about several of your recent trans-
actions.  We are eager to receive these details
so that we can write directly to the contractors.

Would it be possible for us to hear from you by
the first of next week?  While we do not wish to
impose any hardship upon you, we do need to com-
plete this transaction soon.
```

▪ Negative Letters

Often a letter must be written on an unpleasant subject: *complaints* or *claims, refusals, mistakes.* These require special care in composing.

Complaint Letters. A complaint letter can be such a bitter tirade that it is pushed aside by the recipient with a shrug that some crackpot wrote it, or the complaint can helpfully point out a weakness or an area in which improvement is needed. Usually the person or company does not even know there is a reason for dissatisfaction, so complaint letters are generally appreciated.

You have just received delivery of a repeat order of the executive's personal letterheads, many of which are soiled with greasy fingerprints.

As his secretary, you can keep quiet and ignore the poor job, discard
the worst ones, and try to clean up the rest with an art gum eraser.
Instead, you write a letter of complaint similar to the one given below:

```
Mr. Simpson's repeat order of engraved letter-
heads was received today.  We are sorry that
they are not satisfactory.  Many have greasy
fingerprints on them, which, of course, make
them unusable.

I hope that you will be able to duplicate the
shipment early next week and that the letter-
heads will be as carefully and immaculately
engraved as always before.
```

Refusal Letters. Banks often have to reject loans, insurance companies have to refuse life insurance, employers have to turn down
applications for positions, individuals must sometimes refuse to grant
favors. All such refusals require tactful phrasing.

In a refusal letter, you will have to say "no," but try to say it nicely.
If possible, open with an alternative. If there is none to offer, start with
a positive *you*-approach sentence. Try to convince the reader that you
do have his interest at heart. Use *I* with the *we's* to indicate that you
have a personal concern, as in the following opening paragraph:

```
It was very gracious of you to invite Mr. Beamer
and me to show our slides of English cathedrals
at your March meeting.  Unfortunately, I have
loaned them for two months to a friend in Canada;
so we cannot show them again until late May.  If
you wish to select another date, we shall try
our best to arrange to come.
```

If you must apologize, do it in a few simple words—once. "We are
sorry that . . . ." "We sincerely regret that . . . ." Nothing is gained by
reiterating apologetic phrases.

A *no* letter should be longer than the usual concise letter that com-
municates facts. A short *no* letter is like a curt dismissal. An executive's
wife lost a mink stole. The executive reported the loss to his insurance
company, explaining that his wife had no idea when or how the loss
occurred. Shown below is the entire letter he received, which, incidentally, cost the agency his future business.

```
As to your wife's mink stole—your floater policy
does not cover "mysterious disappearance," which
this is.  We regret we cannot reimburse you
for its loss.
```

Mistake Letters. When you must write a letter about a mistake—one of omission or one of commission—admit that it was your fault. Do not beat about the bush with pompous phrases and long words.

Occasionally and unfortunately mistake letters have to be written by the secretary. If, for example, she has neglected to put in an enclosure with a letter and discovers the oversight the next day, she drafts and types a note of explanation, attaches the omitted enclosure, and sends the message in with the rest of the day's mail to be signed so that the executive learns about her error. Psychologically, you want to help a person when he openly admits a mistake. Compare your reactions to the following:

We find on checking our shipping records that through an unavoidable combination of circumstances we inadvertently delayed shipping the special gear you wanted. It has gone out today by airmail.	This morning we discovered that the special gear you requested did not go out with yesterday's shipment.
We hope you have not been inconvenienced.	We had it packaged immediately and sent to you by airmail.
	We are sorry for the inconvenience and delay.

▪ Letters of Business Courtesy

A secretary can, without being told, do much to make the executive appear thoughtful and gracious. She can draft letters for him to his business friends, recognizing their special accomplishments, congratulating them on promotions, extending sympathy when there is need, expressing appreciation for kindnesses to him, and so on.

Recognition. The secretary will come to know many of her employer's friends and will recognize their names when she sees them in print. If one of them has an article in a current magazine, she can scan the article and draft a letter complimenting the friend, using the executive's writing style, as in the following example:

I have just read your interesting article in the current issue of <u>Dynamics</u>. It is informative and shows your skill in organizing usually confusing ideas into a clear, pro-and-con presentation, so that valid conclusions can be drawn. All of your readers, I know, will commend you for your treatment of this complex subject.

Congratulations. If there is publicity about the promotion or professional achievement of one of his friends, she will draft a letter of congratulations in his writing style, such as:

> Congratulations, Bob, on your appointment to the vice-presidency. I should like to add my sincere good wishes to the many you undoubtedly are receiving. From our years of association I know that you will bring to the position the many fine personal qualities and keenness of intellect that the office requires.

Sympathy. If death or tragedy occurs in the family of one of the executive's friends, the secretary can draft a sympathy note for him to write in longhand. Such notes are sincere, and usually brief. The words *die* and *death* are seldom used in sympathy notes, for they seem to be lacking in consideration. Euphemistic phrases such as *your bereavement*, *fatal illness*, *tragic happening*, and *the obituary in the paper* are kinder.

> I was very sorry to read in this morning's paper of your mother's passing away. My thoughts are with you.

> I cannot find words to express my sympathy for yesterday's events. Please know that I am sharing your sorrow.

■ Formal Acceptances and Regrets

When an invitation is received by letter or in formal style from an organization, the answer should be made by letter or telephone. A formal invitation from an individual, however, must be answered in handwriting in a similar formal style on folded stationery. When the executive receives such an invitation, the secretary can help him by drafting his answer in the proper wording and form. Center each line of his answer, and use attractive vertical spacing.

> **Formal Invitation**
> (*Printed or Engraved*)
>
> Mr. and Mrs. William Edwards
> request the pleasure of
> Mr. David Bender's
> company at dinner in honor of
> their silver anniversary
> on Tuesday, the tenth of May,
> at seven o'clock
> Towne Club

In answering, repeat only the last name (not the initials) of those who extend the invitation. In an acceptance include the day, date, and time as an assurance that they are correctly observed. In a regret it is obviously not necessary to include the time.

<table>
<tr><td>

Formal Acceptance
(Handwritten in this form)

Mr. David Bender
accepts with pleasure
Mr. and Mrs. Edwards'
kind invitation for dinner
on Tuesday, the tenth of May
at seven o'clock

</td><td>

Formal Regret
(Handwritten in this form)
The reason in Line 3 may
be omitted.

Mr. David Bender
regrets exceedingly that
because of a previous engagement
he is unable to accept
Mr. and Mrs. Edwards'
kind invitation for dinner
on Tuesday, the tenth of May

</td></tr>
</table>

■ **Guide Letters**

The secretary soon discovers that situations repeat themselves and that many of the letters she composes cover the same circumstances. When she finds an especially effective phrase or sentence, she should preserve it for the next letter. For instance, most adjustment letters from an exclusive ladies' specialty shop close with, "We hope that we can serve you more effectively next time." This sentence suggests further association with the customer, stresses the service motive, and makes a positive rather than a negative approach in admitting error. A gem like this is worth using again and again.

For help in developing guide letters that reflect your employer's language and typical reactions, you may compile a guide-letter reference manual. Although the preparation of such a book takes time, it will be one of your office's greatest timesavers.

Here is how to do it:

1. Keep an extra carbon copy of all outgoing letters for a month.
2. Reread them at the end of the month, all in one sitting. As you reread them objectively, you will recognize words, phrases, and ideas that recur.
3. Separate the letters into categories, making extra copies of those that fit several classifications; underline pet phrases and other keys to your employer's ways of handling situations; and set up a file folder for each group. Ask yourself the reasons for variations among the letters in the amount of detail used, degree of cordiality, language, tone, and style.
4. Make an outline of the points usually covered in a letter in each category.
5. Pick out the best opening and closing sentences and the best key points tailored to specific situations.

6. **Compile a letter guide, using a loose-leaf notebook.** Type the model outline for the category on a heavy sheet to be used as the divider between categories of letters. Type model opening and closing sentences for the category on a separate sheet and model paragraphs on other sheets.

7. **Code the index tabs for each section.** For instance, "Congratulations" could be C and an especially good paragraph could be C4.

8. **When you compose a letter, compare it with the outline to be sure that you have included all necessary parts.**

9. **Keep a record of the form used for each letter sent so that you will not again send the same letter to a person.**

■ Letters to Non-Americans

Most of our corporations now do business abroad. Letter style for foreign correspondence is much more formal and traditional than for domestic correspondence. Although you will probably not compose many foreign letters (too important!), remember if you do: Choose a formal, more "flowery" style of writing. Always observe the social amenities meticulously. Many a business deal has fallen through because the citizen of another country thought the American "direct" style brash and rude—both in personal contact and in correspondence.

When addressing a letter to a foreign correspondent, copy the address *exactly* as it is given. Here, too, style differs. In European and South American countries the street number *follows* the street name, as Nassaustraat 7, not 7 Nassaustraat. In Japanese addresses there are many other designations in addition to the street name and number to locate the section of the city; all are essential.

■ News Releases

If, in your company, publicity is not the responsibility of an advertising department or agency, you will at times be asked to compose or type brief articles for publication. They will probably cover such subjects as new products, new personnel, or new services of your company; or they may relate to activities of organizations in which the executive is interested. These brief articles are called *news releases*.

Content. Since news releases are unsolicited and are sent to editors in the hope that they will be used, editors are flooded with them. About 20 percent are published. A news release, therefore, must be newsworthy in an editor's eyes. It must contain news (not veiled advertising) and be of interest to the readers of the publication.

NEWS *from* TWA

TWA LAUNCHES MARKETAIR SERVICE
TO HELP SMALL BUSINESS EXPORT   For Immediate Release

NEW YORK -- MarketAir, an export program designed primarily to help smaller companies embark on overseas marketing of their products, was announced today by Trans World Airlines.

The service provides foreign market research and marketing newsletters for manufacturers and arrangements for overseas staff assistance and financing.

"MarketAir embraces a comprehensive array of basic tools to enable companies of modest size to enlarge their horizons and improve their profitability by moving into international trade," said Thomas B. McFadden, TWA vice president - marketing. "We believe the economy

Style. A good news item contains all the facts clearly stated *without* opinion. The italicized words in the following are opinions of a writer: *dire* emergency, everyone *should*, *noted* attorney, *signally* honored.

In composing a news release, answer the five W's—*who, what, when, where*, and *why*—plus the *how*. Get the most vital facts into the first sentence, the second most vital into the second, and so on. Such is journalistic style. It is for the convenience of the busy reader and the busy editor. If the release has to be shortened, the editor cuts out sentences beginning with the last one and works upward. This leaves the important news intact without rewriting.

Typewritten Form. A company that submits numerous releases uses a special letterhead form such as that shown at the top of this page. Otherwise, an item is put on a regular letterhead or on an 8½- by 11-inch sheet of good weight paper (editors dislike handling small, odd-size, or thin onionskin sheets). If a plain sheet is used, the name, address, and telephone number of the company are typed across the top. In every case a person whom the editor can call for additional information should be named. If the news stems from an outside activity of the executive the secretary uses a plain sheet of paper and gives the executive as the contact. Other practices to observe are given below.

Give the date that the news may be published—the release date.

Type the release date near the top. Express it in either of these ways: *FOR IMMEDIATE RELEASE;* or *FOR RELEASE TUESDAY, FEBRUARY 2, 19--.*

Give the article a title if possible. This gives the editor an idea of the contents at a quick glance. He will probably not use the title, but it is helpful to him.

Double-space the text. Leave generous margins for editorial use. Confine the release to one page, if possible.

Number each page after the first one at the top center.

Type—*more*—at the bottom of all pages but the last one.

Type # # # at the end of the release.

Send an original copy and type "Exclusive to . . ." on the release if it really is exclusive. A carbon copy indicates you are sending the same release to other publishers, and the editor may be one who uses only what he assumes is an exclusive.

Mail the release direct to the department editor so that it reaches his desk promptly. Go to the trouble of finding out his name and the correct spelling by telephone or from the listings of the editors in the front part of the publication.

Suggested Readings

Aurner, Robert R., and Morris Philip Wolf. *Effective Communication in Business.* Cincinnati: South-Western Publishing Co., 1967, 644 pp.

Hay, Robert D. *Written Communication for Business Administrators.* New York: Holt, Rinehart, and Winston, Inc., 1965, 488 pp.

Himstreet, William C. and Wayne Murlin Baty. *Business Communications, Principles and Methods.* Belmont, California: Wadsworth Publishing Company, Inc., 1965, 433 pp.

Janis, J. Harold. *Writing and Communicating in Business.* New York: The Macmillan Company., 1964, 502 pp.

Mayo, Lucy G. *Communications Handbook for Secretaries.* New York: McGraw-Hill Book Company, 1958, 568 pp.

Shurter, Robert L., and J. Peter Williamson. *Written Communication in Business.* New York: McGraw-Hill Book Company, 1964, 578 pp.

Questions for Discussion

1. If your employer were promoted to a position involving international trade, how could you help him write overseas business letters that build goodwill for your company?

2. What is your reaction to the practice of the Administrative Management Society of typing the reply directly on the letter being answered and

attaching the printed notation quoted in the chapter? For what kinds of letters would AMS adopt this practice?

3. The executive says, "Subscribe to *Business Week* for me, please." These are the only details he gives you. How would you handle this task?

4. If your employer asked you to send a "bon voyage" note to the ship on which one of his friends is sailing, how would you get the sailing date, the name of the ship, the city of embarkation, and where mail should be addressed for embarkation delivery?

5. What is your reader response to these first sentences in letters?

(a) **This is in answer to your letter of July 10. Your ideas . . . .**

(b) **We cannot send the merchandise you wanted until we receive payment for the last shipment.**

(c) **Your ball-point pens are lousy, and we are sending back the whole kit and caboodle of them express collect!**

(d) **It is with extreme pleasure that we send you the catalog you so graciously requested in your welcome letter of May 7.**

(e) **We want action! In fact, we demand it. You promised delivery of our machine the first of this month. Where is it?**

6. The following clauses have the fault of wordiness. Try to reduce them to the most concise phrases possible:

(a) **It is also of importance to bear in mind the following . . . .**

(b) **Consideration should be given also to the possibility of . . . .**

(c) **It is the consensus of opinion of the group that at the present time we should not endeavor to ascertain the reason for the change.**

(d) **We will all join together to make inquiry about the other possible alternatives.**

7. Revise the following sentences to make them more euphonious. Then use the Reference Guide to correct your answers.

(a) **The letter was too abrupt and tactless.**

(b) **The job was just a job to her.**

With what euphemisms would you replace the italicized words in the following sentences?

(c) **Her secretarial work is satisfactory, but she *irritates* others.**

(d) **He *was discharged* last August.**

(e) **He came from a *poor* neighborhood.**

Problems

■ **1.** At a recent secretarial workshop the participants were asked to reduce the text of the following letter to the smallest possible number of words. One secretary got it down to eight words. Can you do as well?

Gentlemen

A copy of your pamphlet of "The Human Side" has been handed to the undersigned and in reading the contents we have been very much impressed and are wondering if this pamphlet can be secured by subscription and if so, what are the charges for such subscription. Might we hear from you in this regard at your earliest convenience.

Yours truly

■ **2.** Below are four exercises in analyzing and composing excerpted by permission from *Changing Times*, the Kiplinger Magazine (July, 1963, issue), copyright 1963 by The Kiplinger Washington Editors, Inc., 1729 H. Street, N.W., Washington, D.C. 20006.

The first three are badly written sentences. Prune them to as few words as possible without losing their meaning; then see how close you have come to the suggested answers. No. 4 is a list of topics to be put in logical order. Your instructor will give you suggested solutions against which you can check your writing ability.

1. "This is to advise you that we have received your letter of April 14 requesting information on the truck bodies we manufacture, and we are sending you the data." (29 words)

1. _____
_____
_____
_____

2. "The committee has examined the question for several weeks. We feel that the best thing to do would be for all of us to get together and send a joint letter to the highway department asking them to install a traffic light at the intersection." (45 words)

2. _____
_____
_____
_____

3. "Although the growth in number of banks during the six decades from 1860 to 1920 did not proceed at an even pace, in all but a few years that growth exceeded the rate of population increase." (36 words)

3. _____
_____
_____

4. You have to write a booklet for your company on "Insurance for the Farmer." It will be distributed to farmers. These are the major points you should cover. Arrange them into a logical outline.

  fire insurance
  life insurance
  where to write for further information
  crop insurance
  why farm insurance
  hail insurance
  annuities
  when to insure
  types of insurance
  liability insurance
  windstorm insurance

4. _____
_____
_____
_____
_____
_____
_____
_____

Related Work Assignments 29-31————————

29. Composing Letters. Mr. Simpson intercepts the following two letters written by his assistant. He asks you to type acceptable letters for mailing in their place. Type each on a half-sheet letterhead. Letterheads are provided in the Workbook.

(a)

Dear Mr. Williams

Replying to your letter of the 21st, we are sorry to advise that we cannot fill your order due to the fact that our factory has been on strike for the past three months.

As soon as possible after work is again resumed, we hope to be able to let you know when we can take care of your valued business.

Be assured that we appreciate your order and will do everything in our power to serve you again just as soon as we get back on our regular schedule.

Yours respectfully

(b)

Dear Mr. Rosenthal

We are sending you a copy of our catalog, and it should reach you by about the day after tomorrow. Mr. Henderson, our new salesman in your territory, will visit you this month. We trust that you will give him orders to fill your requirements. X–Tray Products can meet your packaging needs for a long time, we are sure.

You failed to place an order with us in December. We want your business. Please let Mr. Henderson demonstrate to you again the high quality of goods and services offered by our company.

Yours truly

30. Selecting Letters } The instructions and supplies necessary for the completion of Related Work Assignments 30 and
31. Analyzing Letters } 31 are provided in the Workbook.

Case Problems

3—1 √ work organization

At 9 a.m. Marianna Graham, secretary to the president of the corporation, had a 75-page report to collate and spiral-bind before the Board of Directors meeting at 2 p.m. Since office space is limited, the material bulky, and the meeting scheduled for the Board Room, she planned to go to the Board Room, spread out the sheets on the Board table and work there.

Just then the comptroller came in to her office with a proposal to be sent to the Interstate Commerce Commission about increasing the capital stock of the corporation. He asked if she could possibly type enough copies for the Board. As this was an unusual request, Miss Graham told him that her assistant, Barbara Eastman, could type it if she could stay at her own desk. The comptroller left the work with Miss Eastman, who immediately started on it.

At 9:45 a.m. Miss Graham asked Miss Eastman to answer her telephone. She then went to the Board Room and began to collate. At 10 a.m. M. Burnet, head of the stenographic services, appeared at the door with five new members of her staff and said that she was holding an orientation meeting in the Board Room. (Miss Graham had already checked to see that no meetings were scheduled for the room.) Miss Graham restacked the report pages to take back to her office and made a pencil notation to tell M. Burnet privately that all Board Room meetings must be scheduled on the master calendar.

In the midst of the crisis Miss Eastman came to tell her that the president wanted Miss Graham to take minutes for the remainder of the morning during his meeting with the corporation counsel. Miss Graham then asked her assistant to leave the comptroller's work and take over the collating job. On her way to report to the president, Miss Graham was stopped by Mr. Harvey, the sales manager, who explained that he had an important deal pending and would like an appointment with the president as soon as possible. She explained that the president was starting a meeting as soon as she arrived. She asked Mr. Harvey to call her after lunch so that she could set up an appointment. She then proceeded immediately to the meeting in the president's office, where she took notes for the remainder of the morning.

After a hurried lunch, she came back to the office for last-minute preparations for the Board meeting. The comptroller came in to pick up the finished proposal. Miss Graham said, "Oh, Mr. Brown, I am sorry; but I had to pull Barbara off your job to finish collating the Board report I was working on, because I had to take notes on Mr. West's meeting with the corporation counsel. I'll be glad to ask Barbara to finish it now." The comptroller said, "No, it's too late now. We'll have to mail separate copies to each member."

Mr. Harvey called to find out about the appointment with the president he had requested. Miss Graham told him that the president would be in the Board meeting all afternoon but would be available for an appointment the **first thing the next morning.** Mr. Harvey said that would be too late, for he had to have an answer before 4 p.m. Miss Graham typed a note that she took in to the president, telling him that Mr. Harvey wanted to see him before four o'clock.

What are your reactions to the way Miss Graham handled her work and the situations with which she was confronted?

3—2 √ delegation of responsibilities

Alice Barry, secretary to Edgar Jones, president of a large manufacturing company, was overworked. Her employer gave her heavy responsibility and regarded her as his strong right arm. It never occurred to him to give part of his work to anyone else on the office force. She had been staying long after five o'clock to finish the day's work, and she always felt hurried during the day as she tried to meet the expectations of that human dynamo, her boss. She never seemed to get caught up with the work and always felt pressed for time. Also, she felt indispensable and carried much of the burden of her job in her mind after she finally left for the night.

She decided to discuss the situation with Mr. Jones; however, it always seemed that something more important than her problems occupied their time. Three weeks passed, and she had not broached her problem. One evening just before five, she started to describe the situation and ask for her employer's suggestions for its solution. After one sentence Mr. Jones broke in, "Yes, Alice, I know you have too much to do. Why don't you get some of the girls in the stenographic pool to help you on some of the routine jobs? You know how much I depend on you. I don't want you to work so hard that you get ill. Just work things out, and anything you can do will be fine with me. I want to catch the 5:25, so I'll have to hurry."

With no further comment, Mr. Jones took his brief case and rushed out of the office to catch his train. In fact, Alice felt he was somewhat annoyed that she had brought up the problem.

The next morning Alice went to two young stenographers who had impressed her as competent and assigned fifty form letters for sending out checks for special services rendered by department heads. She was surprised that they seemed annoyed rather than flattered at having to work directly for the president. They indicated that they felt that their regular work had precedence and implied that they would do the work, but only as a special favor to Alice. About half an hour before five o'clock they left the completed letters on her desk (much later than expected). She found many errors for which she knew she would be blamed.

She typed the letters again after work, took a pill for her ulcer, and was heard to grumble, "Well, *that* didn't help matters any; I had to do the work myself after all. I don't know why it is that these kids we get in here can't be depended on for anything."

What principles of supervision did Alice Barry violate in her solution to the problem?

How *can* she solve her problem as her employer seems confident she can?

—American Telephone and Telegraph Company

The secretary-administrative assistant must keep abreast of the numerous and often spectacular developments in transmittal services—postal, shipping, and tele-communications.

Secretarial Use of Transmittal Services

Technological advances in data processing and communication are among the most spectacular in the business world today. Next-day delivery by postal service to any address in the United States is nearing reality. Volumes of information can be transmitted via telephone and telegraph facilities over vast distances within moments. To assure the greatest return on each communication dollar spent, the secretary-administrative assistant must keep abreast of the multiplicity of services being provided in this rapidly changing field.

Postal and Shipping Services

Since it costs only pennies to mail a letter, why should the secretary or administrative assistant be concerned about postal and shipping services? One answer is that no business firm mails just a few letters. Most businesses mail thousands of letters in the course of a year, and the postage adds up to a considerable sum. In fact, postage and shipping costs are big items in a firm's budget—even a small firm.

The greater the secretary's postage know-how, the more the executive gets for his postage dollar. But there is far more involved than merely saving postage pennies. The Post Office Department, the R E A Express, and other shipping agencies offer a wide variety of services. Knowing what services are available, what type of service best fits each situation, and how to handle unusual postal and shipping problems is also important.

Postal rates change from time to time. Services also change. A table showing current postal rates and fees is shown in the *Postal Guide* section on pages 765–768. The content of this chapter, however, has been restricted to basic information that changes infrequently.

The Postal Manual

The *Postal Manual* of the United States Post Office Department explains the postal services that are offered and prescribes the rates, fees, and conditions under which they are available. As a secretary you will

Part 158

UNDELIVERABLE MAIL

158.1   DESCRIPTION

158.2   TREATMENT BY CLASSES

   .21   FIRST-CLASS MAIL

   .22   SECOND-CLASS MAIL

      .221   Change in Local Address

    a. *Delivery for 3 Months*

    b. *Procedure After 3 Months*

      .222   Undeliverable for Any Reason Other....

The decimal numbering system makes it possible to insert added entries without having to renumber the old ones.

230

want to have your own copy of the *Postal Manual* for office reference. You are not expected to know all the ramifications of postal services, but you are expected to be able to find out about them quickly. Your *Postal Manual* is the best source of this information. The manual can be ordered from the Superintendent of Documents, Washington, D.C. 20402, for a nominal amount on a subscription basis. Revised and new pages will be sent you as changes are made.

Whenever you are confronted with an unusual postal service or cost problem that you cannot answer from your *Manual,* call the postmaster or the superintendent of mails at the local post office. He, or one of his assistants, will be glad to give you the latest official information.

Domestic Mail Classifications

Domestic mail matter includes mail transmitted within, among, and between the United States and its territories and possessions; Army-Air Force (APO) and Navy (FPO) post offices; and mail for delivery to the United Nations in New York City.

The Post Office Department divides mailable matter into the following general classes: *first class, second class, controlled circulation publications, third class, fourth class, airmail, official and free mail, mail for the blind,* and *mixed classes.* (Refer to Reference Guide pages 765–768 for detailed descriptions of classes, services, rates, and fees.)

▪ First-Class Mail

Among the kinds of mail sent by *first class* are: letters in any form (typewritten, handwritten, carbon copy, or photocopy); post cards; business reply mail such as that shown at the bottom of this page; and

The postage for such a business reply envelope is guaranteed by the addressee and is paid when the envelope is returned to him. No postage is paid for envelopes not returned.

FIRST CLASS
Permit No. 739
NEW YORK, N. Y.

BUSINESS REPLY MAIL
No Postage Stamp Necessary If Mailed in The United States

Postage will be paid by
READER SERVICE DEPT.

Administrative
Management

212 FIFTH AVENUE
NEW YORK, N. Y. 10010

matter partly in written form, such as bills and checks. Pieces less than 3 inches wide or 4¼ inches long are nonmailable. Airmail up to 7 ounces (sealed or unsealed) is called first-class airmail matter. For methods of sending first-class mail in combination with a larger envelope or parcel of mail of another class, see page 237.

▪ Second-Class Mail

Second-class mail includes printed newspapers and periodicals. Publishers and news agencies are granted second-class rates if they file the proper forms obtained from their local postmasters, pay the required fees, and comply with the regulations. Such mail must bear notice of second-class entry and be mailed in bulk lots periodically.

Newspapers and periodicals that are mailed unsealed by the public are sent at a "transient rate." (See Second-Class Mail, page 766.)

▪ Controlled Circulation Publications

Publications of 24 or more pages circulated free, or mainly free, come under a special class called *Controlled Circulation Publications.* Since only a limited number of secretaries will work with this class of mail, it is recommended that when information regarding it is needed, the secretary study Part 133 in the *Postal Manual.*

▪ Third-Class Mail

Third-class mail is used for matter that cannot be classified as first- or second-class mail and that weighs up to 16 ounces. The same matter in parcels of 16 ounces and over is considered fourth-class mail.

All sealed pieces mailed at the third-class postage rates must be marked THIRD CLASS (or BULK RATE if bulk rate has been authorized). This notation may be printed anywhere on the envelope (front or back), except in the permit imprint or meter stamp. Third-class mail which is unsealed does not require any endorsement.

Mail that may be sent third class includes merchandise, printed matter, keys, and so on. Special rates also apply to books, manuscripts, music, sound recordings, films, and the like.

▪ Fourth-Class Mail

The more common term for *fourth-class service* is *parcel post.* It includes all mailable matter not in the first, second, or third class and with weight of 16 ounces or over.

Parcel-post rates are scaled according to the weight of the parcel and the distance it is being transported. Every local post office charts the country into eight zones. Zone charts showing the parcel post zone of any domestic post office in relation to the sender's post office may be obtained free from the sender's post office.

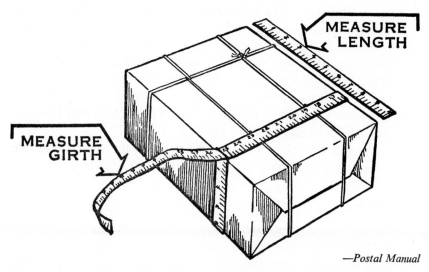

—*Postal Manual*

To determine the size of a parcel, measure the longest side to get the length; measure the distance around the parcel at its thickest part to get the girth; and add the two figures together. For example, a parcel 10 inches long, 8 inches wide, and 4½ inches high, measures 35 inches in length and girth combined (length, 10 inches; girth, 25 inches: 4½ inches + 8 inches + 4½ inches + 8 inches). A free pamphlet on "Packaging and Wrapping Parcels for Mailing" may be obtained from your post office.

There are both weight and size limits for fourth-class packages according to delivery zones. Size limits are given in total inches of length and girth combined. To determine the size of a parcel, see the illustration above. There are also special rates according to weight and zone for catalogs and similar printed advertising matter weighing 16 ounces or over. Refer to pages 766–767 for fourth-class zone rates. Size limits vary by class of post office at the destination. Consult the local postmaster.

Third- or fourth-class packages may be sent unsealed or sealed. Sealing implies that the sender consents to inspection of the contents. This silent assent replaces the old written endorsement: MAY BE OPENED FOR POSTAL INSPECTION. A sealed package is treated as parcel post by the postal sorters no matter what rate of postage has been paid unless the package is conspicuously marked FIRST CLASS.

Certain kinds of packaged mail are given special low rates as follows:

Special Fourth-Class Mail. Books without advertising that contain at least 22 printed pages are eligible for a preferential rate. (See *Special Fourth-Class Mail*, page 766.)

Library Materials. The *Library Rate* applies to materials sent to or from libraries, schools, and certain nonprofit organizations. The secretary is concerned with this rate when, as a borrower, reader, or member, she is returning qualifying material to any of the organizations that are permitted to use this rate. The rate is the same to all zones and applies to books, periodicals, theses, microfilms, music, sound recordings, films, and other library materials. (See page 766.) The package may be sealed, but it must be marked LIBRARY RATE.

It is recommended that the sender consult the local postmaster before mailing special fourth-class mail or library materials.

▪ Airmail

Airmail is carried by air and the speediest connecting ground carriers. For matter weighing less than 8 ounces, postage is charged on airmail according to weight regardless of the distance. For computing postage for airmail weighing more than 8 ounces, both the weight and the zone of address are used. Airmail parcels may be sealed or unsealed. Anything not hazardous may be airmailed except that which is liable to damage at low temperatures or high altitudes.

Airmail may weigh up to 70 pounds and is limited to 100 inches in combined length and girth. The weight and size limitations do not apply to articles addressed to certain overseas military post offices. Generally speaking, it is less costly to send small packages by airmail than by air express (page 252) or air freight (page 253). Airmail, plus special delivery, is the fastest small-package air service available. Letters may be enclosed in packages at no additional cost.

To use airmail service advantageously, obtain from the local post office a schedule showing the times of the day that airmail leaves the post office for the airport. Mail usually must be in the post office thirty minutes prior to the time airmail is scheduled to leave. The secretary will discover that much of her daily mail is sent to the same cities and that it is helpful to have on hand the airmail dispatch schedules. Copies of these are obtainable from the local postmaster or superintendent of mails.

YOUR POSTAL I. Q.

Did You Know That

Airmail is not always faster than regular first-class mail. Between cities that are only 300 miles or so apart a letter with first-class postage will usually be delivered as quickly as airmail.

The addition of the ZIP Code to the address may speed up the delivery of a package by as much as 24 hours or more.

A parcel-post package sent via SPECIAL HANDLING travels with first-class mail and will be delivered nearly as fast as a letter.

A letter mailed by 11 a.m. in any mail box marked with an ABCD sticker will be delivered to any point in the downtown section of the city by 3 p.m. the same day. There are 273 cities with ABCD service.

For 5 cents you can obtain a CERTIFICATE OF MAILING which is evidence that you have mailed a letter or package.

It does not pay to insure a package for more than its true value. In event of loss or damage, the POD will pay only the true value—not an inflated insured value.

Parcel-post packages may be sealed, but the POD has your permission to open for postal inspection of its contents. If you do not wish the package subject to opening by the POD, it must be marked FIRST CLASS and first-class postage paid.

To make certain that an undelivered package is returned, place RETURN POSTAGE GUARANTEED under your return address.

You can send a letter to an address in a foreign country for 13 cents—that is, if you use an aerogramme (air letter). Regular letters sent via international mail cost twice to three times as much.

First-class postage rates to Canada and Mexico are the same as those for the United States.

Airmail does not always assure more rapid delivery. When regular first-class mail is used, you can usually count on next-day delivery within 200 to 300 miles. Letters mailed on Friday will usually reach their destination by Monday regardless of distance (except coast-to-coast letters). The Post Office Department is working toward an objective of next-day delivery to any point in the United States.

Between large cities much of the first-class mail also travels by air, depending upon space available. Therefore, a letter carrying first-class postage might be delivered as soon as one with airmail postage.

HOUSE OF REPRESENTATIVES, U. S.

PUBLIC DOCUMENT

FREE

Mr. Jack Longacre
21294 Aberdeen Road

UNITED STATES POST OFFICE	PENALTY FOR PRIVATE USE TO AVOID PAYMENT OF POSTAGE, $300

N.T. STATION, DENTON, TEXAS 76203

OFFICIAL BUSINESS
P-4

OHIO

Mr. Thomas Church
1717 West Locust Street
Denton, TX   76201

28

Notice the difference between an official franked envelope and a penalty envelope. A franked envelope must show a real or facsimile signature and carry the words PUBLIC DOCUMENT—FREE. A penalty envelope must carry the penalty warning and the words OFFICIAL BUSINESS under a return address.

▪ Official and Free Mail

Federal government offices and personnel send out official mail without affixing postage. There are two kinds of official mail: franked mail and penalty mail.

A *franked* piece of mail must have a real or facsimile signature of the sender in place of the stamp and the words PUBLIC DOCUMENT—FREE on the address side. Only a few persons are authorized to use the frank, such as the Vice President of the United States, members and members-elect of Congress, Resident Commissioners, the Secretary of the Senate, and the Sergeant of Arms of the Senate.

Penalty mail is used for official government correspondence. It travels in penalty envelopes or under penalty labels.

Free mail—mail sent without postage by the general public—is limited to a few items such as matter addressed to the Register of Copyrights, census mail, immigration and naturalization service mail, and absentee ballot envelopes from members of the Armed Forces. For further details, see *Postal Manual*, Part 137.

To enclose a letter, invoice, or other first-class mail inside a third- or fourth-class sealed or tied package, mark the outside of the package FIRST-CLASS MAIL ENCLOSED and add the extra first-class postage required to the regular postage. Place the words RETURN POSTAGE GUARANTEED below the return address. An invoice, instructions, order form, reply envelope, catalog, or other *printed* matter (not typewritten or handwritten) may be enclosed in a package without additional postage.

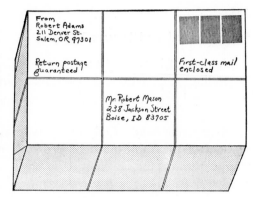

▪ Mixed Classes of Mail

Sometimes it is expedient and reflects better judgment to send two pieces of mail of different classes together as a single mailing to assure their arrival at the same time. A first-class letter may be attached to the address side of a larger envelope or parcel of mail of another class; or it may be enclosed in the larger envelope or parcel. Postage is paid on the two parts at their respective rates. When a first-class letter is *attached*, the correct postage is affixed to each part separately. When a first-class letter is *enclosed*, the postage is computed on each part separately but is affixed together on the outside of the package. The words FIRST-CLASS MAIL ENCLOSED must be written, typed, or stamped below the postage and above the address. A piece of combination or mixed-class mail is handled and transported by the post office as mail matter of the class in which the bulky portion falls—not as first class. (If airmail service is desired, airmail rates must be paid on both parts.)

A piece of mail of mixed classes may be sent special delivery or special handling by paying one additional fee. It may also be insured or sent *COD*.

▪ Mail for the Blind

Some kinds of mail to and from the blind may be mailed free; other kinds may be mailed at nominal rates. If, as a secretary, your work involves sending letters and parcels to or from the blind, you will want to study Part 138 of the *Postal Manual*.

Special Mail Services

In addition to transmitting mail, the post office provides many special services.

■ Registered and Insured Mail

A piece of important or valuable mail can be registered or insured, depending on its nature. For instance, important mail with no intrinsic value may be registered merely for proof of mailing or proof of delivery.

Registering Mail. Only first-class mail can be registered. The full amount of the value must be declared on a piece of mail being registered because the fee charged is based on the full value. There are two sets of fees. The one used depends upon whether the sender has commercial insurance covering the matter being mailed. The rates are slightly lower for values above $1,000 if the sender has such insurance. When the maximum liability of the post office is less than the value of the shipment, special private insurance is usually taken out by the sender for the specific shipment during transit.

Each piece of mail to be registered must be tightly sealed along all edges (transparent tape cannot be used) and bear the complete addresses of both the sender and addressee. The sender takes it to the registry window where the postal clerk computes the fee.

The sender of the registered mail may instruct the post office to change the address should it be necessary. For example, if you sent a registered letter to a company salesman in St. Louis and then learned that he moved on to Kansas City, you should telephone the St. Louis post office and request that the address be changed.

Insuring Mail. A piece of third- or fourth-class mail, or airmail containing third- or fourth-class matter, may be insured up to $200. The package is taken to the post office window where the clerk makes out a receipt for it, stamps the package INSURED, and puts on it the receipt number, if any. An unnumbered receipt is given if the package is insured for $15 or less. After placing the regular and insured postage on the package, the clerk gives the receipt to the sender for filing. If the package is lost or damaged, the post office reimburses the sender according to the amount of the fee. The insurance limits and corresponding fees are given in the Reference Guide on page 768.

If a business frequently sends several insured packages at one time, it may be more convenient to use a mailing book rather than filing a separate receipt for each package. Mailing books will be issued by the post office on request. It provides pages for entering the description of parcels insured. The sheets of this book are officially endorsed at the time of mailing and become the sender's receipts.

Return Receipts and Restricted Delivery. The sender is always furnished with a receipt showing that the post office accepted the piece of insured or registered mail for transmittal and delivery. However, the sender often wants legal evidence that the piece of mail was also actually received by the addressee. For an added fee the sender may obtain a signed receipt, commonly called a *return receipt*, on any piece of certified or registered mail or on any piece of mail insured for more than $15. This service is helpful when the address used is one of several years' duration or when there is reason to believe that the addressee may have moved. The fees for return-receipt and restricted delivery services are given on page 768.

For an added fee delivery may be restricted to the addressee only if the piece of mail is registered, certified, or insured for more than $15.

When the sender wants a return receipt, he fills in the number of the receipt and his name and address on a postal-card form supplied by the post office and illustrated below and writes RETURN RECEIPT REQUESTED on the front of the mail.

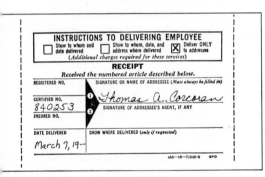

| Ungummed Side | Gummed Side |

This card is pasted (face down) along its two gummed edges to the back of the envelope or package. At delivery the postman removes the card, obtains the addressee's signature on the ungummed (reverse) side, fills in the information required, and mails the card to the sender.

▪ COD

Merchandise may be sent to a purchaser *COD*—that is, *collect on delivery*—if the shipment is based on a bona fide order or on an agreement made with the addressee by the mailer. The sender prepays the postage on the shipment and the COD fees, but they may be included in the amount to be collected if agreeable to the addressee. Otherwise,

U. S. MAIL					C.O.D.		C.O.D.	
C. O. D. Article No.					NO.		No.	
Postmark of	No. of Money Order		Postmark of		Postmark of mailing office			SENDER'S RECEIPT Article accepted by
	Date of Issue							P. M. (Per)
	Date Form 3849-D Sent							Postmark of
Delivery office		Mailing office			RECEIVED C. O. D. ARTICLE: Date and Carrier's Initials			
CHARGES (To be remitted to sender by M. O.)	$ 5 50	M. O. FEE	25¢					
PRINT FROM A. B. JONES Co.								
Street and No. 2240 READING RD.					RECEIVED:		Mailing Office	
City or Town CINCINNATI	(State) OHIO 45202				Charges and M. O. Fee $	Returned Article(√)	C.O.D. FEE 60¢	Postage 40¢
TO MRS. WILLIAM J. O'BRIEN						☐		
Street and No. 225 HEMINGWAY AVE.					Clearing Employee's		DUE SENDER Dollars | Cents 5 | 50	
City or Town LOUISVILLE	(State) KENTUCKY 40207				Initials			

Sender's COD Forms

the addressee pays the amount due on the merchandise, plus the fee for the money order to return the money collected to the sender. The maximum amount collectible on one parcel is $200. Information on mailing COD parcels is found in Part 163 of the *Postal Manual*. Three sections of the form are shown above.

■ Certificates of Mailing

For 5 cents a sender may obtain a very simple proof of having taken a piece of mail to the post office for dispatching. It may be used for any kind of mail. The sender fills in the information required on a certificate blank and pastes on it a 5-cent stamp. This certificate he hands to the postal clerk with the piece of mail. The clerk cancels the stamp and hands it back to the sender as evidence that the piece of mail was received at the post office.

This is an economical service for one who is mailing something that is of value to the addressee but who has no obligation or responsibility to pay the extra expense of having it insured, registered, or certified. It also furnishes a sender with an inexpensive proof of having mailed tax returns.

Certificate of Mailing

▪ Special Delivery and Special Handling

The delivery of a piece of mail may be expedited by use of either special-delivery or special-handling service.

Special Delivery. *Special-delivery service* provides the fastest handling—from mailer to addressee—for all classes of mail. Mail must be marked SPECIAL DELIVERY above the address. Immediate delivery is by messenger during prescribed hours to points within certain limits of any post office or delivery station. Do not send special-delivery mail to post-office-box addresses, military installations (APO, FPO), or other places where mail delivery will not be expedited after arrival.

Special Handling. Most people are not aware of *special handling* for fourth-class parcels—a service that is less expensive than special delivery. It provides the most expeditious handling and ground transportation practicable. Parcels move with first class, but they do not receive special delivery at the destination post office. When airmail (page 767) is used, special handling is unnecessary because airmail also receives priority ground handling.

Since all special delivery mail (including packages) is handled and transported in the same manner as first-class mail, it is not necessary to include SPECIAL HANDLING on a package being sent *special delivery.*

▪ Certified Mail

Airmail or first-class mail that has no real value (such as a letter, bill, or nonnegotiable bond) may, for a 30-cent fee, be certified. The sender is issued a *Receipt for Certified Mail*, like that illustrated below. If at any time within six-months after mailing he needs proof that the letter was delivered, he may use the receipt to obtain a delivery report.

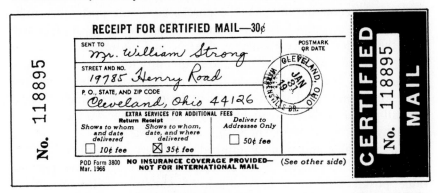

Detachable Receipt   Gummed Stub

Certified mail has the following advantages: (1) It provides the sender with a means of checking on the delivery of the letter. (2) It provides official evidence of mailing if a postmarked receipt is obtained. (3) It gives the letter the appearance of importance and urgency, and for that reason it is frequently used by collection agencies.

Mail received at the post office without sufficient postage will be forwarded to the addressee and postage collected at the time of delivery. It is a breach of business etiquette, however, to send mail without sufficient postage, thus making the recipient pay for your negligence.

▪ Stamps and Stamped Envelopes

Ordinary postage stamps are available in sheet, coil, or booklet form. Everyone is familiar with the 100-stamp sheet from which the postal clerk sells stamps at his window and the little booklets of bound stamps for home use. Coiled stamps are often used in business because they can be quickly affixed to envelopes and packages and because they are less likely to be lost or mutilated than are individual stamps. They are coiled either sidewise or endwise. Postage stamps can be exchanged at full value if stamps of the wrong denomination were purchased or if damaged stamps were received.

Precanceled Stamps and Envelopes. Precanceled stamps and precanceled stamped envelopes may be used only by those persons or companies who have been issued a permit to use them, and then only on matter presented at the post office where the precanceled stamps or envelopes were purchased. Their advantage is the saving of canceling time at the post office.

Stamped Envelopes and Cards. Stamped envelopes in various sizes, kinds, and denominations may be purchased at the post office individually or in quantity lots. For a nominal amount the post office will have the sender's return request and name and address imprinted on them when the envelopes are ordered in quantity lots.

First-class postal cards are available in single or double form, the latter kind being used when a reply is desired on the attached card. Airmail postal cards are available only in single form. To facilitate incompany printing, government postal cards are available in sheets of 40.

Unserviceable and spoiled stamped envelopes and cards (if uncanceled) may be exchanged. Such envelopes are exchangeable at postage value; postal cards are exchangeable at 85 percent of their value. Such exchanges are made in stamps, stamped envelopes, or postal cards.

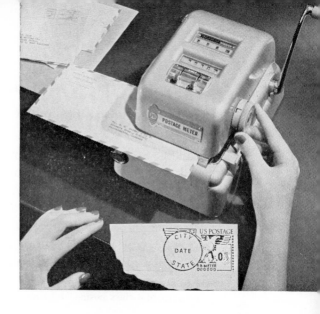

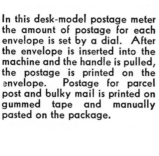

In this desk-model postage meter the amount of postage for each envelope is set by a dial. After the envelope is inserted into the machine and the handle is pulled, the postage is printed on the envelope. Postage for parcel post and bulky mail is printed on gummed tape and manually pasted on the package.

—*F. M. Demarest*

■ Metered Postage

One of the quickest and most efficient ways of affixing postage to mail of any class is by means of a *postage meter* machine. The postage meter prints on each piece of mail the postmark and the proper amount of postage. Consequently, metered mail need not be canceled or postmarked when it reaches the post office. As a result, it often catches earlier trains or planes than does other mail.

The meter machine may be fully automatic, not only printing the postage, postmark, and date of mailing, but also feeding, sealing, and stacking the meter-stamped envelopes. The imprint is usually red and may carry a line or two of advertising. Some models also print the postage on gummed tape which can be pasted onto packages. The meter registers the amount of postage used on each piece of mail, the amount of postage remaining in the meter, and the number of pieces that have passed through the machine.

The machine itself is purchased outright, but the meter mechanism is leased. In order to use a postage meter, a company must first obtain a meter license by filing an application with the post office where its mail is handled. The application must tell the make and model of the meter. A record of use must be maintained in a *Meter Record Book* supplied by the post office.

The meter is taken out of the machine to the post office where the meter is set and locked for the amount of postage bought. When that amount of postage is used up, the meter locks; and it is necessary to take it to the post office again and pay for more postage. Additional postage may be purchased before the meter locks. The operation is very simple, but the meter must be reset each time before it locks.

▪ Forwarding, Returning, and Remailing

Unfortunately mail does not always reach its final destination upon first mailing. Some pieces must be forwarded, returned to the sender, or remailed. Additional postage may or may not be required.

Forwarding Mail. The secretary is often required to forward mail. The following information indicates the extra postage or fee required.

First-Class Mail Up to Thirteen Ounces—No additional postage required. Change the address and deposit in mail.

First Class Forwarded by Air—Change address, affix postage equal to difference between first-class postage (already paid) and airmail postage, and deposit in mail.

Second-Class Publications—Full postage must be paid at transient rate. Change address, affix postage, endorse SECOND-CLASS MAIL and deposit in mail.

Third-Class Mail—Full postage at single-piece rate must be paid. Change address, affix postage, and deposit in mail.

Fourth-Class; Airmail over Seven Ounces—Additional postage at applicable rate is required. Change address, affix postage, and deposit in mail.

Airmail of Seven Ounces or Less—No additional postage is required. Change address and deposit in mail.

Registered, Insured, COD, and Special Handling Mail—Forwarded without payment of additional fees (*registry, insurance, COD, special handling*); however, ordinary forwarding postage charge, if any, must be paid.

Special-Delivery Service—This mail will not receive special-delivery service at second address unless a change-of-address card has been filed.

Return of Undeliverable Mail. A piece of undeliverable first-class or airmail up to seven ounces (with the exception of post cards and postal cards) will be returned to the sender free of charge by ordinary mail.

Undeliverable airmail over seven ounces will be returned to the sender by surface transportation and with return postage due. An undeliverable third- or fourth-class parcel is returned postage due if the parcel is of obvious value.

To assure that postal and post cards and third- and fourth-class packages are returned, place RETURN POSTAGE GUARANTEED conspicuously below the return address.

Undeliverable letters and packages without return addresses are sent to the dead-letter office where they are examined. They may be opened for finding return addresses. Whenever an address is found, the mail is returned for a fee. Undeliverable dead mail is destroyed or sold.

Remailing Returned Mail. The secretary is always chagrined when mail lands back on her desk. Any piece of mail returned with the "pointing finger" rubber stamp RETURNED TO WRITER, with one of six reasons checked, must be put in a fresh, correctly addressed envelope, and postage paid again.

■ Change of Address

The post office serving you must be officially notified by letter or by one of its forms when you change your address. The old and the new address and the date when the new address is effective must be given. Correspondents should be notified promptly by special notices or by stickers attached to all outgoing mail. The post office will supply new address cards free for personal and business use.

■ Recalling Mail

Occasionally it may be necessary to recall a piece of mail that has been posted. This calls for fast action. Type an addressed envelope that duplicates the one mailed. Go to the post office in your mailing zone if the letter is local or to the central post office if the letter is an out-of-town mailing. Fill in Form 1509 (*Sender's Application for Withdrawal of Mail*).

If the mail is an undelivered local letter, on-the-spot return will be made. If the letter has left the post office for an out-of-town address, the post office will wire or telephone (at the sender's request and expense) the addressee's post office and ask that the letter be returned. If the mail has already been delivered, the sender is notified; but the addressee is not informed that a recall was requested.

Mail Collection and Delivery

A number of plans have been inaugurated by the Post Office Department to cope with the increasing volume of mail, to improve service, and to reduce operational costs.

■ ZIP Code and Optical Character Reader

The five-digit *ZIP* (Zone Improvement Program) *Code* was designed to speed mail deliveries and facilitate use of automated equipment to reduce costs. The first digit represents one of ten large geographical areas of the United States. For example, 0 represents the New England States, 1 represents the Middle Atlantic States, and so on. The second two digits represent sectional centers or large cities. The last two digits stand for either a particular postal zone in a city or a particular post office in a small community or rural area. (See the local telephone directory for postal zone numbers for street addresses in your city.)

The *ZIP Code* should be written two spaces following the state on the city-state line. A comma should *not* divide the state name from the *ZIP Code*. To permit the use of addressing equipment with limited line length for bulk mailing, the POD has designed an approved two-letter abbreviation for each state and abbreviations for cities with long names. When these abbreviations are used, the address *must* include *ZIP Code*. The list is also presented on page 769 of this book.

Machines (optical character readers) which electronically read addresses are in use in post offices in several major cities. See page 755 for requirements for addressing mail for optical character readers.

All bulk mailers of second- and third-class mail are required to include the *ZIP Code* on the address. Failure to do so may subject the mail to a higher-postal-rate penalty.

▪ ABCD, NIMS, VIM

The *ABCD* (*Accelerated Business Collection Delivery*) plan is operated to insure prompt delivery of mail in business districts of large cities. Mail placed in a mail box bearing an *ABCD* sticker before 11 a.m. will be delivered to any point in the downtown section of the city by 3 p.m. the same day.

The *NIMS* (*Nationwide Improved Mail Service*) program is designed to curb the great volume of mail pouring into major post offices in the early evening hours. It is a voluntary plan whereby large-volume mailers are urged to space their deliveries to the post office throughout the day and thus avoid the peak mail hours at the end of the day.

VIM (*Vertical Improved Mail*) is a mail distribution system installed in many new large office buildings. In essence, *VIM* is the reverse of the familiar mail chute that drops mail from the upper floors into a collection box. Under *VIM* all incoming mail is delivered to a central mail room in the building. There postal employees sort it into lockboxes by floors. These boxes are then placed on a conveyor belt and keyed by dial to be ejected automatically to the right floor. There the office personnel pick up and deliver the mail. By this process the offices on each floor of the building can have continuous delivery of incoming mail.

SECRETARIAL SUGGESTIONS

To obtain the best postal communication service, the secretary will wish to:

1. Use the *ZIP Code* on all addresses to insure faster delivery.

2. Locate the nearest *ABCD* mail drop, and, when possible, meet the 11 a.m. deadline for rush intracity communications. Postage is usually far less expensive than special messenger delivery service.

3. Obtain time schedules for collection boxes nearest the office; airmail schedules to principal cities; surface mail dispatches to trains, trucks, and buses.

4. Bundle and label *local* and *out-of-town* mail separately. Out-of-town mail should be further subdivided into *airmail* and *first-class* mail. The post office will provide labels to identify bundles.

5. Arrange for letters to be submitted for signature at various times during the day so they can be dispatched to the mailroom and post office throughout the day.

6. Clarify the company's policy of using airmail.

7. Use *mass mailing*—collect all letters going to a branch, the home office, a traveling representative, and the like, and enclose them in one large outer envelope, thereby saving postage.

8. Investigate the desirability of renting a *post office box*. Box holders can obtain mail deliveries more often and at irregular hours.

▪ General Delivery

Mail may be addressed to individuals in care of the *General Delivery* window of main post offices. This service is convenient to transients and to individuals who have no definite address in a city. Such mail is held for a specified number of days and, if uncalled for, is then returned to the sender.

The executive on a touring vacation or a sales representative who is driving for several days and does not have hotel addresses frequently asks to have his mail addressed in care of *General Delivery* to a city enroute. This is the way the envelope address would look:

```
Mr. Gerald R. Robinson
General Delivery
Salt Lake City, Utah  84001
```

The words *Transient* or *To Be Called For* may also be used in the address.

Such a letter would go the main post office in Salt Lake City and be held at the *General Delivery* window for Mr. Robinson for 10 days or up to 30 days if the envelope bore such a request. If not picked up within that time, the letter would be returned to the sender.

Money Orders

Money may be transferred from one person or business to another by use of a *money order*. There are instances in which money orders are the requested form of payment. They are also a convenience to individuals who do not have a checking account.

▪ Domestic Money Orders

Postal money orders may be purchased at all post offices, branches, and stations. The maximum amount for a single *domestic money order* is $100. However, there is no limit on the number of money orders that may be purchased at one time.

▪ International Money Orders

Money may be sent to a foreign country by means of an *international money order* procurable at the local post office. When buying such an order, you are given only a receipt for it by the postal clerk, who then arranges for sending the money order abroad. Exact information is required about the payee and his address; if the payee is a woman, she must state whether she is single, married, or widowed.

International Mail

Information regarding the rates, services, and regulations covering international mail may be obtained from Chapter 2 of the *Postal Manual*, from the local post office, or from *The Directory of International Mail*.

▪ Classifications of International Mail

International postal service provides for *postal union mail* and *parcel post*. Parcel post is a separate category from postal union mail.

Postal Union Mail. This mail is divided into *LC Mail* and *AO Mail*.

LC Mail (Letters and Cards)—letters, letter packages, air letters (aerogrammes), and postal cards

AO Mail (Other Articles)—printed matter, merchandise samples without salable value, commercial papers, small packets, matter for the blind.

The postage for letters and postal cards mailed to Canada and Mexico is the same as for the United States. To all other countries the rates are higher and weights are limited. Letter packages (small sealed packages sent at letter rate of postage) are given letter treatment if they are marked LETTER. A customs label identifying the contents must be attached to each letter or letter package containing dutiable merchandise.

Parcel Post. Parcels for transmission overseas are mailed by *parcel post* and must be packed even more carefully than those delivered within the continental United States. These packages may be registered or insured. Special-delivery and special-handling services are also available. There is now no international *COD* service. A *customs-declaration* form must be attached to the parcel with an accurate and complete description of the contents. As rates, weight limitations, and other regulations are not the same for all countries, the secretary should obtain information from the post office about requirements for her particular shipment.

▪ International Air Postal Services

Rates on letters by air to foreign countries are charged at a fixed rate for a *half* ounce (except to Canada and Mexico where rates are the same as in the United States—a one-ounce basis for fixed rate).

Air Letters (Aerogrammes). The post office sells an *air-letter* sheet which may be mailed to any country with which we maintain airmail service. It is an airmail, prestamped, lightweight, single sheet that is folded into the form of an envelope and sealed. No enclosures, either paper or other kinds, are permitted. Firms engaged in international trade may print, subject to prior approval of the Post Office Department, their own aerogramme letterheads.

AO Mail by Air. Many concerns are not aware of the cheapest and fastest of all international postal services—*AO Mail by Air.* No export forms are required for most shipments. This service is restricted to samples of such items as merchandise, maps, printed matter, and drawings, but it is ideal for shipping small articles and should be investigated by those companies using other air services.

International Air Parcel Post. A minimum of forms is required in shipping by *international air parcel post.* This service is available to nearly all countries of the world and is rated on the first four ounces and each additional four ounces according to the country of destination.

▪ Reply Postage

To enclose reply postage with mail going out of the country, use an international reply coupon, called *Coupon-Response International.* It is purchased at the post office and is exchanged for stamps by the addressee in the country where it is received, whose stamps are then used for postage on mail addressed to this country.

Shipping Services

Shipments are made by means other than the various postal services —by air, rail, ship, bus, and truck. Even pipelines pumping oil and gasoline to refining centers may be considered a type of shipping service. The secretary does not need to know every detail; but she does need to know the kinds of services rendered, the advantages of each, and the sources to turn to for current information. The following discussion deals with two shipping services—*express* and *freight.*

▪ Express Service

Packages may be shipped by rail, air, or bus express. Each service offers advantages. The service to be used would depend upon the specific shipping needs.

Railway Express. *Railway express* service—a widely used shipping service—is provided by R E A Express (formerly Railway Express Agency, Inc.). Speed is an important feature, and there are practically no limitations as to the character or size of shipments—from ladybugs to elephants—from an ounce to a carload. Each shipment is given the care and protection required.

Advantages of Shipping by R E A Express. The advantages of sending shipments by R E A Express are:

1. *Pickup-and-Delivery Service.* There is no extra charge for this service.
2. *Valuation Coverage.* Each package is insured up to a stipulated amount. Additional coverage may be purchased.

—R E A Express

R E A Express gives special care and protection, speed in shipment, and personal attention such as pickup and delivery service.

3. *Care and Protection.* Each shipment is given the special care required. Animals are fed and watered and perishable food kept under refrigeration. Armed-guard protective service can be arranged for highly valuable shipments at reasonable cost.

4. *Speed.* Express intercity shipments travel in fast-moving trains or by R E A Express tractor trailers.

Charges. The express charges are computed on the weight of the shipment, the distance it is to be transported, and the kind of items that are being shipped.

The local office of R E A Express will, upon request, furnish the secretary with a copy of the classification index of items and the rate scales applying to her locality. The local office is also glad to answer telephone inquiries about rates and to look over and estimate charges for a shipment.

Shipping Procedures. An express package should be securely boxed, wrapped and sealed and addressed on two sides. A third copy of the address should be included on the inside. The address should be as complete as possible, giving street, number, building, room, department—any information that would be helpful to the expressman delivering the package.

The shipping forms which accompany the package may be made out ahead of time by the secretary, or the expressman will make them out when he picks up the parcel. A supply of the forms is furnished to frequent users of R E A Express service. Shipping charges may be fully or partly prepaid, or fully or partly collected from the consignee on delivery of the shipment.

Air Express. *Air express* is a joint venture of the air lines in cooperation with the Air Express Division of R E A Express. Service is provided to some 1,800 airports. In addition, over 20,000 off-airline communities are served by combining air service with the trucks and rail facilities of the R E A Express.

Air express has priority after airmail on all passenger and cargo planes and thus provides the fastest means available for transporting packages. Overnight delivery is provided between airport cities and to many off-airline points. Next-day delivery is assured to most points in the United States. Pickup and delivery service is provided (at no extra cost) with a pickup guaranteed within two hours after your call.

When making a rush shipment, the secretary should compare the rates and services of the various air services—*airmail, air express, air freight.* She may discover that air express would be the least expensive and the most convenient.

The local post office and local express agent will be glad to give detailed information about their services. Such references as *Leonard's Guide* and the *Official Air Express Guide* might also be of aid.

Bus Express. If the executive wants speedy delivery of a package to a small town in another part of the state, the secretary should consider *bus express.* This service is particularly useful when destination points are located where there are no airports. Round-the-clock service is offered, including Sundays and holidays—and between many points, same-day service. Pickup and delivery is available at an extra charge. Most bus lines offer this type of shipping, the most widely known being the *Greyhound Package Express.* Items such as films, optical supplies, foodstuffs, medicines, glass, and auto parts are insurable (free up to $50) with a weight limit up to 100 pounds a package and with a size limit of 24 by 24 by 45 inches.

▪ Freight Services

Freight is generally thought of as a shipment sent by any method other than mail or express. It is the most economical service used to transport heavy, bulky goods in large quantities. Because freight shipping is the most complex of all methods, the secretary will probably not be required to select the carrier and to route the shipments. She should, however, know a few of the salient facts.

Railroad Freight. Ordinarily when goods are shipped by *railroad freight*, they must be delivered by the shipper (consignor) to the local freight office. When the shipment arrives at its destination, the addressee (consignee) must arrange for delivery or must call for the shipment. Many railroads, however, have instituted store-door delivery with trucks operated by the railway company in order to meet the competition of the door-delivery service of trucking companies.

A service called *piggyback* is offered by the railroads to trucking firms for long-distance hauls. Here loaded truck trailers are driven to the railway depot in one city, detached from the trucks and placed on railroad flatcars, and moved by rail to another city where they can be unloaded and driven to their destinations. Thus towns and areas not on the regular railroad lines can be reached by this service.

To provide a less-than-carload freight service at a special rate, *freight-forwarding companies* assemble from several consignors shipments that are less than carload and are going to a certain destination. This service is used to gain a carload rate from the railroads.

Motor Freight. *Motor freight* is used for both local and long-distance hauls. Truck companies operate coast-to-coast service and have connecting services with local trucking lines. As described above, they often work in conjunction with railroads. Sometimes shipments are held by trucking companies until they have a paying load destined for the same locality. Specialized trucks also carry single commodities such as milk, gasoline, new cars, chemicals, sand, and gravel in truckload quantities.

Air Freight. *Air freight* differs from *air express* in that air freight is operated by the airlines and air express is operated as a division of R E A Express in cooperation with the airlines. All major airlines have cargo departments which aggressively compete for business with other airlines and other carriers. Some airlines are exclusively cargo-carrying lines.

The volume of freight being moved by cargo planes is growing at an extremely rapid rate. While initially used primarily for rush shipments and for the movement of perishable items such as flowers and foods, air freight is now being used to carry almost every type of item.

The volume of freight being moved by cargo planes is growing rapidly as businesses discover this means of reducing costs of inventory, warehouse space, and packing.

—American Airlines

Businesses are finding that the higher costs of shipment by air are partly offset by reduced costs in inventory and in warehouse space. There is also a saving in packing costs, as air shipments do not require the sturdy crating that surface shipments frequently demand.

Delivery service is provided without charge; however, there is a small charge for pickup service.

Water Freight. *Water freight* is usually considerably cheaper than any other means of freight transportation. River barges and other vessels on the inland waterways of the United States carry such commodities as lumber, coal, iron ore, and chemicals. Bulky items for overseas shipment are carried in freighters, while passenger liners carry mail and items packaged in crates. Information on services and rates can be obtained from shipping companies.

Bills of Lading. For every freight shipment—no matter what kind of freight carrier—a bill of lading must be made out. Two types are used: the *straight bill of lading* and the *order bill of lading*.

When the freight shipment is sent on open account to the consignee, the straight bill of lading is used. It is also used when the freight carrier is to act as the collection agency for a COD shipment. The letters COD and the amount to be collected are written on the face of the bill of lading.

If a bank at the destination of the shipment is to act as the collection agency, an order bill of lading and a sight draft are used. In this case, the consignee pays the bank the amount of the sight draft and obtains transfer of the bill of lading. He then presents the bill of lading to the carrier and receives the shipment.

▪ International Shipments

The market for American products is worldwide. International air cargo service makes it possible to deliver goods to most places in the world within a matter of hours. The bulk of tonnage to foreign markets, however, still moves via *surface* (ships).

International shipments present problems—special packing, complicated shipping procedures, marine insurance, foreign exchange— usually not encountered in domestic trade. Handling communications with a foreign business firm can be a problem in itself. (See page 220.)

Shipping Documents. A foreign shipment involves the preparation of a number of documents, such as forms to obtain an *export license* (some commodities), *ocean bill of lading, consular invoice* or *certificate of origin,* and *export custom declaration.* Large manufacturers doing extensive business abroad usually establish export departments: (1) to market the products, (2) to execute the required export and shipping forms, and (3) to arrange for the actual shipments.

Many smaller firms use the services of an export broker or CEM (Combination Export Management) firm. This firm performs the same functions as an export department; namely, marketing, processing, and shipping of goods.

Some businesses prefer to use the services of a Foreign Freight Forwarder or Cargo Agent, which specializes in processing foreign shipments. The shipper executes the required export and shipping documents and arranges for the actual shipment.

International airlines and steamship companies also maintain departments that assist customers with their overseas shipments.

International Air Cargo. To send a shipment by *international air cargo,* whether one package or a carload, contact the office of an international airline. The airline will provide instructions on packaging and addressing the shipment and completing the necessary documents such as *bill of lading* and *customs declaration.* In many cases, air freight or even express is less expensive than international parcel post.

Suggested Readings ——————————————

The World Almanac and Book of Facts. Formerly edited by the *New York World-Telegram,* which is no longer in print.

Postal Manual. Washington, D.C.: U.S. Government Printing Office.

─────────────────Questions for Discussion

1. Your employer hands you an addressed and sealed envelope for stamping and mailing and says that it contains his income tax return. How would you go about obtaining for him legal evidence that the income tax return was mailed? (The federal government prosecutes a taxpayer whose return is not received, even though the taxpayer has in his files a carbon copy of the return and makes a verbal claim that the return was filed by mail.)

2. Describe the ZIP Code and how it can speed up mail deliveries. Do you think that its use should be mandatory on all classes of mail? Explain your answer.

3. A stenographer who is under your supervision frequently forgets to return or to pay for stamps that she gets from you and uses for personal mail. What would you do the next time she asks for a stamp?

4. What would you do if you assigned to your assistant the job of enclosing, sealing, weighing, stamping, and posting each day's mail and in the morning you found for the third time in two weeks that she had left the mail lying on her desk, ready for mailing but not posted?

5. Why did the Post Office Department develop the ABCD plan for postal delivery? What steps should the secretary take to make maximum use of the plan?

6. Mail from the home office reaches your city post office around 2 a.m. each morning. However, it is not delivered to your office until the time of the regular mail delivery at 10:30 a.m. Your employer would like to have the home-office mail as early as possible so that district salesmen can be told of price changes. What would you suggest to solve this problem?

7. You are sending a request for a free brochure published in Norway. How can you arrange to enclose with your request adequate postage for mailing the brochure?

8. There are three ways of sending a letter about a parcel-post package being mailed out: separately, enclosed with the contents, or in an envelope fastened to the outside of the package. Which do you think is preferable and why?

9. The executive to whom you are secretary is president of a small company that sends out about a hundred letters a day. Each employee keeps and affixes his own postage to his own mail. Discuss whether or not a postage meter (machine) would be worth the rental fee.

10. Fill in the blanks in these sentences. Then use your Reference Guide to verify or correct your answers; tell which Reference Guide subheading entry applies to each point.

    (a) It occurred in the _____ century. (8)
    (b) Refer to page _____. (1,016)
    (c) It happened in the _____. (nineteen forties)
    (d) The trend started in the _____. (mid-60s)
    (e) They now have a _____ workweek. (3 day)

(f) There are _____ users of gas in the area. (186,000)

(g) It cost _____ last month. (876 dollars and 75 cents)

(h) They cost _____, _____, or _____, depending upon grade. (8¢, 18¢, 20¢)

11. See how many of the following questions you can answer. Then refer to the Reference Guide to verify or correct your answers.

(a) **What is the maximum weight of a package that may be sent by airmail to an APO address?**

(b) **Uncovered hotel keys may be mailed to the hotel by what class of mail?**

(c) **What is the difference in pounds between the maximum weight of a package going to a local-zone address and one being sent to an APO address?**

(d) **How much more is the special delivery fee for a 15-pound package than for a 1-ounce letter?**

Problems

■ **1.** Assume that your employer is out of the city on a business trip. How would you go about forwarding each of the following unopened pieces of mail? State whether additional postage is required.

(a) A personal letter

(b) A 1-ounce airmail letter which you wish to forward by airmail

(c) A piece of registered mail requiring a signed return receipt

(d) A letter mailed by your office to the employer but returned because of an insufficient address

(e) A special-delivery letter you wish to have forwarded by special delivery

(f) A parcel-post package

■ **2.** For *each* item listed below and on page 258, tabulate the requested information in appropriately headed columns.

(a) The class of postal service that should be used. If parcel post is chosen, indicate the zone,

(b) The kinds of fees that must be paid in addition to postage, and

(c) Special requirements or secretarial procedures:

(1) A carbon copy of a letter

(2) A pen-corrected copy of a printed price list

(3) A 14-ounce bound copy of a typewritten thesis addressed to a library

(4) A library book you are returning by mail

(5) A letter addressed to a relative of the executive, enclosing bonds valued at $500 and registered for full value. Return receipt required showing address where delivery was made

(6) A magazine addressed to a city 30 miles distant and sent at the request of the executive

(7) An 18-ounce sealed package containing a printing plate and addressed to a city 550 miles distant, with special-handling service

(8) A 480-page textbook weighing 2½ pounds and sent to a city 800 miles away

(9) A 26-ounce sealed parcel containing a gear and measuring 8 inches by 2 inches by 4 inches addressed to a city 700 miles away

(10) A 7-ounce unsealed package of candy sent special delivery

(11) A $20 money order addressed to a city 20 miles distant

(12) A box 3 feet long, 1½ feet wide, and 1½ feet high, weighing 40 pounds, addressed to a city 400 miles distant

(13) A sealed parcel weighing 5 ounces sent airmail

(14) A box of bulbs weighing ½ pound

(15) A monthly statement of a department store to a local customer

(16) An airmail, special-delivery letter weighing 2 ounces

(17) A postal card to a city 300 miles distant

(18) A 1-pound parcel containing clothing sent to a city 95 miles distant and insured for $15 with a return receipt requested at the time of mailing

(19) A check for $8.92 to a city 300 miles away

(20) A 1-pound sealed package containing samples of soap sent special delivery to a city 750 miles away

(21) Sixty individually addressed unsealed envelopes containing 1-page mimeographed price lists

(22) Copyright matter addressed to Register of Copyrights in Washington, registered for $5

(23) A 20-pound box (2 feet long, 10 inches high, and 14 inches wide) containing automobile parts addressed to a city 250 miles distant

(24) A letter sent by certified mail with a postmarked receipt wanted

(25) A 1-pound parcel containing costume jewelry valued at $75 but registered for only $50, being transmitted 2,500 miles

(26) A 1-pound sealed parcel containing costume jewelry insured for $75 and being transmitted 2,500 miles

(27) A certified letter containing notice to an heir of an estate, with return receipt requested showing where envelope was delivered

(28) Thirty mimeographed invitations in unsealed envelopes addressed to out-of-city members

(29) A 5-ounce box of stationery addressed to a town 700 miles distant

(30) A sealed 6-inch by 4-inch by 3-inch parcel containing stationery weighing 12 ounces, addressed to a city 350 miles away

(31) A magazine weighing 10 ounces and sent by an individual to a city 1,500 miles distant.

■ **3.** Obtain the total postage and fees for mailing each of the following: (Use the Reference Guide.)

(a) An airmail letter weighing 2½ ounces sent special delivery return receipt requested, showing the person, time, and address for delivery

(b) A merchandise package weighing 7¼ pounds sent to an address 1,100 miles away (The package is to be insured for $60 and is to receive Special Handling.)

(c) A package containing 16-mm film being returned to a library located 350 miles away (The package weighs 12½ pounds and is to be sent special delivery.)

(d) An aerogramme to Rome, Italy

Related Work Assignment 32-33

32. Special "In-Basket" Project

33. Your Fundamentals

} The instructions and supplies necessary for the completion of assignments 32 and 33 are provided in the Workbook.

Basic Telephone and Telegraphic Services

Business depends upon *rapid* communication. Most innovations in business equipment speed up the collection and communication of business information. Telephone calls supplant or supplement personal visits or letters; telegrams and cablegrams get results not attainable with slower means of communication. With increasing use of both telephone and telegraph services, the secretary or the administrative assistant will want to develop the best possible techniques for handling communication through these media. She often must decide which type of service to use. She may be called upon to recommend new equipment that is best adapted to her communication needs and to those of her employer. This chapter will improve your handling of basic telephone and telegraph responsibilities.

Telephone Conversation

An average of 400 million telephone calls are made every day. Today there is a telephone for every two persons residing in the United States. Naturally, you will want to master good *business* telephone techniques, for being able to represent your employer and your company attractively over the telephone has real dollars-and-cents value.

Some phase of at least 90 percent of all business transactions is conducted by telephone. That is why personnel officers check the telephone performance of applicants before hiring them. It is why companies frequently provide in-service telephone training for all office employees.

What the secretary says in carrying on the telephone conversation is important: tactful choice of words in contrast to blunt statements; offers of help in contrast to plain "noes." Ease in conducting pleasant, effective conversations comes with experience and training.

■ The Phonogenic Voice

Just as your appearance determines whether you are photogenic, your voice determines whether or not you are *phonogenic*. In business

The secretary with the phonogenic voice will sound friendly and interested. She will treat every call as important.

—*H. Armstrong Roberts*

your telephone voice must sound pleasing and friendly because the impression you make is formed largely from the sound of your voice.

A telephone ring is an anonymous thing. The secretary does not know who is calling. It may be an important client, the employer's wife, or the president of the company. It is wise to assume that whoever is calling *is* important and deserves one's best telephone personality.

There are a few simple rules to follow in developing the "voice with the smile" over the telephone:

1. Speak at a normal speed, with rising and falling inflections that avoid monotony.
2. Use a tone suitable for face-to-face conversation, keeping the voice low pitched.
3. Speak directly into the transmitter, which should be between half an inch and an inch from the lips.
4. Try to visualize the caller and speak *to* him—not *at* the telephone.
5. Try to convey a friendly, intelligent interest.

▪ Terminating Conversations

Sometimes a secretary is required to terminate a conversation suddenly for any of several reasons. Use a plausible excuse—for example, "I'm sorry, Mr. Allen has just buzzed for me to come into his office"; or, "I'm sorry, someone is waiting for me in the reception room"; or, "I'm sorry, I must get out a rush letter for Mr. Allen."

▪ Accuracy Techniques

It is often necessary to give or take accurate information over the telephone—names, addresses, amounts, dates, and code words. Sounds do go wrong as they travel over the wires. *F* and *S* are often confused, as are *P* and *B*, *T* and *D* and *M* and *N*. *Five* and *nine* often get mixed up; and strange as it may seem, so do *zero* and *four*.

Telephone Spelling. When word accuracy is needed, telephone spelling is used. To prevent mistakes, use any simple, easy-to-understand word to identify a letter. Telephone operators, who must frequently spell over the telephone, use the words that follow:

A for Alice	J for James	S for Samuel
B for Bertha	K for Kate	T for Thomas
C for Charles	L for Louis	U for Utah
D for David	M for Mary	V for Victor
E for Edward	N for Nellie	W for William
F for Frank	O for Oliver	X for X-ray
G for George	P for Peter	Y for Young
H for Henry	Q for Quaker	Z for Zebra
I for Ida	R for Robert	

To spell *Sphinx* one says, "Sphinx, S-p-h-i-n-x; *S* for Samuel, *p* for Peter, *h* for Henry, *i* for Ida, *n* for Nellie, *x* for X-ray.

Identifying Numbers. When numbers are used in telephone conversations, it is particularly important that the listener understand them correctly. The speaker should exaggerate the enunciation, as "Th-r-ee" (Strong R and long EE). In giving the operator a number, the caller may repeat it. If there is still a question about one digit, give its preceding sequence, as "three-four-FIVE," accenting the final proper number.

Incoming Calls

To handle incoming calls effectively, the secretary must understand the equipment she uses and techniques for answering, screening, and transferring calls, as well as taking messages.

▪ Equipment

The secretary will probably operate some kind of switchboard and possibly several types of desk telephones.

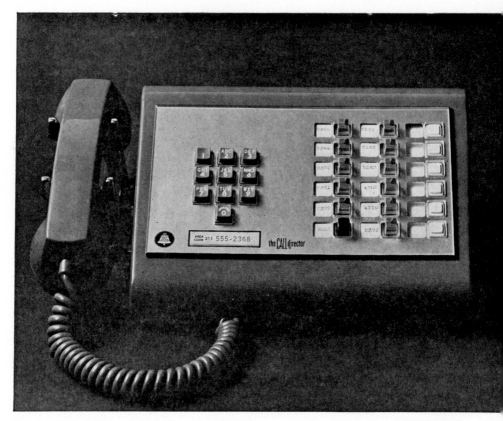

The Call Director telephone enables the secretary to answer many telephones in an office from one location. Associated with other equipment, the Call Director may be used for interoffice communication, to arrange conference calls, to "add on" stations, and so on. Square plastic buttons light up for an incoming call, when a line is in use, or when a call is being held. The buttons are identified in the windows beside them.

The Call Director. This is a desk-size dial station. Two sizes are available: 12-button, expandable to 18; 18-button, expandable to 30. With it the secretary—or her employer—may handle a number of incoming calls at once right from the desk. At the touch of a button a Call Director that is connected to the proper equipment can provide interoffice communication, arrange conference calls, and "add on" other extensions to incoming calls.

Another feature of the Call Director is the *"automatic disconnect"* —a line is available immediately for another call as soon as the receiver is hung up.

Switchboards. The secretary's duties may include relieving the switchboard attendant during the day, operating a simple cordless PBX board. She should, then, become proficient in switchboard procedures. This duty entails screening incoming calls and switching them to proper extensions, dialing certain types of outgoing calls, or completing inter-office connections when direct automatic dialing by number is not done.

A *private branch exchange* (*PBX*) centralizes telephone activity in an office. In office parlance a PBX is referred to as the "switchboard" or just the "board." Switchboards on which connections are made by means of cords are used by some business concerns. Cordless boards are operated by means of keys or buttons.

Desk Telephones. Desk telephones provide telephone service at the fingertips of the executive and his secretary. Most telephones are dial instruments; and with the prevalence of long distance calls by Direct Distance Dialing, the secretary must know how to dial such calls efficiently. She must also know how to use the desk telephone which is equipped with buttons (often referred to as keys) so that it can make or take a number of calls simultaneously from both inside and outside of the office. A button telephone in the hands of an inefficient secretary can create havoc with office procedure.

To answer a call:

1. **Determine the proper line to answer by the location of the ring, the tone, or the signal light on the button.**

2. **Push down the key for the line to be answered, remove the receiver, and answer.**

To place a call:

1. **Choose a line that is not in use (not lighted).**

2. **Push down the key for that line, remove the receiver, and make your call.**

3. **If you accidentally pick a line that is being held, reestablish the hold by depressing the hold key.**

To hold a call:

1. **Ask the person to whom you are talking to hold the line.**

2. **Push down the hold key for about two seconds to assure holding; both the line key and the hold key will return to normal position (with the light on).**

3. **Place or answer another call on another line. The person being held will not overhear your other conversation.**

To transfer a call:

1. **Other telephones in your button system can pick up a call if you depress the key for the line wanted.**

2. **When you hear the called person answer, replace your receiver.**

The desk telephone may also be connected with the central transcription facility so that the executive can pick up his telephone and dictate an item to a voice-writing machine.

Centrex. One of the frustrations of the modern office is the difficulty of getting through the switchboard to the extension wanted. To circumvent this problem, many companies are changing over to *direct in-dialing* to the specific extension wanted (Centrex). The frequent caller is given the extension number and the company number; he can then dial the extension from his outside telephone. Unanswered calls automatically go to the switchboard for handling.

▪ Techniques

The secretary develops two simple but effective habits in handling incoming calls. First, she answers her telephone before the third ring, benefiting everyone concerned. Delayed answering can be a source of irritation to the executive, for when he hears the secretary's telephone ringing several times, he wonders if she is at her desk and whether he should answer. Unfortunately, a call often comes at the busiest possible moment; but the person who answers must avoid implying by tone of voice any feeling that the call is an intrusion.

Secondly, she is ready to take notes. As she answers the telephone, she picks up a pencil and pushes a pad of paper into place.

Identification. The words with which the secretary answers her telephone depend upon whether it is connected directly to an outside line or to the company switchboard; but she always identifies her company or office and herself. If her telephone is on an outside line, she may answer, "Allen and Lovell—Miss Baer." If the call comes through the company switchboard, she will answer, "Mr. Allen's office, Miss Baer," because the PBX operator has already identified the company when she answered. In no case does the secretary say only "hello" or "yes."

For the secretary to recognize his voice and use his name in a telephone conversation is complimentary to the caller. As soon as the caller identifies himself, use his name in speaking with him.

The third or fourth time an individual calls, the secretary may be able to recognize his voice and should then address him by name. In case of any doubt, however, the secretary should not risk the possibility of offending a caller by using the wrong name.

Screening Calls. Employer preference, the nature of the office, and time available determine whether the executive answers his own calls, although there is a trend toward this practice in the upper management echelons.

When the secretary receives a call from among those she learns to recognize as VIP's, she automatically puts it through without question.

When a caller does not identify himself or the secretary is unable to recognize the voice, she may be required to find out who is calling. This procedure requires skillful questioning. The abrupt question, "Who is calling?" sounds rude and discriminating. Tactful secretaries phrase their questions somewhat like these:

May I ask who is calling, please?   May I tell Mr. Allen who is calling,
                                    or   please?

When she does not let the caller talk with the executive, she needs to give a plausible reason and to suggest a substitute person or time. A typical turn-down explanation might be:

Mr. Graham, Mr. Allen is holding an important conference. Perhaps I can help you or transfer you to somebody who can.

Executive Unavailable. The secretary has three responsibilities regarding incoming calls when the executive is not available for answering the telephone:

1. **Giving helpful but not explicit information to the caller about the executive's time schedule and activities**
2. **Getting information from hesitant callers**
3. **Taking messages and keeping a record of incoming calls**

Giving Information. When the executive is not available, the secretary is discreet about giving information. Definite information may be exactly what the executive does not want told to certain callers. *When in doubt, DON'T* be specific. Unless there is a known reason for being specific, the secretary tries to be helpful but not explicit. Note the differences in the responses on the next page.

Specific	Helpful But Not Explicit
He is in conference with the ————→ president.	He isn't at his desk just now. I expect him back soon.
He is in Chicago on business. ————→	He is out of the city today.
He left early this afternoon to play ————→ golf.	He won't be in again until tomorrow morning.

Getting Information. The telephone caller is sometimes reluctant to give information to the secretary. Often he just says, "I'll call back," and hangs up without identifying himself. A secretary can often learn both the identity of the caller and the reason for the call by using an oblique approach. The conversation might develop along these lines: "Mr. Allen is away today. I am his secretary; perhaps I can help you." Notice she does not ask who is calling or what he wants. If the caller is still reluctant, the secretary might ask, "May I have him call you tomorrow?" He may answer, "Yes, will you? This is Tom Snyder, Main 1-6412." She might ask, "Shall I give him any special message, Mr. Snyder?"

Or she might ask, "Will Mr. Allen know what you are calling about?" A positive answer to any such question necessitates the caller's divulging his name or the purpose of his call.

Taking Messages. Always offer to take a message when your employer is out. Ask the caller to explain any details which you do not understand. Take time to repeat the message and verify all spelling and figures. Afterwards, complete the record by adding the date, the time the call came, the name and identity of the caller, and your initials. Some firms use small printed slips for this purpose. It is possible to buy books of telephone message forms interleaved with carbon sheets so that the original message can be put on the executive's desk and the carbon copy retained in the book for reference.

Even if there is no message to report, make a record of the call. Actually, when the executive is away, a helpful secretary keeps a complete telephone diary of all calls received and messages recorded.

Transferring Calls. In a big firm calls must frequently be referred to other persons. In such a case the secretary courteously asks the caller to hold the line while she transfers the call. She may say, "I think you want to talk with Mr. Higgins. Will you please hold the line while I transfer the call to extension 459?" She then transfers the call through her pushbutton telephone or flashes the PBX attendant by depressing and releasing the receiver hook or bar (*flashing*) in the manner appropriate to the type of installation in her office. Some switchboards require several flashes to signal the operator; others, only one. If the flashing is done too rapidly, there is no intermittent flash at the board and consequently no signal. After the attendant acknowledges the signal, the secretary says, "Please transfer this call to Mr. Higgins."

If you are not positive that the person to whom the call is being transferred can really help the caller, offer to find out the information yourself and call back.

▪ Receiving Long Distance Calls

Occasionally when your employer is absent, you will have to take long distance calls. If so, listen carefully and repeat your understanding of the message. Type a full report of the call immediately, so that there will be a correct and complete record for the employer when he returns.

If your employer is not available to answer a person-to-person call, give the long distance operator full information as to when he will be back at his desk. The operator will ask you to have the executive call her and will give you those details of the call that will help her to complete it quickly when he calls back; such as, "Please have him call Operator 18 in Detroit, and ask for 971-1380, Mr. Smith calling."

If the executive can be reached at another telephone, either locally or in another city, and you believe he would not object to receiving a call there, you should tell the operator where he can be reached.

▪ Message-Taking Services

New devices and services that are available assure that telephone calls are always answered, even when the telephone is not covered.

Answering, Recording, and Switching Devices. Automatic answering equipment can deliver any message that the user records. Before leaving the office, the businessman (or his secretary) turns on the machine and makes a recording to tell callers when he will return and asks them to leave a message. The person calling in hears the announcement and then records his message. An innovation made possible by electronics is equipment that enables the businessman to call in and revise his recording. Small businesses, such as real estate and insurance offices, find this service especially advantageous. This equipment has been expanded to attract larger users. For instance, up to six hours of recorded messages capture overnight orders for a meat wholesaler.

With a *Call Diverter*, a thumb wheel is set with the number where the owner subscriber will be, and incoming calls are automatically transferred to that telephone.

Telephone Answering Service. Unlike the automatic recording device which merely recites impersonal messages, the operator in a telephone answering service is able to exercise judgment and understanding in personally assisting the caller. Many business firms invest in such service as a way of personalizing their offices during the hours they are not open. The secretary who finds herself in an office using such service should establish friendly relations with the answering service, check with the operator immediately upon coming into the office after it has been closed, and provide complete information when the office is to be covered by an answering service.

Taped Announcements. Almost every telephone user is familiar with taped announcements that may be dialed: time of day, weather, flight information during inclement weather, market information, movie schedules, and even prayers. It is possible for a telephone user to develop such announcements.

Special Reverse-Charge Toll Service. If a business wishes to make its services easily available by telephone in cities where it has no office, a special listing can be included in the telephone directory of each of the other cities permitting the caller to make the call as a local one. The long distance charge is billed to the listed number. On such incoming calls, the secretary provides complete and cordial help—without waste of long distance time. (See page 270 also.)

Outgoing Calls

In addition to answering the telephone, you will place local and long distance calls. To do this well, you must know how to get maximum service from your telephone directories and telephone operators and how to make the appropriate choices of service.

■ Using Telephone Directories

Before placing a call, the secretary must locate the telephone number, and sometimes that takes quite a bit of skill. The telephone directory has two parts: the *Alphabetical Directory* (white pages) which contains a complete list of subscribers, their addresses, and telephone numbers; and the Yellow Pages (*classified directory*) containing alphabetic listings of names of businesses under headings which are also arranged alphabetically by product or service offered.

Both directories print, in the upper outside corner, the first and last names or headings listed on each page. The conspicuous location of these guide words makes it possible to locate the proper page quickly.

The telephone directory is a mine of information, especially one for a metropolitan area. For instance, the New York City alphabetical directory contains in its introductory pages: emergency numbers; instructions for dialing *Directory Assistance* (*Information*) in any locality; instructions for telephoning locally, nationally, and overseas; special services such as marine and mobile service; a map showing area-code distribution; a local postal-zone map; information about setting up conference calls; explanations of billing; and descriptions of available Picturephone service.

A corporation may find it advantageous to keep in a central location a collection of telephone directories from cities in which it conducts a large volume of business. It is also possible to find out-of-town directories from the larger cities in some hotels and major travel terminals.

The Alphabetical Directory. In the *alphabetical directory* the numbers are usually located quickly, but the exceptions make it necessary for the secretary to know the rules followed in arranging names in alphabetical sequence in filing. For example, there are twenty-one columns of the surname *Miller* in one metropolitan directory. Alternate spellings are suggested as, *Also see MILLAR.*

Locating the various government offices and public services also requires a knowledge of the alphabetical listings. They are generally listed under their proper political subdivisions—city offices under the name of the municipality, county offices under the name of the county, state offices under the name of the state, and federal offices under *United States Government.* Public schools are usually listed under the municipality and then under *Board of Education.* Parochial schools are individually listed. Addresses of identical listings are in the alphabetical order of street names followed by numbered streets in numerical order. (*Eighth Street* would follow rather than precede *Second Street.*)

The Yellow Pages Directory. The *Yellow Pages directory* of business listings is a very helpful source of reference to the secretary. In metropolitan areas a separate Yellow Pages directory contains all classified listings. The executive may want to talk with "that air-conditioning firm on Church Street," but neither he nor his secretary knows its correct name. She looks in the Yellow Pages directory under *Air Conditioning Equip & Supls* and finds that he wants *Tuttle & Bailey, Inc.*

An efficient secretary always circles every frequently called telephone number in the directory so that she can find it more quickly the next time. She may jot the number down on a slip of paper just in case she gets a busy signal the first time she dials it.

When a new number is obtained, it should be listed on the proper directory page or in a desk telephone directory.

Personal Telephone Directory. Every secretary keeps a *personal, up-to-date telephone directory.* In it she lists alphabetically the names of frequently called persons and firms and their telephone numbers. A thoughtful secretary types a condensed list of such numbers for the executive and places it in some convenient spot, such as the back of his daily calendar pad, or inside his office directory of extension numbers.

Some kind of card listing or tab-insertion scheme is preferable to a solid-typed list which makes no provision for the addition of names and changes of personnel or telephone numbers. Any list becomes out of date quickly unless some system is devised that provides for additions and deletions.

The time-and-motion-conscious secretary will be interested in the analysis of the telephone company: You can look up a number in your personal telephone directory in 10 seconds, about a third of the time required for a search of the large directory. A personal telephone booklet may be obtained from the local telephone company for the asking.

Some people prefer not to have their telephone number listed in the directory. This may cost them 50 cents a month because of additional administrative costs. Usually, Directory Assistance (Information) will not have the number in its records. Only in exceptional circumstances, and with the customer's consent, will the telephone company arrange to complete the call. Keeping unlisted numbers in the personal directory becomes doubly important, since they cannot be looked up. Telephone numbers of frequent correspondents may be taken from letterheads and entered in the personal telephone directory for possible use.

Special Reverse-Charge Toll Calls. To stimulate business or to provide wider service, a corporation may make a special listing in the directory of a city in which it does not maintain an office. The listing looks like this:

Link-Hess Finishing Co., Inc.
Philadelphia Pa . . Ask Oper for Enterprise-6782

Charges are automatically billed to the called party; no acceptance of the charges is requested.

Because of the many variations in making Enterprise calls, the secretary should consult the local telephone directory for instructions before using this service.

All-Number Calling (ANC). Nationwide the traditional two-letter, five-digit telephone numbers are being supplanted by All Number Calling (ANC), seven-digit numbers. For example, Ypsilanti 2-2000 becomes 972-2000. The changeover to ANC is being made because:

1. The telephone user will not be puzzled over the correct spelling of the exchange word (for example, whether *YPsilanti* is spelled *YP* or *YI).*
2. Letters and numbers on the dial cannot be confused (the letter *O* for zero; the letter *I* for the number 1).
3. Numbers are easier to find; the telephone user does not have to search for letters on the dial.
4. More telephone number codes are possible under the new system.

■ Placing Local Calls

The procedure in placing calls varies with the kind of telephone equipment. If the desk telephone is a direct outside line, give the number to the telephone operator or dial it. If the line goes through the office switchboard, you either dial 9 for an outside line or ask the PBX attendant for a line by saying "Outside, please." When you get a dial tone, you dial the number.

You will regularly be making two kinds of local calls—reaching someone whom the employer will talk with on his extension, and your own calls. In the first case, after getting the number desired, ask for the person wanted and immediately identify your employer as the caller, saying something like:

Mr. Norman, please. Mr. Allen of Allen and Lovell calling.

To avoid making the person wait on the line, always determine if the executive is ready to take the call before placing it.

If the answering operator or secretary asks you to put your employer on the line before she puts hers on, be gracious and follow her request. The person who must waste a few seconds waiting for the other to respond should be the one who originated the call.

In making your own calls, you will find it advisable to jot down what you want to say before you get the person on the line in order to avoid the embarrassment of having to call back for a point forgotten. You will speak with more confidence and effectiveness and you will make a better impression by knowing in advance what you are going to say.

Introduce yourself properly. Upon being connected, give your own name, and, if desirable, your firm name. For example, "This is Miss Baer, Mr. Allen's secretary, of Allen and Lovell." Making a good impression on people whom you telephone is just as important as is making a good impression on those who call at your office.

▪ Message Units

Within a metropolitan area, calls between widely separated locations are not considered local calls or long-distance calls; however, they are individually charged for as *message-unit calls.*

A message unit is a telephone term describing a standard base rate used in determining the cost of a call. The table of rates in the front of the directory shows the *number* of message units chargeable between telephone exchanges and the length of the overtime period which is charged as a message unit. For instance, from Manhattan Zone 3 to Westchester Zone 6 is four message units (four times the base rate of 5 cents) or 20 cents. Message units are automatically charged and billed in total—not itemized.

▪ Types of Long Distance Calls

There are two general types of long distance calls—*station-to-station* and *person-to-person.* The secretary is expected to know the relative costs, the recommended and permissible practices, and the situation in which to use each type.

Station-to-Station. Because of time saved through Direct Distance Dialing, possible only on *station-to-station calls,* business will probably tend to use this type of service more and more except in cases where there is a question of whether a specific person can be located readily.

All Direct Distance Dialing calls are station-to-station calls, but a station-to-station call may also be placed with the operator. The secretary uses a station-to-station call when she is willing to talk with anyone answering the telephone called or when she is reasonably sure the person wanted is within reach of his telephone. Charges begin at the time the called telephone or switchboard answers even if the person desired is not available. No charge is made if no one answers the telephone called.

Sometimes several valuable minutes are wasted by the efforts of the answering attendant to locate the person wanted. If a secretary were trying to reach a company salesman registered at a hotel, the hotel operator might have to page him in the lobby and the hotel restaurants. If she was unsuccessful in finding him, the call would be fully chargeable; or if it took her two and a half minutes to get him on the line, there would be little of a three-minute initial period left.

Person-to-Person. A *person-to-person call* is made when you must talk to a particular person or extension telephone. Charging begins when the called person or extension answers.

A person-to-person call places on the long distance operator the responsibility for reaching the person or extension wanted. If asked to do so, she will try repeatedly to complete the call.

■ **Relative Costs**

The station-to-station rate is lower than the person-to-person rate between the same points because the connection can be made in less time. The time of day and day of week affect station-to-station rates, as shown below.

One exception should be noted: There is no difference between evening and night rates on station-to-station interstate calls less than 221 miles or on intrastate calls less than 71 miles.

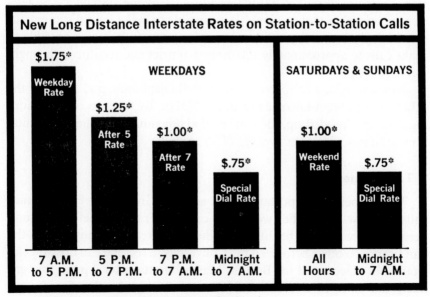

New Long Distance Interstate Rates on Station-to-Station Calls

WEEKDAYS				SATURDAYS & SUNDAYS	
$1.75* Weekday Rate	$1.25* After 5 Rate	$1.00* After 7 Rate	$.75* Special Dial Rate	$1.00* Weekend Rate	$.75* Special Dial Rate
7 A.M. to 5 P.M.	5 P.M. to 7 P.M.	7 P.M. to 7 A.M.	Midnight to 7 A.M.	All Hours	Midnight to 7 A.M.

*Maximum, First Three Minutes Coast-to-Coast

The rates for both types of calls are based on an "initial period," usually of three minutes. No reduction is made if the full initial period is not used. Rates are fixed for time exceeding the three minutes.

A table of long distance rates to many cities is given in the front of every telephone directory. Rates to places not listed are obtainable from the long distance operator.

▪ Which Class of Service?

The secretary must often decide whether to use person-to-person or station-to-station service. She can arrive at the better choice only by considering carefully every factor, including cost and whereabouts of the person called.

If you were asked to reach a salesman at his home office, it would not be good judgment to place a station-to-station call. More likely he would be out in his territory. On the other hand, if you were asked to call the manager of the New York branch office who is usually at his desk, you might place a station-to-station call.

▪ Telephone Systems

More than 83 percent of the nation's telephones belong to the 24 regional telephone companies that comprise the Bell system. In addition, there are almost 2,700 independent telephone systems. The telephone network is truly a giant. It is possible to make long distance calls to all telephones in the various domestic systems. It is also possible to make calls to approximately 120 other countries and territories throughout the world.

Nine out of ten (91 percent) of all Bell telephones, and many of the others, have Direct Distance Dialing (DDD). By this process telephoning is vastly speeded up, for you can dial any number in the continental United States within an average of 15 seconds.

▪ Time Zones

Time zones are important to the secretary in placing long distance calls. A New York office would not call San Francisco before 12 noon because there would be little likelihood of reaching anyone in the San Francisco office before 9 a.m. Conversely, a secretary in Los Angeles would not place a call for Boston, Massachusetts, after 2 p.m., for very likely the office in Boston would be closed very shortly after 5 p.m. During summer months, of course, areas on Daylight Saving will be

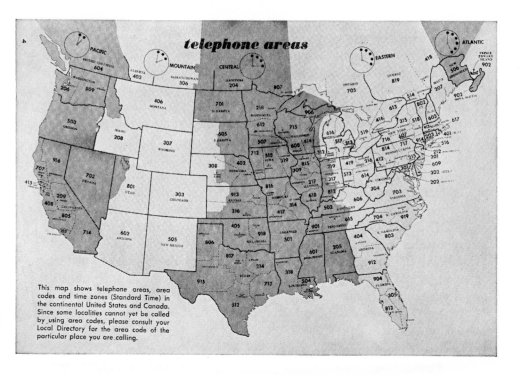

telephone areas

This map shows telephone areas, area codes and time zones (Standard Time) in the continental United States and Canada. Since some localities cannot yet be called by using area codes, please consult your Local Directory for the area code of the particular place you are calling.

an hour later. If placing overseas calls is part of the secretary's job, she should learn the time differences for the cities called.

The map that appears at the top of this page indicates time zones in the continental United States and adjacent Canadian Provinces so that the person placing a long distance call can plan his calls to coincide with the business day in the place called. The time-zone map shows the code zones to be used before long distance numbers. The time at the place where the call originates determines whether day, evening, or night rates apply. Daylight Saving may affect some points during the summer.

▪ Placing Long Distance Calls

Long distance calls may be made by Direct Distance Dialing or through the long distance operator.

Direct Distance Dialing (DDD). Station-to-station long distance calls are dialed direct, without assistance from an operator except in case of difficulty. The caller dials a three-digit *area code*, then the telephone number desired, except when he is dialing a number in his own area.

Specific directions for DDD may be found in the front section of the telephone directory. The general procedures to be followed are described in the next two paragraphs.

Secure the area code from the company letterhead (where it is often included with the address), from your desk telephone directory, the front of the telephone directory, or the operator. If you have the area code but do not know the telephone number of the person to be called, dial the prefix 1 (where necessary), the area code, and the number 555-1212. After you identify to the information clerk the city you wish to call, she can give you the number. There is no charge for this service. If there is even a remote possibility of later calls, record both the area code and the telephone number in your personal directory.

Dial the number carefully, but if you reach the wrong number on any DDD call, obtain the name of the city you have reached and promptly report this information to the operator to avoid charges for the call. If you are cut off before completing a call, inform the operator so that the charges can be adjusted. If it is evident that for some reason your call is not going through, dial the operator for help. Sometimes you get a recorded message telling you that your call has not been completed and asking you to initiate it again.

Placing Long Distance Calls with the Operator. Dial the long distance operator for cities without DDD, collect calls, calls charged to a third telephone, calls from coin telephones, calls on which you require time and charges, and credit-card calls.

A long distance call is completed promptly when the person placing the call first gives the long distance operator the area code and the telephone number being called. Then she can begin to make the connection immediately, while recording the rest of the information. This procedure saves not only the time of the operator but also that of the person calling.

To place a long distance call, the secretary should give the information in 1-2-3 order:

1. Area code (or city and state if area code is not known—state is omitted if no confusion will result.)
2. Telephone number (or name and address)
3. Name of person if person-to-person (or number and station-to-station classification, with the reason for calling through an operator, such as: "This is John Holmes, and I want to reverse the charges," or "... and this is a credit-card call.")

When you have an unusual problem, explain it to the long distance operator and she will try to help you. One secretary had to call an official in Washington, D.C., at two o'clock for her employer who expected to be in the local courthouse near another telephone at that time. She explained the situation to the operator, who placed the call at two o'clock and made the connection to the courthouse telephone, but charged the call to the employer's own office telephone. Another secretary was told to get in touch with Mr. A. J. Dearing who was at some Pittsburgh hotel. She called the long distance operator and told her that was all the information she could give except that she believed he would be staying at one of the better hotels. The operator then began a check of the hotels until she located Mr. Dearing. The secretary should not hesitate to ask for this kind of service.

▪ Paying for Long Distance

The secretary may be responsible for accepting long distance charges, accounting for them, reversing them, or securing her employer's credit card on which he charges calls.

Obtaining Charges on Toll Calls. Charges for long distance calls are referred to as *toll charges*. If you need to know the cost of a call, request the operator *at the time the call is placed* to report the charges. She will then notify you after the call has been completed and the cost has been calculated. This service is not available on DDD calls.

Cost Records of Toll Calls. For accounting purposes most companies charge toll calls in their records to specific departments, clients, or jobs. With memorandum records kept at the secretary's desk showing the date, point called, and the person calling, the correct toll charges can be checked against the bill and charged to the proper departments.

The federal government levies on long distance calls an excise tax which the telephone company collects from the subscriber. The tax rates are shown on the customer's bill. If the secretary is required to keep a cost record of each long distance call for accounting purposes, the tax must be computed and added to the toll charge.

Collect Calls. A long distance call (toll call) can be made *collect*. Charges on person-to-person and station-to-station calls can be reversed —that is, charged to the telephone called rather than to the one placing the call. The request to reverse the charges, however, must be made at the time of placing the call so that the receiving number can have an opportunity to accept or refuse the charge.

Statement B				LONG DISTANCE SERVICE					
TELEPHONE NUMBER	DATE MO	DAY	REF CODE	PLACE CALLED		NUMBER CALLED	ORIGINATED FROM		AMOUNT
622-4264	10	1	CP	CLEVELAND	OHIO	622-4264	DET MICH		95
	10	2	AS	PONTIAC	MICH	332-1216	NY NY		2 10
	10	3	BS	FT LAUDRL	FLA	524-4857	AKRON Ohio		8 90
	10	4	D	ALBANY	NY	246-6642			1 05
	10	4	S	AURORA	ILL	743-3770			1 35
	10	5	P	BOSTON	MASS	534-5000			1 60
	10	6	T	DETROIT	MICH				1 00
THE CALLING AND CALLED CITIES ON COLLECT AND CREDIT CARD CALLS				CITY AND STATE CALLED (IN DETAIL)		THE TELEPHONE NUMBER YOU CALLED			
A. CREDIT CARD CALL P. PERSON TO PERSON				TOTAL U. S. TAX AT 10%					1 70
B. BILL TO 3RD NO S. STATION TO STATION									18 65
C. COLLECT T. TELEGRAM				TOTAL CARRIED TO BILL					
D. CUSTOMER DIALED R. PARTY DESIGNATION									

—The Ohio Bell Telephone Company

From this statement it is possible to allocate toll charges to the proper department. Notice that the calls involved the use of the credit card, direct dialing, a telegram charged to the telephone, and reverse charges. The number of the telephone called is included on each listing as an aid in allocating the charges and verifying the accuracy of the bill.

Telephone Credit Cards. Your employer may carry a telephone credit card that entitles him to charge his long distance calls to his home or business number while traveling. It shows his code number, name, and business affiliation. When making a call, the employer tells the long distance operator that it is a credit card call and gives her the code number and the number of the party he wants to reach. Credit card calls are identified as such on the monthly statement.

Secretarial Responsibility for Telegrams

Once a telegram presaged only disaster. Then it became largely a business tool, the quickest and cheapest method of relaying abbreviated business information. It is still widely used to dramatize the urgency of a situation—to solicit an overdue check or manuscript, to stop an unwanted action, to influence political action, to serve notice of eviction, to relay congratulations, to get attention that might otherwise be denied, and to transact business rapidly when a record of notification is needed. It is still important, therefore, that the secretary learn to use telegraph services for the right occasion and to choose appropriate service.

▪ Domestic Telegraph Services

A secretary works primarily with domestic messages—those communicated within the continental United States. Techniques for sending telegrams to Canada and Mexico, however, are practically the same as those for the continental United States.

The classes of telegrams and other services are standardized; but rates and regulations occasionally change, so it is advisable to secure up-to-date information from time to time from your local Western Union office.

The Two Classes of Telegrams. Just as the Post Office has various classes of mail services, Western Union offers a choice of telegraphic services. The two classes of domestic messages are regular telegrams and overnight telegrams.

Rates for both classes of telegrams are determined by whether the telegram is to be received intrastate (within the same state) or interstate. The rate for an interstate telegram of either class is somewhat higher than that for an intrastate message.

An additional charge of 75 cents is made for delivery by messenger of either class of telegram.

Regular Telegrams. A *regular telegram* is sent immediately at any time, day or night, and takes precedence over all other classes of domestic service. The minimum charge is based on 15 words exclusive of address and signature; an additional charge is made for each additional word. Although deferred service is available at lower rates, the regular telegram is used most frequently.

Overnight Telegram. An overnight telegram can be sent at any time up to midnight for delivery the next morning. It is the less expensive class of service. The minimum charge is based upon a message of 100 words. For longer messages a charge is made for each additional word. An overnight telegram is used when next-morning delivery is acceptable.

The overnight telegram is especially attractive to East Coast companies communicating with the West Coast because of the three-hour time difference. An overnight telegram originating after the West Coast office is closed will be delivered by the time the receiving office opens the following morning.

Selecting the Proper Class of Service. Often a secretary is instructed: "Send a wire." Perhaps she is told to wire Mr. Adams after lunch and

western union				**Telegram**

NO. WDS.–CL. OF SVC.	PD. OR COLL.	CASH NO.	CHARGE TO THE ACCOUNT OF	☐ OVER NIGHT TELEGRAM
	PAID		ACME VENDING CO.	UNLESS BOX ABOVE IS CHECKED THIS MESSAGE WILL BE SENT AS A TELEGRAM

Send the following message, subject to the terms on back hereof, which are hereby agreed to

MARCH 17 19 70

TO JOHN W. SMITH, ACE CANDY MANUFACTURING, INC. **CARE OF OR APT. NO.**

STREET & NO. 125 FIFTH AVENUE **TELEPHONE**

CITY & STATE NEW YORK, NEW YORK **ZIP CODE** 10021

SHIP TEN CASES #27 CHOCOLATE CRUNCH BARS. SUPPLY DEPLETED. NEED

IMMEDIATELY.

ACME VENDING CO.

SENDER'S TEL. NO. 922-3100 **NAME & ADDRESS** ACME VENDING CO.
291 SOUTH AVE., CLEVELAND, OHIO

The charge for this regular telegram is based on the number of words in the boxed message. The information at the bottom of the blank is used for reference purposes. The telegram is typed in solid capitals.

ask him to call on a new prospect, the Atlas Waterproofing Company, Tenth and Greene Streets, before he leaves Boston. By referring to Mr. Adams' planned itinerary, she learns that he is in Boston today and will be there all day tomorrow, so a fast telegram delivered promptly would be no better than a message deferred for delivery until early the next morning. She decides, therefore, to send an overnight telegram and to utilize the extra words in explaining the reason for the call.

In selecting the most advantageous type of telegraph service, the secretary must keep uppermost in her mind not only the cost factor but also the time element—that is, such factors as the speed of delivery, the time of day, the day of the week, the season of the year, unusual geographic or national situations (for example, holidays or disasters), and the difference in time zones in the United States. Some firms make provision for disposition of urgent messages received after the office is closed. They are often telephoned to the home of one of the executives.

Addressing Telegrams. The telegraph company makes no extra charge for long addresses except in unusual cases. For instance, there is no extra charge for "George Harrison, care of Henderson Manufacturing Company, 1 William Street, New York, N.Y." or "Mr. and Mrs. William Schwartz and family" or for the inclusion of a telephone number that will expedite delivery. There is a charge for "or Harry Miller" in the address "John Smithson or Harry Miller."

Sometimes people address a telegram to "Robert Smith, Empire State Building, New York City," forgetting that there are thousands of people employed in that building. Use company or firm names and room numbers. The address "24 Fifty-Second Street, New York City" may necessitate attempts at delivery on both East and West Fifty-Second Street. If, however, the telegram is addressed to a well-known national or local figure, or a nationally known business or bank, it is unnecessary to give the room number, building, and street address.

Typing the Telegram. Telegrams may be typed on long or short blanks obtained from Western Union or on blank paper properly labeled "Telegram." The number of office copies varies among business organizations. You will certainly need at least one file copy, and you may also need an accounting copy and a verification copy. If the message is very important or contains technical information, the verification copy may be mailed to the addressee to make certain that the telegraph message was transmitted correctly. The sample telegram on page 280 provides a model. If an overnight telegram is sent, the box at the right must be checked. Otherwise, a regular telegram will be sent. If the telegram is charged, the account charged is shown. Paragraphs and punctuation are transmitted without charge and should be typed in the telegram to be sent.

The Message. The message should be complete but concise, including only words necessary for clarity. It is better to say, "Arrive International Airport at 8:30 p.m. daylight saving, Thursday, United Flight 241; please meet plane," than "Arrive New York Thursday 8:30 plane. Please meet me." With the latter message, the recipient does not know which airport is meant, whether the plane left the sender's airport at 8:30 or will arrive in New York at 8:30, whether 8:30 in the morning or at night is intended, and at which terminal to expect his guest.

Unnecessary words such as "the," "and," "that," "a," and "I" and minor adverbs and adjectives can be omitted without loss of meaning. Abbreviations, groups of figures, and combinations of letters not forming a dictionary word are counted at the rate of one word for every five letters or fraction of five letters.

In the signature a second identification, such as "Sales Manager," may clarify the telegram and this second identification costs no more than a single name. Street address should be included below the name when it may be needed by the addressee.

When the message is completed, the secretary types the dictator's initials and her own, followed by the sender's street address when the street address is not to be sent. These items are for reference and not for transmittal.

If the addressee is a passenger on a train, bus, or airplane, the telegram can be delivered to him if all the essential information is given:

```
WALLACE BOWMAN
EN ROUTE NEW YORK TO CHICAGO
CARE OF CONDUCTOR (OR LOWER 8, CAR 91)
NYC, TRAIN THREE, DUE 8:10 P.M., BUFFALO, N.Y.
```

or

```
MISS MARY BENTLEY
TWA FLIGHT 402, EASTBOUND
DUE LA GUARDIA AIRPORT, JULY 6, 8:15 P.M.
NEW YORK
```

Whenever the message is in answer to a telegram received and the street address of the sender is unknown, write after the name of the addressee the date of his telegram which you are answering, as "Answer May 29," meaning you are answering his telegram of May 29. Then the originating office will be able to locate the original telegram to facilitate delivery of the answer. Use in place of the regular address the city and telegraph office from which the original telegram was received. The originating telegraph office is the main office in the city unless the name of the city is preceded by identification letters indicating the branch office that transmitted the message. In the following answer address, *MS* identifies the branch office.

```
HAROLD SCOTT, ANSWER MAY 29 MS NEW YORK, N.Y.
```

When you want to wire a person who intends to call at a Western Union office for the message or money order, address the message:

```
R. C. BURTON, CARE WESTERN UNION, COLUMBUS, OHIO
```

When sending a telegram to a person who will register at some later time at a hotel, indicate this information by adding to the message: *Hold for Arrival.*

A "rush message" takes precedence over other typewriting and can be typed without removing material that is already in the typewriter. If you have a carbon pack in your typewriter:

1. Roll the material backward until 1 inch or so is left in front of the platen.
2. Drop a Western Union blank against the paper table and another behind each carbon. Add carbons if necessary.
3. Roll the material forward to position the blank for typing the message.
4. Roll the material backward and remove the telegraph blanks and extra carbons.
5. Position the original material and continue to type.

Code Words. For fewer chargeable words and as a measure of privacy in some cases, code words are devised for names of specific products, stock numbers, titles of publications, names of clients, and so on. It would be quite costly to write these names, numbers, and titles in full each time. Code words are usually of five letters or less, but they may be longer if they are dictionary words.

A public accounting office would not refer to a client by name in a telegram because such identification might divulge confidential information. A code name for the client tells nothing. For example:

```
BACAR INVENTORY $3,250,000.  SURPLUS $950,000.
WARF PAPERS WILL BE SHIPPED FRIDAY.
```

Code systems are classified as private and public. Private code systems are those devised by private business concerns for use in messages with others who are supplied with copies of the code. Public code systems are provided by certain publishers. Messages using code words may be translated by anyone who has a copy of that code system.

■ Filing a Telegram

In telegraph parlance, *filing* a telegram means to get it into the hands of the transmitting agency. A telegraph message can be filed:

Over the counter at the telegraph office
At the teletypist's station in your company
By your Desk-Fax
Over the telephone

The secretary may ask the operator to read the message back so that its correctness can be verified. She should always specify the type of service wanted, for the Western Union operator will send the message as a fast telegram unless some other class of service is specified.

Canceling a Filed Telegram. When the executive wants to cancel a telegram that has been filed, call the transmitting telegraph office immediately. If it is possible to do so, that office will comply with the request. If the message has not left the local office at the time of cancellation, no charge is made. If the message has been communicated to the receiving office before being canceled, however, not only does the original charge for the message stand, but also an additional charge is made for the message to the receiving office regarding the cancellation. In many cases a cancellation is not possible because the message of cancellation can be handled no faster than the original telegram.

Precautionary Measures. Two special services (repeat-back and report-delivery) can be requested on the foregoing types of messages.

Repeat-Back Service. If *Repeat Back* is typed above the address on a telegraph blank, the destination office of the telegraph company will (for an additional charge equal to one half the unrepeated message rate) repeat the message back to the sending office to be checked for possible error. If an error is discovered, the corrected message is then sent at no additional charge. The liability of the telegraph company is increased when this service is used. Although this service is not frequently used, it is advantageous when the message contains technical terms, stock numbers, amounts of money, or code words. The words *Repeat Back* are counted as chargeable words in computing the cost of the message.

A precautionary measure which Western Union provides without charge to business customers such as brokerage houses is to repeat at the bottom of the message received all numbers included. For instance, a telegram notifying a customer that he must pay for 50 shares of stock costing $1343.12 by two o'clock on October 2 would show typed at the bottom of the message "50, $1343.12, 2PM, and 2."

Report-Delivery Service. If the sender wishes the telegraph company to notify him when and to whom delivery of a message is made, *Report Delivery* is typed immediately preceding the address, as "Donald W. Eastman, Report Delivery, Wayne Manufacturing Co., 6012 West...." This instruction counts as two chargeable words. The report stating to whom and when the telegram was delivered is wired back collect from the destination office of the telegraph company to the sender. This service is particularly valuable when you are trying to reach a person who is traveling.

Methods of Paying Telegraph Charges. Several methods of paying for telegraph services are used. Usually those who use these services infrequently pay cash for each message when it is filed. For those who make frequent use of telegrams, the telegraph company keeps a record of the charges and submits a monthly statement. When messages are sent by telephone, they are billed on the telephone company's toll statement, and payment is made to the telephone company, which in turn reimburses the telegraph company. The sender can have the telegraph charges billed directly to his personal account or to the company account.

The telegraph company permits a person to send messages collect —that is, the recipient pays for the sending of the message. A firm may request its customers and sales representatives to send messages collect, in the first instance as a courtesy, and in the second to eliminate handling the charge on the salesmen's expense accounts. Western Union offers a liberal credit policy. A customer need only give his address or telephone number—home or business.

Whether the telegraph charges are billed on a Western Union statement or on the telephone toll statement, the secretary checks them with the file copies of the telegrams. The Western Union accounting office will help in locating discrepancies.

■ Handling Incoming Telegrams

When a telegram comes to your desk, it requires special and prompt handling, for its very use indicates urgency. Therefore, attach to it any pertinent information and give it to the executive at once.

A telegram will come to your desk by one of four ways:

By Desk-Fax

By office teleprinter and delivered to you

By Western Union messenger

By telephone from the Western Union office

If the telephone operator says, "I have a telegram for you," take the message down on your note pad and transcribe to a telegraph blank immediately afterward for easy later identification. It is always wise, however, to ask for a file copy to be sent by mail so that you can verify the message, especially if figures are involved.

If the telegraph company fails to deliver a message or makes an error in the transmission of the message, it is liable for damages. A maximum liability under each of the different circumstances is stated on the back

```
     SYA265 RA383

R FVA253     PD=FAYETTEVILLE NCAR 28 = PM 3 26

SOUTHWESTERN PUBLISHING CO=              19_NOV 28 PM 6 58
      NEW ROCHELLE NY=


PLEASE SEND ME 27 HUNTER PRACTICE SET WITH BUSINESS

PAPERS ( 20TH CENTURY BOOKKEEPING AND ACCOUNTING) 20TH

EDITION. BILL ME.=

        MRS GEORGE DASKAL TAR HEEL SCHOOL TAR HEEL NCAR.
```

of the telegraph blank. The liability is much larger when a message is sent at the "repeat back" rate (page 284).

The form of a delivered telegram is illustrated above. From the second typed line you can ascertain the city from which the message was sent, the day of the month, and the time the message was filed. If it is other than a fast telegram, the type of service in code precedes the name of the city. The first numbers in the line refer to the wire number of the message. The receiving telegraph office time-stamps the message, showing the full date and the exact time the message came into the office.

▪ Other Western Union Services

Western Union renders a number of services other than the transmission of messages. The telegraph company will serve as an intermediary in the transmission of money by means of a *telegraphic money order*. The sender gives the money to the telegraph office, which wires the destination office to pay that amount to a certain person in American Express Travelers' Checks, if desired. The recipient must be able to identify himself. The rates are the same as for a fifteen-word, fast telegram plus a money-order fee. Night-letter money orders are charged at night-letter rates. At a small extra charge a message may be included.

Specialized services include *commercial news service* (such as giving reports on market prices and conditions and news reports) and *time service* (providing clocks that are electrically synchronized with Naval Observatory Time every hour so that they always show official time). Western Union can send *messengers* on business or personal errands.

One of the most useful services to the businessman is the *hotel-motel reservation service* illustrated at the top of page 287. The secretary sends a telegram to Western Union in the city where her employer

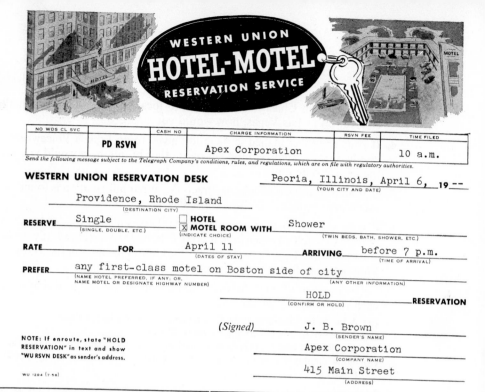

NO WDS CL SVC		CASH NO		CHARGE INFORMATION		RSVN FEE	TIME FILED
PD RSVN				Apex Corporation			10 a.m.

Send the following message subject to the Telegraph Company's conditions, rules, and regulations, which are on file with regulatory authorities.

WESTERN UNION RESERVATION DESK

<u>Peoria, Illinois, April 6,</u> 19--
(YOUR CITY AND DATE)

<u>Providence, Rhode Island</u>
(DESTINATION CITY)

RESERVE <u>Single</u>
(SINGLE, DOUBLE, ETC.)

☐ **HOTEL**
☒ **MOTEL ROOM WITH** <u>Shower</u>
(INDICATE CHOICE)   (TWIN BEDS, BATH, SHOWER, ETC.)

RATE _____ **FOR** <u>April 11</u>
(DATES OF STAY)   **ARRIVING** <u>before 7 p.m.</u>
(TIME OF ARRIVAL)

PREFER <u>any first-class motel on Boston side of city</u>
(NAME HOTEL PREFERRED, IF ANY; OR,
NAME MOTEL OR DESIGNATE HIGHWAY NUMBER)   (ANY OTHER INFORMATION)

<u>HOLD</u>
(CONFIRM OR HOLD) _____ **RESERVATION**

NOTE: If enroute, state "HOLD RESERVATION" in text and show "WU RSVN DESK" as sender's address.

(Signed) <u>J. B. Brown</u>
(SENDER'S NAME)

<u>Apex Corporation</u>
(COMPANY NAME)

<u>415 Main Street</u>
(ADDRESS)

WU 1294 (7-58)

wants a hotel reservation, specifying the type of service wanted (as, "single in first-class hotel"). When the executive arrives at his destination, he telephones the local Western Union office and is told where his reservation has been made.

Operator 25 service localizes national advertising; that is, a national advertiser suggests that the reader, viewer, or listener telephone Operator 25 at the local Western Union office to obtain the names of local dealers handling the product or service advertised.

The secretary may be responsible for sending telegrams of congratulations, condolence, greetings of various kinds, or political endorsement or dissension. Some of these may be special-rate standard-form telegrams for which the suggested messages are available in the Western Union offices. The secretary will want to watch for innovations of new special services which may be attractive to her employer.

Questions for Discussion

1. Think of the business telephone calls you have made. Describe the techniques that have pleased you and those that have annoyed you.
2. The telephone company recommends that executives answer their own Centrex telephones. Which would be most likely to follow this practice: the president of the company or the sales manager?

3. If you were in Chicago and wanted to locate a good hotel and make a reservation in Las Vegas, how would you proceed?

4. If your employer mailed in dictation given to an Edison Voicewriter and you had transcribing equipment of another brand, how would you locate the appropriate unit?

5. Examine your local telephone directory. What information is found in the introductory pages? in the Yellow Pages?

6. If your office is located in Philadelphia, between what office hours would you try to reach an office in Salt Lake City by long distance? If your office is in Salt Lake City, between what office hours would you try to reach the Philadelphia office by long distance?

7. Tell what class of long distance service you would use in trying to reach each of the following persons:
    (a) A buyer in a leather goods department of a department store
    (b) A lawyer who is pleading an important case
    (c) A politician who is staying in a hotel in which you made his reservation
    (d) Your employer's son who lives in a college dormitory not equipped with Centrex

8. In handling incoming local calls, tape record or role-play exactly what you would say if your employer is—
    (a) At the bank to get some papers from his safe deposit box
    (b) In conference with the president of the firm
    (c) On a sales trip in another state and not due back for several days
    (d) At a local print shop to check on a catalog being printed for your company
    (e) At the state capitol working on the phrasing of a bill that is to go before the legislature

9. Criticize or comment upon the secretarial procedure in each of the following situations:
    (a) The secretary is asked to call the executive's home. She locates the number in the alphabetic telephone directory and makes the call.
    (b) When the telephone rings, the secretary picks up the receiver and says, "Mr. Kline's office, Miss Francis speaking." After a moment she says, "Please hold the line while I get a pencil and paper."
    (c) When the executive returns after an hour's absence from the office, his secretary gives him a detailed oral report on five incoming telephone calls.
    (d) An executive asks his secretary to call the telephone company and report that his telephone has not been working satisfactorily. She returns to her desk and dials 411, which is the number for Information.

10. When a call between two executives is being connected by their secretaries, the question may come up as to which executive should be placed on the line first to await the answer of the other executive. What is your opinion?

11. Type the following excerpts of conversation in acceptable form. Then use the Reference Guide to verify or correct your answers.
    (a) The opening part of a telephone conversation which occurred this Monday, shortly before noon. Mr. Lawrence Bell called Mr. Thomas Green.

Bell—Tom, have you come to a decision yet? Green—No, I'd like a day or two more to think it over. Bell—Time is getting short, Tom. I have to know by Wednesday at the latest. Green—I'll sleep on it and let you know the first thing in the morning.

(b) A confidential memorandum to the president of the company, reporting on a conversation which occurred in the executive's office two weeks ago today between Steve Douglas and Charles Duncan.

This is the conversation as I recall it. Steve said I talked it over with Nelson, very confidentially of course, and he thought he could arrange a meeting before the end of this month. Charles said do you think it was wise to expose our hand. Steve said I don't think talking it over with Nelson can be called exposing our hand. He's trustworthy. Charles said well it's done now. What about the meeting?

(c) In the middle of a paragraph—

We have it on good authority that he said I'll be very much pleased if we receive a bid as low as $100,000. (end of direct quotation) For that reason I think we are on pretty firm ground bidding $99,500.

12. What precautionary measures can the secretary take to assure more effective telegraph services, both sending and receiving?

13. Would you suggest establishing a rule that a verification copy be sent to the addressee of every telegram? Why?

14. What advantages do you see to using Western Union hotel-motel reservation service? what disadvantages?

15. What class of telegraphic service should be used in each of the following situations:

(a) At 3 p.m. a secretary in Seattle, Washington, is given a 30-word telegraphic message to send as quickly as possible to an office in Boston, Massachusetts, which closes at 5 p.m.

(b) At 11:30 a.m. a secretary in Albany, New York, has a 40-word message to be sent to a firm in Butte, Montana. The message should be delivered the same day.

(c) At 10:30 a.m. a secretary in Oklahoma City is instructed to send a 120-word message to a firm in Salem, Oregon. A delay of a few hours in the delivery of the message is not important.

(d) At 3:30 p.m. a secretary in Minneapolis is given a 15-word message to be sent to a firm in Montgomery, Alabama. It is important that the message should be delivered as quickly as possible.

16. What instructions would you include, or what service would you request, in sending a telegram:

(a) To a person en route by train

(b) To a person who will register at some later time at a hotel

(c) To either of two persons at the same address

(d) To a person traveling by automobile who is expecting a message at a Western Union office in a specific city

(e) On which you wish to know when delivery was made

(f) Which *must* be delivered exactly as filed

17. Assuming that the following words came at the ends of typewritten lines, indicate those words that you could correctly divide and show where you would make the divisions. Then use the Reference Guide to verify or correct your answers.

freight	profit-taking	science
Anderson	forgotten	February 26
half-brother	holiday	mailable
foundation	selling	into

Problems

■ **1.** Locate in the alphabetic section of your local telephone directory the numbers for the following. Type in tabular form a list showing for each item the organization or department wanted, the name under which the telephone is listed, and the telephone number.

(a) City hall
(b) Western Union
(c) Fire department
(d) Park or recreation department
(e) Police department
(f) Post office
(g) Public library
(h) The nearest hospital
(i) Your college or university
(j) The local office of the state employment service

■ **2.** The purpose of this problem is to help you become familiar with the organization of your Yellow Pages.

Type a list showing the heading in the Yellow Pages under which you would find the names of subscribers for each of the types indicated in the following list:

(a) Agents for calculating machines
(b) Certified public accountants
(c) Dealers in advertising stickers
(d) Dealers in traveling bags
(e) Dealers in window screens
(f) Dealers in window shades
(g) Income tax specialists
(h) Interior decorators

(i) Lawyers
(j) Ministers

■ **3.** Telephone manners require that one use courtesy and tact in phrasing. The following is a list of poor expressions used in telephone conversations. Rephrase courteous statements in typewritten form.

(a) I'll put Mr. Crawford on the wire.
(b) Who's this?
(c) Hold the 'phone.
(d) Who do you want to talk to?
(e) What do you want to talk to Mr. Crawford about?
(f) I can't hear you!
(g) OK, I'll see that it is taken care of.
(h) Mr. Crawford left word that he is not to be disturbed; I'll take the message.
(i) I want you to have him call Mr. Crawford before 2 o'clock.

■ **4.** Assume that your employer, Robert L. Simpson, wishes to make the following out-of-town call from the office telephone, 351-6866, on the current date. Exactly how would you place the call?

A person-to-person call to Dr. E. B. Snyder, of Fort Worth, Texas, relative to a personal matter. You do not know his number or address, but he is a noted eye specialist.

■ **5.** Rewrite each of the following telegraph messages, using not more than 15 words so that the message may be sent as a regular telegram.

(a) THERE WILL BE A SALES
MEETING SATURDAY
MORNING IN THE OFFICE
AT TEN O'CLOCK.
PLEASE ARRANGE TO BE
THERE. BRING RE-
QUESTED ESTIMATES.

(b) MR. WILCOX WIRED
SAYING HE WOULD BE
HERE TOMORROW. IS
IT POSSIBLE FOR YOU
TO COME BACK? MUST
KNOW BY THREE
O'CLOCK.

(c) IN ANSWER YOUR TELE-
GRAM SUGGEST YOU
OFFER A 40% DISCOUNT
TERMS 2% 10 DAYS.
DELIVERY TO BE MADE
FOB NEW YORK.

■ **6.** Type each of the following
telegrams and determine the number of chargeable words. If a word
or a group of letters, figures, and
characters represents more than
one chargeable word, underscore
the item and indicate by a small
figure beneath the underscore the
number of chargeable words
included. Omit spaces where permitted if savings in word counts will
result.

(a) CHANGE CATALOG GROSS
PRICES ON AS123 TO
$117.92; 10B19 TO
$192.21; 15X102128 TO
$85.72.

(b) STOCK EXHAUSTED ON
KNRP, KNRPVO, AND VT.

(c) ENJOYED SEEING LOCKS
AT SAULT STE MARIE.
HEADING FOR CANADA
TODAY. RETURNING TO
UNITED STATES 10 P.M.
WEDNESDAY. FEELING
OK.

(d) CHANGE 1½ TO 7½ IN
17TH LINE ON PAGE 21
OF PLUMBING SPECIFI-
CATIONS.

Related Work Assignments 34-36

34. Reporting Incoming Telephone Calls. The following incoming telephone
calls were received while your employer, Mr. Simpson, was out of the office.
Fill out a brief memorandum for Mr. Simpson on each call.

   (a) Mr. Kiley called at 3:25 p.m. and left a message that he would pick up your
   employer at 5:10 p.m. at the front entrance to the building.

   (b) Mr. Mellon, of the District Sales Corporation, called at 3:30 p.m.; he stated
   he would call back at 4:30 p.m.

   (c) Mr. Wilcox, of National Products, Inc., called at 4 p.m. about their order for
   equipment and wants you to call him back. His number is 243-4891.

   (d) Mr. Roberts, of the Cleveland office, called long distance at 4:10 p.m. to tell
   you that the Fuller Implement Company order is to be canceled. A letter of
   explanation will be put in the mail tonight.

35. Annotating Telephone Calls ⎫ The instructions and supplies necessary for
36. Composing and Typing ⎬ the completion of Related Work Assign-
   Messages ⎭ ments 35-36 are provided in the Workbook.

Special Telephone and Telegraphic Services

Breakthroughs in electronic data processing and transmission are revolutionizing telephone and telegraph services. Potentialities for sending voice, picture, typed or longhand messages and volume data have increased so vastly that telephone and telegraph companies are challenged by newcomers to the data-communication field who are introducing new machines and devices into an increasingly competitive field.

In Chapter 12 the customary uses of the telephone and telegram were described. In this chapter more specialized telephone and telegraph services are discussed. The executive secretary in the modern office will be expected to use at least some of these services and to understand them as part of a system of communication. She may find herself in a position to recommend such services to increase her own or office effectiveness. The Bell System and Western Union, as well as other corporations in the business communications area, provide free consultation service to business customers so that businesses can organize their facilities into a complete, effective communications system.

Until recently each separate department within a branch of a corporation operated as a separate unit, and weekend, month-end, or year-end reports were made to administrators of the branch. Reports from each branch were mailed to headquarters, where they served as bases for decision making. Data processing equipment (fully described in Chapter 18) has changed all this. A transaction becomes part of a cumulative report almost as soon as it is completed. Even more remarkable, this report in whole or in part is transmitted to headquarters or to other operating units immediately.

Improved business-communication telephone and telegraphic services "reduce the distance" between branches or plants and headquarters and lower costs of quantity transmission. They enable management to base decisions on more current and complete information and to control and coordinate operations throughout the company.

Communication systems use both telephone and telegraphic transmission, and the services described next are often a part of a company's total communication system.

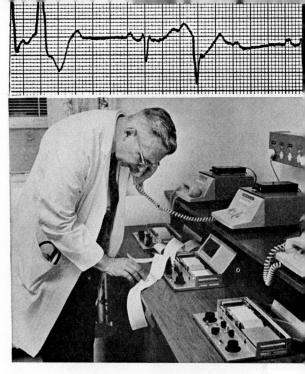

Reproduced at the right is an electro-cardiogram transmitted through Bell System Data-Phone service to a cardiac specialist for his diagnosis.

—Western Electric

The Nature of Today's Communication System

All forms of data may be transmitted from a point of origin with appropriate sending equipment to any distant point with appropriate receiving equipment: handwritten or typed messages, processed or unprocessed data, pictures, or voice.

■ Teleprinting Machines

Western Union and others have for many years used the teleprinter for sending messages. The operator types the message, which is reproduced on perforated tape. The paper tape is then fed into an automatic transmitter that sends a message to a high-speed message center in a nearby central city. There an electronic "brain," acting on codes previously punched into the tape, routes the message through the proper circuits. The words travel across the country at the speed of light. Seconds later another tape—a duplicate of the original one prepared in your local telegraph office—is punched automatically in the destination switching center, where it is quickly translated back into regular characters on the receiving teleprinter, for delivery.

New uses for teleprinters have developed, and businesses have installed teleprinters suited to their own needs. Teleprinters have improved as technology has improved, so messages can now be sent not only by

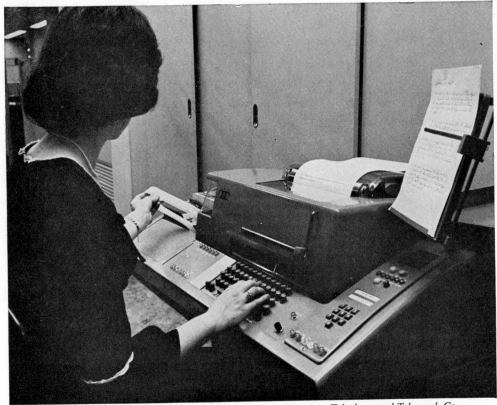

A fast, efficient way to communicate in written form, the TWX dial service gives your business versatile and reliable written communications on a message rate basis. Messages may be transmitted at 100 words a minute.

keyboard but by other means, such as data on punched tape and cards sent via electromagnetic waves. The print-out may be page copy, printed tape, or punched tape.

Teleprinters or teletypewriters are used by large companies for intercompany and intracompany communication. A teletypist calls the other operator in another location. Once the connection is established, operators at the two machines converse by typing back and forth or by feeding paper tape to the equipment for automatic transmission of the message. Teletypewritten communication is similar to a telephone conversation, except that the message is written instead of oral. An advantage over the telephone is that you have a printed record of both the sent and the received message.

Automatic teleprinter exchange switching services are provided by Western Union (*Telex*) and by the Bell System *Teletypewriter Exchange Service* (*TWX*).

▪ Tone Transmission

The key to the development of a business information system is the *compatibility* of equipment used for processing and transmitting information. Most computers being designed are compatible with communication channels or can, by addition of more equipment, be made so. Increasingly, computers will be able both to process and to transmit data or switch it to channels that can transmit it.

Data sets can be used to achieve compatibility between business machines. The data set converts the business-machine signals into tones which can be sent over communications facilities. A similar data set receives the transmitted tones and reconverts them into business-machine signals.

Data-Phone. Data-Phone data sets transmit data over the regular telephone network, using a telephone-like device connected to compatible business machines. The distant telephone is contacted, the Data-Phone data set turned on, and the data converted into tones and sent over telephone lines.

Automatic Calling Unit. A Data-Phone data set may be equipped with an Automatic Calling Unit (Data Auxiliary Set) that enables it to connect and disconnect automatically with a Data-Phone data set at some distant station in a communication network. This allows for a totally unattached arrangement for data transmission.

Touch-Tone Service. Keyboard devices can also generate tones that can be transmitted. One such device is the new Touch-Tone telephone, used for both regular service and data communications. Its electronic keys reduce the average dialing time from nine to four seconds. At the receiving end of this push-button telephone, the tones are converted to the electrical signals that activate a business machine to reproduce the original transmitted data.

The new push-button *Touch-Tone* telephone, unlike its predecessor dial telephone, is thus used for data transmission. With a Touch-Tone telephone, a user may connect with a computer and send and receive

Heralding a new era in communications, on a Touch-Tone telephone the dial is replaced by pushbuttons. As each button is pressed, two simultaneous tones are generated and transmitted to a central switching office, then translated into a series of pulses similar to those made by the standard telephone dial. It is in production by Western Electric.

information. Small business share the use of a computer in preparing and billing orders, in controlling inventory, and in keeping books of account. Depositors can order the computer to charge their bank accounts for purchases. Doctors and dentists can use Touch-Tone telephones to send a computer information for billing purposes.

▪ Xerography

Xerox, too, is experimenting, especially with transmittal of facsimile copies of documents through regular telephone circuits. The operator dials the recipient, places a document in the *Magnafax* unit, and drops the telephone receiver into a cradle. Six minutes later a clear facsimile is reproduced 3,000 miles away by *Long Distance Xerography*.

Incidentally, the suffix *-Fax* refers to transmittal of facsimile copies. For instance, *Desk-Fax* is Western Union equipment designed for the

This especially designed pushbutton telephone is used by subscribers to Western Union's "Broadband Exchange Service" to select bandwidths and make connections, in seconds, with other subscribers to transmit data or facsimile and, alternately, to talk.

—*Western Union*

desk of the secretary for receiving and sending messages to the local Western Union office. *Intrafax* is an interoffice transmittal system for sending pictorial, written, typed, or printed matter. *Ticket-Fax* reproduces an airplane or railroad ticket at a receiving center in eight seconds. *High-Speed Fax* can send a whole 20-page magazine, including illustrations, in a few minutes.

▪ Broadband Exchange Service

Broadband Exchange Service, developed by Western Union, automatically links two subscribers over bands of greater width, providing greater speed and transmission of varying kinds of data that common voice carriers cannot handle with their narrower band width.

▪ The Future of Communication Systems

Today it is possible to communicate from department to department, from branch to headquarters, from company to company, from computer center to and from company, with pertinent information available to the inquirer only rather than displayed to all subscribers simultaneously. Many companies are entering the business-communications

IBM's Tele-Processor makes it possible to supply pertinent information to one subscriber only, rather than display it to all subscribers.

system competition. In addition to Western Union and various components of the telephone system, there are, among many others, Xerox and IBM. IBM has developed two time-sharing computer communications services *Quiktran* and *Tele-processing*—linking computers to isolated customers and computers to computers. Through a "dial-a-document" system introduced by Alden Electronic & Impulse Recording Equipment Co., Inc., it is possible to dial a number and retrieve almost instantly any full-size document stored in a centralized microfilm center.

Most large information systems today are *dedicated* (leased to and serving a single customer). However, equipment in central-processing computer service centers can be made compatible with business equipment already in use so that a company whose volume does not justify purchasing a computer can lease computer service in another location.

Western Union is developing a vast real-time (see page 451) computer communications complex called the National Information Utility, which will distribute information services or computer power needed to conduct its subscribers' business locally, regionally, and nationally, just as an electric utility distributes electrical service to all subscribers.

Extended Services

The preceding section describes technical developments that are to a large extent informational to the secretary. These developments have, however, provided her with extended services which she should be able to handle capably.

▪ Wide Area Telephone Service (WATS)

WATS service enables the user to place an unlimited number of calls within a specific radius of his place of business for a flat-rate monthly fee, unlimited in either number or length of calls. A measured-time service is also available that provides ten hours of unlimited calls.

The country is divided, for WATS service, into six geographic areas ranging in size from Area I, which usually covers only neighboring states, to Area VI, which extends from coast to coast.

One type of company may need expanded long distance service to only one or possibly two zones, while another may need WATS service covering all six areas. One company may want unlimited calls, while another may need only a limited number of calls and may want to restrict the length of calls. With WATS, abuses of the long distance privilege sometimes occur, so each subscriber develops its own means of controlling calls. The secretary should be exemplary in her use of the WATS privilege.

▪ Extended Area Service (EAS)

The concept of Extended Area Service (EAS) reflects the larger community of interest that exists in metropolitan areas. A business located in Washington, D.C., that wishes "local" service to suburbs (such as Alexandria, Virginia; and Silver Springs, Maryland) could purchase reduced-rate EAS at a flat monthly fee. The extent of use of such service is shown by the fact that more than a third of the calls handled as long distance calls 20 years ago now go through as local.

▪ Leased Lines

It is possible for a company to lease telegraph and telephone lines for its exclusive use.

The use of a Speakerphone adds greatly to the efficiency and convenience of conference calls.

—*American Telephone and Telegraph Company*

Tie-Line Service. The tie-line connects different locations within a business complex. The lines may be in different parts of the same city or in different cities. They provide direct contact with separate units of a business and can be used to transmit data.

Foreign-Exchange Service (FX). A local telephone number in a location removed from the site of a plant or company headquarters can be listed so that the call made to the listed number goes through as a local call: The New York City directory might carry the number of a firm located in New Brunswick, New Jersey, as NYC 987-6640.

▪ Conference Call

A *conference call* is placed when the caller wants to talk simultaneously with several persons at different locations. An executive may want to get a group opinion on an idea, or to announce design or price changes or a policy decision. The secretary calls the number for long distance, asks for the conference operator, and gives the locations and names of persons to be talked with, sometimes specifying the time the call is to be put through. From three to fourteen long distance points can be connected for a *two-way* conference call. With specialized equipment such as a Speakerphone shown in the picture above or a loudspeaker, several persons may listen in on a call at any one location. Up to 49 points can be connected for a *one-way* conference call (one in which the voice of only the caller is transmitted).

With recent innovations in equipment, it is sometimes possible to set up conference calls without the services of the operator. Also, with the *Add-On* feature, a caller already engaged in a two-way conversation can add a third person to the call.

An improved mobile telephone service provides all features of regular telephone service. Users can dial directly over the nationwide network, and the need for "push-to-talk" operation has been eliminated. This motor-vehicle service is being extended as rapidly as possible.

—American Telephone and Telegraph Co.

■ Mobile Service

More than 25,000 customers have mobile telephone service. These customers include trucks, news services, private automobiles, buses, planes, and trains and many other mobile users. Anyone can make a call to mobile equipment from any telephone, and any telephone can receive a call from mobile equipment. To place a call to a mobile telephone, either dial the number or contact the mobile service operator. The conversation travels part way by radio and part way by telephone wire.

■ Overseas Service

The extension of American business to foreign countries and the increased interaction between American and foreign companies has made overseas service increasingly common.

Telephone. To call almost any point in the world by telephone, the caller dials the operator and gives the country to be called, the name of the company wanted, and the name of the person to be reached. Of course, it is essential to consult the time zone (page 303) and to check with the local operator or directory for the times during which the various rates apply.

Telegraph. Increased capabilities are available through Western Union International, Inc., which provides *Datel* services, high-speed combined message and data communications; *Telex* world-wide service between correspondents in 100 countries; leased-wire voice-data

Using a Telex, the operator is dialing the number of another subscriber. When each operator has identified himself on the other's typed copy, the sender will type the message on her teleprinter for transmittal and recording on the receiving teleprinter.

—Western Union Telegraph Company

circuits; and Imco, a customer-to-customer metered communication system between the United States and the United Kingdom.

International Telegraph Services

A secretary who uses international service frequently should procure from the nearest telegraph office their literature concerning this service. Overseas telegraph communications are sent either by underwater cables (*cablegrams*) or by radio (*radiograms*). Overseas cables or radiograms are sent through RCA Global Communications. Since RCA offices are not found in all cities, Western Union offices accept overseas telegrams and pass them along to RCA for transmittal.

▪ Classes of International Service

Classes of international services include full-rate telegram, letter telegram, cable money orders, and IMCO service.

Full Rate; Letter Telegram. There are two basic classes of international service—*Full Rate (FR)* and *Letter Telegram (LT)*. These services are summarized in the table on page 304.

Cable Money Orders. Cable money orders are sent in the same way that Western Union money orders are sent. The money is deposited with the local office for payment abroad. Only full-rate service is available.

IMCO Service. *IMCO* (International Metered Communications) is a private customer-to-customer cablegram service between the United States and the United Kingdom for New York and London firms guaranteeing to do cable business costing at least $500 a month.

This world time-zone map will help the secretary in planning overseas communications. Refer also to page 275 for a time-zone map of the United States.

▪ Codes and Ciphers

Because one code word may mean several plain-language words, code language is frequently used in cables. Code words are composed entirely of letters. They may be real or artificial words, but they must not contain more than five letters. In an international message the use of code words lowers the cost of the message. For example, the one code word KALOP may be used to cover the statements "We authorize you to act for us. Will confirm this by mail."

A.B.C., Acme, Bentley's, and the Western Union codes are used most frequently. If you decide to use a private code, check with the telegraph company used to determine whether this code will be acceptable in the country to which the cablegram is sent.

Cipher words are generally composed of figures or of letters exceeding five per group, not fulfilling the requirements of code or plain language. Cipher language is used for secrecy. In a message composed of a combination of code, cipher, and plain language, the code and cipher words are chargeable at the rate of five characters to the word, while the plain language is charged at the rate of fifteen letters to the word. The use of code and cipher is permissible only in the address and signature portions of letter telegrams and is permissible in all parts of full-rate messages.

Obviously, a full-rate message will be chosen only if time and code are of the essence.

	Full Rate (FR)	Letter Telegram (LT)
Indicator Preceding Address	No indicator necessary	LT
Charge for Indicator	——	LT chargeable as 1 word; inserted immediately preceding the address
Precedence of Transmission	Takes precedence over all other messages	Delivery at destination next morning
Language	Plain language, secret (cipher or code), or a combination	Plain language, but code may be used in address and signature
Word Length	Plain language: 15 letters to a word <u>Cipher or code language:</u> 5 characters to a word	15 letters to a word
Minimum Number of Words	5	22
Relationship of Rates	Based on distance message is sent	One half of full rate

▪ Counting Words in International Messages

The basic principles in counting chargeable matter in international messages are as follows:

1. Count each word in address (except country of destination and routing designation for which there is no charge), text, and signature.

2. Count each plain language dictionary word at the rate of 15, or fraction of 15, characters to the word.

3. Count each secret language nondictionary word at the rate of 5, or fraction of 5, characters per word. (Not admitted in letter telegrams or press messages)

4. Count groups of figures, letters, signs, or a mixture of them where authorized, at the rate of 5 characters per word.

5. Place names:
   (a) In address—if destination point is a compound name, join it and count the name as one word, regardless of length.
   (b) In text and signature—count at the rate of 15 characters per word as written by sender.

6. **Punctuation:**
   (a) **In figure or letter groups—count as 1** *character* **each.**
   (b) **In normal sense in text—count as 1** *word* **each (transmitted only on specific request of sender).**
   (c) **Acceptable signs are:** . , : ? ' - — ( ) " /
7. **Special characters or symbols should be spelled out because they cannot be transmitted:** ¢ $ @ & # £

▪ Cable Addresses

Except for the destination country, each word in the name, address, and signature is counted as a chargeable word in a cablegram; therefore, a one-word cable address saves words in both incoming and outgoing messages. For a small annual charge cable address may be registered at any telegraph office. It cannot duplicate another already on file.

Frequently a firm in this country and its foreign correspondent will register an identical cable address and restrict its use to the exclusive exchange of messages between themselves. This procedure is known as a reversible address and obviates the need for a signature on messages, thus saving the cost of one word.

New Services

Special equipment of many types is available so that the telephone can be tailored to the user's needs. In addition to items discussed previously, the following supplementary services may be obtained from the telephone company for a surcharge or purchased from the vendor.

▪ The Speakerphone

The *Speakerphone* has built-in transmitter and volume control so that both sides of a conversation can be amplified. The secretary can leave the telephone, walk to the opposite side of the office, look up information in a file, and read it to the caller from this location. The caller can be heard in various parts of the room; and vice versa, the caller can hear comments and discussions with others in the room. This equipment expands opportunities for full communication during conference calls. It is also possible to telephone lectures that may be amplified for delivery to class and conference groups. The Speakerphone is illustrated on page 300.

The Bell System's new Model II Picturephone set can be used to transmit drawings or charts by setting the camera focus at one foot. In the photograph, the "self-view" option is being used to position the graph while it is being transmitted.

—American Telephone and Telegraph Company

▪ Picturephone

Initial Picturephone service was introduced between New York, Washington, and Chicago so that people can make see-while-you-talk calls from certain locations. As time goes on, there will be a large increase in visual communication — in educational television, in business, and between people who prefer to see each other when they talk.

With Picturephone it is possible to have face-to-face discussion or demonstrations and presentations. To arrange for Picturephone service, the secretary should call for an appointment, for immediate transmission is not yet possible.

▪ Bellboy Service

Bellboy is a personal signaling service. A salesman, for instance, can put the compact, lightweight unit in his pocket. When his associates wish to get in touch with him, they merely dial his Bellboy number as they would dial any telephone number. Bellboy begins to buzz. The salesman goes to a nearby telephone and calls his office for a message.

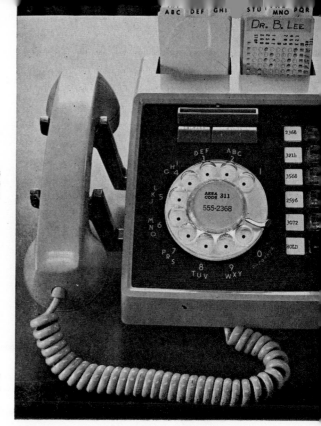

The secretary whose work demands the repeated calling of the same numbers will find the Card Dialer a valuable time-saver.

—American Telephone and Telegraph Company

■ The Card Dialer

The Card Dialer enables a user to reach frequently dialed numbers by placing a punched-hole plastic card into the telephone and pushing the start bar.

Cards are stored at the back of the telephone within easy reach of the user, as illustrated above.

■ Individualized Equipment

Color telephones, light-weight Princess telephones, Trim-line telephones with the dial embedded in the receiver (especially attractive to those who see poorly), in-desk telephones, and panel telephones for side-of-desk or wall placement—all are available to attract the user who wants individualized equipment.

■ Breakthroughs in Improved Telephone Service

In 1965 the Bell Systems started operation of their first completely electronic central office in a small community in New Jersey. In this center is an *Automatic Call Distributor*, which "stores" calls and assigns them to open lines in the order of their reception. Waiting time for open lines is thus virtually eliminated.

—Western Electric

The Call-a-matic enables the user to press a call button to telephone any of 500 numbers listed on the revolving directory at the right side of the telephone. The name of the person to be called is first positioned in the directory's center slot. Magnetic tape is used for rapid electronic dialing.

Fully electronic switching apparatus enables the storage unit to "remember" a personal telephone list so that the caller can reach these numbers by dialing only one or two digits instead of seven. If the number called is already engaged, the person using the telephone at that number hears a "beep" that tells him that a second call is waiting.

All of these innovations and many more are ahead for those communicating by telephone. Undoubtedly, similar improvements, for which the secretary should be alert, will continue to develop rapidly.

It should be noted that all of the capitalized names of telephonic devices given in these chapters are registered and owned by the Bell System.

—American Telephone and Telegraph Co.

The 4A Desk-Top Switchboard controls up to ten trunks and sixty telephones. It is used generally in a medium-sized business where a maximum of 10 trunks and 60 stations will be needed. Direct station selection and busy-station indication are the most outstanding characteristics of this console.

Questions for Discussion

1. What is the difference between special listings such as "Enterprise," tie-line, and Foreign-Exchange service?
2. What is the difference between EAS and WATS?
3. What considerations would affect your decision to send a full-rate international message rather than a letter telegram?
4. How can we say that Western Union is serving business better than it ever has when the telegram is used less than it was?
5. Name two types of business information that might advantageously be transmitted between each of the following business communication points: department to department, branch to headquarters, company to company, and company computer to computer service center?

6. Contrast the advantages of a computer leased to a company versus linkage to a time-sharing computer service center.

7. What recent innovations in equipment have speeded up telephone service?

8. In what ways is the secretary involved in data communication?

9. What considerations would affect your decision to send a full-rate international message rather than a letter telegram?

Problems

■ **1.** If you were employed by a well-equipped corporation headquarters, which type of communication would you probably choose in the following situations? Tell why you chose the medium you did.

(a) A message to the governor requesting that he sign a bill that is on his desk

(b) A message to three sales managers in different locations (A reaction is necessary from each of the three.)

(c) A message informing the payroll department in a branch office that data required for issuing paychecks has not been received

(d) A message containing detailed information about production schedules of a branch factory for the next two months

(e) A message to inquire about prices of a well-known office machine manufactured in a nearby suburb

(f) A message to the president of the company en route to Europe by ship (The message is information about an important interview in London.)

(g) A message to a salesman 500 miles away, asking him to call on a prospective customer

(h) A message to the production manager in a branch factory 500 miles away

(i) A message requesting information of a bank in Englewood, New Jersey from your office in New York City (Englewood is just across the Hudson River.)

(j) A message that must reach 12 salesmen in different locations within three hours

(k) A message to the president of the company en route to Europe by ship (The message requires an immediate answer.)

(l) A message sent on opening day expressing good wishes to the manager of a new restaurant for which your company provided the steel used in construction

(m) A message that will be received after closing hours but must be available when the office opens the following morning

(n) A graph to be used tomorrow in a national sales meeting

■ **2.** Develop a bibliography of ten articles published within the past six months describing innovations in data communication. Of what value was this investigation?

■ **3.** Visit the teletypewriter, Telex, TWX, or Data-Phone installation in one corporation and report to the class the uses being made of the equipment.

Related Work Assignments 37-38

37. **Foreign Telephone Calls**
38. **Measuring Your Secretarial Information and Judgment (Parts 3 and 4)**

The instructions and supplies necessary for the completion of Related Work Assignments 37 and 38 are provided in the Workbook.

PART 4   Case Problems

4—1 √ transmittal of material

Mr. Howard Hart is sales manager of the New Era Publishing Company, whose home office is in Boston. Mr. Hart is preparing for the annual sales conference for 45 salesmen.

This year the meeting is to be held at the Roosevelt Hotel in New Orleans on October 6–10. The meeting has been scheduled at this location in an effort to reduce travel expense. Mr .Hart realizes, however, that getting the necessary materials to the meeting will be difficult. He plans to fly to the meeting, and he asks you, his secretary, to arrange that everything he will need be sent ahead by the appropriate class of service.

Mr. Hart wants the materials sent to Willis Williams, manager of the New Era branch office at 18 Canal Street, New Orleans 70102. Here is the list of items Mr. Hart will need:

50 copies of the September issue of *Sales Management* magazine to be distributed to all salesmen—ready September 10

2 copies of *Mathematics for Today* just received from the printer and not yet seen by the salesmen—ready now

1 copy of the new sales film, *New Era in Selling Books Around the World*—ready September 15

50 copies of the complete sales analysis for the preceding year—ready September 15

50 copies of an 80-page sales catalog to be distributed to the 45 salesmen; 1,000 catalogs to be sent to each salesman at his local address for use upon his return from the conference—ready September 23

50 copies of a 42-page report on 15 new books to be published by March 1. All pages except those covering the last book—ready October 1. The last report—ready October 5

50 copies of a sales-promotion calendar under consideration for December distribution—ready October 1

50 copies of the proposed new sales territory assignment—ready October 1

50 copies of the agenda for the meeting—ready October 2

50 copies of the expense-account form for the annual conference—ready October 2

50 copies of a proposed revision outline of Hughes' *French in the Elementary School* to be undertaken next year—ready October 2

50 copies of an evaluation form for the proposed revision—ready October 2

2 copies of Mr. Hart's speech to open the conference—ready October 4

1 copy of a new manuscript Mr. Hart wants to discuss with the West Coast regional sales manager—ready October 5

2 "Retirement" watches for senior salesmen, to be presented at the final dinner—engraving to be completed October 6

45 bonus checks to be a surprise for the salesmen—ready October 9 (Mr. Hart thinks that presenting them at the final dinner will have a better psychological effect than mailing them to the men.)

Develop a master plan (preferably in table form) for getting the materials to Mr. Hart. Indicate the method and the date for sending each item.

4—2 √ absenteeism

Helen Addison is employed in the law firm of Franklin and Associates. There are four girls in the office; and since Miss Addison is secretary to Mr. Franklin, the senior member of the firm, she is expected to supervise the work of the office. Mr. Franklin generally delegates to Miss Addison the employing of replacements in the office when a vacancy occurs.

Miss Mary Rogers has been on the staff approximately three months. The only criticism of her work is her absenteeism. Mary's time record shows that she is absent an average of two to three Mondays each month.

Mary's regular absence on Monday creates a workload problem in the office. She is assigned to Mr. Rawlings, one of the junior lawyers in the office. Another secretary must take his dictation and handle his appointments on the Mondays Mary is absent.

When Miss Addison discusses the matter with Mary, Mary reports that she is generally tired from the weekend and doesn't feel too well on Monday morning. She uses Monday to rest up so she will be in shape for the rest of the week. Mary points out that she is permitted 30 sick-leave days each year; and if she prefers to take them all on Monday, that should be her prerogative. Miss Addison suggests that Mary curb her weekend activities and possibly relax on Sunday so she will feel like coming to work on Monday. Mary replies that what she does on her own time is her own business. She points out that she shares an apartment with two other secretaries—that they also often miss work on Monday and their employers expect it.

At the next meeting of the National Secretaries Association (International), Miss Addison learns from other members that absenteeism on Monday is a serious problem in a number of offices, especially with the younger, unmarried girls—greater, in fact, than on all the other days put together.

Girls with legal experience and ability to handle legal dictation are difficult to locate. Mary's work is of a very high quality. She is well liked. Mr. Rawlings considers her the best secretary he has ever had—far superior to the girls who do his work when Mary is absent.

When Miss Addison discusses the matter with Mr. Franklin, he instructs her to take any action she feels necessary. If you were Miss Addison, what action would you take?

4 — 3 √ mailing list conversion

Mr. Reed is Vice President (Marketing) for Business Education Publishers, Inc. As his secretary, you have been asked to develop a pilot plan for converting an addressograph mailing list to a computer-assisted one. As the pilot or trial run, it has been decided to convert selected addresses for the four-year colleges in the state of Arizona.

The addresses that are to be converted are given below. The following modifications are necessary:

1. The appropriate two-letter state name abbreviation that has been specified for ZIP must be obtained from the list on Reference Guide page 769.
2. The ZIP Code that is appropriate for the address must be determined from the official *ZIP Code Directory*.
3. An identification number must be supplied, consisting of the ZIP Code for the school address, a school identification number, and a teacher identification number—in that order.

Use the following plan to establish an appropriate identification number for each address:

1. The ZIP Code you determined for the address itself is to be used as the first number for identification.
2. Schools whose names begin with "A" should be assigned numbers from the series 001 through 010; those whose names begin with "B" should be assigned numbers from the series 011 through 020; etc.
3. Addresses in the business teacher education department should be assigned numbers from the series 101 through 200; those in the office and distributive department should be assigned numbers from the series 201 through 300.

When the appropriate identification numbers have been determined, type the address list in appropriate form for evaluation by Mr. Reed. Type the identification number *above* each address to conform to the order required by the optical scanner.

The computer has a maximum capacity of thirty typewriter strokes per line; therefore, abbreviation is necessary.

00000-000-000	00000-000-000	00000-000-000
Dr. Gordon C. Glenn, Chairman Business Teacher Education Arizona State University Tempe, ?? 00000	Dr. Neal R. French, Chairman Business Teacher Education University of Arizona Tucson, ?? 00000	Dr. Adele L. Lewis, Chairman Business Teacher Education Northern Arizona University Flagstaff, ?? 00000
00000-000-000	00000-000-000	00000-000-000
Miss Elizabeth Higgins, Head Office and Distributive Educ. Arizona State University Tempe, ?? 00000	Dr. S. J. Thompson, Head Office and Distributive Educ. University of Arizona Tucson, ?? 00000	Mr. Arnold C. Hill, Head Office and Distributive Educ. Northern Arizona University Flagstaff, ?? 00000

—*The Cincinnati and Suburban Bell Telephone Company*

The secretary should be able to organize and use executive and central files; to control material access, safety, and usability; and to keep in touch with the drastically changing field in record handling.

Secretarial Management of Records

Records control and management involves far more than indexing, storage, and retrieval of business information. It includes setting up filing systems, determining what should not be filed, how long an item should be retained in the file, and what should be retained in the executive's files. It also includes special filing systems as well as filing procedures—releasing, indexing and coding, cross-referencing, sorting, requisitioning, charge out, and follow-up methods. All of these topics are discussed in this section.

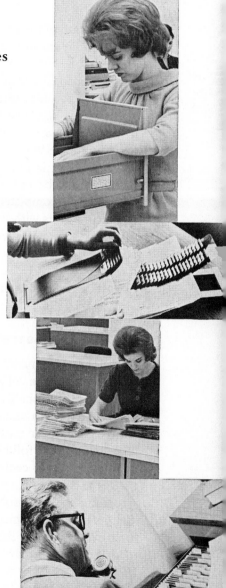

Ch.

14　**Controlling Office Files**

15　**Alphabetic Indexing Procedures**

Ch. 14 Controlling Office Files

The wrath of the employer who is delayed while his secretary searches for a lost document is understandable, for time is money. When he and his telephone caller are both kept waiting because his secretary cannot locate needed information, no wonder he is annoyed. Of all the skills needed on the job, filing is the one the secretary usually knows least about when she comes to work. Yet unless she can find material when it is needed in a form that will make it of maximum value to those requesting it, she has not achieved competency.

Since filing is done by people, many opportunities exist for error. A paper may be put into the wrong folder, inadvertently attached to material in a completely unrelated file, removed from a folder without any record of its withdrawal, or buried in the mass of papers on the desk of the executive or the secretary or in the file clerk's work-to-be-done accumulation. Yet one manufacturer of filing equipment estimates that a misfile costs $61.23—a startling indication of the importance of this facet of secretarial training.

The Secretary's Filing Responsibilities

Files are the memory of a business. They may be *centralized* in one location or *decentralized* in various departments or branches. The secretary will probably maintain a decentralized executive file and also send materials to and secure materials from a larger central file. She and her employer must plan together the executive file if it is to work well, but she will follow company procedures for borrowing and returning documents to central files.

If the company in which she works has a strong records management program, she will probably receive instructions about how to maintain her current files efficiently and how long to keep certain records before destroying them or sending them to a low-cost storage area. Records managers are primarily concerned with reducing the amount of paper to be filed. Since it costs 1½ cents a year to keep one piece of paper in the files, they want to prevent filing anything without reference value,

316

The file supervisor must maintain coordinated use of centralized and decentralized files, adequate control of materials, and reasonably low-cost storage.

—Remington Rand

to reduce duplication of copies in several locations, and to insure that superseded material will be destroyed when a current replacement is filed. To save space, they frequently try to reduce executive files. On the other hand, the executives, fearing that they cannot refer to items easily once the records have left their hands, build "little empires" that take unnecessary space and increase the expense of paperwork within their companies.

▪ Designing and Supervising the Files

Caught between two viewpoints of keeping almost everything or reducing file space, the secretary has the responsibility for reducing executive files whenever possible without interfering with the accessibility of material needed to maintain her employer's efficiency. She must follow accepted filing practices in her own office and also understand the central filing system so that she can readily secure materials not available in her own files. Frequently she supervises, rather than does the filing, in the executive's office. She must create and/or maintain various kinds of files suitable to the needs of her employer and herself, for every situation is different. Possibly she will need card or strip name files, project files, files of catalogs frequently consulted, tickler

Safety, findability, and confidentiality are factors the secretary must consider important in supervising and using the executive's files.

files involving upcoming events, geographic files, and files for storing engineering blueprints or other outsize materials, in addition to traditional drawer files of alphabetic or numeric captions. She will certainly need that very important round file, the wastebasket, to which many, many papers should be consigned, for executive files should be reduced to a minimum of space. She would do well to base file-planning decisions on factors of findability, confidentiality, and safety.

Findability. Unfortunately, files are thought of first as places to *put* papers, not places to *find* papers. Yet the criterion for judging any file system is findability, and the efficient secretary makes her decisions about where to put material after asking herself, "How will it be requested" or "How can I find it?" She must locate materials with dispatch, selecting from a complete file only the papers actually wanted. To do this, she must understand her employer's need for a file so that she will not burden him with 250 pages when he wants only 10—but the right 10.

Confidentiality. The secretary is also responsible for the confidentiality of her employer's files. The degree of security required varies

Particularly at the end of the work day the secretary should see that important papers are safe against fire and prying eyes. Confidential papers must be safeguarded at all times.

—Tommy Weber

from the tight surveillance over top-secret documents required by the air-space engineer to the careful protection required for the less sensitive work of the typical executive. Yet it can safely be said that the records of any high executive are confidential and should be kept so.

Safety. Allied to the need for security is the secretary's ultimate responsibility for the safety of the records in her office. Many of them are irreplaceable, so it behooves her to take especial care of those she handles. Before leaving at night, she should see that all folders are in filing cabinets or a vault as a safeguard against fire and that all files are locked away from prying eyes.

▪ Developing an Index

The secretary in a new position may find in her procedures manual a *table of contents* for her employer's personal file. Chances are, though, that she will have to develop her own index telling *where* in the files to look for materials. Even after the secretary has familiarized herself with the file, she will find the preparation of such a guide advantageous, for it will help anyone (including the executive or a new assistant) to locate material. A simple table of contents that indicates where to look for all types of records follows.

FILE INDEX
NO. 89
CHEMICAL

	Location	
	File No.	Drawer No.
Correspondence		
Company	2	1
Government	2	2
Patents	2	3
Personnel Work		
Applications	1	2
Medical	1	3
Security	1	6
Reports		
Company	5	1
Outside	5	3

If there is no company pattern for records control, the secretary should discuss with her employer his preferences for developing usable files with suitable captions and cross references. He may prefer to code material for his subject files himself or design the index for the file.

Communication between secretary and executive seems particularly bad in the filing area. The secretary feels that she is the one who has to get the material from the file so she should not bother her employer with questions about *her* system. Yet, it is *their* system; and if they work together in planning it, a continuity can be developed that will not be destroyed with the transfer of either of them. Certainly the new secretary should not reorganize the files until she has developed considerable insight into the nature of the office. Equally so, no executive objects to intelligent questions that will improve performance.

The secretary can sometimes get ideas for setting up files appropriate to her type of work from professional organizations and publications. For instance, she may find suggestions in an engineering magazine for filing blueprints. An educational secretary might find a model for pupil attendance records in publications of the National Association of Educational Secretaries. The Life Office Management Association has made studies of office systems for insurance records. Likewise, manuals of the legal profession give directions for developing numeric legal files. The American Municipal Association has developed a list of subject

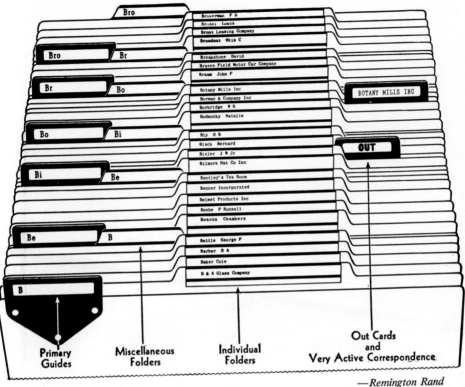

Bro
Broverman F S
Bruni Louis
Brons Leasing Company
Broadman Otis C

Bro
Br
Breakstone David
Braves Field Motor Car Company
Braun John F

Br
Bo
Botany Mills Inc
Borman & Company Inc
Borbridge W R
Bodansky Natalie

BOTANY MILLS INC

Bo
Bi
Bly H B
Black Bernard
Bixler J W Jr
Bilmore Hat Co Inc

OUT

Bi
Be
Bentley's Tea Room
Benner Incorporated
Belmet Products Inc
Beebe F Russell
Beacon Chambers

Be
B
Battle George F
Barber D A
Baker Cole
B & A Glass Company

B

Primary
Guides

Miscellaneous
Folders

Individual
Folders

Out Cards
and
Very Active Correspondence

—Remington Rand

In this illustration of an alphabetic file, four positions are used for the captions.

headings peculiar to municipal activities and problems. The American Institute of Architects has created a standard filing system and alphabetic index for information on the materials, appliances, and equipment used in construction and related activities.

It is also possible to buy prefabricated subject file systems for certain types of offices. For example, Shaw-Walker manufactures a prefabricated Administration file containing main subjects and subclassifications printed on guide and folder tabs. The manufacturer claims this system will provide indexing applicable to 90 percent of all basic executive data.

■ The Nature of the Office Files

Records are usually kept in file folders, on cards, or on pages of looseleaf books. Correspondence, memorandums, invoices, and similar materials are kept in *folders* that are filed vertically in file drawers. Inside the drawers, stiff pressboard cards called *guides* separate the file folders into convenient divisions. On the tabs of these guides are printed the

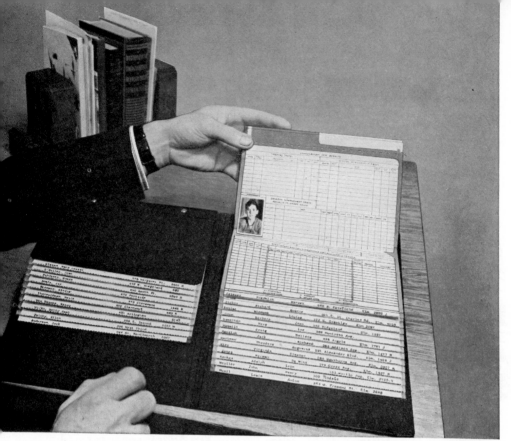

—*Remington Rand*

division captions—that is, the names, letters, or numbers representing the sections into which the drawer is divided. At the tops of the folders, too, are tabs on which the captions for filing are written.

Many types of business records are kept on cards. Standard sizes for cards to be filed vertically are 5 by 3, 6 by 4, and 8 by 5 inches. Cards, too, are separated in the drawers by guides similar to those used for correspondence files.

Cards may also be filed in shallow metal trays or on upright stands so that only the lower edge of each card is visible and the entire card seen only when the preceding card is flipped up. The visible portion of each card contains the name or other designation upon which the indexing is based. The card can be inserted and removed easily; and it is so fastened that the back of the card, as well as the front, can be used for record keeping. *Visible card files*, such as that illustrated at the top of this page, are used extensively for perpetual inventories, purchase records, accounting records, sales records, personnel histories—those situations in which information must be available quickly, as in answer to a telephone inquiry. Colored signals are frequently used as a visible means of control; for example, a blue signal attached to the visible edge of a credit card at a given point may mean "Watch credit closely."

Material should be filed according to the designation by which it will be sought. Many folders are filed in *alphabetic* sequence by name. However, a *numeric* system may be used in which a number instead of a name is assigned to each folder. This system is frequently used for case records or other material of a confidential nature where anonymity is preferable to direct access. Since folders are called for by name, it is then necessary to refer to a master index to discover the number which has been assigned to an item for filing purposes. In some cases the geographic location of a name is more important than the name alone. In that case, a *geographic* file is used. If material will be sought under a subject or title rather than a name, a *subject* file is used.

These are the four bases for filing systems. Manufacturers of filing equipment have devised and patented improvements upon these fundamental systems, such as color schemes to hasten sorting, filing, and finding procedures, or techniques for grouping names spelled differently but pronounced alike. Trade names such as Variadex, Tell-I-Vision, Amberg-Nual, or Safeguard refer to commercial systems available.

Filing Procedures

Many papers that are filed should have been destroyed. Letters of acknowledgment, letters of transmittal, announcements of meetings (placed on the desk calendar), forms and reports filed in another location, duplicate copies, and routine requests for catalogs and information fall into this category. (In some well-run organizations the original request is returned with the material.)

Any document that is superseded by another in the file should be removed. When filing a card giving a change in telephone number, remove the old one. When a new catalog is filed, destroy the old one.

A temporary file may be kept for materials having no permanent value. The paper is marked with a *T* and destroyed when the action involved is completed. The Army has developed this technique to the highest level, and every document receives a date-of-destruction notation before it goes into the file. By continuously purging the files of outdated material, the secretary can painlessly reduce the volume of material appreciably and thus keep her files up to date.

■ Preparing Materials for Filing

Routines for preparing materials for filing should proceed by the steps described on the next page.

Conditioning Materials. All pins, brads, and paper clips are removed, and related papers are stapled or welded together for material to be filed. Clippings or other materials smaller than page size should be attached to a regular sheet of paper with paper cement. Damaged records should be mended or reinforced with tape. If they are not filed in special equipment, oversize papers should be folded to the dimensions of the folder and appropriately labeled so that to unfold them for identification is not necessary.

Releasing Materials. When the secretary places an incoming letter in her filing basket, it should bear a *release mark* indicating that it has been acted on and is ready for filing. This mark may be the executive's initials, a FILE stamp and the secretary's initials, or a diagonal mark across the sheet. A check of all attachments will indicate whether they belong to the document. A release mark is not necessary on a carbon copy of an outgoing letter or on an original to which a carbon copy of a reply is attached. The file copy is usually of a distinctive color.

Indexing and Coding. The term *indexing* means deciding where to file a paper; *coding* refers to noting that decision on the face of the paper either by underlining the name or words that are to be used as a basis for filing, or by writing the appropriate name, words, or number in a prominent place. A colored pencil is commonly used for this purpose.

In alphabetic filing, correspondence is usually filed according to the most important name appearing on it. A letter to or from a business is usually coded and filed according to the name of that business. If a correspondent is an individual, his name is ordinarily used in coding. If, however, he is writing as an agent of a business and the name of that business is known, the business name is used instead. Similarly, if a business letterhead is used by an individual to write a personal letter, the name of the individual is coded rather than the name of the business. Complete rules for alphabetic-filing sequence are given on pages 345–356.

In subject filing, the subject title must be determined from the body of the letter; the letter is then coded according to that title or a number that represents that subject. In numeric filing, the number to be used as a code is determined from a card index file. In geographic filing, coding usually consists of underscoring the city and the state in the heading of an incoming letter or the inside address of the carbon copy of an outgoing letter.

Cross-Referencing. For correspondence or material that could be filed under more than one name, a cross-reference sheet or card should be prepared and filed. For instance, a letter from Allen Rothmore Company poses the problem: Is Allen a given name or a surname? In such a case a used file folder should be cut apart and only the back half used for the permanent cross-reference folder with the caption ALLEN ROTHMORE (*See* ROTHMORE ALLEN) and filed under *Al*. The regular file should be set up for ROTHMORE ALLEN and filed under *Ro*.

A letter may be received from the Modern Office Equipment Co. regarding an exhibit at the Eastern Office Equipment Association meeting in Atlantic City. The file clerk might file all correspondence about this meeting under EASTERN OFFICE EQUIPMENT ASSOCIATION; however, she should also make a cross-reference sheet like the one at the right and file it under MODERN OFFICE EQUIPMENT CO. If a cross-reference form is made out, that fact is indicated by *X* (for cross-reference) written near the name on the letter.

An extra carbon copy of a letter, usually in a color different from the file copy, or a photo copy, might

CROSS-REFERENCE SHEET
Date of Item *May 3, 19--*
Name or Subject *Modern Office Equipment Co. Baltimore, Maryland*
Regarding *Exhibit — Eastern Office Equipment Association — Atlantic City, New Jersey, June 21-26*
SEE
Name or Subject *Eastern Office Equipment Association*
Authorized by *Joyce Replogle*

also be used as a cross-reference. In this case, it would be filed under MODERN OFFICE EQUIPMENT CO. and the cross-reference sheet would not be prepared.

Perhaps a letter should be cross-referenced by subject. If inquiries have been mailed to several printers asking for quotations on new letterheads, a cross-reference sheet labeled "Letterhead Quotations," listing the firms written, may be filed under *Le*, and the correspondence with the printers may be filed alphabetically according to firm names.

Cross-reference forms may be colored sheets imprinted with blanks that are to be filled in; or they may be tabbed colored cards on which the reference information is listed. A good secretary follows the rule, "When in doubt, make out a cross-reference."

Sorting. Sorting is arranging the papers in order for filing. When sorting material, the secretary should first make one or two preliminary

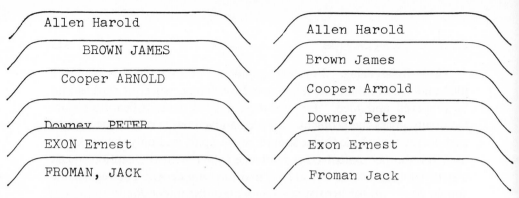

Allen Harold		Allen Harold
BROWN JAMES		Brown James
Cooper ARNOLD		Cooper Arnold
		Downey Peter
Downey PETER		
EXON Ernest		Exon Ernest
FROMAN, JACK		Froman Jack

The captions at the left are inconsistent in their punctuation, capitalization, and placement. Captions may be typed in all capital letters or as shown at the right.

sortings before the final one. For example, she may first place the A–E, papers in one group and then in the second sort put them into A, B, C, D, and E order. It is a simple matter then to put each of these letter groups in correct alphabetic sequence. Sorting for a numeric file should follow a similar efficient procedure.

Typing Labels. Pressure-sensitive labels are easier to attach than others, but the secretary should be sure to press the label down securely at all corners. When using rolls of labels, type the label before tearing it off. To prevent captions from being hidden in the file, type the caption uniformly two spaces in from the left edge of the label as illustrated above. Do not stagger file-guide captions; keep them in perfect alignment. Type the primary reference in solid caps on the top line. Type the secondary reference such as city and state (if any) in mixed caps and lower case on the second line directly under the first line. Use index form—JONES, JOHN L. & COMPANY, not *John L. Jones & Company*. Uniform omission of periods and commas saves time, but it is by no means universal practice. For quicker reference, use different colored labels to designate individual file breakdowns, such as projects and reports.

■ **Techniques for Drawer Filing**

Use an *individual folder* for letters and other materials to, from, or about one correspondent or subject. Use a *Miscellaneous* folder for all individuals and businesses (within the caption designation) with whom correspondence is infrequent. When five records relating to a person or topic accumulate in the *Miscellaneous* folder, open an individual folder. File material in the *Miscellaneous* folder in alphabetic order, then within the alphabetic order file in chronological order, with the most recent date on top. Adopt the following time-saving ideas:

1. Set a definite time for filing every day.

2. File records face up, top edge to the left, with the most recent date to the front of the folder.

3. Place individual folders immediately *behind* the guides.

4. Place a *Miscellaneous* folder at the end of each section of the file, just in front of the next guide.

5. Use a guide for every 6–8 folders (1 inch of drawer space), about 20–25 to each drawer.

6. Leave one fifth of the drawer for expansion and working space.

7. Keep no more than 20–25 sheets in one folder. With heavy loads, use scored (creased-at-the-bottom) folders for expansion.

8. "Break" the files when the folder becomes crowded. Underscore the caption on the old folder in red so that all new material will be placed in the new folder. Date each folder and keep the folders filed together.

9. Use specially scored and reinforced folders for bulky materials such as catalogs.

10. Avoid accidents by opening only one file drawer at a time and closing it when the filing has been completed.

11. Lift the folder an inch or two out of the drawer before inserting material so that the sheets can drop down completely into the folder.

12. Do not grasp guides and folders by their index tabs, or they become dog-eared.

▪ Requisitioning Materials from the Files

When the secretary knows at the time the materials are released for filing that they will be needed at a definite future time, she can mark or stamp on each item the notation "Follow-up" or "Tickler," with the

The secretary may request material from the central file on a standardized form such as this. The filing department records the two dates at the top of the card.

Date Due *April 6, 19--* Charge Date *April 3, 19--*

MATERIAL REQUESTED FROM FILES

Name or Subject *Mohawk Supply Co.*

Address *Boston, Mass.*

Regarding *adj. on Feb. statement*

Date of Material *Latter part of Feb.*

REQUESTED BY

Name *James Morris*

Department *Auditing* Date of Request *4/3/--*

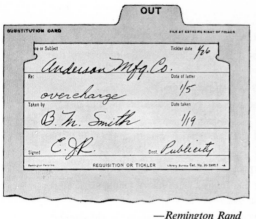
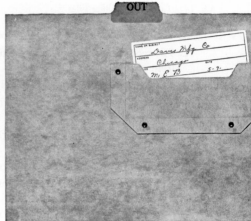

—*Remington Rand*

At the left is a substitution card indicating (1) the item that has been removed from the files, (2) the name of the person who has it, and (3) the date it will be asked for if not already returned. An out guide is shown at the right. Note the pocket provided for an out slip (or substitution card).

date when she wishes the material. More frequently, however, she will not know at that time just when the material will be needed again. In these cases she will make her request for such materials when they are needed, following the usual routine—by telephone, in person, or by *requisition card* sent to the filing department. The request may be for the entire contents of a folder, or it may be for specific items in a folder. A telephone request is, of course, faster than a requisition, especially if the information sought can be given verbally.

The secretary should return materials to the files as soon as she has finished using them. A special problem arises when files that the secretary has received are transferred to someone in another department before they are returned to the filing department. In some companies the secretary reports such a transfer to the filing department on a special form. In any case she should inform central files of the location of the file so that she will no longer be charged for the materials and so that the filing department can locate them if they are needed.

Charge-Out Methods. When an entire folder is taken from the files or when separate items are removed from a folder, a record should be made so that others will be able to locate the materials.

Several charge methods are in common use. When an individual item is removed from the folder, a *substitution card* is usually put in its place in the folder. This card indicates the nature of the material, the name of the person who has the material, and the date it was removed.

328

When an entire folder is removed, an *out guide* may be substituted for the folder; or an out folder with a *substitution card* may be placed in the drawer to take the place of the regular folder. Sometimes the regular folder is retained in the file drawer, and the contents of the folder are transferred to a special *carrier folder*.

In many companies the original requisitioned material never leaves the central filing area. A photocopy is sent to the person making a requisition, and he may destroy the copy when he has finished with it.

Follow-Up Methods. A secretary frequently uses her daily calendar pad as a memory aid or follow-up to filing. She anticipates the due date of a letter and jots down such a notation on the future-date page of her calendar. See page 327 for follow-up steps.

Special Filing Systems

If the secretary works for an executive who deals with *ideas* or the running of the business, she will become involved with subject filing (about 10 percent of all filing). If she works in a sales office where geography is an important factor, she will maintain a geographic file. In a legal office or an insurance office, she will find numeric filing basic.

▪ Subject Filing

With billions of dollars being spent today on research and development, subject filing becomes increasingly challenging. A management consultant said:

> To do subject filing well, the secretary has to think like an executive. She has to be attuned to the thought pattern of the boss. She not only has to know how he is thinking today, but she must be flexible. The file must be built in relation to today's needs; but she must realize that as the projects develop, the pattern in the boss's mind also changes. She should anticipate not only where her employer's area of interest lies today but also where it will lie a few months from now.

If the secretary has only a few materials to file by subject, she may include them in the alphabetic correspondence file. If, however, she has a large volume of reference material to which her employer wishes to refer, she will want to isolate it in a separate subject file.

A subject file is developed for a particular situation, and no specific instructions as to the divisions, subdivisions, and individual captions can be given. Each piece of material to be filed is filed under one

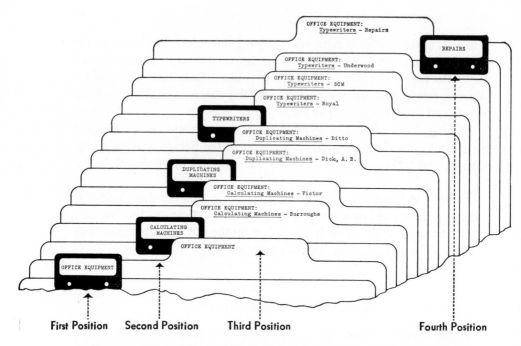

OFFICE EQUIPMENT:
Typewriters – Repairs

REPAIRS

OFFICE EQUIPMENT:
Typewriters – Underwood

OFFICE EQUIPMENT:
Typewriters – SCM

OFFICE EQUIPMENT:
Typewriters – Royal

TYPEWRITERS

OFFICE EQUIPMENT:
Duplicating Machines – Ditto

OFFICE EQUIPMENT:
Duplicating Machines – Dick, A. B.

DUPLICATING
MACHINES

OFFICE EQUIPMENT:
Calculating Machines – Victor

OFFICE EQUIPMENT:
Calculating Machines – Burroughs

CALCULATING
MACHINES

OFFICE EQUIPMENT

OFFICE EQUIPMENT

First Position   Second Position   Third Position   Fourth Position

This subject file would be suitable for the purchasing agent or the office manager.

caption, but a *relative index* must be developed listing all the possible
titles under which the item may be sought. A relative index is a cross-
reference system by which are listed all captions under which the material *may* be filed. The searcher is then referred from each possible
caption to the title under which the item was actually filed.

The executive and his secretary may profitably spend time in developing the relative index—time that will be saved later when the executive
asks for the material under a number of captions. If the executive asks
for the file on wage incentive plans of a rival company, the Green Corporation, the secretary may have it filed under (1) fringe benefits, (2) incentive plans, (3) personnel, or (4) Green Corporation. Reference to the
relative index will help her locate the pamphlet.

A description of a portion of the subject file pictured above will
perhaps best illustrate the principles. This illustration shows only one
of the major headings with its subdivisions.

Each main heading has a number of subheadings. For instance,
OFFICE EQUIPMENT is subdivided into several categories such as:

OFFICE EQUIPMENT: Adding Machines
OFFICE EQUIPMENT: Duplicating Machines
OFFICE EQUIPMENT: Typewriters

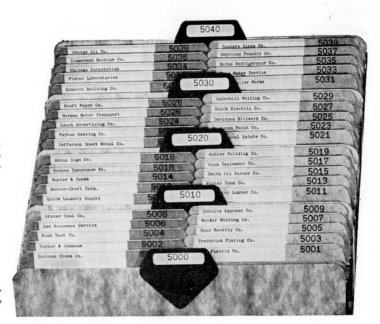

With numeric filing a card index provides the key to the numeric correspondence file.

—*Shaw Walker Company*

Some of these subdivisions are further subdivided. For example, OFFICE EQUIPMENT: Typewriters is subdivided into:

```
OFFICE EQUIPMENT:  Typewriters - Royal
OFFICE EQUIPMENT:  Typewriters - SCM
OFFICE EQUIPMENT:  Typewriters - Underwood
```

The subdivision Typewriters is further subdivided by the special classification guide SERVICE CONTRACTS in the fourth position.

The Dewey decimal system used in library classifications is another example of filing by subject. The subjects are divided into not more than 10 general classifications numbered in hundreds from 000 to 900, inclusive. Each of these major classes may be divided by units of 10, such as 100, 110, and 120. And again these classes may be further subdivided by units of 1, such as 110, 111, and 112. Subdividing can be continued by the use of the decimal point and can be extended indefinitely—for example, 126.1, 126.2, 126.21, 126.22, 126.221, ad infinitum. The pages of printed loose-leaf publications in which additional pages are frequently inserted are usually numbered this way.

▪ Numeric Filing

Numeric files are often developed for professional offices such as those of lawyers. Numeric filing is often used also by contractors who assign a number to each project. This is an indirect filing system, as it

This illustration shows a portion of the 03 drawers of a terminal-digit-file. The terminal digit system assures easier filing and finding.

—Remington Rand

is necessary to refer to a card index to determine the number assigned to a file. There are three parts to the numeric file system: (1) the card index, (2) the numeric correspondence file, and (3) an alphabetic correspondence file for papers about correspondents and subjects too inactive to justify the assignment of a number.

As the files grow in straight numeric filing, the numbers assigned to them become higher. Soon nearly all the work involved in filing is concerned with the highest numbers, since they deal with the most recent work. For instance, in a numeric file of insurance policies, the 102,000th policy sold would be given that number; and the next policy would be 102,001. Obviously, the chances are that more of the file clerk's time would be spent in the files from 100,000 to 102,000 than in the files between 25,000 and 100,000.

To obviate the problems connected with ordinary numeric filing, *terminal-digit* (or *last unit*) *filing* was introduced. With this system, for example, folders numbered *1210, 98,210, 147,210,* and *186,210* would all be filed in the same group and in that order, since all of these numbers have the same terminal group, *210.* Similarly, folders numbered *1743, 13,743, 121,743,* and *942,743* would all be grouped together and in that order, since the numbers all have the same last three digits.

As the same distribution applies to all other numbers, it can readily be seen that this method automatically divides the system into 1,000 separate groups, each group ending in some number between 000 and 999. To see the advantages of terminal-digit filing, assume 1,000 different file drawers, each labeled with a number. The first drawer would be numbered *000;* the second, *001;* the third, *002;* the fiftieth, *049;* the 615th, *614;* and the last, *999.* Folder 246,823 would go in Drawer 823; Folder 21,252 in Drawer 252; and so on. Thus, if any consecutive new files were added, they would be distributed one to a drawer throughout the entire 1,000 drawers.

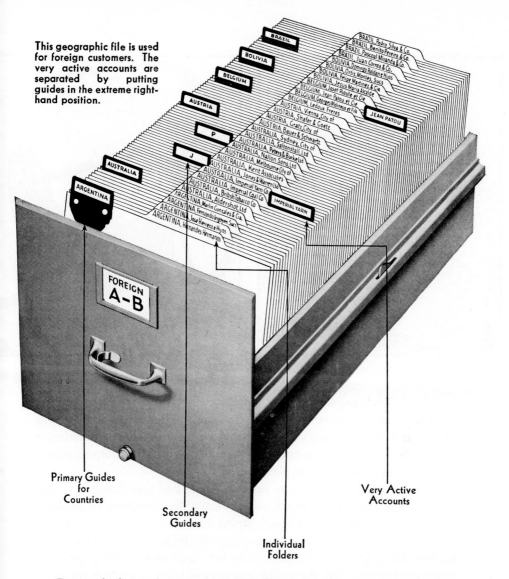

This geographic file is used for foreign customers. The very active accounts are separated by putting guides in the extreme right-hand position.

FOREIGN
A-B

Primary Guides for Countries

Secondary Guides

Individual Folders

Very Active Accounts

Research shows that terminal-digit filing can save up to 40 percent in file operating costs by assuring uniform distribution of workload, better employee relations, unlimited expansion facilities, and fewer misfiles.

▪ Geographic Filing

Geographic filing keeps records by geographic units or territories. Divisions are made in some logical sequence: nations, states or provinces, cities, and so on. Guide cards are used for the larger divisions and subdivisions. Material is filed in miscellaneous folders alphabetically, usually by name of city and then by name of correspondent. Individual folders are filed alphabetically by location, then by name.

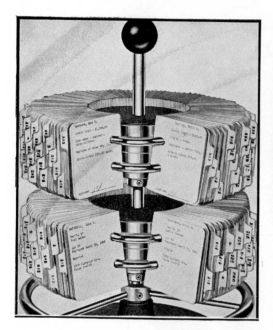 

Special Filing Equipment

The following discussion relates more directly to the filing department than to the secretary's own files. It is presented so that she will understand her company's files. A trip to a business show will indicate the intense competition among manufacturers of filing equipment and the extent of change taking place.

The secretary should try to select supplies and equipment that will improve her administration and supervision of her employer's decentralized files. She should also study innovations in the control of central files because of their effect on her own job. By becoming an expert in records management, she can improve her value as a secretary, and it is not inconceivable that she could be promoted into a records management position through this channel.

Background about filing equipment and supplies can be obtained by visiting business shows or manufacturers' and office equipment showrooms. Books on records management and magazines contain articles and advertisements about equipment and supplies.

▪ Rotary Card Files

A card file on which a great deal of information can be assembled within arm's reach of the operator is the *rotary wheel file*, two of which are illustrated at the top of this page. A wheel file can be small for desk use or motorized and large enough to hold thousands of records.

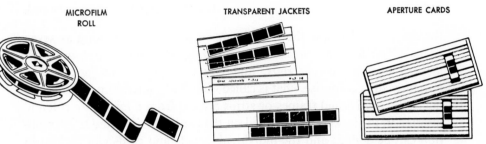

MICROFILM ROLL TRANSPARENT JACKETS APERTURE CARDS

—Charles Bruning Co., Inc.

Three major methods of filing microfilm—rolls, transparent jackets, and aperture cards—are illustrated above. Chips also are frequently used. A 5- by 3-inch card can be used to supplement index information recorded on the microfilm cartons.

▪ Mobile-Tray Card Files

With mobile-tray card files, the file clerk stays in one spot and presses the button which moves the needed file tray into working position.

▪ Open-Shelf Filing

Open-shelf files stacked to the ceiling hold more material per square foot than do vertical or visible filing equipment. Open-shelf files also require less floor and aisle space, cost less, and require less time to file and find records. (See the illustration on page 317.)

Filing Special Types of Records

With the advent of new procedures for recording data, new filing problems emerge. Manufacturers build special equipment for special problems, such as a special suspension file in which to hang mimeograph stencils so that they will be protected against damage. Many manufacturers provide consultant service for their customers.

▪ Punched-Tape Filing

File folders that hold punched tape and edge-punched cards in orderly pocket arrangements are available, as are special desks and files for holding these folders. In addition, special equipment is being built to house magnetic tape and magnetic drums. The filing of punched paper tape is illustrated on page 434.

▪ Microfilming

Microfilming, too, presents a filing problem at the same time it is solving one (see page 109). Microfilming records reduces space in files in a ratio of 99 to 1. But microfilming is expensive—often more so than the space saved unless the records are to be kept for as long as seven years. The four major methods of filing microfilm are *transparent jackets, aperture cards, rolls,* and *chips.* Transparent jackets and aperture cards comprise what is called "unitized" microfilm. In unitized microfilm, individual frames or strips are cut from a microfilm roll and inserted in the jackets or mounted on the cards. Written index information can be added; and the individual jackets and cards can be filed in any order, similar to the manner in which standard files are kept. Because of the time and cost required for unitizing microfilm records, the roll method is the most commonly used for 17 mm microfilm.

For the chip method of filing microfilm, approximately 100 chips are stored in a cartridge. When a chip is wanted, the proper cartridge is loaded into a viewer. The code numbers are scanned by an electric eye; the desired chip is located and projected on a screen or printed out.

Mechanics of Good Filing

▪ Reducing Misfiles

The secretary should vow to avoid expensive misfiles. One cause of misfiles is carelessness—placing a record in a folder without scanning its contents to see if they are related to the paper being filed, fastening materials together with paper clips which often also pick up unrelated papers, or putting one folder inside another one. Another cause for misfiles is not using supplies and equipment as recommended—too many or too few guides, overcrowded folders that sag so much that their tabs are hidden, drawers so overstuffed that there is inadequate work space, and miscellaneous folders crowded with papers for which individual folders should have been opened. The final cause of misfiles lies in coding—captions that are not mutually exclusive, the choice of a wrong title, or too few cross-references.

▪ Places to Search

If only one paper is lost, it is probably in the wrong folder. Check the folders in front and in back and check the bottom of the drawer. Look in Charge-Outs and in file baskets (or on the boss's desk). Look in the index of files transferred to storage areas. Look under similar names, numbers, or titles. For instance, if the name is Brooks Allen, look under Allen Brooks. If 2309 is lost, look under 2390. Look in the relative index for other possible captions.

Good Management Practices

Practices recommended by records-management specialists should be helpful to the secretary in controlling her files and in understanding the management aspects of records control, including retention and transfer.

▪ Retention Schedules

The most efficiently operated companies have an overall file retention plan which the secretary should follow. The retention schedule of a company specifies how long a document can remain in the office flow; if and when it is to be removed to a separate, low-cost records center; and when it should be destroyed. Here is an adaption of recommended practices:[1]

1. **File one month:**
    General correspondence requiring no follow-up

2. **File three months:**
    Incoming and outgoing correspondence with customers and vendors on routine, promptly settled business
    Bank statements
    Stenographers' notebooks
    Expired insurance policies

3. **File two years:**
    Work sheets for financial statements
    Internal reports and summaries, including print-outs from data processing equipment, and all punched cards and tapes
    Physical inventories

4. **File to comply with the statute of limitations in the states affected:**
    Cancelled payroll checks and summaries
    Invoices to customers and from vendors
    Employee data, including accident reports
    Completed contracts and leases, as well as other legal papers
    Duplicate deposit tickets and checks, except as noted below

5. **File permanently:**
    Books of accounts and minutes
    Capital stock ledgers and transfer records
    Cancelled checks, vouchers, and cost data on capital improvements
    Tax returns and related papers
    Perpetual agreements about pensions, group insurance, and other fringe benefits
    All property records
    Maps, specifications, plans

---

[1]Records Controls, Inc., Chicago, Illinois.

▪ Transferring Materials

Plans for storing files are made in relation to the importance of the material and the reduction of costs effected by storing infrequently called-for material in cheaper filing equipment and in cheaper rental areas. Possibility of destruction of vital records by nuclear attack has caused concern for safe storage—in mountain vaults and caves in some instances and in widely dispersed units in others. Some companies have built storage centers, and others have rented file storage space from companies that specialize in providing ready access to stored materials.

Certain types of files can be handled under a perpetual transfer plan. When a case is closed or a project finished, the file is closed and transferred. In other cases periodic transfer is made. By the one-period method all material is taken from the active files and sent to transfer files. New active files are established, but it is impossible to avoid consulting some old records. With a two-period transfer the middle drawers contain current papers, and the upper and lower drawers contain less active material. The semiactive material is eventually transferred.

A variation is the maximum-minimum transfer. Only the inactive material is transferred at regular intervals. If files are transferred on June 30, 1969, no material placed in the files during 1969 would be moved. When the June 30 work is completed, records for the past six months would remain in the active files. On June 30, 1970, materials dated from January 1, 1968, through December 31, 1969, would be transferred.

Effect of Automation on Filing and Records Management

Automation is changing the entire field of record handling. There are fewer individual *paper* records to file. There are new materials to file: punched tapes, cards, reels, printouts, and wired panels. But the greatest innovation is in filing, merging, updating, and recalling information from electronic equipment at lightning speed, automatically. Records are centralized, and data are fed into a computer center from all parts of the organization—from overseas units and branch offices as well as from diverse offices within the headquarters. An example will explain: In billing, information about a customer is accumulated in the billing department on a master tape. Each time that additions and changes are made, they are accumulated on a supplementary tape. The supplementary tape is periodically meshed with the master tape so that every transaction, with credit information and terms, will show on the updated bill. Because information in the computer is not necessarily in the desired sequence, random access to the relevant portion of the data can be secured by optical scanning, and a file can be updated in minutes rather than in the days and even weeks that are often required for copying and handling manual files.

Another example of filing by computer involves providing names and qualifications of college graduates to companies seeking such applicants. Information about 25,000 job seekers who have worked for at least one year is stored in a random-access computer. An employer can query the computer for the names and code numbers of registrants who meet his requirements so that he can examine their résumés from the computer's microfilm files. The student pays $10 to register, and the business representative pays 50 cents for each minute of computer time and $2 for each résumé.[2]

Scientific information is subject filed in computers according to key words describing the nature of each report. If a researcher wants a printout of a list of all articles written on a certain topic (or even short abstracts of them), for a fee he can have a search made in the scientific computer center and thus save himself days of routine search for information relating to his study. The possibilities of automated information retrieval are amazing and are just beginning to be appreciated. Revolutionary changes in business information retrieval, too, are imminent.

Suggested Readings

Bassett, E. D., Peter L. Agnew, and David Goodman. *Business Filing and Records Control*, 3d ed. Cincinnati: South-Western Publishing Co. 1964, 202 pp.

Bourne, Charles P. *Methods of Information Handling*. New York: John Wiley and Sons, Inc., 1963, 241 pp.

Griffin, Mary Claire. *Records Management, A Modern Tool for Business*. Boston: Allyn and Bacon, Inc., 1964, 300 pp.

Guide to Record Retention Requirements. Washington: Government Printing Office, 1962.

Ideas for Management. Systems and Procedures Association, 7890 Brookside Drive, Cleveland. Yearbooks: 1960, "Records Management," John Dethman; 1960, "Records Management," R. Norman Beattie; 1958, "How to File It, Find It, and Get Rid of It," George Derry; 1958, "Records Management," William Benedon; 1958, "Systems in Records Management," James McCabe; 1956, "Cost Reduction through Records Management," John Dethman; 1959, "An Integrated Records Management Program," William Eastman.

---

[2]*Business Week*, March 12, 1966, p. 50.

Johnson, Mina M., and Norman F. Kallaus. *Records Management.* Cincinnati: South-Western Publishing Co., 1967, 362 pp.

Kahn, Gilbert, Theodore Yerian, and Jeffrey Stewart. *Progressive Filing and Records Management.* New York: Gregg Publishing Division, McGraw-Hill Book Company, 1962, 244 pp.

Place, Irene, and Estelle L. Popham. *Filing and Records Management.* Englewood Cliffs: Prentice Hall, Inc., 1966, 290 pp.

Weeks, Bertha. *Filing and Records Management.* New York: The Ronald Press, 1964, 287 pp.

Questions for Discussion

1. In what ways has your concept of the filing part of a secretary's job changed since reading this chapter?

2. Do you think that the appointment of an executive to control all paper work within a company is desirable? why?

3. What can the secretary do to assure good relations with the central filing department?

4. In some companies the executives are permitted only two filing drawers for their personal files. What advantages do you see in this blanket rule? what disadvantages?

5. If you were employed as secretary to the head of research projects in a chemical company, what steps would you take to develop an understanding of a subject file already in operation?

6. If you were working for a company with no records-retention schedule, how would you proceed to establish one?

7. If you started to work in a position during a peak period and discovered that many materials were misfiled, the folders and drawers were overcrowded, the materials were not arranged chronologically in the folders, and the miscellaneous folders contained materials for which individual folders should have been opened, what would you do?

8. Suggest situations in which each of the following types of files would be advantageous:

alphabetic	**subject**	**visible card file**
numeric	**geographic**	**chronological**

9. Type the following sentences in correct form. Then use the Reference Guide to verify or correct your typing of *yes* and *no*.

    (a) The answer is no we are sorry to say.

    (b) On second thought, we will say yes.

10. There is some feeling that quoting an unusual word choice is uncomplimentary to the intelligence of the reader, and in some cases is sarcastic. Discuss the following italicized words. Would you use quotation marks with any of them in a business letter? Would you revise any of the sentences? Is any one of the italicized words an acronym?

    (a) We have your *so-called* revised chapter.

    (b) He is a *VIP*—an extremely important one.

(c) The situation is completely *snafued* now.

(d) Your *complaint* can be taken as a compliment too.

(e) To save time we are sending you a rough draft in which deletions have been X'd out.

(f) It looks as if we *goofed* on your order.

(g) Perhaps you do not know, but he is a *hot-rod* enthusiast.

Refer to *so-called* and to *Coined Words* in the Reference Guide to check your answers.

Problems

■ **1.** You are secretary to the sales manager, Mr. Bert Henderson. The following items have been seen by Mr. Henderson and are ready for your action. Indicate what disposition you would make of each one. For instance, a notice of an intraoffice meeting would be entered on the desk calendar and destroyed.

(a) The program for the next weekly meeting of the Sales Executives Club

(b) A new catalog from Brown and Brown, a firm that services sales-incentive plans (The old catalog is in the files.)

(c) An application for a sales position from William Ainsworth

(d) Copy for the *Weekly Sales Newsletter*, which is sent to the sales manager by Bob Miller, editor, for final approval before it goes to the reproduction department

(e) A letter from an applicant for a sales position thanking Mr. Henderson for his initial interview

(f) An announcement of fall courses at a local college (The company reimburses employees who take job-related courses for their tuition costs.)

(g) A notice that Mr. Henderson's subscription to *Sales Management* has expired

(h) A letter from James Miller asking that his appointment for Wednesday be changed to Friday at the same hour

(i) A completed chapter for a book on *Prognosis of Sales Ability* (The name of the chapter is "Psychological Testing.")

(j) A carbon copy of Mr. Henderson's expense account for the preceding week

(k) A requisition for a new Norelco dictating unit for Mr. Henderson's use on the road

(l) A car-rental contract covering rental of salesmen's automobiles in the Chicago area

(m) A quarterly report of Xerox Corporation in which Mr. Henderson holds stock

(n) An interoffice memorandum from the president of the company approving Mr. Henderson's request to hold a sales training conference at Lake Crystal on September 18–20

(o) A letter from an irate customer complaining about the treatment he received from the Little Rock area salesman, Herman Beckwith

(p) A catalog from Hertz Company about its blanket quarterly service contract for company rentals

(q) Safety regulations applying to all departments in the home office

(r) A computer printout summarizing sales in each district for the preceding quarter

(s) Sales projection figures which you submitted to the Administrative Committee Monday

Related Work Assignments 39-41

39. Preparing a Letter for Filing. Mr. Simpson dictates the letter given below. He then tells you to follow it up in ten days with Form Letter 6 if the account is still unpaid. If no action has been secured in twenty days, you are to send Form Letter 9. Mr. Simpson then says that he has a vague remembrance of a Mr. Powell in Cedar Rapids or Muscatine who formerly dealt with the company and had a bad credit record. He asks you to get any information available from the central files about such a person. Use this procedure:

1. Type the letter and one carbon copy in good form so that you can prepare the carbon copy for filing.
2. Cross-reference the letter if necessary.
3. Release it for filing.
4. Make the necessary tickler file notations.
5. Requisition materials from the central files.

(The carbon copy of the letter and the forms are in the Workbook. If the Workbook is not available, type the letter and draw up the necessary forms.)

CONTINENTAL PRODUCTS
320 Euclid Avenue   Des Moines, Iowa   50313

July 18, 19--

Mr. John R. Powell
415 Cornell Avenue
Waterloo, Iowa 50701

Dear Mr. Powell:

On June 4 you wrote us that you had purchased the L. J. Rees business in Waterloo and that you would assume all of his obligations. At that time Mr. Rees owed us $36.15 on Invoice No. 5301. On June 13 you gave our representative in your territory, H. Barnes, an order for $42.81. The terms on the invoice were 2/10, n/30.

Since the old bill incurred by Mr. Rees is now sixty days past due and your own commitment of $42.81 remains unpaid, we are wondering if something is wrong. We know, Mr. Powell, that you realize the importance of establishing good credit relations with all of the companies from which you make purchases.

Won't you write us at once, either enclosing your check for the two invoices or letting us know what we may expect from you in the way of payment. If you will address your letter direct to me, you will save time in getting your credit record in good shape.

Sincerely yours,

Robert L. Simpson

Robert L. Simpson
General Manager

ble

40. Coding Letters for Subject Filing ⎫

41. Planning a Subject File ⎭
The instructions and supplies necessary for the completion of Related Work Assignments 40 and 41 are provided in the Workbook.

Alphabetic Indexing Procedures

Although she is expected to have filing skill and knowledge far beyond the rules of alphabetic indexing, the secretary, in using her own and company files, must also have a mastery of the rules for alphabetic indexing. Likewise a file supervisor, in guiding the serviceability of a filing system, must know these rules thoroughly, for all filing systems are based directly or indirectly upon them. When either of two rules may be followed, the rule which best fits the needs of the particular office or organization must be selected. This choice should be based on adequate understanding of filing.

Both general and specialized local and national references are helpful in indexing and coding specialized items. Telephone directories and lists

A secretary or a file supervisor, as well as a file clerk, must understand thoroughly principles and rules of filing.

—Remington Rand

Both secretary and file supervisor must work for uniform procedures for indexing and coding throughout the organization.

of civic, business, and governmental agencies are examples of such references. The *Stateman's Yearbook*, the *World Almanac and Book of Facts*, and *United States Government Organizational Manual* may be helpful specific sources for today's large business or governmental organization. The secretary, as well as the file supervisor, should be familiar with such important guides.

In addition, the file supervisor must see that the filing instructions and indexing and coding rules are uniform throughout the firm and are in written form, clear in meaning, and understood by all who have filing responsibilities. Without written explanations and systematic control, files lose their effectiveness.

On the following pages are some rules for alphabetic indexing that constitute a guide for efficient alphabetic filing. The examples under each rule are listed in correct alphabetic order. In each example the underline indicates the first letter or letters used in determining the indexing sequence.

Names of Individuals

■ (1) Basic Order of Indexing Units

Each part of the name of an individual is an indexing unit. Consider the surname (last name) as the first unit, the first name or initial as the second unit, and the middle name or initial as the third unit. Arrange all names in A–Z sequence, comparing each letter in order until a point of difference is reached. *The letter that determines the order of any two names is the first letter that is different in the two names.* Consider first the first unit of each name. Consider the second units only when the first units are identical. When further indexing is necessary to determine the relative position of two or more names that have exactly the same coding units, the relative position of the two or more names is determined by a further *identifying element,* such as *junior* or *senior,* or a part of the address. In such cases, the coder places a check mark above or at the left of the identifying element.

Name	Index Order of Units			Identifying
	Unit 1	Unit 2	Unit 3	Element
[1]John Ander	Ander,	John		
John E. Ander	Ander,	John	E.	
Louis Ander	Ander,	Louis		
Adam Anders	Anders,	Adam		
John C. Anderson, Jr.	Anderson,	John	C.	Junior
John C. Anderson, Sr.	Anderson,	John	C.	Senior
Aaron Andersson	Andersson,	Aaron		
David Lee Andrews	Andrews,	David	Lee	
E. Bennett Andrews	Andrews,	E.	Bennett	
[2]Soo On Bee	Bee,	Soo	On	
Eli J. Dorman, II	Dorman,	Eli	J.	II
Eli J. Dorman, III	Dorman,	Eli	J.	III

Note 1: *Ander* precedes *Anders* because the *r* in *Ander* is not followed by any letter. This is an example of the rule that *nothing precedes something.*

Note 2: An unusual or foreign personal name is indexed in the usual manner, with the last word considered to be the surname and therefore the first indexing unit.

■ (2) Surname Prefixes and Hyphened Surnames

(A) A surname prefix is considered to be a part of the first indexing unit. Among the common prefixes are *D', Da, De, Del, Des, El, Il, La, Le, Les, Los, Mac, Mc, O', Van,* and *Von.* In some cases the first letter of a prefix is not capitalized. Spacing between the prefix and the surname is not significant. (B) When compound (hyphened) surnames, such as *Martin-Ames*, occur in filing, each part of the surname is considered as a separate unit.

| Name | Index Order of Units | | |
	Unit 1	Unit 2	Unit 3
Charles Lemate	Lemate,	Charles	
Francis LeMate	LeMate,	Francis	
Ruth Martin-Ames	Martin-	Ames	Ruth
Wallace Martin	Martin,	Wallace	
Raymond O'Bonner	O'Bonner,	Raymond	
Albert Odell	Odell,	Albert	
[1]Edith St. Marner	Saint	Marner,	Edith

Note 1: Even though *St.* is abbreviated in the name *Edith St. Marner*, it is indexed as if it were spelled in full and is considered to be the first unit. (A variation of this rule is to consider the prefix *Saint* and the part of the surname that follows it to be one unit.)

Note 2: A variation of Rule 2B above is to consider hyphened surnames as one unit.

▪ (3) Initials and Abbreviations

(A) An initial in an individual's name is considered as an indexing unit and precedes all names in the same unit beginning with the same letter as the initial. (B) An abbreviated first or middle name or a nickname is considered as if it were written in full.

| Name | Index Order of Units | | |
	Unit 1	Unit 2	Unit 3
Paul Cameron	Cameron,	Paul	
D. D. Crawford	Crawford,	D.	D.
Dale Crawford	Crawford,	Dale	
Wm. E. Dackman	Dackman,	William	E.
Willis Dackman	Dackman,	Willis	
[1]Bob L. Davenport	Davenport,	Bob	L.
Robert Davenport	Davenport,	Robert	

Note 1: When the brief form of a given name is known to be used by an individual in his signature as his given name, this brief form name is treated as a unit.

▪ (4) Titles

(A) A personal or professional title or degree is usually not considered in filing. When the name is written in index form, the title is placed in parentheses at the end of the name. (B) A title is considered as the first indexing unit only when it is followed by given name only or by surname only.

Name	Index Order of Units		
	Unit 1	Unit 2	Unit 3
Miss Mary J. Fatam	Fatam,	Mary	J. (Miss)
1ᵃFather Delbert	Father	Delbert	
Rev. A. O. Hanson	Hanson,	A.	O. (Rev.)
Ralph Hanson, D. D.	Hanson,	Ralph (D. D.)	
1ᵃFather Robert O. Hanson	Hanson,	Robert	O. (Father)
Madame Mavis	Madame	Mavis	
Capt. Orrin Mason	Mason,	Orrin (Capt.)	
Mrs. Ann Jones Milton	Milton,	Ann	Jones (Mrs.)
Dr. Alfred Miltson	Miltson,	Alfred (Dr.)	

Note 1: For names including the religious titles *Father, Brother,* and *Sister,* Rule 4B may be modified as follows:

(a) To group together within a filing system all names bearing one of these titles, consider the titles themselves of first importance in indexing, regardless of the names that follow them. Names that do not include a surname are indexed in the order written: *Father Delbert.* Names that include one or more given names and a surname are transposed after the title, as explained in Rule 1: *Hanson, Robert O. (Father).*

(b) To set up a separate section to include all such names in the files, consider the name or names following such titles as of first importance, and *disregard the title.* Names that do not include a surname are indexed in the order written. Names that include one or more given names and a surname are transposed. Indexing order for Father Delbert in such case would be *Delbert (Father);* for *Father Robert O. Hanson* would be *Hanson, Robert O. (Father).*

▪ (5) Names of Married Women

The name of a married woman is indexed according to her legal name (her first name, either her maiden surname, or her middle name or initial, and her husband's surname). The title "Mrs." is disregarded in filing, but it is placed in parentheses after the legal name. The husband's name may be given in parentheses below the woman's legal name if it is known; but legally the only part of a man's name the woman assumes when she marries is his surname.

Name	Index Order of Units		
	Unit 1	Unit 2	Unit 3
Mrs. Robert (Becky Mae) Fritts	Fritts,	Becky	Mae (Mrs. Robert)
Mrs. Lucien (Becky Smith) Fritts	Fritts,	Becky	Smith (Mrs. Lucien)

■ (6) Identical Names

When the names of individuals are identical, their alphabetic order is determined by their addresses, starting with the city. Names of states are considered when the names of the cities are also alike. When the city and the state names as well as the full names of the individuals are alike, the alphabetic order is determined by street names; next, house and building numbers, with the lowest first. When it is used, the address is treated as an identifying element.

Names	Index Order of Units			Identifying Element
	Unit 1	Unit 2	Unit 3	
John Hess 314 Elm Street, Toledo	Hess,	John		Elm
John Hess 92 Plum Avenue, Toledo	Hess,	John		Plum
Edward Horton, Akron	Horton,	Edward		Akron
Edward Horton, Columbus	Horton,	Edward		Columbus
Edward Horton, Dayton	Horton,	Edward		Dayton
Edward B. Horton	Horton,	Edward	B.	

Names of Businesses and Groups

■ (7) Basic Order of Indexing Units

(A) Usually the indexing units of a business or group name are considered in the order in which they are written. (B) An exception is made to the usual rule when a business name includes the full name of an individual. In that case the units in the individual name are considered in the same order as if the individual name appeared independently.

Names	Index Order of Units		
	Unit 1	Unit 2	Unit 3
S. Martin Hats	Martin,	S.	Hats
Sam Martin Garage	Martin,	Sam	Garage
Nelson Lumber Company	Nelson	Lumber	Company
1Newsweek	Newsweek		
John Nobee News Corner	Nobee,	John	News
World Almanac	World	Almanac	

Note 1: The name of a magazine or book may be indexed according to these basic indexing rules for the name of a business.

▪ (8) Articles, Conjunctions, and Prepositions

(A) Such words as *the, and, &, for, on, in, by*, and *of the* are generally disregarded in indexing and filing. However, they are placed in parentheses for coding purposes. An initial *the* is placed in parentheses after the last unit. (B) A word normally classified as a preposition but used as the first word in a business name, or a modifying word, or part of a compound name is considered to be a separate indexing unit.

Names	Index Order of Units		
	Unit 1	Unit 2	Unit 3
By the Lane Inn	By	Lane (the)	Inn
Charles of the Ritz	Charles (of the)	Ritz	
Committee on Departmental Reorganization	Committee (on)	Departmental	Reorganization
Emery & Frank Shoes	Emery (&)	Frank	Shoes
End of the Mile Tavern	End (of the)	Mile	Tavern
The Favorite Music Shop	Favorite	Music	Shop (The)

▪ (9) Initials, Abbreviations, and Titles

(A) An initial or letter that is not a common abbreviation precedes a *word* beginning with that letter. (B) A known abbreviation, even though the abbreviation consists of a single letter without a period, is treated as if it were spelled in full, except *Mr.* and *Mrs.*, which are filed alphabetically as they are written. (C) A business name including a title followed by a given name, a surname, or a coined name is indexed in the order in which it is written.

Names	Index Order of Units		
	Unit 1	Unit 2	Unit 3
BB Brakes	B	B	Brakes
Ball Crank Co.	Ball	Crank	Company
B & O Railroad	Baltimore (&)	Ohio	Railroad
Bayard Co.	Bayard	Company	
C and C Dress Shoppe	C (and)	C	Dress
City Cleaners	City	Cleaners	
Dr. Footeze	Doctor	Footeze	
Monsieur Antoine Beauty Salon	Monsieur	Antoine	Beauty
Mrs. Della Knits	Mrs.	Della	Knits

■ (10) Numbers and Symbols

(A) A number in a firm name is considered as if it were written as one word. It is indexed as one unit. Four-place numbers are expressed in hundreds (not in thousands) in order to consider a smaller number of letters in the index unit. (B) A symbol with the number is considered separately as a word.

Names	Index Order of Units		
	Unit 1	Unit 2	Unit 3
A 1 Garage	A	One	Garage
8th St. Bldg.	Eighth	Street	Building
1110 Choices Store	Elevenhundredten	Choices	Store
$5 Bargain Store	Five	Dollar	Bargain
Ft. Evans News	Fort	Evans	News
40th Avenue Laundry	Fortieth	Avenue	Laundry
Fortilair Food Shop	Fortilair	Food	Shop

Note 1: Some file manuals omit the words *hundred* and *thousand* in considering the indexing unit—examples: fiveten for 510 and twelveseventy for 1270.

Note 2: When several names differ only in numeric designations, the order of those names may be based upon the numeric sequence instead of the alphabetic order of those numbers written in words. For example, if several branch stores of the same company are numbered, it might be more convenient in an office to have the names arranged in numeric sequence.

■ (11) Hyphened Names

The hyphened parts of business names (including coined parts) are indexed and filed as separate words.

An exception is made to this rule when the hyphened parts are shown in the dictionary as a single word or as a hyphened word. Both parts of such a word are considered together as one indexing unit.

Names	Index Order of Units		
	Unit 1	Unit 2	Unit 3
A-1 Retail Markets	A-	One	Retail
Read-N-Sew Studio	Read-	N-	Sew
Ready-Built Shelf Shop	Ready-	Built	Shelf
Reedy-Adam Corp.	Reedy-	Adam	Corporation
Charles A. Reedy Corp.	Reedy,	Charles	A.
Reedy-Miller Studios	Reedy-	Miller	Studios
Adam D. Reedy-Smith Corp.	Reedy-	Smith	Adam
Self-Service Laundry	Self-Service	Laundry	
Selfton Voice Studio	Selfton	Voice	Studio

▪ (12) One Versus Two Units

When separate words in a business name are shown in the dictionary as one word, the two should be treated as one indexing unit.

Names	Index Order of Units		
	Unit 1	Unit 2	Unit 3
Semi Weekly Cleaning Service	SemiWeekly	Cleaning	Service
Semiweekly Communication Review	Semiweekly	Communication	Review
Southwestern Machine Products	Southwestern	Machine	Products
South Western Office Supplies	SouthWestern	Office	Supplies
South-Western Publishing Co.	SouthWestern	Publishing	Co.
Southwick Drug Service	Southwick	Drug	Service
Southwick Drug Store	Southwick	DrugStore	
Stephan's Super Repair Shop	Stephan's	Super	Repair
Stephan's Super Market Displays	Stephan's	SuperMarket	Displays

▪ (13) Compound Geographic and Location Names

(A) Each English word in a compound geographic or location name is indexed as a separate unit. (B) A prefix or foreign article in such names is not considered as a separate indexing unit but is combined with the word that follows.

Names	Index Order of Units		
	Unit 1	Unit 2	Unit 3
Le Mont Food Products	LeMont	Food	Products
Los Angeles Actors' Guild	LosAngeles	Actors'	Guild
New York Central R. R.	New	York	Central
North Dakota Curios	North	Dakota	Curios
Old Saybury R. R. Station	Old	Saybury	Railroad
St. Thomas Island Home	Saint	Thomas	Island
Saintbury Publishing Co.	Saintbury	Publishing	Company
[1]San Diego Greenhouses, Inc.	San	Diego	Greenhouses
[1]Santa Clara Lithographers	Santa	Clara	Lithographers

Note 1: The words "San" in San Diego and "Santa" in Santa Clara mean "Saint," and are therefore indexed separately according to their spelling.

Note 2: When it is part of the actual name of a city (as *The Dalles*), *The* is considered to be the first unit.

Note 3: Some plans of filing treat each geographic name as one word regardless of the number of words in the name. *New Orleans* would be considered as one unit in such a filing system.

▪ (14) Possessives

When a word ends in *apostrophe s* ('s), the final *s* is not considered as part of the word for filing purposes, except as part of a contraction. When a word ends in *s apostrophe* (s'), however, the final *s* is considered.

Names	*Index Order of Units*		
	Unit 1	*Unit 2*	*Unit 3*
Girl Scouts of America	Girl	Scouts (of)	America
Girl's Sportswear	Girl('s)	Sportswear	
Girls' Short Stories	Girls'	Short	Stories
Harper's Restaurant	Harper('s)	Restaurant	
Harpers'	Harpers'		

▪ (15) Identical Business Names

(A) Identical names of businesses are arranged alphabetically by address, with address parts treated as identifying elements. (For this reason the word "City" should not be used in place of the name of the city.) (B) If the names of the cities are alike, filing arrangement depends upon names of states. (C) When two or more branches of a business are located in the same city, the names of the branches are arranged alphabetically by streets.

Names	*Index Order of Units*			*Identifying*
	Unit 1	*Unit 2*	*Unit 3*	*Element*
Jones Stationers, Decatur	Jones	Stationers,		Decatur
Jones Stationers, Eureka	Jones	Stationers,		Eureka
Jones Stationers, Sterling	Jones	Stationers,		Sterling
Kastner's, 531 Main Street	Kastner('s),			Main
Kastner's, 1024 Oak Street	Kastner('s),			Oak

Note 1: The name of the building in which the firm is located should not be considered unless the name of the street is not provided or is identical for both branches.

▪ (16) Banking Institutions and Newspapers

(A) When only local banking institutions are involved, their names are indexed as written. (B) When banks from several cities are involved, however, the names of the cities in which the banks are located are considered as the first indexing units with the words in the names of the banks following. If the name of the bank contains the name of the city or state, that geographic location is not repeated in the indexed form. If several states are involved, the names of the states should be considered after the name of the city, as identifying elements. (C) Newspapers follow the same indexing rules as those used for banks.

Names	Index Order of Units			Identifying Element
	Unit 1	Unit 2	Unit 3	
Bloomington Trust Co. Bloomington, Illinois	Bloomington	Trust	Company	Illinois
Bloomington Trust Co. Bloomington, Indiana	Bloomington	Trust	Company	Indiana
Third National Bank Duluth, Minnesota	Duluth:	Third	National	
Wenatchee Times Wenatchee, Washington	Wenatchee	Times		
Times Herald Williamsport, Pennsylvania	Williamsp't:	Times	Herald	

▪ (17) Elementary and Secondary Schools

An elementary or secondary school name is indexed first by the name of the city and then by the name of the school. An individual's name within a school name is transposed in the usual manner. If a school name begins with a city name, the city name is considered only once. State names are treated as identifying elements if a city name is alike in two or more states.

Names	Index Order of Units			Identifying Element
	Unit 1	Unit 2	Unit 3	
Modesto Elementary School Modesto, California	Modesto	Elementary	School	
Muncie Central High School Muncie, Indiana	Muncie	Central	High	
Muncie Southside High School Muncie, Indiana	Muncie	Southside	High	

| Newport High School Newport, Rhode Island | Newport | High | School | Rhode Island |
| Newport High School Newport, Washington | Newport | High | School | Washington |

▪ (18) Colleges, Universities, Special Schools, Hotels, Motels, and Other Organizations

(A) When common usage makes one part of a name more clearly identify the organization, that part is used as the first indexing unit. Otherwise, names of such organizations are indexed as they are generally written. (B) A city or state name as part of the organization name is considered an indexing unit or units. When the name of an organization is the same in two or more cities, city names are considered last as identifying elements.

Names	*Index Order of Units*		
	Unit 1	*Unit 2*	*Unit 3*
University of Idaho	Idaho,	University (of)	
Indiana University	Indiana	University	
Hotel Jolee Florists	Jolee,	Hotel,	Florists
Priest River Kiwanis Club	Kiwanis	Club,	Priest
Los Angeles City College	Los Angeles	City	College
Association of Lumbermen	Lumbermen,	Association (of)	
First Methodist Church	Methodist	Church,	First
[1]Martha Nelson Beauty College	Nelson,	Martha,	Beauty
[2]WLBC	Radio	Station	W
Venovich Motel	Venovich	Motel	

Note 1: An individual's name within the name of the organization is transposed in the usual manner.

Note 2: Preferable way to index a radio or television station is to consider *Radio Station* or *Television Station* as the first two units, followed by each call letter as a separate unit.

▪ (19) Federal Government Offices

The name of a federal government office is considered for indexing in the following order: (1) United States Government, (2) principal word or words in the name of the department, (3) principal word or words in the name of the bureau, (4) principal word or words in the name of the division. Such words as *Department of*, *Bureau of*, and *Division of* are transposed, with the word *of* disregarded and so placed in parentheses.

Names	Unit 4	Unit 5	Unit 6	Unit 7	Unit 8
Bureau of the Census U.S. Department of Commerce	Commerce	Department (of)	Census,	Bureau (of the)	
Weather Bureau U.S. Department of Commerce	Commerce	Department (of)	<u>W</u>eather	Bureau	
Social Security Administration U.S. Department of Health, Education, and Welfare	<u>H</u>ealth	Education (and)	Welfare	Department (of) { *Unit 9:* Security *Unit 10:* Administration	Social
Office of Indian Affairs U.S. Department of the Interior	<u>I</u>nterior	Department (of the)	Indian	Affairs	Office (of)
Federal Bureau of Investigation[1] U.S. Department of Justice	<u>J</u>ustice	Department (of)	Federal	Bureau (of)	Investigation

Note 1: The Federal Bureau of Investigation is so well known by its full name and initials that the name is often filed as known.

■ (20) Other Government Offices

(A) The name of any other government office is considered in the following order: (1) principal word or words in the name of the political subdivision, followed by its state, county, or city classification, (2) principal word or words in the name of the department, board, or office. Such words as *Department of* and *Bureau of* are transposed, with the word *of* placed in parentheses. (B) If two or more political subdivisions within a state have the same first indexing unit, the state name as an identifying element is considered immediately after the first principal word in the political subdivision, to determine relative placement of the items with identical first units.

Names	Index Order of Units		
	Unit 1	*Unit 2*	*Unit 3*
Department of Public Safety California	California,	State (of)	Public
Board of Health Cincinnati	Cincinnati,	City (of)	Health
Tax Collector Cook County	Cook,	County	Tax

▪ (21) Foreign Governments

Foreign-language names are translated into English for indexing, and the distinctive English name of the foreign country is considered first. Next, divisions are considered in the same manner as are United States governmental units.

Names	Index Order of Units		
	Unit 1	*Unit 2*	*Unit 3*
Republique Francaise Armée de l'Air[1]	France	Air	Force
Estados Unidos Mexicanos Secretaria de Industrio y Commercia	Mexico Secretary (of)	Industry (and)	Commerce, ←— *Unit 4*

Note 1: The names of foreign countries may be uniformly filed according to the native spelling, rather than the English translation.

General Guides

The student of alphabetic indexing rules may find it helpful to think in terms of general guides and then to note variations of these general guides. The following items would be among those most important:

1. An individual's full name is transposed, in either a personal or a business name; otherwise a business name is indexed as written.

2. Articles, conjunctions, prepositions, apostrophe addition in possessives, and titles are disregarded and placed in parentheses except where (1) a preposition or modifying word is a coined major part of a business name, or (2) a title is followed by a given name only or by a surname only.

3. Numbers and known abbreviations are spelled in full as one word, except *Mr.* or *Mrs.* or a nickname used as part of the individual's official signature.

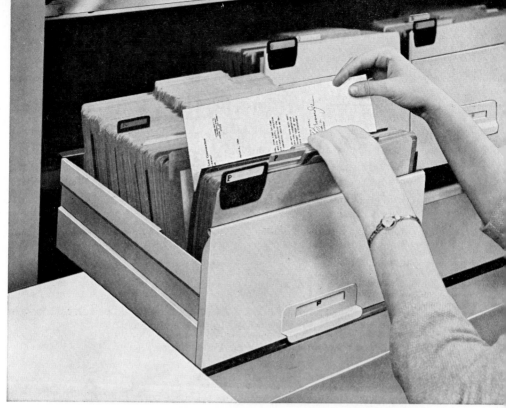

The secretary or file supervisor can assist in selecting a filing system that will help participants to file, withdraw, and refile materials with a minimum of time and error.

4. Initials, hyphened parts of names, and separated words are treated as individual units except where hyphened or separated words are shown by the dictionary to be acceptable as one word.

5. A special organization is indexed first by that part of the name which common usage causes to stand out most clearly in identifying that organization.

6. Elementary and secondary schools, newspapers, and banking institutions may be indexed first by the name of the city.

7. Governmental offices are indexed first by the major governmental unit of which the particular office is a part.

The secretary or the file supervisor, in determining which of several possibilities of filing rules will best fit her office or her organization, should keep in mind major criteria of serviceability: (1) What indexing procedure will provide for filing or refiling of materials with the least amount of error? (2) What indexing procedure will provide for filing or withdrawing materials and refiling materials with least time waste?

Once such a decision is made, definite steps must be taken to assure that, through the manual and whatever other means might be helpful, the procedure will be communicated successfully to all concerned and followed consistently.

Questions for Discussion

1. For what purposes other than filing may the secretary make use of the rules for alphabetic indexing?

2. Why do rules for filing government units, banks, schools, churches, and other organizations differ from the other rules for alphabetizing?

3. Can you think of a good reason why the rule for filing hyphened individual names differs from the rule for filing hyphened business names?

4. In what order are the units of an individual name considered in indexing?

5. Why should the word "City" not be used instead of the city name for local correspondents?

6. In what order are the units of a federal governmental office considered for indexing?

7. Refer to the Reference Guide. What salutation would be correct to use in a letter addressed to each of the following persons:

   (a) The wife of the President of the United States
   (b) The Vice President of the United States
   (c) An American ambassador
   (d) A member of the President's Cabinet
   (e) A priest in the Catholic Church

Problems

■ **1.** You are to set up a portion of a file for the Sales Promotion Department of Ohio Bell Telephone, which is planning solicitation of all business organizations in a small Ohio city for a new type of pushbutton telephone. Arrange the following names in the correct filing form and order:

1. **First National Bank of Athens**
2. **Saint James Church**
3. **Martins' Service Station, Third Street**
4. **South-Eastern Ohio Freezer Co.**
5. **Bank of Ohio, Athens**
6. **First Baptist Church of Athens**
7. **Agricultural Extension Service (Federal Office)**
8. **Board of Education, Athens, Ohio**
9. **Ohio University**
10. **Vocational Rehabilitation Service (Federal Office)**
11. **Athens Chamber of Commerce**
12. **State Highway Department**
13. **C & O Railway**
14. **Martin's Drive-in Theater**
15. **Third National Bank of Athens**
16. **Aaron Jones Retail Outlet**
17. **Martins' Service Station, Elm Street**
18. **Aaron-James Production Credit Corporation**
19. **Cartinson Dress Shoppe**

■ **2.** Rewrite the following business names in index form. Underline the first unit of the name once and the second unit of the name twice.

1. **Stoke's Paper Company**
2. **Mr. Tom's Fur Salon**
3. **The Las Vegas Novelty Shop**
4. **Tom & Joe's Bait Shop**
5. **Top of the Ridge Restaurant**
6. **Russell Stone Camping Equipment**

7. 8th Street Garage
8. John Stokes and Sons
9. S & T Delicatessen
10. Bureau of Labor Standards
    U.S. Department of Labor
11. Stone's Grocery, No. 1
12. South West Auto Supplies
13. San Bernardino Rest Home
14. Stone's Grocery, No. 2

■ **3.** The purpose of this project is to bring your card filing to a skill level. You will need 75 cards (5- by 3-inch).

Standards to Try for:

Type the cards in **15 minutes** (approximately 15 words per minute—**15** *wam*).

File the cards in **30 minutes**—not more than 2 errors.

With practice, reduce your time to 20 minutes—no errors.

Type each of the following names in index form at the top of a file card. (a) Place the number of each name in the upper right-hand corner of the card. (b) Arrange the cards in correct alphabetic order.

1. Paramount Theater
2. K & D Statistics Bureau
3. Mrs. Carl (Ann L.) Sailor
4. El Dorado Saddle Shop
5. Brother Edward Burke
6. N.Y.C.R.R.
7. Bureau of Internal Revenue
   Treasury Department
   U.S. Government
8. Donald Richards Camera Shop
9. No-Run Hose
10. North Western Printing Company
11. W. Walter, Jr.
12. Union Trust Company
    El Paso, Texas
13. National Savings Bank
    Newark, New Jersey
14. Joseph Hall, LL.B.
15. Water Works Department
    City of Glendale
16. Nordell, Inc.
17. Eck Sandwich Counter

18. National Park Service
    Dept. of Interior
    U.S. Government
19. Acacia Mutual Insurance Co.
20. Mt. Carmel Welfare Center
21. Jas. Le Doux
22. South Eastern Carloading Co.
23. Department of Health
    City of Rockdale
24. A & B Welding Co.
25. 19th Hole Restaurant
26. Walter-Woody, Attys.
27. C. C. Walter
28. Adam Salter
29. Paramount Shops, Inc.
    1000 McMillan
    Cincinnati, Ohio
30. A 1 Letter Service
31. Edith Marie Beauty Shop
32. KDKA Radio Station
33. Bureau of Nursing Service
    City of Birmingham
34. Town of Ft. Mitchell
35. Wm. Walter
36. Employment Service
    Department of Labor
    U.S. Government
37. Phillip St. Clair
38. John W. St. Clair
39. Bureau of Public Relief
    City of Rockdale
40. Paramount Shops, Inc.
    918 Glenway
    Cincinnati, Ohio
41. A B Furniture Co.
42. Jerome Rice Newman
43. La Mode Frocks
44. G. Laderman
45. East Hyde Park Market
46. Edith's Dancing Studio
47. Advance Laundry
48. Paramount Shops, Inc.
    Elder and Race
    Springfield, Ohio
49. Commission of Public Utilities
    City of Rockdale
50. South Norwalk Delicatessen
51. Civil Aeronautics Authority
    Dept. of Commerce
    U.S. Government
52. Carl Walter
53. Ann Sailor

54. Paramount Shops, Inc.
    2719 Erie Avenue
    Springfield, Ohio
55. Dr. S. F. Newman
56. Rev. Wm. J. Lekwin
57. J. A. Eckerle
58. Ad-Sales Corp.
59. Mountain Valley Water Co.
60. Newman-Rice Institute
61. B. A. Walterman
62. Fire Department
    City of Rockdale
63. The J. H. Albers Co.
64. Paramount Shops, Inc.
    133 East 5th Street
    Springfield, Illinois
65. St. Charles Hotel
66. Charles G. Walter
67. A & P Food Shoppe
68. Southern Pacific Lines
69. B. A. Walters, Sr.
70. The Abstract Co.
71. 9th St. Baptist Church
72. William E. Walter
73. Paramount Shops, Inc.
    4220 Glenway
    Cincinnati, Ohio
74. Mrs. Anna Adams
75. B. A. Walters, Jr.

■ **4.** Group I is arranged alphabetically. File each Group II name
in its proper position in Group I by
placing the letter at the end of the
line of the name it follows.

Group I

1. AAA Answering and Office Service
2. A & A Window Corporation
3. ABC Vending Corporation
4. A-1 Taxi Service
5. Abbey Floor Waxing Company
6. Abbott, A. C., Company, Inc.
7. Abraham & Straus
8. Abrahamson's Pharmacy
9. Abrams, Norman J. (Dr.)
10. Abrantes, Anthony (Jr.)
11. Academy Auto Wreckers
12. Accessory Shop
13. Ace Auto Service
14. Ackerman, Mary E.
15. Ackermann, Andrew J.

16. Acme Excavating Corporation
17. Acme-Standard Supply Company
18. Acorn Landscape Service
19. Acousticon of White Plains
20. Adam, Mary T.
21. Adams, Leonard C., Company
22. Addressograph-Multigraph
    Corporation
23. Adelman, Murray P.
24. Adelson, Marvin
25. Air Dispatch Incorporated
26. Air-Way Travel Service
27. Al & Nick's Restaurant
28. Albanese's Eastchester Inn
29. Albert Studio (The)
30. Alert Employment Agency
31. Alex's Radio & Television Service
32. Alfredo, A., Nurseries
33. Alitalia Airlines
34. All County Electric Service
35. Allen Brothers Incorporated
36. Allen-Keating Corporation
37. Allen's Supply Company
38. Allevi, Lillian (Mrs.)
39. Allied Van Lines, Incorporated
40. Allis-Chalmers Manufacturing
    Company

Group II

A. Accounting Associates
B. Addressing Machine & Equipment
   Company
C. A & A Automotive Company
D. Acorns' Dress Shop
E. J. B. Allin
F. A-B-K Electric Company
G. Adler Shoes for Men
H. Acme Steel Company
I. Joseph H. Alleva
J. Academy of Aeronautics
K. Air-Step Shoe Shop
L. Mrs. Elizabeth Abbott
M. Alexander Carpet Company
N. A & P Food Co.
O. Al's Glass Service
P. Paul Allen Incorporated
Q. Aladdin's House of Beauty
R. Julian B. L. Allen
S. First National Bank of Alden, New
   York
T. The Alice Ackermann Shop
U. The Allen-Andrews Mailing Co.

■ **5.** If the following names within each group were written in correct alphabetic order, in what order would they appear?

(a) 1. John E. Barnett
2. B & B Bakeries
3. Bakersfield Steel Products Co.
4. Baker, Barnett, and Baker
5. Baden-Morris Products

(b) 1. California Bank, Compton
2. California State Highway Commission
3. University of California
4. California Artcraft, Inc.
5. J. C. Caldwell Co.

(c) 1. McDevitt Bros., Inc.
2. Edward C. Mason, Senior
3. MacDaniels Chemical Corp.
4. Edward C. Mason, Junior
5. Dr. E. C. Mason

(d) 1. Petroleum Refining Co.
2. Sister Petronella
3. Mrs. Ann J. Pennington
4. Pt. Pleasant Barber Shop
5. Port Arthur News

(e) 1. St. Francis Hotel, San Francisco
2. San Bernardino Garage
3. Sacramento Business College
4. Santa Barbara Junior College
5. San Diego Education Association

■ **6.** The following letters are filed in the individual folder for Mary Young. Indicate the order, from front to back, in which the letters should be placed in this folder.

(a) A letter of recommendation from Mr. Wilson, dated April 23.

(b) Our request, dated April 7, to Harry Watson for a reference for Miss Young.

(c) A cross reference dated March 27 to a letter with five suggestions for candidates, including Mary Young.

(d) Our reply to her on April 6.

(e) A letter setting an appointment for Miss Young's interview, dated April 27.

(f) Mr. Watson's recommendation for Miss Young, dated April 10.

(g) Mary Young's application for a position, dated April 4.

(h) Our second request to Mr. Wilson for a reference, dated April 20.

(i) Our request to William Wilson for a letter of reference, dated April 7.

■ **7.** Rewrite the following names of individuals in index form. Underline the first unit of the name once and the second unit of the name twice.

1. Wm. Mier, 381 Shady Lane, Louisville, Kentucky
2. J. L. Meyers
3. Jas. C. Naber
4. John L. Meyer
5. Mrs. Robt. (Debra L.) O'Brien, Akron
6. Tom M. O'Connell, Sr.
7. T. Kenneth MacNab
8. Wm. Mier, 29 Parkland Avenue, Louisville, Kentucky
9. Mrs. J. Clarence Naber
10. Sister Norita
11. Mrs. Robt. (D. Lucille) O'Brien, Springfield
12. Tom M. O'Connell, Jr.
13. Thomas McNamara
14. John Meyers
15. J. L. Meyer, Ph.D.

Related Work Assignment 42

42. Your Fundamentals. This is the fifth in a series of Workbook assignments reviewing English usage, grammar, and punctuation. These assignments are based on the Reference Guide in this textbook.

5—1 √ *reorganizing the files*

Gail King has been secretary to Max Gill, director of in-service training, for three months.

Her greatest problem lies in locating material in his files. The only equipment is a file cabinet and folders. The manila folders are worn and uneven. Captions, either in caps or lower case, are not uniformly positioned.

Outlines for all courses given by Mr. Gill in the four years of his present position are filed chronologically. Outlines from other sources are filed under the company or university in which they were used. All catalogs of training material have been put in one folder as they are received each year. A file, *Teaching Aids*, contains sample charts, instructions for making a flannel board, leaflets on training films, case studies, felt pens, several reels of cases recorded on tape, graph paper, and samples of chart-making materials.

One folder contains class rolls for the four years; another, all requisitions. A folder marked *Retention System* has the company retention schedule.

In the supply closet is a pile of pamphlets and reprints of articles relating to employee training. Two shelves are filled with old magazines whose covers are marked with such notations as, "Use. *Office Discipline*, p. 17."

Correspondence and materials are filed in the same drawers. No correspondence has been destroyed during the four-year period. A letter is filed under *either* the name of the writer or the name on the letterhead.

Miss King drafts a reorganization plan to discuss with Mr. Gill.

Assuming you are Miss King, draft the plan showing materials you want to order, your classification plan, and your work-schedule plan.

5—2 √ *controlling the files*

Mr. Jones, Anne Taylor's employer, often bypasses company rules about only secretaries having access to the files. He takes folders and single items from the files without telling Miss Taylor or charging them out. He leaves material on her desk for refiling or in his desk or attaché case until a search locates the material.

One day, after being embarrassed by Mr. Jones when she can't locate the file on the preliminary budget (BUDGET—PRELIMINARY), she finds it filed behind "P." Hoping Mr. Jones will get the hint, she posts a KEEP OUT sign on the front of the file cabinet.

Do you think this is the way this situation should have been handled? If not, how would you have handled it?

5—3 √ intraoffice relationships

Isabel Boyd had been executive secretary to Mr. Robert Johnson, president of Apex Products, for five happy years. One Monday morning Mr. Johnson said, "I want you to meet Fred Abbott, my new administrative assistant. You will continue to do my confidential secretarial work, and Mr. Abbott will assume some of your responsibility for contacts both inside and outside the office. He was recently graduated from the University of Michigan where he majored in business administration. I am sure you will be glad to help him learn the ropes around here."

Naturally, Miss Boyd was disturbed. She usually knew Mr. Johnson's plans for personnel changes, but she had heard nothing of his adding an assistant. In the back of her mind was the remembrance of a talk which stressed that women cannot usually aspire to management status and that they should reconcile themselves to the fact that men win most of the promotions. She had worked long enough with Mr. Johnson to sense that he was slightly embarrassed and on the defensive. The change was obviously not to be further discussed. She decided against discussing his role with Fred Abbott. She felt it wasn't her responsibility to train somebody in secretarial techniques when he showed he felt superior to secretaries.

Fred seemed to be getting along well with Mr. Johnson. It developed that they belonged to the same college fraternity. Soon Fred was calling Mr. Johnson "Bob," although nobody else in management did so. He greeted all callers and tried to handle their business. He reached for the telephone before it stopped ringing. A typical conversation follows:

Hello. No, Mr. Smith, this is Fred Abbott instead of Miss Boyd. Just a minute and I will look it up. (Aside in a stage whisper: "Miss Boyd, what is the regulation on overtime for supervisory personnel?" Miss Boyd icily gives the information.) They get nothing above their 35 hours unless it is specifically authorized on a Form 11 by Bob. Bob has to sign it. Oh, you're welcome. Any time I can help, just let me know.

The crisis came after six weeks when Fred Abbott stopped at Miss Boyd's desk and said, "Miss Boyd, I am working on some budget figures. I can't seem to locate the file on administrative salaries. Will you get it for me, please." Miss Boyd said, "Mr. Abbott, that is a *confidential* file. Nobody but Mr. Johnson ever sees that file."

Fred Abbott walked away muttering, "Oh, well, if that is the way you want to cooperate! Just keep that chip on your shoulder and see where it gets you." Miss Boyd burst into tears and rushed into Mr. Johnson's office and said, "Mr. Johnson, it is either Fred Abbott or me. I will NOT work with that pipsqueak any longer." Mr. Johnson put down his papers and said, "Why, Miss Boyd, what is wrong? I had no idea you felt this way."

In dealing with this situation, you are to concentrate only on Miss Boyd's behavior, not on that of the administrative assistant.

What should Miss Boyd have done when Fred asked for the file?

In what ways should she have modified her behavior during the six weeks?

Can she do anything about the situation now, or does the correction lie with Mr. Johnson? Ideally, what should he do?

PART

6

—*United Press International Photo*

The executive's secretary or administrative assistant can expect to be constantly involved in planning and reporting meetings, arranging travel, and assuming greater responsibility during the executive's absence.

Assistance with Travel and Conferences

The business executive of today travels extensively—both at home and abroad—and spends many hours attending meetings. His meetings range from those of small intercompany committees and numerous policy-making groups to national and international conventions. Consequently, an increasing amount of the executive secretary's time is spent in planning and following through on travel arrangements, in helping the executive organize the meetings he chairs, and in assisting with reports of those he attends.

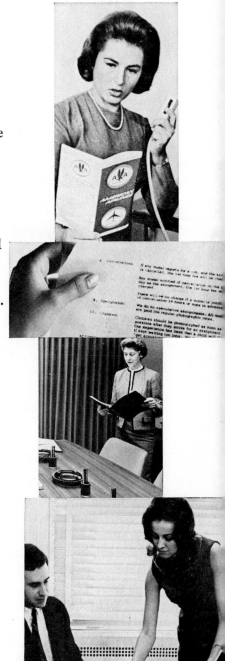

Ch.

16 Handling Travel Arrangements

17 Supervising the Details of Meetings

Handling Travel Arrangements

Top-level businessmen spend about 37 percent of their work year outside the office, according to a recent *Business Week* survey. They average 41 trips a year. A domestic trip usually lasts from one to three days, and their one or two yearly overseas trips usually take two weeks.

You as a secretary will handle some—if not all—of the details connected with your employer's travel. His accommodations will depend on his status in the company, but he has a right to the best equipment available in his category, on convenient time-saving schedules. To secure the best possible arrangements, learn the executive's preferences and your company's policies about travel. Learn, too, about special services to businessmen which cause them to prefer one carrier over another.

When 50 secretaries were asked what change within their companies during the past year affected them most, they listed first that their bosses are away from the office more of the time and that they have greater responsibility for daily operations than they formerly had. While the executive is away, you as a secretary or administrative assistant see that urgent matters are handled, that routine work flows to its completion, that a record of what transpired is prepared for the executive's return, and that, if the trip is an extended one, your employer is kept adequately informed during his absence.

Company Policies Regarding Travel Arrangements

The secretary's first concern in handling travel arrangements is to find out her company's policies. Who handles this responsibility? What airline, hotel, and other credit cards are issued; and what procedures are authorized for their use? How are tickets paid for? How are employees reimbursed for travel expenses? What restrictions does the company have as to per diem travel expenses? How are travel funds obtained?

Travel arrangements may be handled by a traffic department within the company, by an outside travel agency, or by the secretary herself.

▪ Traffic Department

In a very large office actual reservations for travel are expedited by a *traffic department* or *central travel service* that maintains close contact with all carriers; has on hand complete official guides for airlines, railroads, and steamships; and deals with special reservation clerks (at unlisted numbers) serving only such volume buyers. Here, the secretary informs the special department of a proposed trip; the department then suggests possible schedules to be approved by the executive and his secretary. When their decision is made, the department obtains the necessary tickets. The traffic department also secures and distributes credit cards for authorized personnel.

▪ Travel Agencies

In recent years the business world has turned increasingly to travel agencies. Some agencies now work with business travelers exclusively. The "know-how" of the reputable agency is especially helpful to an overseas-bound customer, but it is also a convenience to the domestic traveler.

A travel agency charges the customer no fee; the transportation lines "pick up the tab." The agent plans the entire itinerary, handles all ticketing, and at times provides unusual services.

▪ The Secretary

If a business organization provides neither the services of an intracompany special travel department nor the regular services of a travel agency, the secretary is "on her own" in handling all travel arrangements. She will deal directly with the transportation companies, or she may enlist the services of a travel agency.

The alert secretary arranges travel facilities that conform to the executive's personal preferences. She will soon discover the hotel chain he likes best, the airline he prefers, and even the seat location he enjoys most. By consulting the executive about his preferences or by remembering them from trip to trip, she alleviates the mental and physical stress of traveling.

> ROSE-FOR-A-FIRST-LADY campaign. Recognizing that the secretary usually chooses the plane her executive flies, United Airlines delivers every Monday morning a fresh long-stemmed rose to some 2,500 top secretaries in New York, Chicago, San Francisco, and Los Angeles. It has paid off.

Jet travel, now used by over 115 million passengers yearly, enables the executive to keep in close touch with various phases of his business operations.

Air Travel

Most businessmen prefer to fly, especially on long trips, because travel time is thereby reduced. Today, a passenger can breakfast in New York and lunch in San Francisco. The jet age has given the executive the advantage of keeping closer contact with operations without being away from his desk too long at a time. Air travel, however, has an element of uncertainty with the possibility of a canceled flight due to weather conditions (particularly during the winter). When an executive has a speaking engagement or a meeting where his presence is imperative, alternate transportation by air and rail can be arranged. In case weather permits him to fly, he may redeem his train ticket; but the cost of reserved space in a chair or sleeping car may be forfeited.

▪ Classes of Flight

Most flights between major cities are made by jet planes. A passenger en route to a small city probably will board a smaller feeder-connecting plane at some point. Nonstop service is preferable if available at a convenient hour. Generally, the classes of flight are:

1. **First class—serves complimentary meals during conventional mealtimes, provides refreshments, and has several attendants.**
2. **Air coach (Sky Tourist)—usually serves either a snack or a modest hot meal when the plane is aloft at mealtime.**

3. **Night air coach—usually travels between midnight and dawn, sometimes at reduced rates.**

4. **Executive (*for men only*)—provides extra services and more spacious quarters for an extra fee. For instance, on coast-to-coast flights, the TWA forward lounge is equipped with dictating machines, typewriters, and a curtained section marked "reserved."**

For shuttle service between certain cities (as New York/Boston, and Baltimore/Washington), passengers board the plane without reservations, and the flight leaves as soon as the plane is filled.

Many airlines now use planes that combine coach and first-class facilities on the same flight, with the plane divided into two sections.

Businessmen usually travel on first-class or executive flights. For a short flight not at mealtime a coach reservation may be adequate, but on a longer trip the executive may prefer more luxurious facilities. His executive level may determine his travel level to some extent. At almost all airports, too, the airlines maintain special luxury lounges for passengers who have flown a specified number of miles on the line. An executive who travels frequently is possibly eligible for such red-carpet treatment.

Baggage weight on domestic flights is no longer restricted. The traveler may take two bags of any size or weight and a carry-on case. Regulations differ on need to reconfirm a reservation for a return flight upon arrival at the first destination. Therefore, it is advisable to find out the requirements of the airline whose plane you plan to board. Also, if you leave your temporary phone number when you arrive at your first destination, the return-flight-line office will contact you if weather or other problems cause a change in flight schedule.

We are now on the brink of mass air traffic in planes carrying 250 or more passengers on domestic flights between major cities and on overseas flights, with corresponding fare reductions. Several airlines have ordered giants which carry around 500 passengers and which have cabins so large that they can be partitioned into rooms.

▪ Fares

A schedule of sample one-way first-class and coach fares between major cities is given in the back of the timetable folder. Sometimes there is a surcharge for luxury flights. Family plans are frequently featured, whereby a wife and children may travel with the husband at reduced rates (usually on Mondays through Thursdays only). Currently, a 10 percent federal tax is added to the cost of domestic airline tickets.

The setting of a working session may even be an airplane.

—Lockheed

■ Flight Schedules

Airline flight schedules are not uniform in structure. Most of them, however, contain separate quick-reference tables of all flights between major cities served. From the Trans World Airlines table illustrated on page 371, note that Flight 111 leaves O'Hare Field (which is 23 miles northwest of downtown Chicago) at 4:55 p.m. and arrives in San Francisco at 7:05 p.m. (actual flight time, 4 hours and 10 minutes) after a nonstop jet flight that provides both first-class and coach service. Schedules are always shown in *local* time.

The express tables between major cities served are usually followed by a complete schedule of all flights in each direction.

At the back of a flight folder an alphabetic chart of the cities served by the airline may be found, listing: the telephone number to call for reservations, the ticket office location, name of airport(s), miles from city, travel time to midtown, and fare to airport. (Major cities may have more than one airport. New York is served by three; Chicago by two; and Detroit by two, one of which is 14 miles closer to the city than the other.) Also shown is a table of one-way fares and important requirements for picking up tickets, reconfirming, and checking in on flights.

■ Flight Information

The quickest and best way a secretary can obtain flight information is to telephone the downtown ticket office of the various airlines. For complete information, however, she should consult the current issue of the monthly *Official Airline Guide*, which contains such data as worldwide airline timetables, fares, schedules of each airline as well as connecting schedules, and cities that have air service. As this reference is rather expensive for the infrequent user, a possible substitute called *Combined TDI*[1] *Timetables* (a summary card or folder issued monthly

[1]*TDI* refers to Transportation Displays, Inc., 17 E. 45th Street, New York, New York 10017.

at a modest subscription rate) may be used. This condensation shows the timetables of all direct flights of scheduled airlines between the local city and others frequently served. For instance, the TDI timetable for New York shows flights to and from 26 cities in the United States. A free copy of its timetables and card-size schedules of its flights between major cities may be picked up from an airline at the local airport. Each airline will also send new timetable folders, as they are issued, to the secretary requesting them.

▪ Flight Reservations

Reservations for air travel must be made—by telephone or in person—at the airport terminal, at a central ticket office, or with a travel agency. Usually, the person making the reservation decides upon the accommodations wanted and requests the airline clerk to check the availability of space. The clerk uses electronic equipment that stores all reservations that have been made for a certain flight from all ticketing stations, and he can tell immediately whether the space wanted is available. If the reservation is made in person, the ticket is issued then; otherwise, it is issued later and mailed to a specified address or held for pickup at the ticket office or airport. Messenger service also is available (at your expense) for ticket delivery and fare collection. Payment may be made in cash, by check (if proper identification is carried), or with an airline credit card (used for future billing).

Tickets-by-Mail service enables the customer to make a telephone reservation and then pay the invoice that accompanies the mailed ticket in time for his check to clear before the actual flight.

On many flights the exact seat location is reserved when the ticket is purchased or at check-in time. The location of choice seats depends on the type of plane.

TWA QUICK-WAY SCHEDULES

FROM CHICAGO						For Reservations and Information Call Numbers Shown on Pages 10 & 11	RETURN TO CHICAGO					
Leave O'Hare	Arrive Destination	Frequency	Flight No.	Aircraft	Class	Stops		Leave Destination	Arrive O'Hare	Frequency	Flight No.	Aircraft	Class	Stops

Leave O'Hare	Arrive Destination	Frequency	Flight No. Aircraft	Class	Stops		Leave Destination	Arrive O'Hare	Frequency	Flight No. Aircraft	Class	Stops
9 40 A	11 47 A	Daily	135 Jet	F Y	NON-STOP	SAN FRANCISCO Calif.	8 35 A	2 18 P	Daily	134 Jet	F Y	NON-STOP
11 15 A	1 22 P	Daily	175 Jet	F Y	NON-STOP		0'd 8 40 A	2 20 P	Daily	118 Jet	F Y	NON-STOP
1 15 P	3 25 P	Daily	137 Jet	F Y	NON-STOP		10 15 A	4 01 P	Ex We	818 Jet	F Y	NON-STOP
4 55 P	7 05 P	Daily	111 Jet	F Y	NON-STOP		10 15 A	4 00 P	We	180 Jet	F Y	NON-STOP
6 00 P	0'd 8 05 P	Daily	179 Jet	F Y	NON-STOP		2 40 P	8 26 P	Daily	144 Jet	F Y	NON-STOP
7 15 P	9 23 P	Daily	131 Jet	F Y	NON-STOP		4 00 P	9 45 P	Daily	176 Jet	F Y	NON-STOP
12 50 A	4 30 A	Daily	15 Jet	F/Y/K	One-stop		12 30 A	6 10 A	Daily	138 Jet	F Y	NON-STOP

SYMBOLS
*Next day
**Second day

/ Indicates connection
F—Jet First Class

Y—Jet Coach
(Domestic) or Jet Economy (Int'l)

K—Jet Economy
‡ Change of airport

Complimentary meals at normal meal time
For specific details please call your TWA agent

PAN AMERICAN

TABLE 4B

From Chicago

TO	FREQUENCY	LEAVE CHICAGO	FLIGHT NO.	CLASS	ARRIVE	CONNECTION POINT	LEAVE	FLIGHT NO.	CLASS	ARRIVE DESTINATION
FRANKFURT	DAILY DAILY	15 30 17 00	UA300 PA58	FY FY	18 45	New York DIRECT	19 45	PA72 PA58	FY FY	8 15 9 15
LISBON	DAILY	18 30	AA70	FY	21 25	New York	22 30	PA154	FY	9 55
LONDON	DAILY	17 00	PA58	FY	—	NONSTOP	—	PA58	FY	6 35
PARIS	DAILY	18 00	PA52	FY	—	DIRECT	—	PA52	FY	9 15
ROME	DAILY DAILY DAILY	14 00 16 30 18 30	NW20 UA300 AA70	FY FY FY	16 54 18 45 21 25	New York New York New York	18 30 20 30 22 30	PA110 PA114 PA154	FY FY FY	7 30 11 10 15 40

To Chicago

FROM	FREQUENCY	LEAVE FRANKFURT	FLIGHT NO.	CLASS	ARRIVE	CONNECTION POINT	LEAVE	FLIGHT NO.	CLASS	ARRIVE CHICAGO
FRANKFURT	DAILY DAILY	12 00 13 15	PA59 PA73	FY FY	— 16 45	DIRECT New York	— 18 25	PA59 UA341	FY FY	16 50 19 47
LISBON	DAILY	LEAVE LISBON 13 45	PA155	FY	16 00	New York	18 00	AA67	FY	19 17
LONDON	DAILY DAILY	LEAVE LONDON 14 15 18 30	PA59 PA1	FY FY	— 21 10	NONSTOP New York	— 23 00	PA59 AA239	FY FY	16 50 0 08
PARIS	DAILY DAILY	LEAVE PARIS 11 15 16 30	PA53 PA119	FY FY	— 19 30	DIRECT New York	— 21 00	PA53 AA331	FY FY	15 50 22 17
ROME	DAILY DAILY	LEAVE ROME 11 00 13 45	PA111 PA119	FY FY	15 15 19 30	New York New York	18 00 21 00	AA67 AA331	FY FY	19 17 22 17

A—(Propeller)—First Class.   F—(JET)—First Class Service.   L—(JET)—Standard Service (when used in multiple configuration).
T—(Propeller)—Coach Class.   Y—(JET)—Economy Class Service (U. S. Domestic—Coach Class).

To and from the United States

BETWEEN / AND	Class	New York O.W.	New York R.T.	Boston O.W.	Boston R.T.	Chicago O.W.	Chicago R.T.	Cleveland O.W.	Cleveland R.T.	Detroit O.W.	Detroit R.T.	Pacific Coast Cities① O.W.	Pacific Coast Cities① R.T.	Houston O.W.	Houston R.T.	Miami O.W.	Miami R.T.	New Orleans O.W.	New Orleans R.T.	Philadelphia O.W.	Philadelphia R.T.	Washington O.W.	Washington R.T.
SAO PAULO	F	$429.00	$815.00	445.50	848.00	471.00	904.00	454.00	865.00	461.00	879.00	502.00	954.00	434.00	825.00	377.00	716.00	434.00	825.00	429.00	815.00	429.00	815.00
	Y	330.00	627.00	344.60	656.10	364.00	700.00	349.60	666.10	354.00	675.00	386.00	734.00	330.00	627.00	290.00	551.00	330.00	627.00	330.00	627.00	330.00	627.00
SHANNON	F	346.00	657.40	337.00	640.30	398.30	762.00	378.90	723.20	381.90	730.70	506.90	*979.20	454.30	874.00	446.00	847.40	430.90	827.20	356.80	678.90	366.10	697.50
	Y	191.00	362.90	186.00	353.40	228.40	437.60	214.00	410.50	212.00	406.50	332.30	*647.10	276.00	536.70	276.00	524.40	263.40	507.70	201.10	383.10	207.40	395.70
	YH	230.00	437.00	225.00	427.50	267.40	511.70	253.00	484.60	251.00	480.60	371.30	*721.20	316.10	610.80	321.00	609.90	302.40	581.80	240.10	457.20	246.40	469.80
SINGAPORE ③	F	990.20	1897.40	997.30	1911.50	946.60	1810.10	966.60	1850.20	963.70	1844.40	830.00	1577.00	1005.50	1773.60	1005.50	1928.60	954.40	1825.70	966.60	1890.20	982.80	1882.50
	Y	639.00	1226.00	643.90	1235.90	605.00	1158.00	627.00	1202.00	623.90	1195.80	520.00	988.00	660.10	1268.20	660.10	1268.20	621.60	1191.20	639.00	1226.00	639.00	1226.00
STOCKHOLM	F	447.30	849.90	438.30	832.80	498.60	954.50	480.20	915.70	483.20	923.20	588.20	1133.70	533.00	1012.70	533.00	1012.70	532.20	1019.70	458.10	871.40	467.40	890.00
	Y	282.30	536.40	277.30	526.90	319.70	611.10	305.30	584.00	303.30	580.00	403.60	*782.60	368.40	710.20	368.40	701.20	354.70	681.20	292.40	556.60	298.70	569.20
	YH	327.30	621.90	322.30	612.40	364.70	696.60	350.30	669.50	348.30	665.50	448.60	*868.10	413.40	795.70	393.00	746.70	399.70	766.70	337.40	642.10	343.70	654.70
STUTTGART	F	417.00	792.30	408.00	775.20	469.30	896.90	449.90	858.10	452.90	865.60	577.90	*1114.10	525.30	1008.90	513.00	974.70	501.90	962.10	427.80	813.80	437.10	832.40
	Y	252.00	478.80	247.00	469.30	289.40	553.50	275.00	526.40	273.00	522.40	393.30	*763.00	338.10	652.60	328.00	623.20	324.00	623.60	262.10	498.50	268.40	511.60
	YH	297.00	564.30	292.00	554.80	334.40	639.00	320.00	611.90	318.00	607.90	438.30	*848.50	383.10	738.10	373.00	708.70	369.40	709.10	307.10	584.50	313.40	597.10
SYDNEY ③	F	904.50	1734.70	910.90	1747.40	860.20	1646.00	880.20	1686.10	877.30	1680.30	743.60	1412.90	841.90	1609.50	868.00	1661.60	868.00	1661.60	900.20	1726.10	896.40	1718.40
	Y	649.50	1246.00	654.20	1285.30	635.50	1218.00	635.50	1218.00	635.50	1218.00	530.50	1008.00	615.80	1178.60	670.60	1288.20	632.10	1211.20	649.50	1246.00	649.50	1246.00
TEGUCIGALPA	F	216.00	420.00	228.10	444.20	206.00	400.00	204.10	396.20	207.00	403.00	207.00	§394.00	150.00	285.00	139.00	265.00	139.00	265.00	206.40	400.80	200.10	388.20
	Y	151.90	295.80	161.70	315.40	137.40	266.80	142.90	277.70	143.50	279.00	152.00	§292.00	105.90	203.70	83.00	158.00	83.00	158.00	146.40	284.80	141.20	274.40
TEHERAN	F	759.80	1443.70	750.80	1426.60	812.10	1548.30	792.70	1509.50	795.70	1517.00	920.70	*1765.50	868.10	1660.30	846.00	1607.60	844.70	1613.50	770.60	1465.70	779.90	1483.80
	Y	498.00	946.20	493.00	936.70	535.40	1020.90	521.00	993.80	519.00	989.80	639.30	*1220.40	584.10	1120.00	571.00	1084.90	570.40	1091.00	553.10	1051.90	514.40	979.00
	YH	543.00	1031.70	538.00	1022.20	580.40	1106.40	566.00	1079.30	564.00	1075.30	684.30	*1315.90	629.10	1205.50	616.00	1170.40	615.40	1176.50	598.10	1137.40	559.40	1064.50
TOKYO ③	F	800.20	1536.40	807.30	1550.50	756.60	1449.10	776.60	1489.20	773.70	1483.40	640.00	1216.00	738.30	1412.60	815.60	1567.60	764.40	1464.70	796.60	1529.20	792.80	1521.50
	Y	519.00	998.00	523.90	1007.70	485.00	930.00	507.00	974.00	503.90	967.60	400.00	760.00	472.80	905.60	540.10	1040.20	501.60	963.20	519.00	998.00	519.00	998.00
VIENNA	F	448.30	851.80	439.30	834.70	500.60	956.40	481.20	917.60	484.20	925.10	609.20	*1173.60	556.50	1068.40	533.20	1021.60	533.20	1021.60	459.10	873.30	468.40	891.90
	Y	277.00	526.30	272.00	516.80	314.40	601.00	300.00	573.90	298.00	569.90	418.30	*810.50	363.10	700.10	354.00	672.60	349.40	671.10	287.10	546.50	293.40	559.10
	YH	322.00	611.80	317.00	602.30	359.40	686.50	345.00	659.40	343.00	655.40	463.30	*896.00	408.10	785.60	399.00	758.10	394.40	756.60	332.10	632.00	338.40	644.60
ZURICH	F	417.00	792.30	408.00	775.20	469.30	896.90	449.90	858.10	452.90	865.60	577.90	*1114.10	525.30	1008.90	513.00	974.70	501.90	962.10	427.80	813.80	437.10	832.40
	Y	252.00	478.80	247.00	469.30	289.40	553.50	275.00	526.40	273.00	522.40	393.30	*763.00	338.10	652.60	328.00	623.20	324.00	623.60	262.10	498.50	268.40	511.60
	YH	297.00	564.30	292.00	554.80	334.40	639.00	320.00	611.90	318.00	607.90	438.30	*848.50	383.10	738.10	373.00	708.70	369.40	709.10	307.10	584.50	313.40	597.10

Y—BASIC ECONOMY CLASS JET—Applies any time of the year except for Transatlantic Travel to or from Europe, Africa and the Middle East commencing during the periods when the YH (Peak Economy Class Jet) fares are in effect.
YH—PEAK ECONOMY CLASS JET—Applies when transatlantic travel to or from Europe, Africa and the Middle East commences during the periods:

From the U.S.A.—May 22 through August 3.
To the U.S.A.—July 17 through September 28.

F—FIRST CLASS JET.
KN—NIGHT THRIFT CLASS JET.

K—THRIFT CLASS JET.   ①—These fares apply from Los Angeles, Oakland, San Francisco, Portland and Seattle, except as noted.   ②—These fares are transpacific fares.   ③—Good southward on flights scheduled to depart 11:46 p.m. to 4:59 a.m. inclusive and northward on flights scheduled to depart 11:15 p.m. to 7:30 a.m. inclusive. Not good June 29–September 4 or southward December 15-31 or northward Dec. 31-Jan. 7.

†—These fares also apply for Balboa, C.Z.   ★—Fares apply for Los Angeles and San Francisco only.   ✝—St. Croix only.   §—Fares apply for Los Angeles only.   See Page 34 for fares from Atlanta and Dallas.

FOR A SLIGHTLY HIGHER AMOUNT FARES MAY BE PAID IN MONTHLY INSTALLMENTS IN THE U.S.A. AND CERTAIN OTHER COUNTRIES.

Shown above are portions of a Pan American flight schedule.

■ Ticketing Plans

Because competition among airlines is so keen, especially for the business of heavy commercial purchasers of transportation, numerous ticketing plans have been developed. Undoubtedly, additional ingenious ones will follow rapidly. One airline issues a stock of regular airline tickets and a validator to the commercial customer. After space has been reserved by telephone or teletype, a "ticket office" can thus be set up within the company and tickets can be issued. A company may also arrange for an employee to carry a supply of *Airchecks*, the "write-your-own" tickets. With Airchecks the customer telephones for a reservation, fills in his ticket, presents it at the gate, and boards his flight; the company is billed at the end of the month.

To save pickup time, another airline provides *Teleticketing*. When a telephone reservation is made, teletype transmits the ticket and automatically prints it in the customer's office on a special machine. *Commuter books* are also available between selected pairs of cities for customers having frequent occasion to travel between two cities. The passenger makes a telephone reservation and uses his commuter ticket when he boards his flight.

Reservations may be canceled by the passenger, or purchased tickets may be returned for refunds until certain specified hours before departure times. If equipment failure or weather conditions warrant, the airline also may cancel a flight. All persons with reservations are notified promptly of the cancellation. For this reason the business and home telephone numbers of all passengers are obtained when a reservation is made.

■ Other Airport Transportation Services

An *airport limousine* is available for transportation to and from downtown locations to the airport, usually at a lower rate than taxi service. In some cities the limousine calls for passengers at key hotels; in others it leaves from either a downtown ticket office or a downtown airline terminal. The ticket often shows the location of the limousine pickup point and departure time for the airport. Sometimes it is necessary to reserve limousine space when making a plane reservation. If the limousine leaves from a downtown airport terminal, the passenger checks in at the terminal (checks in his baggage, which then becomes the airline's responsibility, and checks in for the flight); when he arrives at the airport, he has only to board the plane. If the limousine leaves from a point other than a terminal, the passenger checks in at the airport.

Helicopter Service. The airline flight folder indicates whether *helicopter service* is available between airports in cities served by more than one facility or from the airport to downtown points. While this service may be provided without charge to long-distance passengers, it is usually more expensive than taxi or limousine service. The opening page of Part 6 of this book shows the heliport on top of the Pan American Building in New York.

Rent-a-Plane Service. Either *taxi-plane service* (with pilot) or *fly-yourself service* (without pilot) is available in a number of cities. The automobile rental service can provide information.

Company-Owned Planes. In 1965 a *Business Week* study showed that more than half of the companies surveyed owned their own planes—usually two or more. Business is taking to the air in its own craft to reduce travel time even more for executives than is possible by commercial aviation. Many companies, however, limit the number of top officials who can fly in the same plane, either private or commercial, to protect continuity of management in case of a crash.

Train Travel

The businessman who chooses to travel by train does so because he can usually travel at night and have the day free for business. He also appreciates arriving close to the center of the city. Most important, weather does not introduce as much of an element of uncertainty of arrival in time for a crucial appointment. There are two classes of train travel: (1) *coach* and (2) *first class* (Pullman or sleeping car).

■ Coach Travel

A railroad coach ticket, which may be purchased at the station ticket window at the time of departure, entitles the passenger to transportation in a *coach car*—one with standard seats. No reservations are necessary for travel in ordinary coaches. Reservations are necessary, however, on the special, de luxe all-coach trains operated by some lines. The seats in these coaches recline, and the lights are dimmed at night so that the passengers may sleep in their seats. There may be a slight service charge for reservations on a de luxe coach train. Coach service is the least expensive type of train accommodation. On some lines sleeper-coach service is available on coaches at no extra fare but with a flat charge for the sleeping accommodations. An advance reservation must be made for sleeper-coach space.

▪ First-Class (Sleeper or Chair Car) Travel

Either the Pullman Company or the railway company operates the sleeping and chair-car concessions on railroads.

For day travel there is the *chair* (or *parlor*) *car* containing comfortable armchairs. For night travel or day-and-night travel, there is the *sleeper car*. In the traditional sleeper, the seats are converted into berths. Each pair of seats constitutes a *section* that may be made up into an upper and a lower berth; access to the upper berth is by ladder. Other types of sleeping cars provide more expensive accommodations. In the order of increasing cost, these are the *roomette, bedroom, compartment, drawing room,* and *master room.* Most executives prefer the roomette, or better, type of accommodation.

Reservations must be made for all sleeper and parlor-car space. *Space* refers to the actual accommodation and where it is located—for example, Roomette 6, Car 541, Train No. 618. Reservations are usually made by telephone with the central ticket office of the railroad or the ticket office at the railroad station. The railroad clerk will ask that reservations for tickets be picked up and paid for by a certain date.

Railroads also have plans for ticketing by mail. They will accept corporate checks and honor certain credit cards.

▪ Redemption of Train Tickets

When an executive changes his travel plans, the secretary must cancel first-class tickets 24 hours in advance of train departure to obtain refunds (here, full redemption is given for the railroad portion only, less a service charge for the first-class portion). Full redemption is given on coach-travel tickets returned up to departure.

SLEEPING-CAR, SLEEPERCOACH, LOUNGE AND DINING SERVICE
COACH SERVICE AVAILABLE ON ALL TRAINS.
TRAINS NOT INDICATED BELOW CARRY COACHES ONLY.

No. 6—Sleeping Car, Lounge Sleeping Car, SLEEPERCOACH and Diner Lounge Car.
No. 8—Sleeping Car, SLEEPERCOACH, Lounge Car and Dining Service.
No. 15—Sleeping Car and Dining Service.
No. 16—Sleeping Car, Lounge Car and Dining Service.
No. 17—Sleeping Car, SLEEPERCOACH, Lounge Car and Dining Service.
No. 19—Sleeping Car, SLEEPERCOACH, Lounge Car and Dining Service.
No. 25—Observation Lounge Sleeping Car, Sleeping Car, SLEEPERCOACH, Lounge Car and Dining Service. Reserved Reclining Seat Coach.
No. 26—Observation Lounge Sleeping Car, Sleeping Car, SLEEPERCOACH, Lounge Car and Dining Service, Reserved Reclining Seat Coach.
No. 27—Sleeping Car, SLEEPERCOACH, Lounge Car and Dining Service.
No. 28—Sleeping Car, SLEEPERCOACH, Lounge Car and Dining Service.
No. 51—Buffet Service, Buffalo to Cleveland.
No. 57—Sleeping Car and Lounge Sleeping Car, Breakfast Service into Cleveland.
No. 59—Sleeping Car, SLEEPERCOACH Diner Lounge Car and Lounge Sleeping Car.
No. 90—Buffet Lounge Car from Cleveland.
No. 302—Tavern Lounge Chicago to Indianapolis.
No. 303—Sleeping Car (Pullman Operated), Lounge Coach and Dining Service. All Coach Seats Reserved.
No. 304—Lounge Coach, Sleeping Car (Pullman Operated) and Dining Service. All Coach Seats Reserved.

▪ Timetable Folders

Each railroad publishes its own timetable folder (as illustrated on page 378) and supplies it free to prospective travelers and to passengers. It includes a general index, an index to tables, an index to the cities or stations, the specific timetables, a table of fares between important points, and general travel information. The monthly Official Guide of the Railways (National Railways Publications Company, New York), which is available by subscription or single copy, is helpful to a secretary involved in extensive planning of travel.

Railroad timetables are not uniform. To the inexperienced secretary, reading a timetable may seem difficult. Every timetable, however, fully explains the meaning of every symbol and typeface used. For instance, examine the New York Central timetable illustrated on the next page. Every reference mark is important.

Each railway timetable folder includes an *index to stations* giving the numbers or letters of the individual timetables in which service to a city (or railroad station) is listed. To learn which tables list service between two cities, look up both cities in the index and jot down those table numbers or letters that are common to both. For example, to find the service available between Albany and Buffalo in the illustration, look for the table numbers that are common to both Albany and Buffalo—in this case, Tables 1, 2, 3, 4, 5, and 6. Therefore, these tables may be studied to select the service to be used between these two cities. Part of Table 1 is illustrated on page 378.

Rent-a-Car Automobile Travel

There are times when a businessman finds it more convenient to travel by air or train and to rent a car at the destination than to make the entire trip by automobile in order to have the automobile available. Both airline and railroad timetable folders indicate those cities with rent-a-car service. Rental agencies publish directories of companies both here and abroad that rent automobiles, giving daily rates and mileage charges of each station. Reservations for rental cars, including a specification of make and type wanted, may be placed with the ticket agent when the travel reservation is made or with the local office of the rental agency.

Upon arrival, the executive presents his driver's license and makes financial arrangements for renting the car. An especially attractive

Schedules shown on this page are in terms of "LOCAL TIME" (standard or daylight) as observed by each city.

NEW YORK and BOSTON—ALBANY—BUFFALO—CLEVELAND—TOLEDO—CHICAGO

Table No. 1 — WESTBOUND

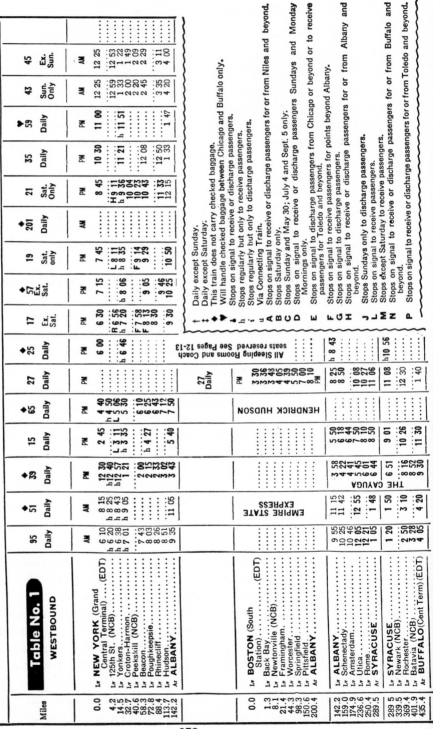

NEW YORK to ALBANY

Miles	Station	95 Daily	◆51 Daily	◆39 Daily	15 Daily	◆65 Daily	27 Daily	◆25 Daily	17 Ex. Sat.	◆57 Ex. Sat.	19 Sat. only	◆201 Daily	21 Sat. Only	35 Daily	▾59 Daily	43 Sun. Only	45 Ex. Sun.
		AM	AM	PM	PM	PM	PM	PM	PM	PM	PM	AM	PM	PM	PM	AM	AM
0.0	Lv NEW YORK (Grand Central Terminal)....(EDT)	6 10	8 15	12 30	2 45	4 40		6 00	6 30	7 15	7 45		8 45	10 30	11 00	12 25	12 25
4.2	Lv 125th St. (NCB)	h 6 20	h 8 25	h12 40		4 50							H9 11				
14.5	Lv Yonkers	h 6 38	h 8 43	h12 57	L 3 11	h 5 06							h 9 36			12 59	12 59
32.7	Lv Croton-Harmon	h 7 01	h 9 05	1 21	3 35	L 5 30		h 6 46	R 6 56	h 8 06	L 8 11		10 04	11 21	h 11 51	1 33	1 22
40.6	Lv Peekskill (NCB)																
58.3	Lv Beacon	7 43			h 4 27	6 10			7 20		h 8 35		10 23	12 08		2 00	1 49
72.8	Lv Poughkeepsie	8 03		2 00		6 25			F 7 58	9 05	F 9 14		10 43	12 50		2 20	2 09
88.4	Lv Rhinecliff	8 26		2 15		6 43			F 8 13		F 9 29					2 45	2 29
113.7	Lv Hudson	8 51		2 33		7 12			8 30	9 46			11 33	1 33	1 47	3 35	3 11
142.2	Ar ALBANY	9 35	11 05	3 43	5 40	7 50			9 30	10 25	10 50		12 15			4 20	4 00

All Sleeping Rooms and Coach seats reserved. See Pages 12-13.

BOSTON to ALBANY

Miles	Station	51 EMPIRE STATE EXPRESS	39 THE CAYUGA	65 HENDRICK HUDSON	27 Daily
					PM
0.0	Lv BOSTON (South Station)....(EDT)				3 30
1.3	Lv Back Bay				3 36
8.1	Lv Newtonville (NCB)				3 43
21.4	Lv Framingham				4 05
44.3	Lv Worcester				4 39
98.3	Lv Springfield				5 50
150.6	Lv Pittsfield				7 00
200.4	Ar ALBANY				8 10

ALBANY to SYRACUSE

Miles	Station	95	51	39	15	27	25
		AM	AM	PM	PM	PM	PM
142.2	Lv ALBANY	9 55	11 15	3 58	5 50	8 25	h 8 43
159.0	Lv Schenectady	10 25	11 42	4 22	6 18	8 50	
174.9	Lv Amsterdam	10 46		4 41	6 44	10 08	
236.6	Lv Utica	12 05	12 55	5 45	7 50	10 08	
250.4	Lv Rome	12 21		6 01			
289.5	Ar SYRACUSE	1 05	1 48	6 44	8 50	11 06	h10 56

SYRACUSE to BUFFALO

Miles	Station	95	51	39	15	27
289.5	Lv SYRACUSE	1 20	1 50	6 51	9 01	11 08
339.5	Lv Newark (NCB)	2 50		8 16		
369.4	Lv Rochester	3 28	3 10	8 52	10 26	12 30
401.9	Lv Batavia (NCB)					
435.4	Ar BUFFALO (Cent Term) (EDT)	4 05	4 20	9 30	11 30	1 40

Reference Notes

† Daily except Sunday.
‡ Daily except Saturday.
◆ This train does not carry checked baggage.
⧫ Will handle checked baggage between Chicago and Buffalo only.
h Stops on signal to receive or discharge passengers.
⋮ Stops regularly but only to receive passengers.
⋮ Stops regularly but only to discharge passengers.
u Via Connecting Train.
A Stops on signal to receive or discharge passengers for or from Niles and beyond.
B Stops Saturday only.
C Stops Sunday and May 30; July 4 and Sept. 5 only.
D Stops on signal to receive or discharge passengers Sundays and Monday Mornings only.
E Stops on signal to discharge passengers from Chicago or beyond or to receive passengers for Toledo and beyond.
F Stops on signal to receive or discharge passengers for points beyond Albany.
G Stops on signal to discharge passengers.
H Stops on signal to receive or discharge passengers for or from Albany and beyond.
J Stops Sundays only to discharge passengers.
L Stops on signal to receive passengers.
M Stops except Saturday to receive passengers.
N Stops on signal to receive or discharge passengers for or from Buffalo and beyond.
P Stops on signal to receive or discharge passengers for or from Toledo and beyond.

feature is the "rent-it-here-leave-it-there" policy of the agencies. Automobile rental costs may be charged to any of a number of credit cards. Rental services provide local information about routes, where to eat and stay, and what to see.

Members of the American Automobile Association may secure travel guides for any contemplated trip. Several oil companies map travel routes on request. There are handy dining and lodging guides that may be purchased to indicate recommended restaurants and motels.

International Travel

"Last week when I was in Rome . . ." is as common in business conversation today as a casual reference to a trip to a neighboring state used to be. A secretary to a top executive will probably plan his international—as well as his domestic—travel and will need to understand its many ramifications.

■ General Considerations

Planning for foreign travel differs in several ways from planning for shorter domestic trips. For instance, time changes can take a great toll on the executive. (See time zones, page 275.) Air Force medical experts suggest that important decisions should not be made either shortly before or after a long jet flight, so the businessman who travels by plane should try to allow one day on arrival in Europe and two days on return to the United States to adjust both physically and psychologically to time differences. Leaving here on a morning flight which arrives overseas at night will force the traveler to rest before he starts his negotiations, and flying home on the first day of a weekend will provide rest before going back to the office.

Another difference between domestic and foreign travel is in arranging appointments. Both because of difficulties in getting around in a foreign city and the slower pace at which European business is conducted, the American visitor will want to keep his appointments to two or three a day.

Fares are standard, so an airline can attract the lucrative American business travel only by providing special services. One airline arranges for conference rooms at the international airport and coordinates flight schedules of participants so that they can meet conveniently, sometimes without ever leaving the airport and going through customs. Other lines help to make business contacts, arrange for secretarial services and conference rooms, or make hotel reservations if they are given at least two weeks to provide these special accommodations.

The business card is an important adjunct to the business call. A card is always presented by a caller; therefore, a business visitor can easily use up a supply of 200 cards if he is attending a business fair. The European business fair has no counterpart in this country. An entire year's output of a product may be sold during such a fair.

Learning the mores of the countries to be visited is important to the success of a business visit. Most of the international airlines now publish guides for conducting business in Europe. These and *Business Week's Businessman's Guide to Europe* are useful references when planning a trip. In them are found dates of important trade fairs, holidays in each country, hotel and restaurant information, addresses of important business contacts in each country, currency information, and invaluable hints for improving business contacts.

▪ Services of a Travel Agency

A company's travel department or a travel agency can be of great help in planning a foreign trip. In fact, without a well-established company travel department, the secretary will find the services of a travel agent almost indispensable to:

Make hotel and rent-a-car reservations.

List available transportation.

Suggest an itinerary or itineraries and procure tickets.

Notify you of the required travel documents and how to obtain them.

Give currency information and secure enough foreign currency for entering the first country on the itinerary.

Explain baggage restrictions.

Secure insurance for traveler and baggage.

List port taxes levied. (Most international airports charge from $1 to $3.)

Give information as to time limitations for visits.

Supply free literature and services.

Arrange for you to be met by a travel representative or a limousine.

Get visas.

▪ Foreign Business Contacts

Half of the work of a successful trip abroad will take place before the executive boards the jet. Locating business contacts and other data must precede the trip. Two of the most practical sources of such help are the U.S. Department of Commerce and the Chamber of Commerce of the United States. The commercial attachés of the countries to be visited (most of them located in New York City) can give detailed information. The nearest field offices of the Department of Commerce (such as Atlanta, Los Angeles, and Milwaukee) will give advice either personally or in writing if a special form, Request for Assistance by American Businessmen Traveling Abroad, is used. The Foreign Trade Handbook (Dartnell Corporation) covers foreign trade organizations, foreign trade management, finance, foreign trade services, technical procedures in foreign trade, international commercial policies, and legal aspects of foreign trade.

■ Passports

The first requisite for foreign travel is a *passport* issued by the Department of State three or four weeks after an application is filed. A passport is an official document granting permission to travel to the person specified in it and authenticating his right to protection. For travel in most countries outside the United States, a passport is necessary; but it is not required in Canada, Mexico, Bermuda, the West Indies, and Central American countries. Application forms are obtainable from the Federal District Court in your city or from the passport agencies of the Department of State in Boston, Chicago, Los Angeles, Miami, New Orleans, New York, San Francisco, and Washington.

The applicant (not his secretary) must appear *in person* at the passport office, before the clerk of the nearest Federal Court, or County Court having jurisdiction in naturalization proceedings with:

Proof of United States citizenship

An identifying witness (American citizen over 21 years of age who has known the applicant at least two years)

Two signed duplicate photographs taken within the past two years

The passport fee

As soon as the passport is received, it should be signed and the information requested on the inside cover must be filled in. It should always be carried during overseas travel. The business traveler should also carry a letter from the business organization represented—stating the where, when, why, and duration of the proposed visit.

▪ Visas

A *visa* is a permit granted by a foreign government for a person to
enter its territory. It usually appears as a stamped notation in a passport indicating that the bearer may enter the country for a certain purpose and for a specified period of time. Anyone in doubt as to the
necessity of obtaining a travel visa for travel in any foreign country
should consult a travel agent before leaving the United States. Consular
representatives of most foreign countries are located in principal cities
and their addresses can be found in the *Congressional Directory*, or in
the Yellow Pages under "Consulates." If the traveler intends to work in
the country to be visited, he should check to see whether he needs a
work permit.

▪ Vaccination and Inoculation Requirements

When applying for a passport, the traveler should ask for an *International Certificate of Vaccination*. Before his return to the United
States, he must present a valid Certificate indicating that he has had
a successful vaccination within the past three years or has been re-
vaccinated within this period. In addition, the traveler will need certain
inoculations before he enters countries where the incidence of certain
diseases is great. (Information may be obtained from the travel agency
or the consulate of the country in question.)

▪ Overseas Flights

Executives with foreign interests frequently take overseas flights.
Jet flights are made in excellent time. For example, the average jet
flies to London in six hours and will soon require no more than two
hours.

Flights have two seasons—the "on" season (from April 1 to September 30) is more expensive than the "off" season (from October 1 to
March 31). The winter schedule to Europe is limited.

There are two classes of flights: *first class* and *economy* (or *tourist*).
On a jet plane these flights are combined, with economy passengers
occupying a different section of the plane. Meals are served, but the
quality may differ. For example, steak may be served to first-class
passengers, while chicken is served to those taking the economy flight.
First-class passengers are allowed 66 pounds of baggage on overseas
flights, and economy-class passengers are allowed 44 pounds.

24-Hour Clock

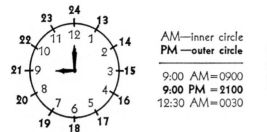

AM—inner circle
PM —outer circle

9:00 AM = 0900
9:00 PM = 2100
12:30 AM = 0030

All international flights in the timetable below are shown by 24-hour-clock time.

▮ NEW YORK - MONTREAL - BOSTON - LONDON - MILAN - ROME

Effective 15th - 31st March, 19--

READ DOWN

FLIGHT NUMBER		AZ 613	AZ 613	AZ 653	AZ 613	AZ 611	AZ 603	AZ 633	AZ 653	AZ 625
CLASS		F/Y	F/Y	F/Y	F/Y	F/Y	F/Y	F/Y	F/Y	F/Y
AIRCRAFT		DC-8	DC-8	DC-8	DC-8	DC-8	DC-8	DC-8	DC-8	DC-8
OPERATION DAYS		MO	TU	WE	TH	FR	FR	SA	SA	SU
		JET	JET	JET	JET	JET	JET	JET	JET	JET
NEW YORK (Idlewild) (♦) .... Lv.		21.15	21.15	21.15	21.15	18.00	21.15	19.30	21.15	21.15
MONTREAL (Dorval) (♦) .... Ar.		......	......	R 22.30	......	D		D....	R 22.30	......
MONTREAL (Dorval) .... Lv.		D....	D....	23.15	D....		D		23.15	R....
BOSTON (Logan) .... Ar.		......	......	......	......			R....	......	22.05
BOSTON (Logan) .... Lv.		R....	R....	D....	R....		B	......	D....	22.50
LONDON (London Airp. Central) (▲) .... Ar.		TU 08.55	WE 08.55	......	FR 08.55	B		SU 07.10	......	D....
LONDON (London Airp. Central) (▲) .... Lv.		F/T 10.05	F/T 10.05	B....	F/T 10.05			08.05	B....	B....
MILAN (Malpensa) .... Ar.		B 12.40	B 12.40	TH 12.05	B 12.40		SA 10.45	B....	SU 12.05	MO 11.35
MILAN (Malpensa) (●) .... Lv.		13.15	13.15	F/T 12.50	13.15		F/T 11.30	......	F/T 12.50	F/T 12.20
ROME (Leonardo da Vinci) (●) (◎) .... Ar.		R 14.20	R 14.20	R 13.55	R 14.20	SA 07.50	R 12.35	11.20	R 13.55	R 13.25
		TU	WE	TH	FR	SA	SA	SU	SU	MO

—Alitalia Airlines

An Overseas Timetable

An examination of this flight schedule reveals that the executive can leave Logan Airport in Boston on Sunday evening at 22.50 on Jet Flight 625, either by first class or by economy; have dinner, breakfast, and refreshments aboard; and arrive at Leonardo da Vinci Airport in Rome on Monday at 13.25 Rome time. (The time in Rome is six hours later than in Boston; refer to the world time-zone map on page 304.) Note that *economy* class becomes *tourist* class after the stop at Milan. Economy class is not used within Europe.

EXPLANATION OF SYMBOLS AND ABBREVIATIONS

MO	= Monday	AZ	= Alitalia
TU	= Tuesday	EV	= Elivie
WE	= Wednesday	SD	= Sudan Airways
TH	= Thursday	☎	= Telephone Number
FR	= Friday	✦	= Telegraphic Address
SA	= Saturday	SL	= First Class with
SU	= Sunday		*«dreamerette»* accommodation
B	= Breakfast	F	= First Class service
D	= Dinner	T (●)	= Tourist Class service
L	= Lunch	F/T	= First and Tourist Class
R	= Refreshments		service
S	= Snack	N/T	= Night Tourist service at
T	= Tea		reduced fare
DC-8	= Douglas DC-8 *JET*	Y (●)	= Economy Class service
CARAV.	= Caravelle *JET*	🛏	= Sleeping accommodation
DC-7C	= Douglas DC-7C		on First Class only, subject
DC-7F	= Douglas DC-7 Freight		to load availability
DC-6B	= Douglas DC-6B	✈	= *«dreamerette»* accommodation
DC-6	= Douglas DC-6		on First Class only, as
DC-3	= Douglas DC-3		indicated

(●) Except for American sectors and for North Atlantic services, the class designators " Y " and " T " refer to the same lower class of service.

Timetables give flight numbers, the classes of service, the kind of aircraft used, and flight operations by days. Twenty-four-hour clock times are used. To convert times after twelve o'clock to p.m. time, deduct 12 hours; thus 19:25 is 7:25 p.m.

The requirements and guides to overseas travel details are in the general-information section of airline folders. Overseas airlines are even more competitive than domestic ones, and the secretary should be alert to frequent changes in fares, accommodations, and special services.

■ Train Transportation

Most foreign railroads provide three classes of service: (1) *first-class* accommodations with four to six persons in a compartment, (2) *second-class* accommodations with six to eight persons, and (3) *third-class* where passengers sit on wooden, unupholstered seats. Seat reservations are necessary for first-class travel.

Sleeping cars are of the compartment type. The class of service indicates the number of passengers per compartment. Reservations well in advance of the trip are recommended, for it is often difficult to obtain sleeping-car (*wagon-lit*) accommodations. Extra-fare trains carrying first- and second-class sleepers only are available on the most important international routes. These de luxe trains with individual seats are also available for day travel.

Restaurant cars are attached to most express trains. Before the meal, the dining-car conductor comes through the train and takes reservations. The meal is served at an announced time at one seating only in most countries.

■ Hotel Reservations

Hotel reservations can be made through the travel agent either in this country or abroad or through the airline used. Businessmen's guides indicate whether secretarial services or meeting rooms are available in listed hotels. Breakfast is included in the hotel charge in Great Britain. In other countries in Europe a "continental breakfast" consisting of a hot beverage and a roll is included.

■ Automobile Rentals

Rented automobiles are as readily available in larger foreign cities as in the United States. Flight schedules indicate whether this service may be secured at the airport. Rental may be arranged by the travel agent here, and it is usually possible to leave the car at a designated point rather than return it to the place of rental.

In most countries a United States state driver's license is sufficient; but to be on the safe side, the traveler may obtain an American International Driving Permit from the American Automobile Association either here or in Europe for $3.

Travel Details Handled by the Secretary

The groundwork for planning a trip will probably be laid during a conference between the executive and the secretary. The executive will mention the places to be visited and the dates, and perhaps he will specify names of hotels. For example, he may tell the secretary that he plans to be in New York on November 2; visit the Upper Darby plant on November 3; spend the weekend with his sister in Paoli; attend a convention in Philadelphia from November 6–8; visit customers on November 9 and 10 (for which definite appointments must be arranged in Pittsburgh and Baltimore); spend Veteran's Day back home in St. Louis, and be back in the office on the morning of November 13.

▪ Planning the Trip

Planning a trip requires checking transportation schedules and making necessary reservations.

Convenient Flights and Trains. In the case just given, the secretary must route the executive to New York, Philadelphia, Baltimore, Pittsburgh, and back to St. Louis. First, she would obtain and study current timetable folders of airlines and railroads to determine convenient times and accommodations for the St. Louis to New York trip, New York to Philadelphia trip, and so forth. From these she would type a list of the convenient flights and trains that could be used, giving departure and arrival times, and other pertinent information. The secretary selects only those flights and trains that fit into the executive's particular business schedule. Especially important would be the location of the airport and its distance from the city. Illustrated on page 386 is a schedule that the secretary might have prepared.

ST. LOUIS TO NEW YORK SERVICES

Via	Flt./Train	Lv SL	Ar NY	Terminal	Type of Serv.
*American (exc. Sat.)	96	6:30 pm	9:20 pm	Kennedy (Intern'l)	Jet, first-class, dinner
**Eastern	406	3:20 pm	10:08 pm	"	Jet, first-class, dinner
*TWA	194	7:00 pm	10:00 pm	"	Jetliner Ambassador, first-class, dinner, compli. beverage
NYC	Southwestern	8:40 am	8:45 am	Grand Central	Roomettes & bdrms., diner from Indianap. at 1:15 pm
Penn	Penntexas	10:15 am	8:15 am	Penn. Station	Roomettes & bdrms., diner from St. Louis

*Nonstop flights
**Stops at Louisville, Ky. (dinner at 5 pm) and Washington, D.C.

~~~~~~

This schedule shows convenient times of departure with respective times of arrival. It is unnecessary and, in fact, inefficient to take the time to write everything in full in memorandum reports.

■ Making Transportation Reservations

After the executive has selected the flights and trains he will use and the accommodations he prefers, the secretary makes the reservations.

■ Making Hotel or Motel Reservations

The secretary is usually asked to make the hotel or motel reservations. If a rented automobile is used, a motel may be preferred. In many cases the executive will provide the names of the hotels or motels, or the secretary may know which ones he prefers. When she is expected to select the accommodations or to provide information about suitable ones, she uses one of the directories, such as the *Hotel Red Book* (published annually by the American Hotel Association) or regional directories (published by the American Automobile Association). These directories give the number of rooms, the rates, and whether (in the case of a hotel) the lodging is operated on the *European* or the *American plan*. Under the European plan the rate represents the cost of the room only. Under the American plan the rate includes the cost of meals as well as the cost of the room. Most commercial hotels are European plan.

Room rates quoted in a directory are for one night's lodging. Many hotels offer a reduced rate for occupancy of a room during the daytime only. This service is desired by some businessmen who use a hotel room as daytime headquarters when they are in the city for only a few hours. Since the time of arrival is often early morning, the executive may want to "register in" a night earlier so he can be assured of accommodations before the midafternoon checkout hour.

Requests for reservations should be specific, indicating:

Kind of Room Desired—air conditioning, cross ventilation, or television; location (away from elevator, above a certain floor, with a view, etc.); a suite of rooms

Type of Accommodations—twin beds or double bed; tub or shower bath

Approximate or Relative Rate—$15 to $20; medium-priced room

Number of Persons in the Party

Date and Approximate Time of Registration (If Known)—after 10 p.m.; 9 p.m. (If the executive may be late in arriving, a "guaranteed-arrival" reservation can be made. The room will be held, but the guest will be billed even if he does not come.)

Type of Transportation—because of uncertainty of time of arrival if by plane

Probable Length of Time Accommodation Is Needed

There are several ways of making a reservation. Hotels in a chain such as Hilton or Sheraton have communication systems that enable them to make reservations with other member hotels with confidence. A telephone call to the local hotel assures the reservation in a member hotel. Out-of-town hotels sometimes maintain in major cities local offices where the reservation can be made. Once again, check the Yellow Pages. The secretary in a company having a teletypewriter may ask its operator to request reservations over that equipment, which a large hotel would undoubtedly have.

If an assured reservation is wanted but no specific hotel is essential, wire the Western Union office in the city to be visited for a guaranteed reservation in a hotel or motel, specifying the type of accommodations desired. (See description and illustration on page 287.) In requesting a hotel reservation, it is important to mention the business connection, as a special commercial rate may be involved.

The secretary may write for the reservation. For a vital reservation, telephone or telegraph the hotel or motel in which space is wanted.

Policy differs as to confirmation; however, it is always safe to request a confirmation so that the executive may have it in his hands when he registers. Rooms are at a premium in many cities, and a confirmed reservation is a good precaution.

Some hotels, to simplify their accounting, request that a deposit *not* be sent. Motels, however, are usually smaller operations, and a deposit may safeguard a reservation.

```
I T I N E R A R Y   F O R   M R.   E.   G.   M A H R

Monday    3.8.--  Check in Copenhagen Airport              20:00 hrs.
                  Depart Copenhagen Airport                20:30
                  Flight SCANDINAVIAN AIRLINES SK.646
                  Arrive Oslo Airport

Tuesday   4.8.--  Check in Oslo Airport                    15:40 hrs.
                  Depart Oslo Airport                      16:10
                  Flight SCANDINAVIAN AIRLINES SK.315
                  Arrive Bergen Airport                    17:20

Thursday  6.8.--  Check in Bergen Airport                  09:15 hrs.
                  Depart Bergen Airport                    09:45
                  Flight SCANDINAVIAN AIRLINES SK.515
                  Arrive Stavanger Airport                 10:30
                  Depart Stavanger Airport                 11:15
                  Arrive London Airport Central            13:10
                  --Transfer to London Airport North
                  Check in London Airport North            20:15
                  Depart London Airport North              21:00
                  Flight TRANS WORLD AIRLINES TW.701

Thursday  6.8.--  Arrive New York International Airport     22:35 hrs.

                  (All times quoted are local times.)

         The following taxes are payable locally in Scandinavia:
              In Copenhagen D.Kr.7 on departure for Oslo
              In Bergen K.Nr.7 on departure for New York
```

Note that *August 3* is expressed as *3.8.--* in a foreign travel itinerary.

▪ Preparing the Itinerary

The secretary can give real secretarial service by preparing a comprehensive itinerary for the executive shortly before he leaves. The usual itinerary covers *when*, *where*, and *how* the traveler will go. An itinerary serves also as a daily appointment calendar. It contains helpful reminders and shows the tickets and business papers taken along. The executive may have his secretary make a number of copies for his associates and his family so that mail or messages can be forwarded to him and so that he can be reached immediately in an emergency. Foresight and analysis are required to be able to prepare this type of itinerary.

A good way to start is to set up a file on the trip as soon as it enters the planning stage. In it, place the memorandum prepared on convenient flights and trains, the purchased tickets, the reservations made, confirmations received, the appointments obtained, the factual material needed for scheduled meetings and appointments—in fact, everything that pertains to the trip. When it is time to prepare the itinerary, the items and notes can be sorted into chronological sequence according to the day and time each will come up. It is then an easy matter to list

MR. ALLEN'S ITINERARY, NOVEMBER 1-10, 19--
New York - Upper Darby - Philadelphia - Baltimore

WEDNESDAY--NOVEMBER 1 (ST. LOUIS TO NEW YORK)

7:00 pm   Leave St. Louis airport on TWA 194 Jetliner Ambassador (tickets in TWA
           envelope).

10:00 pm   Arrive Kennedy International (16 miles from NYC). "Guaranteed-
           arrival" reservation at Hotel Waldorf-Astoria (confirmation of reser-
           vation attached).

THURSDAY--NOVEMBER 2 (NEW YORK)

10 am   See Mr. Hillery, Sales Manager of Argo Products, Room 2431, Seagram
           Building, 243 Park Avenue.

1 pm   Lunch at New York Athletic Club, 61 Central Park South, with Mr. Arthur
           Lyle and Miss Betty Foreman of J. Walter Thompson to discuss advertis-
           ing promotion of Multiflex (Multiflex folder in briefcase).

4 pm   Interview Mr. Roland Sanders for position as Production Manager, your
           room at Waldorf-Astoria (application and job specification in brief-
           case).

7 pm   Dine with Mr. and Mrs. Harold Hargrove at 42 East 62 Street.

FRIDAY--NOVEMBER 3 (UPPER DARBY PLANT AND WEEKEND IN PAOLI)

9 am   Leave New York, Pennsylvania Station, on PRR (no reservation; buy
           coach ticket at station).

10:30 am   Arrive Philadelphia, 30 Street Station. Pick up Hertz Chevrolet
           (arranged for) and drive to Upper Darby plant for rest of day. (File
           on plant proposals will be mailed to you at plant.)
           Drive to Paoli for weekend with sister. Turn in car at Hertz, 39 West
           Lancaster Pike, Paoli.

MONDAY--NOVEMBER 6 (PHILADELPHIA CONVENTION)

9 am   Check in at Sheraton Hotel (confirmation of reservation attached).
           Check with hotel to see that charts to illustrate talk have been
           received (will be mailed 11/1/--; return wrapping, postage, and labels
           in package).

           Convention opens.

2 pm   Your speech (in briefcase; duplicate in package with charts).

7 pm   Annual banquet. Tickets for dais guests will be given to you by
           secretary. White tie.

**This first page of an itinerary contains all of the details of the
executive's travel and appointments, together with reminders on procedure. Note that the secretary has relieved him of many details.**

APPOINTMENT SCHEDULE

CITY	TIME DATE - GMT*	WITH	TELEPHONE	APPT. ADDRESS	REMARKS
London	Thursday Aug. 6	Phillip Morse	Mansion House 3312	To be arranged	Telephone Mr. Morse on arrival. Folder A contains papers for meeting.
"		Hubert Poling	Waterside Savoy 1113	"	Mr. Poling arranging meeting with possible patent lawyer. Folder B contains patent information.

*Greenwich Mean Time

For an overseas (or extended) trip the executive may find it desirable to have two separate forms—(1) a travel itinerary prepared by a foreign travel agent, and (2) an appointment schedule.

and describe each item in order. The first page of an itinerary on page 389 shows the detail and thoroughness with which it should be prepared.

On an extended or foreign trip it may be desirable to separate the actual travel schedule from the appointments and prepare two separate forms. Suggested headings for the travel portion are: DEPARTURE POINT, DEPARTURE TIME, DESTINATION, ARRIVAL TIME, TRANSPORTATION (including airline and flight number), HOTEL RESERVATIONS.

▪ Carrying Travel Funds

Often the executive relies on the secretary to remind him to obtain ample travel funds. She can ask if he wants her to get money from the company's cashier or the bank.

Travelers' Checks. If he plans to carry *travelers' checks* (which he must purchase himself), she can remind him of that need. Travelers' checks are sold at travel agencies, American Express, banks, and Western Union offices. American Express Company travelers' checks are sold in denominations of $10, $20, $50, and $100; they cost $1 per $100. If the executive intends to take $500 on his trip, he may purchase $400 worth in the denominations he wishes, say $50 and $100. Each check is numbered and printed on a special kind of paper. The purchaser signs each check on a line near the top before an agent of the Express Company. In order to cash one of the checks, he takes it to a business concern, bank, hotel, or American Express office and signs the check again at the bottom in front of the person paying out the money. Such checks are as acceptable as cash and constitute almost personalized money, because a person to whom they do not belong would have to forge the purchaser's name on each check in the presence of another person in order to cash it. The secretary should prepare a record in duplicate of the numbers and amounts of the checks issued, one for her files and one for the executive to carry so that reimbursement can be immediate in case the checks are lost or stolen.

Money Orders. Sometimes the secretary acts as an advance money agent who supplies the traveling men of the firm with company funds through *express money orders*. Travelers' checks cannot be used for this purpose because they must be signed at the time of their purchase by the person who is to use them. In order to facilitate the cashing of express money orders, American Express Company furnishes identification cards which include the signature of the bearer.

If the executive should find himself without funds, he can always wire his secretary to send him a *money order by telegraph*. She takes the cash, cashier's check, or money order to the Western Union office, which in turn telegraphs the distant office to pay that amount to the executive.

Letter of Credit. Frequently a *letter of credit* is used when extensive travel is involved or when the amount of travel funds required is relatively large. The cost for a large amount of money through a letter of credit is considerably less than the cost of travelers' checks. This travel fund can be obtained from the local bank. It indicates the person to whom issued, who is identified by his signature on an identification card. It also states the amount the holder is entitled to draw on the issuing bank. To obtain funds, the holder presents the letter of credit to any one of the designated banks in the city where he is traveling. The amounts drawn are recorded on the letter of credit so that the balance that can still be drawn is always known.

An express money order can be cashed only by the designated payee or by someone to whom the payee has endorsed the money order. The sender retains the stub as his receipt.

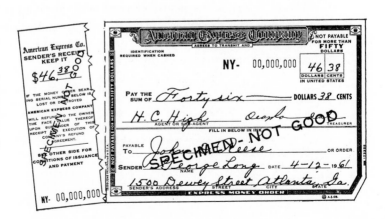

Credit Cards. *Hotel credit cards* are another means of securing cash while traveling. To a guest with an established credit rating, the hotel furnishes a credit card. He may present this with his personal check regardless of what bank it is drawn on, and the check will be honored by the hotel cashier. Often a credit card on one hotel will be honored by another.

A recent trend is toward the use of multipurpose credit cards. *Airline, railway, telephone, Diner's Club, American Express*, and similar credit cards permit the holder to charge practically any service to his own or company's charge account. Credit cards must be carried and ready for presentation when needed. Usually the executive keeps his credit cards in his wallet, and the secretary's only responsibility is in requesting renewals on those which expire and in keeping the serial numbers on file. (See page 544 for credit-card statements.)

Credit-card charges help the secretary in preparing expense reports and enable the executive to verify expenditures.

■ Insurance

The employing company sometimes buys blanket insurance policies covering executives while they are traveling for their companies. In addition, it has rules governing the purchase of trip insurance at the airport. The secretary is expected to inform herself of company policy about travel insurance and follow through to see that the executive is appropriately covered.

■ Speeding the Executive on His Way

The secretary is frequently charged with packing the briefcase that accompanies the executive. The following quotation describing the work of Evelyn Lincoln, secretary to the late President John F. Kennedy, illustrates the importance of this responsibility:[1]

> . . . for this self-effacing, dedicated woman in her middle forties bears one of the most delicate yet little-known responsibilities of any of the people around the President. It is she who packs the President's "little black bag," the 15-year-old black alligator briefcase he takes with him on trips and over the weekends.
>
> On every level of government, New Frontiersmen vie to get their ideas into that black bag. One says, "What goes into that briefcase on any given weekend may affect the course of history."

[1]*Newsweek*, January 7, 1963, p. 16.

Certainly few briefcases would contain such critical subject matter, but the effectiveness of any business trip is determined by the accessibility of relevant material when it is needed. Just as soon as the secretary becomes aware that a trip is "in the making," she should start to assemble materials to be taken along and to procure tickets and other papers necessary for the trip.

Just before his departure, the secretary hands the executive all the documents that she has obtained, prepared, and kept safe:

His travel tickets

Notes about reconfirming reservations for foreign flights

Hotel and motel confirmations

Travel funds (Money packet of foreign currency for first stop, travel checks)

United States driver's license or American International Driving Permit

Car-rental arrangements

Itinerary (both a detailed one and a thumbnail copy on a card)

Address book (including addresses of other people he might wish to see in the area)

Passport, International Certificate of Vaccination, and baggage identification labels for foreign travel

Papers to be taken along (bulky materials may be sent air express on the same plane). A separate envelope for each appointment is recommended, including carbon copies of previous relevant correspondence, lists of people to be seen and their positions in their companies, and memoranda about matters to be discussed.

A personal checkbook and expense-account forms

A supply of business cards for foreign calls

While the Executive Is Away

While the executive is away, the secretary assumes greater responsibility for smooth operation of the office. But she need not shoulder this role alone. Sometimes it is better to discuss some of the problems with the executive's superior or one of his associates, after identifying "who knows what." Routine matters, of course, should be taken care of promptly by the secretary.

The executive who wants to keep in touch with home base usually telephones his secretary daily, especially if his company uses WATS service. (See page 299.) If the secretary expects to hear from the executive by telephone, she should keep notes about events she wishes to discuss with him.

Her performance while the executive is away is just as important as when he is present. Other employees are quick to notice whether she keeps busy or fritters away time. When the executive returns, he will be grateful and pleased if she has taken care of the routine matters, has kept records of office activities for his review, and has arranged the matters that need care in the order of their importance. The material accumulated for him should be separated into two groups:

1. **Matters already taken care of by the secretary or others**
2. **Matters to be handled personally by the executive**

The secretary places the first group in a folder and marks it "Information Only." The second group she puts in a folder marked "Important." Just before the executive's return she sorts the material in each folder into logical order, placing the most important items on top.

The executive also likes to know who telephoned or visited him during his absence, although in some instances it may be of more interest than importance. A list of appointments and engagements made for him should obviously be included in the "Important" folder.

When he is away for some time, he may wish the secretary to send him copies of letters that require his personal attention (refer to page 145 for proper processing of the mail). And an executive always appreciates a letter telling him of interesting developments in the office.

Expense Reports

Some firms advance funds to a traveling executive. Periodically or on his return, he submits a complete report of his travel and the expenses incurred. In other companies executives advance their own funds and are reimbursed later in accordance with the expense report submitted and approved. In either case the executive must keep an accurate record of the dates and times of travel, the conveyances used, and the costs. He sometimes must submit receipts for hotel and other accommodations. His word is usually taken for the amount of taxi fares, meals, and tips; but they must usually be listed or itemized.

If she realizes that it takes $100 a day to keep a company salesman on the road today (and even more to finance an executive's trip), the secretary will understand the importance of this facet of her work.

Expense account forms are usually provided by the company and need only be filled in correctly and completely and totaled. The secretary should, however, check the executive's present accounting with previous reports to make sure that his amounts for such items as taxis and meals are reasonable and that the flight and rail fares are correct. Reimbursement is frequently held up until all items are in line and approved by the auditor's office.

Suggested Readings

Any of the airlines' special periodicals, such as Pan American's *Clipper Cargo Horizons* or Japan Air Lines' *JAL Trade Courier*, are available without charge to possible business customers. Practically every major airline publishes a handbook on business travel and international trade as a service to prospective customers in this highly competitive market. For instance, TWA's handbook is *TWA's Business Travel Tips—Europe*, 190 pp. JAL publishes *JAL's Business Man's Guide to Japan* and *Hong Kong for the Businessman.*

Finney, Paul. *The Businessman's Guide to Europe.* New York: McGraw-Hill Book Company, 1965, 625 pp.

Questions for Discussion

1. How can the secretary find out her company's policies about travel arrangements? How can she find out her employer's preferences?

2. Compare the first page of an itinerary and appointment schedule on page 389 with the appointment schedule on page 390. Which was prepared by the more efficient secretary? Why do you say this?

3. Report any recent plan for airline or railroad ticketing that is not described in the chapter. Compare it with the methods described, in terms of convenience to the customer.

4. If your employer were going to Europe to visit an affiliate of your company, how would he probably carry his funds? Why?

5. If your employer found himself without cash while on a trip, what would he probably do?

6. Who should receive copies of itineraries?

7. Your employer is visiting a dissatisfied customer in a distant city. He telephones you to mail him at once the entire correspondence file relating to his customer. There is a strict company rule that no files can be taken from the building. What would you do?

8. What criteria should the secretary use in determining what mail should be forwarded to her employer while he is away on a business trip? What procedures should she follow in forwarding the mail?

9. Just after your employer left on a somewhat lengthy business trip by train, you discover that he has forgotten to take along his itinerary, reservation letters, and appointment schedule. What would you do?

10. You are asked to write either of your two senators to request a certain report. How would you type the address and salutation? Refer to the Reference Guide to check your answer.

11. Type the following sentences correctly. Then refer to the Reference Guide to verify or correct your answers. Tell which Reference Guide entry you used for each reference.

   (a) The Case Western Reserve library is closed on Mondays.
   (b) Go to room 10 of the library this noon, please.
   (c) U.S. route 4 is within a half mile of our office.
   (d) All we know is: he is a negro who upholds democracy.

Problems

■ **1.** Your employer, Mr. Robert Simpson, raises the following questions. The answers can be found in schedules on pages 371–374. Write the answer to each question in memorandum form; that is, in a brief and clear way to give to your employer in written form.

(a) What flight would you suggest that I take from Chicago to San Francisco to fill a luncheon speaking engagement at the St. Francis Hotel on Wednesday at 1 p.m.? I have a dinner engagement in Chicago on Tuesday night; it cannot be canceled.

(b) What flight should I choose in returning on Friday after the speech? When will I arrive in Chicago?

(c) I have a business appointment in Palo Alto on another trip. What information can you give me about returning to Chicago on Flight 176?

(d) What direct flights from Chicago to London are available?

(e) What is the fastest train between New York and Syracuse?

(f) How much would our company save on each passenger making a round trip by restricting first-class air travel to Tokyo to senior vice-presidents and the president?

(g) What flight should I choose to get back to Chicago from Paris in time for work on Monday? I prefer a direct flight.

(h) I have to be at the airport to meet Harry Morton, the man who heads the French company we are working on to merge with us. What flight should I plan to meet if he leaves Paris on Pan Am Flight 119?

■ **2.** Prepare a schedule of available services for a business trip from your community to the capital and the largest city of each of three neighboring states. Insofar as possible, traveling should be scheduled for overnight and at least six hours in each city should be available for office calls. Include the airplane and train services that might be used.

■ **3.** Prepare what you consider to be the best itinerary based upon the schedule of available services that you prepared in the preceding problem. Assume that all appointments will be typed on a separate schedule.

Related Work Assignment 43

43. Handling Travel Details. The instructions and supplies necessary for the completion of this assignment are provided in the Workbook.

Supervising the Details of Meetings

Much of the executive's time is spent in meetings. His prestige and effectiveness are measured partly by the number of intracompany and outside committees on which he participates. His secretary can, then, expect to be constantly involved in planning meetings, in reporting them, and in doing the follow-up work occasioned by them.

The meetings with which the secretary is concerned may range from informal committee meetings within the company to annual meetings of stockholders, from meetings of a service club of which her employer is president to the yearly meeting of a professional organization for which her employer is partially responsible. Her responsibilities may vary from sending out notices of a meeting to seeing that uncongenial guests are not seated side by side at the banquet.

She may find herself confronted with a problem, too, in reporting what is *done* in a meeting, for she has learned to record only what is *said*. To winnow from the discussion the pertinent facts so that her minutes serve as a record of what has been decided and a guide to what needs to be done by whom challenges her best efforts.

Small, Informal Meetings

Many office meetings do not involve complicated arrangements. The secretary, however, may have to spend considerable time on the telephone with the secretaries of other executives in trying to schedule a possible meeting time. After the time is agreed upon, it is still a precautionary measure to send a confirming note reminding those who are to attend of the time and place. If the meeting takes place in the executive's office, the secretary makes sure that the room is in good order with enough chairs available for all members and that all the materials needed are assembled.

During the meeting the secretary may be asked to take notes. Recommended conference procedure suggests that the chairman summarize the actions and consensus of the meeting. If the secretary

The secretary must make sure that the meeting room is in good order, with all chairs, equipment, and materials needed.

is reporting a meeting for such a chairman, she is lucky. Many office conferences, however, are informal discussions where opinions are exchanged, conclusions are reached, and recommendations are made with no observance of protocol. In these cases the secretary herself is expected to make the summary—subject to the executive's revision, of course—to be distributed to all participants. Certainly, if during the meeting it is agreed that certain conferees take specific action, as a reminder the secretary should send each a copy of the report underscoring the agreed-upon action.

Formal Meetings

Just as soon as you know that a meeting is to be called, you should set up a file folder, listing on the caption the name of the meeting and its date. Into this folder goes every bit of relevant information that crosses your desk during the planning stages. When you prepare the agenda or later attend the meeting, you will derive much help from this folder.

▪ Aids to Planning Meetings

If you are involved in planning a local meeting, the hotel personnel will make useful suggestions about facilities. For out-of-town meetings, various airlines and hotels provide planning service. For instance, in

The meeting room must be reserved as one of the first steps in preparing for a meeting.

major cities the local office of either Holiday Inn or United Airlines' Meet-O-Matic will coordinate flight arrangements of participants and provide rooms, meals, and meeting rooms equipped with necessary facilities such as lecterns and tape recorders. Air France has a similar service at Orly airport (Paris).

■ Reserving the Meeting Room

The first detail to be taken care of by the secretary in making arrangements for a meeting is that of reserving the meeting room. This must be done before notices are sent out. What usually happens is something similar to this. The executive says, "Will you call a meeting on budget requests for next Wednesday afternoon at two." He does not say, "It will be held in the conference room." He always calls his meetings there, and he takes it for granted that the secretary knows that the conference room will be available for his use. It is the secretary's responsibility to make sure the room is not being used that afternoon by another group. It is very embarrassing to the executive—and it is the secretary's fault—if the executive's group tries to gather in a room that is already in use.

In case the meeting is to be held in a hotel, the secretary should be sure also that the meeting place and hour are posted correctly on the announcement board in the lobby and in the elevators. Usually, all participants have traveled a distance to the meeting, and nothing is more annoying than to reach the hotel at the last minute and be unable to locate the meeting. Even if the information about time and place is checked with the hotel, mistakes often creep into the announcements unless the secretary verifies the final results.

■ Notices of Meetings

The secretary's responsibility for taking care of the notices of a meeting frequently involves the five steps listed below:

1. **Making the calendar notations**
2. **Preparing the mailing list**
3. **Composing the notice**
4. **Typing and sending the notices**
5. **Handling the follow-up work**

```
Dr. E. R. Randall              KC
3152 Glenrose Avenue
Sacramento, California 95815
```

```
Randall, E. R. (Dr.)           KC

Dr. E. R. Randall
3152 Glenrose Avenue
Sacramento, California  95815
```

Cards may be prepared for the mailing list so that (1) the address appears in exactly the same form as it will be copied on the notice, (2) the name is typed first in inverted form for easy filing, and (3) some identifying signal indicates the organization for which the card constitutes part of the mailing list. (KC shows that Dr. Randall belongs to the Kiwanis Club.)

Making the Calendar Notations. There must be follow-up notations on the calendar to remind the secretary when to prepare and send the notices. These dates should be far enough ahead to allow time to have the notices composed, reproduced, and delivered several days before the meeting. Notices that are too late reduce attendance; those that are too early may be forgotten. An office conference of staff men could be called one day after the notice is delivered; an office conference of traveling men might require two weeks' notice. A calendar notation should also be made for a date preceding the meeting by several days on which the secretary is to confirm meeting room reservations.

Preparing the Mailing List. If notices are sent out periodically to the same group, the secretary should prepare a mailing list of the names and the addresses in a form that is convenient to use. This list may be kept on loose-leaf sheets in a notebook or desk manual, or on five- by three-inch cards. The first line is typed in filing order, then the names and the addresses are typewritten in envelope-address form because that is the easiest to follow in copying. They are usually arranged in some systematic sequence—alphabetic, geographic, or by groups, committees, teams, and so forth.

Preparing addressing-machine plates for those who receive frequent notices will expedite the notifying process. These plates are classified and filed in drawers marked for easy selection. For instance, tabs on plates for the total membership of an organization might be white; and tabs on plates for the chairmen of committees might be pink. An entire drawer is inserted into the addressing machine, and the entire list of notices can be quickly addressed. The plates are automatically placed back in the drawer for the next addressing session. Envelopes or cards can also be addressed during slack periods so that one set is always ready for use.

An address list MUST be kept up to date. Once a year the secretary should send out double postcards for the membership to use in reporting their current addresses. When a change of address occurs, the secretary corrects her mailing list or has a new addressing-machine plate made and inserted at the proper position in the drawer.

Composing the Notice. Simple notices may be composed by the secretary and given to the executive for approval. The previous notice may be a good model to follow, but it is desirable to vary the form. Instructions for typing the notice are on page 402. Some organizations require that any matter to be discussed at the meeting must be reported to the secretary prior to the meeting so that it may be placed on the agenda. In this instance, the notice of the meeting must carry this request for agenda items.

Before a notice of an official meeting is sent out, the legal department should check the bylaws of the organization for any stipulations that the notice contain certain information before an item can be acted upon at the meeting. For instance, the bylaws may require that the notice include a statement that the question of the payment of dividends will be discussed before dividends can be voted at the meeting. Even in a less formal situation, it is desirable to indicate the purpose and agenda of the meeting.

```
                                                    April 2, 19--

    To the Publicity Committee:

        A. B. Abney          Marvin Lee          S. M. Smith
        Dorothy Babcock      Morris Levy         Vern Toy
      ✓ John Kent            Horace Ralston      Harry Williams

    As you know, we will be required to make our report at the annual
    meeting on August 6.  We will make recommendations for retaining
    our present public relations consultant or for employing another.
    In case we decide to make a change, we should investigate all pos-
    sibilities.  Therefore, we should make the first decision at once.
    Will it be possible for you to meet with the Committee for lunch
    at 12:30 on April 10 at the York Country Club?
```

A duplicated notice of a meeting may list the names of all committee members and give each recipient of the notice the complete list in one operation. The name of the person to receive this copy of the notice is checked.

In case the secretary is preparing a notice of a corporation meeting, she should enclose with the notice a form on which the shareholder may execute a proxy, giving someone else authority to vote his stock in case he does not plan to attend. As this notice must include a detailed list of the business to be transacted, the reasons for soliciting the proxy, and other information specifically required by law, it is usually prepared by the legal department.

Typing and Sending the Notice. For small groups the notice is either typewritten or telephoned. For large meetings the notice is printed or reproduced by some duplicating process.

Post-card notices should be typed attractively, with the message neatly displayed. A simple, double-spaced form is acceptable for short notices. Some secretaries underline the important words.

If the secretary is sending notices of regular meetings, a form may be printed or duplicated at the beginning of the club year so that the date, program topic, or other pertinent information is all that need be filled in to complete the form.

Some meetings or conferences are of such importance that the announcement is typed or duplicated on letterhead paper. If only a few names are involved, a tabular listing of the names of those to receive the letter may be typed, in place of the usual single name, address, and salutation. Without the tabular listing the salutation then is a general one, such as "Dear Member," "Dear Committee Member," or "Dear Mr. . . . .," with the name to be filled in later. Modern usage permits the omission of the salutation entirely. An individual letter to each person is sometimes used, but that is a time-taking procedure.

Keeping a copy of the notice and the date of mailing is a precautionary measure that the secretary should adopt.

▪ Handling the Follow-Up Work

The secretary's follow-up duties consist chiefly of recording who and how many will or will not attend the meeting. If return post cards have been furnished, the notice follow-up is merely a matter of sorting the cards into the "will's" and "will-not's." But usually it means also telephoning several persons for a definite "yes" nor "no."

The executive who is secretary of a civic luncheon club in a large city sends out multigraphed notices one week before the monthly meeting. Two days before the meeting his secretary telephones each member to ask if he will or will not attend the luncheon. She keeps a record on a sheet of three columns—one wide one for names and two narrow ones for the acceptances and the refusals. As soon as answers are in from all the members, she telephones the hotel, giving the exact number of reservations. A quick method is to use a duplicated form that includes the names and the telephone numbers of members. Each name can be checked off as an answer is obtained. The frequency of meetings determines whether or not the preparation and duplication of a special form of this kind is justified.

A helpful secretarial service on meeting day, especially if the group is small, is to make reminder telephone calls to those who should attend. Early in the morning of the meeting day the secretary calls each person, or preferably the secretary, and tactfully reminds of the meeting. A diplomatic way to do this is to inquire of the secretary if the executive plans to attend such and such a meeting called for such and such a time, adding in explanation that you are making a final check on probable attendance. Some members may be unable to attend for last-minute reasons; others may explain that they will be late. Fortified with such knowledge, the chairman can call the meeting to order promptly.

▪ Preparing the Order of Business

Every meeting follows some systematic program, which is planned and outlined before the meeting. This program is usually called the *order of business* in organized groups. It is called the *agenda* in academic and business meetings and conferences. *Calendar* is the term used at meetings of some legislative bodies, such as a city council.

If the executive is to be the presiding officer, the secretary should remind him to prepare the order of business several days before the meeting. If she knows the purpose of the meeting, she can probably prepare this agenda in rough-draft form so that he will merely have to complete and rearrange it to his liking. It is definitely a secretarial duty to see that the order of business is ready on meeting day. A review of the bylaws and the minutes of previous meetings (properly indexed for easy cross reference) will be of invaluable aid in preparing the order of business and in helping the presiding officer to carry out the agenda in an effective manner.

In small groups brought together for discussion of topics, a copy of the order of business or program is given to each person. This may be an especially helpful secretarial service in office conferences, because it gives those attending the conference time to get their thoughts in order on the questions to be discussed. If the meeting has been called to discuss a proposed plan, there is better chance of action if the secretary distributes copies of the proposal prior to the meeting.

The order of business may be set forth by the organization in its bylaws. If not, the usual order is:

Call to order by presiding officer
Roll call—either oral or observed by secretary
Announcement of quorum (not always done)
Reading of minutes of previous meeting (Sometimes the minutes are circulated
     before the meeting, and the body approves them without their being read orally.)
Approval of minutes
Reports of officers
Reports of standing committees   *Copies usually are given to the*
Reports of special committees   *secretary.*
Unfinished business (taken from previous minutes)
New business
Appointments of committees
Nominations and elections
Date of next meeting
Adjournment

In a group that is meeting for the first time, a temporary chairman presides and a temporary secretary is appointed.   Permanent officers

This secretary is getting ready for a meeting in the conference room of the Indianapolis Power and Light Company's new headquarters building in Indianapolis.

are then elected or committees are appointed to nominate officers and
to draw up the constitution and bylaws.

■ Last-Minute Duties

The secretary's first duty on meeting day is to check on the meeting
room to make sure that it is ready; that the air in the room is fresh;
that there are enough chairs, ash trays, matches, paper, pencils, clips,
and pins; and that any special equipment requested, such as a portable
chalkboard or a tape recorder, has actually been brought.

She should take to the meeting minutes of previous meetings, a list
of those who should attend, a copy of Robert's *Rules of Order* for her
employer, the bylaws, a seating chart, blank ballots, and aids similar to
those illustrated on page 408 to help her in taking minutes.

Many small business meetings and conferences are recorded on
tape. If this is the case, the secretary should make arrangements for
setting up the recording machine. One of her responsibilities at the
meeting may be to operate the tape recorder.

Unless she has previously done so, the secretary's next job is to gather together all the material that will be needed at the meeting—notebooks, pencils, a filled fountain pen, the minute book, reports. It is most embarrassing if the secretary must leave the meeting room several times for things that she should have brought along. It advertises that the secretary is not very thorough. On the other hand, offering to get records or material on subjects that are unexpectedly discussed shows eagerness to please. The secretary should never leave a meeting room, however, without first getting permission from the executive or presiding officer. She is there to get the data for the minutes, either through her own notes alone or through verbatim recordings of a professional reporter or tape recorder, supplemented by her own notes which will aid her in abstracting the important points from the mass of material.

The secretary should study the minutes of previous meetings to acquaint herself with the usual procedure and make an analysis of techniques used in television or radio round-table discussion. She may also familiarize herself with parliamentary procedure by reading Robert's *Rules of Order* or other references named at the end of this chapter. If she has noted from the order of business the names of those who are to present certain topics at the meeting, she will be able to record this information easily in the minutes the day of the meeting.

Before the meeting opens, the secretary may have to make introductions, acknowledge introductions, or help the executive on some last-minute arrangements.

▪ Parliamentary Procedure

The secretary can better report a meeting if she understands parliamentary procedure. She can also unobtrusively call the attention of the chair to any violations of parliamentary rules, such as voting on a motion before voting on an amendment to the motion. Therefore, she should review important points of parliamentary procedure before going to the meeting.

Parliamentary law has been defined as "common sense used in a gracious manner." Its purpose is to arrive efficiently and orderly at a group decision. Parliamentary procedure is based on four principles:

1. **Courtesy and justice must be accorded to all.**
2. **Only one topic is considered at one time.**
3. **The minority must be heard.**
4. **The majority must prevail.**

Most business is transacted through main motions, which are handled as described below. A member addresses the chair, is recognized, and makes a motion. Another member seconds the motion. After the motion has been made and seconded, the chairman states the motion, names both the one who made it and the one who seconded it, and calls for discussion. When the discussion ends, a vote is taken, usually by voice. The Chair announces the result, "The motion is carried (or defeated)." If anyone calls "Division," the chair asks for a show of hands or a standing vote. If a majority demands it, the vote may be taken by ballot.

After a main motion has been made, a member of the body may amend the motion. If the amendment is seconded, the amendment is discussed. The amendment must be voted upon before the main motion can again be considered. After the chairman announces the action on an amendment, he says, "The motion now before the house is . . ." and states the original motion plus the amendment if it carried.

In addition to main motions, there are subsidiary, incidental, privileged, and unclassified motions, which are handled according to the chart that appears on page 409.

▪ The Secretary at the Meeting

The secretary's first duty at the meeting is to report to the chairman when a quorum is present. If the secretary is to take full notes, she concentrates on taking minutes as unobtrusively as possible. She should, however, ask to have everything repeated that she does not hear distinctly or that she is unable to get into her notes. She may say, "I did not get that," or she may give a prearranged signal to the Chair, such as raising her left hand slightly. Then the chairman will ask that the point be repeated. An error or an omission in procedure that the secretary observes can be pointed out to the Chair by a brief reminder note tactfully phrased.

It is better to take too many notes than too few. No one turns to the secretary in a meeting and says, "Take this," or "You need not take this." The secretary is simply held responsible for getting everything important in her notes. She must keep on the alert for motions, amendments, and decisions. If she is afraid to decide at the instant whether remarks are important, she should record them. If they are not important, they can be omitted from the final draft.

```
Present No._____
Excused (Names)

_____

_____

_____
```

```
Motion_____

Proposed by_____

Seconded by_____

Vote:      For_____

        Against_____

Summary of Discussion:
```

```
Things to Do After
     Meeting
1.
2.
3.
```

During the meeting the secretary may use skeleton forms similar to those above to aid her in taking minutes. If she wishes, she can put all items on one page for easy handling. Or she may prefer slips that can be clipped to the shorthand minutes. She can type an agenda, if available, on large sheets, leaving ample space for notes covering each item and varying the space given each item according to past experience.

Some essential parts of the minutes may not be specifically recorded at the time of the meeting. The date, time, and place of the meeting and the name of the presiding officer may not be stated. The roll may be called; but if not, the secretary is expected to observe and to record all of the details of attendance—who attended, who did not attend, who came in late, and who left early. The last two items of information are important in recording action on measures voted upon. Those not wishing to go on record with their votes may absent themselves from a part of the session for just that reason. To report the attendance of a person at the entire meeting when he attended only a part of it could have serious consequences.

If the secretary is depending on a verbatim report of the meeting as her source of minutes, she will need to make notes of items which are not likely to appear in the record: the names of those attending, the official title of the speaker, the time of meeting and adjournment, the names of those voting "yes" and "no" to motions, the names of those coming in late and leaving early and possibly the difficult names and words which may cause confusion in transcription. If she outlines the proceedings during the meeting, she can more easily make necessary fill-ins when she works with the verbatim report.

RULES FOR HANDLING MOTIONS

Types of Motions	Order of Handling	Must Be Seconded	Can Be Discussed	Can Be Amended	Vote Required[1]	Vote Can Be Reconsidered
MAIN MOTION						
To present a proposal to assembly	Cannot be made if any other motion is pending	Yes	Yes	Yes	Majority	Yes
SUBSIDIARY MOTIONS[2]						
To postpone indefinitely action on a motion	Has precedence over above motion	Yes	Yes	No	Majority	Affirmative vote only
To amend [improve] a main motion	Has precedence over above motions	Yes	Yes, when motion is debatable	Yes, but only once	Majority	Yes
To refer motion to committee [for special consideration]	Has precedence over above motions	Yes	Yes	Yes	Majority	Yes
To postpone definitely [to certain time] action on a motion	Has precedence over above motions	Yes	Yes	Yes	Majority	Yes
To limit discussion to a certain time	Has precedence over above motions	Yes	No	Yes	2/3	Yes
To call for vote [to end discussion at once and vote]	Has precedence over above motions	Yes	No	No	2/3	No
To table motion [to lay it aside until later]	Has precedence over above motions	Yes	No	No	Majority	No
INCIDENTAL MOTIONS[3]						
To suspend a rule temporarily [e.g., to change order of business]	No definite precedence rule	Yes	No	No	2/3	No
To close nominations[4]		Yes	No	Yes	2/3	No
To reopen nominations	These motions have precedence over motion to which they pertain	Yes	No	Yes	Majority	Negative vote only
To withdraw or modify a motion [to prevent vote or inclusion in minutes][5]		No	No	No	Majority	Negative vote only
To rise to a point of order [to enforce rules or program][6]		No	No	No	No vote, chairman rules	No
To appeal from decision of the chair [must be made immediately][6]		Yes	Yes, when motion is debatable	No	Majority	Yes
PRIVILEGED MOTIONS						
To call for orders of the day [to keep meeting to program or order of business][6]	Has precedence over above motions	No	No	No	No vote required[7]	No
Questions of privilege [to bring up an urgent matter—concerning noise, discomfort, etc.]	Has precedence over above motions	No	No	No	Majority	No
To take a recess	Has precedence over above motions	Yes	Yes, if no motion is pending	Yes	Majority	No
To adjourn	Has precedence over above motions	Yes	No	No	Majority	No
To set next meeting time	Has precedence over above motions	Yes	Yes, if no motion is pending	As to time and place	Majority	Yes
UNCLASSIFIED MOTIONS						
To take motion from table [to bring up tabled motion for consideration][8]	Cannot be made if any other motion is pending	Yes	No	No	Majority	No
To reconsider [to bring up discussion and obtain vote on previously decided motion][9]		Yes	Yes, when motion is debatable	No	Majority	No
To rescind [repeal] decision on a motion[10]		Yes	Yes, when motion is debatable	No	Majority or 2/3	Yes

1. A tied vote is always lost except on a motion to appeal from the decision of the chair [see "Incidental Motions"] when a tied vote sustains the decision of the chair.
2. Subsidiary motions are motions that pertain to a main motion while it is pending.
3. Most incidental motions arise out of another question that is pending and must be decided before the question out of which they arise is decided.
4. The chair opens nominations with "Nominations are now in order." Nominations may be made by a nominating committee, by a nominating ballot, or from the floor. A member may make a motion to close nominations, or the chair may declare nominations closed after assembly has been given a chance to make nominations. The voting is not limited to the nominees, as every member is at liberty to vote for any member who is not declared ineligible by the bylaws.
5. The mover may request to withdraw or modify his motion without consent of anyone before the motion has been put to assembly for consideration. When motion is before the assembly and if there is no objection from anyone in the assembly, the chairman announces that the motion is withdrawn or modified. If anyone objects, the request is put to a vote.
6. A member may interrupt the speaker who has the floor to rise to a point of order or appeal, call for orders of the day, or raise a question of privilege.
7. Orders of the day may be changed by a motion to suspend the rules. [See "Incidental Motions."]
8. Motion can be taken from the table during the meeting when it was tabled or at the next meeting.
9. Motion to reconsider may be made only by one who voted on the prevailing side. A motion to reconsider must be made during the meeting when it was decided or on the next succeeding day of the same session.
10. It is impossible to rescind any action that has been taken as a result of a motion, but the unexecuted part may be rescinded. Notice must be given one meeting before the vote is taken, or if voted on immediately, a two-thirds vote to rescind is necessary.

The presiding officer may ask for corrections or additions after the secretary reads the minutes. The secretary then adds these changes to the minutes as they were originally written.

If it is the secretary's duty to read the minutes of the last meeting, she should read them in a meaningful manner and in a loud enough voice so that everyone in attendance will be able to hear what matters were considered and what decisions were made.

After the minutes are read, the presiding officer asks for corrections and additions to them. Usually this is a mere formality, and the minutes are approved as they have been read. In some cases, however, corrections or additions are made. When this happens, the minutes should not be rewritten. The changes should be made on the copy of the minutes as they were originally written; and, of course, the corrections and additions become a part of the minutes of the meeting at which they are made. In order to save meeting time, some organizations have a *Minutes Committee*, whose function is to examine the minutes prior to the next meeting and report to the membership whether the minutes are in order or what changes should be made.

The order of business follows the agenda. The story of every motion, passed and defeated, must be recorded in the minutes. The name of the person making the motion, the complete motion exactly as stated, the name of the person seconding it, a summary of the pro's and con's given during the discussion, and the decision by vote—all must go into the secretary's notes.

After the meeting, the secretary must restore the room to order and compile a report of the minutes or proceedings.

After the business of the meeting is completed, the date of the next meeting is usually announced. As a rule, this immediately precedes adjournment. After the meeting has been adjourned, the secretary collects copies of all papers read and all committee reports so that they can be made a part of the minutes. (The committee reports are attached to her minutes.) Before leaving the meeting room, the secretary should check and verify all doubtful or incomplete notes (such as the correct spelling of names and the correct phrasing of a motion).

■ Follow-Up Work after the Meeting

There is always a lot of work for the secretary to do after a meeting aside from putting the meeting room back in order and writing the minutes or proceedings. All items that require future attention should be listed on both the executive's and the secretary's calendars. Individual letters should be written to those elected to membership and to those appointed to serve on committees or requested to perform certain tasks—even though they were at the meeting and are aware of the appointments or assignments. If expenses of participants are to be paid by the organization, the secretary should see that necessary forms are completed and reimbursement made as soon as possible. Many executives send a summary of the meeting to all members of the group.

RESOLUTION

Adopted June 8, 19--

WHEREAS, The Administrative Management Society of Boston has had an unusually successful year, being cited at the national convention for having conducted the outstanding research project in the nation; and

WHEREAS, That success has been due in great part to the unstinted efforts of our President, Mr. Lawrence Carmichael, and the Chairman of the Research Committee, Mr. Robert McCormick; therefore, be it

RESOLVED, That the members of this organization go on record as expressing enthusiastically their appreciation to Mr. Carmichael and to Mr. McCormick; and be it

RESOLVED FURTHER, That our Secretary present a copy of this resolution to each of these men.

Clarence M. Depenbrock

Clarence M. Depenbrock, Secretary

A resolution is usually presented as a formal statement. Each paragraph begins with WHEREAS or RESOLVED typed in capital letters or underlined.

Resolutions. Often an organization wishes to send an expression of its opinion or will (such as a resolution expressing sympathy on the death of a member or concurrence in a stated objective) in the form of a resolution to a person or an association. A resolution may be presented at the meeting in writing, or the secretary may be instructed to prepare an appropriate resolution. After the meeting the secretary is responsible for composing or typing the resolution, having it signed and sent out, and incorporating it into the minutes.

Reporting the Meeting. The report of a meeting varies with the degree of formality required. For an office conference, the proceedings are compressed and simple. For a meeting of an organization, it is customary to embellish the report with recognition of the efforts of individual members or with reference to letters from former members, as well as with a record of the formal actions taken. The final minutes do not record the events in chronological order if the secretary finds that regrouping around a central theme is clearer. For official minutes of a formal nature, however, the proceedings are recorded in the order of occurrence in complete detail, including the exact wording of all motions or resolutions.

MEETING OF THE EDITORIAL COMMITTEE

September 4, 19--

The Editorial Committee met in the office of the Chairman, Mr. Perry, at 10 a.m. on Friday morning, September 4, 19--, for its regularly scheduled semimonthly meeting. Those present were Mr. Perry, Mr. Harrison, Mr. Solkol, and Miss Henry. Mr. Richman was absent.

The following decisions were reached:

New Books. The manuscript submitted by Lawrence LeMar will be published in May without major change. The manuscript submitted by Alice Lewis was rejected with the recommendation that she collaborate with James Allison in a revision.

Personnel. The Committee voted unanimously to request that a new editorial assistant be employed to work on the reading series.

Schedules. Mr. Perry discussed at length the necessity for revising publishing schedules for school textbooks. He stated that it is necessary for a book to be available in January if September adoption is planned. Miss Henry suggested that every member of the Committee submit to her by September 10 a written and detailed progress report on every book on which he is doing editorial work so that she can make a report to the Committee at its next regular meeting. The Committee voted to follow this suggestion, Mr. Solkol dissenting.

Cover Designs. Cover designs were submitted for E67 and M14. It was decided to use Murray Brown's design for E67. The Committee voted to reject all designs submitted for M14.

The meeting was adjourned at 12:30.

September 18, 19--
Date

Alex Harrison
Alex Harrison, Secretary

The secretary merely summarizes the major actions of a meeting that follows no formal order of business.

P E R S O N N E L   C L U B

MEETING OF MARCH 10, 19--

Time and Place of Meeting	The regular monthly meeting of the Dayton Personnel Club was held on Tuesday, March 10, 19--, in the Regis Hotel. The meeting was called to order at 8:10 p.m. by the President, Mr. Walker.
Roll Call	There were thirty-four members present.
Reading of Minutes	The minutes of the February meeting were approved as read by the Secretary.
Treasurer's Report	The Treasurer presented his monthly report showing a balance of $51.32. This report, a copy of which is attached, was accepted. Two small bills, amounting to $8.15, were presented and approved for payment by the Treasurer.
Committee Reports	The President called for special committee reports that were ordered for this meeting. The

Minutes of a meeting follow the order of business given on page 404. They indicate whether the meeting was a regular or a special one. Marginal headings aid in locating items.

Sometimes the secretary records the minutes in the secretary's book only. In other cases, however, it may be desirable for her to duplicate and distribute the minutes after they have been officially approved by the chairman. If the minutes are to be referred to at subsequent meetings, duplicated minutes are often prepared with the line numbers typed at the left margin. It is then easy for a speaker to refer to *Page 3, Line 17*, and have the entire group follow him easily.

The minutes should answer the journalistic questions: What? Where? When? Who? Why? The following suggestions apply to writing minutes of all kinds.

1. Capitalize and center the heading which designates the official title or nature of the group which met, as *Committee V*; *Student Personnel Services*; *Recruitment, Guidance, and Placement.*

2. Single- or double-space the minutes and allow generous margins. There is a preference for double-spaced minutes.

3. Prepare the minutes with marginal subject captions for the various sections to expedite locating information. Record each different action in a separate paragraph.

4. Establish that the meeting was properly called and members notified properly. Indicate whether it was a regular or a special meeting.

5. Give the names of the presiding officer and the secretary.

6. Indicate whether a quorum was present and provide a roll of those present. At official meetings and committee meetings, list those absent.

7. Rough out the minutes with triple spacing for approval by your employer before preparing them in final form.

8. Transcribe notes while they are still fresh in your memory. If that is impossible, you may find it desirable to take the notes home and read them through, getting them in mind for accurate transcription the next day. If minutes for a meeting which you did not attend are dictated to you, be sure that you get all the pertinent data from your employer at the time of the dictation and that he interprets his notes to you properly.

9. Capitalize such words as *Board of Directors, Company, Corporation,* and *Committee* in the minutes when they refer to the group in session.

10. Send official minutes to the secretary of the organization or presiding officer or both, for signatures. At the end of the minutes type a line for recording the date of their approval. *Respectfully Submitted* or *Respectfully* may be used on formal minutes.

11. Do not include personal opinions, interpretations, or comments. Record only business actions, not sentiments or feelings. Such phrases as *outstanding speech, brilliant report,* or *provocative argument* are out of place in the minutes. Where gratitude or appreciation is to be expressed, it should take the form of a resolution.

12. Try to summarize the gist of the discussion about the motion, giving reasons presented for and against its adoption. A recently formed organization interested in improving business records for historical purposes decries the lack of helpful information contained in the minutes of company meetings at all levels. This organization stresses the value of such summaries when later discussions of similar proposals are held.

SALARIES	SALARIES
Appointment of Committee for Recommendations	Increases approved
1939 – p. 63 1946 – p. 11 1953 – p. 36 1957 – p. 59 1959 – p. 64 1961 – p. 81 1963 – p. 23 1967 – p. 17	1952 – p. 26 1954 – p. 35 1958 – p. 48 1959 – p. 56 1960 – p. 11 1961 – p. 47 1964 – p. 20 1966 – p. 34

On these sample cards from an index to minutes are found the years of action and page references to actions taken on the subject of salaries. Both of these cards follow the subject guide *Salaries.*

Indexing the Minutes. Because the composition of committees and organizations is constantly changing, sometimes groups find themselves in embarrassing situations because they do not know the regulations which they, as a body, have previously passed. They may take an action contrary to required procedure; they may violate their own regulations; or they may pass motions that contradict each other. The presiding officer takes a look at old minute books, which have been preserved since the beginning of the organization, and decides that it will be impossible to ferret out the separate actions on recurring problems. Nothing that you could do for the harrassed officer could be more helpful than the preparation and maintenance of an index of the minutes by subject, giving the year and page number of each action taken. Sometimes a separate volume is used for the minutes of each year.

If captions are written in the margin of the minute book beside the motions passed, the preparation of file cards for the index is facilitated.

▪ Minutes of Corporations

Corporations are usually required by law to keep a minute book for recording the minutes of meetings of stockholders and directors. Stockholders usually meet once a year, but directors' meetings are held more frequently. Minute books are extremely important legal records. Recorded decisions must be carried out, for they constitute the regulations to which the management must conform.

The records of a corporation are kept by the corporation secretary, a full-time officer of the company, whose duties differ greatly from those of the secretary discussed in this book. He is a company executive and will probably employ a secretary whose duties approximate those described here.

Auditors who examine the accounting records of a corporation read the minutes carefully to see that all financial decisions have been executed. They observe whether all transactions entered into by the corporation—those that are of a nature required by law or by the company's charter to be passed upon by the board of directors or stockholders—are authorized or approved in the minutes. For instance, an item in the minutes to pay a dividend of $1 a share on common stock as of a certain date makes it legally mandatory that such a dividend be paid.

One large company whose success and continued operation depended upon a certain process patented by its founder learned upon his death that the heirs were claiming royalty rights to the patent. The founder had stated verbally his intention of passing the patent rights on to the company itself. A statement to that effect, which was found in the minutes of a meeting held fifteen years previously, was upheld by the courts.

The Minute Book. Two separate books are frequently used for corporate minutes, one for stockholders' meetings as illustrated on the next page and one for meetings of the board of directors. If only one book is used, a portion of it is assigned to each group so that each set of minutes can be entered in consecutive order. A corporate minute book may also contain a copy of the certificate of incorporation and a record of the bylaws adopted.

The minute book may be bound or loose leaf. The latter is preferable, for it permits the typing of the minutes. In order to prevent substitution or removal of sheets, one of the following types of loose-leaf books is used:

> **One with prenumbered pages, with each page signed by the corporation secretary and carrying the date of the meeting**
>
> **One with pages watermarked with a code symbol**
>
> **One with keylock binder, making it impossible to remove or insert sheets without the use of a key**

Papers are seldom made a part of corporate minutes; but if so, they are pasted into the book. The final copy of the minutes is signed by the officers required to do so. Corrections are written in and the incorrect portions ruled out in ink. These changes are initialed in the margin by the signers of the minutes.

Contents of Corporate Minutes. The following information is recorded in corporate minutes:

> **1. Membership of group—directors or stockholders**
> **2. Date and place of meeting**
> **3. Kind of meeting—regular or special**
> **4. Names of those attending**
> **5. A complete record of the proceedings of the meeting**

Ordinarily the responsibility for formal minutes is given to the official secretary of the company. His secretary may help in the routine work of typing the minutes; but he carries the full responsibility of their completeness, accuracy, and legality.

MINUTES OF FIRST MEETING OF STOCKHOLDERS
THE ATOMIC POWER COMPANY

Held March 3, 19--

Pursuant to written call and waiver of notice signed by all the incorporators, the first meeting of The Atomic Power Company was held in the Board Room of the Company's offices at 25 Mission Street, San Francisco, California, at 2:15 p.m., March 3, 19--.

There were present in person: J. A. Barnes, D. E. Barnes, W. J. Howe, H. A. Lomax, and M. A. Miller. Mr. J. A. Barnes called the meeting to order and was elected Chairman by motion unanimously carried. Mr. D. E. Barnes was elected Secretary.

The Chairman reported that the certificate of incorporation had been filed with the Secretary of State on January 16, 19--, and that a certified copy had been filed with the County Recorder on February 7, 19--. H. A. Lomax made the following resolution, which was duly seconded and unanimously carried:

> RESOLVED, That said certificate of incorporation be accepted, the Directors named therein be approved, and the Secretary be instructed to cause a copy of such certificate to be inserted in the minute book of the Company.

The Secretary presented bylaws prepared by counsel, which were read, article by article. Upon motion duly made by W. J. Howe, seconded by H. A. Lomax, and unanimously carried, the following resolution was adopted:

> RESOLVED, That the bylaws submitted be, and the same hereby are, adopted as the bylaws of this Corporation, and that the Secretary be, and he hereby is, instructed to cause the same to be inserted in the minute book of the Company immediately following the copy of the certificate of incorporation.

The Chairman announced the date of the next meeting to be April 6, 19--, to be held in the Board Room of the Company's offices at 10:30 a.m.

There was no further business. Upon motion made and seconded, the meeting was adjourned. The time of adjournment was 4:30 p.m., March 3, 19--.

J. A. Barnes
J. A. Barnes, Chairman

April 6, 19--
Date

D. E. Barnes
D. E. Barnes, Secretary

Formal minutes of a corporation are shown above.

Conferences

Much of the work of a conference precedes and follows the actual event. The secretary is usually involved with details of preplanning and with preparing the conference report.

▪ Conference Organization

Many conferences are held every year, some of them requiring the full-time efforts of a secretary for the entire year. Securing facilities, getting speakers, planning menus and social activities, publicizing and distributing the proceedings, possibly securing registrations by mail, maintaining up-to-date mailing lists, and ironing out the thousand and one details that make things run smoothly when the conference date finally arrives are secretarial duties of a specialized kind.

During the conference the secretary is responsible for seeing that an opaque projector, not an overhead projector, is available if the speaker specified an opaque projector. She is the one who finds out whether the hotel uses AC or DC current so that equipment to be used will be compatible with the wiring. She is the one who sees that the projectionist is on hand at the very minute the speaker wants to show his slides. Above all, she is the one to see that the microphones are operating and that repairmen are on hand during any presentations. (Who can't remember at least one meeting that was ruined by failure of audio-visual equipment because nobody bothered to check it before the meeting started?)[1] She is the one who remembers to send complimentary tickets for the wife of the luncheon speaker, to have ice water at the lectern, to check the number of chairs on the platform, and to provide place cards for the speakers' table and arrange them with some sense of protocol. It is she who must follow through with the gracious gestures that send the participants home happy.

▪ Conference Reporting

At many conferences, the proceedings are of such value that they are preserved in permanent form. For example, the American Management Association may hold a conference on employee appraisal and later publish the proceedings as a service to its entire membership and outside purchasers of the report. These meetings are usually reported by specially trained reporters. Here the secretary's function changes from

---

[1]The 3M Company sells *A Secretary's Guide to More Effective Meetings.* This transparency kit includes materials for making more effective visual presentations. In major cities the company also sponsors secretarial seminars on the same topic.

The secretary as reporter of a conference may have to record a talk, edit it, and write introductions and conclusions.

—Harold M. Lambert Studios, Inc.

reporter to coordinator. If she works in a situation where outside conference reporters are regularly used, she is expected to locate persons who can do excellent work. Keeping a file of possible reporters, printers, lithographers, and artists—along with an appraisal of the quality of their services—will aid her.

The secretary is responsible for all the conference groundwork and probably for all the follow-up work, just as she would be for any other meeting. She should not, however, be concerned with the writing of the conference report—only with the processing of it.

Often registrants at the conference want a copy of the proceedings. This service might be paid for by the registration fee, or an additional charge might be made. In any case the secretary may be responsible for securing mailing addresses of those entitled to the publication.

If papers are read at the conference, each speaker is usually asked to submit his paper prior to (or at) the meeting so that it can be either printed in its entirety or abstracted. It is the secretary's responsibility to obtain a copy of this paper for publication. The conference reporter needs to report only the discussion following the presentation of the paper—either from tape recording or from summary notes. Sometimes the speaker is asked to prepare the summary himself. Then the reporter has to organize the material; edit it for uniformity of style; and write proper introductions, conclusions, or recommendations.

Suggested Readings

Augur, B. Y. *How to Run More Effective Business Meetings.* New York: Grosset & Dunlap, 1964, 157 pp.

Bridge, Lawrence. *Funk and Wagnalls Book of Parliamentary Procedure.* New York: Funk and Wagnalls Company, 1954, 180 pp.

Crumme, Marguerite. *Basic Principles of Parliamentary Law and Protocol.* (Order from author at 3830 Humphrey Street, St. Louis, Missouri, $1).

Cruzan, Rose Marie. *Practical Parliamentary Procedure.* Bloomington, Illinois: McKnight and McKnight, 1962, 92 pp.

Menderson, Melanie F. *Parliamentary Procedure Simplified.* Washington: The National Federation of Business and Professional Women's Clubs, Inc., 1953, 150 pp.

Robert, Henry Martyn. *Rules of Order.* Chicago: Scott, Foresman and Company, 1951, 326 pp.

Questions for Discussion

1. In what ways could an efficient secretary have improved the last organized meeting you attended?

2. When should you send notices for each of the following meetings:

   (a) **A monthly luncheon meeting for which reservations must be received not later than the day preceding the meeting.**

   (b) **A meeting of the board of directors of a large corporation. All committees must present full reports.**

3. What duties must the secretary perform before a meeting is held?

4. While taking notes at an office conference, you feel that the subject being discussed would be clarified by reference to a report filed in your employer's personal file in the next room. Would you (a) write a note to him asking if you should obtain the report? (b) leave the room to obtain it? (c) do nothing?

5. If the telephone in the meeting room rings during the meeting, should the secretary answer it?

6. How can the consensus of a meeting be reflected in the minutes without subjectivity on the part of the secretary?

7. Is a motion voted on before the amendment to a motion? Can an amendment to a motion be amended?

8. What should the secretary do (a) if an unidentified person makes a motion? (b) if a person makes a motion that lacks clarity and that is changed several times in phraseology before it is voted on? (c) if the Chair entertains a new motion before the motion on the floor has been disposed of?

9. Suppose you were sent to a conference to take notes. One of the men at the conference passed cigarettes to the group and offered you one. What would you do? Would you accept an invitation from the men to accompany them to lunch?

10. Why are strict rules followed for keeping corporation minutes? What precautions are taken to avoid substitution of pages in the minute book?

11. What follow-up work should be done by the secretary after the meeting?

12. Capitalize words as necessary in the following sentences. Then use the Reference Guide to verify or correct your answers.

    (a) Attendance declines in the summer.

    (b) The atomic age brings its own wonders—its own terrible fears.

    (c) Mr. Lawson is the new president of our company.

    (d) We heard an address by president Lawson.

    (e) He hopes to become a professor of marketing.

    (f) The professor of mathematics spoke, too.

    (g) I know professor Lawson well.

Problems

■ **1.** Your employer, H. C. Campbell, is secretary of the Pittsburgh Credit Managers Association. The regular monthly meeting of that organization was held on Thursday, June 22. The week before, you had mailed notices of that meeting to be held at 6:30 p.m. at the Hotel Pittsburgher.

Mr. Campbell gives you the following notes for the minutes of that meeting. You are to type the minutes in good form, using marginal or side headings for each paragraph. Mr. Campbell also instructs you to do these things as follow-up work: (a) Notify Harry Shorten of his nomination, as he was absent; (b) Write a note of appreciation to the speaker, enclosing a check for $27.50 which the treasurer drew for his expenses. (Since Mr. Campbell does not have any stationery of the Pittsburgh Credit Managers Association, you will use plain stationery.)

Called to order—8:05 p.m.

Mr. Riopelle, Pres., absent—Mr. Bavin, V.P., presided.

No. present—16. Minutes of May meeting read by secy.—approved.

Treas. report—present bal.—$572.68. Accepted (copy of report given to you by Mr. Steiner). No bills presented for payment.

Budget Com.—Betz, Chairman. Acceptance moved and seconded. Discussion. Motion carried.

Membership Com.—Herbert, Ch., introduced 2 new members—T. E. Gary and R. C. Taylor.

Nominating Com.—Overly, Ch. Officers nominated for year beginning Aug. 1.

President—Shorten, Clevelle

Vice President—Horgan, Steer

Secretary—Bruck, Anderson

Treasurer—Murphy, Hartline

Acceptance of report moved, seconded, and passed. No nominations from floor. Nominations closed by motion. Bavin announced election of officers to be held at next regular meeting as provided in the constitution.

Clevelle, Ch. of Program Com., reminded members of golf tournament and dinner—Oakdale Country Club, afternoon and evening of June 29.

Steer introduced Mr. Donald Durst of Atlanta as speaker. Subject—"Trends in Installment Credit." Question and answer period.

Mr. Bavin announced July 27—date of next reg. meeting.

Motion for adjournment carried—9:37 p.m.

■ **2.** You have been appointed chairman of a committee in the local chapter of The National Secretaries Association (International) to prepare a resolution of appreciation of the services of Miss Janet Godfrey, who founded the local chapter and is retiring as president after serving two terms. Miss Godfrey is also a member of the State Board of the organization and has contributed two articles to the national magazine. Draw up the resolution.

Related Work Assignments 44-47

44. Preparing Notices of Meetings. Prepare the following notices of meetings, sending them in the name of your employer, Mr. Robert L. Simpson, who is secretary of both organizations:

(1)

Send a double postcard notice of a luncheon meeting of the Metropolitan Club at one o'clock at Yeatman's Tearoom, on June 24, to Mr. Charles Steele, 816 East Third Street, Des Moines 50309. The topic of a panel discussion that will constitute the program is: "How to Make Des Moines Schools Better." The return portion of the double postcard will include space for the member to state his intentions about attending the meeting, any plans to bring a guest, and his signature. Experiment with the organization of the material until you feel that you have designed the notice in the most effective and attractive way so that you can use it as a model for each monthly meeting.

(2)

Also send Mr. Steele a notice of the monthly social meeting of the Hobby Club to be held Friday night of next week at 8:30 p.m. at the home of the president, J. C. Garson, at 6118 Grand Vista Avenue. Mr. Garson would like to know how many are planning to attend because refreshments are to be served. Ask that Mr. Steele call your office, 351-6866, by Monday evening. There will be a special display of woodworking projects.

45. Interoffice Notice of Meeting. Compose and type an interoffice communication notifying the key men in the factory of a conference to be held on safety measures. There have been four accidents in the past month, one fatal. Each man is to come prepared with specific suggestions on safety measures and ways to improve the safety record. The meeting will be held in the Foremen's Dining Room at 3:45 p.m. ten days from today. The following men are asked to attend:

N. A. Daniell	John Whitford	James Rahn
Paul G. King	Carl Gates	Clyde Richardson

46. Editing Minutes
47. Measuring Your Secretarial Information (Parts 5 and 6)

} The instructions and supplies necessary for the completion of Related Work Assignments 46 and 47 are provided in the Workbook.

6—1 √ *difficult telephone situations*

Miss Mary Holmes, secretary to Harry Miller, handled the following telephone calls:

(1) Mr. Miller was attending a Kiwanis luncheon meeting at the Terrace Hotel and expected to be back at his desk at 1:30 p.m. At 12:15 a long-distance call came in from his superior, who was in Boston. Miss Holmes said, "Mr. Miller will not be back until 1:30 and cannot be reached until then."

(2) At closing time the long distance operator had not reached a person with whom Mr. Miller must talk before the next morning. Mr. Miller was going to dinner at his brother's home but would be at his own home until 7 p.m. Miss Holmes said, "Operator, try that number again and keep trying until seven o'clock. Mr. Miller will be at 734-8973 in half an hour and will be there until seven."

(3) Mr. Miller was playing golf. The long distance operator informed Miss Holmes that she had a call from his New York broker, Mr. Adams, who wanted to talk to him as soon as possible. Miss Holmes said, "Mr. Miller is out of the office for the afternoon. If you will tell me where Mr. Adams can be reached, I will try to get in touch with Mr. Miller and ask him to call back immediately. I should be able to reach him in an hour."

(4) Mr. Miller was writing copy for an advertising circular and told Miss Holmes that he did not wish to be disturbed under any circumstances before four o'clock. A call came in from George Herman, his assistant, who was in Baltimore attending a sales conference. Mr. Herman was to leave Baltimore on a three o'clock train. Miss Holmes said, "I am sorry, but Mr. Miller can't be reached this afternoon. Ask Mr. Herman if I can help him. I am Mr. Miller's secretary."

(5) Mr. Miller wanted to make a long distance call from the office telephone, 623-2219, to Dr. L. K. Nelson of New Orleans on a personal matter. Miss Holmes did not know Dr. Nelson's number but knew that he was a noted eye specialist. She dialed Long Distance and said, "Operator, this is 623-2219. I want to make a call to Dr. L. K. Nelson in New Orleans. I do not have the number, but he is a famous eye specialist. Will you give me the code and the number, please, so that I can dial him direct."

(6) Mr. Miller wanted to make a person-to-person call to D. L. Chaney of Chaney Construction, Inc., in Birmingham about a back order. He wanted a report on the charges. Miss Holmes said, "Operator, this is 623-2219. I want to place a call to Chaney Construction, Inc., in Birmingham, 298-2313. Will you please call me at the end of the conversation and tell me how much the charges are."

(7) Mr. Miller wanted to call Mr. Houston in the purchasing department of the Acme Company in White Plains, New York, Area Code 914. Mr. Miller wished to say that on Friday afternoon he would call on either Mr. Houston or his assistant about the new service contract. Could one of them be available for a conference? Miss Holmes made a DDD call.

(8) Mr. Miller wanted to call his wife, who was visiting in Akron, Ohio. Her number was 864-0753 and the Area Code 216. He said that it need not be a person-to-person call; but he wanted the call charged to his home number, 266-7106. Miss Holmes said, "Operator, this is 263-2219, Extension 62. I want to place a call to 864-0753 in Akron, Ohio. Don't charge the call to this number. It should be charged to 266-7106. . . What difference does it make whose name the phone is listed under or what time he will be home to verify the charges? You just make the call and charge it to the 266-7106 number. I'm his secretary, and I will guarantee that Mr. Miller pays his bills."

(9) Mr. Miller wanted to call Lawrence Taylor of the Lenox Supply Company in Los Angeles about the cancellation of an order. The number was 823-6501; the Area Code number, 213; the charges were to be reversed. Miss Holmes said, "Operator, this is 263-2219. I want to place a call to Lawrence Taylor of the Lenox Supply Company in Los Angeles. I don't know the number. Tell the switchboard operator there that Mr. Miller won't pay for the call because it is about an order he plans to cancel. Ask Mr. Taylor to pay for it."

(10) While Miss Holmes was on the button telephone, a second call came through. She excused herself and answered the second call, which was for Mr. Miller. She depressed the local button to ask Mr. Miller if he would take the call and then transferred it to his wire. When she returned to the first caller, he had been disconnected.

(11) Mr. Miller asked Miss Holmes to call the Research Center at the State University. She dialed *Information*, obtained the number, and then made a direct (DDD) dialing of the number. Upon connection, she found that she had the wrong Research Center but they gave her the correct number to call. Miss Holmes thanked them, hung up, listened for the dial tone, and dialed the correct number.

(12) Mr. Miller asked Miss Holmes to get Harry Stokes of the Eastern Publishing Company in Boston on the phone. Miss Holmes checked the letterhead of the Eastern Publishing Company, obtained the telephone number, and dialed the number direct (DDD). When Eastern Publishing Company answered, Miss Holmes said, "Mr. Stokes, please." Miss Holmes then waited patiently for approximately six minutes before her connection at the publishing company came back on the line to say, "Thank you for waiting, I am unable to locate Mr. Stokes. He is in the building someplace; I am still trying. Do you wish to wait?"

Mary Holmes was surprised when Mr. Miller told her that he had arranged for her to take a five-hour course to improve her telephone techniques. She had always thought that she was unusually proficient in this area.

Criticize Mary's handling of the twelve calls described above. Indicate what you would have done in the cases that were poorly handled.

PART

7

—*IBM Corporation*

In today's automated office, the secretary can prove her value as an administrative assistant as she uses her ability and imagination in collecting, processing, and presenting business information.

Collecting, Processing, and Presenting Business Data

Increasing dependence upon data is a
phenomenon of modern business.
Information from all parts of an industrial
complex are channeled into the central
offices. Other data are researched
and collected, statistics are organized
into meaningful tables and graphs, and
reports are prepared for others to
study, evaluate, and act upon. Few areas
offer the secretary greater opportunity
to prove her value as an administrative
assistant.

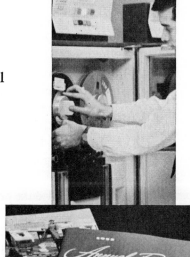

Ch. 18

Data Processing and Communication

The office has been aptly described as the nerve center of the business —the center for planning, recording, and communicating activities. Budgets must be compiled; production schedules developed; raw materials, equipment, supplies, and labor purchased; orders processed; payrolls prepared; records with customers and creditors maintained; costs computed; and financial information communicated to stockholders and others. Most of these activities involve data processing—that is, the coding, sorting, computing, summarizing, recording, and communicating of data for more effective management of the business organization.

High-speed data processing systems have become essential because of the rapid growth of expanding business and markets and the need for better production control and increased office efficiency. In addition, more and more immediate data are required by management in order to keep businesses competitive. Responsible management decisions require that voluminous data be processed and reported in time for action. These requirements have necessitated the constant search for faster and more efficient ways to handle data, so that decisions may be formed on the basis of up-to-date information.

The modern office uses many machines and facilities in *processing data*. Some of them—typewriters, duplicators, copiers and calculators —the secretary uses regularly in her work. Others—punched-card equipment, tape-activated machines, and the electronic computer— may or may not be operated by the secretary, but they are important to her work. The computer and the telecommunication system are revolutionizing office work and present an entirely new method of operation for the executive. It is predicted that the computer in tomorrow's office will be as commonplace as the electric typewriter and the copying machine are in today's office.

The secretary is not expected to be a specialist in office automation. As a key person on the office staff, however, she must understand the concept of office automation, the functions involved, and the various methods of processing data.

Common Machine-Language Media

The volume of paper (forms, statements, reports, communications) in business has been growing at a fantastic rate. This growth continues at an estimated 15 percent increase each year. Billions of pieces of paper are processed annually on a vast array of key-depression machines such as typewriters, teletypewriters, calculating and adding machines, payroll machines, checkwriters, and bookkeeping machines, found in most large offices. They are called key-depression machines because they are activated by an operator who depresses keys.

In processing data the identical information may be written many times; thus the identical key strokes are repeated over and over. For example, a sales order sets in motion the preparation of a variety of other pieces of paper. These include inventory forms, sales-record forms, production forms and reports, shipping orders, bills of lading, customer invoices, accounts receivable records, and company reports. Some identical information is written on each of these.

In one firm a count revealed that in the processing of a sales transaction identical information was recorded nine times; thus nine repetitions on key-depression machines were required, and *each had to be checked for accuracy.*

▪ Work Simplification

Several means have been devised to decrease the manual writing of the same information on different forms and in different offices in the same company and thus keep the business from being drowned in a sea of paper work. Carbon-interleaved multipurpose forms, pegboard one-write systems, and multiple forms produced via duplicating machines (as explained on page 118) permit one writing or one typing to produce several different forms required to process the information.

These methods have reduced, but have not eliminated, repetitive writing. Furthermore, they do not save time and labor in processing repeat orders—orders from the same customer for the same items which comprise the bulk of the business of many firms. The basic need for large-scale paper work production, therefore, is to capture the data on one machine and then reproduce the same data, when needed, by mechanical or electronic means on other machines. This procedure requires the use of common machine-language media—a code system that can be used to communicate between machines—that is, a language that can be read by machines and used to activate other machines.

The teleprinter and teletypewriter can send in tape form and receive in tape or page copy form.

■ Common-Language Tape

Punched or perforated tape was first used to communicate between machines used in telecommunication. It was later adapted for use in other office operations.

Teletype Machine (Teleprinter; Teletypewriter). The *teleprinter* and the *teletypewriter* are equipped to produce punched tape and also may be activated (operated) by tape. When connected through the facilities of the telephone or telegraph company, these machines transmit written conversation to a distant point just as the telephone transmits vocal conversation. Although transmission may be direct from machine to machine, it is frequently done via paper tape, as the tape may be sent at a much faster rate. As the message is typed on the teleprinter or tele- typewriter, a five-channel paper tape is produced. The tape is then used to transmit the message over the wire. The receiving teleprinter or teletypewriter reproduces the communication in page copy; it may also produce a tape as a by-product.

Automatic Typewriters. The automatic typewriter was the first machine to use punched tape for the handling of routine correspondence. Many businesses have a certain number of form letters—letters of acknowledgment, letters of credit standing, collection letters. Standard paragraphs can be recorded on punched tapes or perforated rolls and

By pressing a button, the typist can instruct the IBM tape Selectric to search a magnetic tape on which the typed material is stored and locate the point where a change is needed. Simultaneously, she erases unwanted material and stores new data in its place by retyping in that position.

—IBM Corporation

fed into an automatic typewriter as needed. The operation can be so planned as to provide for an automatic halt of the typewriter at appropriate places to permit manual insertions of inside addresses, salutations, appropriate figures, and other entries necessary to personalize the letter. The finished letters look like individually typed letters, for they are.

Tape-Activated Office Machines. Punched tape is now used to operate other office machines. Typewriters, adding, calculating, billing, payroll, bookkeeping, and other machines can produce tapes as by-products of their normal operations. These machines are also activated by paper tape. Punched tape thus has become a *common machine language*—that is, the tape produced by one office machine can be read by a number of different types of office machines.

Reading Tape. The tape developed by the communication industry for use with the Teletype machine was five-channel tape. The following illustration shows the coding that is used. A single hole punched into the top channel represents the letter *E* or the figure *3*. *A* and the hyphen (-) are coded by holes in the first and second channels.

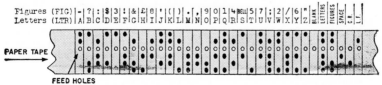

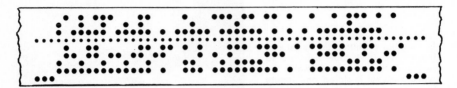

The tape above illustrates the coding for the title of this book, *Secretarial Procedures and Administration.*

The number of different letters, figures, special characters, and tabulations that can be coded on five channels is restricted. This limitation led to the development of six-, seven-, and eight-channel tapes illustrated below. The increased number of channels enables the coding of upper- and lower-case letters and additional special characters. It also permits a mechanical method of checking accuracy of the tape.

| *5-Channel* | *6-Channel* | *7-Channel* | *8-Channel* |

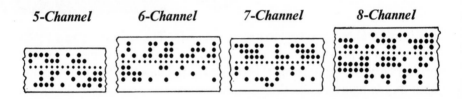

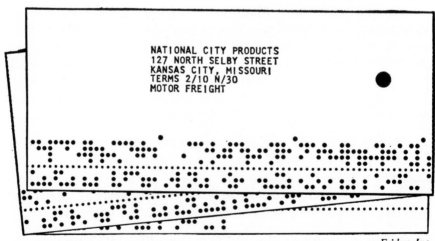

NATIONAL CITY PRODUCTS
127 NORTH SELBY STREET
KANSAS CITY, MISSOURI
TERMS 2/10 N/30
MOTOR FREIGHT

—Friden, Inc.

This common-language card has been edge-punched in eight-channel tape. The cards are sectioned for folding in seven-inch lengths. As many sections as necessary for all the desired data may be used and retained as one unit. For ease of reading the printed information when the card is filed, the lower side of the card is punched.

Punched paper tape and edge-punched cards are filed in a number of ways. One common method is to label and file each tape alphabetically or numerically in a small jacket or pocket card. The jacket can also indicate what is on the tape. The operator removes the jacket just as he might take a letter from a file folder.

—Shaw Walker Co.

▪ Edge-Punched Cards

In addition to tape, edge-punched cards are also used as a common-language medium. They offer the advantage of being easier to file and locate, and the data punched can be reproduced on the card also in words and figures for visual reading by the operator. Many machines that handle tape will also handle edge-punched cards. The cards can be of varying width and may be punched on either side, or on both sides.

Integrated Data Processing (IDP)

The procedure of capturing information in a machine-language medium and then electro-mechanically reproducing repetitive information at any point in the process is known as *integrated data processing*.

In an integrated data processing system:

1. Original data are recorded at their point of origin in a machine-language medium.
2. Once in punched-tape or card form, the data are processed by machines with a minimum of manual intervention.
3. All processing of data is unified so that the original data in tape or card form serve all subsequent applications.

▪ Processing a Sales Order

The processing of a sales order can illustrate IDP procedure.

Typing the Shipping Order. To type the shipping order, a *tape-reading typewriter* reads punched tape by sensing the difference between punched holes and unbroken tape. The typewriter may be operated manually.

—*Cincinnati and Suburban Bell Telephone Company*

Tape for data processing can be stored in built-in racks for easy finding and use.

Since there are many repeat orders from the same customers and since the bulk of the orders also represent business for the same items being ordered over and over, repetitive information is prepunched into paper tape (or *master*) and filed in two files.

One file contains tapes composed of information likely to be repeated for each customer—firm name, location, salesman, shipping instructions, terms, and the standard contractual clauses.

A second file contains tapes for the stock numbers and descriptions of all items that are sold.

When the customer's order is received, the appropriate master tapes are obtained from the two tape files and fed into the tape-reading typewriter to type the shipping order. The tape is so coded as to cause the typewriter to position the information on the order form and to stop at certain points to permit the operator to make manual insertions, such as date, order number, names and addresses of new customers, quantity ordered, and any special instructions.

The typewriter used in typing the order is also equipped with a tape-perforating attachment. As the machine is typing the data on the order form, it automatically prepares a punched tape as a by-product. This tape is used in the next step in the operation, as shown in the illustration at the foot of page 435.

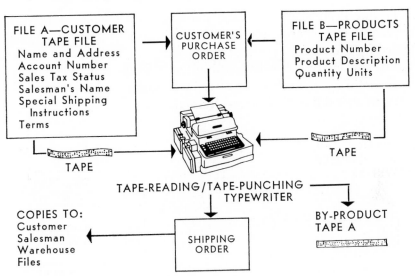

Preparing the Invoice. The by-product tape produced when the shipping order was typed is then used to operate a *computer-typewriter*, such as the Computyper. The computer-typewriter performs the calculations (such as multiplying quantity and unit price, obtaining totals, subtracting discounts) and types the invoice from the tape. Coding on the tape causes the typer to stop at certain points for the operator to type manually data that were not produced on the sales order and, therefore, are not on the tape—shipping date, price, and other items.

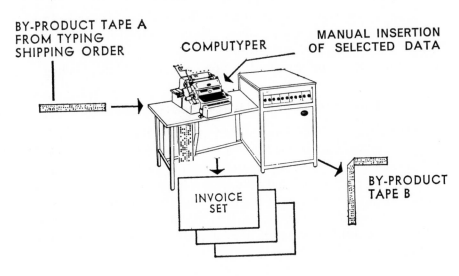

Further Processing. The computer-typewriter prepares a tape as a by-product of preparing the invoice. This tape contains all the data needed for accounting records, inventory control, and reports. If these records are kept by a punched-card system, the tape would then be used to convert the data to punched cards by a *tape-to-card converter*, or the tape may be fed directly into an electronic computer.

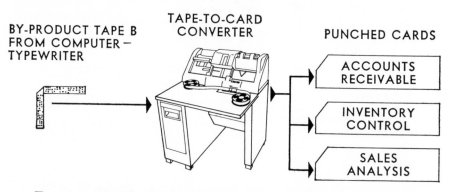

For processing the order, the data were recorded (typed) manually only once. All repetitions of the data were produced from the tape, as illustrated above. This process not only reduced and eliminated repetitive typing, but also increased accuracy because mechanical reproduction is more dependable than manual typing of such details as names, addresses, terms, descriptions, and prices.

▪ Transmitting Data

Tape can be used to communicate between offices. It can be transmitted by wire, or it can be mailed. Thus, tape used in preparing an invoice can be sent to the warehouse in a distant city where it can be used to prepare such forms as the shipping order and bill of lading.

Punched-Card (Unit-Record) System

The principle of the punched-card system is that data (words and figures) are "written" in the form of holes punched in cards according to a predetermined code and location plan. Machines that sense the location of the holes read and act upon the information as the cards are run through. They can sort the cards into desired groups; they can perform required calculations, such as additions, subtractions, multiplications; and they can decode the information back to written words and figures.

■ Punched-Card Equipment

There are four basic machines used in the process: the keypunch, the sorter, the calculator, and the tabulator.

Keypunch. The *keypunch* is the initial machine used to process the data. It is operated manually by depressing keys set upon a typewriter-like keyboard. The operator takes the data from the original document —a sales order, an invoice, or a payroll sheet—and "types" the keys according to an established sequence to enter the data upon cards in the form of holes.

Since there is always the possibility of the operator's making an error, the punched cards are checked for accuracy by using either an *interpreter* or a *verifier*. The machine referred to as the *interpreter* reads back the data recorded by the holes on the card and prints the data on the card where they can be verified by reading. The key *verifier* is similar to a keypunch machine. The original data are again punched on the verifier, which detects any errors that may have been made on the card.

A *reproducer* is used to read all or part of the data in an existing punched card and punch the desired data into duplicate cards automatically. Data from two or more cards also can be combined and punched into one card by the reproducer.

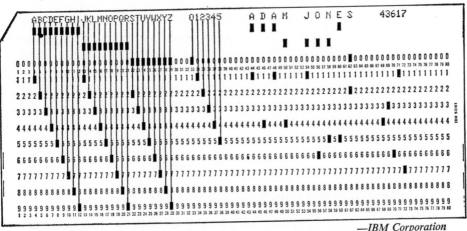

—*IBM Corporation*

The foundation of the punched-card system lies in the representation of data by coded holes punched in a card. Each letter is identified by a punch in one of the three positions at the top of the card and a punch in one of the numbered columns. Each number is identified by a punch in its specific column only. As the cards are fed through the machine, the position of the holes activates the equipment electrically.

Sorter. The punched cards can be sorted in numeric or alphabetic sequence or classified into groups or sequences by a machine called a *sorter*. The sorter consists of a reading device (to pick out holes on the card), a rack of pockets, and a mechanism to shunt the cards into their appropriate pockets. If the sales manager, for example, wished to know the total sales made by a salesman, all the sales orders (on punched cards) would be run through the sorter. This machine would pick out those cards (orders) which had a hole or holes in a certain coded location designating the salesman. All cards with holes in this coded location would be directed by the machine into a separate pocket and thus separated from the rest of the orders.

A *collator* is a special type of sorter that is capable of taking two batches of cards and combining them into one sequenced deck.

Calculator. The *calculator* reads the information on the punched card, performs the calculations required, and produces the result in punched holes on the card.

On a sales invoice, for example, the calculator will multiply the unit price by the number of units for each item, record the extension amount for each item, the total for the order, the amount of discount, and net amount of the invoice.

Tabulator. The principal elements of the *tabulator* are a reading unit, a printing device, and a series of accumulators.

The reading unit senses the holes in the cards and activates type bars which print the data on sheets of paper forms fed through the machine. The accumulators add, subtract, and produce totals. The three components—reading unit, printer, and accumulator—are interconnected through the control panel or wiring unit. The tabulator may be wired to accumulate, summarize, and print all or part of the data for all or part of a group of cards.

The principle of the punched card system is illustrated on page 439 in the processing of a monthly payroll.

▪ Limitations of the Punched-Card and Tape Systems

Punched-card and tape systems greatly increase the speed of processing certain types of data. They also increase accuracy and eliminate a great deal of manual effort. They are, however, restricted in the extent to which they can take alternative courses of action in the processing operation. Each of these systems, therefore, must be conducted in

Weekly Time Cards. The hours worked by each employee are recorded on an individual time card by a time clock. Four weekly time cards are accumulated for each employee.

Keypunch Machine. Using the data on the weekly time card, the operator of the keypunch machine punches a card for each week for each employee. This card shows the employee's name, payroll number, social security number, hourly rate, hours worked each day, income tax exemptions, and any other information necessary to determine the employee's pay.

Punched Cards. Data are transferred from weekly time cards to punched cards. An individual earnings card for each employee is prepared along with deduction cards for such items as government bonds and insurance. Once the data from the weekly time cards are transferred manually by the keypunch to punched cards, all other operations in preparing the monthly payroll are performed by the machines.

Sorter. Punched cards are run through the sorter-collator, which classifies the weekly punched cards for each employee along with his individual earnings record card, and deduction cards for the items such as government bonds and insurance.

Sorted Cards. Cards are classified by employees.

Calculator. As the cards feed through the calculator, the gross amount earned, deductions, and net pay for each employee are calculated.

Tabulator (Accounting Machine). The following operations are performed as the cards feed through the tabulator: (1) the date, payroll period, employee's name, and all salary information are printed on the check; and (2) the payroll journal or register is printed.

Payroll Check. The payroll check is ready for distribution to the employee.

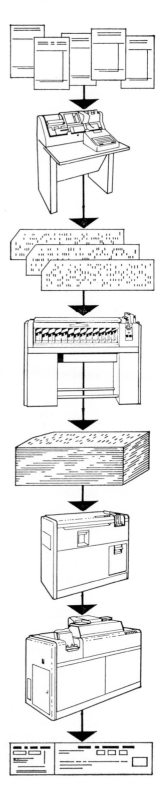

sections, not as one continuous process. The operator makes required decisions between steps and transfers the cards or tape manually from one machine to the next. Although they are rapid as compared with strictly manual methods, they are exceedingly slow when compared with electronic data processing which is described in the following section.

Electronic Data Processing (EDP)

In the *electronic data processing* (*EDP*) system, data are converted into the binary code (basic language of the electronic system) and communicated in the form of electrical pulses through electrical circuits. The speed of processing the data is several hundred times faster than that attainable in mechanical or electro-mechanical systems. The electronic system makes possible a continuous chain of processing from the point where data and instructions are read into the system to the final step of printing out the results.

The electronic system consists of input equipment, a central processing unit, and output equipment.

■ Input Equipment

The term *input* is used to describe the act of introducing data into an electronic data processing system. The *input data* may be any data upon which one or more of the basic data processing functions are to be performed—coding, sorting, computing, summarizing, recording, and communicating. The data may be fed into the system through any one of several types of input equipment.

Punched-Tape and Punched-Card Readers. Data such as sales orders, purchase invoices, or payroll cards are usually converted into punched tape or punched cards and fed into the system by high-speed readers. These readers convert the punched holes into coded electrical impulses which, in turn, are transmitted into the central processing unit.

In order to carry out its work, the central processing system must be given specific, step-by-step instructions as to what it is to do. These instructions are referred to as the *program*. The person who prepares these instructions is called a *programmer*. A program must be written for each operation—to process payroll, to update inventory, to allocate costs. The program is usually recorded on punched cards or tape and fed into the central processing unit by the input equipment.

—General Electric Company, Nela Park

Keypunch data processing at The American Greeting
Card Company in Cleveland, Ohio, is shown here.

MICR (Magnetic Ink Character Recognition) and Optical Readers.
To convert input data into punched tape or punched cards from standard business forms requires a manual keypunching operation unless the tape or card is a by-product of some other operation such as typing of an invoice. To eliminate this time-consuming and error-potential operation of manual keypunch, banks have standardized on MICR equipment. This equipment reads directly from the check or deposit slip the figures written in magnetic ink. Also, optical readers are used for reading characters imprinted from credit cards.

One of the major developments in EDP in the future will be the refinement of optical character readers with the capability of reading any type of material and processing it directly into the EDP system. For instance, the ultimate objective of the ZIP Code is to enable letters to be electronically sorted by optical readers. (See pages 755 and 769.)

Typewriter. Data may be introduced into the system directly from the typewriter keyboard. The typewriter, however, is used primarily for direct communication with the central processing unit (such as asking questions), as it is too slow for volume input. The central processing unit is capable of receiving data at the rate of several hundred characters per second.

The console typewriter permits the operator to communicate to the computer and to receive responses.

—Cincinnati and Suburban Bell Telephone Company

■ Central Processing Unit

The heart of the electronic data processing system is the *central processing unit* called the computer. It is made of (1) *a console*, (2) *an internal memory* or *storage file*, and (3) an *arithmetic component*.

Console. The *console* is the control center of the computer. It is used to supervise the various units and to communicate with the computer. It is made up of a series of lights and switches, and usually includes a typewriter. The lights are visible signals to the operator of the functions the computer is performing. With the switches the operator gives commands to start, to stop, to accept input data, and so on. The console typewriter is the means of communication with the computer. For example, the operator uses the typewriter to ask the balance of an account. The typewriter receives and types the computer's answer.

Storage or Memory File. *Storage* (frequently called memory, or memory file) is where data and instructions (programs) are stored magnetically.

Storage is organized into thousands of individual locations, each with a unique address by which it can be located in the same manner that a house can be located by a street address. The speed with which the processing unit can locate an address in the storage or memory file and transfer the amount in the address to the arithmetic component is referred to as *access time*. Since large processors can perform several hundred operations per second, the access time to stored data is critical.

Most computers have two types of storage, internal and bulk (external). The internal storage is quick-access storage. The quick-access storage holds the program and the data that are being used at the time.

Arithmetic Component. The arithmetic section of the computer performs the calculations (addition, subtraction, multiplication, division) like a calculating machine which functions electronically instead of mechanically. It has two sections, the *adder* and the *accumulator*.

The calculations are performed in the *adder* section. The calculations are made at lightning speed measured in microseconds (millionth of a second) of time. For example, a small computer can multiply a four-digit number by a five-digit number in 1/1000 of a second. Large computers can perform the operation in much less time.

The *accumulator* is that portion of the arithmetic unit where results (answers) of the arithmetic operation are temporarily stored until the calculation is complete. The instructions may direct the equipment to:

(1) Copy a number from a storage location into the accumulator.
(2) Get a second number from a storage location and add it to the number in the accumulator.
(3) Multiply the sum of the two numbers (in the accumulator) by 25 and return the answer to storage.

▪ Output Equipment

Output equipment is used to report out the processed data from the central processing unit into one of two forms (1) records and reports for people to use, and (2) punched cards, tape, or magnetic tape for use in further data processing.

Printers. The print-out is done on high speed equipment by printers that usually print a whole line of characters at one time. An average speed printer can print from 600 to 900 lines (120 characters—24 words a line) per minute. The end product may be a sales analysis, payroll checks, utility bills, statistical reports, invoices, cost distributions, and the like. The system can be programmed to print out hard copy (copy in final form for mailing or distribution).

Punched Tape, Cards, Magnetic Tape. Data may be printed out on tape, cards, or magnetic tape and stored, transferred by telecommunication to a central computer or later read into the same computer.

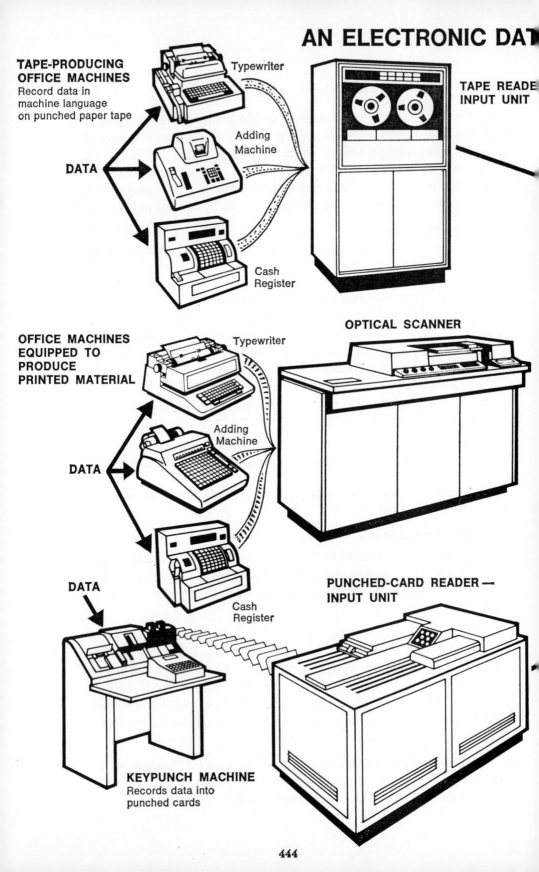

AN ELECTRONIC DAT

TAPE-PRODUCING OFFICE MACHINES
Record data in machine language on punched paper tape

Typewriter

Adding Machine

DATA

Cash Register

TAPE READE INPUT UNIT

OFFICE MACHINES EQUIPPED TO PRODUCE PRINTED MATERIAL

Typewriter

Adding Machine

DATA

Cash Register

OPTICAL SCANNER

DATA

PUNCHED-CARD READER — INPUT UNIT

KEYPUNCH MACHINE
Records data into punched cards

ROCESSING SYSTEM

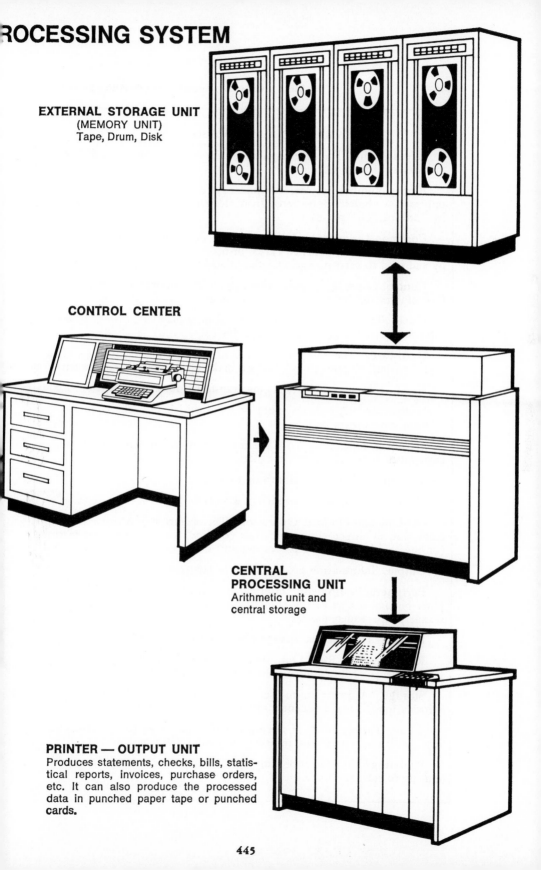

EXTERNAL STORAGE UNIT
(MEMORY UNIT)
Tape, Drum, Disk

CONTROL CENTER

**CENTRAL
PROCESSING UNIT**
Arithmetic unit and
central storage

PRINTER — OUTPUT UNIT
Produces statements, checks, bills, statistical reports, invoices, purchase orders, etc. It can also produce the processed data in punched paper tape or punched cards.

A GUIDE TO DATA PROCESSING TERMS

Access Time. The time required for the computer to locate data in its memory or storage section

Binary Number System. A number system using the base 2 (There are only two symbols: 1 or 0—zero. In an electronic system this is represented by "on" or "off" pulses.)

Common Language. A term used to describe punched paper tape, edge-punched cards, punched cards, or magnetic tape which may be read by and used to activate various office machines

Control Console. A panel through which the operator regulates the flow of data and instructions to the computer

Erase. To remove information stored on a magnetic drum, magnetic tape, magnetic disc, or other storage device

Hardware. The components or configuration of machines (such as input, output, or power units) which make up a system of equipment

Input. Information (data) being transferred into the computer

Instruction. A coded symbol or word which tells the computer to perform some operation

Memory. Devices used for the internal storage of data such as magnetic tapes, magnetic drums, magnetic discs, and magnetic cores

Microsecond. One millionth of a second

Millisecond. One thousandth of a second

Off-Line and On-Line Operation. The operation of peripheral equipment not in direct communication (off-line) or in direct connection (on-line) with the central processing unit of the computer

Output. Information produced by the computer

Peripheral Equipment. Equipment used in conjunction with a computer but not a part of the computer itself; that is, a converter, optical scanner, tape reader, printer

Printer. The machine that prints the output from the computer

Read, Read In, Read Out. The operation of transferring information from one type or location to another type or location

Storage. A general term used for the ability of the machine to hold information (This is frequently referred to as the memory.)

Write. The operation of storing a number on the surface of a magnetic tape, or drum, transferring information to an output medium

Updating. The process of bringing data stored in the computer memory unit up to current value

Visual Display. Computer systems that are now available will produce visual displays based on data stored in the computer. Sales charts, engineering drawings, tables and graphs, and many other forms of visual presentation can be produced almost instantaneously. New data can be fed into the computer and the resulting changes in the charts, graphs, or drawing immediately shown.

Decision-Making Ability. One of the distinctive qualities of the computer is its ability to select among alternate courses of action. This is frequently referred to as decision-making ability. The computer can be programmed to examine a figure and determine if it is above or below a certain amount. If it is above, the computer will follow one set of instructions. If it is below, the computer will follow another set. This decision-making ability makes it possible, once data and a program have been fed into the system, for the computer to complete a sequence of operations automatically. For instance, it can process a payroll without any further human intervention after data on the individual time cards are fed into the computer. It calculates the wage for each employee, searches out his payroll information and obtains the number of withholding tax exemptions and then determines the withholding tax and social security tax, makes other approved deductions, determines the net pay, and prints the paycheck. In addition, it stores the payroll information and produces complete payroll information on each employee and prints the W-2 forms (Withholding Tax Statements). A payroll for several thousand employees can be completed within a few hours.

▪ Computer Applications

Since the computer is capable of making routine decisions, it is being successfully used as an accounting device to perform many types of routine jobs which formerly required clerical workers. Computer installations perform payroll calculations, update accounts receivable and payable, control inventories, process insurance data, prepare dividend checks, keep depositors' checking accounts, distribute costs and expenses, make out bills for telephone and electric utilities, and analyze personnel data. The ability of the computer to do routine work is causing major changes in the office structure and in the clerical occupations.

▪ Long-Range Planning

Part of the guesswork in long-range planning is being eliminated through the use of the computer. The expected activities of a business

Shown here is the data processing room in the
People's Savings Bank in Bridgeport, Connecticut.

for one, two, or three years in advance can be simulated and fed into the
computer. Within minutes the computer can report back the results,
completing calculations that would take man with paper and pencil a
century to do.

Data Communication

Developments in data communication are making it possible to
coordinate people, data processing equipment, and communications
into a *business information system.* This system supplies timely information to both management and nonmanagement people so that they can
plan and operate a business wisely. It permits the moving of both processed and unprocessed data from the point of origin to the point of
need or effectiveness.

■ Information Flow

Formerly it was not possible to communicate data from location to
location except at intervals. Since the flow of information was restricted
to one segment of an organization, to one plant, or to one location, it
was necessary to decentralize operations and management. Decision
making had to be delegated to management at the local level.

Improvements in the computer and in telecommunication are now
making it possible to achieve a flow of information through the entire

business system. Each corporate branch, regardless of its geographical location, can be connected "on line" with a central computer. Thus, the branch has a direct connection and can feed data into and receive answers back from the computer. An illustration of the on-line process is the reservation system used by some airlines. Each ticket sales office of the airline throughout the United States has an on-line connection with the computer center. In a matter of seconds, a ticket agent can question the computer on space available on any flight, receive the reply, and ticket (reserve) the space.

In one company payroll, records are typed into a teleprinter and transmitted to a teleprinter at the central accounting center, where the data are converted to punched cards and processed. At the end of the weekly payroll period, the processed data are transmitted to the local plant and automatically printed on checks that have been inserted into the keyboard printer. Then they are signed by authorized personnel.

A department store with several branches accumulates data from the cash register in each department into a central processing center. When a sale is recorded on any register, it is automatically and simultaneously transmitted to the processing center. The center answers with voice response all requests for credit information, provides management with a daily report of sales in each department plus a comparison with last year's figures for the same day, analyzes sales trends, and compares the daily performance of each sales person with the records of his previous sales.

▪ Centralization of Management

Telecommunication is bringing about important changes in management operational patterns. First, it is making all relevant facts immediately available to management. Management can now know what is happening inside the company as soon as it happens. Secondly, it is getting the information to management in "real time"; that is, in time to do something about it. For example, the production costs of a branch operation may be gradually increasing. Without the assistance of the computer, these costs could get far out of line before coming to the attention of management. With the computer, coupled with data communication facilities, however, any change in costs can be known immediately, in time to take corrective action.

Management can now measure the immediate effect of management decisions. This is known as "information feedback." A familiar illustration of the principle of feedback is the interaction between the thermostat and the air conditioner, which constantly interact to keep the room at a predetermined temperature. In a similar manner, the feedback through the computer permits management to regulate and initiate changes in costs, prices, profit margin, inventories, production, and so forth, in line with a predetermined plan.

Telecommunication is also making it possible to centralize management. Top management in the central office can now have access to everything important that is happening at any corporate outpost as soon as it happens. An executive in the central office can have data on each branch at the same time that the branch manager can have the data. Decisions can be made and fed back to the branch as rapidly as they could be made at the branch. Centralized control of decentralized operations is now a reality.

▪ Data Processing Service Centers

To provide the advantages of modern data processing to businesses that are too small to justify an expensive data processing installation and also to handle overflow loads of those businesses that have their own installations, data processing service centers have been established. These centers provide their services for a fee.

Most service centers have ready-made programs to do such routine jobs as (1) payroll, (2) inventory, (3) receivables, (4) payables, (5) labor distribution, and (6) sales analysis. However, they will also prepare financial reports, complete marketing data, and perform complicated scientific calculations.

Business firms using a service center usually record the data on punched tape or cards. The data are then transferred to the processing center by a direct hookup via data transmission equipment.

One alert secretary saved her company $2,000 by suggesting that, instead of adding a new employee to handle the payroll overload, it use the services of a local data processing center. The difference between the cost of an additional clerk and the service center's charge was slightly over $2,000 a year.

Computer Networks. Manufacturers of data processing equipment and communication carriers are developing time-sharing computer centers interconnected by a complex of telecommunication facilities. For example, the National Cash Register Company has established a computer center to process data from several hundred savings and loan associations over a network of several states. Western Union is developing a vast real-time computer communications complex called the National Information Utility, which will distribute information services or computer power needed to conduct a subscriber's business locally, regionally, and nationally, just as an electric utility distributes electrical service to all subscribers.

Information Retrieval and Exchange. Information service centers provide subscribers with scientific and technical information by direct connection with a computer over telecommunication facilities. For example, the Western Union Telegraph Company and the Law Research Service, Incorporated, have developed a legal service whereby law offices across the country can have access to files of legal citations stored in a central computer in New York City. Subscribers to the service install Telex teleprinters in their offices. Inquiries from the subscribers go by Telex to the computer center. The computer sorts out the appropriate citations and returns the information to the subscriber over the same Telex hookup. Similar services are developing in other professional and scientific fields.

Business services are also available. For example, a business can subscribe to a local credit rating service which, in turn, has an affiliation with a regional or national credit service. The credit ratings of most businesses and millions of individuals are stored at geographically located main service centers. The local credit center can obtain the credit rating on a business or individual in any part of the country within minutes.

The Labor Department recently disclosed plans to develop a computer system to rapidly match unemployed workers with available jobs or training opportunities, first on a state and regional basis and then for all states.

Automation and the Secretary

Automated methods of data processing coupled with developments in data communication are producing many changes in office work. A major shift in the composition of office personnel is evident. Fewer typists, clerks, and stenographers are required, as many of the functions they perform are being taken over by machines. On the other hand, the demand for persons trained in automated data processing is greatly increasing. There is also an increasing demand for highly trained secretaries. Technology has not devised a way to replace the secretary for, as one person said, "Machines will never charm the boss' guests or cover up for him when he goofs. What they will do is free the secretary from petty jobs and make her a more important person."

Technology is changing the role of the secretary. As office work becomes more automated, the work of the secretary is becoming less routinized and clerical in composition and more supervisory and administrative in nature. Many of the routine duties involving copying, calculating, sorting, and recording that have consumed so much of the secretary's time can now be done by automated processes. The secretary has more time to devote to supervisory and administrative functions and to tasks requiring imagination and initiative. Thus, her position becomes more stimulating and challenging, as well as more important.

The computer has, in part, changed the secretary's role of compiler of data to one of screener of data—a role that involves decision making on an administrative level. The centralization of data—made possible through the computer with its interconnections with all the branches and divisions of a company—brings a flood of data into the executives' offices. These data pass over the top-level secretary's desk. The secretary must perform the decision-making function of deciding what data are to be fed to the executive. This screening function is necessary to conserve the executive's time.

In a large company, the secretary inevitably becomes the liaison person between her executive and the data processing department or center. Consequently, she must understand both management and data processing in order to interpret what data her employer requires.

The introduction of automated equipment into the office demands that the office personnel adjust to new procedures—a problem complicated because of the natural tendency to resist change. New knowledges and skills must be developed. Old ways must be abandoned and new procedures accepted. Thus, the supervisory role of the secretary becomes increasingly important. The staff, under the supervision of the secretary, must be conditioned to accept the new procedure. Training must be provided and new work standards developed. Changes in personnel may be required. All of these factors add to the responsibilities of the secretary, but also add to the prestige of her position.

As the secretary becomes more involved in decision making and administrative and supervisory responsibilities—a trend that automation is accelerating—her preparation must be equal to the demands. A broad understanding of economics and business organization and management is essential.

Suggested Readings ─────────────────────────

Burck, Gilbert. "The Boundless Age of the Computer," *Fortune*, March, 1964, p. 101.

───────. "On Line in Real Time," *Fortune*, April, 1964, p. 141.

Electronic Data Processing Written for the Layman, Books 1, 2, 3. National Cash Register Company, Dayton, Ohio.

Gentle, Edgar C., Jr. *Data Communications in Business*. New York: American Telephone and Telegraph Company, 1965, 163 pp.

Neuner, John J. W., and B. Lewis Keeling. *Administrative Office Management*, 5th ed. Cincinnati: South-Western Publishing Co., 1967, pp. 667–738.

Questions for Discussion ─────────────────────

1. What does the term "common machine-language media" mean? Describe the various media in use in offices and identify the advantages and disadvantages of each.

2. Explain how a tape file on customers and on products sold could save time, reduce repetitive work, and improve accuracy in typing sales invoices.

3. What does integrated data processing mean? Illustrate how it might be applied in processing a sales order.

4. What are the major advantages of automated data processing? Which do you consider to be the most important advantage?

5. A company has a letter explaining an important change in credit policy to be sent to approximately 500 regular customers. What advantages, if any, would there be in having the letter produced on an automatic typewriter, rather than having it printed?

6. Since messages may be sent directly from one office to another by teletype machines through a direct machine-to-machine connection, why do many offices convert the message first to paper tape and then transmit the tape, as opposed to direct machine-to-machine connection?

7. What special advantages does electronic data processing provide in comparison with other systems of processing office data?

8. Illustrate ways electronic data processing and developments in telecommunications are revolutionizing management processes in business.

9. It has been stated that top management in business in the future will be less concerned with personnel relationships and more involved in problem solving and abstract relationships. What is your reaction to this statement?

10. What is the relationship between data processing and data communication?

11. In what ways, if any, do you think improvements in telecommunications and electronic data processing will change the work of the secretary to a top executive in the future?

12. Decide whether you would use the words italicized in the following sentences dictated by your employer. Then use the Reference Guide to verify or correct your answers.

(a) The *balance* of the order was shipped this afternoon.

(b) The *balance* of the report will be prepared by my assistant.

(c) Mr. Downs acted as chairman during the *remainder* of the meeting.

(d) The *remainder* of the fund will be used for research.

Problems

■ **1.** Obtain information and prepare a report on each of the following types of automatic typewriters: (a) Flexowriter, (b) Justowriter, (c) Auto-typist. Include in your report the following:

(a) A description of the machine and how it operates (Include an explanation of the code system used to activate the machine.)

(b) An explanation of how the machine is used in office work

■ **2.** Visit a company that has one of the following types of equipment. Prepare a report showing how the use of the equipment has reduced the amount of repetitive labor involved in the work of the office.

(a) Automatic typewriter

(b) Punched-card equipment

(c) Punched tape- or card-activated machines

(d) Electronic data processing equipment

■ **3.** Select one of the following and prepare a demonstration for presentation to the class explaining:

(a) Coding pattern in punched card tabulation

(b) Coding pattern used with the seven- or eight-channel tape

(c) A pegboard payroll system

Related Work Assignments 48-49

48. Data Processing. The following procedure is used in filling an order by your company.

Chicago Office. Sales order is typed and copy sent by mail to central accounting office in St. Louis.

St. Louis Office. Order is approved for credit and invoice is typed. A copy of the invoice is sent to the customer, and a copy is forwarded by airmail to the factory in Portland, Oregon, for filling.

Portland Office. Shipping order and label are typed and merchandise forwarded to customer.

Two weeks are frequently required to process an order.

Prepare an interoffice memorandum to your employer, Mr. Simpson, outlining a plan that will (1) reduce the repetitive work, and (2) speed up the processing of the order. An interoffice communication form is provided in the Workbook.

49. Systems Analysis. The instructions and supplies necessary for the completion of this assignment are provided in the Workbook.

Ch.
19   Collecting Business Information

"Getting the facts" can be both exciting and rewarding—for those who know information sources and how to use them. It is exciting because it challenges initiative and resourcefulness. It is rewarding because it provides the secretary or administrative assistant with opportunities to demonstrate this important contribution she can make to the executive.

The administrative assistant or the executive secretary is expected to be qualified to work with resource materials. In some instances it is up to the secretary to anticipate the needs; in others, these research-and-find assignments may be delegated by the executive.

The following are illustrations of assignments that an administrative assistant or executive secretary might be expected to do:

Check out a proposal by gathering the pertinent data the executive will need in his evaluation.

Verify the accuracy of data submitted in support of a proposal.

Gather the data the executive will need in preparing a proposal.

Examine possible solutions to a problem, advantages and disadvantages, opinions of authorities, ways others solve the problem.

Do the library research required by the executive in contributing to a project.

Gather and organize information the executive will need in preparing a speech or an article for a professional magazine.

In such activities, the secretary has a look-it-up function and a presentation function. This chapter discusses the sources to which the secretary can turn to find the information. Chapters 20 and 21 discuss ways that the secretary may organize the data to make the most effective presentation.

Sources of Business Information

Business information is being updated constantly. Sources are revised and new materials published regularly. It is necessary, therefore, to supplement any guide (including this chapter) with new sources as they appear.

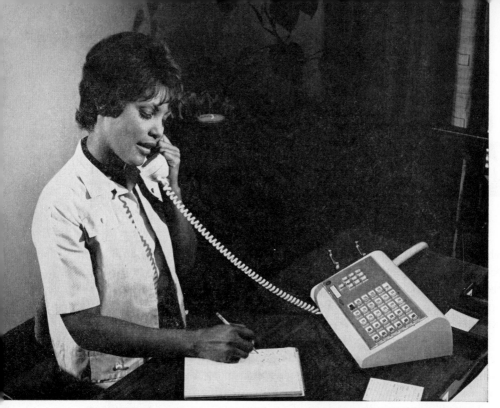

—*American Telephone and Telegraph Company*

Often information gathered by telephone will save extensive time and energy. The secretary pictured here is using Bell Telephone System's Touch-Tone telephone.

■ Places to Look for Information

Needed information may be found in the *office of the executive or of the secretary*, in a *company library*, or in an *outside library*. An executive undoubtedly subscribes to publications devoted to his field; other materials are collected through his memberships in trade or professional organizations. What the employer reads is often his top aide's cue to what she should read. The executive often secures specialized reference books for his personal office library. The company also may provide materials for the reference shelf of the secretary or office supervisor—if she is enterprising enough to request the indispensable ones and to watch for pertinent new publications.

In addition to quick-reference materials kept in the executive's office, many large corporations maintain a company library staffed with a technically trained librarian. In addition to a librarian, many companies have a research staff that locates information requested by each office. In this case the function of the secretary is to provide an accurate and exact request for information. In other situations the secretary must locate the information in the company library.

It may be necessary to go outside the organization for needed information. The first logical outside source is the public library. A number of cities have public libraries with specialized business departments and branches that provide invaluable assistance to the business interests in their area.

Another source for information is the specialized library. *The Directory of Special Libraries and Information Centers* (published by Gale Research Company, Detroit) lists over 10,000 special libraries, their location, size, and subject of specialization. The local Chamber of Commerce, for instance, frequently has a library on commercial and industrial subjects. Many business, technical, and professional societies or associations maintain excellent libraries. Use of these facilities is limited, generally, to members. Law libraries are often located in county and federal court buildings or at the local university or college of law. Many cities provide municipal reference libraries for the use of the public as well as city employees. Medical and surgical libraries are maintained by hospitals or by the local college of medicine. Art, historical, and natural history museums have specialized libraries, as do colleges and universities. Some newspaper offices have large library collections that may be open to limited public use. The United States Department of Commerce maintains regional offices in the principal cities. In these offices, files of the publications of the Department are available for consultation.

The public or special library (through its reference department) may answer questions over the telephone. Naturally, only questions that can be easily answered are accepted. If the public library in the secretary's community renders telephone reference service and if the secretary has frequent need for such service, it is courteous for her to visit the library and introduce herself to the person in charge of the reference desk.

> "EVERY MAN has a right to his opinion, but no man has a right to be wrong in his facts."
>
> —*Bernard Baruch*

▪ Abstracting Services

So vast is the volume of technical literature published in many areas that engineers, scientists, and business executives find it difficult to keep abreast of new developments. To help bridge this information gap, some large companies subscribe to an abstracting service that specializes in a specific field. An example is the American Petroleum Institute's Abstracting Service. Highly trained specialists abstract thousands of journals, publications, and scientific papers from all parts of the world. The abstracts are distributed to subscribers.

Some of the abstracting services feed abstracts and selected references into a computer. The computer arranges the material alphabetically by subject. A computer-driven phototypesetter prints out indexes periodically and can provide an immediate print-out of all abstracts on a specific subject. The recipient can determine from the abstract whether he wishes to read the original and complete document.

The National Federation of Science Abstracting and Indexing Services, Washington, D.C., publishes a *Guide to U. S. Indexing and Abstracting Services in Science and Technology.*

▪ Subscription Information Services (General)

Management often subscribes to information services relating to business conditions in general. These services present information from more direct and limited sources than those found in popular publications. The service may be in loose-leaf form so that superseded pages can be destroyed and new and additional ones inserted easily. It may be the secretary's duty to see that the new material is filed in its proper place in the service, according to the instructions sent by the publisher. These services include:

Babson's Business Service. Three bulletins are issued: *Business Inventory— Commodity Price Forecast* (monthly), *Business Management—Sales and Wage Forecasts* (monthly), and *A Confidential Barometer Letter* (weekly).

The Bureau of National Affairs, Inc. This privately owned company reports government actions affecting management, labor, law, taxes, finance, federal contracts, antitrust and trade regulations, international trade, and patent law. It publishes a *Daily Report for Executives.*

The Kiplinger Washington Letter. This weekly confidential letter analyzes and condenses economic and political news for subscribers.

The National Industrial Conference Board. Over 3,800 subscribers support research in the field of business and personnel practices, business, economics, and statistics. Included in the service are two monthly magazines—*The Business Record* and *The Management Record,* an annual—*The Economic Almanac,* a weekly desk sheet in Bulletin form—*Desk Sheet,* and several major reports a year.

Research Institute Recommendations. This weekly newsletter analyzes economic and legislative developments and makes tax recommendations.

■ Subscription Information Services (Specialized)

The secretary should be acquainted with the subscription services for specialized fields described below:

The Bureau of National Affairs, Inc. In addition to providing general business services, this organization publishes *Antitrust and Trade Regulation Report, Federal Contracts Report, International Trade Reporter, Export Shipping Manual, The United States Patents Quarterly*, and *Daily Labor Report.*

Commerce Clearing House Services. These services are especially useful to lawyers and accountants. The CCH Topical Law Reports (over 100 loose-leaf publications) provide assistance on such problems as federal tax, labor, trade regulation, state tax, social security, securities, bankruptcy, trusts, insurance, and aviation.

Dun and Bradstreet Credit Service. This service collects, analyzes, and distributes credit information on retail, wholesale, and manufacturing companies.

Most brokerage houses provide investment information to prospective and present customers.

Investment Services. Many investment services are available, as a cursory look at the advertising on the financial pages of newspapers will attest. Two of the best known are reported here: Moody's Investors Service publishes *Moody's Stock Survey, Moody's Advisory Reports, Moody's Investors Advisory Service, Moody's Dividend Record, Moody's Bond Record*, and *Moody's Handbook of Common Stocks.*

Standard and Poor's Corporation publications include *Corporation Record, Dividend Record, Listed Stock Reports, Over-the-Counter and Regional Exchanges Stock Reports, Stock Guide, Industry Survey, Foreign Securities Survey, The Outlook, Transportation Service Stock Summary, Poor's Investment Advisory Survey, Called Bond Record, Status of Bonds, Bond Reports, Bond Guide, Municipal Bond Selector, Register of Corporation Directors and Executives*, and *Fitch Survey.*

Prentice-Hall Services. These loose-leaf current publications cover the latest laws, rules, and regulations with interpretations and comments. All aspects of federal and state laws are covered. In addition, *Accountant's Weekly Report, Insurance and Tax News* (a biweekly newsletter), *Lawyer's Weekly Report*, and *Executive's Tax Report* (weekly) keep subscribers up to date.

Real Estate Analyst Reports. These monthly, loose-leaf reports include: *The Real Estate Analyst, As I See It, The Agricultural Bulletin* (farm sales and values), *The Appraisal Bulletin, The Construction Bulletin, The Mortgage Bulletin, Trends Bulletin*, and *Real Estate Tax Bulletin.*

The *Directory of Business and Financial Services*, compiled by the Special Libraries Association, lists 1,500 bulletins, newsletters, and reports (both general and specialized) that are distributed periodically on a service basis to subscribers.

■ Periodicals for Executives

The periodicals that come to the office can be divided into two types —general and specialized.

General Periodicals. The alert secretary scans general business magazines received at the office or at her employer's desk for material that may be of immediate or possible interest to the executive and also to her. Typical business magazines are:

> *Business Week.* This periodical covers factors of primary interest to the business executive on the national and international scene. Statistics reflect current trends.
>
> *Dun's Review and Modern Industry.* This monthly covers finance, credit, production, labor, sales and distribution.
>
> *Fortune.* This monthly magazine features articles on specific industries and business leaders. It also analyzes current business problems.
>
> *National Observer.* Factual articles on world affairs and economic and political developments of special interest to the business executive are provided by this monthly published by Dow Jones and Co., Inc.
>
> *Nation's Business.* Published monthly by the Chamber of Commerce of the United States, this business magazine concerns topics that are political and general in nature.

School of Business Publications. In addition, the executive may subscribe for the business magazines published by some of the larger university schools of business. Well-known magazines of this type are the *Harvard Business Review* (bimonthly) and the *Journal of Business* (quarterly), University of Chicago.

Special Articles. In the business sections of such weeklies as *Time* and *Newsweek* and the special articles in *The United States News and World Report*, the reader can learn a great deal about current business trends.

Specialized Periodicals. It is common for a company to belong to several trade associations, each of which helps it with a different aspect of its business. In addition, the executives may belong to several professional associations. These associations issue regular magazines to their members, publishing articles and statistics of current interest. *The Standard Periodical Directory* lists over 20,000 United States and Canadian periodicals.

The *Business Periodicals Index* is the primary source of information on a wide range of articles appearing in business periodicals.

Specialized periodicals and digests provide much information of value to the executive.

—Cincinnati and Suburban Bell Telephone Company

When seeking data on a specific magazine, the secretary might consult *Ayer's Directory of Newspapers and Periodicals* (annual), providing such information as name of publication, editor, publisher, date established, technical data, and geographic area served. Another source of specialized magazines is the *Readers' Guide to Periodical Literature*. More than one hundred well-known magazines (such as the *Architectural Record, Changing Times, Consumer Reports, Foreign Affairs, Monthly Labor Review,* and *Time*) are indexed in each issue and their articles cataloged under appropriate headings.

■ Government Publications

Our government is a prolific publisher and a major source of information for the businessman. Some government publications may be subscribed to or purchased by the company. Others will be found on file in the reference department or business section of the public library, or in the municipal reference library of a city hall—all depending upon the subject matter. If the secretary works in a city that has a depository library (usually located in a larger library) designated by law to receive all or part of the material published by the government, she might turn to it for reference. Otherwise, she would go to one of the libraries or departments just described; or she would purchase the publications.

In *The Monthly Catalog of U.S. Government Publications* the secretary will find a comprehensive list of all publications issued by the various departments and agencies of the United States Government, including those for sale by the Superintendent of Documents and those for official use only. A semimonthly list of *Selected United States Government Publications* is sent free to persons requesting the Superintendent of Documents to include their names on the mailing list.

Proceedings and debates of Congress are given in *The Congressional Record. The Congressional Directory* provides names and biographical facts of Senators and Representatives, composition of Congressional committees, information about special agencies and commissions of the government, and listings of our diplomatic representatives abroad and of foreign representatives here.

Publications of the U.S. Department of Commerce, Bureau of the Census, are based on data from censuses taken in various years including information on population, housing, business, manufacturing, and agriculture. Full census reports provide complete information. *The Statistical Abstract of the United States* (annual), however, presents summary statistics about area and population, vital statistics, education, climate, employment, military affairs, social security, income, prices, banking, transportation, agriculture, forests, fisheries, mining, manufactures, and related fields. Data on all cities over 25,000 in population are given in the *City Supplement* to the *Statistical Abstracts*.

The U.S. Department of Commerce, Bureau of Foreign and Domestic Commerce, publishes the annual *Foreign Commerce and Navigation of the United States* that gives detailed statistical records of the foreign commerce of the United States: articles exported and imported, rates of duty and duties collected, and a complete registry of vessels involved in foreign trade. *Foreign Commerce Weekly* provides information for those engaged in trade with other countries. The *Survey of Current Business* (issued monthly) reports on the industrial and business activities of the United States.

Publications of the Department of Agriculture provide agricultural and marketing statistics and information for increasing production and agricultural efficiency. Department of Labor publications deal mostly with labor statistics, standards, and employment trends. Their official publication is the *Monthly Labor Review*.

Economic and agricultural data on many subjects may be acquired from various state governments. The secretary should address inquiries to the departments of health, geology or conservation, and highways; to the divisions of banks, insurance, and statistics; to industrial and public utilities commissions; or to the research bureaus of state universities. Pertinent information about executive, legislative, and judicial branches of state governments is given in the *Book of the States* which is published every two years by the Council of State Governments.

■ City Directories

A secretary to a lawyer or to an insurance man may be asked to locate or trace the address of an individual by a search through city directories when the name of the person is not listed in the telephone directory. Current and back issues of city directories are kept at libraries for the convenience of business users. The library collection of directories might contain the local city directory and also directories of all the cities in the state and of the major cities over the country.

City directories are not published by cities but by commercial enterprises for profit. Some of the very largest cities, such as New York City and Los Angeles, no longer have city directories.

■ Special Directories

There are also hundreds of classified directories serving many fields —so many, in fact, that a special guide to directories is published. The latest edition of *Guide to American Directories* lists more than 4,000 directories in over 300 major fields of public and private enterprise. Some of them are listed below.

1. Those that list individuals engaged in the same occupation—for example, the *American Medical Directory* which gives education and field of specialization of all physicians in the United States and Canada.

2. Those that provide biographical sketches of *selected* individuals. *Who's Who in America* is a biographical directory, reissued biennially, of notable living men and women. *Who's Who*, an international annual biographical dictionary published in London, contains mainly prominent English names. There are also many selective *Who's Who* references, such as *Who's Who in Labor, Who's Who in Commerce and Industry, Who's Who in the South* and *Who's Who of American Women.*

3. Those that list all the businesses or service institutions engaged in similar or related enterprises in the United States, such as *Thomas' Register of American Manufacturers*, and *Polk's Bankers Encyclopedia.*

4. Those that list businesses in foreign countries, such as *Australasian Manufacturers Directory; Canadian Trade Index;* and *Japan Register of Merchants, Manufacturers, and Shippers.* The United States Department of Commerce publishes *A Guide to Foreign Business Directories.*

5. Those that serve as buyers' guides. The best known is *MacRae's Blue Book*, a buying guide published annually. It also lists trade names and firms owning such names. Other typical buyers' guides are *Hardware Retailer Buyers' Guide, Green Book Buyers Directory* (chemical), and the *Hospital Purchasing File*. The *Buyers Laboratory Incorporated* publishes newsletters and reports on the ratings of office machines, furniture, and supplies.

6. Those that provide such information as *Where to Find Statistical Information, Encyclopedia of Associations, A Businessman's Guide to Washington* (governmental agencies and their services), and *A Businessman's Guide to Europe*.

▪ Atlases

An atlas is a collection of maps and statistical information regarding populations and geographic areas. *Rand McNally Commercial Atlas and Marketing Guide*, subscribed to by most libraries, contains not only geographic maps but also many economic maps. It really constitutes a map service, because new and revised editions are furnished throughout the year. When a subscription is stopped, all material must be returned to the publisher.

▪ Dictionaries

One would naturally expect a dictionary to be a reference source frequently used by secretaries. The office may have a large unabridged dictionary; but the efficient secretary will also want an up-to-date, desk-size dictionary within arm's reach. *Webster's New Collegiate Dictionary, The American College Dictionary*, and *New College Standard Dictionary* are all acceptable in the latest edition.

There are also innumerable specialized dictionaries such as bilingual ones for use in writing and translating foreign correspondence. There are also technical ones, such as *A Dictionary for Accountants, A Dictionary of Foreign Trade, A Dictionary of Modern Economics, A Dictionary of Occupational Titles, A Dictionary of Scientific and Technical Words, Hackh's Chemical Dictionary, A Dictionary of Statistical Terms, Encyclopedic Dictionary of Real Estate Practices, Thomson's Dictionary of Banking, Black's Law Dictionary, Encyclopedic Dictionary of Business, International Business Dictionary, Modern Dictionary of Electronics, Hawley's Technical Speller, The Van Nostrand Chemist's Dictionary, Dictionary of Physics and Electronics, The Condensed Chemical Dictionary*, and *Chambers Technical Dictionary*.

New developments outdate technical dictionaries rapidly. Only the most recent editions can be considered dependably up to date.

▪ Yearbooks

Yearbooks are annual reports of summaries of statistics and facts. *The World Almanac and Book of Facts*, which is the most popular book of this type, was published annually by the *New York World-Telegram and The Sun*.[1] One reference librarian has said, "Give me a good dictionary and *The World Almanac*, and I can answer 80 percent of all questions asked me." *The World Almanac* contains many pages of statistics and facts, preceded by an excellent index. It covers such items as stock and bond markets; notable events; political and financial statistics of states and cities; statistics on population, farm crops, prices, trade and commerce; educational data; and information on the postal services. Because of its wide coverage and low price, the secretary might request the executive to purchase a copy of *The World Almanac* each year for office use. Another yearbook of this type is the *Information Please Almanac*, published by Simon and Schuster.

The *Statesman's Yearbook*, published in London, provides factual and statistical information on countries of the world. Data are provided on type of government, area and population, religion, education, justice, defense, commerce and industry, and finance. The *Yearbook of World Affairs* analyzes developments of international significance.

▪ Handbooks

Handbooks have been published in many areas of business. They are highly factual and are written to give a general survey knowledge (with the minimum use of time and effort) about a field. A few of the many handbooks that have been published include: *Handbook of Business Administration, Business Executive's Handbook, Accountants' Handbook, Business Finance Handbook, Financial Handbook, Handbook of Tax Techniques, Foreign Trade Handbook, Manager's Handbook, Handbook of Employee Selection, The Marketing Handbook, The Sales Manager's Handbook,* and *Production Handbook*.

Among a number of handbooks written for the secretary employed in a specialized office are handbooks for the legal secretary, medical secretary, school secretary, and others. (See pages 202–203.)

▪ Secretary's Reference Shelf

In addition to the secretarial handbooks and reference materials needed for transcription (pages 201–204), the secretary may collect

---

[1]This publisher is now defunct. The new publisher is *Newspaper Enterprise Association, Inc.*, 230 Park Avenue, New York 10017.

other worthwhile reference books; or she may be asked by the executive to purchase them for the office. What is on the secretary's reference shelf should depend on the nature of her job and the background information she will need. A useful, inexpensive reference is *How to Use the Business Library*. This manual is revised periodically and would be a valuable adjunct to the office library or secretary's reference shelf. Among other source books of information are the following:

> Abridged encyclopedias—such as *The Columbia Encyclopedia* (one volume), comprised of very brief articles. It is particularly strong on biography and geography; or the *Lincoln Library of Essential Information* (two volumes), that classifies information into twelve broad subject fields, rather than alphabetically.
>
> An annual book of statistics—such as the *Statistical Abstract of the United States, The Economic Almanac, The World Almanac,* or the *Commodity Yearbook.*
>
> An atlas or gazetteer—such as the *Rand McNally-Standard World Atlas* or *Webster's Geographical Dictionary.*
>
> A book of quotations—such as Bartlett's *Familiar Quotations* or *The Concise Oxford Dictionary of Quotations.*

The secretary's reference shelf should surely include a technical handbook that covers the area of work of the executive.

Using Library Sources

When a subject requires extensive searching or considerable listing and copying, the secretary usually goes to the library to do the work; but she needs considerable skill in finding the information about published materials from which she will make selections.

▪ Finding the Information

Her first task is to select material to examine from the various library indexes, guides, and catalogs.

Books. The index of books is the *card catalog*. This is a card file that shows the contents of the library just as a book index shows the contents of a book. In the catalog there are at least three index cards for each book; one card is filed by the author's name, one by title, and one or more by subject classification. Many of the cards contain "See also" notes, which indicate where similar or related information may be found. The cards are uniformly printed and available to libraries from the Library of Congress.

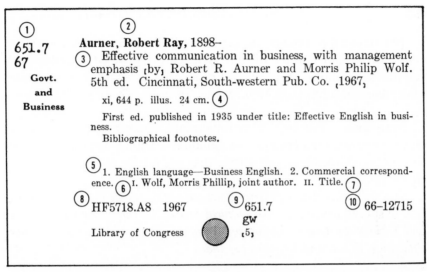

① 651.7
67
Govt.
and
Business

② Aurner, Robert Ray, 1898–
③ Effective communication in business, with management
emphasis ₍by₎ Robert R. Aurner and Morris Philip Wolf.
5th ed. Cincinnati, South-western Pub. Co. ₍1967₎

xi, 644 p. illus. 24 cm. ④
First ed. published in 1935 under title: Effective English in busi-
ness.
Bibliographical footnotes.

⑤ 1. English language—Business English. 2. Commercial correspondence. ⑥ I. Wolf, Morris Phillip, joint author. II. Title. ⑦

⑧ HF5718.A8 1967   ⑨ 651.7   ⑩ 66–12715
                              gw
Library of Congress   ₍5₎

An author's card in a library catalog shows: (1) the classification and book number; (2) the
author's name; (3) the title of the book, author and joint author, edition, publisher, and date
of publication; (4) text pages and the size of the book in centimeters; (5) the subject entry;
(6) the joint-author entry; (7) other listings of the same book; (8) the Library of Congress call
number; (9) the Dewey Decimal classification number; and (10) the serial number of the card.

The *Cumulative Book Index* (or the CBI as it is familiarly identified)
is an index of all the books printed in English all over the world and
still available from publishers. The CBI lists each book in three ways—
author, title, and subject. These king-sized volumes are normally shelved
in the catalog department of the library.

Pamphlets and Booklets. Much valuable information is now published in pamphlet, booklet, or leaflet form. Such material is cataloged
by subjects in the *Vertical File Index* (a subject and title index to selected
pamphlet material) which is published monthly. The following is a
typical listing:

Business and Professional Women
    Opportunities for women workers in business
    4 p il '65 chronical guidance pubrs Moravia
    N Y 13118 35¢

This source of information can easily be missed during research on
a topic because the material may not be indexed in the library's catalog
nor shelved. It is usually stored vertically in file drawers.

News. *Facts on File* is a weekly world news service published as a
one-volume, loose-leaf booklet with a cumulative subject index.

For newspaper references, the *New York Times Index* should be consulted. Supplements of this index are published monthly and cumulative editions, annually. Entries are arranged alphabetically under name or subject. *The Wall Street Journal* publishes a similar index.

Magazines. The best index on general magazines is the *Readers' Guide to Periodical Literature*—a cumulative author and subject index to articles appearing in periodicals that are on file in almost all main public libraries.

Other indexes that will help the secretary to locate current information in special fields are: *Agricultural Index, Art Index, Applied Science and Technology Index, Bibliographic Index, Business Periodicals Index, Education Index,* and *Engineering Index.*

▪ Preparing Bibliography Cards

The first consideration in selecting material for examination is its *date of publication.* If current information is desired, an article on missiles published ten years ago would be of little value; but twenty- or thirty-year-old biographies of Benjamin Franklin would be worthwhile.

The second consideration is *content.* Some listings describe the types of information in the publications. Such descriptions help in selecting material to be researched.

For each reference selected for study, prepare a bibliography card. On a 5- by 3-inch card record the library call number, the author's name, the title of the publication (and article if it is in a periodical), the publisher, the date of publication, and the page reference.

Number the cards in the upper right corner in sequence, according to each new source used. The number that is thus assigned to a source is used to identify all notes that are taken from it. This method saves a great deal of time in identifying the sources when the references are copied or abstracted; besides, the cards serve as a permanent and detailed record of the sources used.

▪ Taking Notes

The secretary is now ready to study, evaluate, accept or reject material, and record the references on individual sheets or on cards six by four inches or larger. With cards or sheets of uniform size, instead of a shorthand notebook, the complete set of references can be sorted for use in drafting the outline and the report.

rkhurst, Charles Chandler (6)

se Studies and Problems in
Business Communication

entice-Hall, Inc.
glewood Cliffs, N.J. — 1960

. viii + 140   651.75
                                P246

P. 3 of reprint

Paperwork Controls Yardsticks (10)

"Misfiles cost an average of
    $61.23 each."

One of the key facts and figures
reported by the National Records
Management Council.

The bibliography card (left, above) identifies the book as source No. 6. The card at the right shows a convenient way to collect pertinent material, organize it, and possibly reorganize it before doing the actual writing of a paper.

Each reference should give the following information in a standardized form similar to that illustrated above:

Page Number—written in the top left corner (If this is done first, there is less likelihood of omitting it.)

Source—indicated by the number on its bibliography card

Topic—given a conspicuous position as it describes the nature of the reference

Information—written either as a direct quotation or as a summary statement (If the information is a direct quotation, copy it word for word and enclose it in quotation marks. Indicate each omission from the original by an ellipsis.)

Abstracting. A reference in abstract form should be identified as such, and the source and page number from which it was taken should be indicated. The secretary can save the executive a great deal of reading time by preparing good abstracts. She must develop the ability to pick out the salient points and to express them in summary form.

▪ Copying Material

Fortunately, libraries often provide typewriters for researchers. Copying machines are available if a duplicate copy is wanted. If the secretary is taking verbatim notes on a single article or copying a statistical table, she probably will find it advantageous to use her stenographic notebook. The text matter can be written in timesaving shorthand, and the notes can be filed as a permanent record.

When library publications are circulating, the material may be taken to the office and typed or reproduced on a copying machine. Even if copies are not circulating, the librarian will often permit the secretary to borrow them for a limited time, for libraries are eager to cooperate with business people and to have them make fullest use of their collections. Public libraries all over the country are trying to make available to the businessman publications which are of interest and value.

Suggested Readings

Coman, Edwin T., Jr. *Sources of Business Information,* Revised ed. Berkeley, California: University of California Press, 1964, 330 pp.

Johnson, H. Webster. *How to Use the Business Library with Sources of Business Information,* 3d ed. Cincinnati: South-Western Publishing Co., 1964, 160 pp.

Murphey, Robert W. *How and Where to Look It Up—A Guide to Standard Sources of Information.* New York: McGraw-Hill Book Company, Inc., 1958, 750 pp.

Perrin, Porter G. *Writer's Guide and Index to English.* Chicago: Scott, Foresman and Company, 1965, 907 pp.

Questions for Discussion

1. Distinguish between general and special subscription information services. Give illustrations of each. Why might a business executive subscribe to both types of services?

2. Does the reference department of your public library render telephone service? If so, what limitations are placed on it? Is there a special business department or branch?

3. If your employer is involved in scientific research and gives highly technical dictation, where would you turn for help in learning the vocabulary?

4. If your employer disagreed with the rules of good usage that you follow in your transcription, what would you do?

5. It is difficult to determine how long reference material should be retained in an office. In each of these cases, what factors would determine your decision?

   (a) Catalogs from suppliers
   (b) Back numbers of professional and technical magazines
   (c) Advertisements of competitive items
   (d) House organs of your company
   (e) Copies of *The Statesman's Year-Book*

6. In the following sentences insert the proper word for those enclosed in parentheses or rephrase the sentences so that there is no doubt as to the meaning. Then use the Reference Guide to verify or correct your answers.

   (a) New statistics are published (every two years).
   (b) Data are requested (twice a month).
   (c) Summaries are compiled (every two months).

7. Show how you could, in a piece of formal writing, avoid the use of *above* in the following sentences:

   (a) The interpretation of the above statistics is important to any conclusion we reach.
   (b) The above is subject to more than one interpretation.

   Use the Reference Guide to verify or correct your answers.

Problems

■ **1.** A number of books list famous quotations and their source. Some are indexed by subject and others by their source. Make a list of these books that are available in your library. Indicate which one you prefer and give your reason.

■ **2.** Compare the table of contents of *Webster's Third New International Dictionary, Unabridged*, with that of *Webster's Seventh New Collegiate Dictionary*.

(a) What types of information are included in the abridged edition that are not included in the unabridged?

(b) What types of information that are included in the unabridged edition are not included in the abridged?

■ **3.** The college-type dictionaries published by Random House and Merriam differ in their content arrangement. Examine both dictionaries and explain the differences.

■ **4.** Examine a copy of *Information Please Almanac*. Write a description of the general classes of information. Include one or two examples of interesting facts you found it to contain.

■ **5.** Assume that in your work you are called upon to seek the following information. Prepare a list of the answers (identify by letter) and your source of information.

(a) Who is chairman of the board of American Telephone and Telegraph Company? Where would you find biographical data about him?

(b) What is the address of the national headquarters of Kiwanis International? What is the total membership?

(c) What was the population of New Orleans at the last official census?

(d) Who are members of the Interstate Commerce Commission?

(e) What is the total circulation and the advertising rate of *Fortune*?

(f) What is the annual crude petroleum production of Indonesia?

(g) What products are manufactured by Harold L. Palmer Company, Inc., Farmington, Michigan?

(h) What are the five principal business centers in the state of Arkansas?

(i) Who said "The man who makes no mistakes does not usually make anything"?

■ **6.** For Problem 3, page 520, you will be asked to prepare a business report on one of the following subjects. You are now to do the necessary reading, prepare bibliography cards, and take the necessary notes.

(a) Turnover of office personnel

(b) Evaluation of the work of office employees

(c) Professional organization for business women

(d) Marriage and a career—are they compatible?

(e) Improving interoffice communication

(f) Supervision in the office

(g) Salaries of office workers

(h) The unionization of the white collar worker

(i) Employment tests used in the selection of beginning office workers

(j) The electric versus the manual typewriter in the office

(k) The effects of automation on the field of secretarial work

(l) Promotional training for office workers

Related Work Assignments 50-51

50. Your Fundamentals

51. Special "In-Basket" Project

The instructions and supplies necessary for the completion of assignments 50 and 51 are provided in the Workbook.

Presenting Statistical Information

The reliance upon quantitative data is the most significant change that has taken place in business decision making in recent years. The computer is capable of providing data in volumes hitherto impossible. The business executive today can have immediate access to data pertinent to each detail of the business's operations. The task still remains, however, to convert the data to meaningful information that a reader can readily comprehend. Tables, charts, and graphs are extensively used for interpretation. A well-constructed table or chart can convey a picture of business operations more quickly and more clearly than words or numbers. Thus, business management relies heavily upon visual media to convey information.

Chapter 19 pointed out that the executive secretary, in her role as administrative assistant, has the function of gathering data and also of organizing the data for effective communication to others. For example, to support a proposal to change the retirement age of employees, the executive needs data on retirement practices in various types of industries, retirement ages within the company, attitude of employees, and so forth. Gathering the needed data is but the first step. The second is organizing the data. Tables and graphs are effective devices for communicating. The administrative assistant who has the ability to take masses of figures and organize them into meaningful tables and graphs is of exceptional value to the executive.

Giving life to figures, which well-planned tables and graphs really do, calls for a thorough knowledge of the techniques of table and graph construction, good planning, and imagination. The several steps involved in this type of work—compiling, classifying, and presenting data in tables and graphs—are discussed in this chapter.

Compiling and Organizing Data

The data with which the secretary works come from many sources. Some of the data are compiled within the organization. Other data,

National Insurance Corp.
Life Policies and Amounts
December 31, --

Districts	Agents	Policies	Amount (Thousands$)
Atlanta			
Florida	14	1950	6240
Georgia	9	1089	3049
North Carolina	25	2046	10744
South Carolina	18	1926	3659
Total	66	7011	23692
Boston			
Maine	8	608	1276
Massachusetts	7	588	2387
Vermont	19	1957	6262
Total	34	3153	9925

From Annual Report of District Offices
Compiled by R.C. 1/21/-- Checked by L.H.

The data work sheet should indicate the source of the data, who compiled the data, and and who checked them. The work sheet should be filed with the finished tabulation, with the adding-machine tape attached as proof of totals.

however, must be obtained from such secondary sources as magazines, yearbooks, and reports of outside agencies.

The data must be assembled onto a working form or forms so that totals can be obtained, averages and percentages calculated, and the information summarized. This process of transferring the data from the source documents to working forms is called compiling the data. The simplest compilation of data is a pencil-written tabulation similar to the one illustrated at the top of this page.

```
                    CONTINENTAL PRODUCTS

                NUMBER OF ACCOUNTS AND TOTAL SALES
                       OF WILLIAM MOYLE
                IN 5 LARGEST CITIES IN EASTERN IOWA

                FIRST AND SECOND QUARTERS OF 19--

                                              SALES
     NAME OF CITY    NAME OF ACCOUNT     1/01/-- - 3/31/--    4/01/-- - 6/30/--

     BURLINGTON      GRAYS DRUG COMPANY       349.16            1,214.62
                     MILLERS VARIETY          430.11              237.46
                     PURITY DRUGS           1,113.02              899.34
                     A. J. WALKER              46.39
                     RICHARD WESSELS        2,304.19            3,321.76
                                           4,242.87*           5,673.18*


     DUBUQUE         CAMERON PHARMACY          88.62            1,114.05
                     DRAGER BROTHERS           83.23               34.77
                     EVERYBODYS MARKET        442.89              233.84
                     ZEISS BROTHERS           134.77
                                             749.51*            1,382.66*


                                          43,376.07**         47,418.38**
```

— IBM Corporation

In many offices the manual compilation of information is being supplanted by machine tabulation. The data are tabulated by machines from punched cards or tape on printed sheets. These sheets are then available as a basis for later tables or graphs.

▪ Methods of Classifying Data

The objective in compiling data is to organize information into some type of meaningful classification. Data can be classified in any of five ways: (1) alphabetic sequence, (2) kind, (3) size, (4) location, or (5) time.

1. An *alphabetic sequence* of data is often used when the data are compiled for reference. For instance, the data on the worksheet compilation might list the names of the district offices in alphabetic sequence and the names of the states in each district, also in alphabetic sequence.

2. A *kind grouping* of data is used when the items are kinds of objects, characteristics, products, and so on. An example of kind of grouping is a table entitled, "Retail Trade in U.S., 1966, by Kind of Business." The number of stores and the year's sales are broken down into several main groups, such as food stores and apparel stores. Under each of these are listed the data for each of the types of stores included in the group.

3. *Size variations* may be shown in two ways: (a) in an *array*—that is, with the items listed in ascending or descending order, such as a table of the fifty greatest ports in the world with the ports arranged in the order of net tonnage in descending order; (b) in a *frequency distribution*—that is, according to the number in each size class. A frequency distribution is used instead of an array when

the size classes can be grouped advantageously. Tables of age distribution are usually shown in this way; for example, the number of persons between the ages of 10 to 14, 15 to 19, and on as far as needed, instead of the number of persons 10 years old, 11 years old, and so on.

4. A *location listing* is used to show the data by geographic units—such as cities, states, and countries. Real-estate data are often listed this way, as are commodity sales on a national scale.

5. *Time-of-occurrence or time-series listings* are very common. The listing may be made by days, weeks, months, years, decades, and so on.

After data have been collected, they may be translated into either averages or percentages so that comparisons can be made. To say that sales in Clinton were 35 percent greater this month than last month is easier to interpret than to say that sales last month were $50,000 and this month, $67,500.

In some instances, it may be more helpful to know the average salary of clerks in the purchasing office than to know the highest and the lowest salary paid. The use to be made of the data determines which figures would be of most value.

■ Averages

One way to help the reader understand a set of figures is to indicate averages of some type. (An average is a single value used to represent a group.) But which of the averages in common use should be chosen? The one used most often is the *arithmetic average* or, more technically, *arithmetic mean*. It is determined by adding the values of the items and dividing that total by the number of items. If the weekly payroll for 119 employees is $9,282, for example, the average pay would be $78.

The *mode* is a second kind of average. It is the value that recurs the greatest number of times. The data are arranged in a frequency distribution to determine the mode. For example, the mode in the following distribution is the class interval $90.01 to $100.00, because the greatest number of earned amounts fall in that range.

Weekly Earnings	No. of Employees
$80.01 – $ 90.00	2
90.01 – 100.00	26
100.01 – 110.00	19
110.01 – 120.00	9
120.01 – 130.00	5

The *median* is an average of position; it is the midpoint in an array. In order to determine it, the data must be arranged in an array; that is,

AVERAGE BUSINESS LETTER COSTS
FOR THE YEAR 1967[a]

Cost Factor	Average Cost per letter	Percentage of Total Cost
Stenographic Cost	$ .94	37.8[b]
Fixed Charges[c]	.61	24.5
Dictator's Time	.42	16.9
Nonproductive Labor[d]	.20	8.0
Mailing Cost	.15	6.0
Materials	.07	2.8
Filing Cost	.10	4.0
Totals	$2.49	100.0

[a]Based on data supplied by the Dartnell Corporation, Chicago
[b]Expressed to the nearest 1/10 of 1%
[c]Depreciation, supervision, rent, light, and similar items
[d]Time lost due to waiting, illness, vacation, and other causes

An array may list items in descending or ascending order. Vertical lines may be used to separate columns and the ends of the table may be left open. The footnotes are placed directly under the table and are identified by use of lower-case letters.

in either ascending or descending order. Then it is necessary only to count the number of items and find the mid one, which is the median. For example, assume that five students have the following amounts in their checking accounts:

Student A............ $500
Student B............ 190
Student C............ 175 ←——MEDIAN
Student D............ 160
Student E............ 5

The median is $175; on the other hand, the mean is $206. Obviously, the mean is affected by extreme cases (the student with an abnormally large checking account and the one who is almost "broke"). This kind of influence is why the median is usually selected as the average that comes nearest to indicating the true state of affairs when there are extreme cases in the data.

▪ Percentages

Percentages help in making numbers understandable and the relation of various items to one another and to the total more easily grasped.

In the table on page 476, the last column shows the percentage each cost factor represents of the total cost. The statement, "The stenographic cost in producing a business letter is 94 cents," has less meaning than "The stenographic cost in producing a business letter is 94 cents or 37.8 percent of the total cost of producing the letter."

Percentage relatives or *index numbers* are used to compare the extent or degree of changes. They are relative because they are based on a value at some specific time and that base must be clearly defined. For example, in 1929 there were approximately 20,000,000 telephones in the United States; in 1934, 17,000,000 telephones; in 1940, 22,000,000; in 1952, 45,000,000; in 1960, 66,500,000; and in 1964, 84,167,000. The percentage relatives, based on the 1929 figure as 100, are 85 for 1934, 110 for 1940, 225 for 1952, 332.5 for 1960, and 420.8 for the 1964 index.

Presenting Data Effectively

One of the problems that confronts the secretary when she works with numeric data is to decide on the most effective presentation. She may choose to present the data through a table or a graph. The table and graph have the advantage of presenting figures in concise form. Furthermore, they help in identifying relationships.

▪ Tables

Statisticians classify tables into two kinds: *general-purpose tables*—those to be used for reference; and *special-purpose tables*—those that direct the eye and mind to specific relationships of significance. The very large, comprehensive tables of census data are general-purpose tables. Most tables of statistical data that are included in business reports are special-purpose tables.

A table should be kept simple and designed for rapid reading. The incorporation of too many elements in one table detracts from its readability and effectiveness. When planning a table, keep one question in mind, "Precisely what is this table to show?" All data that do not apply should be excluded.

Another word of caution is that statistics should not distort the true situation. To avoid misrepresenting facts when you present statistics you may want to read *How to Lie with Statistics*.[1]

---

[1]Darrell Huff, *How to Lie with Statistics* (New York: W. W. Norton & Company, Inc., 1954).

After the table has been developed, it may be well to dramatize the material presented in it by a chart or graph. In other words, the chart does not replace the table; it supplements it. Tables provide details; charts present relationships but not minutae and would not be satisfactory to the reader who seeks exact data.

■ Planning the Table Layout

It is almost impossible to type a well-balanced table, allowing sufficient space for all items and margins, unless the work is carefully planned. The facts and the figures to be tabulated must be analyzed carefully before the various headings and column arrangements are determined. The best method of planning a table is to make a penciled rough draft.

After this plan is drawn, the secretary can save herself time (and often grief) by using the backspace-from-center method when tabulating.

■ Suggestions for Typing Tables

Additional suggestions will help you plan and type an effective table:

Title. The title should be complete and clearly worded. The title, subtitle, and column headings should make the table self-contained. If the data represent a period of time, either the title, the subtitle, the column headings, or the reference to the data source should indicate the period covered. Type the title in all capitals with no terminal period. Break a title too long for one line at the division of a thought.

POOR:	ANNUAL SALES OF ELECTRONIC EQUIPMENT BY MAJOR MANUFACTURERS IN THE UNITED STATES TO LATIN AMERICAN COUNTRIES
BETTER:	ANNUAL SALES OF ELECTRONIC EQUIPMENT BY MAJOR MANUFACTURERS IN THE UNITED STATES TO LATIN AMERICAN COUNTRIES

If there are several tables presented in a report, it is advisable to number the tables to facilitate reference.

Abbreviations. In order to save space, abbreviations may be used in column headings; but they should never be used in titles.

Columns. For easy reference, the column headings may be numbered consecutively from left to right. Columns of related data should be placed closer together than other columns. Major divisions of groups of columns can be indicated by wider spaces or by double vertical rules.

For ruling lines on the typewriter, place the pencil or pen point at an angle in the cardholder notch. For horizontal lines, move the carriage from left to right. For vertical lines, release the variable line spacer and turn the platen forward or backward.

—IBM Corporation

Alignment. In tabulated words and phrases, the left margin should be kept even. In tabulated figures, the right margin must usually be kept straight. When decimal fractions involving different numbers of places to the right of the decimal point are listed, the decimal point must be kept in vertical alignment.

Incorrect	*Correct*	*Incorrect*	*Correct*
Adding machine	Adding machine	1,476	1,476.0
Calculator	Calculator	32.7	32.7
File cabinet	File cabinet	11,148	11,148.0

Amounts. A comma should be used to separate every three digits in amounts, but it should not be used with the digits after a decimal point. For example: *1,125.50* and *21.16184.*

For sums of money the dollar sign should be used with the first amount in a column and with each total.

INCORRECT:		*CORRECT:*	
	$1,456.26		$1,456.26
	$ 362.35		362.35
	$ 18.46		18.46
	$1,837.07		$1,837.07

Readability. *Leaders,* or lines of periods, aid the reader by carrying the eyes across a wide expanse of space from one column to another. Leaders are usually typed with a single space between periods. Periods on successive lines should be in vertical alignment. When long columns are single-spaced, the skipping of a line every three, four, or five rows improves readability.

Rulings. Rulings may improve the appearance of a table. They may be typed with the underline key or made with pencil or a ball-point pen.

A double ruling is used at the top of the table two lines below the title. Single rulings should divide the stub and box headings from the rest of the table. A single ruling should also end the table. Vertical rulings should separate the columns. Rulings may be omitted at the sides.

NATIONAL INSURANCE CORPORATION
LIFE POLICIES IN FORCE
DECEMBER 31, 19—

District	Number of		Total Amounts (Thousands)
	Agents	Policies	
Atlanta.	66*	7,011	$ 23,692
Boston	34	3,153	9,925
Chicago	18	1,016	5,017
Cleveland.	9	2,114	10,170
Dallas	21	4,118	12,375
Dover	7	846	8,751
Kansas City.	5	718	9,278
Omaha	20	3,875	18,117
Newark	16	2,110	13,476
Totals	196	24,961	$110,801

*Includes South Carolina, added since last year.

This table was prepared from the work-sheet compilation on page 473. Leaders and skipped lines have been used to improve the readability of the table. To avoid confusion of reading large figures, the amounts are shown in thousands. Thus 23,692,000 is shown as 23,692.

Avoid beginning a column heading on the line immediately below a rule or ruling immediately under a heading. Leave space.

Special Notes. If the meaning of any item in the table is not clear or must be qualified, an explanation should be given in the form of a footnote. Footnotes are also used to indicate the source of secondary data.

Instead of numbers (146^1, 371^2), use symbols (146^*, $371^\#$) or lowercase letters (146^a, 371^b) to identify footnote references for figures. A number may be confused as being part of the numeric data.

Reference. The name of the person responsible for the preparation of the table should be indicated on the file copy at least. When the data come from a secondary source, such as a publication, the source should be indicated on the table.

Variety and Emphasis. Both variety and emphasis on relationships may be attained in the typed copy by using italics, bold face, and different type sizes and styles. Two typewriters, one with pica type and the other with elite type, may be used. Footnotes and column headings can be typed on the elite-type machine, while entries in the body may be typed on a pica-type machine. Even wider variations may be obtained on the IBM Selectomatic by merely changing the typing element. A wide-carriage typewriter may be used for tables having numerous columns.

▪ Checking the Typed Table

Every typewritten table must be checked for accuracy. This proofing requires the help of another person, who should read the original draft while the secretary checks the typed copy. Reading figures for check purposes is an oral technique that has a fairly definite prescribed routine, indicated by the examples given below. The words in the examples that are connected by a hyphen should be read as a group; the commas indicate pauses:

> 718   seven-one-eight
> 98,302   nine-eight, comma, three-0 (oh)-two
> 24.76   two-four, point, seven-six
> $313.00   three-one-three even (or no cents) dollars
> 77,000   seventy-seven thousand even

For copy in columnar form it is usually advisable to read down a column rather than across the page. This procedure provides a double check because, in most instances, the typing work has been done across the page. If the table includes totals, the amounts in each column should be added and checked against the total.

After the accuracy of the typed table has been checked and errors corrected, the original draft of the table should be filed in a personal folder kept by the secretary or attached to, and filed with, the typed file copy of the final draft. If anyone who reads the typed copy discovers an error, the filed copy of the original data will enable the secretary to determine whether the error occurred in the original material, which may have been supplied to the secretary, or whether the error was made in the process of typing the table.

▪ Graphic Presentation

A graph is a statistical picture. It presents numerical data in visual form, making them more easily analyzed and remembered. The average person can remember a graph, yet he is unable to remember the columns of figures upon which the graph is based. Taking the hard facts of business and organizing them in visual form to make comparisons easy, to emphasize contrasts, and to bring out the full force of the message that figures can tell is a challenging opportunity. The secretary may construct graphs on her own typewriter or with the help of commercially available aids. The most widely used commercial graphing material is found in the Chart-Pak kit, which contains self-adhering bar and line tapes in various designs and colors. With such a kit the amateur can make charts that are very effective—even dramatic. Then there are the professional chart makers. Believe it or not, the Yellow Pages in New York City alone contain over thirty listings under *Charts, Business*.

Alphabet packs, such as Prestype, can also help the secretary produce an effective graphic presentation. The line graph on page 483 was prepared by a secretary untrained in art, using such materials. The secretary needs a basic knowledge of the various types of graphs. An "Idea" folder can be set up in which examples of each type (both typewritten and commercially prepared) can be placed, with notes concerning their suitability for certain data.

Minnesota Mining and Manufacturing Company holds seminars in major cities to teach secretaries the techniques of charting data.

Line Graphs. A commonly used type of graph is the *line graph*. It is most effective in showing fluctuations in a value or a quantity over a period of time, such as variations in production, sales, costs, or profits over a period of months or years. Thus, the line graph is an effective way to depict a comparison of trends over a period of time.

The line graph on page 483 emphasizes the positive relationship that existed between net profit and the amount spent for advertising over a particular five-year period.

Follow these suggestions for preparing line graphs:

1. **Prepare a working copy on printed graph or coordinate paper and the final or presentation copy on plain paper.**

2. **Place periods of time on the horizontal scale at the bottom of the graph; record variations in quantities or numbers on the vertical scale.**

3. **Always show the zero quantity. To avoid placing the curve too high on the chart, a break in the chart may be made to show that part of it has been omitted.**

4. **To avoid distortions, plan the size of your graph. It is good practice to make the width at least one and one-half and not more than one and three-fourths times the height. A rise can be made to appear very steep and thus sharp or quite gradual, depending upon the relation of height to width.**

5. **If possible, position all lettering horizontally on the chart.**

6. **If more than one line is used, make each one distinctive in character by the use of different colors or by the use of the following lines: heavy solid (—), light solid (—), dash (---), dots (. . .), or dot and dash (.__.__.).**

Bar Graphs. The bar graph presents quantities by means of extended bars. Variations in quantity are indicated by the lengths of the bars, which may be drawn horizontally or vertically. The bar graph is most

COMPARISON OF NET PROFIT WITH ADVERTISING EXPENDITURES

In Thousands of Dollars

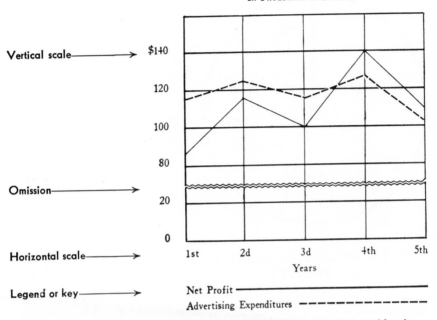

Vertical scale ————————→ $140

120

100

80

Omission ——————————→ 20

0

Horizontal scale —————→ 1st   2d   3d   4th   5th

Years

Legend or key ————————→ Net Profit ————————————

Advertising Expenditures — — — — — — — —

As in this line graph, a zero line should always be indicated on a vertical chart. Note how a break in the chart conserves space and avoids placing the plotted data too high upon the grid (the crossed guide lines). Although only two items are plotted on this chart, as many as four or five may be plotted provided the lines are not too close together.

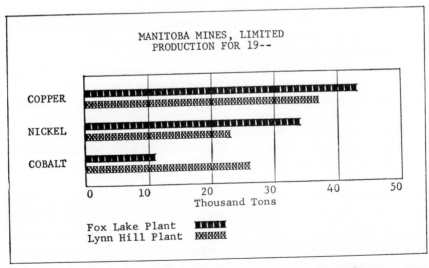

MANITOBA MINES, LIMITED
PRODUCTION FOR 19--

COPPER

NICKEL

COBALT

0   10   20   30   40   50

Thousand Tons

Fox Lake Plant
Lynn Hill Plant

For this typewritten horizontal bar graph, the heavy bar was typed by striking over upper-case *M, W, A,* and *V.* The light bar was typed by striking over upper-case *X* and *O.*

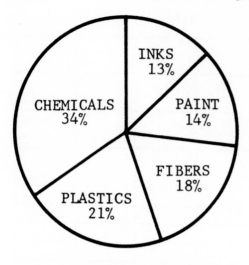

This partially typewritten circle graph shows the relationship of the sales of each product to each other product and to the total sales volume.

SALES VOLUME BREAKDOWN
BY PRODUCT

effectively used to show comparisons of a limited number of values, generally not more than four or five.

Follow these suggestions for preparing bar graphs:

1. For best appearance, when space is left between single bars, space the bars so that there is a distance between them ranging from one half to a whole bar width.

2. Except for time series, the quantities indicated on the chart should begin with *zero* (0). In a chart where starting at 0 makes the chart too tall or too wide, omit that portion after 0 on which all bars would appear and indicate the omitted portion by a pair of break lines.

3. When possible, arrange bars in ascending or descending order. If they are arranged according to time, chart the earliest period first.

4. Bars may be in outline form or solid. If the bars represent different items, shade or color them for contrast.

5. Bars may be made on the typewriter by using upper-case letters (*X, W, N, $*), a heavy strikeover (*X* over *O*), or a combination of letters and characters (as shown in the typewritten graph on page 483).

Circle Graphs or Charts. The circle chart is an effective way to show the manner in which a given quantity is divided into parts. In this type of graph the complete area of the circle represents the whole quantity, while the divisions within the circle represent the parts. Thus, the illustration shows not only the relationship of each part to the whole, but also of each part to every other part.

THE EFFECT OF RECORDS LOSS BY FIRE

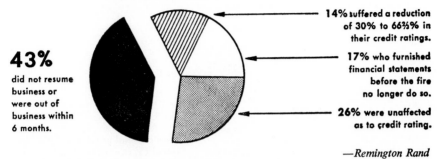

43%

did not resume
business or
were out of
business within
6 months.

14% suffered a reduction
of 30% to 66⅔% in
their credit ratings.

17% who furnished
financial statements
before the fire
no longer do so.

26% were unaffected
as to credit rating.

—Remington Rand

Notice how, in this commercially prepared circle graph, the black section dramatizes the effect of records loss by fire and indirectly promotes the sale of fireproof files and safes.

The circle chart may be used to present such data as how the sales dollar is spent; how taxes paid by a firm are divided among local, state, and federal governments; or the percentage of store purchases made by men as compared with the percentage of store purchases made by women. Follow these suggestions for preparing circle graphs:

1. **Convert the data to be presented into percentage form. Let the circumference of the circle equal 100 percent.**

2. **Arrange the elements to be plotted according to size, largest first.**

3. **Mark the top center of the circumference of the circle. From this center point on the circumference, mark off that percentage of the total which each segment represents, usually starting with the largest segment. The sequence, however, may be changed to permit emphasis on a specific element.**

4. **Determine the size of each segment.** *If a protractor is used,* **the circumference of the circle equals 360, or a total of 100%; thus a segment representing 10% would be 36°.**
   If a protractor is not available, **divide the circumference of the circle into four equal parts (each part representing 25%). Each fourth part may in turn be divided into halves (representing 12½% segments). Follow this division plan until the size of segment desired is obtained.**

5. **If space permits, identify each segment by a caption inside the segment. Shade or color the segments to provide contrast.**

6. **Type the titles of the sections horizontally.**

Pictorial Charts. One of the more interesting developments in graphic representation is the use of pictorial charts. They are generally an adaptation of one of the other types of graphs in which drawn symbols are used to represent the types of data being charted.

For example, a bar chart showing fire losses may be illustrated with streaming fire hose, the length of the stream varying with the amount of

MEDIAN WEEKLY WAGE FOR OFFICE WORKERS
EMPLOYED IN CLEVELAND, OHIO
JANUARY, 196–

120		
100		$$$$$$
80	$$	$$$$$$$$$$ $$$$$$$$$$
60	$$$$$$$	$$$$$$$$$$ $$$$$$$$$$	$$$$$$$$$$ $$$$$$$$$$ $$$$$$$$$$
40	$$$$$$$$$$ $$$$$$$$$$	$$$$$$$$$$ $$$$$$$$$$	$$$$$$$$$$ $$$$$$$$$$
20	$$$$$$$$$$ $$$$$$$$$$	$$$$$$$$$$ $$$$$$$$$$	$$$$$$$$$$ $$$$$$$$$$
	$$$$$$$$$$ $$$$$$$$$$	$$$$$$$$$$ $$$$$$$$$$	$$$$$$$$$$ $$$$$$$$$$

Typist   Stenographer Secretary

In this pictorial graph the dollar-sign symbol ($) in each bar represents $1. When larger amounts are being presented, each $ can represent $100, $1,000, $10,000, or more.

the loss. The growth of telephone service may be represented by cradle telephones arranged in a line, each telephone representing so many thousand telephones. It is not considered good practice to represent increases by enlarging the size of the object symbolized, such as augmenting the size of the telephone to indicate an increased number; it is difficult to compare like objects of different sizes. It is easy to determine that one is larger than the other, but to estimate that one is twice or three times as large is difficult. Furthermore, the symbol frequently gives the impression that the item and not the quantity increased in size. Indicate size or growth by more symbols rather than larger symbols.

■ Preparing Charts and Graphs

In making any chart or graph, no matter how simple, it is best to rough out a working copy first. When the final copy is prepared, the graph should be framed on the paper. The bottom margin should be slightly larger than the top margin. The margins on the sides should be even unless the pages are to be bound on the left side. If the necessary guide points are marked lightly in pencil, they can be erased with an art gum eraser after the inking in is completed.

The title of the chart or graph should indicate its nature concisely. It should be centered above or below the chart, and its lettering should be the largest or the most heavily emphasized on the chart. The use of lettering guides is recommended. The source of the data and the date of compilation can be placed in one of the bottom corners at either

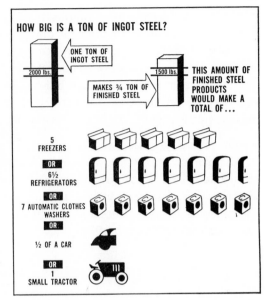

HOW BIG IS A TON OF INGOT STEEL?

ONE TON OF INGOT STEEL

2000 lbs.

MAKES ¾ TON OF FINISHED STEEL

1500 lbs.

THIS AMOUNT OF FINISHED STEEL PRODUCTS WOULD MAKE A TOTAL OF...

5 FREEZERS

OR
6½ REFRIGERATORS

OR
7 AUTOMATIC CLOTHES WASHERS

OR
½ OF A CAR

OR
1 SMALL TRACTOR

The secretary would not be expected to do the drawings necessary in the preparation of a pictorial graph. She may, however, do much of the planning for the graph and be responsible for seeing that the drawings are prepared by a commercial artist.

*—American Iron and
Steel Institute*

margin. Although this information may be omitted from the presentation copy, it should certainly be recorded on the working copy.

▪ Limitations

While charts or graphs are useful in presenting comparative data, they have certain limitations. The number of facts presented on any one graph is usually limited to four or five. It is best to use a table when six or more items are involved. A second limitation is that only approximate values can be shown on charts or graphs.

A third limitation is that it is possible for a graph to be drawn with mathematical accuracy and still give a distorted picture of the facts being presented. For example, the overall width of a line graph determines the angles of the plotted lines. A graph that is too narrow may indicate a much sharper rise and fall in the lines than the data indicate. In the same way, a graph that is too wide may tend to give the impression of a much more gradual fluctuation than may have actually occurred.

▪ Process and Flow Charts

One of the most widely used tools in office management is the process or flow chart. It is used to determine the most effective, simplest, and least expensive means of accomplishing a task. The flow chart traces a unit of work as it flows through the office. Symbols with connecting lines are used to trace a step-by-step sequence of the work from point of origin to point of completion. The basic symbols are shown on page 489.[2] While the meaning of each symbol has become fairly standardized, a key may be provided to prevent any misunderstanding. A template may be purchased for drawing these symbols.

Graphic data processing equipment is now available which makes it possible for man and machine to exchange graphic information at electronic speed. The equipment is designed to help businessmen work directly with graphics—charts, curves, sketches, and drawings. The equipment generates tables and graphs on a display tube. The graphic image can be recorded on film.

▪ Organization Chart

An organization chart is a graphic presentation of the organizational structure of a business. It points out responsibility relationships and answers two basic questions: (1) What are the lines of authority (who reports to whom)? (2) What are the functions of each unit (who is responsible for what)?

A business organization is seldom static. It is changed by new personnel, new divisions, new responsibilities, and realignment of old responsibilities. The organization chart, therefore, is frequently revised. The technique of preparing and updating an organization chart is part of the "know-how" that every secretary should bring to an office. Here are suggestions to help in preparing an organization chart. (Other suggestions worthy of study can be found in references named at the end of this chapter.)

1. **The chart should be simple. A complex chart can confuse more than it can help.**

2. **Responsibility should flow downward in the chart with each level clearly identifiable. Lines of authority should be easily identified.**

3. **When the intersecting of a line is unavoidable, the *pass symbol* (a half-circle "detour" in an otherwise straight line) is used.**

4. **Different symbols differentiate policy-making positions (line) from support positions (staff).**

---

[2]Clarence B. Randall and Sally Weimer Burgly, *Systems & Procedures for Business Data Processing* (2d ed.; Cincinnati: South-Western Publishing Co., 1968), pp. 167–171.

FLOW CHART SYMBOLS

SALES – ORDER FLOW CHART

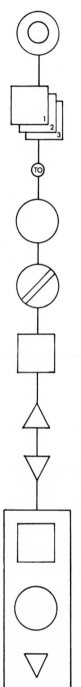

Origin. To create a document (such as filling in a sales invoice or writing a check)

Document. In multiple copies

Transport. To move a document from one desk or operator to another

Operation. To change a document; to sort; to collate (such as stapling two forms together or separating multiple copies)

Add. To add to a document (such as entering amounts, recording extensions, or completing shipping directions)

Inspection. To check the accuracy of a document (such as verifying invoice extensions or comparing the purchase order with the purchase invoice)

Temporary Storage. To hold the document temporarily (such as the receiving clerk's holding the purchase order pending receipt of merchandise)

Filing. To send to storage or permanent file

Boxed Symbols. To indicate a series of steps performed by one person at one time (such as *inspect, sort, file*)

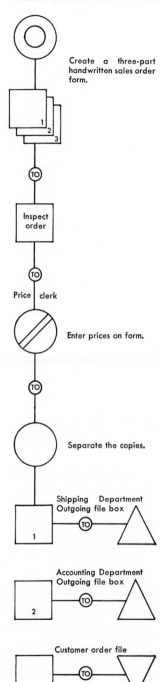

Create a three-part handwritten sales order form.

Inspect order

Price clerk

Enter prices on form.

Separate the copies.

Shipping Department Outgoing file box

Accounting Department Outgoing file box

Customer order file

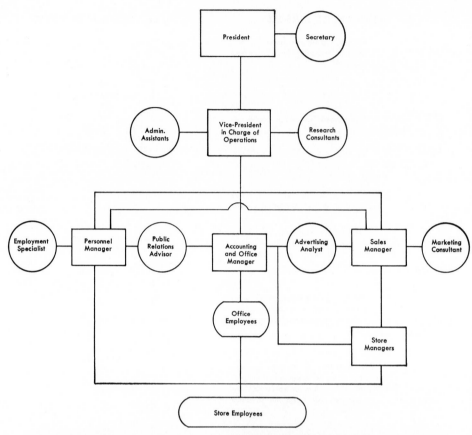

On this organization chart, the four levels of administrative authority are clearly identified. The administrative staff is differentiated from the support staff. Note that the secretary to the president is not under the supervision of the office manager.

The organization chart shown on this page shows a line-and-staff relationship. Such a chart would be supplemented with a functions chart on which the responsibilities of each position would be identified. To show on one chart both authority relationships and functional responsibilities detracts from its visual simplicity.

Suggested Readings

Balsley, Irol Whitmore and Jerry W. Robinson. *Integrated Secretarial Studies*, Jubilee ed. Cincinnati: South-Western Publishing Co., 1964, pp. 324–326.

Rogers, Anna C. *Graphic Charts Handbook*. Washington, D.C.: Public Affairs Press, 1961, 189 pp.

Stockton, John R. *Introduction to Business and Economic Statistics*, 3d ed. Cincinnati: South-Western Publishing Co., 1962, pp. 65–121.

Questions for Discussion ————————————

1. What is meant by the statement "Business decisions are not based on raw data, but on information derived from data"?

2. What kind of graphs should be prepared to present the following data:

   (a) **The number of men employees as compared with the number of women employees of a company for each year of a five-year period**

   (b) **The amount paid in one year for taxes to the city and county governments compared with the amount paid to the state and federal governments**

   (c) **The average consumption of electricity over a 24-hour period in order to identify peak-load periods**

   (d) **Amounts two companies spent for research over four years.**

3. Corporations usually use graphs extensively in their annual reports to stockholders. Financial tables and statements, however, are generally used in presenting data to boards of directors and to banks. Why are graphs used in the one case and tables in the other?

4. The secretary to the vice-president in charge of research is often charged with the responsibility for reports written by the scientists in her division. She can make graphs by using typewriter characters, she can buy commercial materials for use in making improved charts, or she can contract for professional charts. What factors will influence her decision?

5. A consultant firm with a total of 35 employees reported in a community wage study that its average wage (arithmetic mean) was $11,200. An examination of the records revealed that the firm had ten high-paid executives, each receiving over $25,000 a year. What would be your criticism of the reported average wage figure?

6. What is the secretary's responsibility in a situation in which she is aware that her employer is issuing false statistical information? Would it make any difference whether the information was going to an outside agency or to another official in the firm? What should she do if the information is misleading but not illegal?

7. Tell how you would indicate the following kinds of omissions in quoted matter. Then use the Reference Guide to verify or correct your answers.

   Research has barely begun, **(words omitted here)** and no fair estimate of additional time required can be given **(closing words of sentence omitted here)**. We hope three months will be sufficient but can make no promises. **(sentence omitted here)** Two of the technicians begin new assignments October 1.

8. Tell how you would punctuate the following kinds of changes in quoted matter. Then use the Reference Guide to verify or correct your answers.

   (a) **To show a correction:**
   This material is of excellent *actually inferior* quality.

   (b) **To show an uncorrected error:**
   The *author's* styles are similar.

   (c) **To show an interpolation:**
   Since publication *1960* the situation has changed.

Problems

■ **1.** Mr. Simpson tells you that Continental Products is considering the establishment of a new branch office. The proposed location has narrowed to:

Phoenix, Arizona

St. Petersburg, Florida

Grand Rapids, Michigan

Charlotte, North Carolina

Elyria, Ohio

Nashville, Tennessee

He asks you to make a comparison of the 1950 and 1960 population reports for these five cities as one of the bases on which the Board of Directors will make its final decision.

(a) Prepare in pencil a tabulation of the data that you secure from a reference source. Compute the percentage of increase or decrease in population during the ten-year period, and arrange the table in descending order. In calculating your percentages, round your population figures to the nearest thousand.

(b) Type the table in good form, making one carbon copy. If necessary, prepare a pencil layout.

(c) Keep a record of the time you spend on this project and prepare an itemized report of the cost of preparing this table for your employer. Assume that your salary is $126 for a 40-hour week.

■ **2.** Preparatory to establishing a policy on sick leave, Mr. Simpson asks you to make a study of the number of days of absence from work because of illness and other causes (excluding vacations) of the 70 employees in the Des Moines office. From the records, you obtained the total number of days each employee was absent. They are as follows:

26	8	17	15	17	14	13
16	7	5	47	20	25	19
12	20	11	15	9	4	41
18	27	19	11	19	12	13
8	3	44	18	24	17	15
18	14	13	10	2	37	20
28	16	15	15	14	11	9
1	32	19	30	18	11	12
10	6	13	15	33	17	21
16	11	13	8	7	14	12

(a) Prepare a frequency distribution of the days absent. Use a class interval of five days (one work week), such as 11 to 15, 16 to 20. Include in the table the percentage of employees who were absent in each frequency class.

(b) Determine the modal class interval.

■ **3.** The following amounts are the June sales per day of a product.

Amount	Amount
$118.23	$ 9.61
41.32	18.23
91.73	107.16
63.24	26.31
36.74	83.17
18.92	67.92
87.65	74.26
27.11	68.31
16.94	17.08
78.26	10.66
124.36	94.33
97.08	101.09
	89.31

(a) Prepare in pencil a tabulation of the sales so that you can determine the median. What is the median sale for June?

(b) Calculate the arithmetic average or mean of the June sales.

Related Work Assignments 52-55

52. Preparing Graphs. The following figures represent the sales volume for Continental Products for each month of a two-year period.

	First Year	Second Year
January.....................	$86,857	$114,273
February....................	69,623	92,526
March......................	38,972	64,159
April.......................	34,284	60,844
May........................	40,485	69,273
June........................	37,737	76,294
July........................	40,852	74,858
August......................	46,085	82,437
September...................	49,592	80,158
October.....................	55,846	83,628
November...................	54,249	87,859
December...................	61,292	94,958

Your employer, Mr. Simpson, wishes you to prepare for a board of directors' meeting a curve or line graph of the data for the two years. Prepare the graph. What implication can you present about seasonal fluctuations and general performance for the two years?

53. Determining Letter Costs. Mr. Simpson is interested in comparing letter costs in the office with those reported in the national study shown in the table on page 476. He asks you to collect and report the data.

To obtain data, you keep a production record for one week for Miss Wright who devotes full time to taking dictation and transcribing. She recorded and transcribed 120 letters during the week.

The cost division of the Accounting Department provides you with the following cost information:

Miss Wright's salary...$90 a week

Dictator's time...........................14 hours at a cost of $4.50 an hour

Fixed charges (depreciation, supervision, rent, light, interest, taxes, insurance, pension, and similar overhead).........................40% of labor cost
Labor cost: Miss Wright's salary plus cost of dictator's time

Nonproductive cost (time lost by Miss Wright and dictator due to waiting, illness, vacation, and other causes)......................15% of labor cost

Materials (amount used during week)................................$9.60

Mailing cost for 120 letters (postage and labor).....................$14.40

Filing cost for 120 letters (labor and materials)......................$9.60

Prepare the report. It should contain the following tables and graphs:

(a) A table showing
   (1) The total cost of producing the 120 letters, with a breakdown (such as stenographic cost, fixed charges) showing how the total was obtained
   (2) The cost per letter, with a breakdown showing the amount and percentage that each factor represents of the cost

(b) A circle chart showing the distribution of the costs per letter

(c) A bar graph comparing the costs per letter at the office with the average cost as reported in the table on page 475

54. Interpreting Statistical Data ⎫ The instructions and supplies necessary
                                                  ⎬ for the completion of these assignments
55. Preparing a Flow Chart ⎭ are provided in the workbook.

Assistance with Reports, Procedures Writing, and Publications

You may work for top management whose primary function is to make planning decisions involving the long-range goals of the firm. You may work for middle management which is primarily concerned with short-range planning. Or you may work for, or even be, a front-line supervisor, concerned mainly with operating decisions—the day-to-day problems that must be solved under existing policy. All of these employers are constantly involved in some kind of report writing, varying from the informal interoffice memorandum to the formal bound report. Many of them will prepare manuscripts for publication. More and more front-line supervisors realize the importance of preparing clearly stated step-by-step "how to . . ." instructions for performing the numerous operations they oversee. So you may be involved frequently in procedures writing, either for your employer or for yourself as a supervisor of office employees.

The employer will probably compose his own reports, relying on you to assist in collecting data, to revise and edit, and to organize and present the document in the most attractive way. A very able employee, capable of functioning at the administrative assistant's level, though, organizes the ideas collected and may even draft the preliminary report which the employer can use as a base from which to develop the final form. Whether your employer or you have the responsibility for initiating the writing, you will help in polishing the material into final form, in arranging it for improved readability, and in typing it in approved style (which you, not he, are expected to know and to assume responsibility for).

This chapter deals with reports, procedures writing, and manuscripts for printing. It gives specific instructions for format and organization, with illustrations of techniques for making material more interesting. Surely the importance of employer-secretary teamwork is nowhere better exemplified than in their business-writing relationship. Each has a contribution to make; the work of the assistant complements the work of the executive.

A business report may present information and recommended courses of action that influence executive decisions.

Report Writing

A business report is written primarily to transmit objective information which stimulates management action. It is only an instrument of diagnosis; like a doctor's stethoscope, it shows up the facts so that proper treatment can be given, but it is not the cure. It may, however, present recommended courses of action that influence executive decisions. It should usually follow the army "staff-work accomplished" concept: Dumping a problem in the lap of a superior is not enough; staff work has not been accomplished until courses of action are recommended and their possible consequences assessed.

▪ Trends in Report Writing

According to an American Management Association survey, the typical business executive spends four office hours a day and an extra hour at home reading the reports, correspondence, and publications sent to him. Naturally, a major consideration is how to reduce this time.

The form and purpose of business reports are being affected by the rapid acquisition of information through the modern communication system.

One way is through using information immediately available as the result of automation. Since modern computers can give real-time information (data when it originates—not days later), the traditional business report is obsolete just because of the lag between the time the information is collected and the time that a report can be prepared. Charts have supplanted many periodic written reports. Some large corporations maintain chart rooms in which computerized data are used daily to update charts that aid executives in performing their functions. One secretary to a company president says that she spends at least one third of her working hours in maintaining the charts in the executive suite of her company. With extensive use of charts, written communication is limited to special reports to explain unusual fluctuations, for what is called "management by exception."

More and more management decisions are based on computer solutions to management games. Simulated business situations are fed into the machine, and possible results of various courses of action emerge. As management is thus reduced to scientific analysis, fewer formal reports suggesting courses of action and setting forth expected results will be written.

Another way to reduce executive report-reading time is to use more informal reports such as interoffice memorandums and send them as soon as information is available. The interoffice memorandum has been facetiously described as "management's confidential bulletin board," but it is business's favorite means of keeping people informed and of exchanging information leading to business decisions. One item to the memorandum, points numbered for easy reference, and lots of white space, these are aids to cutting reading time by making easy the reading and identification of points.

Better reports, too, will aid in keeping the executive from bogging down in a sea of paper. Topical headings, outlines, and summaries are used to improve reports. A former secretary of state and a university president ruled that all reports brought to their attention must be summarized in a one-page memorandum. Many executives look first at the summary or at the conclusions and recommendations and then decide whether the whole report warrants study.

Yet reports are still essential as an aid to management, and many routine reports will continue to be written and many special reports authorized to support business decisions.

▪ Report-Writing Routine

There is considerable difference in the routine for writing a report and the routine for writing a letter. The executive writes and rewrites a business report until he has presented the subject matter with precise clarity. His routine is something like this:

He formulates a broad or detailed outline of the contents.

He drafts the report in longhand or dictates it. The secretary types it in rough-draft form.

He (and perhaps the secretary, too) reorganizes the material for better structure and edits it sentence by sentence for clarity and correctness. The secretary types another draft.

He reorganizes it and edits it again. The secretary types it (or supervises its typing) in final form.

Executives vary in their skill and procedures in writing reports. Every executive, however, edits and polishes successive drafts until the final report is clear, concise, and logical. The secretary with an aptitude for analyzing and arranging subject matter often helps in organizing and editing. But, *all* secretaries are responsible for the typewritten presentation of the report; they are expected to make the report attractive, easy to read, and consistent in form.

▪ The Form of a Report

Some companies have developed style sheets for all or for special reports. If such is the case, the form indicated in the style sheets will be used as standard practice. In other cases, the writer follows his own preference.

A short report may consist of only the body or informative text. A comprehensive report may have, in addition to the body of the report, introductory and supplementary parts arranged in the order shown in the following outline.

Introductory Parts:	**Cover or title page (or both)**
	Preface or letter of transmittal, including acknowledgments
	Table of contents
	List of tables, charts, illustrations
Body of the Report:	**Purpose of the report or statement of the problem**
	Summary, conclusions, and recommendations
	Main body of the report
Supplementary Parts:	**Appendix or reference section**
	Bibliography
	Index

Notice that the summary, conclusions, or recommendations often precede the main body of the report because they are the most important and interesting to the reader.

The body of the report is most frequently developed first and put into final typewritten form; then the other parts are completed. For that reason the specific parts of reports are discussed in this chapter in the order of their preparation rather than in the order of their occurrence in a report.

Developing the Body of the Report

The body of the final report is the responsibility of its author. The preparation of the other parts and the typewritten form of the report are usually assigned to the secretary.

▪ The Outline

A methodical executive first sets up a topic outline or framework of the report. He may make and use only a pencil draft of it; however, if the outline is to be a part of the final report or if it needs to be submitted

```
I.   TYPING THE BODY OF THE REPORT        I.   Typing the Body of the Report

     A.  Laying Out the Typed Page             A.  Laying out the typed page
         1.  Margins                               1.  Margins
         2.  Indentions                            2.  Indentions
             a.  Paragraphs                            a.  Paragraphs
             b.  Quoted Matter                         b.  Quoted matter
     B.  Preparing Manuscripts             B.  Preparing Manuscripts
         1.  Magazine Articles                 1.  Magazine articles
         2.  Press Releases
                                                2.  Press releases
II.  PREPARING AND TYPING OTHER PARTS
     OF THE REPORT                     II.   Preparing and Typing Other Parts
                                             of the Report
     A.  Typing the Table of Contents
         1.  Top Margin                       A.  Typing the Table of Contents
         2.  Page Numbers                         1.  Top margin
                                                  2.  Page numbers
```

In this first outline form, identifying numbers or letters are followed by a period and two spaces; and they begin just below the first word of any line immediately above. Succeeding lines of any point follow this same placement. This form is frequently used for outlining.

This second outline form shows several variations from the first, any one or combination of which might be used. Differences include vertical spacing, use of capitals and underlines, and indention for succeeding lines.

to a superior for approval, the secretary is responsible for seeing that it follows the principles of good outlining and for typing it in proper form, on one page if possible. No main heading or subheading ever stands alone. For every "I" there is at least a "II"; for every "A," a "B." This outline may later serve as the table of contents and the heading framework for the report.

Phrasing Main Headings and Subheadings. The main headings and subheadings should be phrased accurately and concisely in parallel form. When the executive expresses them in wordy, varied constructions, the secretary should suggest improved phrasings if the outline is to be read by anyone else.

In the following partial first-draft outline of an article on executive-secretary teams, notice the wordy and nonparallel phrasings of the main headings and subheadings.

```
  I. Worst traits of a typical secretary
     A. Search me--I don't own the place
     B. Has to be told to do everything
     C. Can't remember

 II. What secretaries dislike most about bosses
     A. Treats me like a piece of office scenery
     B. Too many five-minutes-to-five emergencies
     C. Doesn't realize I have a good mind too
```

In the revised draft below, the main headings and subheadings are phrased in concise, parallel form—each subheading begins with a verb and is followed by its object.

```
  I. Worst traits of secretaries
     A. Gives impression of I-don't-care
     B. Shows very little initiative
     C. Forgets details and instructions

 II. Worst traits of executives
     A. Treats secretary too impersonally
     B. Has needless five-minutes-to-five emergencies
     C. Ignores intellectual capacity of secretary
```

■ The Rough Draft

Any piece of careful writing is typed one or more times in rough-draft form. A rough draft is generously spaced and accurately transcribed, but little thought is given to final form or appearance. The purpose of the rough draft is to get the writer's thoughts on paper and to give him something tangible to edit and improve. Rather than a waste of time, this is a vital and essential step.

In typing rough drafts these practices are followed:

1. **The paper used is less expensive than letterhead quality but is sufficiently strong to withstand erasing. Many offices use colored or manila paper.**

2. **Carbon copies are not made unless they are expressly requested or unless the secretary wants an extra copy to cut into strips for reorganization of the material.**

3. **Plenty of room for write-ins and transfer indications is provided by use of triple spacing and wide margins on all four sides.**

4. **Each successive draft is given a number and dated. Each page is numbered in sequence and sometimes carries the draft number and date also.**

5. **Typing errors are X'd or lined out rather than erased if time is short and if the executive approves.**

The secretary using IBM'S desk-size 1130 data processing system must check galley proof resulting from this computer's automatic type composition. Helpful in the preparation of reports, the 1130 can read, format, and justify copy, schedule priorities, and generate paper tapes to run automatic linecasting machines.

—*IBM Corporation*

6. Quoted matter, if several lines in length, is single-spaced and indented in the same form as in the final copy because there is little likelihood of its being changed.

7. Footnotes are typed at the bottom of the page, on a separate sheet, or as shown in the excerpt illustrated on page 502.

All successive rough drafts are saved until the report is completed and presented. A rough draft is not destroyed, even though it is superseded, because the executive sometimes decides to use material from an earlier draft.

■ Secretarial Editing of the Rough Draft

If there is time, a helpful secretary always edits each rough draft before giving it to the executive—carefully reading each page and lightly penciling in her suggestions of more descriptive or exact words and of improvements in typing form. Editing includes pointing out

A simple method of incorporating a footnote in a
rough draft is shown in this example[1]—that is, to put

---

[1]J Marshall Hanna, Estelle L. Popham, and Esther
Kihn Beamer, Secretarial Procedures and Administration
(5th ed.; Cincinnati: South—Western Publishing Co.,
1968), p. 513.

---

the footnote immediately following the reference and
to separate the footnote from the textual matter by
lines across the page.

conspicuous repetition, inconsistencies, ambiguities, illogical order,
and errors in fact, grammar, or typing. Standard proof marks can be
found on page 756, in a typing book, or in a dictionary.

Typing the Body of the Report

The final version of the report is evidence of the executive's skill in
concise, logical writing and of the secretary's skill in sustained, attractive, meticulous typing. As the secretary begins the final typing, she
should vow to make haste slowly, taking time to design an attractive
page layout. Keeping a dictionary and a punctuation guide within arm's
reach is also a must.

Most reports require multiple copies. Carbon copies may be made
as the original is typed, the secretary may photocopy the original copy
material for distribution, or the copy may be typed on a duplimat for
reproduction.

■ Page Layouts

There are two kinds of typed page layouts: the *traditional* which
looks much like a standard printed page of a textbook; and the *nontraditional* in which the units of typing are creatively arranged and
displayed. A traditional page layout is conservative; a nontraditional
layout, however, may be an effective means of attracting attention to a
report or of highlighting significant material. The successful secretary
must be alert to ways of presenting facts in nontraditional layouts as
well as in traditional ones. By varying margins, line spacing, indentions,
capital and small letters, spacing between letters and words, underlining,

placement of various parts, using white space generously, and devising charts, drawings, and graphs, she can achieve results that will greatly enhance the effectiveness of a report.

1. To leave the correct ½-inch margin between the page number and the edge of the paper, type top-positioned numbers just below the short line at the top of the paper and bottom-centered numbers just above the short line at the foot of the page.

2. The vertical ruling on the left indicates the left margin of the copy and is 1½ inches from the left edge of the page. This margin includes ½ inch for binding.

3. The vertical ruling on the right indicates the right margin of the copy and is 1 inch from the right edge of the page. The right margin should be as even as possible. Not more than two or three letters should extend beyond this right vertical line. Avoid having more than two consecutive lines end with a hyphenated word, and never end a page with a hyphenated word.

4. The two horizontal lines at the top, 1 inch and 2 inches respectively from the top edge of the paper, indicate the upper margins for the copy. The lower of these two lines is used only for the first page of a part of the paper (e.g., preface or letter of transmittal, table of contents, chapter, etc.). The upper margin is for the second and subsequent pages of a part. The typed letters should touch but not extend above the appropriate margin.

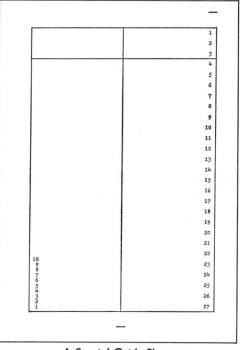

A Special Guide Sheet

5. The horizontal line at the bottom, 1 inch from the edge of the paper, indicates the placement of the last line of copy or footnote. At least two lines of a paragraph must appear at the bottom of a page, and at least two lines of a paragraph should be carried forward to a new page.

Spacing. Reports may be single- or double-spaced, depending upon their length, type, and purpose. Letter reports, memorandums, bulletins, and routine intraoffice reports are usually single-spaced. If a report is longer than three pages, it is frequently double-spaced.

Indentions. Paragraphs may be typed flush with the left margin or indented 5, 10, 15, or even 20 spaces. For single- and double-spaced reports with paragraph indentions, double-space between paragraphs. In blocked double-spaced work, triple-space between paragraphs.

Margins. The suggestions that follow will help the secretary to secure uniform margins.[1] The typewriting job is considerably simplified and expedited by placing a *special guide sheet* immediately behind the page being typed. Ordinary bond or other serviceable paper may be used for this guide sheet; onionskin may be used if carbon copies are being made. The special sheet (shown on page 503 for a manuscript to be bound at the left) should be ruled with India ink, other dark ink, or colored pencil so that it will be visible through the top page of typing.

Titles. Notice the differences in impact weight of the titles at the right. Which do you like best? Why?

Every typewritten title is a part of a black-and-white picture. Therefore, select a style that is attractive in width and weight and that is in satisfying proportion to the dimensions of the typed page. It is hard to *visualize* which form of title is best. But you can try them out for size, weight, and appearance by typing several experimental arrangements of the title, cutting them out, and laying each one on a full page of similar typing. The best one will become evident.

```
TRADITIONAL TITLE or
TRADITIONAL TITLE


Upper and Lower or
Upper and Lower


S P R E A D   H E A D   or
S P R E A D   H E A D


EXTRA   SPACING   or
EXTRA   SPACING

            or

 .   .   .   .   .   .   .
 .  A  F R A M E D   T I T L E
 .  F O R   D I S T I N C T I O N  .
 .   .   .   .   .   .   .

            or

- - - A n   U n u s u a l
      A r r a n g e m e n t
      o f   T i t l e - - - -
```

Headings and Subheadings. Headings and subheadings are used to guide the reader through the report. The criterion for their use is: Would a heading clarify the content and increase readability?

---

[1]Erwin M. Keithley, *A Manual of Style for the Preparation of Papers and Reports* (Cincinnati: South-Western Publishing Co., 1959), pp. 4–5.

In general, headings and subheadings parallel the outline. Note their arrangement in this book and their usefulness in preparing the reader and in showing the relative importance of subject matter.

Both headings and subheadings can be varied by placement, by use of capitals and small letters, and by indention, as shown in the illustrations at the right. The styles illustrated here are unusual and would be used only where there was a need for an eye-catching, dramatic effect.

Before the secretary types the report, she plans a guide to the form and position of each heading and subheading, of each

```
      T I T L E   O F   R E P O R T


             A MAIN HEADING

Text begins here without indention.  It
is single-spaced.  Four line spaces are
above this heading and two below it.

             A Subheading
```

```
      T I T L E   O F   R E P O R T

A MAIN HEADING      The text begins five
APPEARS HERE        spaces beyond the long-
                    est line of the heading.
There are four line spaces above the center
title and three line spaces below it.
The side heading must be broken into two
or three short lines.

             Subsequent paragraphs are
indented fifteen spaces as this one is.

A FIRST SUBHEADING

             For attention value it is
best to have this heading stand on a sepa-
rate line.  Three line spaces are above
it and two line spaces are below it.

             A Second Subheading.  The
text follows on the same line.  Two line
spaces are above the heading.
```

margin and indention, and of all line spacing. This plan, typed in a form easily referred to, is called a style sheet.

■ Quoted Matter

Material from other sources is often quoted in reports. If an idea is used, either quoted indirectly or directly, credit must be given. In indirect references, a footnote suffices. Direct quotations are handled in the following ways:

1. Quotations of *fewer than four lines* are typed in the body of the paragraph and enclosed in quotation marks.

2. Quotations of *four or more lines* are usually single-spaced and indented from the left margin or from both margins.

3. When a quotation of *several paragraphs* is not indented, quotation marks precede each paragraph and follow the final word in the last paragraph.

4. A *quotation within a quotation* is enclosed in single quotation marks.
5. *Italicized words* in the quotation are underscored.
6. *Omissions* are shown by ellipses—three spaced (or unspaced) periods within a sentence and between sentences; four periods at the end of a sentence.
7. *Inserted words (interpolations)* are enclosed in typewritten brackets, using the underscore and diagonal: $\underline{/\ \ /}$. Parentheses cannot be used, as they often occur naturally in the context and the reader could not identify matter enclosed in them as inserted matter.
8. A *footnote reference* showing the source should be made for the quotation unless the source is identified adequately in the text.

Permission to quote copyrighted material must be obtained from the copyright holder when reports are to be printed or duplicated and given public circulation, except for material published by a governmental agency. Full information should be sent with the request including the:

1. Text leading up to the quotation
2. Lines to be quoted, or page and line locations in the publication from which lengthy material is being quoted
3. Credit line or complete footnote reference
4. Title and publisher of the publication in which the quoted matter will appear

▪ Footnotes

Footnotes are numbered in sequence on each page, throughout each section, or throughout the entire report. There is an advantage in numbering footnotes anew with each page or section—if footnotes are inserted or deleted, only the numbers on the page or within the section need be changed. Practices for typing footnotes may be reviewed in the Reference Guide on page 757.

▪ Numbering Pages

Usually the typist saves time by waiting until the body is typed before typing page numbers. Changes are likely, so she pages the top sheet of each carbon assembly in pencil as it is completed, thus keeping unpaged copy in order. After the supplementary sections and the preliminary pages have been typed, the entire report is paged at the typewriter.

Arabic numerals without punctuation are placed at the upper right corner of the body and supplementary parts of the report. The preliminary pages preceding the body are numbered in small Roman numerals at the bottom center.

▪ Checking the Typed Copy

Each typed page of the final copy of the report is checked word for word and figure for figure. Some offices require that the last carbon copy be used for checking, that all corrections be boldly marked on it, and that the checked copy be permanently filed. The careful worker goes through the material at least twice—the first time for comparison with the original and for catching errors in sense, and the second time for inconsistencies in form.

Preparing and Typing the Other Parts

The order in which the other parts of a report are prepared varies, but paging of the table of contents is usually the last, or one of the last steps. In the following discussion the concluding supplementary parts and then the introductory parts are considered.

▪ Appendix or Reference Section

In a comprehensive report an *appendix* or *reference section* devoted to supplementary information, supporting tables and statistics, or reference material follows the body of the report.

▪ Bibliography

A report that is based upon a study of published materials frequently includes a bibliography, listing the source material. Such a bibliography is called a *selected bibliography*. Many business reports are based on factual information within the company, and there is no need to refer to outside source material.

Sometimes the secretary is requested to prepare a *comprehensive bibliography* listing all the material published on a subject for a selected period of time. An *annotated bibliography* contains an evaluation or a brief explanation of the content of each reference.

A bibliography reference is very similar in form to a footnote in that it cites the author's name, the title of the publication, the publisher, and the date. If there is an editor, a translator, or an illustrator, his name may be included. The price and complete details on the number of illustrations, plates, diagrams, and so on can be included if this information will be of value to the ones who will use the bibliography. Specific chapters or sections and their inclusive page numbers should be stated if the entry refers to only a certain part of the book or periodical. A typing book or examples from "Suggested Readings" at the end of chapters throughout this book will provide a more specific review of form for a footnote or bibliographical reference. (See also page 757.)

■ The Index

An *index* is included only when it is felt that there will be occasion to use it. A detailed table of contents usually suffices. When an index is necessary, use a copy of the report and underline in colored pencil each item on each page that should be included in the index. Each underlined item and its page number are written on a separate slip. The completed slips are then sorted into alphabetic order, and a typed index is prepared from them.

■ The Letter of Transmittal

Frequently a *letter of transmittal* is bound into the report and performs a function similar to the preface of a book. It gives authorization for the report, details of its preparation, the period covered, or other such information that will help the reader understand the depth and breadth of the report and arouse his interest in studying it. (See page 509.)

The letter of transmittal is typed on the regular business letterhead and is signed in ink. It is reproduced on the same kind of paper used for the other pages of a duplicated or printed report, and the signature is duplicated rather than handwritten.

■ Title Page

The *title page* may provide an opportunity for artistic typing. Even a report of five or ten pages is improved with a title page. One designed by the secretary should be simple if the report is typed in traditional form. If the report is typed in nontraditional form, the secretary should try for distinction and artistic display of the information. Notice the contrast of the two title pages on page 510. The traditional title page merely identifies the report and the author. The nontraditional one is designed to present the same information in an eye-appealing manner.

The title page must contain the essential facts for identifying the report—the title, the author, the date, the place of preparation. The essential facts vary with the contents and the readers of a report. An

August 19, 19--

To the General Manager and Board of Directors:

Here is the report by the Committee on Standardization of Forms, appointed by you on June 15 to make recommendations about standard communication forms for all departments of this organization.

The conclusions were reached after consulting the head and two members of each department, after studying fifteen style manuals published after 1960, holding conferences with three university teachers of business writing and three professors of industrial management, and analyzing the forms used in five companies that manufacture the same type of product which we make.

On the basis of its findings, the Committee classifies forms now in current use in the company as follows: (1) recommended, (2) accepted, and (3) disapproved. It also submits forms not now in use in this company with either of two recommendations: (1) for immediate adoption or (2) for consideration with a view to future adoption if practicable.

Each member feels that working on this Committee has given him a better insight into the problems encountered by our management and a better understanding of work simplification processes. It has been a privilege to compile the report.

Respectfully yours,

COMMITTEE ON STANDARDIZATION OF FORMS

Harold J. Zahl, Chairman
Joan Matthews
Edward Evanston
Carline Winters

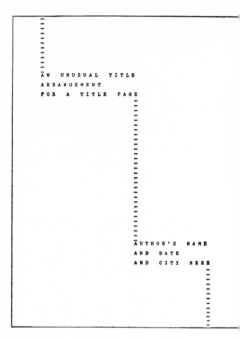

interoffice report may require only the title and the date. The executive should approve the title page because he may have definite opinions on the inclusion of certain items and their placement and arrangement.

■ Table of Contents

After paging the report, the secretary prepares the table of contents which precedes the report and consists of a list of the main topics or chapter titles and page numbers, possibly conforming to the original outline. It may be more useful, however, if subheadings and their page numbers are also listed. Usually the table of contents is roughed out to get an idea of its length and width before the final form is decided upon.

Reports often contain tables and charts, and occasionally illustrations, which are listed and paged at the end of the table of contents. A table of contents should be checked for correctness of titles and page numbers should be cited before final typing is done.

Assembling, Final Checking, and Binding

After all the typing is finished, the report is ready for assembly, final checking, and binding.

TABLE OF CONTENTS

Aligned dots
as leaders

Page

Recommendations 1

I.   Outline of Procedures 12
     Scope of Inquiry 13
     Assignments of Phases to Committee Members . . . 15

II. Analysis of Forms Used by Other Companies 28
     Companies Interviewed. 28
     Departments Studied. 29

Spread title ⟶   C O N T E N T S   Spaced hyphens
                                              as leaders

Page

Letter of Transmittal - - - - - - - - - - - - - - i

Table of Contents - - - - - - - - - - - - - - - - ii

List of Forms - - - - - - - - - - - - - - - - - - iv

Recommendations - - - - - - - - - - - - - - - - - 1

                                              Main parts
               OUTLINE OF PROCEDURE ⟵   centered

Scope of Inquiry- - - - - - - - - - - - - - - - - 13
Assignments of Phases to Committee Members- - - - - 15

Double   ANALYSIS OF FORMS USED BY OTHER COMPANIES
space

Companies Interviewed - - - - - - - - - - - - - - - 28
Departments Studied - - - - - - - - - - - - - - - - 29

▪ Assembling

The typed pages are assembled in reverse order—that is, the bottom page is laid out first, face up. By following this procedure, the secretary can discover blank or mutilated pages during assembly. The assembled sheets should then be joggled several times to line them up exactly.

▪ Final Checking

The final report is submitted by complete sets, with the ribbon copy on top. A final check is made after the pages are assembled into sets. Use a final check sheet and go through the report once for each item listed. This final checking has caught many an embarrassing error and is a device, in fact, that can well be used for any task involving detail and accuracy. The secretary might check the following items on each set of the report:

1. Page numbers in proper sequence
2. Indicated corrections made on every page
3. Correct references to page numbers, tables, or figures
4. Correct figures and computation of figures

▪ Binding

Binding is the last step of preparing the report. The most popular kind of binding is stapling. When only one staple is used, it is placed diagonally across the upper left corner (like /, not |). When two or three staples are required, they are spaced along the top or left edge of the report, where a larger margin has been left for this purpose.

If the report seems a little too thick for stapling, but stapling is the only convenient method, use double stapling; insert the staples in their proper positions on the top of the report, and then insert a second set of staples in the same positions from the back.

Some offices prefer sturdier and more permanent types of binding. These bindings require special supplies and equipment, such as metal eyelets, punches, or spiral binding. The technique of using them is easily learned.

Preparing Copy for Printing

When typewritten work is to be sent out of the office for printing or duplicating, the secretary types the copy in a complete, accurate, and easy-to-follow form. Since the copy is to be followed exactly, she does not rely on others for necessary punctuation, for correct spelling, or for the improvement of the copy in other ways. Of course she retains a file copy for ready reference.

If possible, however, she should discuss styling with the person who is to be responsible for the work. Together they should develop a style sheet showing the type to be used for main headings and subheadings, for footnotes, for bibliography, and for captions.

▪ Manuscript

A manuscript which is to be sent to the printer should be prepared according to the following guidelines:

1. Type all copy double-spaced on one side of 8½- by 11-inch sheets, with one or preferably two copies. Leave generous side margins. Quoted material or other text matter to be set apart should be single-spaced and indented on both sides.

2. Key all typewritten copy to its exact position on a page layout.

3. Number all sheets in the upper right corner. Two or more compositors may work on the same assignment, so correct numbering is imperative.

4. Type incidental changes, or write them clearly in ink, between the lines or in the margins.

5. Typewrite a long addition on a separate full-sized sheet and give it an inserted page number, as 16a; indicate on page 16 the point at which the insertion is to be made.

6. Draw a heavy line through words to be omitted.

7. Give explicit directions. With the help of a compositor, specify size and style of type faces and amount of leading (space between lines) desired.

8. Use a single underline to indicate *italics*, a double underline for SMALL CAPS, and a triple underline for REGULAR CAPS. To indicate bold face, use a wavy underline.

9. Number footnotes consecutively. They may be typed on the page to which they pertain; between full-width rules directly under the line in which the reference occurs; or at the bottom of the page but separated from the text by a short line; or all in sequence on a separate sheet.

10. Provide titles and number tables and illustrations consecutively with Arabic numerals. Send with the manuscript a full list of all tables and illustrations.

11. Include a title page showing the title, the author's name and address, and perhaps the date.

12. Send the original copy to the printer. Do not fasten the sheets together. Keep them flat by placing them between strong cardboards or in a strong box. Wrap the manuscript in strong paper.

13. Send the manuscript by first-class mail, by R E A Express, or by fourth class, Special Handling, if time is not a factor.

▪ Magazine Articles and Press Releases

At times the executive may be asked to submit an article for magazine publication. The secretary simplifies the editor's job of judging the space needed for the copy by typing a sample paragraph from a recent issue of the magazine line for line. She can then determine the average line length and the number of lines to an inch of printed material. She can then type the material to conform to this gauge. Headings for the copy should be consistent with those used in the magazine. A covering letter giving the approximate number of words in the article also aids the editor.

If the approximate length requirements of the article are known in advance, the secretary types a rough-draft version with double spacing in the average line length of the magazine copy. This copy is given to the executive with a close estimation of the amount of space presently accounted for. As he revises the copy, the executive can lengthen or shorten the article. Copies of the published material should be kept in a file so labeled.

Press releases should be addressed to the City Editor unless a definite person (such as the Financial Editor) is specified. Publicity and news releases are discussed on pages 220 and 221.

▪ Reading Proof

It is customary for the printer to submit proofs. The secretary usually does the checking for errors, but the executive should be given an opportunity to approve revisions.

The first proof is usually in galley form—long sheets containing one column of printed copy, the column width as on the final printed page. Each kind of error or change to be made is indicated by a proofreaders' mark (illustrated on page 756). The place of the correction is indicated in the text, and the kind of correction to be made is written in the margin on the same line. If there is more than one correction in a line, the proofreaders' marks in the margin are separated by conspicuous diagonal lines as shown in the illustration on page 515.

The printer submits the second proof in page form. This new proof must be again meticulously read and corrected. Page numbers and page headings are shown in this proof and are usually checked as separate individual operations. This is often the final opportunity for the author to catch errors and to make changes.

It does not appear that the earliest printers had
any method of correcting errors before the form
was on the press/ The learned The learned cor-
rectors of the first two centuries of printing were
not proof/readers in our sense/ they were rather
what we should term office editors. Their labors
were chiefly to see that the proof corresponded to
the copy, but that the printed page was correct
in its latinity/ that the words were there, and
that the sense was right. They cared but little
about orthography, bad letters or purely printers'
errors, and when the text seemed to them wrong
they consulted fresh authorities or altered it on
their own responsibility. Good proofs, in the
modern sense, were impossible until professional
readers were employed/ men who [had][first] a
printer's education, and then spent many years
in the correction of proof. The orthography of
English, which for the past century has under,
gone little change, was very fluctuating until after
the publication of Johnson's Dictionary, and capitals, which have been used with considerable reg-

Anyone charged with responsibility for reading proof should adopt standard proofreading marks, which can be found in a dictionary or in a typewriting book. Proofmarked copy is illustrated above.

Procedures Writing

Procedures writing has been called "verbal flow charting." It lists step by step the logical sequence of activities, so that an employee can perform an operation by following written instructions. Writing good procedures looks deceptively simple; to eliminate extraneous material is extremely difficult. Effective procedures writing is one of the most valuable forms of business writing because it saves time and money.

Procedures for a department or for an operation are usually collected in a loose-leaf notebook that can be updated by adding and deleting pages as new procedures are issued.

▪ A Sample Procedure

Assume that several mix-ups occurred because there was no standard procedure for reserving the board room for special meetings. Finally, your employer decides to put you, his administrative assistant or secretary, in charge of scheduling the room. He wants your help on writing a procedure to be sent to all office employees, outlining the steps to be taken in reserving and using the room.

There are at least four formats that can be used: *traditional, improved traditional, job breakdown,* and *playscript.*

Insert in Section IV, <u>Use of Special Rooms</u>, following page 16 and label 16a, <u>Board Room</u>.

The person requesting use of the Board Room files a written request with the administrator of office services at least ten days before the date of the proposed meeting, indicating the name of the group involved, the exact time of the meeting, its expected duration, and expected attendance.

The administrator of office services immediately notifies the applicant in writing as to whether the room is available and, if so, notifies the custodial staff in writing of the necessary room setup and the duration of the meeting and gives instructions for any special cleaning necessary.

The person requesting the room checks the room one hour before the meeting and provides any special supplies needed.

Insert in Section IV, Use of Special Rooms, 16a.

<u>Board Room</u>

<u>The person requesting use of the Board Room</u> files a written request with the <u>administrator of office services</u> at least ten days before the proposed meeting, indicating:
1. The name of the group involved,
2. The exact time of the meeting,
3. Its expected duration, and
4. Expected attendance.

<u>The administrator of office services</u> immediately notifies the applicant in writing as to whether the room is available and, if so, notifies the <u>custodial staff</u> in writing of:
1. The necessary room setup,
2. The duration of the meeting, and
3. Instructions for any special cleaning necessary.

<u>The person requesting the room</u> checks the room one hour before the meeting and provides any special supplies needed.

Traditional. The traditional format shown on the opposite page uses little, if any, variation in spacing or other features of format that are shown by the format below.

Improved Traditional. In contrast with the traditional format (bottom of page 516), the improved traditional has variation in spacing, emphasis of the performers by underscoring, and tabulation of points.

Job Breakdown. With the job breakdown the logical sequence of action is reflected in the *Steps*. The *Key Points* represent cautions to the worker at the points where he is likely to make mistakes. The *Steps* tell the worker what to do; the *Key Points* tell him how to do it. Every *Step* does not have to have a *Key Point*, and there may be more than one *Key Point* for one operation.

Insert in Section IV, Use of Special Rooms, 16a.

B O A R D   R O O M

STEPS	KEY POINTS
1. File a written request with the administrator of office services.	1a. Do this at least ten days before the date of the proposed meeting.
	1b. List name of group to use room, time of meeting, duration, and expected attendance.
2. On day of meeting, check the room one hour before the meeting.	2. Be sure that room is clean, the air is fresh, and enough chairs are positioned for participants.
3. Distribute necessary supplies.	3. Provide water and glasses, ash trays, sharpened pencils, and note pads.

Playscript. The playscript format answers the question, "Who does what?"[1] The actor is easily identified, and what he does starts with an

[1]Leslie Matthies, *The Playscript Procedure* (New York: Office Publications Inc., 1961).

action verb in the present tense. According to the man who developed this technique, playscript is really a form of flow chart, and any step that backflows rather than proceeds by forward action can immediately be spotted, and gaps in the logical steps can also be quickly detected.

                              Insert in Section IV, Use of
                                Special Rooms, p. 16a.

Subject: RESERVING BOARD ROOM FOR SPECIAL MEETINGS

  Responsibility   Action

Requesting Employee   1. Prepares a written request
                          at least ten days before the
                          date of the proposed meet-
                          ing, including name of
                          group, time of meeting, du-
                          ration, and expected attend-
                          ance.
                       2. Sends request to the ad-
                          ministrator of office ser-
                          vices.

Administrator of   3. Notifies the applicant in
Office Services   writing whether the room is
                          available.
                       4. Notifies custodial staff in
                          writing of necessary room
                          setup, duration of meeting,
                          and need for any special
                          cleaning.

Requesting Employee   5. Checks the room one hour
                          before the meeting.
                       6. Distributes necessary sup-
                          plies.

▪ Selecting the Format

A traditional person or a traditional company would probably adopt the improved arrangement of the traditional format. A more venture-some author in search of eyecatching appeal would probably choose the job breakdown or the playscript. In a procedure involving one operator, the job breakdown might be chosen, for it has the advantage of caution-ing against wrong moves. It looks more complicated than the playscript, however. The playscript would probably be selected for writing proce-dures involving more than one worker.

Suggested Readings

Anderson, Chester R., Alta G. Saunders, and Francis W. Weeks. *Business Reports*, 3d ed. New York: McGraw-Hill Book Company, 1957, 407 pp.

Aurner, Robert R. *Effective Communication in Business*, 5th ed. Cincinnati: South-Western Publishing Co., 1967, pp. 485–526.

Brown, Leland. *Effective Business Report Writing*. Englewood Cliffs: Prentice-Hall, Inc., 1963, 420 pp.

Graves, Harold. *Report Writing*. Englewood Cliffs: Prentice-Hall, Inc., 1965, 286 pp.

Hay, Robert D. *Written Communications for Business Administrators*. New York: Holt, Rinehart, and Winston, Inc., 1965, pp. 253–406 and pp. 441–467.

Himstreet, William C., and Wayne Murlin Baty. *Business Communications, Principles and Methods*. Belmont, California: Wadsworth Publishing Company, Inc., 1965, pp. 205–268.

Keithley, Erwin M. *A Manual of Style for the Preparation of Papers and Reports*. Cincinnati: South-Western Publishing Co., 1959, 96 pp.

Menning, Jack, and C. W. Wilkinson. *Communication Through Letters and Reports*, 3d ed. Homewood, Illinois: Richard E. Irwin, Inc., 1963, pp. 440–600.

Sigband, Norman B. *Effective Report Writing*. New York: Harper and Brothers, 1960, 688 pp.

Questions for Discussion

1. Why might a written procedure be called a "verbal flow chart"? Why is it difficult to write procedures?

2. What is meant by "management by exception"? Does it seem superior as a management policy to periodic reporting? Why?

3. Do you favor a management policy of appointing a vice president in charge of paper-work control? Why?

4. If you were responsible for getting a company brochure published, how would you prepare for a conference with the printer?

5. Consider the illustrations of page layouts and heading guides on pages 504 and 505. Suggest a situation in which you might use each type.

6. Suppose your employer is in conference with his superior, going over a report which you and he have prepared. He discovers an error in an amount and calls you in and says that you made the error. He petulantly asks if you failed to check the figures. You remember distinctly that the amount is one which he took from a statement prepared by someone else in your department. How would you answer?

7. If you had obtained all the data available on a certain subject and an executive had drafted a report based on this information, what would you do if in the morning's mail you received a business magazine containing an article which covers a new angle of the subject? Would you call the executive's attention to the new material, knowing that it would mean a rewrite job?

8. In the printed copy of the lecture "The Care and Feeding of the Mind" by Professor Jacques Barzun there appears the following paragraph. Punctuate it as you would if it were dictated to you. Then use the Reference Guide to check your answers.

> The lesson is don't be afraid to *lend* your mind. It is a perfectly safe loan you are sure to get it back possibly with interest and in any case the very act of wrapping it around an alien thought will keep it in stretching trim. Give heed to any idea that is proposed to you and see where it leads. Don't judge by first appearances and don't fear a permanent imprint on the pure white page of your mind. You can always wind up with Euclid's favorite conclusion you remember how he starts by saying Let ABC be larger than DEF. You let him foolish as his idea appears from the diagram and pretty soon he reassures you by exclaiming Which is absurd!

9. Type the information in the blanks in the following sentences. Then use the Reference Guide to verify or correct your answers.

(a) The typewriter is _____ years old. (8)

(b) We are asking _____ for the typewriter which is _____ years old. ($20, 14)

(c) To be exact, the Mimeograph is _____ years, _____ months, and _____ days old. (15, 8, 4)

Problems

■ 1. Type each of the following titles twice (eight different arrangements). Divide the titles into two or more lines if necessary, and center each line horizontally on the page. Allow six line spaces between titles.

(a) Opportunities for Women in Business Management

(b) How Data Communication Creates Total Business Systems

(c) Women Who Work

(d) Secretarial Work—Is It Really a Profession?

■ 2. Using information in the Reference Guide type correctly as a footnote and as part of a bibliography the following information:

(a) An unsigned article, "Pan American's Boeing 747 Order Heats up Jumbo Jet Competition," on pp. 80–81 of *Air Travel*, June, 1966.

(b) A book written by Sydney Clark called *All the Best in Mexico*. The seventh edition of this book was published by Dodd, Mead & Company of New York. It was published in 1966. It contains 284 pages. The footnote refers to page 34.

(c) A chapter entitled "How to File It, Find It, and Get Rid of It," by George Derry in *Ideas for Management*, the 1958 yearbook of the Systems and Procedures Association of 7890 Brookside Drive, Cleveland, Ohio. The chapter appears on pages 48–57.

(d) An article by Carol J. Loomis called "The 500: A Decade of Growth," in the July 15, 1966, issue of *Fortune*. It appears on pages 213 to 215 and is continued on pp. 268, 271, 272, 274, 278. The footnote refers to material appearing on page 271.

■ 3. From the bibliographical notes that you prepared for Problem 6 in Chapter 19, page 471, develop a business report on one of the ten topics given (or a topic of your own choice which your instructor has approved). Use graphs or tables if you think they will improve your presentation.

Related Work Assignments 56-59 ─────────────

56. Interpreting Proofreaders' Marks. To provide some practice for yourself in using proofreaders' marks, indicate the method of marking both the text and the margins when the following changes are desired. If you are not using the Workbook, set up three columns across the page heading *Change Desired, Mark in Text,* and *Mark in Margin.*

(1) Insert the word *more.*
(2) Change the word *readnig* to *reading.*
(3) Delete the word *usually.*
(4) Show a space in *ofthis.*
(5) Even up the left margin where the letters have been set a space too far to the left in one line.
(6) Write the word *think* in solid capitals.
(7) Show an apostrophe in the word *womens.*
(8) Capitalize the word *congressional.*
(9) Insert a hyphen in *selfemployed.*
(10) Indicate a new paragraph in the copy.
(11) Italicize the word *usually.*
(12) Use lower case for the words *History, Algebra,* and *Social Studies.*
(13) In marking the copy for the preceding question, you inadvertently indicated that the word *English* should be written in lower case too. Show that you want the original capitalization to stand.
(14) Transpose *two only* to *only two.*
(15) Use less space between words.
(16) Use small caps for the paragraph heading, *Characteristics of the New Process.*
(17) Use quotation marks around *shot in the arm.*
(18) Indicate no paragraph.
(19) Indicate that type does not match.
(20) Delete the hyphen in *readily-available service.*
(21) Insert a comma between *pens* and *and.*
(22) Center and type in solid caps the main paragraph heading: *Introduction.*
(23) Change *thimk* to *think.*
(24) Indicate leaving two spaces after a colon.
(25) Increase the size of the space between lines.
(26) Move copy to the right to align.
(27) Delete the hyphen in *state-room.*
(28) Delete the apostrophe in *it's.*
(29) In the title *A Manual of Style for the Preparation of Papers and Reports,* the words *for the Preparation of Papers and Reports* have been crossed out. Indicate that these phrases should be retained.
(30) Delete the comma: *He finished the report, and got it on his superior's desk before leaving the office that afternoon.*

57. Copying from Rough Draft. The instructions and supplies necessary for the completion of this assignment are provided in the Workbook.

58. Your Fundamentals. This is the seventh in a series of Workbook assignments reviewing English usage, grammar, and punctuation. These assignments are based on the Reference Guide in this textbook.

59. Measuring Your Secretarial Information and Judgment (Part VII.) This is the fourth in a series of Workbook assignments providing practice in answering types of questions used in an examination for professional secretaries.

7—1 √ conference planning

Jeanne Kistner is secretary to Bill Murray, sales manager for General Products, a national corporation located in Newton, Massachusetts, selling packaged frozen foods. The six division sales offices have the following number of regional salesmen doing the following amounts of business:

	No. of Salesmen	% of Volume
Houston, Texas............	16	25
San Diego, California.......	12	21
Tacoma, Washington.......	12	16
Kansas City, Missouri.......	9	15
Columbia, South Carolina...	8	13
Newton, Massachusetts......	3	10
	60	100

Last year the annual sales conference was held in Boston and included a visit to Newton because Mr. Murray wanted the salesmen to see the new methods of processing food which had been developed. No startlingly new processes, however, were introduced during this year. Mr. Murray decides to hold this year's conference in Houston to "give a shot in the arm" to the lagging sales force there. Six weeks before the conference, however, he receives this memorandum from the president: "Last year's conference costs were exorbitant. Remember our austerity budget. Cut expenses by 40 percent, but don't give the boys a cheap conference."

Mr. Murray decides to visit all sales offices at once so that he can plan a more effective conference. He wants to visit the one with the poorest record first and plan the most economical itinerary from there on.

As a new secretary, Miss Kistner reads the files on last year's conference and discovers that:

One salesman arrived at the Boston hotel at the last minute and could not locate the meeting room.

One salesman asked to be excused because he and his wife had completed all travel arrangements for a trip to Europe during his month's vacation before he found out the date of the conference.

The charts Mr. Murray wanted to use in illustrating his opening talk were not delivered to him in the meeting room because he was not registered at the hotel but commuted from Newton.

Considerable effort was needed to get expense reports from two salesmen.

Something happened to the tape recorder, so no record was made of the report on new products to be marketed.

Some of the salesmen paid for their rooms themselves, and the hotel inadvertently charged the company for them again.

Some of the salesmen could not get into their rooms until 4 p.m. on the first afternoon of the conference although they arrived at 8 a.m.

In preparation for this year's conference, Mr. Murray asks Miss Kistner to:

(1) Suggest his itinerary for the trip to sales offices.

(2) Recommend for the annual sales conference a location that would reduce expenses and also provide attractive facilities, easily accessible.

(3) Obtain comparative figures on entertainment costs for two evenings outside the hotel.

(4) Submit a plan for "handling the details before and during the conference [which Miss Kistner will attend] so that everything will run smoothly."

7—2 √ *employment commitment*

Upon graduation from college, Edith Harvey was employed by the Beckwith Chemical Corporation. At the time of the employment interview, the personnel manager asked her if she intended to stay with the firm for a period of time, as induction of new employees is very expensive and the company wants to employ only permanent staff. She said "yes."

She was assigned as secretary to William Brower, one of four district sales managers, and felt that the position offered unusual opportunities for promotion.

After she had been on the job for three months, she overheard the following conversation: "Did you know that Jim Lucas is going to be appointed all-company sales manager? I guess that Bill Brower will be pretty disappointed." "Why should he be? Everybody knows that he isn't going anywhere in this company."

Even though Edith was happy working with Mr. Brower and liked both the company and the chemical world, she resigned at once to look for another job.

During the customary exit interview, she evaded the question of the reason for her leaving because she felt that she should be loyal to Mr. Brower. She replied that a personal problem had arisen that made it necessary for her to work nearer home.

Did Edith have a responsibility to the company to remain? Is she right in resigning to find a job in which she can go along with her employer on the promotion road?

— *E. I. Du Pont de Nemours & Co., Inc*

The executive secretary may have responsibilities for handling company funds and for other financial and legal aspects of executive and company business

Financial and Legal Facets of Secretarial Work

A secretary-administrative assistant may be involved with activities related to finances. Common among these activities are handling the employer's bank account, taking care of investments and insurance, processing or checking the payroll, and compiling personal tax data. A close relationship frequently exists between the financial and legal aspects of secretarial work. Thus, both are included in this section.

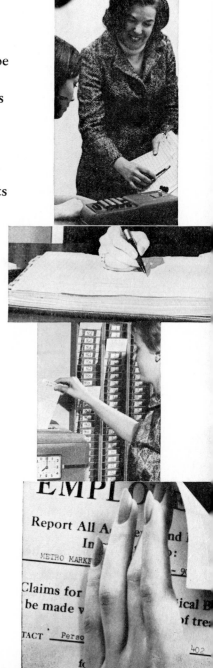

The executive for whom you work will be one of the fifty million persons in the United States who maintain a personal checking account and collectively write over twenty billion checks each year. Many an executive secretary may have the dual responsibility of handling not only company funds but also the personal checking accounts of her employer. Some executives turn over to their secretaries all of their personal financial records—checkbook, salary check, dividend checks, and personal and family bills. Others prefer to keep their personal finances confidential and delegate only those fiscal matters that relate to the company.

Whether a secretary's financial duties are extensive or restricted, she may expect to perform some, if not all, of these functions: making bank deposits, writing checks, reconciling bank statements, handling petty cash funds, cashing checks, paying bills, and recording incoming funds. A knowledge of banking terminology and procedures, therefore, is necessary. Although practices and processes vary with different banks to some extent, the basic banking functions are similar in all banks.

The Checking Account

The new secretary with financial responsibilities must be identified at the bank as representing the executive or his business. If the executive wishes the secretary to sign checks for the withdrawal or payment of funds from his account, or to indorse and cash checks made out to him, he must authorize the bank to honor her signature. The bank may require the executive to sign a special authorization form, or to arrange for the secretary to add her signature to his signature card on file at the bank. Some banks require that the secretary be issued a power of attorney (page 606) to perform these functions.

■ Accepting Checks

When accepting a check that is given in person or received through the mail, the executive secretary should exercise precautions to assure that the check has been properly prepared. The check needs to be examined to be sure that it meets the obligation for which it is being tendered and that it is written in a form which will make it acceptable by the bank for payment. To have a deposited check returned by the bank because of an error is time consuming and an inconvenience to the accounting department.

These points should be examined: (a) date—to see that the check is not post dated, (b) amount—to determine that the correct amount of payment is being received, (c) figures—to be sure that the amount written in figures is the same as the amount written in words, and (d) indorsement—to see that an indorsement, if required, has been properly made.

Before checks are deposited, the secretary should make certain that the information needed for entering the receipt in the accounting records has been recorded, perhaps by the preparation of a receipt or an entry in a form or book while the details are available.

▪ Making a Deposit in a Checking Account

To make a deposit, the secretary presents to the bank teller a deposit slip (See page 530.) listing in detail the amounts to be deposited, a duplicate deposit slip or a passbook, and the deposit itself, consisting of currency, coin, indorsed checks, and money orders.

Receipt of a deposit is evidenced by the bank in one of several ways: (1) The teller stamps the duplicate deposit slip and returns it to the depositor (the stamped duplicate slip is the depositor's record and receipt); (2) the teller enters the deposit in the depositor's passbook; or (3) the teller imprints by machine the details of the deposit onto a duplicate deposit slip or separate receipt form. The secretary retains receipted records of deposits for use in reconciling the bank statement.

Preparing Coins and Bills for Deposit. Banks prefer that coins and bills, if in sufficient quantity, be put in the money wrappers that the banks furnish. Coins are packed in paper rolls as follows:

DENOMINATION	NUMBER OF COINS TO A ROLL	TOTAL VALUE OF COINS IN ROLL
Pennies	50	$ .50
Nickels	40	2.00
Dimes	50	5.00
Quarters	40	10.00
Halves	20	10.00

Bills of each denomination are made into packages of $50, $100, and so forth. The packages are separated into all-of-a-kind groups with each bill laid right side up and top edge at the top. A paper bill wrapper—a narrow strip with the amount printed on it—is wrapped tightly around the bills and securely glued.

The depositor's name should be stamped or written on each roll of coins and package of bills. Receiving tellers of banks do not stop to count packaged money when taking deposits, but they do count it later in the day. A mistake can easily be charged to the proper account if the depositor's name is put on each roll or wrapper.

Extra currency is counted out, right side up, the largest denominations on the bottom and the smallest ones on top. The entire packet of bills should be encircled with an elastic band. Extra coins are counted out, placed in an envelope, identified, and sealed.

Preparing Checks for Deposit. In order to deposit a check, the payee indorses it on the back; however, banks accept checks for deposit that are indorsed by a representative of the payee. The indorsement may be rubber-stamped or written in ink. In fact, a bank may accept an occasional check that lacks an indorsement. Some banks stamp the back of such a check with a statement such as, "Credited to account of payee named within—absence of indorsement guaranteed."

Notwithstanding the last sentence, it will be the secretary's responsibility to indorse every check for deposit. If the name of the payee is written differently on a check from the account name, indorse the check twice: first, as the name appears on the face of the check, and again, the exact way the account is carried. A rubber-stamp indorsement (showing the name of the bank, the branch location or number, the name of the account, and the account number), obtained from the branch where the executive banks or from an office-supplies dealer, is the most time-saving method. A pen signature does not need to be added to a rubber-stamp indorsement if the check is to be deposited.

There are several standard indorsements:

1. *A restrictive indorsement* (shown on page 529) is one in which a condition attached to the indorsement restrains the negotiability of the check or renders the indorser liable only upon a specified condition or conditions, such as "For deposit," or "Upon delivery of contract." A restrictive indorsement is commonly used when checks are being deposited. Checks indorsed "For deposit" need not be signed personally by the depositor but can be indorsed or stamped by the secretary. The "For deposit" qualification automatically keeps the check from being used for any purpose other than for deposit to the account of the depositor whose name appears in the indorsement.

FOR DEPOSIT AND
CREDIT TO ACCOUNT OF

57   APR ▮7 6-

APEX CORPORATION

Cleveland, Ohio_____ *April 1* _____ 19--

ELITY TRUST CO. $\frac{6\text{-}12}{410}$

rporation _____ $ *481.65*

eighty-one $^{65}/_{100}$ ⁓⁓⁓⁓⁓⁓ Dollars

Eugene H. Taylor

Indorsements are properly made across the back of the left end of checks and money orders, as is shown on the restrictive indorsement illustrated here.

2. An *indorsement in full* or *special indorsement* (shown first below) gives the name of a specified payee, written before the indorser's signature. This indorsement identifies the person or firm to which the instrument is transferred. A check indorsed in this way cannot be cashed by anyone without the specified payee's signature.

   The words "Pay to the order of First National Bank" in the illustration at the right identify the name of the bank to which the check is being transferred. For further transfer, the First National Bank must indorse the check again.

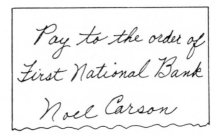

3. *A blank indorsement* consists simply of the signature of the payee, making the check payable to any holder. This indorsement, therefore, should never be used except at the bank immediately before the check is being deposited or cashed. A check should never be indorsed at the office or sent through the mail with a blank indorsement, because if the check is lost, the finder can turn it into cash.

4. A *qualified indorsement* shows the words "Without recourse" above the signature of the indorser. This indorsement passes title to the instrument without rendering the indorser liable if the maker is unable or refuses to pay. Normally, a bank would not accept for deposit a check indorsed in this manner.

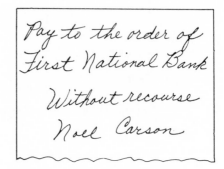

Making Out a Deposit Slip. Many types of deposit slips are in common use. Some banks have specially designed deposit slips planned for use with automated equipment. Those banks that encourage depositors to use duplicate slips in place of a passbook may provide deposit slips that have the duplicate attached to the original with interleaved carbon. A bank that gives the depositor a machine-prepared receipt will use a deposit slip designed for that purpose.

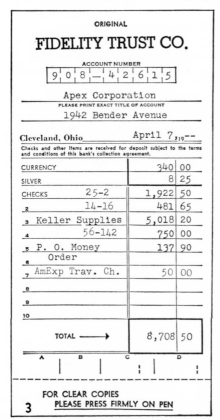

←DEPOSITOR'S ACCOUNT

←BANK ACCOUNT'S EXACT TITLE
  AND ADDRESS

←DEPOSIT DATE

←TOTAL PAPER MONEY

←TOTAL COINS

←CHECKS IDENTIFIED
  SEPARATELY
  (Listed here by the ABA transit number or by the name of the person from whom the check was received)

←MONEY ORDERS AND
  TRAVELERS' CHECKS ALSO
  IDENTIFIED

←TOTAL

←ORIGINAL COPY
  (Second copy for teller, third copy for customer)

Account Numbers. Most banks now identify depositors by account number. In banks that use automated equipment, all posting to accounts is done by number, rather than by name. Even banks that do not use automated equipment prefer to post by account number. The account number is printed on the deposit slip in magnetic ink, or space is provided for the depositor to record his account number.

Check Numbers. Each bank in the United States has been assigned an ABA (American Bankers Association) transit number. This number is usually printed in small type in the upper right portion of the check, to identify the bank for clearing-house functions. Illustrated, the numbers mean:

City or State $\longrightarrow$ **25 - 2** $\longleftarrow$ **Specific bank in the city or state**

412 $\longleftarrow$ **(4) Federal Reserve District**

(1) Branch in the district

(2) Number of days required to clear the check

Each check listed on the deposit slip should be identified by using the two top ABA transit numbers, in this case, 25-2.

Some banks prefer that if the check is drawn on the same bank in which the deposit is made the check be identified by writing the name of the maker of the check in place of the ABA transit number. (See illustration, page 530.)

Listing Checks. When a large number of checks are regularly deposited, it is common practice to list the checks on an adding machine and to attach the tape to the deposit slip, listing only the total. Some banks, however, prefer that all checks be shown on the deposit slip; they provide "long" deposit slips for such use.

Listing Other Items. Money orders and travelers' checks may be listed with the checks on the deposit slip. The check from Keller Supplies, shown on the deposit slip on page 530, was drawn on the bank where the deposit was being made (Fidelity Trust Co.); it is identified by the name of the maker of the check and not by the ABA transit number of the bank.

▪ Automation in Banking

To reduce the manual clerical work involved in handling checking accounts, many banks have installed data processing equipment. A

ARO PNEUMATIC TOOL CORPORATION	CHECKING	CASH		48	25
2216 Madison Avenue	ACCOUNT	CHECKS 6-68		22	50
Cleveland, Ohio 44106	DEPOSIT	LIST SINGLY 13-39		49	25

CHECKING
ACCOUNT
DEPOSIT

CASH	48	25
CHECKS 6-68	22	50
LIST SINGLY 13-39	49	25
• 6-83	18	20
BE SURE EACH 13-31	112	60
ITEM IS ENDORSED 56-43	37	90

DATE: *April 13, 19--*

OFFICE WHERE ACCOUNT IS CARRIED:

TERMINAL SQUARE OFFICE   **2**

| TOTAL | 288 | 70 |

SUBJECT TO RULES AND REGULATIONS GOVERNING CHECKING ACCOUNTS

THE NATIONAL CITY BANK

⑆0410⑈0012⑆ 6009946⑈

① ─────────── ②

At the bottom of the deposit slip for a magnetic-ink system, the numbers have been pre-printed in magnetic ink that remains "dead" until the slip is put into the electronic reading-and-sorting machine. The symbols between the numbers separate the fields of information for the machine. The *bank identification (ABA) number* needed for clearing-house exchanges is (1) 0410 0012; the *account reference number* is (2) 6009946. Later, a bank clerk will imprint in the blank space remaining along the bottom edge an indicator symbol of the date and the amount of the deposit.

uniform system of MIRC (Magnetic Ink Character Recognition) has been adopted by the American Bankers Association. Under this system, the bank's transit number and the depositor's account number are printed in magnetic ink characters at a uniform position at the bottom of the check. Optical Character Recognition (OCR) equipment (machines that read magnetic ink characters) can sort the checks at the rate of several hundred a minute.

Banks that have a computer installation also record at the bottom of each check when the check is received, the date, amount of the check, and other coded information. When this is done, the entire process (sorting of checks by issuing banks, sorting by account numbers, totaling, and posting to accounts) is done electronically and at very high speeds.

A preprinted deposit slip for a MICR system is illustrated above; a check identified by magnetic-ink characters is illustrated on page 533.

When an automated system is in use, the depositor can use only those deposit slips and checks that have been specifically printed to show his account number. If a depositor does not have his deposit slip or check at the time of a deposit or withdrawal at the bank, the bank clerk can handle the transaction.

Check-Stub Entries   **Bank-Check Entries**

	DOLLARS	CENTS
AL. BRO'T FOR'D	8,604	81
MT. DEPOSITED	913	40
TOTAL	9518	21
MT. THIS CHECK	325	27
AL. CAR'D FOR'D	9192	94

No. 832   ,325 27

TE April 15, 19--

Apex Corporation

OR Machinery
Parts

ARO PNEUMATIC TOOL CORPORATION
2216 Madison Avenue
Cleveland, Ohio 44106

No. 832

9-12
410

April 15, 19--

PAY TO THE ORDER OF *Apex Corporation* $325 27

Three hundred twenty-five 27/100 ———— DOLLARS

TERMINAL SQUARE OFFICE **2**

THE NATIONAL CITY BANK
CLEVELAND, OHIO   *Marion L. Owens*

⑆0410⑆001 2⑈ 600994 6⑉

Note that the series of magnetic-ink identification numbers at the bottom of this bank check are the same as those of the preprinted deposit slip on page 532. As a convenience to left-handed persons, checkbooks are also available with the stubs at the right.

□ Banking by Mail

Depositing by mail has become very popular because of the time it saves. The secretary in a small office may make most or all of the bank deposits by mail. Various kinds of mail-deposit slips and envelopes are provided by different banks. All checks must be indorsed "Pay to the order of (name of bank)" or "For Deposit Only," signed, and listed on the mail-deposit slip. The deposit slip and indorsed checks are placed in an envelope and mailed to the bank. Currency should never be deposited in this manner unless sent by registered mail. By return mail, the bank sends the depositor a receipt, along with a new mail-deposit slip and envelope.

▪ Night Depository

Some businesses use the *night depository* to protect funds collected after banking hours. The bank provides the depositor with a bag in which the deposit may be locked and dropped through a slot on the outside of the bank at any time during the night. On the next banking day, the bank teller unlocks the bag and makes the deposit. The depositor stops at the bank sometime during the day and picks up the empty bag and his deposit receipt. If the depositor prefers, however, the deposit bag will remain locked until the depositor goes to the bank and makes the deposit personally. For the convenience of depositors, many banks have established branches. They may also remain open at least one evening a week.

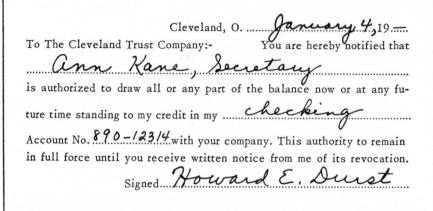

Cleveland, O. ....*January 4*,19.—

To The Cleveland Trust Company:-   You are hereby notified that

........*Ann Kane, Secretary*................................

is authorized to draw all or any part of the balance now or at any fu-

ture time standing to my credit in my ....*checking*..........

Account No. *890–12314* with your company. This authority to remain

in full force until you receive written notice from me of its revocation.

Signed....*Howard E. Durst*

When an account holder wishes to authorize a person to draw on his account for the time being, the bank may stamp the back of his signature card with an authorization form similar to the one shown above and have him fill it in and sign it. Such authorization may be withdrawn at any time.

▪ Making Withdrawals from a Checking Account

A withdrawal from a checking account is made by check. Checkbooks with one or more checks to a page are furnished by the depositor's bank. Many business offices use prenumbered checks with the name of the business imprinted on the face of each check. No matter what kind of checkbook is used, it is the secretary's responsibility to order new checkbooks before the old ones are completely used.

Writing Check Stubs. Writing out stubs and checks is an exacting responsibility. The record on the stubs must be kept accurately in ink and reconciled periodically with the bank statement. The stub should be filled in *before* the check is written, or too often the stub is forgotten.

All the information to be shown on the check itself, plus any other data that will help in classifying or breaking down the disbursement in bookkeeping or tax records, should appear on the stub. The number of the check, the date, the name of the payee, and the amount must appear on the stub. If the amount represents several items, these should be listed individually. If the check represents a part payment, an installment payment, or final payment, that fact should be noted. If the check represents a premium on an insurance policy, the name of the insured and the policy number should be listed.

The amount of the check must be accurately deducted from the previous stub balance with each subtraction and addition verified. Deposits should be entered on the check stubs promptly.

COMMERCIAL ACCT. NUMBER

890–12314

The undersigned hereby assent(s) to and agree(s) to be bound by the present and all future Rules and Regulations of **THE CLEVELAND TRUST COMPANY** governing commercial accounts, and ACKNOWLEDGE(S) RECEIPT OF A COPY OF SUCH PRESENT RULES AND REGULATIONS.

SIGNATURES	BIRTH DATE
1. *Howard E. Durst*	*3/8/20*
2. *Howard E. Durst*	BIRTH DATE *6/1/39*
by Ann Kane, Secretary	HOME PHONE NO. *671–2459*

MAIL ADDRESS AND ZONE NO. *236 Euclid Road, Cleveland, Ohio*

OTHER ADDRESS *1283 State Bldg. Cleveland*

BUSINESS OR EMPLOYER *Attorney – Durst & Durst*

INTRODUCED BY OR BANK REFERENCE

MOTHER'S 1ST NAME 1. *Nina*

MOTHER'S 1ST NAME 2. *Maude*

BUSINESS PHONE NO. *341–3478*

PLACE PAYING INSTRUCTION STAMP HERE

THIS SPACE FOR BANK USE ONLY	DATE OPENED	1ST DEPOSIT	OPENED BY	CLOSED
B-94 4-59		$		

On this signature card for a checking account, note how the form of the secretary's signature shows that the account is the executive's and that she is merely signing for him. In addition to the exact signatures needed for verification in honoring checks, the birth dates and mothers' first names are required so that the bank has on ready file identifying information about the account holder. When a request for information about the account is made, the bank can ask these two questions. This procedure helps to prevent divulging information to the wrong person.

Writing Checks. A check is a negotiable instrument and imposes certain legal responsibilities on the maker. Therefore, it must be written with care to insure that no unintended liability is created. For example, an altered check is not cashable. If a bank cashes such a check, the bank must assume any resulting loss. However, if it can be shown that the maker failed to use reasonable precautions in writing the check, thus making alteration difficult to detect, the maker must assume any loss that would result if the check were altered. Consequently, always type all checks or write them in ink—never in pencil. Follow these steps:

1. Be sure that the *number* of the check corresponds with that on the stub. If the checks are not numbered in printing, number all checks and check stubs upon starting a new checkbook.

2. *Date* the check on the exact date that the check is being written. Occasionally checks are postdated—that is, dated ahead to a time when sufficient funds will be in the checking account. This is a questionable practice, however.

3. The name of the *payee* should be written in full and correctly spelled. If you are not sure of the correct spelling, the information may be obtained from bills, letterheads, or the telephone directory. Omit all titles such as "Mr.," "Mrs.," "Miss," "Dr." On checks payable to a married woman, her given name should be used—make out the check to "Ruth Hill," not to "Mrs. John R. Hill."

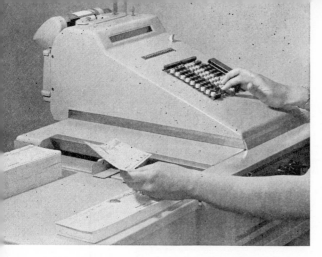

For businesses issuing many checks, complete automated check control is available. In addition to writing, protecting, and signing checks at rates up to 2,000 an hour, the machines date, count, add, and list the checks—then deposit them in a locked vault.

—Burroughs Corporation, Todd Division

4. In writing the *amount*, use large, bold figures written close to the dollar sign and sufficiently close together to prevent the insertion of other figures. In spelling out the amount, start at the extreme left, capitalizing the first letter only, and express cents as fractions of 100:

Three hundred forty and no/100————————————————Dollars

Two hundred thousand eight hundred sixty-four and 65/100—————Dollars

Two thousand seven hundred and 35/100————————————Dollars

Businesses that write a large number of checks usually use a check-writing machine. This machine imprints the amount on the check in such a manner that alteration is impossible. Some businesses, to save time, use specially designed checks that do not provide for the spelling out of the amount.

If a check must be written for less than $1, circle the figure written following the dollar sign. Precede the spelled-out amount with the word "Only," and cross out the word "Dollars" at the end of the line.

5. Fill in with hyphens, periods, or a line all *blank spaces* before and after the amount.

6. The *purpose* of the check, such as "In Payment of Invoice 6824," may be written in the upper left corner, if space permits, or across the end of the check.

Never cross out, erase, or change any part of a check. If an error is made, void the check by writing "VOID" very conspicuously across the face of both the check and the check stub. The voided check should be saved and filed in numerical order with the canceled checks when they are returned from the bank. To type checks, your ribbon should be fresh; it is easy to alter impressions made by a worn ribbon.

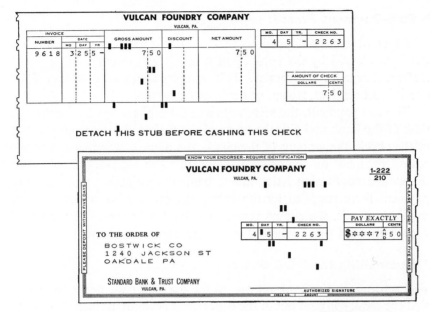

—*IBM Corporation*

A voucher check consists of the check and a detachable stub which shows its purpose. Note that the amount is written only in figures on this check. The punched holes permit the check and the stub to be processed through punched-card equipment that will sort the canceled checks and total and record amounts in appropriate accounts automatically.

Writing Checks for Cash. For a withdrawal from the checking account for the depositor's use, a check is usually written to *Cash* as the payee and signed by the depositor. Such a check is highly negotiable and can be turned into money by anyone into whose hands it may fall. For this reason, utmost care must be taken of checks made out to *Cash*. The bank asks the person receiving the money to indorse the check.

The executive may expect the secretary to see that he is always supplied with cash. On banking days she simply asks, "Do you need money?" If he does, she can write the check and give it to him for signing, unless she is authorized to sign checks. The executive need not indorse these checks if they are payable to *Cash*. His signature as maker is sufficient.

The executive's funds should always be kept separate from the secretary's. One secretary, in order to be sure of the funds she receives from cashing a check, places the money in a pay envelope requested from the teller. This she seals and drops into her purse for "intact" delivery. She takes no chances of spending any of this money.

■ Stop-Payment Procedure on Checks

Payment may be stopped on a check after it has been issued if it has not been cleared by the bank upon which it was drawn. Most banks make a charge for this service. This procedure may be necessary if the check has been lost, stolen, or made out incorrectly.

To stop payment, the secretary should telephone the stop-payment desk of the bank and give the name of the maker, the date and number of the check, the amount of the check, the name of the payee, and the reason payment on the check is stopped. The secretary should then dispatch a confirming letter to the bank immediately or use a stop-payment form supplied by the bank. Before writing a corrected or duplicate check, she should request the bank to examine the canceled checks on hand to see whether or not the check has cleared.

■ Reconciling the Bank Balance

Each month the bank returns to the depositor the canceled checks that the bank has paid out of the depositor's account, a statement listing each deposit and withdrawal, and the service charge for the period. This procedure permits the depositor to check the accuracy of his checkbook with bank records and file his canceled checks as proof of payment.

When the statement and canceled checks are received, the final balance on the statement and the bank balance in the checkbook are compared and the difference between the two records accounted for. This process is called *reconciling the bank balance.*

Procedure. The following is a systematic procedure for making the reconciliation:

1. Compare the amount of each canceled check returned by the bank with the amounts listed on the bank statement. The canceled checks are generally returned in the same order in which they appear on the bank statement so that any bank error in recording a check can be discovered.

2. Arrange the canceled checks in numerical sequence.
   (As a service to customers with large check volume, some banks print the check number in magnetic ink characters. Before returning the canceled checks to the depositor, they run the checks through the sorter, which arranges them in numeric sequence. A bank statement is then printed electronically with checks listed in numeric order and missing check numbers identified. This procedure greatly speeds the bank reconciliation process. There is a small charge for this service.)

3. Compare the returned checks with the stubs in the checkbook. Indicate on the stubs by check mark those checks that have cleared (been returned).

4. Make a list of the outstanding checks—those that have not been paid. Show the number of each such check, the payee, and the amount. Total the outstanding checks.

CUSTOMER'S STATEMENT

THE NATIONAL CITY BANK
CLEVELAND, OHIO

"Good Neighbor Banking"

ACCOUNT NUMBER	CODE	DATE
513-68120	2	APR 30, 19—

HOWARD E. DURST
1283 STATE BUILDING
CLEVELAND, OHIO 44101

NUMBER	CHECKS PAID AMOUNT	OTHER CHARGES	DEPOSITS AND OTHER CREDITS	DATE	BALANCE
			FROM PREVIOUS STATEMENT		1,300.00*
⊣⊣⊣⊣	125.00 7.16 21.65 17.87			4/1/— 4/6/—	1,175.00* 1,167.84* 1,146.19*
⊣⊣	46.20 18.40		184.75	4/9/— 4/12/— 4/13/—	1,128.32* 1,313.07* 1,266.87* 1,248.47*
⊣⊣	75.00 33.65		100.00	4/19/— 4/23/—	1,348.47 1,273.47* 1,239.82*
⊣⊣⊣⊣	66.80 5.30 208.85 33.19	1.21SC	288.70	4/27/— 4/28/— 4/30/—	1,528.52* 1,461.72* 1,456.42* 1,247.57* 1,214.38* 1,213.17*

NUMBER	CHECKS PAID AMOUNT	OTHER CHARGES	DEPOSITS AND OTHER CREDITS	ITEMS ENCLOSED	BALANCE THIS STATEMENT
12	662.07	1.21	573.45	12	1,213.17,

DO 100   SC – SERVICE CHARGE   RV - REVERSED ENTRY   OD - OVERDRAFT

PLEASE RECONCILE THIS STATEMENT ON THE REVERSE SIDE AT ONCE. IF NO ERRORS ARE REPORTED WITHIN TEN DAYS THE ACCOUNT WILL BE CONSIDERED CORRECT.

The monthly bank statement shows the checks paid, the deposits received, and any other deductions made from the account, such as the $1.21 service charge.

MONTH _April_ 196—

THIS FORM IS PROVIDED TO HELP YOU BALANCE
YOUR BANK STATEMENT

* CHECKS OUTSTANDING – NOT
  CHARGED TO ACCOUNT

No.		
41	$	19.25
52		26.80
53		49.95
TOTAL	$	96.00

BANK BALANCE $ 1,213.17

ADD +

DEPOSITS NOT CREDITED
IN THIS STATEMENT $ 200.00
(IF ANY)

TOTAL $ 1,413.17

SUBTRACT –

→ CHECKS OUTSTANDING $ 96.00

BALANCE $ 1,317.17

CHECK BOOK BALANCE $ 1,318.38

DEDUCT:
SERVICE CHARGE   1.21

OTHER CHARGES NOT
PREVIOUSLY ENTERED   —
IN CHECK BOOK

CHECK BOOK BALANCE $ 1,317.17

* OUTSTANDING CHECKS ARE CHECKS WHICH HAVE NOT YET BEEN RECEIVED BY THE BANK.
  THEY CAN BE DETERMINED IN THE FOLLOWING MANNER.
  1. SORT CHECKS ENCLOSED INTO NUMERICAL ORDER ACCORDING TO CHECK NUMBER.
  2. OBTAIN AMOUNTS FOR MISSING NUMBERS (OUTSTANDING CHECKS) FROM YOUR
     CHECKBOOK RECORD AND ENTER ABOVE.

Printed on the back of many bank statements is a convenient form for reconciling the bank balance.

5. **Deduct the total of the outstanding checks from the balance as shown by the bank.** The remainder should be the balance appearing on the last stub for the period being reconciled, unless a service charge is involved.

6. **If a service charge has been made, it is listed among the withdrawals on the bank statement, and a form itemizing the charge will be among the canceled checks.** Subtract the amount of the service charge and any other deductions made by the bank from the checkbook stub balance on the computation sheet. The resulting figure should agree with the adjusted bank balance.

As shown in the illustration on the right, an entry must now be made in the check stubs *deducting this service charge*, preferably after the last written check (not after the last check written during the period being reconciled, because that would mean changing the stub balance on all of the subsequent checks).

Many banks print, on the back of the bank statement, instructions and a form for reconciling the bank balance. This printed form may be used, or the reconcilement may be typed on a separate sheet and attached to the bank statement.

No. 53		$32.50
Date May 3, 19--		
To Lenox Opticians		
For Prescription sunglasses		

	DOLLARS	CENTS
Bal. Bro't For'd	840	30
Amt. Deposited	93	00
TOTAL	933	30
Amt. this Check	32	50
Bal. Car'd For'd	900	80
LESS SERVICE CHG.		.95
CARRIED FOR'D		899.85

Locating Errors. If the two adjusted balances—statement and stub—do not agree, first check the computation on the reconciliation sheet to make sure there is no error. If there is none, make sure that:

No check has been omitted in the reconciliation. Go through the check stubs (one by one) and see that each one is included among the checks either cleared or outstanding.

No deposit has been omitted. Cross check the deposits in the check stubs with those on the bank statement.

If deposits are made by mail, a deposit in the mail on the date your bank statement is prepared would not appear on the statement. This deposit should be added to the bank statement balance on the reconciliation sheet.

If there is still an error, either the bank has made an arithmetical error in the statement, or more likely there is an error in the stubs. First check the accuracy of the amounts forwarded on each check-stub page. If these are correct, the arithmetical computations for each stub should be examined. When the error is located, mark the stub where it occurs: "Error—should be $_____; corrected on Stub #_____." Then make the compensating adjustment on the last stub.

Enter the amount of the error on the reconciliation statement and show where the error occurs and where it is corrected in the check stubs. After the proper check stub (the last transaction covered by the bank statement), write "Agrees with bank statement, (*date*)." The beginning of the next month's work of reconciliation will then be easily found.

Filing. The bank reconciliation must be readily available so that, when the next reconciliation needs to be made, the record of outstanding checks at the beginning of the preceding month can be checked to see if the checks have been returned. Canceled checks may be kept inside the folded bank statements with the reconciliations and filed chronologically. Another filing procedure is to file the statements and reconciliations separately and to file the canceled checks numerically. Canceled checks must be saved, as they are evidences of payment; they constitute legal receipts. (A recommended retention is for six years, but many companies retain checks for fifteen years or more.)

■ Bank Safe-Deposit Boxes

Frequently the executive rents a *safe-deposit box* from his bank. This is a metal box locked by two keys into a small compartment in the bank's safe-deposit vault. The bank has very strict ru.es about access to safe-deposit boxes. The customer must register each time he goes to his box; a bank guard accompanies him to the box, opens one of the locks with his key, and opens the other lock with the customer's key. The box itself is then removed and taken by the customer to a private room. Ordinarily securities, wills, insurance policies, notes, gems, and other small valuable articles are protected by safe-deposit storage. Rent is usually billed annually and is deducted from the customer's checking account if he has one.

The executive must sign a special banking form if he wishes his secretary to have access to his safe-deposit box. She may have two responsibilities relative to safe-deposit-box work: (1) to maintain a perpetual inventory of its contents in duplicate, one copy to be kept in the box, the other in her office; and (2) to guard the key carefully.

■ Special Bank Services

Some banks provide a number of special services that are available to the bank's checking-account customers.

One-Check Payroll Service. If a number of employees maintain checking accounts at the same bank, a one-check payroll plan may be used. In place of writing a separate check for each employee, the employer sends the bank one check covering several employees. A list of the employees and the amount to be deposited to each account is attached to the check. The bank then deposits the amount to the employee's account.

Dividend Deposit Plan. Banks will collect dividend payments for customers. Under this plan, the stockholder requests the companies in which he holds stock to send all dividend payments directly to the bank for deposit in his checking account.

Freight Payment Service. Companies that have a large number of freight bills find it difficult to process the paper work and make payment within the time limit established by the Interstate Commerce Commission. Some banks provide a freight-payment service. The carrier sends the freight bill directly to the customer's bank. The bank deducts the amount of the bill from the customer's account and credits it to the carrier. Monthly, the bank sends to the customer a complete listing of all freight bills paid and charged to his account. Corrections for overcharges and unapproved bills are made at that time.

Paying Bills

An executive seldom turns over his personal bill paying to a new secretary. It is one of the responsibilities that a secretary earns. Frequently the responsibility is a gradually assumed one. First, the secretary may be asked to address the envelopes. Then when the executive is rushed, he may say, "Will you write these checks for me?" It is then that the secretary has a chance to show that she is capable of handling this responsibility. *Bill paying* consists of:

1. Verifying the items and checking the computations on each bill
2. Filling in the check stub, being sure to itemize and identify the expenditure so that the stub record will be usable in preparing accounting records or income tax returns
3. Making out the check
4. Writing on the face of the invoice or the statement the date, the number, and the amount of the check used in payment

5. Addressing the envelope
6. Tearing off the stub of the bill that is to be mailed with the check
7. Attaching the stub from the bill to the check and inserting both under the flap of an addressed envelope ready for presentation to the executive for signature

▪ Verifying Bills

When the executive gives bills to the secretary to pay, she can assume that he approves their payment; but she should verify the prices, the terms, the extensions, and the additions. The bills may be invoices, statements, or just plain bills.

Invoices—itemized listings of goods purchased from another business firm—should be checked with the prices and terms quoted or with records of previous prices paid. The secretary should also carefully check monthly statements showing the amount due at the beginning of the month, purchases and payments made during the month, and the unpaid balance at the end of the month. She should compare figures on the monthly statements with invoices covering purchases during the month and the record of payments made on the account.

RICE SUPPLY COMPANY, INC.

146 Ohio Avenue
Cleveland

Sold to Continental Products
320 Euclid Avenue
Des Moines, Iowa 50313

Terms Net 30 days

Date January 11, 19--

No. 48639

Shipped Via Delivered

	DESCRIPTION	UNIT PRICE	AMOUNT
5 gals.	Excello Paint - White	5.20	26.00 ✓
2 qts.	Excello Varnish	1.90	3.80 ✓
			29.80 ✓

Paid 2/8/--
Check # 86

This invoice is ready for filing. The check marks indicate that the extensions have been checked. The number and date of the check sent in payment has been noted.

Bills for services (utility companies, for example,) are usually accepted as they are, although the toll statement with the telephone bill is checked very carefully. Before paying bills for professional services such as those of doctor and lawyer, the secretary should obtain the personal approval of the executive.

▪ Credit-Card Statements

Many business and professional men use credit cards. They are especially convenient to the executive while he travels because he doesn't have to carry so much cash. (See also page 391.) Credit-card charges also are helpful in preparing expense reports and in verifying expenditures for income tax reporting.

When a purchase is made with the credit card, the purchaser signs a bill or receipt and is given a copy. Later a monthly statement for all credit-card purchases, accompanied with the signed receipts or bills, is mailed to the executive. The executive may delegate to the secretary the responsibility for checking his monthly credit-card statement. If he does, she should carefully examine the signature on each receipt or bill that supports each charge on the statement and compare each amount with that shown on the copy received at the time the purchase was made.

▪ Filing Paid Bills

Some logical system should be set up for filing paid bills, for they provide the key to the canceled checks. If there are only from ten to twenty bills each month, the secretary can place all of them in one file folder. If there are many, she may set up an alphabetic file for them; or she may use a subject file, keeping together all of the utility bills, the insurance bills, the bills for supplies, and so on. Whenever a question arises concerning the payment of a bill, the secretary should be able to locate the annotated bill giving the check number and then to get the canceled check from the files for evidence.

▪ Other Forms Used for Making Payments

Although most of the payments handled by the secretary will probably be made by ordinary check, she may on occasion use one of several special checks or money-order forms that can be obtained at the bank (usually at a nominal charge).

No. 263   The Southern Trust Co.   69-371 / 515

Charleston _May 18_ 19--

Pay to the order of _Penwood Supply Company_ $65.25

Sixty-five and 25/100 ———————— Dollars

CERTIFIED
THE SOUTHERN TRUST CO.
N. A. Clarke CASHIER

L. R. Harris

⑆ 0515⑆0371⑈ 9992⑈52071⑈

Certified checks are used when payment of a sum of money is required to bind a contract, to guarantee fulfillment of a contract, or to make settlement between stock brokers, bond dealers, and others. A stop-payment order cannot be issued against a certified check.

Certified Check. A regular depositor's check that is guaranteed by the bank on which it is drawn is called a *certified check*. To obtain such a check, the secretary takes the executive's personal check to the bank and asks that it be certified. After investigating the account to see that sufficient funds cover the check, a bank official stamps on the face of the check "CERTIFIED," adds an official signature, and immediately charges the account with the amount of the check.

Official Check. A check written by the bank on its own funds is known as an *official check* (sometimes known as a cashier's or treasurer's check). Such a check may be issued to a bank customer who does not have a checking account. The amount of the check plus a service fee is paid to the bank clerk, who then writes the check to the payee requested and gives it to the customer. This form is most frequently used to transfer relatively large sums of money. Banks use official checks to pay their own expenses.

In making a payment to another firm or individual, the secretary should request that the official's check be made payable to the executive or his firm; it should then be endorsed in full over to the other person. The check then stands as a receipt that payment has been made.

Official Check

NEW YORK, N. Y. _April 11,_ 19--   № 2492

Union National Bank   1-30 / 210

PAY TO THE ORDER OF _David A. Stewart_ $178.50

The sum of $178 and 50 cts ———————— DOLLARS

OFFICIAL CHECK   _Raymond P. Bateman_ CASHIER

⑆0210⑆0030⑈ 323   940 8⑈

Bank Draft

No. 195   **First National Bank**   13-1
                                                    420
                  Camden, Ohio___ June 20, ___19__

PAY TO THE
  ORDER OF _Consolidated Lamp Co_ $ 1247. 55

          The sum of $1247 and 55 cts _____DOLLARS

TO
FIRST NATIONAL BANK   } Charles L. Grosvenor
  CINCINNATI, OHIO   CASHIER

I:0420—000 I: I03—404—7I"

Bank Draft. A *bank draft* is a check written by the bank on its account in another bank located in the same or in another city. A purchaser pays the bank the exact amount of the draft plus a small fee for issuing the draft. Properly indorsed, the bank draft can then be cashed at the bank on which it is drawn. It is used for the same purpose as an official check and differs only in that the bank draft is drawn by the bank on funds it has on deposit in another bank while an official check is drawn by the cashier on funds in his own bank.

When there is need to transfer funds quickly, the bank can telegraph (cable, if to a foreign country) its corresponding bank in another city directing it to transfer funds to a designated person or company.

Bank Money Order. A *bank money order* (*personal money order* or *registered check*) is similar to that issued by the post office but less expensive. It is also similar to an official check, except that it is sold to the general public, rather than to customers of the bank only. This form may normally be cashed at any other bank—at home or abroad; it is negotiable and may be transferred by indorsement. The amount of a single bank money order is generally not more than $200, but there is no restriction on the number of bank money orders that may be issued to the same person to be sent to the same payee. The purchaser is given a receipt for his records.

Bank Money Order

PERSONALIZED MONEY ORDER

THE FIRST NATIONAL BANK   50-31
                                      213

PAY TO THE   SYRACUSE, N.Y. May 9, 19___ NO. 299003
  ORDER OF   _The Collier Corporation_
NOT VALID FOR AMOUNT OVER 1 NO HUNDRED DOLLARS

          The sum of $22 and 5 0 cts

                          Richard Dean
                                SIGNATURE
                621 Carey Ct., Syracuse, NY
                                ADDRESS

I:0213—003 I: I36   I8904"

PERSONALIZED MONEY ORDER

The bank money order is more frequently used than an official check or a bank draft when the amount of money transferred is relatively small. It differs from an official check in that the names of both the purchaser and the payee appear on the money order.

In addition to the forms discussed here, payments may be made by other money orders (postal, telegraph, or express); or cash may be sent by registered mail under special circumstances. Refer to the index of this book for further explanation of these methods of payment.

Payment via Telephone. Automated Credit Exchange (ACE) Systems are being developed whereby it will be possible for bank customers to pay bills by telephone. Special card-dialing telephones and dialing cards will make it possible for the bank customer to transfer funds from his checking account to the business to whom the payment is to be made without writing a check. When this system comes into wide use, it will greatly reduce the volume of checks that are handled daily in business.

The Petty Cash Fund

Payments of small amounts for postage, bus and taxi fare, collect telegrams, donations, delivery charges, and incidental office supplies are frequently made from a *petty cash fund*. In many instances the fund is entrusted to the secretary.

The size of the fund will vary according to the demands made upon it. If the fund is large, it should be kept in a locked cash box and stored in the office safe or vault at night. If it is a small amount, it can be kept in a small box or an envelope. In any event, the fund should be locked at night in a desk drawer, a file drawer, or the safe.

▪ Petty Cash Records

The petty cash fund is usually set up with a stipulated amount, such as a $10 fund. Each replenishment of the depleted fund brings it up to $10 again. For example, after the secretary has disbursed $8.50 from the fund, she has on hand $1.50. The reimbursement check to the petty cash fund is for $8.50. The executive may prefer to write a check for a full $10 each time, or he may give the secretary $10 one time, $5 another, and $15 still another. As long as the fund is purely personal, its size can be kept as desired.

Each expenditure should have a receipt covering it for an accounting record. If receipts are used consistently, the total money in the cash box plus the total of the receipts should equal the amount of the fund.

PETTY CASH VOUCHER   No. 56

$ *3.00*   Date *January 4, 19--*

PAID TO *Post Office*

FOR: *Stamps*

Received Payment *R. L. Reed*

Pads of petty cash vouchers (or receipt forms) may be obtained at a stationery store.

A record of the receipts and the disbursements must be kept. The record should be balanced whenever the funds get low, or periodically if the executive prefers. Some of the expenses itemized in a petty cash record may be deductible on the income tax return, and for that reason the records are filed for examination at tax-return time. A record of petty cash is usually kept in the form similar to that illustrated.

Petty cash entries should be made at once, for they are quite difficult to recall if postponed.

PETTY CASH RECORD

Date		Explanation	Received	Paid
Jan. 19--	4	Check #15	10 —	
	4	Stamps		3 —
	8	Book on flower gardening		3 25
	20	Contribution to flowers for R. J.		50
	26	Magnifying glass		1 75
	26	Totals	10 —	8 60
	26	Balance		1 50
			10 —	10 —
	26	Balance	1 50	
	26	Check #34	8 50	

There should be a receipt for each item listed in the Paid column of the petty cash record.

■ Petty Cash Report

When the petty cash fund is replenished, the secretary should prepare a summary report of the payments that have been made.

```
        PETTY CASH REPORT (JANUARY 4-26, 19--)

Balance on hand (1/4/--) . . . . . . . . . . .  $10.00

Expenditures:

    Stamps . . . . . . . . . $3.00
    Book . . . . . . . . . .  3.25
    Flowers. . . . . . . .     .50
    Magnifying glass . . . .  1.75          8.50
Balance on hand (1/26/--). . . . . . . . . . .  $ 1.50
```

Credit and Collection Instruments

The executive secretary's financial responsibilities may extend to such credit and collection instruments as notes, drafts, and certificates of deposit. Because these papers can be transferred or negotiated by the holder to someone else, they (together with checks and other substitutes for cash, such as bank drafts and money orders) are known as *negotiable instruments*.

■ Notes

A *promissory note*, more commonly referred to as a note, is a promise by one person (known as the *maker*) to pay a certain sum of money on demand or at a fixed or determinable future date to another person or party (known as the *payee*). A promissory note is illustrated below.

$660 00   Phoenix, Arizona   August 7,   19.

Four months   AFTER DATE I PROMISE TO PAY TO
THE ORDER OF James Bailey
Six hundred sixty 00/100   DOLLARS
PAYABLE AT Second National Bank
VALUE RECEIVED WITH INTEREST AT 6 %
NO. 13   DUE December 7, 19.   Robert Shaw

Frequently collateral is requested to pledge the payment of a note. In this case the instrument is called a *collateral note*. Collateral can be salable securities (stocks, bonds), a real estate mortgage, or anything that represents ownership and is exchangeable. When an obligation is fully paid, the collateral is returned to the borrower. If it is not paid, the creditor can convert the collateral into cash.

Some notes are interest bearing. On these the interest is paid at maturity when the *face* of the note is due. If a note is noninterest-bearing, the agency making the loan deducts the interest in advance (known as the *discount*) from the face of the note. The remainder is called the *proceeds*. For instance, a borrower who gives a bank a three-month, noninterest-bearing note for $1,000 would receive $985 if the discount is figured at the rate of 6 percent.

The amount and the date of a partial payment on a note are written on the back of the note. When the secretary makes a partial payment on a note for the executive, she should make certain the payment is recorded on the back of the note in her presence, for the note is held by the lender until it is paid in full. If she makes the payment in full, the indorsed note should be turned over to her, for then it is a legal record that the obligation has been discharged.

▪ Drafts

A draft is a written order by one person on another to pay a sum of money to a third person. There are two major types—commercial drafts and trade acceptances.

Commercial Drafts. A commercial draft is largely used as a collection device. In the commercial draft illustration on this page, Ankromm and Son owe $539.62 to King and Wilson, who give this draft to their bank in Topeka for collection. The bank forwards it to their correspondent bank in St. Louis, which presents it for payment to Ankromm and Son. When the draft is paid, the proceeds are forwarded to the Topeka bank and thence to King and Wilson.

This draft is a *sight draft* for it instructs that it is to be paid "at sight." A *time draft* is payable at some future time and reads "thirty days after date" or some other stipulated period of time.

Drafts are frequently used as a means of collecting before delivery of goods shipped by freight. The merchandise is shipped on an order bill of lading, which requires that the receiver present the original copy of the bill of lading to the railroad company before obtaining possession of the merchandise. The bill of lading with the draft attached is sent to the bank in the town of the buyer. When the merchandise arrives, the purchaser pays the draft at the bank, obtains the bill of lading, and claims possession of his goods at the freight office.

Trade Acceptances. When a commercial time draft is drawn upon a customer at the time of a sale, the instrument is known as a *trade acceptance*. It differs from other drafts in three respects:

1. **The trade acceptance always grows out of the purchase of merchandise.**
2. **The trade acceptance is always accompanied by a bill for the goods sold.**
3. **The trade acceptance is never given in payment of old accounts or in return for a loan.**

A trade acceptance is illustrated below.

TRADE ACCEPTANCE

No. 62 Jackson, Mississippi, March 17, 19--

TO The Hall Hardware Co. Lansing, Michigan

ON April 16, 19-- PAY TO THE ORDER OF Ourselves

Five hundred forty-seven 28/100---------------------- DOLLARS ($547.28)

The transaction which gives rise to this instrument is the purchase of goods by the acceptor from the drawer. The drawee may accept this bill payable at any bank, banker, or trust company in the United States which he may designate.

ACCEPTED AT Lansing ON March 19, 19--

PAYABLE AT Lansing State BANK

BANK LOCATION Lansing, Michigan

BUYER'S SIGNATURE The Hall Hardware Co.

BY AGENT OR OFFICER C. R. Tate, Sec'y.

Long & Humphrey

BY D. M. Long

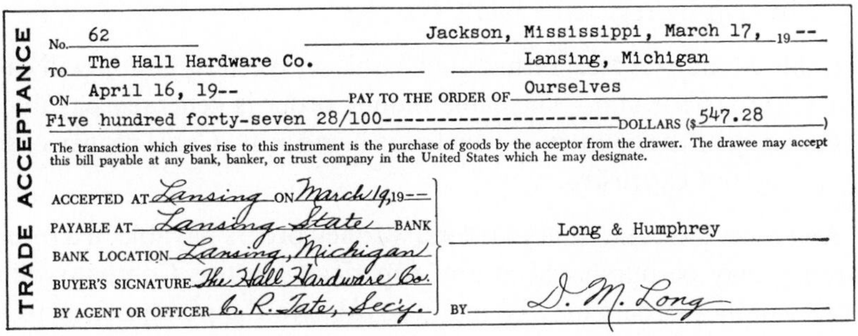

■ Certificates of Deposit

A certificate of deposit is a promissory note issued by a bank to a depositor. It is negotiable (ownership may be transferred from one party to another by indorsement and delivery) as it contains the five basic elements of a negotiable instrument, which are listed on page 552.

1. **It must be in writing and be signed by the maker or drawer.**
2. **It must contain an unconditional promise or order to pay a definite sum.**
3. **It must be payable on demand or at a fixed or at a determinable future time.**
4. **It must be payable to order or to bearer.**
5. **It must identify the drawee with reasonable certainty.**

▪ Discounting Notes and Drafts

Many business firms accept notes, time drafts, and trade acceptances from customers in payment for merchandise and convert these instruments into cash before they are due for payment. This is done by "selling the paper" to the bank. The bank deducts interest (discount) and gives the business firm the cash proceeds. The bank, in turn, holds the paper until maturity and collects from the customer.

The ownership of notes and drafts is transferred by indorsement in the same manner as for checks.

▪ Foreign Remittances

When a payment or remittance is to be made to a person or business firm in a foreign country, the following forms of payment may be used.

Currency. United States currency, or foreign currency purchasable through your local bank, may be sent abroad. Most foreign countries regulate the amount of currency that may be so transferred. Your bank will advise you as to the legal restrictions. Currency payments, of course, would be sent by registered mail.

Cable Money Order. Either your bank or Western Union will cable money abroad for you. The cable money order is generally payable in the currency of the country to which it is being sent. Cable money orders are speedy but expensive.

American Express Money Orders. Money orders payable in a foreign currency may be purchased at any American Express Company office. Express money orders may be made payable to the purchaser or to another person or firm. American Express will arrange for the transfer of the money order to the person or firm in the foreign country to whom it is payable by cable, airmail, or mail; or the purchaser, if he elects, may receive the money order and transfer it by mail or some other means. Express money orders are payable in the foreign country at the office of the American Express Company or at the bank in the foreign country identified in the money order.

Foreign Bank Draft. A bank draft payable in a foreign currency may be purchased at your local bank. As with currency, most foreign countries limit the amount of money which may be transferred. The bank will arrange for the transfer of the draft; or the purchaser, if he elects, may transfer it by mail or by some other means. This method of payment or transfer of funds would be used when large amounts are involved.

Suggested Readings ─────────────

Office Work in the Field of Banking, Manpower White Glove Training Manual. Milwaukee: Manpower Inc., 1965, 48 pp.

Savage, William G., and others. *Business Review for Professional Secretaries.* New York: Pitman Publishing Corporation, 1959, pp. 111–119, 149–158.

Turner, Bernice C. *Private Secretary's Manual.* Englewood Cliffs, New Jersey: Prentice-Hall, Inc., 1963, pp. 158–179.

Questions for Discussion ─────────

1. As Miss Hill, a secretary, was leaving for lunch her employer, Mr. Roger, asked her to deposit his salary check in the bank. Mr. Roger indorsed the check by writing his name on the back of the check. Miss Hill placed the check in her purse. While at lunch and before the deposit was made, Miss Hill's purse was either lost or stolen.

   (a) What poor business practices were evident in this situation?
   (b) Upon discovery of the loss, what should the secretary do?

2. What precautions or safeguards should a secretary observe in writing checks? Explain why each precaution is important.

3. A secretary follows the practice of placing all personal bills (home expenses, charge accounts, and so forth) of her employer on his desk when received. She makes no follow-up on them on the basis that she has no responsibility for her employer's personal financial matters. Would you agree with the secretary's evaluation of her responsibility?

4. In preparing a reconciliation of the bank statement, the secretary notes that one check for $1.50 has been outstanding for several months. What, if anything, should the secretary do in relation to this check?

5. On a check stub certain items are added to the previous balance and other items are subtracted from the previous balance. Name as many plus items (additions) and as many minus items (subtractions) as you can.

6. Indicate the steps that should be followed in replenishing the petty cash fund. Include (a) method of proving the petty cash fund, (b) procedure for determining the amount required to replenish the fund, and (c) description of the check that would be written to replenish the fund.

7. Do you think that the secretary is ever justified in borrowing for her personal use from the petty cash fund?

8. Explain the difference between (a) a certified check and a personal check, and (b) a commercial draft and a trade acceptance. In what business situations would you use a certified check?

9. When a bank draft is purchased, it may be drawn in favor of the person or business to whom payment is being made, or in favor of the person making the payment and indorsed by him to the creditor. Which do you think is the better method? Why?

10. A fruit grower located in Portland, Oregon, is shipping by railway a large quantity of fruit to a dealer in Chicago. He wishes to be certain of obtaining payment for the fruit before it is delivered to the dealer. The dealer, in turn, wants the fruit delivered in Chicago before he makes payment. Outline the procedure that would be followed by the shipper and by the buyer (dealer) in handling this transaction.

11. If necessary, correct the following. Then use the Reference Guide to check your answers.

   (a) Deposits reached a new high during the month of May.

   (b) Working together in such close proximity caused friction between the two tellers.

   (c) The posting machines are both alike in appearance.

   (d) The action of the court bars out the possibility of our obtaining an early settlement.

   (e) Enclosed herewith is our certified check in payment of the account.

Problems

■ **1.** A deposit includes the following checks, bills, and coins:

Checks

27-10	$124.80
45-12	16.25
27-10	115.25
14-8	76.10

Bills

4	$20 bills
16	$10 bills
21	$5 bills
155	$1 bills

Coins

19	Halves
62	Quarters
73	Dimes
45	Nickels
103	Pennies

(a) Indicate how the checks should be indorsed for deposit in the First National Bank by Continental Products.

(b) For each denomination of bills give (1) the number of bills that would be wrapped, (2) the value of the wrapped bills, (3) the number of unwrapped bills, (4) the value of the unwrapped bills, (5) the value of all bills of all denominations.

(c) Follow the same instructions for the coins.

(d) Determine the total amount of the deposit.

(e) Indicate specifically how the bills and coins in the deposit would be presented to the bank teller.

■ **2.** Prepare the reconciliation of the bank statement.

The bank statement showed a balance of $948.39 on March 31. Examination of the bank statement provided the following information: A deposit for $211.80 made by mail on March 31 was not shown on the statement. A service charge for $3.50 had been deducted by the bank. The bank had also deducted $12 rent for a safe deposit box and $6.50 for printing of checkbooks. All checks written were returned with the bank statement with the exception of checks No. 87 for $118.20, No. 96 for $178.48, and No. 97 for $1.92.

The check-stub balance on March 31 was $883.59.

Related Work Assignments 60-63 ────────────

60. Preparing Deposit Slips. Prepare duplicate deposit slips, listing the checks, bills, and coins given in Problem 1 to the account of Continental Products. If possible, type the deposit slip and use carbon paper for making the duplicate. Use the current date.

61. Writing Checks. Assume that you are employed in the branch office of Continental Products located in your community. Write the checks listed on this page. Use the current date, and sign the checks with your own name. If possible, type the checks. The checkbook balance is $4,851.25.

Check No. 1000 — $5 to the gas company for connecting the gas meter
  "   " 1001 — $100 to the Reliable Plumbing Company for repairs
  "   " 1002 — $15 to the water company for the water assessment for the year
  "   " 1003 — $50.50 to Miss Julia Blackburn for special decorating services
  "   " 1004 — $6.50 to the light company for the electric bill
  "   " 1005 — $2,070.85 to the National Building and Loan Association of
             Chicago for payment on a loan
  "   " 1006 — $3.50 to the telephone company for a telephone connection
  "   " 1007 — $.75 to Mrs. Elsa Hill for Continental Products' contribution
             to a benefit

62. Keeping a Petty Cash Record. Your office had the following petty cash transactions during the month of May:

May   1. Had cash on hand, $10.
      3. Paid 20¢ for insuring a parcel-post package.
      4. Paid the Modern Office Supply Company $2.15 for miscellaneous office sup-
         plies.
      8. Purchased flowers for the bookkeeper, $2.50.
     10. Paid postage due, 15¢.
     12. Purchased a bottle of ink, 25¢; and a diary for Mr. Robert L. Simpson, 75¢.
     16. Purchased stamps, $3.
     17. Cashed a check for $9 to reimburse the petty cash fund.
     19. Paid $4 for having the windows washed.
     21. Paid postage due, 10¢.
     24. Paid $1.23 for express charges on merchandise returned.
     26. Paid $3.50 for typewriter repairs.
     29. Paid 50¢ for a duplicate office key.
     31. Cashed a check to bring the balance of the petty cash fund up to $10.

   (a) Rule a simple petty cash record form similar to that illustrated on page 548.
   (b) Record the petty cash transactions. Rule and balance the record, and carry
       forward the balance each time that the fund is renewed. Prepare the May 17
       and May 31 petty cash reports.

63. Reconciling the Bank Account. The instructions and supplies necessary for the completion of this assignment are provided in the Workbook.

Ch. 23 Assisting with Investments and Insurance

Accurate records of all securities, real estate, and insurance transactions are important to an employer. He must report on his tax return all the income he received from such sources. The dates when securities are bought and sold, as well as the amounts, are necessary to determine whether there has been a long-term or a short-term capital gain. Supporting papers must be retained for tax-liability proof.

The insurance portfolio of an executive usually includes several types of insurance and may involve a number of policies. Premium payments must be made when due, to avoid lapsing of the insurance. Thus, records are required.

Securities and insurance policies represent valuable documents that must be kept in a safe place and their whereabouts carefully recorded so that they may be obtained immediately when needed.

The executive may delegate many of these responsibilities to his secretary. He may expect his secretary to share his interest in the market fluctuations and his enthusiasm for the financial section of the newspaper. Even if an employer handles his own security and insurance records, a secretary should be familiar with investment procedures and insurance. She should also familiarize herself with the market "lingo" used in financial reports of stock market activities.

Securities

Many executives have investments in securities—stocks and bonds. *Stocks* are evidence of ownership in a company. *Bonds* are evidence of creditorship—that is, a loan to a company.

▪ Stocks

Ownership in a corporation is divided into units known as shares of stock. A stockholder is an owner of one or more shares of stock, and his ownership is evidenced by a certificate known as a *stock certificate*.

The stockholder receives *dividends* in return for his investment in the corporation. Dividends are paid from the earnings of the company and are paid in cash or in additional stock referred to as a *stock dividend*.

Kinds of Stock. Stocks fall into two general classes, *common* and *preferred*. Holders of common stock are usually the only ones who have the right to vote in the stockholders' meetings. The rate of dividends paid on common stock is not fixed.

Preferred stock has a fixed dividend rate. It also has a preference over common stock in first payment of dividends and in the first distribution of assets if the company is liquidated. Preferred stock may be *cumulative* or *noncumulative*. When the stock is cumulative, any dividends on preferred stock that are not paid accumulate and must be paid before any distribution can be made to common stockholders. Noncumulative preferred stock does not contain a provision to pay dividends in arrears.

Preferred stock also may be *participating* or *nonparticipating*. It is participating only if the stockholder is entitled to share with the common stockholders in any additional dividend disbursement after an agreed rate is paid on the common stock.

Some preferred stock is *convertible*; that is, the owner has the privilege of converting it into a specified number of shares of common stock at any time he chooses. Most preferred stocks are *callable*; that is, they are redeemable at the option of the issuing corporation.

Stock may be *par-value* or *no-par-value* stock. *Par value* refers to a value ($5, $10, $100) printed on the stock certificate. This printed value has no significance in determining the market price of the stock. Many companies today, therefore, do not print any value on their common stock. It is then known as *no-par stock*.

Stockholders' Meetings. Stockholders' meetings are held annually. Members of the board of directors are elected at this meeting by the stockholders present in person or by proxy. The board, in turn, elects the officers of the company at one of its regular meetings.

A notice of the stockholders' meeting, accompanied by a proxy form and a proxy statement, is sent to each stockholder entitled to vote. The notice gives a description of the business that is to be transacted. A *proxy* is a legal instrument assigning one's voting privilege to a specified person or persons. If directors of the corporation are to be elected, the proxy statement indicates the names of the persons nominated for whom the stockholder's proxy will be voted.

P
R
O
X
Y

PLEASE MARK, SIGN ON
REVERSE SIDE AND RE-
TURN PROMPTLY IN THE
ACCOMPANYING ENVELOPE.

PROXY   PHILLIPS PETROLEUM COMPANY   PROXY

ANNUAL MEETING – APRIL 26, 19—

The undersigned hereby appoints K. S. ADAMS, PAUL ENDACOTT, STANLEY LEARNED and RAYBURN L. FOSTER as proxy holders with power of substitution, or, if all do not act on a matter, those who do act, to vote all stock which the undersigned could vote at the Company's annual stockholders' meeting to be held in the Adams Building, Bartlesville, Oklahoma, on April 26, 19—, at 10:00 A. M., and at any adjournment thereof:

(1) For the election of fifteen Directors as specified in the Proxy Statement.

(2) FOR ☑ AGAINST ☐ approval of the proposal to increase the Company's authorized capital stock as described in the Proxy Statement. (Management recommends a vote FOR)

(3) In their discretion on any other matters presented to the meeting not known or determined at the date of the Notice and Proxy Statement, a copy of which has been received by the undersigned.

In the absence of voting instructions for item (2), this proxy will be voted FOR adoption of the proposal.

THIS PROXY IS SOLICITED ON BEHALF OF THE MANAGEMENT
(Continued, and to be signed, or other side)

A proxy is sent to the stockholder for his optional use. The form usually indicates the names of the persons to whom the voting rights are being assigned and, in some cases, provides the stockholder with a place to indicate whether he wishes his stock to be voted for or against certain proposals that are to be decided at the stockholders' meeting.

The stockholder may attend the meeting and vote in person; he may sign and send in the proxy and thus cast his vote; or he may simply choose to do neither and thus fail to vote his stock.

If the executive usually attends the stockholders' meeting, the secretary should see that the date of the meeting is recorded on his calendar. If the meeting is to be held out of town, she should discuss travel arrangements with him.

Annual Reports. Most companies send an annual, and usually also a quarterly, report to stockholders. Such a report usually includes a review of the company's activities and its financial statements.

Some executives study these reports carefully and then have them filed. If this is your employer's habit, file them with other such reports or in the separate folder for that stock.

■ Bonds

A *bond* is a certificate containing a written interest-bearing promise to pay a definite sum of money at a specified time and place. The interest due must be paid to bondholders before stockholders can share in the profits of the company, and for that reason bonds are considered safer investments than stocks. The ownership of bonds does not give the investor voting rights in the company.

There are two general classes of bonds—coupon bonds and registered bonds. *Coupon bonds* are payable to the person holding them. If the bond or the interest coupons are lost or stolen, they can be converted into cash by the holder. Coupon bonds, therefore, present a great responsibility to the secretary who is entrusted to care for them. Bonds should be kept in a safe-deposit box.

Coupons are cut from the bonds on or after their due date and presented at a local bank for collection. Most banks make a small charge for this collection service. Bond coupons can be listed on a bank-deposit slip.

Registered bonds are decidedly less worry to the secretary. Such bonds are registered by the issuing corporation, which mails the interest and principal payments to the registered holders. If the bond is lost, the owner still receives his payments; and the bond certificate can be replaced.

Corporate bonds are usually issued in $1,000 units. The selling price, however, is quoted as though they had a $100 denomination. Thus, if a corporate bond is said to sell at 97⅝, it actually sells at $976.25, a discount of $23.75 from its maturity value.

▪ Stock Market Trading

Most stocks and bonds are purchased and sold through a stock exchange such as the New York Stock Exchange (known as the "Big Board"), the American Stock Exchange (Amex), the Midwest (Chicago) Stock Exchange, the Pacific Coast Stock Exchange and the Toronto Stock Exchange. A number of smaller organized exchanges are found in different parts of the country in large cities. On the New York Stock Exchange only securities listed on the exchange are traded on its floor; the American Stock Exchange and other exchanges permit trading in unlisted securities.

Some stocks and bonds are purchased in the *over-the-counter* market, which is not a place but a method of doing business; that is, the transaction is handled privately through a bank, a broker, or a securities dealer and does not go through any of the stock exchanges. A buyer or seller of the security is located, and the sale price is arrived at by negotiation. Most over-the-counter transactions are limited to unlisted securities (stocks and bonds of relatively small local companies that are not listed on an exchange).

Buying and selling of stocks and bonds on the stock exchange is handled through a *broker*. Stock certificates sold through brokers are not passed from owner to owner; the seller turns in his certificates to the broker who sends them to the transfer agent for cancellation. The transfer agent employed by the corporation is usually a bank, which keeps a

record of the specific owners of stock certificates by names and numbers·
The agent fills in a new certificate with the name supplied to him, writes
in the number of shares the certificate represents, has it signed and
countersigned, and forwards it to the broker for delivery to the new
owner or for deposit to the credit of the owner's account at the brokerage firm. As a service to investors, some brokerage firms will hold all
stock owned by an investor and send him a monthly statement showing
an inventory of his stock and listing the amounts received as dividends
that month.

The term *mutual funds* is used to identify investment companies (or
investment trusts). These investment companies sell shares to individual investors and use capital raised in this manner to purchase
securities in other companies. These stocks and bonds are known as the
portfolio of the investment company. The individual with limited funds
is offered a chance to own (indirectly) an interest in many companies
and types of securities because these investments are diversified among
bonds, preferred stocks, and common stocks, and also among many
corporations.

Specialized mutual funds are available to investors wanting to purchase specialized securities—for instance, insurance, chemicals, or
other stocks offering growth possibilities or high income.

Stock Market Information. The financial pages of leading newspapers print daily the stock transactions at major exchanges. The
number of shares sold and the selling price for all stocks listed and
traded in that day on each exchange are reported. Sales and prices of
bonds are also reported in separate tables.

Stocks listed on the exchange on which there was no trading—that
is, no sales were made of the stock on the day being reported—are
printed under a special "Bid and Asked" section. This section gives the
closing bid and asking price for the stock. For example, AmBak bid
42½, asked 44½. This means no American Baking stock was transferred and that there was an offer to buy at 42½ and an offer to sell
at 44½.

In addition to the daily stock market report and financial news that
appear in the newspapers, information on security prices, trends, and
business conditions may be obtained from such sources as *Wall Street
Journal, Business Week, Barron's, Financial World, Forbes, Magazine of
Wall Street, The Exchange, American Investor, Moody's Stock Survey,*
and *Commercial and Financial Chronicle.* Several large brokerage firms
and some banks also publish special reports on securities.

There are a number of investment advisory services, such as American Investors Service, Babson's Reports Inc., United Business and Investment Service, and Financial World Research Bureau. Most of these organizations analyze the stock market and for a fee provide investors with detailed information on companies, lists of stocks to watch, stocks that represent "good buys," stocks to "sell." They also analyze the individual's stock holdings and provide other data that an investor may need. For detailed information on the type of services available, see the *Directory of Investment Advisory Services*.[1] Such service is also available from the broker with whom an investor identifies.

Market Averages. A number of stock averages are designed to serve as barometers of the stock market—that is, whether the market is moving up or down. Probably the best known are the Standard and Poor's Index and the Dow-Jones Average. The Standard and Poor's Index is based on the price of 500 stocks and is computed hourly each trading day. The Dow-Jones Average is actually four averages—one for industrials (stock of industrial corporations), one for rails, one for utilities, and a composite average which is supposed to measure trends in all divisions of the market. The market averages are published in leading newspapers and are reported on television and by radio.

Market Terminology. In placing orders for the purchase or sale of stock, certain standard terminology is used.

Market Order. A *market order* instructs the broker to buy or sell a security at once. No price is indicated and the order is executed "at the market"; that is—at the best price obtainable.

Limited Order. A limited order instructs the broker to buy or sell a security at a certain price only. If the transaction cannot be consummated at the designated price, the order is not executed.

Day Order. The day order is good only for the day on which it is given; *GTW Order* is "good for this week"; a *GTM Order* is "good this month"; and an *Open Order* (GTC Order) is "good till canceled."

Stop Order. The investor using a stop order instructs the broker to buy or sell "at the market" whenever the security moves to a specified quotation.

---

[1]H. C. Walker, ed., *Directory of Investment Advisory Services* (Rochester, New York: Fir Publishing Company, 1963).

NEW YORK STOCK EXCHANGE TRANSACTIONS

19— High	Low		Sales in 100s	Open	High	Low	Close	Net Chg.
50 ¼	44 ½	Abbott L .90	82	49 ⅛	49 ½	48 ⅛	48 ¼	+ ⅛
118 ½	112 ¾	Abbott L pf 4.50	8	116 ½	116 ⅜	116	116 ¼	− ¼
23 ⅝	17 ⅛	ABC Con. .70	21	22 ⅛	22 ⅛	22 ½	21 ¾	− ¾
93	77 ⅝	ACF Ind 3a	23	88	88 ¼	85 ⅞	85 ⅞	−2 ¼
73 ½	64	Acme Mkt 2b	7	68 ⅛	68 ⅛	68	68	− ⅛
28 ¾	27 ¼	Adam E 2.05g	27	27 ⅞	28 ¼	27 ¾	28 ¼	+ ¼
18 ¼	13 ⅛	Ad Millis. 40a	9	15 ¼	15 ⅜	15 ¼	15 ⅜	− ⅛

| 1 | 2 | 3 | 4 | 5 | 6 | 7 | 8 |

Key

1 The price range (high and low) of the stock in the year to date

2 The name of the company and a description of the stock. The rate of annual dividend paid per share based on the last quarterly or semiannual declaration is listed next. Special and extra dividends are not included unless noted by a legend letter following the dividend rate. Check the legend at the end of the stock listing for interpretation of the letters. The following legend explains the letters used in the illustration above:

    a — Also extra or extras   b — Annual rate plus stock dividend
    g — Declared or paid so far this year   pf — preferred stock

3 The number of shares of stock sold during the day (in hundreds)

4 The price of the first (*opening*) sale of the stock for the day

5 The *highest* price the stock reached during the day. Stock quotations are in eighths of a point (dollar). Thus 76⅛ means a price of $76.125 per share; 76¼ ($76.25); 76½ ($76.50); 76⅝ ($76.625).

6 The *lowest* price for which the stock sold during the day

7 The *last* (*closing*) price for the stock at the end of the day

8 The difference between today's last price and the last price of yesterday. The plus sign (+) indicates an increase in the last price today over yesterday's last price; the minus sign (−) indicates a decrease.

The stock-market-page illustration shown above provides the following information: To this date this year, Abbott Laboratories common stock has sold at a high 50¼ ($50.25) and a low of 44½ ($44.50). The stock paid 90 cents in dividends last year. During the day 8,200 shares were sold. The stock opened at 49⅛ ($49.125). It reached a high of 49½, and the lowest amount for which it sold was 48⅛. The last sale for the day was at 48¼. This was up ⅛ from yesterday's closing.

Short Sale. The investor sells short—that is, sells securities that he does not own in anticipation of buying them later at a lower price. To negotiate the sale, he, or his broker, borrows the stocks temporarily.

Bid and Offer. The price at which a prospective buyer will purchase and the price at which a prospective seller will sell is called *bid and offer.* This quotation involves over-the-counter sales.

Yield. The annual percentage of return that the security will yield if purchased at the current market price is known as the *yield.*

Round and Odd Lots. Most stocks listed on the stock exchanges are traded in 100-share units, called *round lots.* An order for anything less than 100 shares is known as an *odd lot.* A small additional commission charge is made for handling *odd-lot* transactions.

Stock Split. A company may split its stock to lower the market price. In a *stock split,* the company issues to each stockholder a specified number of additional shares for each share he now owns. For example, if it is a three-to-two split, the stockholder will receive three shares in exchange for each two shares he owns.

A Brokerage Transaction. To understand the procedure of a brokerage transaction, let us follow through a hypothetical one in which the secretary shares responsibility.

1. **The purchaser, or his secretary, places an order with the broker to buy 25 shares of U.S. Steel common "at the market," (generally by a telephone call.)**
   (The secretary makes a full memorandum of the order; the date, the time, and the order placed. The broker *executes* the order on that date—the trade date.)

2. **When the broker has made the purchase through the stock exchange, he sends an invoice called a *confirmation* for the purchase of the stock to the buyer.**
   (The invoice or bill for the purchase or sale of securities is called a *confirmation* because the broker is acting as an agent, and he confirms by means of the invoice the instructions given to him. The confirmation lists the name of the stock and description, the number of shares, the price per share, extension, commission charge, tax, postage, and total.
   The *secretary* compares the confirmation with the memorandum of the order to make sure the order has been carried out correctly.)

3. **The purchaser, or his secretary, sends a check to the broker by the settlement date (which is five business days after the trade date).**

4. **The broker arranges for the transfer of the stock to the purchaser.**
   (If the executive has the brokerage company retain the stock, his account will be credited and the stock will be reported on the next monthly inventory statement. If he retains his own stock certificates, the certificate will be forwarded to him by registered mail. If delivery is made to the executive, the secretary, upon receipt of the stock, records the stock certificate number on the confirmation. She transfers all the information from the confirmation to the executive's permanent record.
   The secretary may attach the confirmation to the stock certificate, or she may file the confirmations chronologically under the broker's name so that they will be available when the stock is sold. The sales confirmation may be filed with the executive's copy of his income tax return.)

JAN	FEB	MAR	APR	MAY	JUN	JUL	AUG	SEPT	OCT	NOV	DEC

(Dividend Date)

STOCK: Detroit Edison, common
BROKER: Merrill Lynch   DIVIDENDS: Mar., June,
FILED: Safe deposit box, City National   Sept., Dec.

Date	Certificate Number	How Acquired	No. of Shares	Cost per Share	Total Cost*
1/18/--	H21601	Purchased	100	41 1/2	4,189.75
5/20/--	H29861	New cert. for H21601 after sale 40 shares	60		
12/4/--	H32504	5% stock dividend	3		

*Includes postage, insurance, and commission.

RECORD OF SALES

Date	Shares Sold	Selling Price	Gross Amount	S.E.C. & Taxes	Commission Paid	Net Amt. Received
5/20/--	40	43 3/4	1,750.00	2.43	22.50	1,725.07

A separate record card or sheet for stock transactions should be kept for each lot of securities. Purchases and sales are recorded on the front of the card as illustrated. Dividends are recorded on the ruled form on the back of the card. A metal tab can be used to indicate the dates when dividends may be expected. The card should show where the securities are kept.

Delivery of Securities. When securities held personally by the executive are sold, they are ordinarily delivered to the broker's office by the secretary or by messenger, or are sent by registered mail. Any securities sent by registered mail should be accompanied by a covering letter describing the securities in full, with the owner's name and with such items as the company name, amount, and certificate number for each stock certificate or bond enclosed. A return receipt should be requested at the time of sending the registered letter.

Records of Securities. One good rule for the secretary to follow in keeping financial records for securities is to use a separate page or card for each lot. The illustration given above shows a convenient form and indicates the information that would be recorded on each group of securities.

The "where kept" notation is one of the most valuable bits of information recorded about any valuable paper. Papers tucked away in

```
┌─────────────────────────────────────────────────────────────┐
│               CURRENT LIST OF SECURITIES                     │
│                                                              │
│  Date                      No. of  Cost per                  │
│  Pur.      Security Name    Shares  Share    Total Cost      │
│                                                              │
│  2/12/-  Garrett Industries  200   27 1/2    $2,813.00       │
│                                                              │
│  4/19/-         "            100   29 3/4     3,008.88       │
└─────────────────────────────────────────────────────────────┘
```

Executives usually appreciate having a typed alphabetic list of securities they own immediately available for reference. The secretary may wish to prepare three copies: one for the executive's desk, one for the files, and one for her own records. On such a list, each block of stock acquired at a different date or price is listed separately.

unusual safekeeping spots known only to the owner often remain hidden when they are desperately needed in his absence.

Stock Certificate Numbers.   When all the stock covered by one certificate is sold, the certificate is surrendered to the broker as part of the sale.   When only a portion of a block of stock covered by one certificate is sold, the certificate is also turned over to the broker; but the investor receives a new certificate for a total of the unsold shares. This procedure requires a change in the certificate number on the stock records.   For example, in the stock record illustrated on page 564, the 40 shares that were sold were from the block of 100 shares covered by Certificate Number H21601. This fact was indicated. The new certificate number for the 60 unsold shares is also recorded.

Real Estate

A secretary may be commissioned to do any or all of the tasks incident to the executive's real-estate activities—to care for the valuable papers necessary to real-estate transactions, to do the banking work, and to keep simple, complete records of income and expenses.

▪ Buying Property

When real property is purchased, the title of ownership is transferred by means of a properly executed written instrument known as a *deed*.

Deeds.   There are two types of deeds—warranty deed, and quitclaim deed.   In a *warranty deed* the grantor or seller warrants that he is the true and lawful owner, that he has full power to convey the property, and that the title is clear, free, and unencumbered. In a *quitclaim deed* the grantor quits his claim to the property, that is, relinquishes his claim, but he does not warrant or guarantee the title.

A deed must be signed, witnessed, and acknowledged before a notary public. It should be *recorded*—that is, entered on public record, at the courthouse in the county where the property is located. Deeds, mortgages, and leases are valuable legal documents and should be kept in a bank safe-deposit box or a fireproof office vault or safe.

Legal Terms. Other legal terms frequently used when the title to real estate is transferred are:

Amortization—mortgage or loan repayment plan that permits the borrower through regular payments at stated intervals to retire the principal of the loan

Appurtenances—rights of way or other types of easements that are properly used with the land, the title to which passes with the land

Easements—privileges regarding some special use of another person's property, such as right of way to pass over the land, to use a driveway, or to fish in a stream

Fixtures—those articles that are permanently attached to real estate, such as buildings, fences, and electric wiring in a building

Foreclosure Proceedings—legal process used to satisfy the claim of the lender in case of default in payment of interest or principal on a mortgage

Junior (Second) Mortgage—a mortgage that is subordinate to a prior mortgage

Land Contract—a method of payment for property whereby the buyer makes a small down payment and agrees to pay additional amounts at intervals (The buyer does not get a deed to the property until a substantial amount of the price of the property is paid.)

Mortgages—formal written contracts that transfer interests in property as security for the payment of the debt (Mortgages must be signed, witnessed, and recorded in the public records the same as a deed. The law considers the mortgagor [the borrower] as owner of the property during the period of the loan.)

Option—an agreement under which an owner of property gives another person the right to buy the property at a fixed price within a specified time

▪ Property Records

Permanent records of property owned are kept for several reasons: to determine the value of the property, to show the outstanding debt, to use in tax reporting, and to use as a basis for setting a satisfactory selling price. The records are used over a period of years.

A separate record should be kept for each piece of property owned and should include information similar to that shown on page 568.

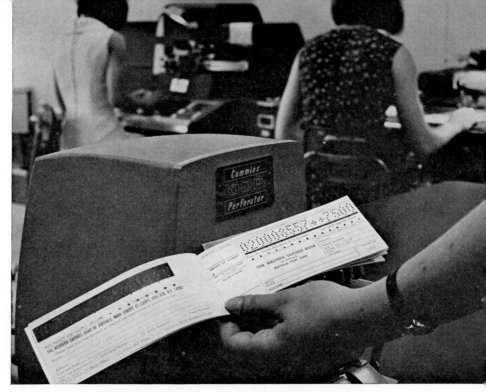

Investment-property records can be planned in advance so that every deposit or payment can be quickly and specifically identified.

Investment Property. Property held for rental income or to be sold at a hoped-for profit is *investment property*. The secretary's employer may own several such pieces, or he may be employed to manage such property for other owners, for which service he receives a fee. Managing property means negotiating with the tenants, keeping the building in repair, and handling certain of the finances—collecting rentals, paying expenses, and so on.

Tenants may be required to sign *leases* prepared by the secretary. Printed lease forms (see Chapter 25, page 614) are obtainable in stationery or legal-supply stores. The pertinent facts must be filled in on the form and the signatures affixed. These forms should be checked with an attorney to be certain they set forth the exact conditions desired.

The secretary keeps full detailed records of expenses on each piece of investment property, since all expenses are deductible on income tax returns; and full detailed records of income, since all income must be reported.

To keep accurate data on each unit, the secretary can follow the plan suggested on pages 568 and 569.

—Pfening & Snyder,
Columbus, Ohio

A property record similar to this form would be kept on each piece of property. At the end of each year all the income and expenses related to each piece of property could be conveniently organized in preparation for the income tax reports.

REAL ESTATE

TITLE IN NAME OF Steve M. Thomas and Helen F. Thomas

LOCATION AND DESCRIPTION Two-family dwelling at 285 Summit Road
Bexley, Ohio

LOT NO. 7 BLOCK NO. PARCEL NO. 1-5910 TAX NO.

RECORDED IN Franklin COUNTY, STATE OF Ohio

DEED BOOK NO. 15 PAGE NO. 256 DATE April 1, 19--

ACQUIRED FROM S. Walter Sims and Mary Sims

PURCHASE PRICE $32,000 CASH PAID $ 17,000 BAL. $ 15,000

MORTGAGEE 1ST. First Trust Company AM'T $ 15,000

PAYMENT DUE 10th day each month AM'T $ 140

MORTGAGEE 2ND. AM'T $

PAYMENT DUE AM'T $

ASSESSED TAX VALUE 19 -- $ 20,000 $ 19 $ 19 $

REMARKS Deed--First Trust Company

USE HEADINGS GIVEN OR WRITE IN SPACES PROVIDED ACCORDING TO YOUR NEEDS

TAXES · INSURANCE · DEPRECIATION · REPAIRS			INCOME FROM RENTALS			PAYMENTS ON PRINCIPAL AND INTEREST		
DATE 19--	ITEM	AMOUNT	DATE 19--	ITEM	AMOUNT	DATE 19--	ITEM	AMOUNT
4/8	Ins.	80 —	5/1	Rent	280 —	5/10	P & I	140 —
5/10	Taxes	250 —	6/1	"	280 —	6/10	"	140 —
5/20	Repairs	75 —	7/1	"	280 —	7/10	"	140 —
6/10	Paint	125 —	8/1	"	280 —	8/10	"	140 —

(Margin text, vertical:) PFENING AND SNYDER, COLUMBUS 8 OHIO — PRICE COPYRIGHTED 1958

1. Set up an individual file folder for each rental unit, such as each suite of offices, each apartment in a building, or each house. As each unit would be identified on the file folder by the number or address, an alphabetic index of tenants' names giving their rental location would serve as a helpful cross reference.

   In this folder would be filed everything pertaining to the unit of rental such as correspondence, the lease, bills for repairs or improvements, lists of any special fixtures or furniture provided, rental amount.

FILE DATE: 12th day of each month

MORTGAGE PAYMENT DUE: 15th of each month
 (Mail check no later than the 12th)

Duplex, 906 Fourth Street

AMOUNT: $125

MAKE CHECK TO: Estate of Frank Freeland
SEND CHECK TO: Thompson and Wills
      Room 148, Briggs Bldg.
      1845 South Kane Avenue
      Fort Worth, Texas 76006

FINAL PAYMENT DATE: April 15, 1972

The tickler card for monthly mortgage payment indentifies the property; it also indicates the file date, due date, amount of payment, to whom payment is to be made, and where the check is to be sent.

2. A miscellaneous folder (or folders) would be used for the building in general to take care of the items that cannot be charged to a specific rental unit, such as janitor service, repairs to the exterior of the building or corridors, taxes, and other such items.

The record of all receipts and expenses paid can be written right on each folder, or on a card or sheet filed inside each folder. Preferably, such records are kept on separate sheets in a loose-leaf book where the chance of their being lost is considerably reduced.

The banking of money collected from investment property and the payment of bills for such property should be handled carefully. It is extremely important that the deposit slips be completed so that every deposit can be identified and that every check stub be labeled to be charged against a specific rental unit or building.

Personal-Property Records. To provide necessary information in event of death or other contingency, the secretary is often asked to keep a file of the executive's personal property, such as an inventory of household goods, a description and the location of family jewels and heirlooms, insurance policies, and the names and addresses of certain key people involved in his personal affairs. Such information and materials should be placed in sealed envelopes, labeled, and kept in the safe-deposit box or fireproof office safe.

▪ Tickler Card File

There are many recurring expenses on property, such as mortgage payments (usually due monthly), tax payments (due annually or semi-annually), and insurance premiums (due quarterly). On income property, the rent is usually due on a certain day each month. To make sure that income is received when due and that recurring expenses are paid on time, a tickler card should be prepared for each item so that the card can be continually used—refiled under the next pertinent date after it comes to the front on the current reminder date.

In addition to interest and mortgage payments, use tickler cards for:

Taxes—On the tickler card indicate for each kind of tax payment: the kind of tax, the payment date, the amount, to whom to make the check payable, where to send the check, and whether or not a return must accompany the payment.

Insurance Premiums—See page 572 for information to be shown.

Rent Receipts—For each rental unit show location, amount of rent, the name and mailing address of the tenant, and any special information that may assist in collecting or interpreting the rent payment.

▪ Source Materials

If the secretary's employer has extensive real-estate holdings or is engaged in the real-estate business, he may subscribe to an information service, such as the *Prentice-Hall Real Estate Service* or the *Real Estate Analyst.*

There are a number of periodicals that specialize in providing current information on real estate, a few of which are *American Building, The Appraisal Journal, National Real Estate and Building Journal, Journal of Property Management,* and *Building Reporter and Realty News.*

The *Handbook of Real Estate Forms*[1] would be a valuable addition to the secretary's reference shelf.

Insurance

Insurance can be grouped into three general classes—personal, property, and liability. *Personal insurance* includes the many kinds of life, accident, and health insurance. *Property insurance* covers loss from impairment or destruction of property, such as fire, earthquake, burglary, and automobile collision. *Liability insurance* protects the insured against losses resulting from injury to another, such as public liability, workmen's compensation, and employer's liability.

The individual or business purchasing the insurance is called the *policyholder.* The *policy* is the written contract that exists between the policyholder and the insurance company. The insurance company may be referred to as the insurer or the *underwriter.* The policyholder makes periodic payments to the insurance company for the policy. These payments are called the insurance *premium.*

The secretary has three responsibilities regarding the executive's insurance; namely, to see that the premiums are paid promptly so that there will be no lapse in protection, to keep summary records on each kind of insurance for the executive's information, and to store the policies in a safe place.

▪ Premium Payments and Renewals

Insurance premiums are payable in advance. Those on property insurance are usually paid annually or for a term of three or five years. Premiums on life insurance may be paid annually or in monthly, quarterly, or semiannual installments.

---

[1] E. J. Friedman, *Handbook of Real Estate Forms* (Englewood Cliffs, New Jersey: Prentice-Hall, Inc., 1957).

It is a responsibility of the secretary to follow up on payment of insurance premiums, as well as cancellations and additions.

Many life insurance policies allow a 28- to 31-day grace period in making premium payments. If the premium is due and payable on August 16, payment of the premium may be made any time before September 16. If the premium notice does not specify the grace period, the secretary should inquire from the insurance company if a grace period is allowed.

Checks in payment of premiums must be drawn in sufficient time to have them signed and sent to the insurance company or agent before the expiration date. It is the secretary's responsibility to avoid any insurance policy lapse caused by failure to make premium payment.

In addition to seeing that premiums are paid, the secretary should also arrange for the cancellation of policies when the protection is no longer needed. A policy can be canceled by telling the insurance company or agent of the cancellation and returning the policy. The premium for the unexpired period of the policy is refundable.

■ Insurance Records

When a secretary begins working with an executive, she will know nothing of his personal insurance commitments, and he probably will

LIFE INSURANCE PREMIUM RECORD

Company	Policy No.	Amount of Premium	Payable	Due Dates
Pacific Mutual	1222470	$ 76.65	Annually	Jan. 17
Massachusetts Mutual	1120857	213.61	Quarterly	Aug. 24 Nov. 24 Feb. 24 May 24
Prudential	1004094	120.44	Quarterly	June 9 Sept. 9 Dec. 9 Mar. 9

This life-insurance record provides ready information on premium-payment dates and amounts and a record of the life insurance carried by the executive.

not take time to explain them to her. If she is lucky, she may inherit a summary record from the previous secretary. More likely, however, she will have to set up this record herself from the notices of premiums due as they are received. It takes at least a year to complete the insurance records from premium notices, for insurance might include many of the types named in the illustration that follows.

When the premium notice is received, the secretary should record information about the policy in whatever form of insurance summary record she is keeping and establish a tickler card (See page 574) which may be filed by premium-payment date.

From the information listed on the premium notice for a life insurance policy, the following facts can usually be determined: the name of the insurance company, the name of the insured, the policy number, the amount of premium, frequency of payment, and present due date. These data are sufficient for the records the secretary should keep.

Policy Number	Day of Mo. Due	DISTRIBUTION OF LIFE INSURANCE PREMIUM PAYMENTS											
		Jan	Feb	Mar	Apr	May	June	July	Aug	Sept	Oct	Nov	Dec	Total
548721	5	48.50			48.50			48.50			48.50			194.00
231770	25		128.10						128.10					256.20
701809	3						88.45							88.45
		119.60	128.10		78.40	21.50	88.45	119.60	128.10		119.60		86.40	889.75

A premium-distribution record will assist the executive in planning for his premium payments.

TYPES OF INSURANCE

Personal Insurance—Protects against the effects of illness, accident, and loss of income because of illness, accident, or death.

Life: Endowment
    Limited payment life
    Ordinary life
    Term

Health: Hospital care
    Medical fees
    Surgical fees
    Loss of income

Property Insurance—Protects from financial loss if your own property is damaged.

Automobile collision
Burglary and employee theft
Fire
Fire—Extended Coverage (windstorm, lightning, riot, strike violence, smoke damage, falling aircraft and vehicle damage, most explosions)
Plate glass
Standard boiler
Valuable papers
Vandalism

Marine: Barratry
    Burning
    Collision
    Mutiny
    Piracy
    Sinking
    Standing

Liability Insurance (Casualty)—Protects against claim of other people if you injure them or damage their property.

Automobile liability
Bailee insurance
Elevator insurance
Libel and slander

Premise and operations liability
Public liability
Product insurance
Workmen's compensation

Credit, Fidelity, and Surety—Protects against losses from:

Bad accounts (Credit)
Title (Surety)

Employee embezzlement
    (Fidelity)

```
FILE DATE:   December 26, 19—

EXPIRATION DATE:   January 4, 19—
TYPE OF INSURANCE:   Fire on office
                     furniture
AMOUNT:   $5,000

COMPANY:   Mutual Insurance Company
           5321 Main Street, City
POLICY NO.:   X438621
DATE OF ISSUE:   January 5, 19—

PREMIUM – TIME:   $48.20 for five years

POLICY FILED:   First National Bank
```

Some secretaries find it conven‹
to prepare an index card for e‹
insurance policy. The index ‹
is filed in a tickler file a few d
before the expiration date (or ‹
premium-payment date).   ⁊
the card provides a record of ‹
insurance and also serves a‹
reminder notice for renewals ‹
premium payments.

Property-insurance records should show all the information provided on the illustrated insurance index card. The information may be placed on a separate card or may be included in an insurance register.

▪ Safe Storage of Policies

Insurance policies (especially fire and life) should be kept in the executive's safe-deposit box, office safe, or home safe. In event of fire, if the policies are kept in the office, they might be destroyed along with the insurance records; thus, all records of the insurance would be lost. If the policies are to be retained in the office, a record of each policy should be given to the executive to keep in his home safe.

For a claim for losses resulting from fire or theft, a description of the items lost will be required. The secretary should maintain a list of the office furnishings and equipment. This list should show the cost of each item and the date purchased. It should be kept up to date and filed with the insurance policy.

▪ Fidelity Bonds

A *fidelity bond* is insurance on an employee's honesty. Most employers carry such insurance on those employees who handle money. The company to which application is made for a fidelity bond investigates the employee's character and the supervisory and control methods in force in the employer's business. No bond is sold if the applicant's character is found wanting or if the situation is such that it would be easy to embezzle funds from the employer.

Blanket fidelity bonds covering the entire personnel are bought by banks and other financial institutions. They protect against losses by embezzlement, robbery, forgery, and so on.

To be asked to take out a fidelity bond is no reflection on your character. Actually it indicates that you are considered competent to be entrusted with company funds.

▪ Action in Emergency

When disaster strikes, the secretary has an opportunity to prove that she is the cool-headed, responsible type that can think and act quickly. Others may be so excited and involved in the emergency that they fail to think of procedures. Insurance companies make these suggestions:

When a fire breaks out, notify the insurance company immediately by phone and confirm the call by wire. The insurance company may be able to have an inspector on the scene to witness the damage and save a lot of paper work later on.

Keep accurate and separate records for cleanup, repairs, and charges made by outside contractors. The items are all part of the insurance claim.

When an accident occurs, interview witnesses on the spot. Signed statements carry a lot of weight and refresh memories in settling claims. If possible, take pictures at the scene.

Where-Kept File

In event of the sudden death of an executive, his widow and family will need immediately certain financial information. The secretary can be of great assistance in such an emergency if she maintains a folder containing up-to-date information that will be needed. The following information might be included:

Bank Accounts—the name and address of each bank in which an account is kept, the type of account, the exact name of account, and the name of bank contact (if the executive has one)

Birth Certificate—where it can be found

Business Interests—list of the executive's business interests

Credit Cards—record of names and account numbers

Income Tax Record—where past returns are filed; the name and address of the tax consultant

Insurance Policies—location of insurance records (If these records do not contain detailed information on life, health and accident, hospitalization, and medical insurance policies, the information should be placed in the folder. The name and address of the insurance adviser should be filed also.)

Real Estate Investments—location of detailed property records

Passport—where it can be found

Safe-Deposit Box—the name of the bank, the box number, and where the key can be found

Social Security—the social security number

Stocks and Bonds—location of detailed investment records

Will—where the original and copies of the will may be found; name and address of the attorney who prepared the will; date of the last will; the executor's name and address

Administrative Functions

The administrative assistant to an executive may be expected to perform a number of administrative functions related to the property, investments, and insurance coverage of the company and of the executive for whom she works. The college-trained secretary brings to her position a background of courses in economics, accounting, business law, and, in some cases, real estate and insurance. All of these courses contribute to her competency.

As an administrative assistant she may be asked to:

1. Prepare an investment prospectus on stocks that are under consideration for investment. This activity would involve checking investment service reports for gathering data on products, past performance, background of company officials, forecasts for the area and for the company, comparison with competitors, and so forth. Such data are available in the business section of a public library and in special libraries.

2. Update the investment portfolio of the company or of the executive. The updating process would involve analyzing (1) the rate of yield on each investment, (2) profit trends, and (3) the outlook for the company. For some classes of stock, charts showing the fluctuations in the market may need to be prepared and updated at regular intervals.

3. Supervise and follow through on repairs and improvements made to investment property. Frequent visits to the location of the property and careful study of the repair or construction contract would be necessary.

4. Handle the details related to processing the sale or purchase of real estate. This activity involves such details as having the title searched for liens and mortgages, obtaining title insurance, and processing and recording the deed.

5. Review at regular intervals the insurance policies in force and arrange for revision in insurance coverage in keeping with changing values of the property. The responsibility includes cancelling unneeded policies and being alert to new insurance needs.

6. Process an insurance claim. This responsibility involves compiling the records necessary to support a claim—cost records, appraisal of loss, and proof of loss.

Suggested Readings

Barnes, Leo. *Your Investments.* Larchmont: American Research Council Inc., 1964, 228 pp.

Business News Staff of the New York Times. *How to Read and Understand Financial and Business News.* Garden City: Doubleday & Company, Inc., 1963, 96 pp.

Doris, Lillian. *The Real Estate Office Secretary's Handbook.* Englewood Cliffs, New Jersey: Prentice-Hall, Inc., 1953, 401 pp.

Engel, Louis. *How to Buy Stocks.* New York: Bantam Books, 1962, 209 pp.

Low, Janet. *The Investor's Dictionary.* New York: Simon and Shuster, 1964, 218 pp.

Officework in the Field of Insurance, White Glove Training Manual No. 7. Milwaukee: Manpower Inc., 1965, 64 pp.

Rosenberg, Claude N., Jr., *Stock Market Primer.* Englewood Cliffs, New Jersey: Prentice-Hall, Inc., 1962, 276 pp.

Stable, C. Norman. *How to Read the Financial News.* New York: Harper & Brothers, Publishers, 1965, 233 pp.

Questions for Discussion

1. A company issues both preferred and common stock. What factors should be considered in determining whether to purchase preferred or common stock?

2. Your employer asks you for a report on United Airlines (UnitAirLin) stock for his consideration as an investment. What type of information would you include in the report? What would be your information sources?

3. Assume that you keep the records of your employer's personal financial investments. In the event of his death, would you turn these records over to his widow, or would you wait until the executor of the estate is appointed and turn the records over to him?

4. What information, in addition to stock prices, does the financial section of the newspaper contain? Should the secretary read this section regularly?

5. In the event of fire or theft, all financial records (including stock certificates, bonds, and insurance policies) may be lost. What precautions should a secretary take and/or suggest to her employer that would minimize such losses?

6. An owner of a small grocery store with six employees wishes to protect himself against all possible insurable losses. What types of insurance would he obtain? (He owns the building in which the store is located.)

7. Your employer asks you to have a mortgage recorded. What does this mean, and how would you carry out his instructions?

8. Your employer owns several pieces of rental property. You are responsible for keeping the records. What records would you keep?

9. Write the following years in Roman numerals.

1900   1918   1945   1950   Current year

Convert these Roman numerals to Arabic numbers:

D   M   MDCDXLVIII

Consult the Reference Guide to correct your answers.

10. Type the information in the blanks in the following sentence.

One historian thinks it dates back to _____ and another to _____. (*anno Domini* 175, before Christ 200)

Consult the Reference Guide to verify or correct your answers.

Problems

1. Your employer owns the following securities:

200 shares....American Potash and Chemical, common, (A Potash)

100 shares....Coca Cola, common, (CocaCola)

75 shares....Consolidated Edison, preferred, (ConEdis)

500 shares....Imperial Oil, Limited, common, (ImpOil)

200 shares....Standard Oil (Indiana), common, (StdOilInd)

5 $1000 Pan American World Airways, cv 4½s84 bonds (PanAmA)

(a) Prepare a report showing the current market value of your employer's security holdings. (Use the closing price of the security on the day of the date of the report.)

(b) Your employer purchased the American Potash and Chemical stock when it sold at 25. He receives a quarterly dividend of 30 cents per share. Determine the rate of yield that he receives on his investment and the rate of yield at the current market price.

2. When you obtain employment as a secretary, you may be able to participate in some form of employee group insurance. So that you may know something about these arrangements and how they operate, investigate the employee insurance plan maintained by some company and report to the class the details of the plan.

Include in your report the types of insurance available, how the premiums are paid, and the status of the insurance upon termination of employment with the company.

3. Financial jargon includes many terms with which a secretary should be familiar. Using reference sources, prepare a short report explaining:

bear market
"blue-chip" stocks
book value
bull market
ex dividend
float
growth stocks
industrials
investment companies
margin
market value
mutual fund
option
"over-the-counter" securities
rails
sleeper
stock dividend
stock rights
utilities

Related Work Assignments 64-67 ─────────────

64. Property Records. Your employer, Robert L. Simpson, owns a small apartment building. One of your responsibilities is to keep a record of all income and expenses on the building.

Four-Apartment Building, 17 Avenore Drive. Cost: $60,000. The rentals are:

> **Apartment 1 — $130, due on the 8th of the month**
> **"   2 — $115, due on the 27th of the month**
> **"   3 — $110, due on the 21st of the month**
> **"   4 — $100, due on the 11th of the month**

Apartment 4 was empty during August, September, and October; the other three were rented through the year.

In April, the floors in Apartments 1 and 3 were sanded at the cost of $47.50 and $35, respectively. The living rooms in all four apartments were painted in September at costs of $80, $80, $75, and $65, respectively. Janitor service is $95 a month, payable on the first. Quarterly water bills for the entire building were: January, $40.62; April, $41.67; July, $45.71; October, $29.32.

Semiannual real estate taxes are $500, due June 15 and December 15. The annual insurance premium of $345 was paid on January 30.

Other expenses were: April 10, repairing driveway, $35.00; August 12, installing front door lock, $12.50.

> (a) On a sheet of paper or on a card, construct a property-record form for the apartment. The form should provide space for descriptive information and for the recording of each income and each expense.
> (b) Record the information given above on the record form for the current year.
> (c) Prepare a report for submission to Mr. Simpson at the end of the year summarizing the incomes and expenses for the building.

65. Keeping an Insurance Record. Mr. Simpson maintains a number of ordinary life insurance policies. (a) Prepare a record form similar to the one on page 572, and record the following policies:

> **Metropolitan—Policy #3711962 on Mr. Simpson; quarterly premium, $311.16; first premium for the year due February 16.**
> **New York Life—Policy #3618922 on Mr. Simpson; annual premium, $416, due July 30.**
> **Union Central—Policy #761309 on Mrs. Simpson; quarterly premium, $13.61; first one due January 6.**
> **Prudential—Policy #1007091 on Mr. Simpson; semiannual premium, $152.50; first one due on May 10.**

(b) Prepare an insurance index card similar to the one on page 574 and record the first policy (#3711962) on the card.

(c) Prepare a "Distribution of Life Insurance Premium Payments" form similar to the one on page 572, and record the premium payments.

66. Applying for a Fidelity Bond. You handle the firm's banking account, and the management wishes you to make application for a $10,000 fidelity bond. Obtain a fidelity-bond application form and fill in the required data.

67. Recording Stock Transactions. The instructions and supplies necessary for the completion of this assignment are provided in the Workbook.

Payroll and Tax Duties

In all businesses payroll functions must be performed—time records maintained, earnings and deductions computed, and tax reports submitted. In a business employing many workers, these functions are centralized in a payroll division. In a small office, the secretary may be required to assume these responsibilities; so her involvement in payroll records depends largely upon the size of the business.

Regardless of what her payroll responsibilities may be, every secretary should play an important assist role in the preparation of her employer's income tax return. She can systematically collect throughout the year pertinent income tax data so that, when income tax return time comes, the facts and figures are readily available. No employer expects his secretary to assume the role of a tax expert, but the "assist" role that she can assume is a real plus value that he appreciates.

Payroll Responsibilities

Payroll work is detailed and demands mathematical accuracy. In addition, it requires an understanding of the forms and reports that are legislated by Social Security provisions, the Fair Labor Standards Act, income tax laws, state unemployment compensation acts and any pertinent local legislation.

The payroll is also a security responsibility. Payroll information is confidential. The secretary, therefore, must guard all payroll facts. Not only must the actual payroll checks and records be secured, but all payroll computation sheets must be destroyed because they provide the inquisitive person with a source of information. When working on the payroll, the secretary should place all information in a desk drawer if an interruption requires her to leave her desk.

▪ Social Security

Under the Social Security system most business, farm, and household employees and self-employed persons are provided an income in old age and survivor benefits in event of death. Social Security also provides a nationwide system of unemployment insurance and hospital and medical insurance benefits (known as Medicare) for persons of age 65 or over.

To pay most of these social security benefits, both employees and employers share equally in a tax or contribution. Medical insurance (for persons of age 65 or over) is optional and is financed jointly by contributions from the retired insured person and from the United States government.

Social Security Numbers. Each employer and employee must obtain a social security number to identify himself in the government records. These numbers are the only method of unquestioned identification. For the employer the number is called an *identification number*, while the employee must obtain an *account number*.

To obtain an account number, a person files an application form (Form SS-5) obtained from the nearest social security office or post office. After the filled-in blank is sent in, the applicant will receive a card stamped with his account number. If the card is lost, a duplicate can be obtained. When an employee's name is changed or if incorrect information is put on the application form, report the change on Form OAAN-7003 to the Social Security Administration. The secretary may find it convenient to have social security forms on hand.

Forms needed for social security records are as follows:

SS-4 . . . . Application for Employer Identification Number
SS-5 . . . . Application for Employee Account Number
OAAN-7003. . . . . Request for Change in Social Security Records
OAR-7004 . . . . Request for Statement of Earnings

The social security card shows the account number that is assigned to each individual protected under the Social Security Act. Note that it has two parts—the upper part to be carried by the employee in his billfold, and the lower part to be detached and filed with other valuable papers for reference if the other half is lost. The individual retains the same account number throughout his life.

The social security administration recommends that every three or four years each employee request a statement of his account (Use Form OAR-7004) to make sure that his earnings have been reported properly.

F.I.C.A. Tax Deductions. Under the Social Security Act both the employer and employee pay *F.I.C.A.* (Federal Insurance Contribution Act) *taxes* at the same rate. A summary of the present tax rates and those scheduled for the future (subject to change by Congress) is shown in the table at the right.

Each employee's tax is deducted from his wages each payday; the employer accumulates these amounts for each employee and forwards them (together with his own tax payment) to the District Direc-

PRESENT AND FUTURE F.I.C.A. TAX RATES			
(In Percentages)			
Year	Employer	Employee	Self-Employed
1967–68	4.40*	4.40*	6.40*
1969–72	4.90	4.90	7.10
1973–75	5.40	5.40	7.55
1976–79	5.45	5.45	7.60
1980–86	5.55	5.55	7.70
1987– ?	5.65	5.65	7.80

Levied on the first $7,800 of a person's earnings each year.

tor of Internal Revenue. To illustrate, assume an employee earns $90 a week and is paid at the end of each week. At the rate of 4.4 percent the employer deducts $3.96 for the employee's F.I.C.A. tax and contributes an equal amount for his share. At the end of the quarter (13 weeks), the employer remits to the government a total of $102.96.

Self-employed persons (such as farmers, architects, and contractors) are required to pay the entire tax. The rate is approximately three fourths of the total paid by the employer and the employee on the same income. A self-employed individual reports and pays his F.I.C.A. tax simultaneously with his income tax.

Unemployment Compensation Tax Deductions. Under the Social Security Act, employers of four or more workers must pay a federal tax levied to pay the administrative costs of the state unemployment laws.

Most employers are also subject to a state unemployment tax. This tax, in most states paid by only employers, provides funds from which unemployment compensation can be paid to unemployed workers. The tax rate in most states is 2.7 percent of earnings up to $3,000 yearly on each employee. The employer's contributions to state unemployment compensation funds are reported on special forms filed quarterly.

In some states the unemployment tax is levied on employees as well as employers. In these states, the tax is deducted by the employer from the employee's wage. The employer submits quarterly to the state amounts deducted along with his contribution.

▪ Withholding (Income Tax) Deductions

The federal government requires most employers to withhold a certain amount from each wage payment to an employee as an advance payment on his income tax. The amounts withheld are remitted to the District Director of Internal Revenue at the same time the F.I.C.A. taxes are paid. The term *wages* used in this connection includes the total compensation paid for service such as wages, salaries, commissions, bonuses, and vacation allowances.

The amount of income tax withheld depends upon the amount of wages received and the number of personal exemptions to which the taxpayer is entitled. Each employee must file with his employer, immediately upon reporting to work, an Employee's Withholding Exemption Certificate (Form W-4) to indicate the number of personal exemptions to which he is entitled. The amount of tax withheld is then computed from a table provided by the Internal Revenue Service.

Each employee is entitled to the following withholding exemptions:

An exemption for himself
An exemption for his spouse (unless his spouse claims her own exemption)
An exemption for each dependent (unless his spouse claims them)

A number of cities and states tax personal income. The percentage of deduction and the form of payment vary; for example, one city may have the employer deduct 1 percent from every payroll check issued and remit the total deductions at the end of each quarter of a calendar year. A state may require an individual to file an annual income tax return.

The following forms are needed for payroll records:

W-2 . . . . Wage and Tax Statement
W-3 . . . . Reconciliation of Income Tax Withheld from Wages
W-4 . . . . Employee's Withholding Exemption Certificate
450. . . . . Federal Depository Receipt
940. . . . . Employer's Annual Federal Unemployment Tax Return
941. . . . . Employer's Quarterly Federal Tax Return
State Unemployment Return . . . . .Varied rates of contributions

■ Other Payroll Deductions

In addition to the deductions required by federal and state legislation, other payroll deductions—such as hospital care insurance (hospitalization), group insurance premiums, stock and bond purchases—may be made. In most firms these deductions are voluntary, and usually the authorizations may be canceled by the employee at any time.

Most employers furnish with each wage payment an itemized listing of all deductions made for taxes or other purposes from the employee's wage. This information is usually provided on a form attached to the check, to be removed and retained by the employee when the check is cashed. At the end of each year, the employer is required to furnish each employee with a Withholding Tax Statement (Form W-2) that shows the total earnings and tax deductions.

■ Fair Labor Standards Act

There are primarily two classes of remuneration—*wages* at a rate per hour and *salaries* at a rate per week or month. Persons receiving wages are usually paid only for the hours they work; persons receiving salaries are usually paid for the full pay period even though they may be absent from work for brief periods. To differentiate, employees are called "hourly" and "salary" employees respectively. Office employees are almost always paid salaries although record-keeping requirements may make practical the payment of office employees on an hourly basis.

Most hourly and salaried employees come under the provisions of the *Fair Labor Standards Act*, which sets a minimum hourly wage and requires that each employer keep a record of the hours worked by each employee and that each employee must be paid at a rate at least 50 percent greater than his regular hourly rate for all time over forty hours during a work week. Professional workers and executives are excluded from the provisions of the act.

Some companies pay overtime for all work beyond a specific number of hours a day. In other companies no overtime is paid salaried workers, but compensatory time off is given instead.

The Fair Labor Standards Act does not require the filing of overtime reports to any governmental office, but records must be kept on file for four years in the employer's office on nonexempt employees for the perusal of a government examiner at any time he chooses to look them over. Detailed information about this legislation may be obtained from the nearest office of the Wage and Hour Division, Department of Labor.

CALENDAR OF PAYROLL RESPONSIBILITIES

√ On Hiring a New Employee:

Have employee complete Form W-4 (Employee's Withholding Exemption Certificate). Record employee's social security number and number of exemptions. File the certificate for safe keeping.

√ On Each Payment of Wages to an Employee:

Withhold the proper amount of income tax and F.I.C.A. tax (refer to the instructions and tables supplied by the Internal Revenue Service and also to city and state information, if necessary). Make all other deductions.

As part of the payroll check or as a separate statement, a detailed record of total wages, amount and kind of each deduction, and net amount should be furnished to the employee.

√ Within 15 Days after the Close of Each of the First Two Months of Any Calendar Quarter:

If income and F.I.C.A. taxes withheld total more than $100 monthly, use *Form 450 (Federal Depositary Receipt)* and deposit the full amount in a Federal Reserve bank or authorized bank. Keep validated receipts.

> A deposit may be made for the last month of a quarter, but it should be made in sufficient time so that it can be attached to and filed with Form 941 on or before the 10th day of the second month following the quarter.

√ On or Before Each April 30, July 31, October 31, and January 31:

File *Form 941 (Employer's Quarterly Federal Tax Return)* with the District Director of Internal Revenue. Remit with it the full amount due; that is, the total amount of income and F.I.C.A. taxes withheld during the quarter less total of Federal Depositary Receipts (Form 450).

The *State Unemployment Return* is usually filed at this time.

√ On or Before January 31 and at the End of an Employee's Employment:

Prepare *Form W-2 (Wage and Tax Statement)* showing the total wages, total wages subject to withholdings for income tax, the amount of tax withheld, the total wage subject to F.I.C.A. tax, and the amount of tax withheld.

> The government-prepared Form W-2 consists of four copies—two copies given to the employee (for his own record and for his annual income tax return); one copy for the District Director of Internal Revenue; one copy for the employer's record. To save paper work, many large firms print their own W-2 forms with five or six copies. The additional copies are given to the city and state (that is, for records of income tax withheld) if they require them.

√ On or Before January 31 of Each Year:

File *Form 940 (Employer's Annual Federal Unemployment Tax Return)* to report payment of federal unemployment taxes under the Federal Unemployment Tax Act.

File *Form W-3 (Reconciliation of Income Tax Withheld from Wages)* to provide a summary statement that enables a comparison of the total income taxes withheld as reported on all Form W-2s and the total amount of income tax withheld as reported on the four quarterly Forms 941.

Retain payroll records for a period of FOUR YEARS.

The employee takes her time card from a card rack and slips it into an electrically operated time-recording clock. The exact time of entering or leaving is stamped on the card.

▪ Time Records

Hourly workers, such as factory and department-store employees
and some salaried workers, "punch in" and "punch out" each time they
enter and leave their places of employment. The time is stamped on a
time card. At the end of the payroll period the cards are collected and
the pay is computed from the time stampings. A time card is illustrated
on the opposite page.

Instead of using a time clock, salaried employees may sign in and
out on a ruled sheet; or the secretary may be responsible for checking
each person in and out daily on such a time sheet. Time records are
not necessary in computing salaries, but it is advisable to keep them. The
psychological effect in itself tends to cause employees to be more
punctual. A second reason is that such records may be the basis of
paying overtime earnings or balancing time off with overtime worked.

Then, too, there are various reports to be made that may require records of the time off or overtime of his salaried employees.

▪ Payroll Records

Federal legislation requires employers to keep payroll records. These usually include a columnar form similar to the one that is shown on page 588.

An annual permanent summary of payroll data is usually kept for each employee. This record is a sheet or a card to which the information from the payroll record is transferred periodically, preferably each payday. The Employee's Earnings Record illustration on page 588 shows a form that provides quarterly totals as well as the annual total because certain federal and state forms must be submitted each calendar quarter. Even though the laws affecting payroll taxes are changed from time to time, a comprehensive record similar to the type illustrated will provide the basic data from which to adapt almost any type of payroll tax report.

SOC. SEC. NO. 696-44-2878				
			PAY PERIOD ENDING 4/30/--	
CLOCK NO. 12			WITHHOLDING TAX EXEMPTIONS 1	
NAME Nancy Daniels				
REG. HOURS 35½	RATE 2.10	AMOUNT 74.55	F.I.C.A. TAX 3.83	TOTAL EARNINGS 87.15
O.T. HOURS 4	RATE 3.15	AMOUNT 12.60	INC. TAX WITH. 10.40	TOTAL DEDUCTIONS 18.08
TOTAL HRS. 39½			GROUP INS. .50	NET PAY 69.07
			HOSP. 3.35	
			OTHER	

Days	IN MORNING	OUT	IN AFTERNOON	OUT	IN OVERTIME	OUT	Hours
1	M 8^{04}	M 12^{01}	M 12^{48}	M 4^{32}			$7\frac{1}{4}$
2	T 7^{54}	T 12^{02}	T 12^{52}	T 3^{58}			$6\frac{3}{4}$
3	W 7^{58}	W 11^{30}	W 12^{54}	W 4^{36}			7
4	T 7^{59}	T 12^{03}	T 1^{28}	T 4^{31}			7
5	F 7^{46}	F 12^{02}	F 12^{49}	F 4^{30}	F 5^{00}	F 9^{05}	$11\frac{1}{2}$
6							
7							TOTAL $39\frac{1}{2}$

▪ Requesting Salary Check

If a secretary is the lone employee in a firm, her payroll duties include reminding the executive that it is payday—a somewhat embarrassing necessity for the new or young secretary. A not-so-obvious way is to ask, "Shall I write out my salary check for your signature?" or "Do you want me to cash a check this noon for my salary?" Never wait until two minutes before leaving time and meekly and hesitatingly say, "This is payday." Remind him at a timely moment. The lawyer, doctor, or branch-office representative under whom the secretary is likely to be the only employee is a matter-of-fact businessman who wants to pay his secretary promptly but who frequently forgets that important day and may not wish to be delayed at the last minute.

PAYROLL RECORD

FOR PERIOD ENDING April 15, 19--

	EMPLOYEE	EXEMP-TIONS	EARNINGS			DEDUCTIONS					NET PAY	CHE No
			REG.	OVER-TIME	TOTAL	FICA TAX	WITH. TAX	GROUP INS.	HOSP.	TOTAL	AMOUNT	
1	Allen, John	1	200.00	15.00	215.00	9.46	38.30	.50	3.35	51.61	163.39	12
2	Bauer, Thomas	2	220.00		220.00	9.68	37.40	.50	8.85	56.43	163.57	12
3	Cowan, Robert	1	200.00		200.00	8.80	35.80	.50		45.10	154.90	12
19	Scott, Kevin	2	200.00		200.00	8.80	32.40	.50	8.85	50.55	149.45	14
20	Weyer, Louis	1	220.00	10.00	230.00	10.12	43.80	.50		54.42	175.58	14
	TOTALS		4,160.00	140.00	4,300.00	129.00	638.30	10.00	64.35	831.64	3468.35	

EMPLOYEE'S EARNINGS RECORD

	19-- PERIOD ENDING	EARNINGS			DEDUCTIONS					NET PAY
		REG.	OVER-TIME	TOTAL	FICA TAX	WITH. TAX	GROUP INS.	HOSP.	TOTAL	AMOUNT
1	1/15	200.00		200.00	8.80	27.40		3.35	39.55	160.45
2	1/31	200.00		200.00	8.80	27.40	.50		36.70	163.30
3	2/15	200.00		200.00	8.80	27.40		3.35	39.55	160.45
4	2/28	200.00		200.00	8.80	27.40	.50		36.70	163.30
5	3/15	200.00	15.00	215.00	9.46	29.20		3.35	42.01	172.99
6	3/31	200.00		200.00	8.80	27.40	.50		36.70	163.30
	QUARTER TOTALS	1,200.00	15.00	1,215.00	53.46	166.20	1.50	10.05	231.21	983.79
	YEARLY TOTALS	4,800.00	30.00	4,830.00	212.52	661.20	6.00	40.20	919.92	3,910.08

NAME	ADDRESS	SOC. SEC. NO.	KIND OF WORK	DEPT.
Dunn, Gail C.	261 Rose Avenue	561-245-4800	Secretary	Sales
NO. DED. 1	Atlanta, Georgia			

■ Administrative Responsibilities

In her supervisory and administrative role, the executive secretary may be involved in salary administration. For example, she may be asked to perform such administrative functions as to recommend promotions and salary increases for members of the office staff, to assist in determining compensation for office personnel, to determine work standards, to examine and propose incentive plans for the office, to evaluate office employees, and to make recommendations for transfers and dismissals. The manner in which these functions are carried out plays an extremely important role in determining office morale.

An essential to a sound salary-administration plan is that each employee be paid a fair and reasonable compensation for work done. This requires some form of job analysis. Before making recommendations involving salary administration, the secretary needs to be thoroughly familiar with the competencies required for each position under her supervision and to have some measure of the quality and quantity of the work produced by each staff member. Job analysis and employee evaluation are two administrative areas in which the secretary may need to develop competence.

The executive secretary also may find an awareness of union and legislative regulations regarding labor to be helpful.

The Executive's Income Tax

The secretary can assist the executive in the preparation of his annual income tax return by:

Being alert to items that he must report as income and items that he may take as deductions

Accumulating such items throughout the year with supporting papers and records for use at income tax time

Following up to see that returns are filed and payments are made

The performance of these duties demands certain basic understandings as to what constitutes taxable income, what deductions are allowable, and how to organize the material to make it readily accessible.

■ Income Tax Files

The *income tax files* generally consist of income and deduction records, supporting computations and memorandums, previous years' tax returns, and a current income tax file folder or portfolio. To avoid the possibility of filing current tax materials with those of previous years, large expansion portfolios may be used and all the income tax material related to a given year filed in that portfolio and labeled "Federal Income Tax, 19—." All supporting records of income tax returns should be retained indefinitely.

At the beginning of each year a folder should be established for income tax materials for the year, and all such data (bills, canceled checks, reports, itemized listings, receipts) should be filed in this folder. Thus, when the executive is ready to prepare his tax report, all the essential records and materials will have been accumulated and will be ready for convenient reference.

■ Records of Taxable Income

A record of the executive's personal income may be maintained in a special record book where each item is individually recorded. In most instances, however, no separate record book will be kept. The tax information will consist mainly of deposit slips to which identifying notations have been attached, copies of receipts, statements of earnings and deductions from salary checks, dividend statements, notations of entries for interest in savings accounts, and other notations which the secretary files in the income tax portfolio. As personal income may be derived from many sources and be received at irregular intervals, the secretary must be able to identify taxable income and must be alert in seeing that a notation on each income item gets into the tax portfolio.

The following items are *taxable income:*

Wages, Salaries, and Other Compensation. The gross amount (amount before deductions for such items as income tax, old-age benefit contributions, employee pensions, hospitalization, and insurance) received from wages, salaries, commissions, fees, tips, and similar sources is taxable. In addition to these items, awards and prizes of money or merchandise, amounts received in reimbursement for expenses that are in excess of the actual business expenses incurred, and bonuses are also taxable income.

Dividends. Cash dividends on stock when paid in cash are generally taxable. Stock dividends, however, may or may not be taxable depending on whether the stockholder had the privilege of electing to take either stock or cash. Since some dividends may be wholly or partially exempt from taxation, a complete record of all dividends received should be maintained. Those dividends which are not taxable can be eliminated at the time the tax return is prepared.

Corporations usually advise stockholders at the end of the year of the total amount of dividends per share paid during the year. The secretary should watch for and see that the corporation-tax information statements are placed in the income tax portfolio.

Interest. With the exception of interest on state and municipal bonds and some U.S. Government bonds, all interest received is taxable. Thus, interest received from corporate bonds, mortgage bonds, notes, bank deposits, personal loans, accounts in savings and loan associations, and most U.S. Government bonds should be itemized and recorded.

Gains on Sale or Exchange of Property. Profit from the sale of property is fully or partially taxable depending upon the length of time the property was owned and upon other circumstances. In order that the exact profit may be determined, it is essential that detailed property records be kept on each property item. Real estate, stocks, and other securities are property items.

Proceeds from Annuities and Endowment Life Insurance. A portion of income from annuities and endowment life insurance is taxable.

Rents Received. Income received from rents is taxable. The owner of property from which rents are received is entitled to deductions for depreciation, mortgage interest, taxes, repairs, insurance, agent's commission, and other ordinary and necessary expenses of operating the property. Property records should be kept on each rental unit owned (See page 568).

Royalties. Royalties include income received from writings, works of art, musical compositions, and from inventions and patents.

All expenses incurred in producing property (such as patents and books) that provide a royalty income are deductible.

Income from a Profession or a Personally Owned Business. All income from a profession or a personally owned business is taxable after deductions for all ordinary, necessary operating expenses have been made.

Nontaxable Income. Even with nontaxable items, the secretary should strive to keep as complete a record of all income as her working situation permits. The data will then be available when the tax return is being prepared. Incomes which are not taxable or incomes from which deductions are allowable can be examined and properly excluded or recorded by the tax consultant at the time of preparation of the tax return. On the basis of her limited knowledge of tax laws, the secretary should not assume the responsibility for excluding income items from the tax data she compiles.

▪ Records of Tax Deductions

A detailed record of each of the following allowable tax deductions should be kept in the tax portfolio for aid in the preparation of the income tax return.

Alimony. Periodic alimony or other payments in lieu of alimony under a decree of divorce or of separate maintenance are allowable as a personal deduction by the husband in the year of payment.

Bad Debts. Uncollectible and uncollected debts resulting from either business or personal relationships are deductible.

Casualty and Theft Losses. Losses resulting from fire, storm, flood, or theft are deductible if not reimbursed by insurance. Damage to the taxpayer's automobile resulting from an accident would be deductible to the extent not covered by insurance.

Child Care. Expenditures for child care up to a certain amount are deductible by widowers and employed women under certain special circumstances.

Contributions. Contributions to organizations or institutions devoted primarily to charitable, religious, educational, scientific, or literary purposes are deductible. Examples would be contributions to schools and colleges, churches, hospitals, American Cancer Foundation, Girl Scouts, Salvation Army, and United Appeal. Charitable gifts to individuals, political organizations, social clubs, or labor unions are not deductible.

Nonreimbursed expenses (use of automobile, postage, out-of-town telephone calls) incurred while serving in a campaign to collect funds for a charitable, religious, or educational organization are considered a contribution to the organization and are deductible as such.

Interest. All interest paid on personal debts may be deducted. This deduction includes interest paid on such items as bank loans, home and property mortgages, and installment loans on family automobile.

Medical and Dental Expenses. Medical and dental expenses are not restricted to those of the taxpayer but may also include his family and dependents. Medical expenses over a certain amount are deductible. To claim this deduction, the taxpayer is required to furnish the name and address of each person to whom such expenses are paid, the amount, and the approximate date paid.

Taxes. Such personal taxes as the following are deductible: state or local income taxes, personal property taxes, real estate taxes, state or local sales taxes, and state gasoline taxes.

The Executive's Business Expenses. *Traveling expenses* incurred by the executive when he is away from home in connection with his business or profession and for which he is not reimbursed are deductible. These

---

TRAVEL EXPENSE REPORT

<u>From</u>: Des Moines   <u>To</u>: Chicago   <u>Date</u>: February
                                                  5, 6, 7
                                                  19—

<u>Purpose</u>: To attend convention, National Bar As-
            sociation

		Cost
<u>Trans</u>: Plane		$ 35.80
<u>Hotel</u>: Palmer House—2 nights		28.00
<u>Meals</u>:	2/5 $6.00	
	2/6 9.50	
	2/7 5.00	20.50
<u>Other</u>: Tips	3.75	
Taxi	8.20	
Reg. at Convention	6.00	
Airport Parking	4.00	21.95
	Total	$106.25

<u>Receipts Attached</u>: Hotel, Plane, Reg. Fee

Travel expenses may be forgotten if they are not recorded promptly. The secretary should obtain from the executive at the completion of each business trip the data needed to complete a report to support travel expense. The report with attached receipts should be filed in the tax portfolio.

expenses include such items as railroad, airline, steamship, and bus fares, automobile expenses, baggage transfer costs, excess baggage charges, porter charges, car fares, meals (if away overnight), taxi fares, telephone and telegraph expenses, hotel and motel expenses, tips, and laundry.

Entertainment expenses for business purposes (customers, agents, clients, professional advisers) are deductible. The wife of an out-of-town guest may also be included. Meals, including tips, theatre and other tickets are recognized entertainment costs. Even club dues are deductible provided the club is used primarily for entertaining business guests. Deductions for entertainment, however, are subject to detailed examination by the Internal Revenue Service. A detailed record similar to the one illustrated on page 595 should be prepared, identifying each guest and his business connection, and supported by receipts if the total cost is $25 or more.

Gifts up to $25 in value are deductible when given for a business purpose. Each gift deduction, however, must be supported by a record showing cost, reason for giving, and the name and business connection of the recipient.

Many executives use credit cards in paying for travel and entertainment expenses. The monthly statement provides a receipt for each expenditure. When credit cards are used, the secretary should identify each travel and entertainment expenditure on the monthly statement and file it, or a copy, in the income tax portfolio. This record should be kept current.

Other Deductions. Other allowable deductions that apply in specific cases are: safe-deposit-box rental when income-producing items are stored in the box, cost of uniforms and their upkeep when they are essential, and repairs of business property. The secretary should add to her master list of deductible items those items that are pertinent to the executive's situation.

▪ Tax Guides and Forms

The secretary can be of more assistance to the executive in handling his income tax materials if she has studied an income tax guide. She should be familiar with the various tax forms and know how to choose the proper ones and where and how to file them. Such familiarity will help her to follow intelligently the instructions regarding completion of the forms.

BUSINESS ENTERTAINMENT GUEST LIST

<u>Date</u>:   April 10, 19—

<u>Guest</u>	<u>Business Connection</u>
Frank Sayer	R. M. Vessy Co. Atlanta
Robert Ramsey	" "

<u>Explanation</u>:
    Lunch at University Club. Discussion of renewal of contract.

<u>Total Cost</u>: $12.40

A record is essential to support each entertainment expense. If the total cost is $25 or more, a receipt should be attached. The secretary should check her appointment book at the end of each day and flag each appointment which involves deductible expenses, obtain the needed information from the executive, and prepare the report. The report with attached receipts should be filed in the income tax folder.

Tax Guides. For a nominal charge, the following publications may be obtained from the office of the District Director of Internal Revenue Service: *Your Federal Income Tax; Tax Guide for Small Business; Employer's Tax Guide* (Circular E); *Farmers' Tax Guide; Tax Guide for U.S. Citizens Abroad;* and *Casualties, Thefts, Condemnations.* Inexpensive tax guides can also be obtained at book stores.

Tax Forms. One set of blank forms is mailed to each taxpayer; additional copies needed for drafting the return may be obtained from the local office of the Internal Revenue Service and usually from banks and post offices. The forms used for filing individual income tax returns are discussed above.

Making Copies. Income tax forms printed on translucent paper may be purchased at a stationery supply store for use in making duplicates on photocopy machines. The Internal Revenue Service has ruled that reproduction of tax forms, schedules, and supporting data made on office copying machines may be submitted. Forms may be prepared in pencil and reproduced on a copying machine, thus avoiding the necessity of recopying or typing the form.

Copies for the files should be made on a copying machine of all supplementary information and supporting data such as receipts, statements, expense reports, and other items that may be attached and mailed with the tax return.

A CHECK LIST FOR COMPUTING INCOME TAX

In keeping a tax portfolio or before preparing the final copy of an income tax return, check the following list of common items which are deductible and nondeductible from adjusted gross income in computing taxable income.

	Deductible	Non-deductible
Alimony and separate maintenance payments taxable to recipient.	√	
Automobile expenses (car used exclusively for pleasure) —		
Gasoline taxes imposed on consumer.	√	
Interest on finance loans.	√	
License fees.		√
Ordinary upkeep and operating expenses.		√
Burglary losses (if not covered by insurance).	√	
Casualty losses not covered by insurance (fire, flood, windstorm, lightning, earthquakes, etc.).	√	
Charitable contributions to approved institutions.	√	
Domestic servants (wages paid).		√
Dues, social clubs for personal use.		√
Employment fees paid to agencies.	√	
Federal income taxes.		√
F.I.C.A. taxes withheld by employer.		√
Fines for violation of laws and regulations.		√
Funeral expenses.		√
Gambling losses (to extent of gains only).	√	
Gift taxes.		√
Gifts to relatives and other individuals.		√
Income tax imposed by city or state.	√	
Inheritance taxes.		√
Interest paid on personal loans.	√	
Life insurance premiums.		√
Medical expenses in excess of 3% of adjusted gross income (including the cost of artificial limbs, artificial teeth, eye glasses, hearing aids, dental fees, hospital expenses, premiums on hospital or medical insurance) to extent not covered by insurance.	√	
Political campaign contribution.		√
Property taxes, real and personal.	√	
Residence for personal use —		
Improvements.		√
Insurance.		√
Interest on mortgage loan.	√	
Loss from sale of.		√
Rent paid.		√
Repairs.		√
Taxes.	√	
Sales taxes, state and local.	√	
Traveling expenses attending professional meetings.	√	
Traveling expenses to and from place of business or employment.		√
Uniforms for personal use including cost and upkeep, if not adaptable for general use (nurses, policemen, jockeys, baseball players, firemen, trainmen, etc.)	√	
Union dues.	√	
Use taxes imposed on consumers under state law.	√	

FORMS USED FOR FILING INDIVIDUAL INCOME TAX RETURNS

File on or before April 15 Following the Close of the Calendar Year:

Form 1040 (U.S. Individual Income Tax Return)—a two-page return (called the "long form") that may be used for *any* amount of income. All deductions can be listed in full, and all computations are made by the taxpayer.

Form 1040A (U. S. Individual Income Tax Return)—a "punch-card" form used only if an individual's gross income (or the combined income of husband and wife on a joint return) is less than $10,000 and consists entirely of wages on which tax was withheld and not more than $200 total of other wages, dividends, and interest. Standard deduction must be claimed as no provision is made for itemizing actual deductions.

Form 1040-ES (U.S. Declaration of Estimated Income Tax)—filed by persons whose income is not subject to withholding (business owners; professional people; and those receiving income from dividends, interest, rents, royalties, and other such sources). This form is usually submitted along with the individual income tax return.

The estimated unpaid tax may be paid in full at the time of filing the declaration form; or it may be paid in four equal quarterly installments (payable on April 15, June 15, September 15, and January 15). The first installment payment must accompany the declaration. Immediately prior to each installment-payment date, the taxpayer will receive a reminder notice.

▪ Typing and Mailing Tax Returns

The tax return contains information that the executive wants held confidential. The secretary, therefore, will do the typing work herself even though she may have someone to whom she normally turns over typing assignments. The return must be typed carefully, and each figure must be checked for accuracy. Before mailing the form, the secretary should examine it to see that it has been properly signed and that materials accompanying the return have been securely attached to the finished form.

As the mailing of all tax returns is a very important responsibility, the secretary should see to the mailing of them herself. Do not put them in the regular office mail, send them through the mailing department, or trust them to a clerk or anyone else to post. The secretary should note on the file copy the exact time and place where she personally mailed each return. A certificate of mailing may be obtained from the post office as legal proof that the return was mailed. If such a certificate is obtained, attach it to the file copy of the return.

A penalty for late filing is levied if the return is lost in the mail and if there is no proof of mailing.

Suggested Readings

Doris, Lillian, and Besse May Miller. *Complete Secretary's Handbook.* Englewood Cliffs, New Jersey: Prentice-Hall, Inc., 1960, pp. 408–439.

Niswonger, C. Rollins, and James B. Bower. *Income Tax Procedure.* Cincinnati: South-Western Publishing Co., 348 pp.

Pendery, John A., and B. Lewis Keeling. *Payroll Records and Accounting.* Cincinnati: South-Western Publishing Co., 246 pp.

Questions for Discussion

1. Some businesses observe the policy of making information on salaries paid available to all employees. Other businesses keep all salary information highly confidential. Which policy do you think would build the best employee morale?

2. You are responsible for preparing the payroll and distributing salary checks to members of the office staff. How would you answer questions directed to you regarding the salary of a fellow employee? regarding your own salary?

3. The F.I.C.A. tax a person pays is approximately 50 percent higher if he is self-employed than if he works for someone else. Can this procedure be justified?

4. Your assistant, who is your senior in age and tenure with the company, has the habit of arriving at work late in the morning. How would you tactfully correct this situation?

5. You are employed in a small office with eight employees and are assigned the responsibility for keeping payroll records. In the past, office employees have not registered in or out on a time sheet when arriving and departing from work. Would you institute such a time sheet? Give your reasons.

6. Secretaries are usually classified as "salaried" as opposed to "hourly" workers. Explain the difference. What are the advantages, if any, of being a salaried worker as opposed to an hourly worker?

7. Assume that an employee's salary is $610 a month.
   (a) **In what month will his last F.I.C.A. tax be deducted?**
   (b) **On how much of the employee's salary for that month will the F.I.C.A tax be calculated?**

8. Identical information is written on the statement that accompanies the employee's pay check, the payroll record, and the employee's earning record. Suggest a way of recording this information in one writing.

9. In what ways can the secretary assist in the preparation of her employer's income tax return? Suggest a plan that she could follow. When in doubt as to whether or not an item may be an allowable deduction, what should the secretary do?

10. You are secretary to a minor official in a company. When your employer returns from a business trip, he regularly submits to the company for reimbursement expense reports far in excess of his actual expenses. Having made many of the out-of-town arrangements, you are fully aware that he is "padding" his expense reports. What is your responsibility to the company?

11. Type the information in the blanks in the following sentences. Then consult the Reference Guide to correct your answers and tell which reference entry you used in each case.

    (a) They sell for _____ each. ($0.50)
    (b) Your letter of _____ was delayed. (September 25)
    (c) He mailed it on the _____ of September. (25)
    (d) You have _____ _____ grace. (thirty-one days)
    (e) Production has increased _____ _____. (thirty-three and one-third %)
    (f) Production has increased _____ _____. (8%)
    (g) Everything is at _____ and _____. (6's and 7's)
    (h) There is a _____ _____ grace period. (25 day)
    (i) There is a _____ _____ interim. (3 day)
    (j) His _____ _____ vacation began Monday. (3 week *or* 3 weeks)

12. Tell what terminal punctuation mark is used after each item in an enumeration if the units are:

    (a) Run-in words or phrases   **(d) Run-in sentences**
    (b) Tabulated words or phrases   **(e) Tabulated sentences**
    (c) Run-in clauses

Consult the Reference Guide to verify or correct your answers.

13. Tell when you use a comma to separate units in a series. Then consult the Reference Guide to verify or correct your answers.

Problems

■ **1.** Obtain one of the following payroll forms, study the instructions for completing it, and be prepared to present to the class a description of the form and the method of completing it.

SS-4 ..... **Application for Employer Identification Number**
SS-5 ..... **Application for Employee Account Number**
941 ...... **Employer's Quarterly Federal Tax Return**
W-2 ...... **Wage and Tax Statement**
W-4 ...... **Employee's Withholding Exemption Certificate**
OAAN-7003 ... **Request for Change in Social Security Records**

■ **2.** To accumulate information for a tax file, a secretary must have some understanding of taxable income and allowable deductions. From the following list, select those income items that are taxable and those expense items that are deductible. Arrange the items alphabetically and type them in a form convenient for reference. You may need to check reference sources to identify the tax status of certain items.

Income Items	Expense Items
Payment for writing magazine article	Contribution to an old friend
Interest from municipal bonds	Tips paid to waitresses while on business
Bonus from employer	trip
Prize — paid vacation to a resort as a prize for the "Best Idea" contest	Federal income tax paid during year
	Interest on loan on family automobile
Rent received on property inherited from a relative	Contributions to Girl Scouts
	Contributions to a political party
Dividends on corporation stock	Interest on loan on home
Interest on U.S. Government bonds	Driver's license fee
Merchandise received from employer	State income tax
Interest on deposits in savings and loan association	Property loss resulting from theft
	Federal Social Security tax
Payments from accident insurance	Retail sales tax (state)
Property inherited from a relative	Employment fees paid to agency
Payment for a speech to a service club (not related to business or profession)	Life insurance premiums
	Traveling expenses to and from employment
Royalties received from a patent	Union dues
Profit from sale of building lot originally planned for home	Repairs on home
	Gift to a customer
	Expenses incurred in acting as chairman of United Appeals fund drive

Related Work Assignments 68-71

68. Calculating Hours Worked. You are to keep a daily time record for the following six employees in the advertising department of Continental Products. Prepare a time record sheet showing the number of hours worked each day and the total for the week for each employee, for the week ending Saturday, February 14. (Office hours are from 8:30 a.m. to 12 noon and 1 to 5 p.m. from Monday through Friday and from 8:30 a.m. to 11:00 a.m. on Saturday.)

Louis Albers (artist)—came and left on time each day.

Douglas Michaels (student-artist)—left at 3:30 on Tuesday (headache); worked until 6:30 on Wednesday to make up the time lost on Tuesday; worked until 8 p.m. on Thursday (rush job on Closson account); otherwise worked regular hours.

Charles Breckel (student-artist)—came on time each day. He worked until 7 p.m. on Thursday and Friday, and until 12:45 p.m. on Saturday (rush Closson advertisement).

William Meyer (copy writer)—worked regular hours Monday through Friday and 4½ hours on Saturday.

Eloise Kistner (stenographer-clerk)—was 30 minutes late Monday morning; worked until 5:30 Wednesday to make up time lost on Monday; worked until 6 p.m. on Thursday to get out some correspondence.

Janice Moser (secretary)—on time every day; worked until 6 p.m. Wednesday and Thursday nights on correspondence and records; worked until 7 p.m. Friday night and until 1 p.m. on Saturday (Closson job).

69. Calculating Net Pay. Complete a weekly payroll sheet calculating the net earnings for the week for the six employees in the preceding project. Use the current F.I.C.A. tax-deduction rate and the current withholding tax table. (These tables may be obtained from your nearest District Director of Internal Revenue or from your post office.) A 50-cent weekly deduction is made from each employee for group insurance. All employees claim two withholding tax exemptions with the exception of Eloise Kistner and Janice Moser, who claim only one exemption. All employees are paid for overtime work at the rate of one and one-half times their regular rate for all hours in excess of 40 worked in any one work week. Salary or wage rates for the employees are:

Louis Albers...	$160.00 per week
Douglas Michaels.....................................	2.00 per hour
Charles Breckel.......................................	1.60 per hour
William Meyer..	120.00 per week
Eloise Kistner..	80.00 per week
Janice Moser...	100.00 per week

70. Income Tax Worksheet. The Income Tax file contained receipts and notations showing that Mr. Simpson had the following personal income and expenditures during the year.

Prepare a worksheet or statement listing (a) each taxable income and the total and (b) each allowable deduction and the total.

Income Folder

> Salary: $15,000 less F.I.C.A. tax, $660; Federal Income Tax, $2,000; State income tax, $300; hospitalization, $80; United Appeal, $120; net pay, $11,840
> End-of-Year Bonus from company, $1,000
> Rent (after expenses) on investment property, $800
> Interest: From deposits in Savings and Loan Association, $110; City Water Bonds, $70; Life insurance policy, $22
> Dividends on company stock, $350
> Inheritance from estate, $2,000

Expenditures Folder

> Contributions: University Scholarship Fund, $50; Chamber of Commerce Building Drive, $100; First Avenue Church, $200
> Taxes: State sales tax, $180; State gasoline tax, $50; Property tax on residence, $350; Street assessment (new pavement), $500; Federal gasoline tax, $30; Auto license, $20
> Dues: Rotary Club, $70; National Bar Association, $100
> Interest: On mortgage on residence, $400; on installment purchases, $60
> Repairs: Cost of repairing automobile resulting from accident (no insurance payment), $250
> Gifts: College tuition for nephew, $750

71. Preparing Wage Checks. The instructions and supplies necessary for the completion of this assignment are provided in the Workbook.

Legal Facets of Secretarial Work

Business is regulated by law, and a secretary can expect to encounter legal terms in dictation and to prepare common legal documents in the course of everyday routines. In addition to terminology and form, though, there are other facets to the legal work of all secretaries.

The decisions made and the actions taken by the secretary with outside people (in the name of the executive or his office) will often be contractual agreements—enforceable by law—so that she must be well informed about the basic essentials of contracts.

The executive may ask his secretary to witness legal papers, to increase her usefulness to the company by becoming a notary public, or to exercise power of attorney for him, possibly when he is out of the country on a business trip. He may want her to type his will or a codicil to be added to it. Such legal functions of the lay secretary are covered in this chapter.

It may be that the secretary finds her legal duties so attractive that she decides to become a legal secretary in a law firm, in the legal department of a large corporation, or in government. In that case she will be interested in the suggestions given for specializing in this lucrative and challenging field. Certainly the legal background she obtains will be invaluable as she is given increased responsibilities and authority for administration.

Documents Frequently Encountered by the Secretary

Business transactions such as sales, negotiable instruments, or formation of agencies involve parties from different jurisdictions. Naturally, complexities and problems arise in preparing the legal documents to cover conflicting laws of the federal government and the 50 states. To expedite legal procedures, a number of uniform statutes have been enacted, the most recent and most important one from the standpoint of the businessman being the Uniform Commercial Code. The legal documents described here conform to this code.

▪ Contracts

Many people in the business world are concerned with the legal relations pertaining to buying and selling of goods, property, and services. Every buying and selling activity may constitute a contract between or among the persons concerned. A *contract* is an enforceable agreement, either oral or written, which involves legal rights and responsibilities. Some contracts, such as those for the purchase of real estate, must be in writing; but all important contracts should be written even though this is not a legal requirement. A contract may be in the form of an oral agreement, a sales slip, a memorandum, a contract form, a promissory note, or a letter.

Content. In typing a contract, the secretary should check to see if the following essential information is included:

Date and place of agreement
Names of parties entering into the agreement
Purpose of the contract
Duties of each party
Money, services, or goods in consideration of contract
Time element or duration involved
Signatures of the parties

Prepare enough copies of each contract so that each party will have one for his file. When the executive sells his services by contract (as do engineers, architects, builders, and real-estate representatives), the secretary may have a standard form to use as a model; but usually there are items peculiar to each contract that make it necessary to vary the fill-ins each time. Forms are available for most common legal documents. Since some contracts must follow a statutory model or must contain specified provisions, it is recommended that the secretary use them or follow legal advice when preparing specified provisions.

Care Before Signing. All contracts should be carefully read by all parties before they are signed. Not only will mistakes, misunderstandings, and fraud be prevented, but also information can be determined such as: what responsibilities are assumed by each party, exactly what is offered at what price, how payment is to be made, whether or not material can be returned, and when and how the contract can be terminated.

Contracts Made by the Secretary. As has already been pointed out, the secretary often acts (in a legal sense) as the deputy of the executive; that is, she knowingly—and sometimes even unknowingly—executes contracts. This situation places responsibility on the secretary to exercise caution in making commitments, in requesting work to be done by outside agencies, in quoting prices or making offers to purchase, and in signing purchase or repair orders, sales orders, or agreements on her own initiative, for such commitments may be contractual.

The executive naturally relies on his secretary's recommendation on many orders or agreements (contracts) that he signs. The mere fact that the secretary presents the contract for machine repair service to him for signature implies her indorsement of its contents. For example, the secretary makes all the arrangements for redecorating the office or for the purchase of a new office machine. The executive signs the contract on the presumption that his secretary has checked all details and verified that the contract is correct and understood. A secretary may save her employer the time of reading "the fine print" if she annotates the important points of the contract and attaches this annotation to the contract when it is submitted to him for signature.

Filing Contracts. A contract copy should be filed carefully, for it is a legal instrument necessary to prosecuting any deviation from the contract. It is well to place the contract in a No. 10 envelope and mark plainly on the outside, "Signed contract between . . . ." This can be filed permanently in the company's or person's file or in a separate "Signed-Contracts" file; or if it is important enough, in a safe-deposit box. In some companies, such legal papers are kept in asbestos envelopes as a protection against fire.

▪ Wills and Codicils

The requirements regarding the drawing of wills and codicils are very technical and vary with states. Hence, they should not be drawn without proper legal supervision or direction.

Wills. A *will* is a legal instrument whereby a person provides for the disposition of his property after his death. A *testator* (man) or *testatrix* (woman) is the one who makes the will. One who dies without having made a will is said to die *intestate*. A *nuncupative* will is an oral one and is valid only as to personal property and when made by soldiers or sailors in distress; land may not be devised by a nuncupative will. A will in the handwriting of the testator is called a *holographic* will.

A will may be *revoked* by mutilation, cancellation, destruction, or the execution of a new will. Every will should contain a provision stating that any and all previous wills are revoked even though the testator does not remember ever having made another will.

Codicils. A *codicil* is a supplement that makes a change in the will, deletes or adds something to it, or explains it. It must be signed and witnessed with all the formalities of the original will.

To *probate* a will is to prove its validity to the court for the purpose of carrying out its provisions. An *executor* (man) or *executrix* (woman) is the one named by the testator to carry out the provisions of a will.

A person asked to *attest* (witness) a will does not try to read the provisions. He is merely witnessing the signature of the testator and assuring the beneficiaries that the testator was in sound mind when he signed the will. A will presented for witnessing should have only the signature area visible, thus preventing any chance reading of the contents.

▪ Copyrights

Creative work reproduced for sale or public distribution may be *copyrighted.* Copyrighting applies not only to printed matter, such as books and periodicals, but also to photographs, pictorial illustrations, musical compositions, maps, paintings, and movies.

To copyright is to register a claim with the federal government to a piece of original literary or artistic work. A copyright grants the exclusive right to reproduce a creative work or to perform it publicly. Registering is done either by the originator of the work or the one reproducing and marketing copies. Copyrighting tends to prevent a dishonest or careless person from stealing another's creative work and marketing it as his own. Increased use of photocopying equipment increases the necessity for the protection of a copyright.

Copyrights run for 28 years and may be renewed once for 28 more years. A copyright may be obtained by filing the proper forms with the Register of Copyrights in Washington, D.C.

▪ Patents

A *patent* may be obtained by a person who has "invented or discovered a new and useful art, machine, manufacture, or composition of matter, or any new and useful improvement thereof—not known or used by others in this country before . . . ." The following pamphlets on patents may be obtained from the Superintendent of Documents, U.S. Government Printing Office, Washington, D.C. 20402:

General Information Concerning Patents
Patent Laws
Patents and Inventions—An Information Aid for Inventors

Legal specialists usually are employed to prepare the patent application, the first step in negotiations between the Patent Office and the inventor.

A patent grant gives the exclusive right to make, use, and sell the patent. A patent must be applied for by the inventor. After the patent has been granted, it can be sold outright or leased, in which case the inventor is paid a royalty for its use. A patent expires at the end of seventeen years and can be renewed only by an act of Congress.

■ Trademarks

The Patent Office also registers trademarks for goods moved in interstate commerce, giving evidence of the validity and ownership of the mark by the registrant and of his right to use the mark. The registration term covers 20 years. However, during the sixth year of registration, an affidavit must be filed with the Patent Office showing that the trademark is being used or that its nonuse does not signify intention to abandon the mark.

■ Power of Attorney

The executive may vest his secretary with a *power of attorney*—the power to act for him. The document itself sets forth the powers given. It may authorize the secretary to sign checks and other legal documents for the executive. It may be made for an indefinite period, for a specific period, or for a specific purpose only. Only a tried-and-true secretary whose business integrity is unquestioned earns this decidedly weighty responsibility of acting as her employer's agent.

Should the executive have power of attorney for someone else, the secretary sets up a special file and records all executions.

■ Affidavit

An *affidavit* is a written declaration made under oath that the facts set forth are sworn to be true and correct. The word itself means "he has made oath." An affidavit, made by an *affiant*, must be sworn to before a public officer (such as a notary, judge, or a justice of the peace).

For example, evidence of citizenship is required before an applicant can obtain a United States passport. If the person seeking a passport has no birth certificate, he may use an affidavit from a relative declaring that the passport applicant was born in the United States.

PEOPLES UTILITIES COMPANY
PROXY FOR ANNUAL MEETING OF SHAREHOLDERS

KNOW ALL MEN BY THESE PRESENTS that the undersigned, a shareholder of Peoples Utilities Company, does hereby constitute and appoint Richard L. Rose and Milton S. Gold, and each of them, the true and lawful attorneys, agents and proxies of the undersigned, with full power of substitution or revocation, to vote in the name, place and stead of the undersigned, with all of the powers which the undersigned would possess if personally present, all the shares of stock of Peoples Utilities Company standing in the name of the undersigned, at the Annual Meeting of Shareholders of Peoples Utilities Company, to be held at 300 Main Street, Stamford, Connecticut, on Thursday, June 10, 19___, at 2:00 P. M. (E.D.T.), and at any and all adjournment or adjournments thereof.

Either of the said attorneys as shall be present at said meeting, or any adjournment or adjournments thereof, may exercise all the powers of said attorneys and proxies hereunder.

Date_____   _____
                                        Signature

(When signing either as executor, trustee, guardian, or attorney, give full title as such.)

▪ Proxy

A *proxy* is a written authorization (similar to that shown above) empowering another to vote or act for the signer. Proxy forms are solicited from all stockholders prior to annual or special meetings of a corporation. The secretary may be responsible for collecting proxies for the company in which she works, or she may call to her employer's attention a proxy form from a corporation in which he holds stock.

Possible Responsibilities for Legal Papers

The secretary may type legal papers completely, or she may fill in printed legal forms from dictation. She may also *witness* the signing of completed papers. She may extend her legal responsibility so that it is necessary for her to become a notary public. As a notary public she will acknowledge that a document was actually executed by the persons who sign it. She may also witness a verification. Finally, she may be responsible for recording legal papers.

▪ Notary Public

Notarial commissions are issued by the secretary of state, the governor, or other designated official in the various state capitals. Application blanks will be furnished upon request by the appropriate official in the state in which the commission is sought, or they may be bought at a stationery store. (See page 611.) There are usually a fee, an examination, and certain citizenship qualifications. Most states also require bond, which may be applied for on forms obtained along with the application. It is possible for a notary public to purchase Error and Omission insurance to protect herself against liability for her acts.

The notary's appointment states the county or counties in which she is authorized to perform and the date of expiration of commission. It is necessary for her to buy a notary-public seal and a rubber stamp. The former is used to press into the document the seal showing her name, the county in which she is commissioned to act, and the seal of the state. The rubber stamp shows the date when the commission expires. Each notary must comply with the rules of the state according to the instructions furnished her. Ordinarily the executive pays her cost of becoming a notary when the secretary is doing so at his request.

A notary does not scrutinize the document she is to certify. She gives the oath and verifies that the signature or signatures are genuine. If you should become a notary, remember not to be curious about what is in the paper you are certifying.

If the secretary is not a notary public, one of her responsibilities may be to arrange for the details related to having papers notarized. The names of two or three notaries public convenient to the office should be obtained. In some instances, it may be necessary to arrange a meeting time with the notary public and to notify all parties involved.

The notary public witnesses affidavits. She also signs *acknowledgments* and *verifications*, which are executed under oath. In an acknowledgment the person swears that his signature appearing on a document is genuine and was made of his own free will. A verification is a sworn statement of the truth and correctness of the content of a document to which the signer affixes his signature. All necessary signatures must be completed before the notary public signs the document.

▪ Preparing Legal Papers

Legal papers may be divided into two classes:

1. *Papers to be used in a court case*—These vary considerably and must follow the specifications of the particular court in the city, county, state and federal government. In general, a lawsuit is initiated by the service of a summons and a copy of the complaint. The defendant replies by filing an answer. Motions, stipulations, and petitions are filed after the case is moving. After suit is in progress, the lawyer usually serves the opposing counsel with a copy of the document he proposes to file in court. If either party is dissatisfied with the verdict, he may file an appeal.

2. *Papers such as wills, leases, agreements*—These give formal expression to legal acts and could become legal evidence if court action or litigation were later necessary.

The form of legal papers is standardized in some respects; in others, it varies with the jurisdiction and with personal preference.

Legal documents are usually typed on 8½- by 13- or 14-inch, hard-to-tear white paper (called "legal cap") with a red or blue double rule the length of the sheet 1⅜ inches from the left edge and a single rule ⅜ inch from the right edge. Unruled sheets of the same sizes are also in common use. For some documents the lines are numbered on each sheet.

If two or more parties sign a legal paper, each must have a copy. Carbon copies may be used and are referred to as duplicate originals; this means that the copies are to be signed and treated in all respects so that they are just like (conform to) the original copy. The paper used is of the same quality as the original. Distribution and office file copies are often on lighter weight, less expensive paper. The file copy may be on a different colored paper.

After a paper is *executed* (that is, the original and duplicate originals made valid by necessary procedures including signing, witnessing, perhaps notarizing, and recording), distribution copies and the office file copy should be *conformed* by typing in the signatures, dates, and other information that were added to the instrument to execute it.

An instruction to type "three and four" means that the secretary is to type an original, two duplicate originals, and four copies. If a copy of a legal paper is needed for information only, a photocopy will suffice.

Many legal documents that the secretary types are adaptations of previous ones. She can make extra copies until she has developed a legal-form reference file.

Type. For legal papers pica type is preferred. In any case, do not use the fancy type faces.

Spacing, Margins, and Center Headings. For most legal papers use double spacing. *On ruled paper:* Set the margin one or two spaces within the left rule and several spaces inside the right rule to stay inside the rulings. *On unruled paper:* Use a left margin of 1¼ to 1½ inches; a right margin of ¾ to 1 inch; a 2-inch top and a 1-inch bottom margin.

Two inches from the top of the first page, center the heading between margins in solid capitals; then triple-space. (You may also triple-space between paragraphs on double-spaced work.)

Paragraphs. Indent ten spaces for paragraphs. To make difficult any unwarranted insertion of pages, do not end a page with the last line of a paragraph. Carry over several lines to the second page.

Quoted Matter and Land Descriptions. Indent five to ten spaces from the left margin; retain the right margin if desired, or indent five spaces.

Indent an additional five spaces for a new paragraph within the material. Indented quoted material may be single-spaced.

Page Numbers. Center page numbers ½ inch from the bottom edge.

Dates. Single-digit dates are spelled out. Examples: *first day of June, nineteen hundred and sixty-nine; 15th day of June, 196–.*

Numbers. When there is an actual transfer of money (such as contract or bill of sale), or if the document is a contract specifying quantities or a period of time, the amount of money should be written in both words *and* figures. Examples: *Five Thousand Dollars ($5,000); Ten (10) barrels of oil; Sixty (60) days.* In corporate resolutions, figures only suffice.

Use the dollar sign with a number only if it follows the word "dollars," as *Sixty Dollars ($60)*, but *Sixty (60) Dollars.* Capitalize each word of the amount except *"and"* as *Three Hundred Seventy-Five and No/100 Dollars ($375).*

Reference Notations. On the first page of the file copy in the upper left corner, type the reference notations as shown at the right. The *3-4* indicates that an original and two duplicate originals were typed for executory use and that four extra carbon copies were made. Underneath these notations indicate the recipients of each of the six copies.

```
3-4
2/8/--
JWR/jc
```

Names and Signature Lines. Three blank lines are provided at the end of legal papers for required signatures. Such lines cannot stand alone on a page; arrange the body of the instrument so that at least two lines will appear on the page with the signatures.

Begin signature lines for the names of the principals slightly to the right of the center of the page and extend them to the right margin. Witness signature lines should begin at the left margin and extend almost to the page center. Provide one or two blank lines between the lines used for the signatures.

Each name is typed in the body of the document exactly as it will be signed if the secretary knows the signature that will be used. When the regular signature is not known, the secretary uses the legal name—the full two or three names of the individual without abbreviations or initials. The legal signature of a married woman preferably combines her maiden name with her married name, such as Dorothy Keller Brown. Personal titles—*Mr., Mrs.,* and *Miss*—are not used; ordinarily professional titles are not used either.

Some secretaries lightly pencil in the respective initials at the beginnings of the lines on which each is to sign. Other secretaries use a small "X" to mark the spot. In some jurisdictions the names must be typed under the signature lines. Names are typed on file-copy signature lines after some indication for *signed*, such as *Sgd*.

Seals. The abbreviation *L.S.* (*locus sigilli*, meaning "place of the seal") frequently appears at the end of lines on which parties to a paper sign their names. These letters have the legal significance of a wax seal. State laws determine whether or not a legal paper requires a seal.

Insertions. At the time of signing a legal paper, an insertion may be requested. An insertion is valid if the signers indorse it by writing their initials in ink near it. At the time of typing, however, an omission may not be inserted between the lines to avoid retyping the page.

Erasures and Corrections. Each page should be typed accurately, for an erased and corrected error can cast doubt on the validity of an item if it occurs in a vital phrase. For example, *"four* thousand acres" erased and changed to *"forty* thousand acres" (or "June *6*" changed to "June *5*") might raise a question of validity. An error in a single word in the straight text can usually be erased and corrected without question.

Proofreading. The secretary unfamiliar with legal work should be particularly careful in proofreading her work, questioning terms that she does not understand. Novices have typed "the plaintiff praise" for "the plaintiff prays" and referred to the "Court of Common Please" or the "Court of Common Police" rather than the "Court of Common Pleas." They have embarrassed themselves by referring to a "notary republic." FIND OUT if you are not sure of your ground!

▪ Standard Legal Forms

Undoubtedly your employer will engage legal counsel when preparing important legal papers. If, however, certain types of papers are often used, such as leases or deeds, the forms given in legal reference books can be used as guides. Avoid indiscriminate copying of such forms because the laws vary from state to state, and laws also change.

Legal Blanks. Stationery stores that supply legal offices carry printed legal forms that concur with local laws. These are called *legal* or *law blanks*. Sources of supply are shown in the Yellow Pages under one of those two headings for printed blanks of such common documents as affidavits, agreements, deeds, leases, powers of attorney, and wills.

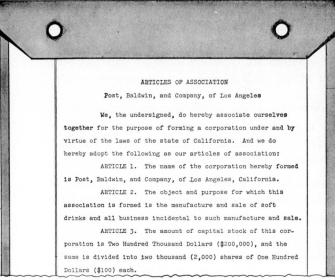

ARTICLES OF ASSOCIATION

Post, Baldwin, and Company, of Los Angeles

We, the undersigned, do hereby associate ourselves together for the purpose of forming a corporation under and by virtue of the laws of the state of California. And we do hereby adopt the following as our articles of association:

ARTICLE 1. The name of the corporation hereby formed is Post, Baldwin, and Company, of Los Angeles, California.

ARTICLE 2. The object and purpose for which this association is formed is the manufacture and sale of soft drinks and all business incidental to such manufacture and sale.

ARTICLE 3. The amount of capital stock of this corporation is Two Hundred Thousand Dollars ($200,000), and the same is divided into two thousand (2,000) shares of One Hundred Dollars ($100) each.

To protect a legal document, a single backing sheet ("le back" or "cover") with dim sions that are about 1 inch w and 1½ inch longer than the strument. This sheet is usu blue and of tough, heavy-qua paper. After the back is prop folded, the indorsement is ty The typed pages are then inse under the inch fold at the to the backing sheet, and an ey or staple is placed at each (about 1 inch from the top the sides). Back sheets may color coded to differentiate ty of documents.

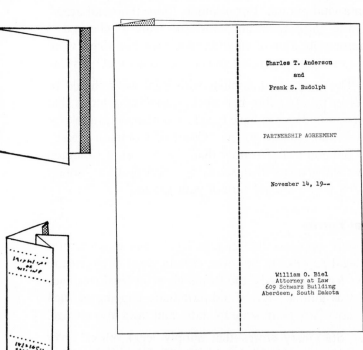

Charles T. Anderson
and
Frank S. Rudolph

PARTNERSHIP AGREEMENT

November 14, 19--

William O. Biel
Attorney at Law
609 Schwarz Building
Aberdeen, South Dakota

No. 5610479

Mortgage

FROM

HARRY K. MORROW and
LOIS J. MORROW, his wife

TO

THEODORE M. MANCHESTER

State of Ohio,   Stark   County, s
Presented for record on the   16th
of   September   19--, at 1:
o'clock, P.M.
Recorded   September 16,
in Mortgage Book No. 4619 Page 39

Robert L. Stageman
County Recorde

A description of the legal paper, called the *indorsement,* is typed on the outside of cover as illustrated above. The indorsement at the right is typed on a printed legal b that provides lines and spaces for recording data. At the left is shown the method of fold a legal paper so that documents may be kept upright in tall, narrow files with the indo ment on the back in reading position. (Some offices use file drawers 16 inches wide that unfolded legal papers with the first page to the front. The indorsements are not visib

Many printed legal forms consist of four pages, printed on both sides of one sheet of 8½- by 28-inch paper and folded once to make four pages of 8½ by 14 inches. The form for the indorsement is printed on the fourth page. With this arrangement, binding of the pages at the top is unnecessary, and a cover is not used. When the front page (Page 1) is turned, Pages 2 and 3 really constitute one continuous page down the full inside length of the document.

Fill-Ins on Legal Blanks. Fill-ins may range from a single letter or figure to words, phrases, or long lines of text. Printed lines are usually not provided in the blank spaces; the typist, therefore, must align the typing line with the printing line. Use the printed margins for typing full lines. As a precaution, rule a *Z* in ink to fill deep unused space.

Carbon Copies of Legal Blanks. To align typed information on carbon copies of printed forms, check the forms to be sure that all copies were printed at the same time. The legend 60M 7/6/6– indicates that 60,000 copies were printed on July 6, 196–. Roll the matched set carefully into the typewriter and then insert the carbons (as shown on page 90). Because aligning is sometimes difficult, the secretary may prefer to type an individual copy of each blank and read each one back against the master for correctness. If all copies typed are originals, type the word *COPY* on all but one.

Riders. When the space allotted for filling in conditional clauses or other provisions in a legal blank is not large enough for the typewritten material, leave sufficient space after the last line to permit a slip of paper containing the rest of the typewritten material (called a *rider*) to be pasted to the document. Use legal cap for the rider, and cut off any unused part of the sheet. Fasten the rider securely to the document.

Aids to Improvement as a Legal Secretary

Following are sources of information about legal secretarial work:

Local Information: directory of legal profession; local law bulletin (daily or weekly), a record of court calls and current news about meetings of interest to the legal profession; catalog of stationery-store printed forms; rules of courts, including the form in which papers are to be prepared (available on request from clerks); meetings and workshops of the local chapter of the National Association of Legal Secretaries, including their annual A Day in Court; and library access to the *Martindale-Hubbell Law Directory,* a four-volume reference listing

This Lease Witnesseth:

THAT   David R. Fisher and Alice G. Fisher, husband and wife,

HEREBY LEASE TO Robert C. Davidson

the premises situate in the   City   _of_   Tampa   _in the County of_

Hillsborough   _and State of_   Florida,   _described as follows:_

Building to be used as a hardware store located at 5101 Madison Road, Tampa, Florida,

with the appurtenances thereto, for the term of   ten (10) years   _commencing_

May 1,   19 -- , _at a rental of_ one hundred (100)

dollars per month   , _payable_ monthly.

SAID LESSEE   AGREES _to pay said rent, unless said premises shall be destroyed or rendered untenantable by fire or other unavoidable accident; not to commit or suffer waste; not to use said premises for any unlawful purpose; not to assign this lease, or underlet said premises, or any part thereof, or permit the sale of_ his _interest therein by legal process, without the written consent of said lessors; not to use said premises or any part thereof in violation of any law relating to intoxicating liquors; and at the expiration of this lease, to surrender said premises in as good condition as they now are or may be put by said_ lessors , _reasonable wear and unavoidable casualties, condemnation or appropriation excepted. Upon non-payment of any of said rent for_ ten _days after it shall become due and without demand made therefor; or if said lessee or any assignee of this lease shall make an assignment for the benefit of his creditors; or if proceedings in bankruptcy shall be instituted by or against lessee or any assignee; or if a receiver or trustee be appointed for the property of lessee or any assignee; or if this lease by operation of law pass to any person or persons; or if said lessee or any assignee shall fail to keep any of the other covenants of this lease, it shall be lawful for said lessors ,_ their _heirs or assigns, into said premises to re-enter, and the same to have again, repossess and enjoy, as in_ their _first and former estate; and thereupon this lease and everything herein contained on the said lessors behalf to be done and performed, shall cease determine, and be utterly void._

SAID LESSORS AGREE   (_said lessee   having performed_ his _obligations under this lease) that said lessee   shall quietly hold and occupy said premises during said term without any hindrance or molestation by said lessors ,_ their _heir or any person lawfully claiming under them._

Signed this tenth _day of_ April   _A. D. 19 -- ._

IN PRESENCE OF:

Mildred Van Horn   _David R. Fisher_

---

lawyers and counties and towns in which they are located, as well as a digest of the laws of the 50 states and patent, copyright, and trademark laws; and _Ballentine Law Dictionary_ with pronunciations.

Government Publications (Superintendent of Public Documents):   _Glossary of Legal Terms for Secretaries_ and _The United States Courts_

Periodical: NALS _Docket,_ a magazine published for members of the National Association of Legal Secretaries, 854 Northwestern Bank Building, Minneapolis

Dictionary: Legal Secretary's Encyclopedic Dictionary (Prentice-Hall, Inc.)

Forms Manual: Sletwold's Manual of Documents and Forms for the Legal Secretary (Prentice-Hall, Inc.)

The National Association of Legal Secretaries provides a contact with other legal secretaries and promotes interest in professional development. Those who qualify for and pass its six-part examination become Certified Professional Legal Secretaries.

Suggested Readings

Leslie, Louis A., and Kenneth B. Coffin. *Handbook for the Legal Secretary.* New York: Gregg Publishing Division, McGraw-Hill Book Company, 1958, 378 pp.

Miller, Besse May. *Legal Secretary's Complete Handbook.* Englewood Cliffs: Prentice-Hall, Inc., 1953, 662 pp.

National Association of Legal Secretaries. *Manual for the Legal Secretarial Profession.* St. Paul: West Publishing Company, 1965, 576 pp.

Sletwold, Evangeline. *Sletwold's Manual of Documents and Forms for the Legal Secretary.* Englewood Cliffs: Prentice-Hall, Inc., 1965, 193 pp.

Questions for Discussion

1. If upon graduation from college you were employed as a secretary in an attorney's office, what could you do to prepare yourself for the work? Be specific.

2. What is the difference between the secretary's action in signing an acknowledgment in her capacity as notary public and in signing a service contract for office machines? in witnessing a will and in signing a lease for an apartment?

3. The suggestion has been made that in typing a will, each page prior to the final page be terminated with a hyphenated word. This is contrary to recommended manuscript- or letter-typewriting procedure. Why would this exception be appropriate for this legal instrument?

4. The secretary in an adjacent office asks you to witness the signatures on a contract. When you reach her office, you find that the signatures have already been affixed; and you are asked to sign as a witness. What would you do?

5. If a student wanted to protect himself against plagiarism of material in an unpublished thesis, how could he do so?

6. Your employer asks you to rush out a legal paper that must be signed by persons waiting in his office. You type it quickly, check it even more quickly, and hand it in. After the signers leave, you notice you have made a serious error in a date. What would you do?

7. How many copies of a lease would you type? of a will? of an employment contract?

8. What precautions are required with signatures to legal documents?

9. If an executive gives a power of attorney to his secretary, can she bind him on all contracts that she signs?

10. Select the words in these sentences that have been converted to unconventional parts of speech. Then consult the Reference Guide to check your answers.
    (a) **Take care of that rush first.**
    (b) **She has a secretary look about her.**
    (c) **The building inspector comes next week.**
    (d) **He powers the invention with gasoline.**

Problems

■ **1.** It has been recommended that a secretary should accumulate a file of legal forms for reference purposes. Prepare a typing instruction sheet that could be inserted in the front of such a file. Include typing instructions for:

(a) Margins
(b) Spacing
(c) Paragraph indention
(d) Writing dates
(e) Paging
(f) Writing figures
(g) Typing names
(h) Typing quoted matter
(i) Preparing forms for signatures
(j) Fill-ins in legal blanks
(k) Correction of errors

■ **2.** Type the following affidavit; make one carbon copy.

State of Ohio, County of Franklin. Richard L. Cummings, being duly sworn, deposes and says that he has been employed by and has worked for the Majestic Furniture Company, 5813 North High Street, City of Columbus, County of Franklin, State of Ohio, continuously for the past fifteen years.

Sworn to before me this
(*use current date*)

_____
Notary Public
My commission expires (*Date*)

■ **3.** Use a manual listed on page 203 or another source as a guide in typing a power of attorney. Prepare one and two, using the information given below and the current date. Below the signature line, type an acknowledgment to be signed by a notary public in San Diego. Prepare legal backs for the first two copies.

Mr. Frank R. Wright, of San Diego, California (San Diego County) wants to make his brother, George L. Wright, of the same city, his attorney for the purchase of the residence and land at 2342 Camino Del Rio in San Diego.

■ **4.** Type the following agency contract; make one and two and use the current date.

AGENCY CONTRACT

(¶) This agreement, made and entered into on this, the _____ day of _____, 19--, by and between the **GENTRY PRODUCTS CORPORATION,** a corporation of Butte, Montana, the party of the first part, and PETER S. ELLIOT, of Boise, Idaho, the party of the second part, (¶) WITNESSETH: That, whereas, the party of the first part is about to open a branch office, to be located in Boise, Idaho, for the sale of its products, the said party of the first part hereby engages the services of PETER S. ELLIOT, the party of the second part, as manager of that office.

(¶) The party of the first part hereby agrees to pay to the party of the second part a monthly salary of Eight Hundred Dollars ($800), payable on the last day of every month, for a period of one year from the date of this contract. (¶) The party of the first part hereby agrees to pay all reasonable office expenses, including rent and salaries of such help as shall be agreed upon from time to time between the parties hereto.

(¶) The party of the second part agrees to give his undivided time and attention to the business of the party of the first part and not to engage in any other business or occupation while in the employ of the party of the first part. (¶) The party of the second part also agrees that he will be governed at all times by the instructions of the party of the first part with regard to all contracts entered into with third persons for the party of the first part, that he will render a report of each and every sale at the time of such sale, giving a detailed account of the products sold, the prices, and the terms of the sale; and that he will submit each month to the party of the first part an itemized list of office expenses. The party of the second part agrees also to make all collections for products sold by his office and to make remittances of funds on hand as directed by the party of the first part from time to time.

(¶) IN WITNESS WHEREOF, the parties have hereunto affixed their hands and seals on the day and in the year first above written.

GENTRY PRODUCTS
CORPORATION

_____(SEAL)
Paul K. Singleton, President

_____(SEAL)
Peter S. Elliot

Witnesses:

_____

_____

■ **5.** Now that you have completed your study of the secretary's financial and legal duties, put the finishing touches on the materials you have collected for your secretarial handbook. Organize the material collected in some systematic manner and see that it is properly identified and filed.

Related Work Assignments 72-74

You will need printed legal forms for the first three assignments. (These forms are in the Workbook, or they may be purchased from a stationery store specializing in legal supplies.) Prepare a carbon copy of each legal form.

72. Preparing a Lease. Mr. Simpson asks you to prepare and notarize a lease. On a printed lease form, use the following information:

Lessor: Robert L. Simpson and M. J. Roth, partners

Lessee: Harry Benson

Property Leased: Building to be used as a garage, located at 210 South Main Street, Seattle (King County), Washington

Term of Lease: Six years to start January 1

Monthly Rental: $125 to be paid on the first day of each month.

73. Power of Attorney. So that you may take care of certain banking and financial matters in connection with his business, Mr. Simpson wishes to give you power of attorney to act in such matters. He asks you to prepare the necessary papers and states that you are to be given the power to:

(a) Draw checks against his account in the Central Trust and Savings Bank, your city.

(b) Indorse notes, checks, drafts, or bills of exchange that may require his indorsement for deposit as cash or for collection by the bank.

(c) Accept all drafts or bills of exchange that may be drawn upon him.

Use printed forms and make one carbon copy. Use the current date and your city as the location of the business.

74. Your Fundamentals. This is the eighth in a series of Workbook assignments reviewing English usage, grammar, and punctuation. These assignments are based on the Reference Guide in this textbook.

PART 8 Case Problems

8—1 √ preparing conference proceedings

The director of research at American Chemical Company assigned his secretary, Mary Johnson, to supervise the preparation of the proceedings of a special national conference on enzymes. The conference was attended by scientists from industry and education. At the conference the research director asked that each of the fifteen participants who had read papers give Miss Johnson a two-page summary of his paper for the conference records.

Miss Johnson finished the necessary post-conference chores and opened her brief case to start her editorial work. She found that she had:

8 summaries that required very little work
3 summaries that were written in first person
1 summary that was in outline form
1 summary that filled 15 pages
1 summary with neither name nor title
18 unmarked reels of tape (recording the complete program)
60 conference registration cards with no addresses

She remembered that the German participant whose summary was missing planned a three-month sightseeing trip in the United States and Canada.

What is your evaluation of Miss Johnson's preplanning? How can this year's experience be utilized in planning for next year's conference?

8—2 √ responsibility without authority

Edna Greenfield is secretary to Harry Allen, manager of a small branch office which operates in an exemplary way when he is there; however, he travels over the entire territory and is frequently away for several days at a time. He always leaves Edna in charge. The rest of the staff—several young men and their secretaries—regard his absence as a time to vacation. They come in late, take two hours for lunch, and leave early.

Edna is the only one who covers the office. She is in on time, has a sandwich at her desk so that all telephones are answered, and works overtime to finish her own work.

Although Edna is theoretically in charge, she has no real authority. She must secure the cooperation of the staff but is reluctant to tell her employer the situation. She knows that the other employees would resent her "tattling."

What should Edna do?

8—3 √ handling a supervisory problem

The office of the Regal Manufacturing Company has grown from a small office of three employees supervised by Mr. Thompson, president of the company, to an office staff of 20 employees. Up to now, the office staff was responsible to certain officials of the company; that is, certain staff members were responsible to the sales manager, others to the production manager, and so forth. Mr. Thompson has decided to reorganize the office and place the entire staff under the direct supervision of an office manager. Mary Adams has been Mr. Thompson's secretary for the past ten years and has grown with the company. She knows almost all of its operations and policies; she is company-minded and loyal. She knows all of the employees well and is well liked. Mr. Thompson decides that she would be the logical one to place in the newly created position of office supervisor. Mary accepts the position.

Mary's attitude is that she has not changed merely because her title has changed; therefore, she will continue her very close personal friendships with certain members of the office staff. It is Mary's plan to continue to identify with the secretarial and clerical staff, and not with the supervisory staff of the company. Thus, she will continue to eat lunch with the girls in the office and be concerned with their personal problems as she has in the past. The one thing she isn't going to be is high-hat or basically changed in her relationship with her fellow workers.

When a new employee comes to the office, she always makes it clear that, although she is technically the office supervisor, she wants to be treated and considered just as a member of the office gang. Her function is to help them, not to supervise them.

Mary is very hesitant to delegate difficult or unpleasant duties to other members of the staff. She feels that she should not ask others to do things that she herself would not like to do; as a result, she herself does many of the really tough jobs and more unpleasant chores. Whenever she assigns responsibilities, she always does it in the name of some other company official, such as "Mr. Thompson would like you to do this"; or "Mr. Franklin asked me to ask you to do this."

Working on the assumption that most problems will take care of themselves, if just given time, she avoids becoming involved in arbitrating personality problems that arise among the office staff except when the situation becomes extremely serious. She is determined that she is not going to meddle in the petty frictions that are certain to arise when people work together.

How successful do you think Mary Adams will be as a supervisor?

Is Mary the kind of person for whom you would like to work?

Is it possible for a supervisor to maintain close personal friendships with her working staff?

Should a supervisor ask a subordinate to do a task that she would not wish to do herself?

To what extent should a supervisor become involved in attempting to solve the petty personality problems of the office staff?

— *Ewing Galloway*

Ability, good judgment, initiative, imagination, and continued study provide the secretary with opportunity for an exciting career in the business world.

Your Professional Future

The emphasis in the preceding sections
has been on preparation for employment
on the executive secretarial
level. This section looks to
the future. Wide differences exist
among secretarial positions. Obtaining a
position that offers both job satisfaction
and a promising career results from
careful planning. Advancement depends
upon continued study and an awareness
of administrative and supervisory
procedures. This section has special
interest to those who look upon
secretarial training as providing the
entering wedge into an exciting career
in the business world—a career with
almost endless opportunity.

Selecting the Right Position

All secretarial positions have common elements, but wide differences do exist. Such factors as location and size of office, type of business organization, and differences in personnel policies have an impact on secretarial opportunities. There are also areas of specialization within the secretarial field. This chapter has a two-fold purpose: first, to point out some of the differences that exist among offices, and second, to help you think through and organize a workable plan for obtaining the position of your choosing.

Types of Offices

One of the advantages of secretarial work is that employment opportunities exist in almost every type and size of community. Although the largest number of secretaries are employed in the downtown areas of cities, there are many attractive secretarial positions in suburbs, in industrial complexes adjoining cities, and even in smaller towns and communities. From a secretary's viewpoint each type of location offers certain benefits.

▪ Downtown Locations

Although many large offices are concentrated in the downtown area, there are also innumerable small offices. Many of these small offices are located in large office buildings. As a secretary working downtown, you would be expected to dress attractively, perhaps smartly. Your clothing cost will probably be higher than in a suburban position or in a smaller community. There will be lunch-hour opportunities to browse and shop. You will see and be tempted to buy more of everything—clothes, accessories, and gadgets.

Though travel time and parking rates for private automobiles present problems, public transportation is more likely to be available. There is a wide choice of eating facilities and after-work entertainment.

The secretary in a large office will probably work in an area
surrounded by numerous other offices—both large and small.

▪ Suburban Locations

In the industrial suburbs there are predominantly large manufacturing concerns located along public transportation routes. Also in each suburban community there are usually a real estate office or two, an insurance agency, offices of several doctors and dentists, a school board, small stores, a city hall, and similar small offices.

More casual dress than in the downtown area is acceptable. As a secretary you will be expected to dress in good taste, but you may find that your clothes allowance can be considerably less.

The suburban position may be very close and convenient to your apartment or home, or it may be located miles across town. There will be far fewer choices of restaurants than in the downtown area, but lunch costs will probably be lower. Your company may operate a restaurant serving food at cost. It may even be the practice to take your lunch and eat in the girls' lounge.

▪ Outlying Locations

Many large industrial plants are located on main highways on the edges of cities but in rural-like open spaces. To get to them, employees must drive or ride in a car pool, which can be expensive.

Dress requirements are the same as in the suburbs. Employee restaurants are often operated at or below cost. Sometimes attractive recreation rooms are available to the employees.

—Atlas Powder Company

Working in an outlying area, the secretary may
be in a more relaxed family-type atmosphere.

▪ Small Communities

Secretarial positions in small communities offer many advantages
including lower living cost, and little or no transportation cost. However, salaries in such communities tend to be lower than those paid in
the urban centers.

▪ Small Offices

Many secretaries choose to work in a one-girl office or where there
are only a few persons—such as offices maintained by attorneys,
architects, engineers, accountants, doctors, dentists, insurance agencies,
real estate agencies, suburban banks, employment agencies, churches,
schools, and company branches. The secretary in the small office has a
wide variety of duties. There is no one else to do the filing, handle the
cash, make long distance calls, duplicate materials, sort and send out
mail, and purchase supplies.

Personnel Policies. One of the advantages of working in a small
office is the freedom offered. The hours of work are usually established,
but the secretary knows the volume of work and when time permits may
take longer lunch hours, leave early, or take a day off.

Small offices usually have general personnel policies rather than
clearly defined ones. This may or may not be to the advantage of the
secretary. There may be no limit to sick leaves and emergency absences,
or there may be no provision at all for them.

The secretary in a small office may find more variety in noontime activities outside the office than she would in a large, self-contained company building.

There are a few definite disadvantages to working in a small office. Generally, there is a limit to the amount of salary a small office can pay. The ceiling may be set by circumstances of the business and not by the competence of the secretary. Instead of giving specified salary increases at definite intervals, the employer is likely to consider each salary increase individually when he gets around to it.

Administrative Opportunities. In some small offices, the secretary must assume a great deal of administrative responsibility, but rarely is she given an administrative title or status. The employer, depending upon the nature of his work, may be out of the office much of the time and the responsibility for running the office falls on the secretary. In such situations, the secretary is pretty much her own boss.

Three- and four-girl offices frequently provide excellent opportunities to gain supervisory experience. In such situations, the secretary usually is the most knowledgeable person on office routines and may supervise the work of the office staff along with her other duties.

■ Large Offices

The work of the secretary in the large office tends to differ in many respects from that of the secretary in the small office. In the large office many of the business routines are performed by special departments. Telephone duties are handled by switchboard operators; postal and shipping chores, by the mailing and shipping department; the purchasing

The secretary who works in a large office will need an understanding of specialized activities such as data processing for her intracompany contacts.

department orders supplies—to mention a few. On the other hand, the secretary in the large office may handle travel details, locate business information for the executive, draft reports, sit in on conferences and write the proceedings, and perform many other services. She may also have many more administrative and supervisory responsibilities.

The impact of automation is more evident in the large office. Automation is adding to the decision-making responsibilities of the secretary and relieving her of many routine duties. (See Chapter 18.)

Personnel Policies. Personnel policies must be clearly defined and followed in large offices. Singling out an individual employee for special privileges can be damaging to office morale. The personnel policies of a large company usually cover such matters as:

> Hours of work, lunch hour, rest periods
> Overtime pay or compensatory time off
> Eligibility for vacation; length of vacation
> Number of days allowed annually for emergency sick leave
> Days considered as holidays (days off with pay)
> Salary range for each job; frequency and extent of salary increases
> Fringe benefits

There is opportunity for advancement in a large organization. There are many secretarial positions up the ladder. In addition, there are supervisory and administrative positions to which the secretary can advance. Secretaries to top management are frequently administrative assistants both in duties and title.

Fringe Benefits. Many companies offer fringe benefits to their employees. They are called "fringe" because they are outside the realm of salary, and sometimes outside the realm of taxable income. In some instances, the fringe benefits cost the company an additional 25 to 30 percent of the wages paid to the secretary.

Group Life Insurance. An insurance policy may be taken out on the employee. The employer and the employee may each pay part of the premium. Every employee is usually eligible, and rates are lower than for individual insurance of comparable coverage. The policy usually terminates when the employee leaves the company, but some policies have conversion features.

Hospitalization Insurance. Insurance for hospital and medical costs is offered to employees covering the employee and the members of his family. The company may pay the premium or may deduct the premium periodically from the employee's salary and pay it to the insurance company for him.

Credit Union. A credit union is a kind of employee-operated bank in which the employees can make savings deposits and from which they can obtain loans. A user must be a member since a borrower must purchase at least one share of stock.

Stock-Purchase Plan. A stock-purchase plan provides an opportunity to buy company stock from one's earnings. The employee may choose to have a set amount deducted from his salary toward the purchase of company stock.

Pension Plan. In recent years, company pension plans have become more and more sophisticated. Sometimes a company purchases an annuity for an employee or sets aside funds from which to make pension payments to him when he retires. Often both the employer and employee contribute.

Bonuses. Some companies give employees bonuses at the end of profitable years, often substantial amounts. This is sometimes a better management policy than to increase and decrease wages to correspond with fluctuating profits. These bonuses may be in the form of cash or of company stock.

Office Divisions .

In order to know which particular office in a company will offer the most stimulation and satisfaction to you as a secretary, you need to know the company divisions and their functions—in short, the office structure. That structure will depend partly upon the nature and the size of the business. The following is a description of an office organization pattern typical of a large manufacturing business.

▪ Company Officers

The top administration of a company usually consists of a president, one or more vice-presidents, a secretary, and a treasurer. Each of these officers will have a staff including a secretary to assist him in his work.

President. The *president* is responsible to the board of directors for the profitable operation of the business. His secretary naturally has the highest prestige rating, and she usually commands the highest salary among the secretaries. Her work consists of taking confidential dictation, handling appointments, arranging travel details, working on addresses and papers, sitting in on conferences and reporting the proceedings, handling personal finances and banking, and perhaps supervising a stenographic assistant who transcribes the president's dictation and that of the secretary.

Vice-Presidents, Secretary, and Treasurer. Often there are two, three, or more *vice-presidents*. Each one is responsible for some phase of administration, such as research or marketing. The *secretary* of a company is almost always an attorney, for he is responsible for the legal actions of the business. His office staff works with legal papers, corporate minutes, and so on. The *treasurer* is, of course, responsible for handling the accounting and credit. His secretary works with financial records and reports. She may handle stocks and bonds.

The prestige rating of the secretaries to these company officers is high. Openings for secretarial positions of this level are usually filled by promotions from within the company. They are positions that are earned, not acquired.

▪ Divisions

The office in a large company may be organized around such operational divisions as production, purchasing, sales, finance, and service.

Production. The production division is responsible for making the company's products. The work of the secretary to the production manager is unique, because her employer's position is a bridge between management and labor—a bridge that is carefully and jealously guarded. She must understand production processes, for she will spend much of her time working with the people who report to her manager—plant superintendents, supervisors, foremen, labor union officers, and plant employees. Her office may be in the factory.

Purchasing. The *purchasing division* usually has responsibility for purchasing materials, machinery, and supplies. In small offices, the department may consist of only the purchasing agent and his secretary. In that case the secretary handles all correspondence and all steps of the purchase routine. She receives the requisitions for the purchase of specific material, locates sources of supply, types the purchase orders, checks to see that the goods are received as ordered, and verifies the correctness of the bill. In larger companies other office workers in the department handle many of these steps in the purchasing procedure so that the secretary is free to handle the executive's voluminous correspondence and his special requests.

The proper filing of catalogs and other information from suppliers is very important to the work of the purchasing department. Another important responsibility of the secretary is the greeting, scheduling, and handling of salesmen. Salesmen representing suppliers provide one of the most important sources of information for the purchasing department. The finesse with which the secretary handles the many salesmen who come into the office has a direct bearing on the efficiency of the department.

Sales Division. Because a business survives only if it sells its products, there must be an effective selling organization. The sales division may be divided into two or more departments.

Sales Department. The sales manager usually directs a staff of salesmen. The department may employ the salesmen, give them special training, assign them to territories, supply samples and literature, introduce new products, and perform a myriad of other functions.

The work of the secretary is usually exciting—even hectic. She corresponds with the salesmen and customers, handles the expense reports of the salesmen, arranges the details of sales meetings, and so on. The sales department often seems to be the hub of office activity.

—*American Telephone and
Telegraph Company*

Concerned with selling as well as creating, the secretary in the advertising department will work extensively with people, both personally and by telephone.

Advertising Department. The advertising department is also concerned with selling. In some instances it turns over the advertising entirely or partly to an agency which plans and executes the program. In other companies the advertising department formulates and carries out its own plans. It is a creative and active department. The advertising manager and his trained assistants plan and develop magazine and newspaper advertisements, radio and TV shows or commercials, and sales campaigns by mail.

The secretary works with creative people who usually dislike detail. The keeping of almost all records falls on her. A lot of her work is on drafts of advertisements and brochures. She learns much about printing processes, printing limitations, and paper qualities. There is likely to be a mailing list of customers and prospects to keep up to date—a monotonous but necessary task. She may keep statistics on the pulling power of advertisements and campaigns.

Market Research Department. The work of a market research department is statistical and interpretive in nature. It is concerned with gathering useful data to guide the business in the marketing of products or launching new ones. The secretary prepares such material as statistical reports, graphs, papers, and articles.

Financial. The financial division concerns itself with the handling of moneys and accounting. Often the financial vice-president is in charge, directing the work of the treasurer and the controller.

The *controller* (sometimes spelled *comptroller* but always pronounced CONtroller) usually directs all phases of accounting—the *general*

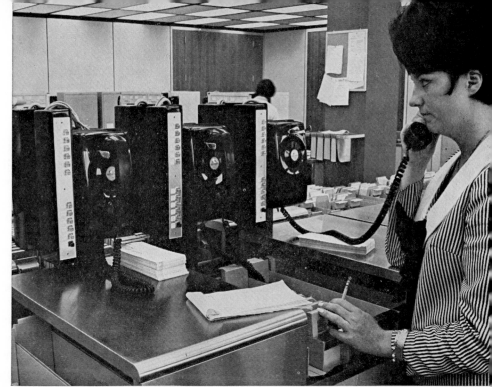

The secretary may have financial responsibilities relating both to customers and to employees. In the picture above she is involved with customer records.

accounting department, cost accounting department, and the combined *tax, internal auditing, and procedures department.*

The secretary to the controller handles correspondence dealing with accounting matters and policies. An important, highly confidential job often assigned to her is the preparation of the office and executives' payroll. She need not be an experienced bookkeeper, but she will enjoy the work more if she knows the principles of accounting. Like an accountant, she should like figures and have a high regard for accuracy. Opportunities for contact with the public are limited.

Research. Large companies are spending an increasing percentage of their annual budget on research because they recognize that survival in the competitive future is contingent upon success in developing "new and better things for people through research." The research division in a business organization, thus, is usually considered an area of prestige. The scientists, the engineers, and the secretaries who work with them occupy a position of high status in the company cadre. Some of the secretaries who work in the research department are classified as technical secretaries, an area of secretarial work which offers unusual opportunities to those who can qualify. See page 637 for an analysis of the qualifications and duties of the technical secretary.

Services. Those departments that serve all others and work almost autonomously are discussed together here as service departments.

Personnel Department. The interviewing and hiring of employees is a function of the *personnel department.* This responsibility involves the exploring of labor sources, processing and filing application forms, organizing and conducting interviews, and administering tests.

The secretary in the personnel department comes in contact with many different types of people, so she must have a genuine interest in people. The applicants who come to the firm for employment, the employees, and the supervisors must be made to feel that the personnel department is concerned about working with them to solve their personnel problems.

The nature of the secretary's work in the personnel department will vary with the size of the company. She may perform some or all of these duties: interview applicants, administer tests, process application forms, update personnel records, compile job specifications, assist in the organizing and planning of company recreational activities and recognition dinners, and report labor-management conferences.

The personnel department is an excellent place to learn the organization of the company, as this department has close communication with all divisions of the company. This experience is invaluable to the secretary who plans to advance to an administrative or supervisory position in the organization.

Office Services. Certain tasks such as filing, typing, stenographic work, duplicating, mailing, machine transcription, calculating work, and messenger service may be handled partially or entirely by a centralized *service department.*

The service department relieves the secretary of a great deal of routine work. To make full use of it, the secretary acquaints herself with the work it does and the equipment it has. By knowing, for example, the types of duplicating equipment available, she can plan her duplicating work around those facilities.

In a company not having centralized office services, each functional division or department operates as a complete, self-sufficient unit. It handles duties that are otherwise turned over to a centralized department.

Many offices have centralized office services but permit departmental operation to some extent. For example, the secretary may keep the executive's personal files close at hand rather than send them to the central filing department. She may choose to type stencils herself rather

—General Electric Company, Nela Park, Ohio

All or many secretarial office services may be centralized, as in the central office bay at the Airport Parking Corporation of America, Cleveland, Ohio.

than wait for them to be typed in the duplicating department. She may keep a supply of postage stamps in her desk for after-office-hours needs rather than hold up mail until the next day when the services of the mailing department are available.

Working for the Government

There are more secretaries working for the government than for any other type of business or organization. Government positions offer certain advantages, such as assured annual increments, job security, a sound retirement system, and the opportunity for advancement based on merit. Working for the government, however, can lack the excitement and stimulation that is associated with a business involved in a competitive market. The work is frequently highly routinized, and imagination and initiative are not always appreciated and rewarded. However, a college-trained secretary who has initiative and ambition and who is highly selective when entering government service can advance to a position involving great responsibility. The large number of women holding high-level executive positions in the government attests to the opportunity there.

▪ Federal and State Service

Being a Government Girl does not necessarily mean working in Washington, D.C., or for the United States Government. In fact, only 10 percent of the Federal Government employees work in the District of Columbia. Wherever there is a military installation, veteran's hospital, weather station, or federal bureau office, there are federal employees, including secretaries. State and local governments (combined) employ far more office workers than does the federal government. Thus, government jobs are found in villages, towns, and cities across the United States, and in foreign lands.

The Federal Government, all states, and many municipal governments have a civil (meaning civilian) service merit system, which means that jobs are classified and appointments made on examination results. Stenographic posts are classified in the Federal government as GS3 (General Schedule 3), secretarial posts as GS4, and private secretaries to executives are GS5 and GS6. There is a standard base salary with annual increments for each GS rating.

The United States is divided into ten regions with a U.S. Civil Service Office in each. To obtain information about a position, write to the regional office in which you wish to obtain employment. If you are interested in working in Washington, D.C., write the U.S. Civil Service Commission, Washington, D.C. You may also obtain information about Federal Civil Service examinations from your local post office.

▪ Foreign Service

Does the prospect of serving as a secretary in the American Legation in Istanbul, Tokyo, Paris, Rio de Janeiro, or Copenhagen excite you? If so, you should examine the employment opportunities in the Foreign Service of the Department of State, United States Information Service (USIS), Agency for International Development (AID), and the Departments of Army, Navy and Air Force.

Working in a foreign country can be thrilling, but also exacting, and calls for a special kind of person—one who is willing to live in an exemplary fashion, for our foreign service personnel are on display 24 hours a day. Each staff member represents the United States and contributes to the success of our program. The Department of State, USIS, and AID, therefore, carefully screen all of their foreign-service personnel. Requirements are high.

The basic requirements for a secretarial position in the Foreign Service of the Department of State are as follows: 21 years of age; single without dependents; a high score on a qualifying examination covering a clerical aptitude, verbal ability, spelling, typing, shorthand; and four years of office experience or the equivalent. Each year in college is generally equated as being equivalent to one year of work experience. However, a minimum of one year of full-time secretarial experience is required in all instances.

Competency in a foreign language is not required. If, however, you should have ambitions to advance to the position of a Foreign Service Staff Officer in the Department of State (there are many women in these posts), ability to speak and write a foreign language is required. Extensive study of a foreign language in college would be a strong plus factor in evaluating your application.

The pay is comparatively good. In addition to a base salary, allowances are provided for housing, cost of living, and special compensation for hardship posts.

A booklet entitled *A Career in the U.S. Department of State—The Foreign Service Staff* can be obtained by writing the Employment Division, Department of State, Washington, D.C. 20402. Information about foreign employment in the U.S. Information Service and Agency for International Development can be obtained by writing to these agencies in Washington, D.C.

Specialization in the Secretarial Field

Specialization—a sign of our times—has justifiably entered the secretarial field. Every secretary is, in a sense, a specialist, but may perform duties that require unique qualities and training.

▪ Medical Secretary

One of the long-established areas of specialization in the secretarial field is that of the medical secretary—the girl who works in the doctor's office or in the hospital. Special training is not essential; learning on the job is always possible. There are also excellent handbooks available for the medical secretary; however, programs for the training of medical secretaries are offered by some colleges. These programs usually concentrate on (1) secretarial training as needed by most secretaries and (2) medical procedures.

Familiarity with medical terminology is essential for a doctor's secretary. The American Association of Medical Assistants sponsors training programs for the medical secretary in which vocabulary is stressed.

In the one-doctor office, the secretary may serve as receptionist, bookkeeper, transcriber of case histories, secretary, office manager, and medical assistant to the doctor. She may be the only employee in the office so the whole show is hers. So, too, is the responsibility for a smoothly run office.

In the larger office, more of her work may be secretarial in nature. In a hospital, she may do only secretarial work. But regardless of the size of the office or the organization, the secretary must be familiar with medical terms, including meaning and spelling, and with medical procedures. In addition, she must understand medical and hospital insurance forms and be familiar with the type of medical records and filing procedures used by her employers.

All medical secretaries who have had three years of employment in the office of a doctor, hospital, or clinic are eligible to take a two-day examination administered by the American Association of Medical Assistants (AAMA). The examination consists of five parts: Medical Terminology; Personal Adjustment and Human Relations; Medical Law and Economics; Office Skills; and Accounting. Those who successfully pass the examination are issued a certificate for professional status as a medical secretary.

636

▪ The Legal Secretary

Many secretaries are employed in legal offices, for there are nearly 300,000 attorneys in the United States. Not all secretaries employed by attorneys, however, could claim the title *legal secretary*. For the most part, legal secretaries reach their status through advancement—that is, they start as stenographers and, through a combination of outside study and learning on the job, advance to the earned title of legal secretary.

To give status to the legal secretary, the National Association of Legal Secretaries (NALS) sponsors, through its local chapters, free training programs, an employment service, and a Professional Legal Secretary examination. This examination consists of four parts: Written Communication Skill and Knowledge; Human Relations; Legal Terminology, Techniques, and Procedures; and Legal Secretarial Skills. To be eligible for the examination, an applicant must be a member of NALS and have at least five years of experience as a legal secretary.

Many of the peculiarities of the work of the legal secretary were described in Chapter 25. Actually, the legal secretary's work is highly varied and involves extensive contacts with people—the clients of her employer.

The professional legal secretary receives a salary that is among the highest in the secretarial field. Many a legal secretary has studied law at evening classes, passed the bar examination, and proudly changed the desk plate from "Secretary" to "Attorney."

▪ The Technical Secretary

The technical secretary serves the engineer and the scientist—men who are at home in the laboratory but not in the office. The shortage of scientific and engineering personnel has prompted companies to provide each top-level scientist and engineer with assistants to perform routine functions and to free him for creative work. The secretary is a member of this "assist" team. Her function is to assume the office burden and to minimize the distractions and interruptions necessitated by office detail.

The "tech-sec" is probably as much an administrative assistant as she is a secretary. Her work includes not only the usual secretarial duties but such additional responsibilities as handling all or most of the correspondence from composition to mailing, maintaining the office technical library, at times gathering materials from other library resources, and proofreading and frequently editing scientific papers, as well as handling all details incident to their publication. She prepares engineering reports, checks materials against specifications and standards, and

The work of the technical secretary or administrative assistant involves scientific and technical understanding as well as secretarial abilities.

—E. I. Du Pont de Nemours and Co., Inc.

orders materials in compliance with specifications. The work is demanding and exacting, but the pay is exceedingly rewarding.

A strong background in mathematics and science is an asset to the "tech-sec." To grow with the position, however, requires continued study. TESTS, Inc. (Technical-Engineering-Scientific Training for Secretaries) has organized a curriculum for the in-service training of secretaries for the National Aeronautical and Space Administration that includes engineering and scientific terminology, mathematics, drafting, statistical typing, and report writing.

When you work as a technical secretary, you may expect to undergo security clearance if you are to be employed in a company having contracts with the Department of Defense of the United States Government. The maintenance of strict security control is becoming important to other companies as well, because of pirating of formulas, research findings, advanced designs, and so forth. The secretary must know how security is maintained for each classification from restricted data to top secret.

The demand for technical secretaries far exceeds the supply.

▪ The Educational Secretary

Employment opportunities for educational secretaries exist in every community. The type of work that the educational secretary performs tends to vary widely among positions. The secretary to the top school officials in the central office of a large city system will have duties similar to those of the secretary in business and industry. On the other hand, the secretary in the office of the local school will perform vastly different duties. For example, she will probably have less dictation, but may keep many more records, order materials and supplies, supervise duplicating, schedule facilities, work on master schedules, and plan group meetings. She will also meet school visitors and have close contacts with students, teachers, and parents.

The National Association of Educational Secretaries is a department of the National Education Association and has offices in Washington, D.C. The NAES is constantly working for the improvement of salaries, retirement benefits, and tenure coverage for educational secretaries. A magazine (*The National Educational Secretary*) is published along with handbooks and other materials written exclusively for the education secretary. The NEAS also sponsors a Professional Standards Program which issues five kinds of certificates based on education, experience, and professional activity. A college degree is required for the Professional Certificate.

▪ The Public Stenographer

The secretary who must be her own boss may find her niche in public stenography. A word of caution is necessary, however. The public stenographer must be a "jack of all secretarial trades." Only a secretary with a broad education, a wealth of office experience, and the highest level of skills should attempt to enter the field.

As the title implies, the public stenographer works for the public— that is, for anyone who comes along with secretarial work to be done. For this reason, her office is usually located in a hotel or off the main foyer of a large office building. She charges by the hour or job and may work for as many as half a dozen persons each day. The work ranges from taking highly technical dictation to recording speeches and testimony of witnesses, to typing legal documents, to purchasing a gift for the wife of a busy executive before he catches the four o'clock plane for home. A public stenographer is usually a notary public.

In the right location, the income is high, but much of the work is under time pressure. It is no position for the ulcer prone.

▪ Temporary Office-Help Service

One of the fastest-growing and unique services today is that of providing part-time help for offices. The Kelly Girl, The Girl in White Gloves, and Olsten's Temporaries are all images developed by advertising of national organizations having offices in all large cities and specializing in providing part-time help. These organizations establish a corps of temporary workers to be deployed wherever required. They help the office that experiences intermittent periods of heavy workload, they fill in for regular employees who are on vacation or ill, and they provide the one-half secretary for the office that needs one and one-half secretaries.

In addition to providing a service to business, these organizations provide a means of organized part-time employment to a large number of women who are unable, because of family obligations or other duties, to devote themselves to year-round full-time jobs or who return to work after rearing a family.

The work of the "temporary" is as varied as is business. Calls for assistance come from all types of offices. The agency attempts to match the requirements of the job with the competencies of the temporary worker. Many a secretarial trainee in college has found that being a Kelly Girl for the summer has been profitable both financially and experience-wise. This is one way to cram a wide variety of experience into a short summer period.

▪ Work-Travel Plans

For several years secretaries from Europe, primarily England, have invaded the United States secretarial market, giving the office an international image. Conversely, an increasing number of secretaries from the United States are seeing Europe via a work-travel plan. International units of temporary office-help services and employment agencies are recruiting secretaries for work in Europe.

There are also work-travel plans for the United States and Canada. One temporary office-help service with offices in over 300 cities in the United States has a work-travel plan which will permit the secretary to work two or three months in one city and then move to another.

Surveying Employment Opportunities

A review of the help-wanted advertisements in the newspaper will show that the highly qualified, college-trained secretary is in a position to pick and choose. The problem, then, is one of job selection. There are many dimensions to the selection process, as the following questions indicate.

Do you want to work in your local community, or do you hope to find employment in a new location—a large city, a different part of the country, or abroad?

Are you the one-girl office type, or will you be happy only in an office crowd?

How well does the business relate to your special interests in art, music, sports, medicine, accounting, social work, research, writing, politics?

Will you be satisfied with the position one year from now? five years from now?

Psychologists advise that the key items in job satisfaction are a sense of responsibility, satisfaction of achievement, opportunity for growth, and an awareness of being needed. Making the right choice is not the result of luck but of careful analysis and action.

▪ Evaluating a Company

How do you judge a company as to whether or not it would be a good employer? There is no sure test, but answers to the following four questions may help.

What is the reputation of the company in the community? The community image of a company is the sum of many things—employee relationships, reputation for progressive management, sponsorship of community projects, and general leadership in civic and business activities.

How satisfactory are the employer-employee relationships (company morale)? Do the employees seem to be one big family with a common bond of enthusiasm, or are there undercurrents of distrust and backbiting?

Is the business profitable? A business that is not economically sound cannot give its employees a feeling of financial security. Its wage policies and employee benefits will always have to be adjusted to the profit picture.

What opportunities for training and advancement are provided? Some administrators of some companies continue to have a mind set against women in executive positions. Sad but true. Such a company is no place for the executively ambitious type—unless she wants to be a crusader.

In your haste to make a connection with a large, established company, don't overlook the opportunities in the small office—you may be happier there—and in the new company that is just getting under way. Being on the beginning team can be exciting and rewarding.

■ Developing a Job Prospect List

No good sales campaign is ready for action without a *prospect list*. Your job prospect list should include potential employers who could offer the kind of employment opportunity you are seeking—location, size, interest appeal, permanence, and job satisfaction.

School Placement Office. The placement office of the school you have attended for your secretarial training can give you expert help in developing your prospect list and can assist you in making job contacts. Complete all forms necessary for registration promptly. Get acquainted with the personnel in the placement office. Discuss with them freely and often about your employment needs. If they arrange a job interview for you, always report back after the interview. Solicit their advice and let them know you appreciate their assistance.

Free Employment Agencies. Employment agencies are a good source of prospective positions. Any person seeking employment may register without charge with one of the Employment Service offices of his state. Registration includes a comprehensive interview and a skills test so that you can be properly classified according to your abilities, personality traits, training, and experience. In order to keep on its active list, you must communicate with that office regularly.

Other free employment services are maintained by certain civic and religious organizations. YMCA's, YWCA's, and YMHA's usually offer free employment service. In some cities the Chamber of Commerce gives a great deal of help in securing employment.

Private Employment Agencies. Private employment agencies charge a fee for each placement. Usually this fee is the first week's salary or 25 to 35 percent of the first month's salary. It is becoming common practice for the employer to pay the fee. The agency usually tests the applicant's skills and conducts careful interviews. Some companies depend upon the private agency to screen prospects for them. Thus, many highly desirable positions may be obtainable only through the private agency.

A private employment agency should be selected carefully. For a directory of reputable agencies, write to the National Employment Association, 2000 K Street, N. W., Washington, D.C. 20006. Agencies listed in the directory subscribe to a code of ethical practices. The directory will be especially helpful in locating an agency in a distant city where you would like to obtain employment.

Newspaper Advertisements. One source of positions is the classified or help-wanted advertisements of your newspapers. Firms that advertise for help in the classified columns use either a *signed* or a *blind* advertisement, such as the one at the right.

A blind advertisement is one in which a key or box number is used for your reply and the firm name is not mentioned. A legitimate blind advertisement is usually inserted that way because the firm does not want to be bothered with interviewing large numbers of applicants. On the other hand, blind advertisements are sometimes used just to get names of sales prospects by someone who has something to sell.

> # SECRETARY
> ### TO THE
> ### PRESIDENT
> We are seeking exceptional girl skilled in all phases of secretarial work. In addition should possess skill and charm in dealing with people, be well organized, capable of mature judgment and have an excellent appearance. Previous experience important.
> You will be joining a highly progressive and growing organization with full range of company benefits as well as opportunities for increasing responsibility and salary.
> ### IT'S WORTH A LETTER.
> Z7126 Times

Friends, Relatives, and Associates. You may wish to enlist the assistance of your friends, friends of your family, the businessmen with whom you have had some kind of contact, firms for which you have worked temporarily, people you have met through group contacts, and your teachers. Inform all of them that you are in the market for a position and that you would appreciate their help. Naturally, you should never make a nuisance of yourself. A report to the person who referred you to an opening, no matter what the outcome, is a matter of courtesy.

Other Sources. The Yellow Pages of the telephone directory provide a classified list of the local businesses to which you might apply. For instance, if you are interested in a position in an insurance company, you would find listed under *Insurance* all of the local companies.

Become an avid reader of the daily newspaper and watch all news items that would give you a clue to a possible job contact. New businesses are constantly opening, and items relating to jobs, changes, or expansions in business frequently appear in the newspaper.

Job Prospects in Other Locations. There are a number of information sources you may use to obtain job prospects in a distant city or area. The names of reputable private employment agencies in the city or area can be obtained from the directory of the National Employment Association (See page 642). Copies of the leading newspapers in the city or area can be examined at your local library. Names of companies can be obtained from the Yellow Pages of the telephone directory. Telephone directories for all major cities are kept in many public libraries. The employment service of the YWCA and the Chamber of Commerce can be contacted.

A nationwide computerized employment service called PICS (Personnel Information Communication System) is offered by Western Union. An applicant's qualifications, interests, and objectives are stored in the memories of the PICS computer. They are checked against incoming job opportunities that flow in daily from employers. Each time the applicant's computer profile matches an opening, the applicant receives a detailed description of the opening. At the same time, the employer gets the applicant's confidential career profile. The service costs the applicant a small monthly fee. Such a service could be very valuable in obtaining information about the more highly desirable positions in other locations.

▪ Learning about the Job Prospect

After two issues had been published, a magazine, using its name, advertised for a secretary. Of the applicants who appeared for an interview, only two had taken the trouble to examine a copy of the publication. Naturally, one of those two got the job.

You should exhaust all means of getting information on each of the firms on your prospect list. Telephone to find out the employment manager's name. Inquire of your friends, acquaintances, and instructors about the firm. Examine the company's advertisements that appear in papers and magazines. Study the annual report of the firm. A copy can usually be obtained by sending a request to the company.

Many large companies publish brochures describing job opportunities and employment policies of the company. Your college placement office may have them on file. If not, send a request to the company. If it is a small firm, you may inquire of its reputation from the Chamber of Commerce and the Better Business Bureau. Use separate file folders to accumulate pertinent material on each company.

Many firms will be eliminated as you proceed in this information-gathering campaign. When your prospect list is as complete as you can make it, check it and group your prospects by jobs you are best fitted to fill. Select the prospects with which you think you have the best chances for employment and which provide an interesting future.

Making Application

A fundamental step in preparation for making an application for a position is to analyze your strengths and weaknesses in terms of the requirements of the position. What skills, understandings, and special qualities will the employer be seeking? What type of experience background will be expected? Do you have unique qualities that would be an asset in the position? What weaknesses in your preparation and background might the employer note? Do you have a plan to correct these weaknesses?

The preparation of your résumé will assist you in making this analysis.

■ Your Résumé

A *résumé* (sometimes called a *data sheet, personal history*, or *dossier*) is merely a short review of your background and ability. Its objective is to help open the door for a personal interview. It should, therefore, arouse interest in your unique qualifications—be an "appetizer." If too long, it dulls the appetite. Keep it short, preferably one page, as illustrated on the following page.

You will use your résumé in a number of ways. It will accompany your letter of application in answer to want ads and in probing for job openings. Copies may be given to friends, relatives, and business acquaintances to pass on to a prospective employer. Your college placement office will need one or more copies. Always take a copy to each interview. It enables you to list accomplishments and some of the extras that can't be included in an application form.

Your résumé should be individually typed (not duplicated), and it should contain the following fundamentals:

Personal Data. Every employer wants to know certain personal items about an applicant. He will want to know your:

Full name	Age
Address	Height and weight
Telephone number	Marital status

Education. Include complete pertinent information about your educational background.

Personal Résumé

NAME: Carol Weber   DATE: April 10, 19--

ADDRESS AND TELEPHONE: Kappa Delta House, 783 North Lake Shore
Drive, Evanston, Illinois 60201, telephone 337-2374

PERSONAL DATA
Age: 21 years   Permanent residence: 127 Far
Height: 5' 3"; weight: 112   Hills Road, Peoria, Illinois
Marital status: Single   61611

EDUCATION
College: Northwestern University School of Business (A.B.
degree in June of this year, major in secretarial studies,
minor in English)
High school: Peoria High School (graduated fifth in a class
of 173 in 19--)
Major courses: Accounting   Economics
                Business communications   Marketing
                Business law   Office machines
                Business mathematics Office organization
                Business statistics   Secretarial studies

Secretarial skills:
Shorthand dictation rate, 120 words a minute
Shorthand transcription rate, 35 words a minute
Typewriting straight-copy rate, 75 words a minute
Office machines:
Can operate the mimeograph and direct-process duplicator
Have operating knowledge of key-driven and rotary calcu-
lator, adding machines, and offset duplicator

EXPERIENCE
Clerk in office of John Hancock Mutual Insurance Company dur-
ing past three summers
Clerk in office of Dean of Women, Evanston campus, junior year
Business manager of sorority for compensatory room and board

EXTRACURRICULAR ACTIVITIES
President of Secretarial Studies Club
Member of Alpha Pi Epsilon, honorary secretarial fraternity
President of Future Business Leaders of America
Member of Kappa Delta sorority; chairman of social committee

REFERENCES (by permission)
Dr. Harold Ames Head of Secretarial Studies, Northwestern
University, Evanston, Illinois 60201, telephone 866-9832
Mr. Louis Ahearn, Personnel Manager, John Hancock Mutual
Insurance Company, Wrigley Building, Chicago, Illinois
60611, telephone 473-3021
Dr. Louise Draddy, Dean of Women, Northwestern University,
Evanston, Illinois 60201, telephone 866-9845
Dr. Robert Kester (my minister), 1804 Woodstock Avenue,
Kenilworth, Illinois 60043, telephone 542-2020

Letter of Application

783 North Lake Shore Drive
Evanston, Illinois 60201
April 10, 19--

Mr. Harold Murray, Vice-President
Harmon Advertising Company
104 North Michigan Avenue
Chicago, Illinois 60202

Dear Mr. Murray:

The Placement Office at Northwestern University tells me of the
opening in your office for a college graduate with some stenographic experience who can handle a large volume of dictation
and relieve you of routine details. Since your own work involves
primary contacts with prospective advertisers, you require of
course, the services of someone who can meet the public well.
In the belief that I have the potentialities for developing these
three qualifications, I should like to apply for the position.

You will see from the enclosed résumé that I have developed to a
superior level the stenographic skills involved in secretarial
work. At the John Hancock Mutual Insurance Company, I worked for
a month in the stenographic pool. Ability to operate the office
machines mentioned should be useful in the statistical work required in your office. One course in business statistics and two
courses in business English have provided me with tools for helping in the interpretation and the preparation of the reports
incident to your work.

Experience in extracurricular activities has helped me learn to
meet people well. As business manager of a social sorority, I
have learned to live with forty girls and to consider and implement their requests for better organization of the physical facilities of the house. As a clerk in the office of the Dean of Women,
I was assigned to the reception desk. I try to be sensitive to
the reaction of the other person in my contacts, and I can say
truthfully that I like best working with people.

When you have analyzed my qualifications in terms of your needs
and have checked my references, I should like very much to come
to your office to talk with you about the position. I shall
telephone you on Wednesday morning.

Sincerely yours,

Carol Weber

Miss Carol Weber

Enclosure

Schools Attended. List all the colleges and universities that you have attended and the high school from which you were graduated. List the most recent schools first and give dates of graduation, diplomas received, degrees conferred, awards, and scholarships.

Major Subjects. The business courses that you completed should be listed. Include also courses related specifically to the position for which you are applying. For example, in applying for a secretarial position in an advertising office, you would list the English, art, and psychology courses taken.

Secretarial Skills and Abilities. Give your speed in shorthand dictation and transcription. List separately the business machines that you can operate, stating your operating ability. Say, for example, that you have operating knowledge on a machine, or expert ability if you have had considerable experience and can operate a certain machine well. Overrating your ability, however, may give your application a tone of superiority which may impress your potential employer unfavorably.

Work Experience. List your work experience in the order of recency or in the order of importance to the position for which you are applying. For example, in applying for a secretarial position, office experience—both full and part-time—should be listed first. A brief description of your duties should follow each position you have held. If your work involved the supervision of others, be sure to include that information. Don't forget promotions.

You will need to exercise selectivity in preparing your list. If you have had extensive full-time office experience, it is not necessary to list all the part-time positions you may have held. If, however, as with most students, your work experience has been largely limited to summer and part-time employment while in school, you may wish to list all such work whether or not it was office work.

Special Interests, Abilities, and Accomplishments. Your extracurricular activities, special interests, and achievements may give the prospective employer an indication of what kind of person you are and how you would fit into his office; therefore, you should list:

1. *The extracurricular activities in which you have participated and the offices you have held.* Holding responsible offices in one or more activities or groups may be more impressive than parading evidence of membership in virtually every organization on the campus.

2. *Special honors received.* **Recognition by awards and scholarships is evidence of your ability and perseverance.**

3. *Special achievements if they have implications for the position you are seeking.* **Your ability to read or speak a foreign language, awards for English composition or original writing, or special training in some field of science may be the specific point that influences the employer in your favor.**

References. From four to six reliable references are adequate. Business people are best; and the longer and better they have known you, the more valid will be their evaluation of your abilities.

If you have had no experience, list teachers or administrators, preferably teachers of business subjects, who know you well. Always secure permission to use anyone's name as a reference before you list it.

The full name and full address (business address preferred) of each reference should be given with business title, if any, and the telephone number, if he can be reached by telephone. An indication of the circumstances under which each person has known you adds to the value of references.

Résumé Related to Situation. In addition to being brief, attractively arranged, and flawlessly typed, the résumé should be constructed, if possible, to fit the particular position for which you are applying. For instance, if you did considerable work on school publications such as the newspaper, yearbook, or literary magazine and are applying for a position in the advertising or magazine world, arrange the résumé to accentuate this experience.

A Few Don'ts. It is recommended that you do not mention your religion or race in your résumé, and a simple indication of your marital status is sufficient. Details can be given in the interview, if they are important. Also save for the interview salary talk, as well as your reasons for leaving previous employment. If you think your photograph will enhance your chances of being interviewed, attach one to the back of the résumé form—but be sure it is suitable for use in applying for employment.

Remember that your résumé is a visible sample of your own work. It should indicate to the interviewer that you are businesslike and know how to present yourself in a complete, accurate, and well-organized way.

▪ Your Application Letter

An application letter is only a means to an end—the obtaining of a personal interview. It is usually wise, therefore, to eliminate the letter whenever possible. Try to make a personal contact by way of an interview. If an interview is not feasible, write the best possible letter of application—one that is certain to create a favorable impression.

Solicited and Unsolicited Application Letters. The application letter may be either *solicited* or *unsolicited*. It may be solicited in that you are writing in response to a help-wanted advertisement or upon an employer's request, which is frequently a part of the screening process.

Unsolicited application letters may be written as "feelers" to discover a vacancy or to follow up news of a vacancy. The same unsolicited-letter form may be used repeatedly, although you will need to adapt it to firms having special requirements about which you know. The adaptation should be done carefully.

Basic Parts of an Application Letter. Whether solicited or unsolicited, your letter should include the following four basic parts:

1. An appropriate opening sentence:

> The position of secretary described in your advertisement in today's issue of the Columbus Dispatch is a challenging opportunity. May I be considered for the position?
> Mr. Frank Johnson of your Sales Department suggested that I write to inquire whether you have . . . .
> Have you a place in your office for a college graduate who possesses good stenographic skills, who majored in English, and who . . . .
> Dr. Martha Adams, Head of the Secretarial Science Department at Western State University, tells me that you have a secretarial position open for a college graduate with stenographic and accounting training. Will you please consider me an applicant.

2. An appraisal of your qualifications in the light of the needs of the position—not complete but just enough to convince your reader that he should see you:

> You will see from the enclosed résumé that I have developed to a high level the stenographic skills involved in secretarial work . . . .

My interest in working in a publications
office started in high school where I edited the
school paper and yearbook. In college I completed
a minor in English and journalism, along with my
secretarial studies. Work on the <u>Review</u>, the
college paper, ...

3. A statement identifying where additional information on your qualifications may be obtained:

Additional information on my qualifications
may be obtained by examining my credentials that
are on file at the University Placement Office
(give address).

The persons listed as references on the enclosed résumé can provide you with additional information as to my qualifications.

4. A closing ("selling") paragraph suggesting an appointment and definite action:

Because I cannot be called by telephone during
business hours, I shall telephone your office on
Friday morning to ask if I may come for an interview.

I should like very much to come to your office
to talk with you about the position. I shall
telephone you on Wednesday morning . . . .

Application-Letter Guides. There is no one formula for writing an
effective application letter, but observance of these eight guides will be
of great aid:

Letter Addressed to an Individual. A letter directed "To Whom It
May Concern" may never concern anyone. Find out the name and title
of the person in charge of employment and use them. This information
may be obtained from the switchboard operator of the company. The
use of the name (correctly spelled) and title personalizes the letter and
makes a favorable first impression.

Box H-816
The <u>Columbus Dispatch</u>
Columbus, Ohio 43212

Gentlemen:

Obviously you cannot address your letter
to an individual when you are replying to a
blind advertisement. The correct address
form and salutation for such a letter is shown
at the left.

"You" Approach. One employment director estimates that nine
tenths of the letters he reads begin with "I want . . ." or "I am interested

in . . ." The potential employer feels like saying, "So what?" He wants to know whether you have a service for sale that fits *his* requirements. Your first objective, then, in both the letter and the interview is to show him that you understand the requirements of the position and to demonstrate to him how your qualifications meet his needs. If you adopt this attitude, your problem of enumerating a long list of "I did this" and "I did that" will be solved.

Honesty and Confidence. Your application letter should show a proper but not overemphasized appreciation of your ability. Above all, be *honest*. Your letter should be neither boastful nor begging. Employers are experts in detecting insincerity. Be specific about the position you want and the things you can do, but do not exaggerate. You may be called upon to prove your claims.

Do not be apologetic. If you have had limited experience, it is not necessary to call attention to it. Use the space to build up your positive qualities.

Original Letter. Examine and study as many effective application letters as possible to get ideas and suggestions, but write your own letter —in your own words and in your natural way of saying things. NEVER copy a letter of application and present it as your own.

Brevity. A great deal of thinking but comparatively little writing should go into an application letter. Remember that a famous letter writer once said, "I wrote a long letter because I didn't have time to write a short one."

A detailed treatment of your education and experience is not given in your letter, since your résumé is enclosed. Your letter, however, must invite reading the résumé. The statement, "I am enclosing information about my training and experience," does little to sell the reader on inspecting your résumé. Stimulate interest by such statements as: "An examination of my résumé will show that I am well prepared by training and experience for secretarial work," or "My extracurricular activities, described in the enclosed résumé, have prepared me to work with other people."

Making Action Easy. You may get an interview more readily by saying, "I shall call you on Friday morning to see if you wish to arrange a personal interview," instead of saying "May I hear from you?" The purpose of the application letter is to get an interview. If you obtain one, your letter has done as much as you can expect it to do.

Letter Eye Appeal. Your letter must be attractive to the eye and absolutely faultless in conformity with the best rules of business-letter writing. Anything you say will be worthless if your message contains a typographical error. There must be no flaws in spelling, grammar, punctuation, typing, arrangement, spacing, placement, or wording. You should use a good quality of white bond paper of standard letter size. Your envelope should match the paper in quality. Letterhead paper should not be used, but your complete address (but not name) should be typed in the heading.

Signature. Type your name—in the form you prefer—after the complimentary close. A woman should indicate marital status by typing *Miss* or *Mrs.* before her name. Remember to sign your letter, in ink.

The Interview

In preparation for the interview, you should go back to the front of this book and reread the discussion of traits requisite for success in secretarial work. The interviewer wants to know whether you have the traits discussed there. Put yourself in his place. What would *you* want to know about the applicant?

Though the time you spend with the interviewer may be short, you will be giving him a volume of information about yourself. He will form opinions based on your general appearance, your voice, diction, posture, attitude, and personality. Your conduct and manner during the interview and the written materials you present to him in your résumé and application blank also tell him a great deal about you.

▪ Guides to a Successful Interview

Tend toward the conservative side in dress and appearance. Secretaries who hold the top jobs are natural looking, well groomed, and smartly but simply dressed. They shun extremes in hair style, makeup, and dress. Avoid wearing new apparel to which you are not adjusted. Although wearing a hat is becoming less essential in today's business world, to be on the safe side, wear one. Gloves, however, are on the essentials list. It is a good idea for you to hold a dress rehearsal before going for the interview.

A PREINTERVIEW CHECK LIST

Are you properly dressed and groomed for an interview? . . . . . ☐

Have you gathered all the information you can about the company —its products, its policies, its status in the community? . . . . ☐

Do you know the interviewer's name? If not, obtain it from the receptionist before the interview. . . . . ☐

Have you mentally formulated answers to the usual factual questions and also to possible unusual questions that the interviewer may ask? ☐

Are you prepared for an interview? Be sure to take—

• Your résumé . . . . ☐
• Your Social Security card . . . . ☐
• A complete school record showing "To" and "From" dates . . ☐
• A tabulated summary of your college courses . . . . ☐
• Your employment record including dates, names, and addresses of employers . . . . ☐
• Your residence addresses for the past several years . . . . . . ☐
• A pen and well-sharpened pencils . . . . ☐
• A small notebook for dictation . . . . ☐
• A good pocket-sized dictionary . . . . ☐
• An eraser and erasure shield . . . . ☐

Anticipate the questions the interviewer may ask. If you have thought through the possible questions, you will be less likely to be caught off your guard during the interview. So plan your answers to talk not too much nor too little; strive for the happy medium.

A card, a letter, or a note of introduction to someone in the organization is usually helpful. It may be a referral card from your placement office or a note on the back of a personal card, but it puts you in contact with the one you want to see.

Before leaving for the interview, use the preinterview check list at the top of the page to be sure you are well prepared.

The Application Blank. You may be asked to complete an application blank before you are interviewed. The application blank is as vital a part of your application as the interview. Many applicants are eliminated entirely on the basis of the way they fill out the application. Therefore, never treat it casually.

> AN OLDER woman didn't get a job because she gave her correct age on an application blank. The next time she was confronted with the question, she wrote: "I refuse to answer on the grounds that it might eliminate me."

Application blanks have usually been planned with care to make every single question on the blank serve a purpose for the interviewer. You may not know the motive for asking certain questions or the use to which the information will be put, but it is up to you to answer every question exactly the way you are asked to answer it and to omit nothing. Draw a wavy line, write the word "none," or make some comment in blanks for which you have no answer. Think before writing any answer. Be certain that you write only in the space designed for each answer. Be careful that you follow instructions. For instance, print your name when the instructions tell you to print; put your last name first if you are so requested. The way you fill out the blank reveals far more about you than you realize.

The general neatness of the blank is important. Good handwriting is desirable because there is always need for longhand writing in office work, and no one in any office wants to decipher a scrawly, illegible hand. An application blank to be typed may be a disguised part of the typing test, so it should represent your best work.

The Interviewer's Method. For a successful interview, keep in mind the interview pointers listed at the left.

The interviewer will ask questions and encourage you to talk. Many of the questions will be routine and, although answered on your résumé, may be asked again to put you at ease and to give you an opportunity to express yourself.

INTERVIEW REMINDERS

Refrain from smoking while being interviewed. ✓

Keep your voice well modulated. ✓

Look directly at the interviewer when speaking or when being spoken to. ✓

Control your nervous actions and maintain good posture. ✓

Refrain from overtalking or undertalking. ✓

Be pleasant to everyone you meet in the office. ✓

At the end of the interview, leave at once—first thanking the interviewer for his time and consideration. Thank the receptionist also when you leave. ✓

Immediately after the interview, make a memorandum of pertinent facts to remember with an evaluation of how you conducted yourself during the interview. ✓

Some of the usual questions are:

What is your education?

What is your special training for this work?

Do you live at home? Do you have any dependents?

**What business experience have you had? By what firms have you been employed?
Why did you leave them—particularly the last one?**

**Why do you want to work for this company? (What an opportunity to show that
you know something about it!)**

What salary do you expect? What do you consider to be your strong points?

In addition to these typical questions, the interviewer may include
a few that are designed to throw an applicant off his guard and obtain
a true picture of his personality. Some of these questions may seem to
be unusual and perhaps personally presumptuous, but they are all part
of the interview technique and have a purpose. Some questions of this
nature are shown in the box that follows.

If you have had business experience, it is quite logical that your
previous employment will be a point of discussion in the interview.

You will probably be asked why you left your last position. Be
prepared to answer this question and, whatever your reason for leaving,
be sure to emphasize positive—not negative factors. Be truthful but
brief. It is tactless and unethical for you to say anything detrimental
about any former employer or firm for which you have worked, regardless of any personal feelings you may have. Always speak well of former
employers. Nothing is gained by doing otherwise.

HOW WOULD YOU ANSWER THESE QUESTIONS?

1. If you were starting college over again, what courses would you take?
2. Are you engaged? Do you expect to make a career of business?
3. Do you think that your extracurricular activities were worth the time devoted to
   them?
4. What kind of employer do you prefer?
5. How did your previous employer treat you?
6. What have you learned from some of the positions you have held?
7. Did you change your major field of study while in college? Why?
8. Do you feel you have done the best scholastic work of which you are capable?
9. What special interests do you have?
10. Which of your college years was the most difficult?
11. What type of people seem to "rub you the wrong way"?
12. Do you think that grades should be considered by employers?

The Salary Question. Salary is always important, but don't pass up an interesting position for one that pays a few dollars a week more. If your work is challenging and interesting, your performance will soon merit a salary increase.

Your college placement office can give you information about salaries. The Administrative Management Society[1] publishes an annual survey of office salaries, fringe benefits, and working hours. The United States Department of Labor makes an annual occupational wage survey in the larger cities. The survey reports may be obtained from your Regional Office, Bureau of Labor Statistics.

Most large businesses have a salary schedule about which you can become informed before applying for a position. When the salary question comes up in the interview—and it usually does — the best response is "I am willing to start at your scheduled salary for a person with my background."

If, before leaving the interview, you are not told what the salary would be, it would be appropriate to inquire "What would be the starting salary for this position?" If the application blank asks "Salary Desired" and you do not wish to state a salary figure, write "Open" or "Your Schedule" in the space.

Asking Questions. An interview is a two-way street, and you will be expected to ask questions. In fact, your failure to do so may be interpreted as indicating a lack of genuine interest on your part. What will be the scope of your work? With whom would you be working? What opportunities will the position provide for advancement? Does the company promote from within? Is there a company training program for self-improvement? These are all thoughtful, intelligent questions that are of concern to you. Even questions regarding vacation schedules, working hours, coffee breaks, and so forth are appropriate provided you are careful not to give the impression that you are more interested in what you will get than in what you plan to give.

If you are not shown, you should feel free to ask to see the prospective work station.

Concluding the Interview. You will probably know quite definitely when the interview is coming to an end. If the interviewer has shown interest and in any way has encouraged you but has not committed himself definitely about a position, it is permissible to ask directly,

[1]Administrative Management Society, Maryland Avenue, Willow Grove, Pennsylvania 19090.

SOME COMMERCIALLY AVAILABLE STANDARDIZED TESTS COMMONLY USED IN PERSONNEL TESTING*		
	Name of Test	**Examples of Jobs for Which Used**
Intelligence	Wonderlic Personnel Test	Clerical, factory, maintenance,
	Adaptability Test	and sales jobs
	Wesman Personnel Classification Test	
	Concept Mastery Test	Managerial or executive jobs
	Otis Test of Mental Ability	
Multi-Aptitude Batteries	General Aptitude Test Battery	United States Employment Service Programs
	Employee Aptitude Survey	All types of jobs from executive to unskilled
Clerical Skills	Minnesota Clerical Test	Office jobs
	SRA Typing Skills	Typists
	The Short Employment Tests	Office jobs
Personality	Gordon Personal Profile and Inventory	Office workers, computer programmers, and others
	Guilford-Zimmerman Temperament Survey	Office workers
Interest	Strong Vocational Interest Blank	Administrative and sales jobs
	Minnesota Vocational Interest Inventory	Various skilled jobs

*Adapted from *Personnel Management*, 3d ed., by Herbert J. Chruden and Arthur W. Sherman, Jr., p. 181.

"When will your decision be made?" If this does not seem to be a fitting question, you might ask, "May I call back on Friday at two?"

The interviewer may rise, and that will indicate that the interview is at an end. You should rise too and thank the interviewer for his time. Do not offer to shake hands and do not delay when the time has come to depart. Make no attempt to prolong the interview. Leave at once, gracefully, pleasantly, and with dignity. Remember to thank the receptionist as you leave.

■ Tests for Selecting Employees

If you have gained favorable consideration, you may be asked to take some form of test. It may be merely a letter or two to ascertain your ability in shorthand and typewriting. It may be a more general test or one designed to detect a wide variety of abilities. The main thing to remember is that you know how to do these things and can do them quietly, confidently, and efficiently.

Many organizations give a battery of tests (including a mental test) to all applicants who are considered likely possibilities for employment.

There is no last-minute preparation possible for such tests and no advice for the taking of them except to follow directions carefully and to proceed systematically and as rapidly as possible.

See a recent edition of *Psychological Abstracts* for a description of these tests.

▪ The Follow-Up of the Interview

Your follow-up letter, arriving within two or three days after the interview, may put your application on top. Include in the follow-up letter additional selling points, such as qualifications not completely covered in the interview or additional emphasis of your strong points related to the position.

For some reason you may decide not to accept a position that has been offered. Certainly this situation demands a prompt, courteous, and straightforward letter of explanation and appreciation. The day may come when you may need the goodwill of that company or of that individual.

Suggested Readings

Adler, Kenneth R. *Pathway to Your Future—The Job Résumé and Letter of Application.* Cambridge, Massachusetts: Bellman Publishing Company, 1964, 33 pp.

Aurner, Robert R., and Morris Phillip Wolf. *Effective Communication in Business.* Cincinnati: South-Western Publishing Co., 1966, 644 pp.

Becker, Esther R., and Peggy Norton Rollason. *The High-Paid Secretary.* Englewood Cliffs, N.J.: Prentice-Hall, Inc., 1967, 233 pp.

Chamber of Commerce of the United States. *Employment Abroad, Facts and Fallacies.* Chamber of Commerce of the United States, 1615 H Street, N. W., Washington, D.C., 13 pp.

Hall, Delight. *How to Become a Government Girl.* New York: MacFadden Books, 1964, 191 pp.

Kelly, William Russell, and Richard H. Kelly. *Work Smartly.* New York: Charles Scribner's Sons, 1963, 114 pp.

Laird, Eleanor Schremser. *The Engineering Secretary's Complete Handbook.* Englewood Cliffs, N.J.: Prentice-Hall, Inc., 1962, 223 pp.

Maule, Frances. *Executive Careers for Women.* New York: Harper & Brothers, 1961, 240 pp.

Mayo, Lucy Graves. *You Can Be an Executive Secretary.* New York: The Macmillan Company, 1965, pp. 1–46.

McLean, Beth Bailey, and Jeanne Paris. *The Young Woman in Business.* Ames, Iowa: The Iowa State University Press, 1962, pp. 1–55.

Myers, Katie Lea. *The Church Secretary*. New York: The Seabury Press, 1966.

Rollason, Peggy Norton. *How to Find the Right Secretarial Job*. New York: McGraw-Hill, Inc., 1964, 63 pp.

Questions for Discussion

1. In some instances, large offices pay a lower beginning salary than can be obtained in smaller offices. In such cases, the fringe benefits offered employees in the large company are emphasized. What fringe benefits are offered that would be of value to the secretary with the following plans:

   (a) To work only a few years until marriage
   (b) To work only to obtain money to continue her education
   (c) To make a career in business

2. After carefully considering your training, interests, and special aptitudes, indicate in which department (purchasing, personnel, research, sales, advertising, statistics, accounting) you prefer to have your first position. Give the reasons for your choice.

3. What are the major advantages of decentralized office services? Discuss the advantages of:

   (a) A centralized filing department
   (b) A centralized mailing department
   (c) A centralized duplicating department

4. Temporary-help services report that the average temporary worker is thirty-seven years old and married, has seven years of office experience, has 1.75 children and comes from a family with above-average income, indicating that there are reasons other than financial that motivate married women to enter the part-time employment market. What, in your opinion, are some of these reasons?

5. Assume that you are considering a foreign-service assignment with the Department of State. Give an evaluation of your interests, training, and experience for such an assignment.

6. What would you consider to be the most important factors to job satisfaction?

7. Some authorities say that references should not be listed on the résumé, but a statement such as "References available upon request" should be included. What reasons, if any, are there for not including the references?

8. The following introductory paragraph was used in a letter of application. What is your criticism of the paragraph? How would you suggest it be restated?

   "I have been looking for some time for a secretarial position similar to the one described in your advertisement in the paper, and I believe that I may have found just the opening that I have been searching for. You may consider this letter an application for the position."

9. Some applicants resent certain questions asked in interviews. They consider the questions to be prying into their personal affairs and to be irrelevant to their application. What would be your answers to such questions as:

"Are you engaged?" "Do you have any debts?" "How do you usually spend Sundays?" "Do you use liquor?" "How do you feel about your family?" "Do you believe in sit-in demonstrations?"

10. A highly qualified job counselor recommends that if, at the time of the interview, you are offered the position, you should ask for time to think it over—even though you definitely plan to accept. The delay is suggested so that the company will not think you make hasty decisions. Do you agree? Why?

11. Is it ethical to accept, without advising your potential employer, a position which he considers to be permanent but which you consider to be temporary, such as a position for the summer only, a position you intend to keep only until another position comes along, or a position to gain experience to qualify for a position in another company?

12. A compound word may be written as a solid word, joined with a hyphen, or written as individual words. Explain why the following groups of words are written as shown. Then consult the Reference Guide to verify or correct your answers.

(a) shell-like, heel-less, re-employ, pre-establish
(b) twenty-five, eighty-four, one-fourth, fifty-five
(c) re-collect, re-form, fruit-less diet, re-count
(d) S-curve, X-ray, U-turn, T-square, H-bomb
(e) a make-believe plan, a two-hour session, a well-known enemy
(f) ex-President, pre-Easter, semi-Dutch, anti-Freudian

13. Show which words you would capitalize in the following sentences. Then use the Reference Guide to verify or correct your answers.

(a) I am sorry that I have not studied biology, chemistry, or physics; perhaps I can take a night course in one of them.
(b) I received straight A's in secretarial practice and also in human relations in business.
(c) I majored in languages: french, german, russian, and spanish.

Problems

■ **1.** Prepare a report on one of the following topics. Include in your report the information indicated under each topic.

Topic A—Federal Civil Service Employment for Secretaries

(1) The GS ratings and pay scale
(2) Fringe benefits
(3) The Civil Service Examination (topics covered, standards)
(4) Source of information about positions and examinations

Topic B—Services of the National Association of Legal Secretaries

(1) Objectives of the association
(2) Services provided to members
(3) Professional standards program

Topic C—Services of the National Association of Educational Secretaries

(1) Objectives of the association
(2) Services provided to members
(3) Professional standards program

Topic D—The Technical Secretary

(1) Nature of work
(2) Preparation requirements
(3) Advancement opportunities

■ **2.** Suggest situations in which each of the following experiences would be an asset in getting a position as secretary:

(a) Treasurer of student government
(b) Camp counselor in summers
(c) Beauty queen in college
(d) Salutatorian of high school class
(e) Checker at chain grocery
(f) Sunday School teacher
(g) Reared on a farm
(h) President of college club of secretarial students
(i) Summer in Europe
(j) Waitress in summer resort
(k) Editor of high school annual
(l) Major in chemistry
(m) Phi Beta Kappa
(n) Part-time worker in registrar's office
(o) Member of social sorority
(p) Voted "most original" by senior class

(q) Advertising manager of college newspaper
(r) Sales clerk in department store
(s) Member of glee club
(t) Member of production staff of Little Theater
(u) College champion in women's tennis singles

■ **3.** Assume that you are applying for a specific position and are asked the following questions. Type your replies on a sheet of paper. In preparing your answers, try to analyze the motive behind the question.

(a) Why do you want to work for this company?
(b) What skills do you have?
(c) What salary do you expect?
(d) Do you intend to stay in the position permanently?
(e) Are you engaged?
(f) What hobbies interest you?
(g) What books have you read in the past three months that interested you?
(h) How much will your living cost you?
(i) What experience have you had?
(j) What kind of grades did you make in college?

■ **4.** A list of the most frequently used employment tests is given on page 657. Prepare a report for presentation to the class describing the nature of each test. One source of information for your report would be a recent edition of the *Mental Measurements Yearbook*.

Related Work Assignments 75-77 ————

75. Office Services Department

76. Completing an Application Blank

77. Applying for a Position

The instructions and supplies necessary for the completion of Related Work Assignments 75–77 are provided in the Workbook.

Ch. 27 Planning for a Professional Future

Everyone who starts a new position does so with mixed emotions—and you will be no exception. Naturally, you will be excited. It is always exciting to start something new. The fact that you are moving into the dynamic business world and that you will be right in the middle of things adds to the anticipation. It is like opening an attractively wrapped gift package; you can't help being excited and curious about what is inside. On the other hand, you will take this step with some anxiety and apprehension. You will be concerned about your ability to make good.

The Success Formula

Formulas for success in business are as varied and legion as there are types of successful executives. If you are to succeed, you will have to develop your own formula. There are, however, certain basic rules that may help you to make good and to achieve professional status in business. These rules do not differ greatly from those followed in your college program. Briefly stated they are:

1. **Get off to a good start.**
2. **Learn all you can about the company, the people with whom you work, and the requirements of your position.**
3. **Plan and systematize your work.**
4. **Accept responsibility willingly.**
5. **Maintain a wholesome, positive attitude.**
6. **Continue to grow professionally.**

▪ Making a Good Start

Some companies have a well-planned program for inducting new employees into their positions. If you obtain a position in such a firm, someone will be assigned to welcome you, introduce you to your colleagues, show you your work area, take you to lunch, tell you something of the history of the organization, possibly show you a movie about your new company, and provide you with both the company manual and the departmental procedures manual.

Many companies, however, have no organized induction program. If you are fortunate, the secretary whose place you are taking will remain on the job for a few days to train you. In many cases, though, you will report to an executive whose secretary has already left, and you "sink or swim alone."

First Impressions. Everyone in the office will form first impressions of you, just as you will of them. The very same things you considered important when you made your application for the position will continue to be important as you try to make good on the job. You can assume that you made a satisfactory first impression on your employer when you were given the job. Now you must make a satisfactory first impression on all of those with whom you work, and then see that this impression becomes permanent.

You will be under critical and detailed inspection that first day. Your dress, your grooming, and everything you do and say will be observed. It is a trait of human nature to be on the defensive against an outsider or a newcomer until that person has won goodwill and approval. There may even be a slight attitude of antagonism or opposition toward you as long as you rank as an outsider. That should not be disconcerting to you. If you understand it, you will be encouraged to make your associates like you and accept you as one of them. Remember that their approval is most important to your future welfare and your happiness.

Learning Names. Certainly one way to create a good first impression is to learn promptly the names (correctly pronounced) of the people with whom you work. An effective plan is to write the name and practice pronouncing and associating it with a mental picture of the person at the very first opportunity after being introduced. Then use the name to address the person at every appropriate occasion.

Observing Ground Rules. New employees are expected to learn quickly the company's regulations relative to rest periods, lunch hours, personal telephone calls, coffee breaks, smoking, and other similar activities. Some of these rules may be in writing; others will have been established by custom but are nonetheless binding. One of the surest ways to get off to a poor start is to be a rule breaker. Ignorance is a poor excuse. The only safe policy is to find out the rules and customs of the office and observe them.

Office Friends. Every office of any size has its cliques. You will want to move slowly in identifying yourself with any one particular group. The secretary who has friends in many sections of the company and who varies lunch dates to include people from all departments is not only popular but is also better able to serve the executive whom she assists. Friendliness should extend to all employment levels—the goodwill of the custodian and the elevator operator as well is important to your success.

▪ Surveying the Work

Your problem from the very first moment will be to learn as much as you can, about everything you can, as soon as you can.

In some companies the job analysis, job description, and job specifications for your new position may be made available to you in the office manual in order to give you an idea of the scope of your duties. If you are to serve your employer effectively, you need to learn about the organization as quickly as possible so that you can interpret his wishes and carry out his instructions without depending on him for elementary information.

It is an asset to learn as quickly as possible the names of customers, the names of people with whom your employer deals, the telephone numbers that he is likely to want most often, the technical language of the firm, and the most frequently used phrases of your employer's dictation. The more you know and the more readily you have this information at your command, the more quickly you will become valuable to your employer and the organization.

In the beginning, you will be expected to adapt to the old routines that you find when you take over. Later, you can determine whether there are reasons these procedures should be followed strictly, or whether they can be improved. Some employers welcome new methods; others do not care to make changes. All of them prefer to get thoroughly adjusted to a new secretary before new courses of action are considered.

The Office Manual. Many organizations have one or more office manuals or instruction sheets about office routine for the use of employees. A general office manual will usually explain the organization of the company, the relationships of the various offices and departments, and general rules, regulations, and information affecting all employees, such as time and method of payment, benefit plans, and holidays observed by the company. Some manuals contain instructions about the

The secretary studies files of correspondence, the office manual, and the advertising matter of the employing company. She learns to know the people with whom she works through reading the house organ.

work of one department; others are manuals of instructions for specific types of work. Separate operating manuals are often available for various machines and equipment in the office. A good many firms have uniform rules about setting up correspondence or arranging specific kinds of typed material. If your office has such rules, you will spend many of your extra moments studying and thoroughly digesting everything that has a bearing on the work you have to do, almost to the point of memorizing them.

The Office Files. Background information can be learned from records and letters in the files. The previous correspondence, both incoming and outgoing, will indicate the type of correspondence you can expect. It will also be an excellent source of terminology and technical language that will occur in dictation. As you look through the files, observe where and how each letter and record is filed.

Other Sources of Information. Almost every office has special types of records which may be helpful to the new secretary. Scrapbooks or collections of clippings about the organization, the executive, or the products of the firm are sources of information on the company's background. Many organizations publish a weekly or monthly paper or magazine (known as a *house organ*) written by and about its employees. Back numbers of these will tell you a great deal.

Questions. Of course, you must ask questions; but there are really two kinds of questions. "Learning" questions help you find out things you need to know; they are excellent questions to ask. "Leaning" questions, which are asked about something you really ought to know or could find out for yourself, are the kind of questions that you should avoid. If there are ways that you can find out something without asking a question, then do not ask. But avoid taking chances and possibly being wrong in your decision because you hesitate to ask questions.

There is a time and place for questioning. Whenever possible, accumulate your problems and questions by making notes, and ask them all at a logical time during the first few days of your work in one session with the executive or with the one who is helping you get started.

The other employees will usually be helpful in answering questions, but you must remember that they have full-time work to do themselves. Sometime later you will probably have an opportunity to repay those who have helped you by returning the favor when they need extra help.

■ The Secretary's Desk Manual

Every secretary needs to develop her own *secretarial desk manual*—a loose-leaf notebook in which she has compiled detailed instructions on the correct procedure for handling the duties peculiar to her desk. Such a manual is not only a real time-saver but a most helpful aid to the executive in training a new or a temporary secretary, for in it can be found the answers to the vast number of questions that would ordinarily be asked of him.

Begin to build your desk manual as soon as you acquire the necessary information. Some sections, such as correct letter form and mailing

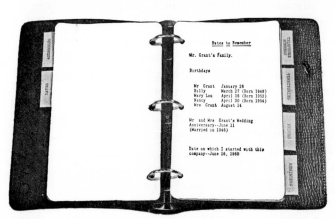

An arrangement of a typical secretarial desk manual is shown here. Note that the loose-leaf page contains "Dates to Remember" for both the executive and the secretary.

procedures, can be started immediately. Others will require time and experience to accumulate the needed data. If you are busy throughout every day, it may be necessary to do the bulk of the preparation after office hours. The first draft will be the most time consuming. After it is once written, the manual, helpfully indexed, can easily be kept up to date.

Who's Who Directory. One section in the book will probably be a directory of the persons with whom the executive has dealings. The names should include:

1. Those with whom he frequently corresponds
2. Those to whom he frequently talks over the telephone
3. Those who call upon him
4. Key persons throughout his organization
5. Those who serve him, such as his lawyer and doctor

To build up the set of names for the directory, jot down each one as it comes to your attention. Then write out a card for each name, listing the following information:

1. The correct name of the person
2. The name and address of his company or organization
3. The telephone number (area code, extension number)
4. The salutation and complimentary close for correspondence, if different from standard ones
5. The way the executive signs his name, if other than the usual way
6. The identity of the person in relationship to the executive (such as relative, school friend, attorney)

There are always a few favored correspondents with whom the executive uses more friendly and intimate forms of salutations and closings. To know who is so treated and what forms to use is of real help to anyone unfamiliar with handling the executive's dictation. A person customarily addressed "Dear Charles" or "Dear C. J." does not relish receiving the formal salutation, "Dear Mr. Giles."

To be of the most use, the manual should include generous cross references of affiliations and identifications. For example, if you have Mr. Ericson's name as sales manager of Acme Metal Company and Mr. Curry's name as advertising manager of the same company, make up a cross-reference slip for Acme Metal Company and list on it the address of the company, and the names of Mr. Ericson, Mr. Curry, and any others in that company with whom the executive has contacts.

Likewise, if Mr. Robert Nolan is the executive's attorney, make out a cross-reference slip headed "Attorney—Mr. Robert Nolan."

A new secretary (or an experienced one) should save herself and her employer time by building one or more directories of names with which she should be acquainted. Such "Who's Who" information should include executive positions and lines of authority within her own organization.

After all of the name and cross-reference cards have been made out, sort them into letter groups. Type the names and cross references on the loose-leaf pages, using at least one page for each important letter of the alphabet. Then insert the page with the proper index tab in the book.

A change of address may be typed on a slip of paper and stapled over the permanent entry until time permits the retyping of the page.

In many offices the "Who's Who" information is kept in a card file or a small Rol-Dex file rather than in a section of the secretary's desk manual.

If the executive is a member of a large company, an organization chart showing the lines of authority and the person in each executive and supervisory position is helpful to a new secretary in learning whom to contact about what.

Clients and Projects. A special section in the secretary's desk manual is needed when the executive is a professional man with a succession of important clients, customers, projects, or jobs. A page should be given to each person or project, listing such information as the title of the job, the work to be performed, pertinent data, terms, and special procedures the secretary must follow. A list of the names of all of those persons connected with the job is also helpful.

Procedures Sections. The rest of the desk manual can be divided into topical sections explaining how to handle the duties of the secretary. The sections in the outline on pages 670 and 671 cover some of the routine duties common to most secretarial positions. Additional sections would be needed to cover the duties peculiar to a particular position.

Personal Data Section. In addition to the major items that comprise the basic office manual, many secretaries add a personal section. This section contains the unusual reminders—dates and events of special interest to her executive:

> *Information on Club Membership*—dues, meeting dates, committees he serves on, and so forth.
>
> *Birthdays and Anniversaries*—of people in the company and in the executive's family

▪ The Executive's Personal Work

The line between what is personal and what is business related is usually hard to distinguish. The higher the level of the executive, the more he will be involved in activities of a social and community nature. While many of these activities may appear to be personal, such as entertaining, serving as chairman of the social committee of the country club, heading the cancer drive, or directing an investment club, they are business related. In fact, many corporations insist that their executives assume leadership roles in all types of community activities.

The secretary certainly should make no attempt to classify her executive's work into personal versus business. By taking care of her executive's personal files and correspondence and by assisting him with his outside activities, she is making more of his time available for the vital business of his company.

▪ The Executive's Private Office

Some men are naturally neat; others, naturally careless. If the executive is of the former kind, the secretary's task of keeping his office neat will be an easy one; but if he is of the latter kind, she will have a never-ending and, probably, a thankless task. A person doing creative work ordinarily has his desk piled high with all-and-sundry items that he wants to keep or use. The accumulation just grows and grows. The secretary in an earnest effort to straighten up the place may "clean house" and be accused forever after of having lost this and that.

TOPIC OUTLINE FOR A DESK MANUAL

<u>Correspondence</u>
    Procedure for handling:

        Incoming mail
          Model interoffice memorandum form
          Number and distribution of carbons
        Outgoing mail
          Model letter form(s)
          Number and distribution of carbons
          Stamps—procedure for obtaining
    Mail schedules

<u>Directory</u>
    (For information, refer to pages 667–668 of this
    book.)

<u>Filing</u>
    Centralized filing system
        Materials that go to centralized file
        Procedure for release of materials for filing
        Procedure for obtaining materials from file
    Secretaries' files—full explanation of filing
    system

<u>Financial Duties</u>
    Bank accounts
        Procedure for
          Making deposits
          Reconciling the bank statement
        Disposition of canceled checks and bank state-
        ments
        Location of bankbook and checkbook
    Payment dates—recurring items such as association
    memberships and subscriptions
        Dates of payment
        Procedure for payment
    Petty cash
        Location of funds
        Procedure for replenishing funds
          Filing of receipts
        Regulations governing expenditures from fund

<u>Legal Forms</u>
    Copies of all forms regularly used
    Instructions for completing
    Number and distribution of carbons
    Name and address of notary public used

Office Machines

Inventory—serial numbers and purchase date of all
machines
Whom to call for repair services (service contracts; other)
Names and number of supplies needed for each
machine
Procedure for obtaining supplies

Public Relations—Procedure for Handling

News releases
Announcements of vacancies
Personal data on executive

Publication Subscriptions

Names, number of copies, renewal dates
Routing of publications in office
Method of renewal

Supplies

Names, addresses, telephone numbers of suppliers
Procedure for obtaining supplies
Procedure for office controlling supplies

Telegrams

Model telegram form
Number and distribution of carbons
Procedure for sending
Procedure for recording charges

Telephone Call Procedures

Placing a toll call
Recording toll calls
Accepting collect calls

Travel

Names and telephone numbers of persons contacted at
travel agency or airlines office
Location of timetables
Model itinerary
Notes on employer's travel and hotel preferences
Method of ticket pickup
Expense report form
Number and distribution of copies
Receipts required

The personality and habits of the executive should be considered before any serious house cleaning of his desk or office is started. If he is a possessive sort of person who wants to keep his things to himself, it is best to leave them alone. If he is the careless type, the secretary can tactfully suggest a house-cleaning period once in a while. Such cleaning may best be done when he is away for a day or two—if he will agree to your undertaking the task.

▪ Promote Your Boss

The more important your executive appears in the eyes of others—his boss, his customers or clients, his friends—the more important you become too.

1. Keep your executive's personal data sheet up to date. Many executives have a prepared data sheet which they may submit when applying for membership in a professional organization or when supplying a biographical sketch prior to a speech or publication. This sheet needs to be updated regularly.

2. Watch the newspaper and magazines for press notices that mention your executive. See that they are clipped, identified, and filed. They can be rubber-cemented into a scrapbook. Many men are too modest to handle or supervise such a task, so the secretary should take the initiative. If the executive is very much in the public eye, he may subscribe to a clipping service. Incidentally, posting clippings about your executive on the bulletin board is one way of letting everyone in the office know that your boss, too, is important.

3. Keep his committee folders in good order and up to date so when he rushes off to a meeting he presents a good image in the eyes of the other committee members.

4. Watch the news for items concerning your executive's business associates and friends. When they are honored or promoted, draft a letter of congratulations for your executive's signature and give it to him with the clipping.

5. Look for news reports about new firms or plants that might be potential customers. Your executive will be watching for these items also, but it does no harm for you to say "Did you happen to see this in yesterday's paper?"

As a secretary, however, do not forget that there is no better way to promote the image of your executive than to see that all work that goes out from his office is flawless and is turned out with dispatch. Mistakes, delays, and sloppiness type a man as well as his secretary.

Professional Growth and Advancement

The business world makes heavy demands on those who would get ahead. Only those who believe with sustained dedication in what they are doing can meet the demands. Your attitude toward your work and your point of view come from within yourself, but you will have a difficult time keeping others from discovering them and mentally labeling you accordingly.

Some girls enter the business world with the idea that they are merely marking time and earning a paycheck until marriage. You cannot feel very enthusiastic about your work if you think of it as being only temporary. It is far better to take a long-range attitude. Actually a high percentage of women work after marriage. According to a release of the United States Labor Department, 51 percent of the women who graduate from college are in the labor force seven years after graduation. John Ruskin once said:

> We are not sent into this world to do anything into which we cannot put our hearts. We have certain work to do for our bread, and that is to be done strenuously; other work to do for our delight, and that is to be done heartily; neither is to be done by halves or shifts, but with a will; and what is not worth this effort is not to be done at all.

▪ Professional Status

Your activities while you are in your initial position will determine your development toward professional status. You will need to learn all that you can while you are in the office, but you can also make your out-of-office activities contribute to your growth.

Programs leading toward professional certification in various areas of secretarial work were described on pages 636–639. All secretaries may work toward becoming a Certified Professional Secretary. To attain professional status, the experienced secretary passes an examination in areas of business administration such as law, management, accounting, and business psychology, as well as secretarial competencies.

Certified Professional Secretary (CPS). A Certified Professional Secretary is one who has completed an examination administered by the Institute for Certifying Secretaries of the National Secretaries Association (International). The examination is divided into six sections: Personal Adjustment and Human Relations; Business Law; Business Administration; Secretarial Accounting; Secretarial Skills; and Secretarial Procedures. The twelve-hour examination is administered once each year. It may be taken only by secretaries with a minimum of three years of experience who meet required educational qualifications.

—Cincinnati and Suburban Bell Telephone Company

The secretary who is competent, alert to new opportunities for responsibility, and conscientious about assigned tasks can expect advancement in her job.

Associations. You are urged to join professional organizations such as the National Secretaries Association (International), The Business and Professional Women's Clubs, and, if you are eligible, the American Association of University Women. Depending upon the nature of your employment, you may wish to affiliate with one of the following organizations:

American Association of Medical Assistants, Inc.

Association of Administrative Assistants or Private Secretaries

Association of Desk and Derrick Clubs of North America (Oil)

Executives' Secretaries, Inc.

National Association of Bank-Women Inc.

National Association of Educational Secretaries

National Association of Legal Secretaries

As you advance up the business ladder, you may become eligible to join the Administrative Management Society, the Altrusa International, Soroptimist Club, or Zonta International.

If you are not a joiner, you can, of course, derive many of the same benefits from self-directed reading and study.

■ Working to Get Ahead

If you stay in your own little niche, doing only the work that has been assigned to you, you are quite likely to remain in the same position and at about the same salary indefinitely. Advancement is very much up to you. Every time you find a way to free your employer of some task, the more valuable you become. Every time you assume a new responsibility and prove yourself equal to the task, the better qualified you will be for that coveted advancement.

This statement does not mean that you barge in before you are sure or that you muscle in or infringe on the work of your co-workers—a sure way to insure your being thoroughly disliked—but it does mean that if you expect to get ahead, you must be a "self-starter," alert to opportunities to prove your value by assuming more responsibility.

Jane Manette emphasized this point in the following statement:

> When a male worker is offered additional responsibilities he usually grabs them. They expand his territory. If he's successful at them perhaps he can give up some other tasks, those he dislikes. But the stock reply from a girl is, 'That's not my job.' She has heard other girls say that and thinks she's acting big, asserting her authority. She limits her sphere and even tries to cut down on her list of duties. Actually she's pulling the fences closer about her, and someone else is glad to get those extra jobs—the person who will ultimately have her job or outdistance her.[1]

In your rush to get ahead, however, don't overlook that there are no substitutes for competence and confidence. Competence comes at a high price—a price paid in hard work, study, and dedication. A capacity for growth must be coupled with the self-discipline necessary to carry out a sustained effort toward growing with a job. Confidence is not only what you believe you can do, but also what others believe. If those up the ladder get the impression that you are striving for their jobs or standing on their shoulders in your climb, you will have destroyed the first rung on the ladder of advancement.

There is also an all-too-prevalent belief in business that the college-trained secretary is more obsessed with "getting ahead" than with demonstrating her worthiness for promotion. While ambition is a highly desirable quality, it is sometimes misinterpreted. A highly respected woman bank president who started as a secretary has this advice: "You reach the executive suite by the road called Hard Work, a trail often littered with carbon paper and typewriter ribbons. Prove your worth, and someone in the organization will discover you."

---

[1]Jane Manette, *The Working Girl in a Man's World* (New York: Hawthorn Books, Inc., 1966), p. 85.

Reading such magazines as *Fortune, Business Week,* and *Office Management* will help the secretary or administrative assistant orient herself to the management point of view.

■ Identifying Yourself with Management

The position of secretary to a major official of the business is not one that you step into or inherit because you have completed a college program or degree. These positions must be earned and are usually filled from the inside. Therefore, you will probably start on a lower level, but your goal is eventually to associate yourself with top management.

To work effectively on this level, the secretary must develop the ability to look at problems from the management point of view. This trait requires an orientation into management thinking through reading the same magazines that management reads, such as *Fortune, Nation's Business, Business Week, Wall Street Journal, Forbes, Office Management, Administrative Management,* and others; through becoming concerned with management problems; and through studying management books and taking management courses, if available.

The emphasis of much of your secretarial training has been on following instructions, observing directives, carrying through on decisions that have been made, and assuming the initiative in a relatively narrow range of operation only. The management point of view, however, involves determining courses of action, making decisions, giving directions, and delegating authority and responsibility. To shift to the management outlook, the secretary must view problems basically from the "other side of the desk." This transition cannot be made easily. It requires a carefully planned program of self-education, orientation, and discipline.

You will need to grow every day of your working life. If the time comes when you cannot keep up with your employer, he will probably begin to look for a secretary who can. If you continue to grow with the man for whom you work, you will have a position as long as you want it; and the possibilities for advancement become limitless.

As you grow into your management role, you will gradually be performing more supervisory functions. The higher up the management ladder you climb, the greater your supervisory responsibilities will be. Chapter 28, the final chapter in this text, will discuss management and supervisory problems.

Suggested Readings

Burke, Marylin C. *The Executive Secretary*. Garden City, New York: Doubleday & Company, Inc., 1959, pp. 11–18, 52–106.

Engel, Pauline. *Executive Secretary's Handbook*. Englewood Cliffs, New Jersey: Prentice-Hall, Inc., 1965, 205 pp.

Flynn, Patricia, *The Complete Secretary*. New York: Pitman Publishing Company, 1965, pp. 1–36.

Manette, Jane. *The Working Girl in a Man's World*. New York: Hawthorn Books, Inc., 1966, 223 pp.

Mayo, Lucy Graves. *You Can Be an Executive Secretary*. New York: The Macmillan Company, 1965, 260 pp.

Popham, Estelle L. *Opportunities in Office Occupations*. New York: Vocational Guidance Manuals, Inc., 1964, 110 pp.

Questions for Discussion

1. Assume that you are employed to replace the secretary to an executive in a large company. The secretary whom you are replacing has already left when you report. What are the various sources you could use to obtain information about the organization of the company? the names of customers? the technical language of the firm? the preferences of your employer in matters of style? the mailing routine? the procedure for requisitioning supplies? the names of other office employees? the lines of authority in the office? the form for writing business reports? the products manufactured by the company? the form for preparing an itinerary?

2. Getting off to a good start with fellow employees is important to success. What would you include in a listing of "Do's and Don'ts for New Employees"?

3. Some personnel departments are skeptical about hiring recent college graduates because they are too anxious to get ahead. Do you think that this criticism is warranted?

4. To what extent is a secretary justified in deviating from the established pattern of dress or customs which are traditional in the business where she is employed?

5. The suggestion is made that if you wish to leave a position, quit gracefully. What does this suggestion imply?

6. Is merit always rewarded in business? Justify your answer.

7. Male skepticism about women in administrative positions is evidenced by such statements as:
  a. Women try to promote two careers simultaneously—business woman and homemaker. Their interest and time are divided.
  b. The absenteeism rate of women in business is triple that of men.
  c. Women approach problems emotionally rather than intellectually. They are too sensitive to criticism and are too gossipy. They crack under strain.
  d. Women bosses are over-critical slave drivers. They have clawed their way up the success ladder and tend to be overbearing to their subordinates.
  e. Women dislike working for women. They much prefer to work for a man.
  How accurate are these criticisms? Recognizing that these attitudes do exist, what can the secretary do to overcome them?

8. Secretaries are warned not to be "too ambitious." What are some of the ways that a secretary might appear over ambitious and thus create an unfavorable impression in the office?

9. Do you think that an executive should load his secretary with work that is entirely of a personal nature and not related to the company? Is he justified at the expense of leaving some of the company work undone?

10. It has been said that a secretary to top management in business must think like top management. What does this mean to you?

11. Explain the difference in meaning between the two words in each set, and illustrate the correct meaning of each word in a sentence. Then consult the Reference Guide to verify or correct your answers.

advice; advise	descendant; descendent
allude; elude	disillusion; dissolution
amount; number	disinterested; uninterested
appraise; apprise	illusion; allusion
comedian; comedienne	ingenious; ingenuous
complement; compliment	practical; practicable
confidant; confidante	predominant; predominate

12. Use the proper form of *alumnus* in each of the following sentences. Then consult the Reference Guide to verify or correct your answers.

(a) The _____ of the University of Wisconsin presented a scholarship. (men and women graduates)

(b) The Princeton _____ of this region will hold their annual picnic. (men graduates)

(c) The Vassar _____ of each city meet regularly. (women graduates)

(d) She is an _____ of Swarthmore.

(e) He is an _____ of Dartmouth.

Problems

■ **1.** Throughout this course you have collected materials for a secretarial handbook. Give each item in your collection a careful final appraisal, keeping it if you now feel that it will be helpful to you for reference purposes, but discarding it if it does not pass that test. Organize your materials in the form of a handbook and submit it to your instructor. Although this handbook serves a different purpose than a secretarial desk manual, you should be able to use many of the materials you have collected when you prepare your first desk manual.

■ **2.** Select the professional association with which you would most like to affiliate as a secretary. Write a report, including a description of the organization, its objectives, activities, membership requirements, and services to members.

■ **3.** An annual examination given by the Institute for Certifying Secretaries leads to the certificate of Certified Professional Secretary. Prepare a report on the CPS examination. Your report should include how the examination is administered, areas covered, eligibility for admission, location of test centers, and advantages of securing the CPS designation.

Related Work Assignments 78-80

78. Checking Your Development. At the beginning of the course (page 21) you checked yourself against a chart of secretarial traits and abilities. You then made a plan for improvement. To see whether you are developing in secretarial personality, complete the chart again. You may wish to ask a friend to discuss your ratings with you. (A chart is provided in the Workbook.)

79. Evaluating Office Manuals. The instructions and supplies necessary for the completion of this assignment are provided in the Workbook.

80. Your Fundamentals. This is the tenth in a series of Workbook assignments reviewing English usage, grammar, and punctuation. These assignments are based on the Reference Guide in this textbook.

Fulfilling Your Administrative Role

One of the facts of business life that cannot be ignored is that business has traditionally been a man's world. Of the 250,000 business executives in the United States, fewer than 5,000 are women. Fortunately, this situation is changing—partly because job discrimination on the basis of sex has been outlawed and partly because the critical shortage of supervisory and administrative talent is forcing business to tap the reservoir of the womanpower that is available.

The barriers have not all been removed, however. As long as you remain on the secretarial level, the masculine bias will not affect you, for you are filling a position traditionally reserved for women. But as soon as your responsibilities begin to give you semiadministrative status, you may meet resistance stemming from what is called male prejudice against women in positions of authority. Incidentally, this resistance frequently comes as much, if not more, from women workers as from men.

It is not unusual for the secretary to top management or a woman who attains the supervisory or administrative level to have one or more assistants to help with her work. In some cases, she may supervise the office staff. Often she has a dual role such as secretary and supervisor.

This dual role is extremely difficult to fulfill because the secretary-supervisor is all too frequently the "girl caught in the middle"—caught between management who determines policy and staff who carry out policy. Often her authority is not so clearly defined that she can assume a managerial role, yet she is expected to get work done through others.

The dual role of secretary-supervisor is complicated by several factors, for she must plan all her supervisory duties around her executive's schedule. His work and demands must have first priority, and all other duties may be immediately interrupted at his beck and call. Therefore, she is not free to plan or supervise in the same way that a full-time office supervisor can.

Part of her time she operates on the same level as those she supervises. She performs the same kinds of tasks. Thus, her subordinates tend to think of her as one who is on their own work level and not as an administrator, so they may not readily accept her authority.

The administrative assistant may spend part of her time in planning and decision-making activities, but at times work also at tasks on the same level as that of her subordinates.

Frequently, those whom the secretary supervises have bosses of their own—executives to whom they consider they have first allegiance. They treat the sharing of the general office duties as secondary and as an intrusion on their time.

Finally, members of the administrative staff frequently bypass the secretary-supervisor in their dealings with the office staff. This situation plays havoc with any plan of operation.

While these factors tend to make the secretary-supervisor's life rather hectic at times, they can be surmounted, as proven by the many highly successful executive secretaries and administrative assistants who are cast in this dual role. Your ability to cope with such situations may well determine how far up the executive ladder you may expect to aspire.

Throughout this book the supervisory and administrative aspects of the secretary's job (and there are many of them) have been integrated at appropriate points, but this final chapter discusses supervision and administration as the primary rather than as the secondary responsibility. If, after you have assessed your potentialities for the role of supervisor or administrator, you think that you would like to try your hand at an administrative job, this chapter will be helpful in preparing you for such a promotional opportunity. In addition, it will increase your usefulness so long as you combine the executive-secretarial duties with those of administrative assistant.

In order to accomplish her goals, the woman supervisor or administrator will continually need to improve her ability to work with and through others.

Four areas of administrative responsibility are discussed: how to develop the potential of your employees, how to facilitate smooth human interactions, how to improve work operations, and how to continue your own development so that you become increasingly capable of managing and supervising.

Richest Use of Human Potential

As a supervisor or administrator, you will need to work *through other people* to accomplish your goals. That is why some people who are excellent practitioners themselves are not good supervisors or administrators—although a person who is not a natural leader may, through effort and education, develop competencies for these responsibilities. The importance of learning how to work through people accounts for the increasing emphasis on the behavioral sciences in college curriculums in business administration, in business books and magazines, and in management seminars.

In the first place, it is necessary to recruit the best possible people for the jobs to be filled. After that, ways must be found for developing those selected so that they can realize their greatest potential.

▪ Recruiting the Best Possible People

Initial recruitment is customarily the responsibility of the personnel department. Potential employees who have met screening standards are then sent to the immediate supervisor for final approval or rejection. (Note that the word "rejection" is used, for it may be that as the person actually in a job you may recognize valid reasons why the proposed candidate would not fit effectively into the work situation. It is easier to say "No" now than later.)

Everyone in management should consider himself a recruiter for his company. Through professional associations and through colleges and universities, it is sometimes possible to interest outstanding prospective employees (those with special capabilities) in making application to the personnel department for a position.

An objective of every company is promotion from within, so as an effective supervisor or administrator you should include as one of your objectives the development of replacements and personnel for new jobs. It has been said, and wisely, that every executive, administrator, and supervisor should have an understudy (in training). No division, department, or section of a business should be left to press the panic button upon the promotion, retirement, or demise of its director.

The problem of applying a functional system of promotion from within is closely allied to the following discussion of growth of employees' potential. When office workers at a day-long seminar on work performance were asked to list their expectations from the job, high on the list was "the feeling that I have some place to go—that I'm not in a dead-end job."

▪ Developing Employee's Potential

If the employees for whom you are responsible achieve optimum performance, the human resources in your segment of the organization are tremendously multiplied. All of your supervisees' capabilities, not just yours alone, are at work for you. To put it selfishly, your success depends on their growth as well as your own.

The great challenge in management is how to induce in the employee an involvement in his job—a feeling that what he does is *our* or, better, *my* responsibility, not *yours* or, even worse, an indefinable *theirs*. The ideal is to generate in every employee the feeling: What I do IS important to MY organization. I *matter*.

The suggestions that follow for increasing the employee's sense of involvement may be helpful.

The supervisor and administrator should be concerned with both physical and emotional climate, for the employee who enjoys his place of work will usually strive to do his best.

Areas of Freedom. In your supervisory or administrative role, assure yourself that you have given instructions and training commensurate with the job; then allow the employee reasonable areas of freedom within which to work, remembering that all people do not work alike. You are interested in the end result, and the employee will produce better if you do not "breathe down his neck" while he is carrying out his assignment. He must have an area of freedom in which to develop his own work patterns. The measure of the supervisor's effectiveness is this discernment of the degree of supervision that an employee needs.

Expanded Responsibility and Authority. As an employee develops and requires less supervision, give him more responsibility and authority —as much as he can take. You are the one finally responsible for his work, however; and you cannot delegate your own responsibility.

Pleasant Working Conditions. Do everything possible to make the physical and emotional climate conducive to good work. Actively try to make the office so attractive as a place to work that employees will enjoy being there. Provide the best possible tools. Treat everyone under your supervision as a person worthy of respect and consideration.

Recognition. Praise good work within the department, and give credit when due. Let your employees know that you support their best interests when you report to management and that you can be treated as their representative.

Upgrading Opportunities. In addition to increasing the responsibilities of employees, solicit ideas for improvement (theirs, yours, the company's) from workers and give them a chance to rub elbows with new ideas and sometimes with plans still in the formative stage. Call their attention to educational opportunities inside and outside the organization and the company's policies regarding tuition reimbursement. Encourage personal development and technical improvement at every opportunity.

The Team Approach. The behavioral science researchers have come up with a new idea for continued development of experienced managers, the organization development plan. The usual pattern for management training has been to bring together individuals on the same level of management from various departments and positions. The new concept involves training all members of a work team together. With vertical (rather than horizontal) training, all levels of management right up the line participate together in staggered, rather than continuous, concentrated sessions. For instance, training sessions might be conducted in three parts: a half-day briefing session on the problems to be solved and two subsequent sessions in which basic principles of management are applied to the problems peculiar to the operation in which the training group is involved.

Workers at all levels come to the realization that problems in a work situation are common to all participants even though the responsibilities at different levels vary. Each participant grows in understanding of the interrelationships of the different jobs. An adaptation of this training technique would improve job effectiveness and increase job satisfaction at the departmental level as workers plan and establish targets together.

Facilitation of Smooth Human Interaction

An essential contribution of the administrative assistant or supervisor is the facilitation of smooth human relationships and the prevention of deterioration in personal interactions. In this role, you may be called upon to get the facts in cases where personalities clash and to make recommendations for restoring harmony.

▪ Effective Communication

In one management study, supervisors and managers at all levels were asked to appraise communication within their organizations. Overwhelmingly, they reported that communication from above was appallingly ineffective but that their own communication downward was excellent. The importance of effective two-way communication is conveyed in the slogan used in one company: *You're down on what you're not up on.* Only if people understand what is happening will they support it. Middle management has a dual responsibility: to keep the people upstairs informed of their performance and to keep their supervisees apprised of what management is doing.

Work Instructions. Work instructions may be given orally or in writing. Preferably oral instructions are supported by written ones. The supervisor may be involved in writing job instructions or work procedures. As a supervisor, you should certainly concern yourself with updating office or departmental manuals and seeing that instructions are available, understood, and followed. Important here is not only *how* to perform but also *why* a certain type of performance is desirable and important.

Personnel Policies. A supervisor is responsible for interpreting management policy to workers in such a way that whatever conformity is needed is secured. Usually this means explaining the reasons behind such policy and the benefits that will accrue from its enactment. A problem arises if the supervisor is not in sympathy with the policy, but it must be stated unequivocally that there is an unavoidable obligation to support all company policies. Conversely, there is an equal obligation to communicate to management suggestions for change—either your own or those of your supervisees.

The Administrative Assistant's Communications. Much of the administrative assistant's work involves effective communication. You may need to collect and to supply information verbally; to write letters for your employer's signature; and to compose reports and memorandums for transmittal vertically throughout the organization. The administrative assistant frequently represents the company to outsiders and is often responsible for the company image.

Daily Challenge. Presenting a daily challenge is the problem of influencing other people to interact for the benefit of the company. Whether dealing with personnel above your own level, on your level, or under your authority, your ability to communicate facilitates human interaction that results in increased productivity. Such ability is not necessarily innate, but it can be learned. Thousands of dollars are going into management programs that have this as a major objective.

▪ Dual Role Position

Secretaries who have succeeded in filling a dual role in a business organization make these suggestions:

1. Work with the other administrative personnel in the office in establishing clearly defined lines of authority and operate within this framework.
2. Know thoroughly what you want done. Make definite assignments. Be specific in your instructions and take the time *to explain why.*
3. Organize the work to be done. This means planning ahead and avoiding—insofar as possible—emergency deadlines and "pressure" situations.
4. Understand and develop fair standards of performance. If your standards are fair, your subordinates will accept them and expect you to enforce them.
5. Be a ready and good listener. Many a problem has been solved by simply letting the person describe it.
6. Solicit ideas and suggestions. After all, there may be a better way. Give full credit to staff members when passing ideas up the administrative channel. Never, never claim their ideas as your own.
7. Openly praise good work but criticize in private.
8. Delegate responsibility. To assume all the responsibility yourself may be a good trait in a secretary but a bad one in a supervisor.
9. Remember that everyone has basically the same needs and drives as you—namely, the satisfaction of *achievement*, the need for *recognition*, the opportunity to *create*, the challenge of *growth*, a sense of *belonging*, and a feeling of *security*.

Facilitation of Work Flow to Achieve Production Goals

In addition to human relationships, other factors are involved in achieving work goals: sound business decisions; provision of the best possible physical environment through scientific utilization of space, selection and maintenance of appropriate equipment, choice and control of supplies best suited to the job; control of the quality and quantity of work; and systems and procedures analysis.

Anyone aspiring to a managerial position must understand business and office organization, labor-management relations, and business law and ethics. Business administration courses—especially business law,

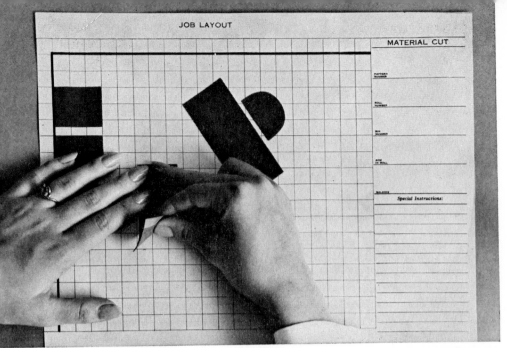

Both the job analysis and the carefully planned use of space are important to production goals and therefore of concern to the supervisor and administrator.

business psychology, and labor relations—will now become functional rather than theoretical. What are the provisions of *your* company's union contract? What is the legal implication of *this* decision? How can I apply the principles of business ethics and psychology to *this* situation? Do my attitudes contribute to good relations among my fellow workers?

■ Lines of Authority

People are jealous of position and are often insecure in their jobs. The surest way to arouse the animosity and suspicion of colleagues—but one frequently used by the novice—is to ignore lines of authority and bypass someone when working out a problem. Strict adherence to office protocol and to lines of authority is essential to business harmony. Even if you think you know "who knows what," and it is not the person designated on the organization chart with that responsibility, don't make the serious error of ignoring the existing line of authority. Many a bright young potential manager has cut his career short by violating this imperative dictum.

■ Sound Business Decisions

Sound decisions are usually based on facts, and facts are secured from reading about research conducted by others or through conducting your own. After a certain procedure has been followed in a project, the outcomes should be evaluated. Objective analysis of results is essential to sound business decisions—application of research techniques to business problems, in other words. Using research as a basis for sound business decisions, though, requires the ability to read, develop, and interpret *raw* data as well as classified or statistical data such as that found in charts and graphs.

Computers are helping in the collection of business data upon which to base management decisions. The latest applications lie in the field of business simulation: If we take this action, what will be the result? By feeding into the computer various proposed courses of action, management can secure a quantitative estimation of results.

Recommendations to Superiors. One of the first evidences of management potential is your reluctance to dump your problems in the lap of your superior for solution. On the Army staff, all problem interviews are handled on a "staff-work-accomplished" basis. The person with the problem is required to present all data along with a recommendation of at least one solution, but preferably several alternate ones—not a bad technique for business to follow too. After a problem is once identified, the person closest to it should be in the best position to work out a solution and to recommend a course of action.

Your Own Decisions. You will have to learn what decisions to make on your own initiative and which ones you should refer to your superior along with all pertinent supporting data that will help him to make a wise choice. Experience will guide you, for employers vary. Some like to delegate as much work as possible and will give a free hand once you have proved your capability. Others just naturally cling to authority and their prerogatives in decision-making. Learn to adjust to the type of employer with whom you find yourself working.

In general, though, you should make routine decisions, keeping the employer informed of them but releasing him for more important jobs. Your freedom to make decisions will probably increase when he develops confidence in your decision-making ability.

▪ Physical Environment

Systems analysts, office design specialists, and office management groups provide a reservoir of help for the uninitiated in office layout. Recommendations for dimensions of each work station, for width of aisles, and for grouping of workers can be used as a standard.

If you have the opportunity to improve the physical environment of your office, review the wealth of articles in business periodicals and the discussions of office supplies and equipment in Chapters 4 and 6. Solicit the help of equipment salesmen and management groups. Develop a sound trade-in rotation plan so that you can stay within your budget and still keep equipment up to date. Investigate rental and leasing plans, as well as purchase. Study office layout and design in current magazines and books.

You have already developed a fund of information about office supplies (See Chapter 4). You will probably be responsible for ordering them. Get competitive prices, and save money for your company by choosing wisely. Plan far enough ahead for delays in deliveries without inconveniencing your staff. You will also control the supplies procured. As you know, pilferage is a serious factor that can be curbed only by careful surveillance. Supplies should be issued only on requisition, and it is your responsibility to review the requisitions periodically to see whether any employees are filing requests out of proportion to their reasonable needs.

▪ Work Measurement

Output in highly repetitive clerical operations has been successfully measured, and realistic quantitative standards have been established. In the management literature you can find standards for such processes as straight-copy and letter typing, addressing envelopes, filling in form letters, or cutting stencils. Your own systems and procedures staff will help you in setting standards. Qualitative standards are not as easy; just remember that the quality of every piece of work from your department is your responsibility. Until an employee demonstrates that her work is consistently usable, proofread EVERYTHING from her typewriter.

▪ Systems and Procedures Analysis

Management of office work is becoming scientific, with the greatest advances being made through the systems approach. In many companies a systems and procedures staff is available for the scientific study of problems in individual offices. Although these specialists may be called upon for studies of a particular problem, the office administrator will want to become familiar with recent developments in this field and learn to make applications of recent developments. An example will suffice.

In evaluating job performance, the manager may choose to make the managerial grid analysis which measures on a 1-9 grid the worker's human relations effectiveness against concern for the task. Low (1) in human relations and a High (9) in concern for the task would pinpoint the training needs if the employee is to be retained on the job.

Advancement in systems and procedures techniques can in part be attributed to increased use of the computer. Unless data are processed systematically, the computer cannot function. Men were forced to analyze the flow-of-work processes into orderly sequences before they could tell the computer what to do (program a process). Such analysis is being carried over into noncomputer operations.

■ Computer Applications

Anyone concerned with office operations today MUST consider computer applications and understand how the flow of business information is facilitated through computer applications to more and more business problems. New opportunities to harness its capabilities must continually be sought.

Carrying Your Own Weight

As you achieve administrative status, you will be expected more and more to carry your own weight—to be able to act "on your own." But you can ruin your whole future unless you demonstrate that you are primarily concerned with implementing your supervisor's goals and developing his objectives, not your own. In a way, your role resembles that of the understudy; do not upstage the star. This final section will discuss ways in which you can become more helpful to him.

■ Idea Development

Try to develop your own creativity. Look at a problem from as many angles as you can find and search out all possible sources of information about it through readings, company files, college and intra-company courses, visits or telephone calls to related organizations, and active participation in professional organizations.

If you do have an idea, share it with your employer. A written memorandum is usually the best medium, for writing the idea forces you to clarify it and to express it succinctly. Also, the written memorandum can be used for later referral.

Do not be jealous of the idea. Sometimes if you make a suggestion, it may be modified greatly before it is finally adopted. Your adaptability may result in the decision of a group or a person to do what you basically want done even though compromise is necessary. And, finally, you may not be given credit for your ideas. The question becomes: Which is more important, to have your idea adopted—or to get credit for it even though it is not accepted? Usually, you will decide that you prefer having the idea accepted.

■ Communication

You will try to improve your communication skills, for even presidents of companies and countries continue to search for clearer and more persuasive ways of telling their story.

You will find yourself on committees where you will want to influence the actions of others. Remember the "staff-work-accomplished" approach (page 689); and make sure that when you speak, you are making a constructive suggestion.

Reduce your superior's reading time through your own improved communications. Write and rewrite to reduce verbiage. Learn how to abstract material and to present it graphically. Become a master at preparing the memorandum that presents the heart of the matter in one succinct paragraph. Learn how to arrange material to highlight all the salient points.

Consider the possibility of expressing your ideas in articles and talks. Too many people are afraid to attempt public speaking or writing for publication. Yet these are tremendous aids to personal development and creativity, primarily because they make you clarify and organize your thoughts more effectively.

■ Your Specialties

You should develop one or more specialties for which you are known throughout the organization. For instance, maybe you have talent in chart-making and have a collection of materials for dressing up graphic presentations. Maybe you are the departmental authority on records management and have recently visited a demonstration in retrieval of computerized business data. Maybe you are studying for an advanced

**The secretary is the liaison between the executive
and both in-company and outside administrators.**

degree in labor relations. Your specialty can be used not only to the
department's advantage but also to your own.

▪ Aid to Your Employer

This entire chapter has been devoted to ways of assisting your employer. These final suggestions summarize what has been said. They are
designed to speed you on your way to supervisory or administrative
success.

Your superior is probably primarily concerned with establishing
policy. But companies do not just run themselves once the policy is
established. Your most important function may be to implement the
policy established and follow through to see that it functions. This
means systematic reporting to your employer so that he knows what is
going on. He must be apprised of results so that he can make modifications that seem desirable or are essential.

You will also relieve your employer of as much administrative detail
as possible, representing him at certain meetings, seeing callers, answering letters, preparing memorandums and reports, making arrangements
for travel and meetings, ghostwriting.

At the heart of your success, though, lies your answer and his to the
questions: Are you carrying out instructions? Are you representing

him? If he frequently says, "Never mind; I'll handle it myself," you can be sure that you are not carrying your own weight. If he hands you a sheaf of papers and says, "Handle these for me, will you please," you may be sure that, for the moment at least, you are his *alter ego*.

Suggested Readings

Better Secretaries Series. *How to Train an Assistant or Substitute.* Englewood Cliffs, New Jersey: Prentice-Hall, Inc., 1962, 47 pp.

Manette, Jane. *The Working Girl in a Man's World.* New York: Hawthorn Books, Inc., 1966, 223 pp.

Maule, Frances. *Executive Careers for Women.* New York: Harper & Bros., 1961.

Mayo, Lucy Graves. *You Can Be an Executive Secretary.* New York: The Macmillan Company, 1965, 260 pp.

Neuner, John J. W., and B. Lewis Keeling. *Administrative Office Management,* 5th ed. Cincinnati: South-Western Publishing Co., 1967.

Terry, George R. *Office Management and Control,* 4th ed. Homewood, Illinois: Richard D. Irwin, Inc., 1965.

Questions for Discussion

1. What problem is presented when the executive hands his secretary a letter and says, "Tell Mr. K's secretary to get an answer to this from K and draft a reply that I can sign."

2. Should the secretary isolate herself socially from those she supervises so that she can achieve an aura of authority?

3. Is your ultimate ambition to secure a position in which supervisory and administrative duties are of primary importance, or would you prefer a position in which these responsibilities are secondary?

4. What is the difference between being a good practitioner and a good supervisor of practitioners?

5. Cite an example of a situation in which the quality of supervision caused you to feel involvement in not only your own work but in the composite of several people's efforts. Cite an instance in which the quality of supervision discouraged your involvement beyond an immediate task. (You may cite educational or social situations if you have had no work experience.)

6. Give an example showing that "You're down on what you're not up on."

7. If the secretary has developed a new procedure for reporting credit information to the sales department, would it be better to present the idea to her employer, the vice-president in charge of sales, or to the head of the credit department?

8. Give an example in which you either used or did not use the "staff-work-accomplished" technique, and evaluate the results.

9. Give an example from your experience (or from the Workbook In-Baskets) of a routine decision that the secretary should make herself. Give another example of a decision that should have been referred to the employer—along with all available data for reaching the decision.

10. What is the relationship of a systems and procedures staff to an operational unit?

11. What specialty do you have that might be developed into a plus asset in your job?

12. How can you be sure that you are representing your employer as he wishes when you carry out your administrative duties?

Problems

■ **1.** Organize a committee of not more than five members, each of which will interview an administrative assistant, a supervisor, or an executive secretary. (You might wish to tape their comments.) Present a panel discussion of their evaluation of their roles in their companies—their successes and frustrations. After you compare notes, draw conclusions about your own level of aspiration.

■ **2.** Organize a committee of not more than five members who will survey local opportunities for study beyond the level of your present college. Include both in-company and out-of-company educational programs, professional seminars, and professional organizations open to women. Present an oral group report.

■ **3.** Join a committee of not more than five members who will interview employers of secretaries, administrative assistants, and supervisors. Present an oral team report of their suggestions to the beginning secretary. (Don't overlook interviewing members of your family.)

■ **4.** Prepare a bibliography of at least seven articles that have appeared within the past two years on how to improve supervision or administration. Do you detect any trends?

■ **5.** In an oral interview with your instructor, demonstrate for your class the staff-work-accomplished technique in suggesting changes in this course or in the curriculum you are following.

Related Work Assignments 81-83

81. Special "In-Basket" Project ⎫ The instructions and supplies necessary for the completion of Related Work Assignments 81 and 82 are provided in the Workbook.

82. Certified Professional Secretary Examination ⎭

83. Measuring Your Secretarial Information and Judgment (Parts IX and X). This is the fifth and last in a series of Workbook assignments providing experience in answering the types of questions used in an examination for professional secretaries.

9—1 √ wage policies

Helen Rutledge is secretary to Mr. Macon, president of the Macon Processing Company. She worked her way up, having started as a file clerk, advancing to secretary to the comptroller, and then to her present position with the president. There are 12 employees in the office, and as secretary to Mr. Macon she is in charge of the administration of the office.

One of her responsibilities is to recommend the starting salary of all members of the office staff and all salary increases. The company has no personnel department. Miss Rutledge employs all office personnel; the factory superintendent employs all other employees.

In establishing wage policies for the office, Miss Rutledge has surveyed wage patterns in other offices, compared office salaries with those of factory employees, and set higher wages than those of other offices in the area. Each year she examines the Administrative Management Society's annual salary report.

Miss Rutledge believes that she is completely fair and democratic in her wage policies. She attempts to reward achievement but resents criticism of her wage policy and resists any effort on the part of the staff for discussion or cooperative efforts in establishing wage policies.

There is a great deal of unrest in the office over Miss Rutledge's wage practices. Her employees claim that (a) no one dares question her policy and those who do are discriminated against in wage increases, (b) she frequently employs inexperienced new employees at higher wages than some members of the experienced staff, (c) she uses wages to force patronage, and (d) she gives wage increases on bases of favoritism.

Assume that you were called in to examine the situation and make recommendations. What recommendations would you make?

9—2 √ employee evaluation

The personnel department of J. L. Simmons Company asks each supervisor to give a yearly composite rating on each of his employees. The rating is on a 100-point scale, with a maximum of 70 points for job performance and 30 points for personality.

As secretary to Mr. Simmons, Betty Kappes is the immediate supervisor of the following three clerical and stenographic employees:

Helen Jackson:

Has a pleasant disposition and is popular with the other workers.
Is always willing to interrupt her work to help others.
Produces only an average quantity of work.
Is generally well dressed and usually fairly neat in appearance.
Does work that must be carefully checked; not always accurate.
Plans to be married soon, but wishes to continue working.
Is taking a night course in college to improve her skills.
Grasps instructions quickly; carries out her assigned duties.
Arrives at work on time. Frequently is early and begins work immediately.
Leaves her desk only normal amount of time. Rarely misses work.
Quits promptly at 4:30 p.m. to meet her fiancé; resents overtime work.

Mary Hillman:

Is reserved, mixes little with other employees, talks little, and volunteers little infor-
  mation about herself. Has no close office friends.
Is punctual in attendance; arrives early, but does not start work until the regular
  time. Quits promptly at 4:30, but will stay overtime.
Does not appear to have any boy friends.
Appears to be satisfied with her work, but her future plans are not known.
Produces work of high quality once she understands what is to be done.
Is slow in learning a routine, but then does a far-above-average quantity of work.
Resents being interrupted to help others; never seeks their assistance.
Dresses conservatively but appropriately.

Jane Watson:

Produces far-above-average volume of work but frequently has errors.
Arrives late to the office an average of one morning each week.
Uses Monday to recover fully from weekend activities.
Is gregarious and inclined to gossip with the other employees. Has to be called
  from the rest room frequently after extended periods of time. She does not resent
  being reprimanded for abusing rest-period rules.
Tends to interrupt others; has no hesitancy about asking for help.
Is well liked by most of the office force, but some think she is a gossip and try to
  avoid her.
Is satisfied to stay in present position and has no ambition to advance.
Learns very rapidly, anticipates instructions, and can be depended upon to do a
  difficult and responsible job.
Is erratic in her dress. Usually dresses very appropriately but at times must be
  reminded that she is working in a business office.
Has many boy friends and occasionally has to be reminded that she is not to receive
  unnecessary personal telephone calls at the office.

**Assuming you are Miss Kappes, rate each employee and indicate how you
would use this rating to improve their performance.**

PART 10 Reference Guide

How to Use the Guide

To locate one of the nine major divisions in this Guide, look for the identifying strip in direct alignment with the division title at the right on this page. Except for the Correspondence and Postal guides, items in each division and subdivision are arranged in alphabetical order.

EXAMPLE: Are commas used to set off the word *too* in a sentence?

Step 1. Turn to PUNCTUATION.
Step 2. Find subdivision COMMA.
Step 3. Under COMMA, find *Too.*

How to Use the Cross-References

▪ *A Cross-Reference to Another Item in the Same Division:*

dissolution—See **disillusion; dissolution.**

Such a cross-reference has but one part directing you to the alphabetic location of that entry within the same major division.

▪ *A Cross-Reference with Two Parts:*

Esq.—See **Abbreviations—Esq.**

The first part (**Abbreviations**) indicates the major division of the Guide; the second (**Esq.**), the subdivision located alphabetically within the major division (**Abbreviations**).

▪ *A Cross-Reference with Three Parts:*

Jr.; Sr.—See **Punctuation—Comma, Jr.**

The first part (**Punctuation**) indicates the major division; the second (**Comma**), the first subdivision located alphabetically within the major division (**Punctuation**); the third (**Jr.**), the second subdivision, arranged alphabetically under the first subdivision (**Comma**).

Introduction

English in all its forms (usage, vocabulary, punctuation) is ever changing. Its study is fascinating and challenging. No part of this book can be of more value to a secretary than the English-usage section of this Reference Guide.

Handbooks and dictionaries *report* usage at different levels. They are not arbitrary authorities. Nor does this Guide presume to be authoritative. It, too, *reports* current acceptable business usages.

When more than one usage is reported in this Guide, it is because there is *divided usage*—dictionaries and handbooks do not agree. A secretary, therefore, cannot assume that her reference books stand alone as supreme authorities on usage.

Formal English usage is followed in reports, dignified letters, papers for publication, and the like.

Colloquial English usage often occurs in friendly business letters. A word marked colloquial in the dictionary means that it occurs in spoken English, in conversation at an educated level. Because most spoken English is informal, colloquial usage suggests the informal level. In this guide colloquial expressions are labeled *INFORMAL*.

Standard business English usage occurs in business correspondence. Such correspondence is distinctly different from other writing. It is direct and to the point in the interest of economy. It saves time. A business letter is frequently concerned with obtaining a favorable result or creating a friendly reaction. This result can often be achieved by a conversational, spoken-English tone. Thus colloquial English is frequently appropriate and suitable to business writing.

Business English often gives an additional meaning to an old word or uses it as a different part of speech, such as to *power* your engine. An executive often coins a needed word, such as *finalize* and *know-how*. The secretary must decide whether she will call attention to such words by quoting or underlining them.

Punctuation practices are always changing. Less punctuation is used now at the informal level; but full, correct punctuation is still required at the formal level.

GENERAL RULE: Spell out all words that would be conspicuous if abbreviated in formal typewritten text. Use abbreviations in informal writing and in tables, footnotes, records, billing, and technical writing. Use periods after abbreviations in formal writing. The periods are often omitted in informal writing.

Ampersand

Use *and* rather than *&* unless you know that the particular company's style preference is for the ampersand.

```
Building and Loan Association
American Telephone and Telegraph Company
Norfolk & Western Railway
```

At Beginning of Sentence

Do not use. Spell out instead.

```
Number (not No.) K71 came out in 1968.
```

Capitalization

Do not capitalize abbreviation unless word it represents is usually capitalized.

```
versus; vs.                Fahrenheit; F.
ante meridiem; a.m.
```

Coined Verb Forms

Add an *apostrophe* and *s, d,* or *ing.*

```
She c.o.d.'s everything.  He c.o.d.'d it.
```

Degrees—See **Capitalization—**Degrees.

Dimensions and Weights

Do not abbreviate designations nor use symbols in typewritten text except in specifications, quotations, etc.

```
2 feet 6 inches; 10 by 18 feet;
8 pounds 6 ounces
```

Esq.

This courtesy title, always in abbreviated form, follows a man's name. No other title or college degree is used with it.

```
Alan R. Kane, Esq.
        NOT:
Mr. Alan R. Kane, Esq.
Alan R. Kane, Esq., Ph.D.
```

Geographic Names

Do not abbreviate: *County, Fort, Mount, Point,* and *Port.*

Government Agencies and Labor Organizations

Government agencies, international organizations, and labor groups are often abbreviated without spaces and without periods.

```
WHO    World Health Organization
ICC    Interstate Commerce Commission
UN     United Nations
AFL    American Federation of Labor
```

Honorable

Do not abbreviate when preceded by *the.* See **Usage—Honorable.**

```
the Honorable A. R. Kane
```

Jr.; Sr.

Such seniority designations are used in combination with titles and college degrees. Comma may be omitted before the abbreviation.

```
Mr. Alan R. Kane, Sr., President
Prof. Alan R. Kane Sr.
Alan R. Kane Jr., M.D.
```

See **Punctuation—Comma, Jr., Sr., II, III**; see also **Usage—Junior; Senior.**

Months

Do not abbreviate names of months or days of the week except in tabulations, citations, references, and the like.

Names of Companies

Follow company's form as to abbreviations and signs.

```
Wm. Taylor & Sons; Saks Fifth Avenue
```

Names of Persons (Initials, Contractions)

A. Copy the way person writes name, spacing after initials.

```
Jay R. Penske; R. Floyd King; E. A. Rex
```

B. With more than two initials, internal spacing may be omitted.

```
A.R.J. King (or A. R. J. King)
```

701

C. When an initial does not stand for a name, omit period unless person uses a period.

J Marshall Hanna; Harry S Truman

D. When the name is a contraction, do not use a period.

Rob't S. Von Wenchstern

Organizations

Names of well-known associations and societies are often abbreviated. The space between the letters is usually omitted. The periods are included.

A.M.S.   American Management Society
Y.W.C.A.   Young Women's Christian
            Association

Period with Another Punctuation Mark

A. Period at end of abbreviation precedes other punctuation within sentence.

Call at 10:15 a.m., or . . . .

B. Use only one period when abbreviation ends a sentence unless abbreviation is enclosed in parentheses.

Please call at 10:15 a.m.
The price is $18 (f.o.b.).

Plurals

A. For most abbreviations, add *s*.

gals.; yds.; Drs.; bbls.

B. For capitalized abbreviations, add *s*.

C.P.S.s; CPSs

C. For uncapitalized abbreviations consisting of single letters, add '*s*.

p.m.'s; f.o.b.'s; c.o.d.'s

Possessives

To form singular possessive, add '*s;* to form plural possessive, add *s*'.

CPS's salary; CPSs' salaries

Publications, Parts of

Spell out in typewritten text. Abbreviate in references and footnotes. Follow capitalization of spelled-out word.

Vol. II; Vols. II and V
Ch. 3; Chs. 3 to 6
p. 17; pp. 17-26
Art. VII; Arts. I-VI

Reverend

Do not abbreviate when preceded by *the.*

Rev. A. R. Kane; the Reverend Mr. Kane

II, 2d, or 2nd

Seniority designations are combined with titles and degrees. A comma is generally used before the designation. When known, follow form person uses.

Mr. A. R. Kane, II (or Kane II)
Prof. A. R. Kane, 2d (or Kane 2d)

Periods are not required for *2nd* or *2d*. They are shortened forms rather than abbreviations.

Spacing Within Abbreviations

Trend is to omit internal spacing except between initials and abbreviated titles before a name.

CBS show; C.B.S. show
L. C. Mason; Lt. Cmdr. Henry Hill
Frank Adams, M.D.

States and Territories

A. Do not abbreviate in typewritten text.

B. Abbreviate in tabulations, footnotes, listings, and the like.

C. May be abbreviated in inside letter addresses for balanced line length. In envelope addresses the Post Office Department prefers they be spelled out, unless the two-letter abbreviation and ZIP Code for bulk mailings and mail to be electronically sorted is used. See **Postal Guide—ZIP Code.**

Street Addresses

A. *Street, Building, Road, etc:* Do not abbreviate in typewritten text. Avoid abbreviating in inside and envelope addresses unless balance requires it.

B. *Compass Designations:* Do not abbreviate compass designations.

210 North Tenth Street; 210 Plaza North

EXCEPTION: It is customary to abbreviate the two-part compass designations at the end of street names.

```
210 Sixteenth Street, N.W.
```

Time

A. Abbreviate a.m. and p.m. in expressions of time, preferably in lower case.

B. Standard time zones are abbreviated in capitals, without period or space.

```
EST; EDST; CST; MST; PDST
```

C. A.D. precedes the year.
B.C. follows the year.

```
A.D. 1900
200 B.C.
```

Titles

A. *Courtesy Titles:*

```
Mr.; Mrs.; Ms. (Miss or Mrs.)
Messrs.; M.; MM.; Mme; Mlle.
```

B. *Position in Business:* Do not abbreviate titles (such as *president* or *general manager*) in textual matter or in addresses. Trend is to omit title if it takes a separate line which makes address longer than four lines.

C. *Rank or Profession:* May abbreviate if title is followed by a first name or initials except in formal writing.

```
Prof. A. R. Kane, (but) Professor Kane
```

GENERAL RULE: When you can find no rule or example to guide you, do not capitalize.

Ages (Eras)

Capitalize historical ages only.

```
Dark Ages; Middle Ages; atomic age;
   stone age; Renaissance period;
   the Victorian era
```

Astronomical Bodies

Capitalize names of the solar system except *earth, moon, stars,* and *sun.*

```
Mars; the North Star
the Southern Cross; the Big Dipper
```

Bible

Capitalize *bible* and its derivatives when it refers to the Scriptures, but not when it refers to a handbook.

```
a Biblical reference; the Bible
That dictionary is my bible.
```

Buildings

A. Capitalize names of *office buildings.*

```
the Stowe Building; Carew Tower
```

B. Capitalize names of *public buildings* only when full or proper names are used.

```
Go to the Erie County Courthouse.
I'll be at the courthouse.
```

Business Names

Follow form the business uses.

```
South-Eastern Tool Co.
tish evans, decorator
```

Compound Words—See Words—Compound Words

Congress

Capitalize.

```
the United States Congress; Congress;
the Senate; the House; Eighty-fifth
Congress, second session
```

Countries, Regions, and Directions

A. Capitalize names of countries and their derivatives.

```
the United Kingdom; the Continent;
European travel; French cuisine
```

B. Capitalize regions when used as proper nouns or adjectives.

```
people of the Far East
a Far East trouble spot
He lives in the West
```

C. Do not capitalize points of the compass when used merely to denote direction.

```
His home is north of Seattle.
```

Courses of Study

Capitalize the specific names of a course, but not of a field of knowledge (except English and foreign languages).

```
He passed Algebra III.
A secretary must know spelling.
He majored in French.
```

Degrees

A. Capitalize abbreviations of degrees. Capitalize a spelled-out degree if it immediately follows a name; otherwise, capitalize or not, as preferred.

```
Professor J. William Knapp, Ph.D.,
  will. . . .
Dean J. William Knapp, Doctor of
  Philosophy, will . . . .
The degree of Doctor of Science (or
  doctor of science) is . . . .
```

B. When typing degree abbreviations, omit spaces after internal periods. Set the degrees off with commas.

```
Alan J. Kane, B.S., is . . . .
```

C. Bachelor, master, and doctor degrees are *earned*, and in that order; honorary degrees are *conferred* as honors.

D. In biographical references, list all degrees in chronological order; or give earned degrees chronologically, then honorary degrees chronologically.

E. In letter addresses, the only degrees commonly used are *M.D.* and *D.D.*, and then only if *Dr.* is omitted.

```
Michael Gavlak, M.D.
Dr. Michael Gavlak
Dr. Stewart McDougald
        NOT:
Dr. Michael Gavlak, M.D.
Dr. Stewart McDougald, D.D.
```

F. In textual matter degrees may follow a name. Use only the highest degree in each field. Set degrees off with commas. Use any title before the name except *Mr.* (and *Dr.* if one of the degrees is a doctor's degree).

```
Professor Grace Weber, Ph.D., is . . . .
Dean Russell Olderman, M.B.A., is . . .
Mrs. Marian Linderme, B.S. '53, is . . .
        NOT:
Mr. A. J. Black, Ph.D., is . . . .
```

Epithets

Capitalize when used as or with a proper name, as *Golden Rule Smith; the Rock*.

Federal; Government; National; State; Etc.

Capitalize each of these words when it is part of a proper name. Otherwise, follow your preferred authority. Dictionaries and handbooks disagree. Non-capitalization has a slight edge.

```
the Federal Reserve Bank; a federal tax;
  a Federal tax
```

First Words

A. *Of Direct Quotations:* Capitalize as follows:

```
He said, "That's fine."
"That's fine," he said, "for you."
"That's true," he said. "You're right."
He explained: There is a reason . . . .
```

B. *Of Clause-Type Questions:* Use lower-case letters for the first words; separate with single typewriter spaces.

```
What will happen if you are not
  ready? if you miss the plane?
```

C. *Of Phrase-Type Questions:* Use lower-case letters for the first words; separate with single typewriter spaces

```
How is the sailing? the swimming?
  the fishing?
```

D. *Of Internal Independent Clauses or Phrases:* Capitalize as follows:

```
The problem is, How can we do it?
The fact is--Too little, too late!
```

E. *Of Lines of Poetry:* Capitalize first word of each line.

```
I ask of thee, beloved Night--
Swift to thine approaching flight,
  Come soon, soon!
                    --Shelley
```

F. *Of Sentences:* Always capitalize.

G. *Of Thoughts:* Capitalize as follows:

```
I thought: He knows now.
```

Freshman; Sophomore; etc.

Do not capitalize such a word unless it is a part of a proper name.

```
As a sophomore you will . . . .
The Junior Class plans . . . .
```

Government—See Federal.

Governmental Agencies

A. Capitalize the official or shortened name of a department, bureau, commission, etc.

```
the Civil Service Commission
the Commission
```

B. Do not capitalize department, bureau, and the like when used generally.

```
Which bureau handles this?
```

Holidays and Holy Days; Days of Special Observance

Capitalize all holidays and holy days.

Christmas	Passover
Easter	Yom Kippur
New Year's Day	Fourth of July
Memorial Day	Labor Day
Mother's Day	Valentine's Day

Locations with Identifying Numbers

A. Do not capitalize page, line, or verse.

```
See page 18, verse 6, line 3.
```

B. Handbooks vary on other location words. Secretarial handbooks recommend capitalizing as in Column 1; printing stylebooks prefer the forms in Column 2.

Room 10	room 10
Column 3	column 3
Figure 8	figure 8

Measurements

Do not capitalize units of measurement.

6 ft.	3 qts.
4 lbs.	5 tons

Military Units

Capitalize, as Twenty-first Division.

Months

Always capitalize.

Nation

Capitalize nation when used as a synonym for the United States.

```
The honor of our great Nation is....
```

National—See Federal

Organizations; Clubs

Capitalize the proper name of an association, club, order, etc.

```
the National Association of...; the Uni-
versity Club of.....; the Independent
Order of Odd Fellows; the Urban League
```

Do not capitalize when used alone unless it has the value of a proper name.

```
He belongs to a bowling league.
We will meet at the Club for lunch.
```

Personifications

Always capitalize.

```
My Girl Friday wrote you.
```

Persons' Names

Follow form the person uses.

```
Anne Obrien
Mr. de Rossett
```

Political Groups

Capitalize as follows:

```
Democrat(s); Republican Party;
a Communist; communism
```

Races and Peoples

Always capitalize, as French; Negro(es); Caucasian(s).

Relatives

Capitalize uncle, aunt, etc. when used with a name.

```
I met your Uncle John.
I have not met your uncle.
```

Religious Faiths and Denominations; Sacred Books; Hallowed Beings

A. Capitalize all such words and their derivatives.

Catholic(s); Jewish; Protestantism; the Bible; the Scriptures; Allah; Old Testament; the Koran; Blessed Virgin

B. Handbooks vary regarding capitalizing a pronoun referring to the Deity. Usually it is capitalized only if it is far removed from its antecedent.

God commanded his people.
We knew He loves his children.

River; Lake; Ocean; Mountain; Etc.

Capitalize when part of a proper name but not when used in plural form.

The Atlantic Ocean
The Atlantic and Pacific oceans

Roads, Routes, Streets, and Thoroughfares

Always capitalize.

U.S. Route 4; the Freeway; Ohio Turnpike; State Route 17; Lincoln Tunnel

Schools

Capitalize *school, high school, Sunday school, college,* or *university* only when part of a proper name.

Seasons

Do not capitalize except when personified.

spring; summer
Old Man Winter

Ships' Names

Capitalize or capitalize and underscore.

Michael sailed on the Castel Felice.
He returned on the Seven Seas.

State, County, City, District, Ward, Etc.

A. Capitalize when part of a proper name.

the State Tax Division   the Loop
New York State   Fountain Square
Boone County   Queens Borough
the County Clerk of   Eleventh District
Courts

B. Do not capitalize when one of them precedes a proper name.

the state of Ohio; the city of Troy

C. Capitalize or not when they stand alone or are used as adjectives.

your state (State) tax return
a County (county) election

Titles of Books, Magazines, Newspapers—See Punctuation—Titles of Published Matter.

Titles of Persons

A. Capitalize *president* when referring to a president of a sovereign country.

the President's speech
former President Truman

B. Capitalize *vice-president* when it refers to the Vice President of the United States or when used as a title with a proper name. (Although most authorities hyphenate *vice-president*, common usage tends to omit the hyphen in a *title designation* before a proper name.)

In 1945 Vice President Truman...
In Vice President King's note....

C. Capitalize title if joined to person's name. Some handbooks capitalize title when alone if it refers to a specific person.

Read President Kane's letter.
Mr. Kane, vice-president of Iron Age, said . . .
Our president (President) says . . .

D. Do not capitalize the following when they stand alone.

priest	rabbi
pastor	cantor
minister	superintendent
rector	judge
consul	professor

Titles of Plays, Songs, Articles, Speeches, Laws, Acts, Etc.—See Punctuation—Titles of Published Matter.

Trademarks

Capitalize all trademarks unless the

manufacturer uses lower-case letters as a distinctive style or the word has become a generic term.

Vaseline	Life Savers
Coca-Cola	Pyrex
Pentothal	Sealtest
Dacron	Crisco
Thermo-Fax	mimeograph
Scotch (tape)	cellophane
	nylon

Weeks of Special Observance

Always capitalize, as *Holy Week*, *National Secretaries Week*.

Whereas; Resolved

Capitalize and punctuate in one of the following ways:

```
WHEREAS, The....
WHEREAS the....
WHEREAS, THE....
Resolved, That....
RESOLVED, That....
Resolved, That....
```

GENERAL RULE: In typewritten text, spell out all numbers under a certain specified one. Usage varies as to what this number should be. Follow the rule of your office or select one of those below; make it your General Rule to be followed consistently.

Spell out:

Numbers under 10 (all agree on this)
Numbers under 11 or 13
Numbers under 100 that do not require hyphens
Numbers under 100 (this is commonly followed)
Numbers under 101
All numbers under 100 plus those over 100 that can be written in three words or less (as *one hundred nine*, *twelve hundred eighteen*)

Addresses

A. *House Numbers:* Always spell out the number *1*. (Some handbooks spell

out numbers *1* through *10*.) Otherwise use numerals.

```
One Fifth Avenue
Ten Park Terrace or 10 Park Terrace
182 Dearborn Street
```

B. *Street Numbers:* Spell out small numbered streets according to the General Rule. Handbooks vary on the

NUMBERS—Page 707

use of ordinals with street numbers and on the way to separate house and street numbers. Use an intervening compass indication if possible.

PREFERRED:

```
22 North 72nd Street
22 North 72d Street
```

WITHOUT COMPASS INDICATION:

```
22 Seventy-second Street
22 - 72nd Street; 22 - 72d Street
22, 72nd Street; 22, 72d Street
```

Ages (Years)

A. Spell out approximate ages, as *about sixty-five years old*, *nearly twenty-one*.

B. Use numerals for exact ages.

```
He is 62 today.
He is 62 years 3 months 11 days old.
```

C. When an age precedes a noun, follow the General Rule, as *a two-year-old will*, *a 20-year-old letter*.

Approximations

As a general rule approximate numbers are written out when they can be expressed in one or two words.

```
Approximately eighty people attended.
```

Beginning of Sentences

Spell out, as *Sixty-three passed.*

Centuries

Spell out (according to most handbooks), as *in the twentieth century*.

Chapters, Sections, Pages, Paragraphs, Verses, Lines, Etc.

Express in Arabic or Roman numerals according to the way the unit is numbered. (Note the usage of capitals.)

```
Chapter IX      Paragraph 2
Chapter 6       Lines 3 to 11
Volume II       Page vi
Section 4       page 1002
Part 7          verse 18
```

Comma

A. Comma may be omitted in four-digit numbers in typewritten text, as *We sent 1475 units*.

B. Separate with a comma, two adjacent numbers.

```
Out of 22, 14 agreed.
In 1955, 1325 students passed.
```

EXCEPTION: See **Consistency Within a Sentence (B).**

Compound Adjectives

A. Hyphenate a number-noun combination occurring before a noun. Follow the General Rule for expressing numbers.

```
a 210-page book; a 54-inch map;
40- and 50-yard bolts (or forty- and
fifty-yard bolts)
```

B. When the dimension is written before the noun, the figure is hyphened to a singular word. If written after the noun, the figure is not hyphened to the word, and the word is plural.

```
a 40-foot line      a line 40 feet long
5- x 3-inch cards   cards 3 x 5 inches
```

Congress, Sessions of

Spell out and capitalize, as the *Eighty-sixth Congress, first session*.

Consistency Within a Sentence

A. Treat alike all numbers in a group.

```
Your three orders of 8, 25, and 110
   dozen . . .
Eight, 25, and 110 dozen were . . .
```

B. Spell out only one of two consecutive small numbers, as *two 6-inch boards*. It is usual to spell out the smaller and to express the larger in figures.

C. Spell out a small number when it is dissimilar in context to a large number.

```
We sold 625 units in nine months.
```

Dates

A. Express and punctuate dates as shown in the examples. (A comma enclosed in parentheses below shows that its use is optional.)

```
On May 22, 1968, we . . . .
On May 22(,) we . . . .
On May twenty-second(,) we . . . .
On the 22d we . . . .
On the twenty-second we . . . .
On the 22d of May(,) we . . . .
On the 22d of May, 1968, we . . . .
```

B. Express two or more consecutive dates as follows:

```
On May 22, 23, or 26 we. . . .
In May, June, and July 1968 we . . . .
From May 4 to May 11 the . . . .
In our letters of May 4 and 7, we . . .
```

C. In legal documents dates are often spelled out.

```
On this tenth day of May in the year
   of our Lord one thousand nine hundred
   and sixty-eight . . . .
. . . this tenth day of May, A.D.
   1968 . . .
```

See **Years**

Decades

Express in numbers or spell out as follows:

```
the 1950s; the 1950's; the fifties;
the mid-fifties; the '50s or '50's
```

Decimals

A. Express in numbers. With numbers less than *1* use a cipher before the period unless decimal begins with a cipher.

```
22.33; 0.56; .045
```

B. No commas are used to the right of a decimal point.

    1,007.604361

Degrees (Temperatures, Angles)

Express in numbers.

    8 degrees below zero; 4°; a 45-degree
    angle

Distances

Express in numerals except fractions under *1.*

    an 825-mile flight
    a distance of 825 miles
    about one-third mile away

End of Line

Figures should never be divided at the end of a line. Avoid dividing spelled-out numbers.

Fractions

A. *As a Subject:* As a subject, fraction takes singular or plural form according to the noun or pronoun following it.

    Half the work is checked.
    Half the units are checked.
    Half of them are checked.

EXCEPTION: In a mixed fraction of one, the noun following is plural, and the verb singular.

    Probably 1 1/2 tons is enough.

B. *Fractions of Less than 1:* Spell out; hyphenate only when used as an adjective. Do not hyphenate when either element contains a hyphen.

    a one-third share
    one third of the shares
    a seven twenty-fifths share

C. *Key (or Made) Fractions:*
(1) In multiple-copy work, make the fractions (key fractions may be illegible on carbons).

    1/2 (not ½)

(2) Type all fractions in a piece of writing the same way.

    1/2 and 3/4 (not ½ and 3/4)

(3) Do not use a comma in *1/1000.*

D. *Mixed Fractions:* In mixed fractions, space before a made fraction, not before a key fraction.

    46 1/4; 46¼

Market Quotations

Express in numbers, as *4s at 102 3/8.*

Measurements

Express in numerals except for fractions under *1* and sometimes small whole numbers which would ordinarily be spelled out.

    36 miles on two gallons of gas
    8½" by 11" or 8½- by 11-inch paper
    three-fourths bushel to the acre
    8 ft. 10 in. by 12 ft.

Note that an exact measurement is written without commas.

Millions and Billions

Million and *billion* may be spelled out after a number in place of ciphers.

    7.9 million; $25 million; 6 billion

Military Units

Spell out and capitalize, as *the Eighteenth Division.*

Money

A. *Amounts in Even Dollars:*

Express in numbers. Omit ciphers (except for appearance where a small amount ends a sentence). Spell out small amounts if preferred.

    a price of $6,000; a saving of $125
    It cost $2.00. It cost two dollars.

B. *Amounts in Dollars and Cents:* Always express in numbers.

    Our estimate is $1.13 each.

C. *Amounts in Cents:* Spell out *cent* or *cents;* use numbers or spell out the amount.

    a 2-cent tax   6 cents
    a one-half-cent increase   six cents
    a ½-cent increase   88 cents
    an increase of one-half cent

D. *Amounts in Legal Documents:* Spell out and follow with amount in numerals in parentheses.   Words are usually capitalized.

```
price of two hundred dollars ($200)
price of Two Hundred Dollars ($200)
price of Two Hundred (200) Dollars
```

Percent

Dictionaries and handbooks vary on the use of numbers, the % sign, and the spelling of *percent*.

```
6 percent; six percent
6 per cent; 6%; six per cent;
```

Periods of Time

Express periods of time that include the year, the month, and the day in figures without commas.

```
Interest for 1 year 6 months and 12 days
```

Plurals

A. Form plurals of numbers by adding *s* alone or *'s.*

```
1900s or 1900's
20s and 30s or 20's and 30's
```

B. Form plurals of spelled out numbers in the usual manner, as *tens*.

Political Subdivisions

Spell out and capitalize, as *the Fourth Ward.*

Possessives

Form singular possessive by adding *'s;* form plural possessive by adding *apostrophe* to plural form; or rephrase to avoid the possessive form for inanimate objects.

```
the building's appearance
the appearance of the building
60 days' option; a 60-day option
$25's worth; ten cents' worth
```

Roman Numerals

A. The following upper or lower case letters are equivalent to the Arabic numbers listed:

```
I -- 1          L -- 50
V -- 5          C --100
X -- 10         D --500
      M -- 1,000
```

B. A bar over a letter multiplies it 1000; thus $\overline{V}$ is *5,000.*

C. Numbers are formed by adding subtracting the values of adjacent ters.
(1) If a letter is followed by one of les or equal value, it is added, as *XI* is *XX* is *20.*
(2) If a letter is followed by one greater value, the first is subtract from the second, as *IX* is *9; XL* is *CM* is *900.*

Room Numbers

Always express in numbers. Do r use commas in numbers of 1000 a over,   as *Room 8;   1620 Williams Building.*

Round Numbers

In typewritten text, use numbers spell out in fewest words possible. very large numbers, you may combi numbers and spelled out words.

```
1500; 4600 (no comma when number is to
   be read as hundreds)
62,000; or sixty-two thousand
600,000; six hundred thousand; or
   600 thousand
```

Serial and Policy Numbers

Express in numbers.   Copy intern spacing if known.   Commas are n used within the number, but the read may be helped if number is separat into arbitrary units by internal spacin Use symbols in technical writing only

```
No. 3718960
No. 3 718 960
#3 71 89 60
```

Sequence

The hyphen may be used to indicate t omission of the word *through* betwe two numbers.

```
on pages 37-65
during August 21-26
```

Time of Day

A. Express even hours as follows:

```
11 am; 11 a.m.; 11:00 a.m.; 11 A.M.
11 o'clock; eleven o'clock;
Come at eleven, please.
12 pm; 12 p.m.; 12 midnight
12 noon; 12 N.; (12M, while
    correct for 12 noon, can be mistaken
    for 12 midnight.)
```

B. Express other than even hours as follows:

```
a quarter to ten
1:20 p.m.
a quarter of ten
    NOT:
1:20 o'clock
one twenty o'clock
```

C. Write military clock time as follows:

```
0045 (12:45 a.m.)
0715 (7:15 a.m.)
1530 (3:30 p.m.)
```

Weights

Express in numbers except for fractions under *1* and sometimes small whole numbers which would ordinarily be spelled out.

```
3 pounds; three pounds
3 pounds 14 ounces
Send one-half pound more
5,760 grams equal one pound
```

Years

Express as follows:

```
A.D. 1961;  A. D. 1961
400 B.C.;  400 B. C.
class of '68
mid-1966; the winter of 1967-68
```

PLURALS

GENERAL RULE: Consult the dictionary for irregularly formed plurals of words. When there is a choice between a foreign and an English plural, use the English.

EXCEPTION: The plural that is the most familiar for the subject matter may be used (i.e., advertising men use the plural *media* rather than *mediums* when referring to modes of advertising.)

The italicized words in the following list are the preferred usage according to *Webster's Unabridged Dictionary.*

ENGLISH PLURAL	FOREIGN PLURAL
appendixes	appendices
criterions	*criteria*
curriculums	curricula
focuses	foci
gymnasiums	gymnasia
indexes	indices
maximums	*maxima*
mediums	media
memorandums	memoranda
minimums	*minima*
radiuses	*radii*
referendums	referenda
spectrums	*spectra*
tempos	*tempi*
ultimatums	ultimata

```
┌─────────────────────────────┐
│ PLURALS AND                 │
│ POSSESSIVES  —Page 711      │
└─────────────────────────────┘
```

Abbreviations

See **Abbreviations—Plurals**

Capital Letter

Add *'s* or *s* alone.

```
A's; Bs
```

Compound Words

A. Pluralize the main word.

```
attorneys general; major generals;
judge advocates; notaries public;
trade unions; assistant postmasters
general
```

B. Pluralize the main word in a compound ending in a prepositional phrase.

```
chambers of commerce; commanders in
chief; attorneys at law; powers of
attorney; points of view; bills of
lading
```

C. Pluralize the noun when a preposition is hyphened to it.

```
lookers-on          passers-by
hangers-on          runners-up
listeners-in        goings-on
```

D. Pluralize the last word when neither word is a noun.

```
also-rans           go-betweens
come-ons            higher-ups
follow-ups          trade-ins
```

Cupful, Handful, etc.

Add *s* to the end, as *cupfuls*.

Numbers—See   **Numbers—Compound
    Adjectives   (B);   Fractions (A);
    Plurals**

Proper Name

Add *es* to names ending in sibilants,
s to other names, as *the Jameses, the
Americas*.

Small Letter

Add *'s*, as *m's and n's*.

Word Used as a Word

Add *'s* or form plural regularly.

```
10 yes's and 3 no's
10 yeses and 3 noes
```

POSSESSIVES

GENERAL RULE: Whenever a possessive form looks or sounds displeasing,
rephrase the sentence to avoid it. *The
climate of Kansas City, Kansas, is more
pleasing than Kansas City, Kansas',
climate.*
Ordinarily, possession is not shown in
reference to inanimate things. Avoid a
contract's terms. A *pen's* top.

Abbreviations—See **Abbreviations—Pos-
    sessives**

Alternate Possession

Each noun should be possessive.

```
man's or woman's handwriting
the mayor's or commissioner's office
```

Appositives

To indicate possession where there is an
appositive, add the possessive ending to
the appositive, or rephrase the sentence.

```
Pay Dale the Printer's bill.
It is Mr. Kane, our manager's, idea.
```

Compound Words

Add the possessive ending (usually *'s*)
to the last word.

```
SINGULAR:   son-in-law's
            passer-by's
PLURAL:     sons-in-law's
            passers-by's
```

"Else" Phrases

Add *'s* to *else*, as *no one else's grade*.

Gerunds

Gerunds require possessives. See **Usage—Gerund (2)**

```
Allen's thinking; the girl's coloring
```

Money's Worth

Use possessive form in this idiom, as
five dollars' worth, $20's worth.

Numbers

Form singular possessive by adding *'s;*
form plural possessive by adding *apostrophe* to plural form; or rephrase to
avoid the possessive form.

```
$12's worth
24 hours' service
page 8's centering
30 days' option; a 30-day option
```

Proper Names

A. In proper names of several words
add the possessive ending to the last
word according to the **Sibilant Sounds**
(page 713), or rephrase sentence to avoid
possessive form.

```
Haskins & Sells's reports
the Scott Company's letter
John, Jr.'s graduation
the Senator from Idaho's speech
```

B. In proper names some words are
considered descriptive rather than possessive. Follow official style if known.

```
Artists Supplies, Inc.
```

C. To indicate individual ownership,
add possessive ending to each one; to
indicate joint ownership, add possessive
ending to the last name.

```
Erf's and Flynn's sales
Erf and Flynn's sales
```

Sibilant Sounds

A. *Words Ending in Sibilant Sounds (Plural):* Add *apostrophe* only.

    the Jameses' dinner

B. *Words Ending in Sibilant Sounds (Singular):*

(1) For one-syllable words and those whose final syllable is accented, add *'s.*

    Mr. Jones's efforts

(2) For words whose final syllables are not accented, add *'s* or *apostrophe* only.

    the princess's (princess') gown
    J. C. Roberts's (Roberts') car

C. *Words Not Ending in Sibilant Sounds (Singular or Plural).* Add *'s.*

    the senator's vote

Time Phrases

Form possessives regularly or convert to adjectival phrases, as *a three weeks' trip,* or *a three-week trip.* See **Words—Compound, Adjective Modifiers (b)**

Elements of Punctuation

APOSTROPHE

1. Use an apostrophe to indicate possession.

See **Plurals and Possessives—Possessives; Abbreviations—Plurals.**

2. Use an apostrophe to indicate the plural of abbreviations, letters, figures, and words.

See **Plurals and Possessives—Plurals; Abbreviations—Plurals; Numbers—Plurals.**

For other uses of the apostrophe, see **Abbreviations—Coined Verb Forms, Names of Persons; Number—Decades, Time of Day, Years.**

3. Use an apostrophe to indicate omitted letters. Do not use a period after a contraction.

    ne'er
    Rob't not Rob't. (with a period)

4. An apostrophe is not used in a shortened or clipped word such as *phone, photo, plane.*

BRACKETS

Make typewritten brackets by typing the underline in regular line spacing above and below diagonals, /thus/.

Inner Parentheses

Use brackets for an inner set of parentheses.

    It is in her biography (A Secretary
    Reports /2d edition only/, page 7)

Quoted Matter

A. *Copied Errors (sic).* Use enclose *sic* (meaning *th* that an error has been

    "The Rosevelts /si

B. *Corrections*. Use brackets to enclose a correction in quoted matter.

"Mr. Wilson /Willson/ stated . . . ."

C. *Interpolations*. Use brackets to enclose an interpolation (matter inserted to clarify or question) in quoted matter.

"They /his brothers/ claim it."

"Testimonial letters /solicited?/ are said to be on file."

COLON

Use a *colon* to indicate that something follows.

After a Clause

A. Use a colon after a clause to indicate that a restatement or amplification follows.

My intuition says: Stop now.

B. If a complete sentence follows a colon, it may or may not begin with a capital letter, according to the emphasis that is desired.

To succeed is not easy: it takes constant effort.

C. A quoted sentence after a colon always begins with a capital.

The inscription read: "Time goes, you say? Ah, no, time stays; we go."

Before an Enumeration

A. Use a colon before a run-in enumeration when the introductory words form a complete thought.

They will use three criteria: (1) the importance of the topic, (2) the purpose . . . .

The three criteria are (1) the importance of the topic, (2) the purpose . . . .

B. Use a colon before a tabulated enumeration.

The three criteria are:
1. The importance of the topic
2. The purpose of the study
3. The scope of the findings

C. Do not use a colon after *namely* o *such as* unless a tabulation follows.

. . . a number of aptitudes; namely, loyalty, honesty, and vitality.

. . . legal tender, such as coins, bills, and checks.

Before a Quotation

A colon is used before a quotation (a sentence or more. See **Quote Matter—Poetry; Several Paragraph Several Sentences (A); Single Sentence**

Before a Series or List

A colon, comma, or dash may introdu a series or list. See **Series (6).**

With Other Punctuation

The colon follows closing quotatio marks.

COMMA

Because the comma is often necessary make the meaning clear, its use is t least uniform of all punctuation mark

In formal writing observe all the comma rules. In each piece of business wring use the comma to the same exte throughout—follow all the rules every sentence, or limit the use commas to those necessary for clarit

Appositives

An appositive gives additional inform tion about the word which precedes

A. Use commas to set off nonrestricti appositives, as *Mr. Kane, our manag is ill.*

EXCEPTIONS:

Do not set off one-word appositives, *My partner Clark is ill.*

Do not set off an appositive that quoted, underscored, or typed in capitals.

The phrase "by your leave" is . . . .
The warning mail early was . . . .
The book TIME WILL TELL tells . . . .

B. Use dashes to set off an emphatic appositive. See **Dash—Appositives.**

Breaks in Continuity

Use a comma to set off matter that breaks the continuity of the sentence.

```
It is the most unusual, if not the most
    difficult, problem we face.
```

But

A. Use a comma before *but* when it joins short main clauses that are contrasted in meaning.

```
The idea is good, but it is costly.
```

B. Use a comma after *but* at the beginning of a sentence or clause only if it is followed by a parenthetical phrase.

```
But, as you know, we agreed . . . .
```

Cities and States

In a sentence use a comma after both the city and the state.

```
In London, Ohio, there stands . . . .
```

Clauses (Compound Sentences)

Use a comma or a semicolon between the main clauses of a compound sentence. For examples of the use of commas and semicolons, see **Semicolon—Clauses (Compound Sentences).**

Clauses (Subordinate)

Use a comma after a subordinate clause that precedes a main clause and is not closely connected to it. Subordinate clauses often begin with such words as *if, when, unless,* etc.

```
If you do not hear today, please wire.
```

OPTIONAL EXCEPTION:

A. When the subordinate clause is short, is closely related to the main clause, or has the same subject as the main clause, the comma may be omitted.

```
If we hear today we will telephone.
```

B. Set off nonrestrictive clauses with commas.

Nonrestrictive (only one book to consider):

```
She needed the book, which was lying on
    the desk.
```

Commands Within a Sentence

Use a comma to set off a mild command within a sentence.

```
Remember, we guarantee it.
```

Contrast, Emphatic, Emphasis

A. Use commas (discriminately) to set off elements that are in emphatic contrast to the rest of the sentence. They usually begin with *not* or *but not.*

```
It is to be used, not abused.
It may be certified, but not insured.
```

B. A comma may be used to set off a single word that is to be emphasized.

```
We must be prepared, always.
Again, let me say that I agree in
    principle.
Many, rightfully, insist on being
    heard.
```

Dates—See **Numbers—Dates**

Degrees (Academic)—For usage examples, see **Capitalization—Degrees.**

Dimensions, Weights, Etc.

Do not separate the parts with commas.

```
10 feet 2 inches by 12 feet
```

Direct Address

Commas set off words in direct address.

```
Thank you, Miss Nixon, for helping.
```

Etc.

Commas set off *etc., and so forth, and so on,* or *and the like* in a sentence.

```
Art, drama, music, etc., are evidences
    of cultural advancement.
All statements, and the like, must be
    carefully audited.
```

Exclamations (Mild)

Use a comma to set off a mild exclamation within a sentence.

```
Hooray, vacation is here.
```

Gerunds

Use a comma after an introductory phrase containing a gerund unless it is the subject. (A *gerund* is a verb form used as a noun.) See **Usage—Gerund.**

```
On studying your proposal, we . . . .
The studying of your proposal was . . . .
```

Identical Consecutive Words

When clarity demands, use a comma between identical consecutive words.

```
If you will call in, in a few days . . . .
We felt that that was right.
```

Inc., Ltd.

Use a comma after *Inc.* and *Ltd.* within sentences.

```
Perhaps Tressel, Inc., stocks it.
```

Infinitives

Use a comma after the beginning infinitive phrase unless it is a subject.

```
To study your proposal, we . . . .
To study your proposal is a . . . .
```

See **Usage—Infinitives**

Jr., Sr., II, III

Use a comma *before* any of these seniority designations if the person uses a comma in his signature. In sentences, use a comma after the designation if it is preceded by one.

```
Write Robert Kane, II, about it.
Write Robert Kane II about it.
Notify Ralph Miller, Jr., to come.
```

Do not follow the possessive with a comma.

```
Call Ralph Miller, Jr.'s home.
```

See **Abbreviations—Jr.; Sr.**

Like

When *like* introduces a nonrestrictive phrase, set off the phrase with commas.

```
The future, like the weather, is
  unpredictable.
A leader like Wilson has world-wide
  influence.
```

Myself, Himself, Yourself, Etc.

Do not set off intensive pronouns with commas.

```
Mr. Kane himself approved it.
```

Numbers—See Numbers—Comma; Decimals; Measurements; Periods of Time; Room Numbers; Round Numbers; Serial and Policy Numbers.

Of (Before Locations or Affiliations)

A comma may precede *of*.

```
Senator Dirksen, of Illinois, said . . .
Senator Kennedy of Massachusetts replied
  that . . .
```

Omitted Words

Use a comma in place of omitted words that are clearly understood.

```
Mr. Kane sails on Sunday; Mr. Baker,
  on Tuesday.
```

Opinion Expressions

Use a comma after an expression such as *fortunately*, *naturally*, *obviously*, etc. when it occurs at the beginning of a clause.

```
It was raining; fortunately, I had my
  umbrella.
```

Parenthetical Expressions

If a pause is required, set off with commas parenthetical expressions, such as *however*, *therefore*, *nevertheless*, *accordingly*, *consequently*, *moreover*, etc.

```
The trend, however, is to use fewer
  commas; nevertheless, we should know
  the rules.
```

When these parenthetical expressions are used as transitional words joining main clauses, a semicolon is required.

See **Semicolon—Clauses (F).**

Participial Phrases

Use a comma after an introductory participial phrase.

```
Studying your proposal, we find . . . .
```

Questions Within Sentences—See Question Mark—Questions Within Sentences (A).

Restrictive; Nonrestrictive Elements

A. A *restrictive element* defines, limits, or identifies the noun it modifies. It is essential to the meaning of the sentence. Do not set it off with commas.

```
The person who composed that letter
    needs to develop tact.
```

B. A *nonrestrictive element* describes or amplifies the noun it modifies. It can be dropped without changing the meaning of the sentence. Set it off with commas.

```
The writer of that letter, which is a
    prize example of how to lose cus-
    tomers, needs to develop tact.
```

Series; Lists—For use of commas, see **Series.**

Such As

When *such as* introduces examples, use a comma before it, but not after it.

```
Order office supplies, such
    as paper, ribbons . . . .
```

Do not punctuate if the phrase contains essential information that cannot be omitted.

```
An excuse such as this cannot
    be accepted.
```

To Prevent Misunderstanding

Use a comma wherever it will prevent misunderstanding.

```
After all, the effort is secondary.
As you know, nothing is more important
    than your goodwill.
```

Too

When *too*, meaning *also*, occurs within a sentence, use a comma before and after it. When it occurs at the end of a sentence, use a comma before it in formal writing.

FORMAL AND INFORMAL:
```
His new book, too, is excellent.
```

FORMAL:
```
His new book is excellent, too.
```

INFORMAL:
```
His new book is excellent too.
```

Transitional Expressions

Set off with commas a transitional expression that serves as a bridge between sentences or clauses. Typical phrases are *in short, in fact, in any case, after all,* etc.

```
Beige is very popular.  On the other
    hand, you may prefer green.
```

Transposed Elements

Set off with commas elements that are out of their natural order in sentences.

```
That he talks convincingly, we agree.
```

Two Consecutive Adjectives

Separate with a comma two consecutive adjectives if the words can be reversed or if *and* can be inserted without changing the meaning.

```
It is a brilliant, intense color.
We have a new alkyd paint.
```

With Other Punctuation

The comma is placed inside closing quotation marks but outside a closing parenthesis.

Words that Answer

Set off with commas such words as *yes, no, certainly, well,* etc.

```
Certainly, you may count on us.
```

Yet (Conjunction)

Use a comma or a semicolon before *yet* when used as a conjunction meaning *but*.

```
We approve it, yet we wish it were
    better designed.
We approve it; yet we . . . .
```

DASH

Appositives

Use dashes to set off an emphatic appositive or one that contains internal punctuation.

```
Speed--the desire of every typist--
    comes with practice.
Even though the facts--their change of
    mind, their reasons, and their new
    plan--seem valid, we . . . .
```

See also **Comma—Appositives.**

Change in Thought or Structure

Use dashes to set off abrupt changes in thought or sentence structure.

```
The typist turned in thirty perfect
letters--isn't that amazing?--on
her first day.
```

Credit Lines, Reference Sources—See Quoted Matter—Credit Lines, Reference Sources.

Emphasis

For special emphasis, set off a word or phrase with dashes.

```
These are the newest--and the best--
available.
```

Hesitancy

Use dashes to join a hesitant, faltering statement.

```
We expect--hope that--that is--we count
on your support.
```

Incomplete Sentence

Use a dash to indicate that an unfinished sentence trails off into nothingness or that the meaning of the omitted portion is obvious. See also **Ellipses (4).**

```
Your kindness so overwhelms me that--
Telephone Mr. Kane today or--!
```

Repetition of a Word or Phrase

Use a dash before an emphasized repetition of a word or phrase.

```
We are introducing a new lubricant--
a lubricant that . . . .
```

Series; Lists—For punctuation with dashes, see **Series.**

Summation

Use a dash before a summation of preceding series or list.

```
Her willingness to try, her friendly
approach, her sincere attitude--
all tend to . . . .
```

With Other Punctuation

Place the dash after an internal excl mation point or question mark.

```
We recall the plan--made in 1945,
perhaps?--when you . . . .
As to your promotion--Congratulations!
you are . . . .
```

ELLIPSES

Ellipses (or omission marks) consist three spaced (or unspaced) perio within a sentence and between se tences. Four periods are used at the e of a sentence. Ellipses are used:

1. To indicate an omission from quot matter—a phrase, sentence, or se tences.

```
". . . because it is so well written . .
and so timely. . . we should like to
reprint . . . ."
```

2. To show that a series continues (place of *et cetera*).

```
Answer every fifth question (3, 8,
13, 18 . . .).
```

3. To show passage of time in narr tive.

```
He rose slowly . . . tried to steady
himself . . . fell forward.
```

4. To show that a statement is u finished or dies away.

```
Your reason makes us wonder . . . .
```

See also **Dash—Incomplete Sentence**

ENUMERATIONS

An *enumeration* is a series or list identified units. It may be run into t text or tabulated. (See also **Series**

Capitalization of Units

A. *Run-In Enumerations:* Capitali units only if they follow a colon a form sentences.

```
We cited three objections:  (1) Time i
limited.  (2) The cost is . . . .
We cited three objections:  (1) limite
time, (2) excessive cost, and . . .
```

B. *Tabulated Enumerations:* Capitalize units—See **Introductory Colon (B).**

Introductory Colon

A. Use a colon before a run-in enumeration when the introductory words form a complete thought.

```
There are three colors:  (1) a light
   beige, (2) a very pale yellow, . . . .
The colors are (1) a light beige,
   (2) a very pale yellow, and . . . .
```

B. Use a colon before a tabulated enumeration.

```
The colors are:
   1. Light beige
   2. Very pale yellow
   3. Stark white
```

Punctuation after Items

Use the same terminal punctuation after each item in an enumeration. If units are:

Run-In Clauses—use semicolons.

Run-In Sentences—use periods.

Run-In Words or Phrases—use commas.

Tabulated Sentences—use periods.

Tabulated Words or Phrases—omit punctuation marks at end.

EXCLAMATION POINT

Exclamatory Elements

A. Use an exclamation point after a forceful remark or command.

```
Ouch!  Your logic hurts.
Mail it today!  You'll be glad.
```

B. A comma may be used after expressions of only mild force or surprise.

```
Good work, but we expected it from you.
Truly, it is not as impossible as you
   think.
```

Extreme Emphasis

Indicate the extreme in emphasis by using an exclamation point. Note the decreasing emphasis in these examples:

```
This means a 200% profit!
This means a 200% profit.
This means a 200% profit.
```

Irony

Use an exclamation point enclosed in parentheses to intensify an expression or word used ironically.

```
Your conscientious (!) follow-up caused
   us to lose the order.
```

For other ways of indicating irony, see **Usage—Irony.**

O, Oh

A. *Oh* may be followed by an exclamation point or comma depending upon the degree of forcefulness intended.

```
Oh! What a surprise your letter was.
Oh, that reminds me, you are . . . .
```

B. *O* is always coupled with a name in direct address and is found only in solemn or poetic writing.

```
O Hamlet, what a tragic day . . . .
```

Rhetorical Questions

Use an exclamation point for emphasis.

```
How can we ever convince him!
```

With Other Punctuation

Place the exclamation point inside or outside closing punctuation marks, depending upon the relation of the enclosed matter to the sentence.

```
"Don't be a litterbug!" is clever.
What a clever "riposte"!
His first book (Hey There!) is best.
He must never return (at least, we
   hope he never returns)!
If we fail--Heaven forbid!--we may . . . .
```

HYPHEN

Capitalization—See **Capitalization— Titles of Persons (B)** *Civil and Military Titles*

Civil and military title designations of official positions are not usually hyphenated.

Lieutenant General   Secretary of State
Sales Manager   Attorney at Law

Clarity

The hyphen is used to improve the clarity of writing.

A little-used car is not the same as a little used car.

Compound Words—Adjective Modifiers

A. Hyphenate two or more words that *precede* a noun when they are considered to be a single modifier. When the modifier follows the noun, in most instances no hyphen is needed.

on-the-job training   Training on the
                      job is provided.
up-to-date report   The report is up
                      to date.

B. In modern usage the hyphen is omitted from *frequently used* one-thought modifiers that are instantly clear without the hyphen.

civil rights movement
long distance call
data processing equipment
post office employees

C. Do not hyphenate:

(1) An adverb-adjective combination.

highly technical paper
unusually warm day
hardly legible copy

Note, however, that some adjectives end in *ly* and therefore would not come under the rule.

surly-looking employee
friendly-appearing candidate

(2) An adjective-possessive combination.

a six months' vacation

(3) A two-word proper noun used as an adjective before a noun.

Scotch Irish descent

Mason Dixon Line

(4) A combination that is a forei phrase.

our per diem rate

(5) A combination enclosed in quot

"brain trust" idea

(6) A combination in which one of t adjectives in a compound modifier en in the comparative *er* or superlative *e*

higher ranking officer
shortest appearing sentence

See **Numbers—Compound Adjective**

Compound Words—Capitalized

A. Whenever the base word is capit ized, the compound is hyphenated.

pre-Christmas; anti-Hindu; pro-French
un-American; ex-President Adams

B. In titles and headings, capitalize ea part of a hyphenated compound nor ally capitalized.

An Off-the-Record Report

Identical Words

To prevent a compound's being m taken for an identical word, use hyphen.

re-cover, re-collect, not the same as
recover, recollect

Letter Prefixes

A compound with a letter prefix hyphenated.

L-shaped, U-curved

Numbers

A compound number is hyphenated, thirty-second.

Also See **Numbers—Ages**
                    —Consistency Wi
                     in a Sentence
                    —Fractions (B)
                    —Sequence

Prefixes—Hyphenated

Compounds with the prefixes on pa 721 are almost always hyphenated.

by	by-record
self	self-praise
ex	ex-golfer
vice	vice-director

Prefixes—Joined

A compound with any of the prefixes below is usually written as one word.

anti	antifreeze
bi	bimonthly
book	bookmark
circum	circumnavigate
co	coplanner
dis	disadvise
fore	foreknown
hyper	hypertension
in, un	uninspired
inter	international
mis	mistold
non	nonatom
out	outdistance
over	overcoat
pre	premeeting
pro	proexercise
post	postdate
re	restyle
trans	transcontinental
tri	tricity
un	unsuitable
where	whereas
semi	semicircular
	but semi-independent
under	underexplain
up	update

EXCEPTIONS: See **Identical Words, Prefixes—Hyphenated (B)**; **Compound Words**

Prefixes—Two-way

Any one of the prefixes below is detached or hyphenated in a compound word according to its part of speech

| air | half | high | ill |

A. *Noun compounds* are usually written as two words.

the air way, a half frown, a high spot

B. Adjective compounds are usually hyphenated.

an air-mixed liquid; a half-sincere offer

C. Verb compounds are usually hyphenated.

to air-mix, to half-approve

Series

In a series of repeated compounds the hyphen is repeated, but the base word is used only in the last compound.

two-, three-, and four-time winners

PARENTHESES

Capitalization Within

The first word within parentheses is not capitalized unless it is a proper name or the beginning of a quoted expression.

He subscribes to the Columbus (Georgia) Blade.
We played basketball (have you ever played it?) for many hours.
The family was watching television (What Makes It Happen?) when the explosion occurred.

Explanations

Enclose in parentheses any words, phrases, clauses, or sentences that explain, verify, illustrate, define, identify, etc.

Inner Parentheses

Use a set of inner parentheses or typewritten brackets to enclose parenthetical matter within parenthetical matter. See **Brackets—Inner Parentheses.**

With Other Punctuation

A. No punctuation mark ever precedes an opening parenthesis.

B. Necessary punctuation may precede and follow a closing parenthesis, depending upon context.

At the meeting (April 2) we . . . .
At the last meeting (April 2), we . . . .
At the next meeting (April 2?), we . . . .
Were you at the last meeting (April 2)?

PERIOD

The period is used after declarative and imperative sentences, commands phrased as questions, abbreviations, initials, and numbers or letters in enumerations. Refer to:

QUESTION MARK

Direct and Indirect Questions

Use a question mark at the end of a direct question, a period at the end of an indirect question.

DIRECT:

```
When is your vacation?
Why not order it today?
```

INDIRECT:

```
He asked why you ordered it.
```

Doubt, Conjecture

Use a question mark in parentheses after a fact to question its accuracy or to indicate that it is but a conjecture.

```
He worked there five (?) years.
```

Questions Within Sentences

A. Use a question mark at the end of a sentence containing a clause that questions the rest of the sentence. Set off the clause with commas.

```
He promised, didn't he, to call?
```

B. Use a question mark immediately after a query that questions the preceding part of the sentence. Enclose the query with dashes.

```
As a graduate of Yale--or is it
Harvard?-- he has . . . .
```

C. Use a question mark immediately after a question that is quoted or is in apposition with the word *question*.

```
One question "Can you finish it
in time?" must be asked.
The question, Can you finish it in
time?, must be asked.
```

Requests Phrased as Questions

A question mark is used at the end of a direct question to which an answer is expected. A polite request in question form to which no direct answer is expected is followed by a period.

DIRECT QUESTION:

```
What should we plan for tomorrow?
```

POLITE REQUEST:

```
Will you please send me your latest
catalog.
```

Several Questions Within One Sentence

Use a question mark after each question within the sentence. See **Capitalization —First Words (B, E).**

Unusual Use of a Word

To indicate that a word is used in a sense other than its true meaning, use a question mark in parentheses after the word or quote it, but do not underline it.

```
Prepare for a shock (?); you have won!
Prepare for a "shock"; you have won!
```

***With Other Punctuation**—Refer to the specific mark involved in this section.*

QUOTATION MARKS

Conversation

A. *Conversation with Description.* In literary writing, the speeches of one person are often grouped with description in a paragraph.

```
"Right you are, Buck. I'll watch my
step." Tod nodded slowly, his gray
eyes thoughtful. "It's No. 2 they
are after, isn't it? More money
there."
```

B. *Direct Conversation, Dialogue.* Direct conversation is enclosed in quotation marks and punctuated as follows:

```
He said, "That's fine."
"That's fine," he said, "for you."
"That's true," he said. "You're right."
"When can you come?" he asked.
"Oh, come now!" he said.
```

C. *Quoted Verbatim Conversations.* A word-for-word personal or telephone conversation is typed in any form that is easy to read and quick to type. It must be fully identified.

```
Telephone call - 6/10/68 - 2:50
    Mr. Alan King called Mr. Burt
K--Hello, Willis, how are you?
B--Fine, Alan.  What can I do for you?
K--I need some steel rods fast!
B--I'll try my best.  What sizes?
```

Familiar Sayings

While it is not necessary to call attention to sayings, it enlivens the typed text if they are quoted or underlined. If the saying is used as an adjective, however, hyphens are sufficient.

```
If "good things come by threes," I am
    especially blessed, for I have four
    to report.
This is a good-things-come-by-threes
    report.
```

Quoted Matter

For the use of quotation marks, see **Quoted Matter** in this section.

Titles of Published Matter

For proper typewritten forms, see **Titles of Published Matter** in this section.

With Other Punctuation

A. Place closing quotation marks:

(1) After a comma or period.

(2) Before a semicolon or colon.

(3) Before or after other marks, depending upon context.

B. Use only one punctuation mark at the end of a sentence even though the sentence structure suggests two.

```
I read that article "Why Punctuate?"
```

C. When there is a double question, use one question mark inside or outside the closing quotation mark.

```
Have you read "Why Punctuate?"
Have you read "Why Punctuate"?
```

Words Different in Tone

A. Enclose in quotation marks (do not underline) words that are different in

tone from the rest of the text or words used uniquely. These may be popular terms, unusual meanings, slang expressions, unusual spellings, and the like.

```
A "man of distinction" like you . . . .
Your "invitation" arrived . . . .
```

B. Do not quote a word when *so-called* precedes it.

```
Your so-called invitation arrived . . . .
```

See **Question Mark—Unusual Use of a Word; Usage—Irony.**

Words Referred to as Words

Enclose in quotation marks or underline words that are defined or pointed out.

```
The term coffee break means . . . .
His pet word is "dynamic."
She spelled "practice" with an "s."
```

QUOTED MATTER

To identify the exact words of a speaker or writer as such, enclose them in quotation marks, set them apart by indention, or both.

Copied Errors (Sic)

To indicate errors copied per se from quoted matter, see **Brackets—Quoted Matter (A).**

Corrections

To indicate corrected matter in quotations see **Brackets—Quoted Matter (B).**

Credit Lines, Reference Sources

The source of quoted matter is given (1) within the text, (2) in a footnote, or (3) in a credit line on the line following the indented quotation as shown below.

```
The article "English for Americans"
in the July, 1955, Holiday says:

    "Many words are stressed differently
    in Britain: laboratory and financier
    take the stress on the second . . . ."

        Four be the things I am
            wiser to know:
        Idleness, sorrow, a friend,
        a foe.

                --Dorothy Parker
```

Inserted Words (Interpolations)

Enclose in brackets any words inserted in the quoted matter. See **Brackets—Quoted Matter (C).**

Omissions

Use ellipses to show omission of words or sentences in quoted matter. See **Ellipses.**

Poetry

Separate quoted poetry from the text by line spaces and centering. Copy line lengths, indentions, and capitalization. The use of quotation marks is optional. If used, place them at the beginning of each verse and after the last word quoted. Use a colon to introduce the quotation.

Quotation Within a Quotation

Enclose the inner quotation in single quotation marks.

```
"My worthy opponent claims 'black is
  always black,' but I wonder if he
  means that."
```

Sentence Fragments

Enclose them in quotation marks.

```
Her reference said that she is
  "pleasant and conscientious" but
  that she "lacks initiative."
```

Several Paragraphs

Indent quoted matter of several paragraphs. The use of quotation marks is optional. If used, place them before each paragraph and after the last word quoted. Introduce the quotation with a colon.

Several Sentences

A. Use a colon to introduce several quoted sentences.

```
He said in his address:
No stone will be left unturned.
Every effort will be made.  We
hope to find the answer in time for
the next meeting.
```

B. Indent four or more lines of quoted matter, using or omitting quotation marks; or type less than four lines within the paragraph using quotation marks.

```
He said in his address: "No stone will
be left unturned.  Every effort will
be made.  We hope to find the answer."
```

Single Sentences

Enclose single sentences in quotation marks. Use a colon before the quoted sentence.

```
He recently wrote: "Our letters must
  have crossed in the mail."  They had.
```

Single Words

```
He said, "Think!"
```

Words in Italics

When copying printed matter in type-written form, underline words that are printed in italics.

```
"We gave him carte blanche so . . . ."
```

SEMICOLON

Clauses (Compound Sentences)

A. If a main clause contains commas, use semicolons between clauses.

```
A good dictionary, they say, is a
  secretary's best friend; and a good
  grammar is her loyal pal.
```

B. If no conjunction joins long main clauses without commas, use semicolons between them.

```
A good dictionary is a secretary's
  best friend; a good grammar is her
  loyal pal.
```

C. If a conjunction joins long main clauses without internal commas, use a comma before the conjunction.

D. If no conjunction joins short main clauses, use commas between them.

```
We ordered it Tuesday, they shipped it
Wednesday, we were using it Friday.
```

E. If a conjunction joins short main clauses that are closely related, do not use a comma before the conjunction (usually *and*).

```
We have considered it and it seems
workable.
```

F. (1) If a transitional word joins main clauses, use a semicolon before it. Such words are:

also	consequently
hence	furthermore
still	moreover
then	nevertheless
thus	therefore
yet	whereas

(2) A comma usually follows a transitional word except when the word is short, like those in the first column of F(1) above or where no pause occurs.

```
The need is pressing; therefore, we . . . .
The need is pressing; hence we . . . .
```

Namely; For Example; That Is

Use a semicolon or a dash before such an introductory expression and a comma after it when it introduces a clause explanation, illustration, or series. In the second example, the comma replaces the understood words *it is.*

```
There are several personnel policies
  that need study; for example, our
  salary ranges must be. . . .
We have an important personnel policy
  to consider; namely, a pension plan.
```

See also **Series, 6.**

Series; Lists—For the use of semicolons in series and lists, see **Series.**

With Other Punctuation

The semicolon arbitrarily follows a closing quotation mark. It may not precede a parenthesis.

```
He said, "There will be no increase";
  however, we hope he is wrong.
Use red, orange, and green (light shades
  only); however, be sure to stir each.
```

SERIES

1. Use commas between units in a series if none contain internal commas.

2. Use semicolons between units if one or more contain internal commas, or if commas would confuse the meaning.

```
Please send copies to Mr. A. J. King,
  Peerless Foundry, Dayton 3, Ohio;
  Mr. E. O. James, Kaymar, Inc.,
  Atlanta 10, Georgia; and Mr. Bruce
  Parish, Nutwood Farms, Medina, Ohio.
```

3. Some writers omit the comma before the ending connective.

```
a choice of tan, ivory, and gray
a choice of tan, ivory and gray
```

4. Do not use commas or semicolons between units if they are all joined with connectives.

```
It comes in tan or ivory or gray.
```

5. Use a comma before and after *etc., and so forth,* and *and the like.*

```
He is scanning books, articles, reports,
  etc., for information.
```

6. To introduce a series or list use either introductory words properly punctuated, or punctuation alone, as follows:

```
. . . many colors; for example, beige,
    ivory, gray, and cream.
. . . many colors--for example, beige,
    ivory, gray, and cream.
. . . many colors, such as beige, ivory,
    gray, and cream.
. . . good colors, for example, are
    beige, ivory, gray, and cream.
. . . many colors:  beige, ivory, gray,
    and cream.
. . . many colors--beige, ivory, gray,
    and cream.
```

See also **Dash—Summation.**

TITLES OF PUBLISHED MATTER

Books, Magazines, Newspapers

Type in all capitals, or capitalize important words and underline entire title. Even though *the* is a formal part of the title, it is often ignored.

```
in yesterday's NEW YORK TIMES
in the New York Times of
in THE NEW YORK TIMES of
```

EXCEPTION: Do not type in all caps or underline the word "Bible."

Compound Words, Capitalization of

See **Words—Compound, Capitalized Parts (C).**

Parts of Published Works (Chapters, Articles, Features Columns, Etc.) and Movies, Songs, Plays, Lectures, Sermons.

Capitalize important words and enclose title in quotation marks.

```
In the "Reference Guide" in SECRETARIAL
PROCEDURES AND ADMINISTRATION . . . .
In the "Reference Guide" in Secretarial
Procedures and Administration . . . .
```

Do not enclose in quotation marks the books of the Bible.

UNDERLINING

Familiar Sayings—See Quotation Marks —Familiar Sayings.

For Emphasis

Underline words that should be emphasized by the reader.

```
Now it is my turn.
```

Italics

Underscore typewritten words to indicate that they are printed, or are to be printed, in italics.

```
Data can be either singular or plural.
```

Titles of Published Matter

For underlining of titles, see **Titles of Published Matter** in this section.

Words Referred to as Words—See Quotation Marks—Words Referred to as Words in this section.

The entries in the following section of the Reference Guide are limited to those words or phrases that are often misused or inappropriately used in business and about which information is not commonly available in standard dictionaries.

a; an

Now commonly used as follows:

```
a historical event; an honor;
a hotel; a habitual trait;
a humble (if you pronounce the h);
an humble (if you do not).
```

ability

Ability *to*, plus verb; as *ability to influence*, not *ability of influencing*.

about; at about

Use either *about* or *at*—not both.

```
Leave at noon.
Leave about noon.
```

above

This word is used in all levels of writing as a preposition and an adverb.
In business writing it is sometimes used as an adjective or a pronoun.

```
It is above the file.
The boxes are shelved above.
The above price is net.
Consider the above seriously.
```

absolve

To absolve (free) *from*, as *to absolve from blame*.

accede

To accede (assent) *to*, as *accede to your request*.

accept; except

1. *Accept* means to agree, to receive. It is always a verb.

```
I accept your offer.
```

2. *Except*, the preposition, means but.

```
All except Mr. Slade replied.
```

3. For *except*, the verb, see **except.**

accompany

To be accompanied *by* a person; otherwise, to be accompanied *with*.

acquiesce

To acquiesce (agree) *in* (not *to*), as *to acquiesce in the matter*.

acronyms

Acronyms are words formed from the initial letters or syllables of two or more words as *Wac, snafu, motel,* and *radar.* They are not enclosed in quotes or underscored. Plurals, possessives, and tenses are formed regularly.

A.D.—See Numbers—Years.

adapt

To adapt (change and make suitable) *to, from,* or *for.*

```
He adapted the device to our needs.
The device is adapted from a standard
    model for experimenting.
```

adept

To be adept (expert) *in* (not *at*), as *adept in training beginners.*

adhere; adherent

To adhere (hold fast) *to,* as *adhere to our policy;* an adherent *of,* as *an adherent of that policy.*

advice; advise

Advice is a noun and means a recommendation as to a decision or course of conduct.

Advise is a verb and means to counsel or to recommend.

```
I can advise you, but will
    you follow my advice?
```

adverse; averse

To be adverse (antagonistic) *to,* as *adverse to change. Averse* means unwilling.

affect; effect

1. *Affect* means to influence. It is always a verb.

```
Weather affects attendance.
```

2. *Effect* (verb) means to accomplish or produce.

```
They tried to effect a compromise.
```

3. *Effect* (noun) means result.

```
It had an adverse effect on sales.
```

agree

Agree *to* or *on* a plan, *with* a person, *in* principle. One thing agrees *with* another.

a la or à la

The accent is dropped in typewritten text except in formal or in specialized writing.

all; all of

Use *all* with nouns, *all of* with pronouns.

```
Check all the reports.
Check all of them, please.
```

all right

This is the only correct spelling. *Alright* is incorrect.

all together; altogether

All together means in the same place, while *altogether* means entirely.

```
The correspondence is all together in
    one folder.
He is altogether too casual in his
    manner.
```

allude; elude

Allude means to refer indirectly; *elude* means to avoid.

```
Allude to a possible wage
    increase, but elude making
    a positive statement.
```

USAGE—WORDS AND PHRASES —Page 726

allusion—See **illusion; allusion**

almost all; most

To indicate number, use *almost all* in written English instead of the shortened, informal *most. Most* is correctly used as a superlative.

```
Almost all of them replied.
```

already; all ready

Already (adv.) means previously.
All ready is an adjectival phrase.

```
He has already left.
They are all ready.
```

altar; alter

Altar is a noun and refers to worship.
Alter is a verb meaning to change.

```
They decorated the altar.
He will alter the assignment.
```

alternative

In strict usage *alternative* is one of *two* possibilities. It is defined and commonly used as one of *several*.

alumna, alumnae; alumnus, alumni

Alumna is a woman graduate or former student (plural, *alumnae*).
Alumnus is a man graduate or former student (plural, *alumni*).
Graduate or *graduates* is often a good substitute word.

among; between

Generally, *between* implies two; *among*, more than two. However, in choices, comparisons, distinctions and interrelationships, *between* is used with more than two.

```
Differentiate between to, too, and two.
Choose between these four colors.
Games between the six schools ....
```

amount; number

Amount is commonly used of money and of things which cannot be counted; *number*, of things which can be counted, as *amount of speculation; number of speculators*.

amounts; quantities

An amount or quantity takes plural forms except when it refers to one unit.

A UNIT: Ten yards makes one cover.

NO UNIT: Ten yards more are needed.

ampersand (and, &)

Use & only when it is a part of a proper name or abbreviation, or in tabulations.

```
King & Jones; B & 0
```

and (*in compound subjects*)

Two or more subject words joined by *and* take plural verbs and pronouns unless the words together describe one person or thing.

TWO PERSONS:

```
Our sales manager and advertising
   director have sent in their requests.
```

ONE PERSON:

```
Our sales manager and advertising
   director, Mr. Allen Kane, has sent in
   his request.
```

TWO THINGS:

```
A pen and a pencil were found.
```

ONE THING:

```
A matching pen and pencil makes a
   welcome gift.
```

and/or

This phrase indicates a three-way choice. *Come Monday and/or Tuesday* means to come Monday, come Tuesday or come both days. It is conspicuous in typewritten text. To avoid, say: *Come both Monday and Tuesday or either day.*

and sign—See **ampersand.**

angry

To be angry *at* or *about* a thing, *with* or *at* a person.

```
He is sure to be angry with (or at)
   Mr. Kane at (or about) the oversight.
```

antipathy

An antipathy (dislike) *toward* or *for*, as *antipathy toward (or for) misrepresentation.*

any

This word takes singular verbs and pronouns.

anyone; any one

1. *Anyone* is written as one word when *any* is accented; as two words when *one* is accented. *Any one* is usually followed by *of*.

```
Anyone is welcome.  (ANYone)
Send any one of your men.  (any ONE)
```

2. This hint also applies to *anyway— any way; everyone—every one;* and *someone—some one.*

anxious; eager

Both *anxious* and *eager* mean earnest desire. *Anxious* denotes worry.

```
We are eager to please.
We are anxious to please (but worried
    that we may fail).
```

appraise; apprise

Appraise means to set a value on, while *apprise* means to inform.

```
The adjustor will appraise the
    damage and apprise you of his
    estimate.
```

appropriate

To appropriate (take) *something;* to appropriate (set aside) *for;* to be appropriate (suitable) *to* or *for.*

```
The city appropriated the land.
They appropriated money for the land.
The cover is appropriate to the book.
A suit is appropriate for office wear.
```

apropos

To be apropos *to* or *of* (with respect to).

```
Apropos of our contract, can you arrange
    a conference for tomorrow?
```

apt; likely; liable

Apt is often incorrectly used for *likely* or *liable.*

Apt means suitable (*apt phrasing*) and talented (*apt at organizing*).

Likely means probable (*likely to refuse*).

Liable means susceptible to something unpleasant (*liable to break*), and responsible (*liable for damages*).

as

This word may be used as:

1. An ADVERB:
    A. To mean *extent.*
```
Write as often as possible.
```

    B. To introduce an appositive.
```
Spell it with a capital, as X-cel.
```

2. A PREPOSITION:
```
Webster shows as as a preposition.
```

3. A CONJUNCTION:
```
As you were talking, he was observing.
```

In a clause of reason, *since* or *because* is more exact than *as.* (See **like,** 2.)
```
Because (as) he is away, I . . . .
```

as . . . as; not so . . . as

In regular comparisons use *as . . . as*; in negative comparisons in formal writing use *not so . . . as.*

REGULAR COMPARISON:
```
This design is as chic as that one.
```

NEGATIVE COMPARISON:
```
This design is not so chic as that one.
```

EMPHATIC NEGATIVE COMPARISON:
```
This design is not nearly so chic as
    that one.
```

as to

Usually a single preposition like *in, for, of, about,* etc., is better than *as to.*
```
He commented about (as to) your idea.
```

as to whether

Use only *whether.*

as well as; together with

The noun or pronoun preceding either phrase is the subject. Subsequent nouns or pronouns do not affect the verb.
```
The report, as well as the schedules,
    is finished.
The schedules, as well as the report,
    are finished.
```

aversion

An aversion (dislike) *to* or *toward*.

His aversion to orderliness frustrates
his systematic secretary.

B. C.—See Numbers—Years.

bad; badly

1. Use *bad* when an adjective is required as with a linking verb. (See
Linking Verbs.)

He feels bad; he looks bad; it sounds bad.

2. Use *badly* when an adverb is required (even though some dictionaries now give *bad* as an adverb, too).

He played badly in the tournament.

bail; bale

Bail means security, to dip; *bale* is a
bundle, package.

The prisoner was released on bail.
There is a bale of paper. . . .

balance; remainder

Balance means the amount of money
in an account: the balance in a bank
account, the balance due in a credit
account. *Balance* for *remainder* is colloquial. (See **colloquial.**)

FORMAL:

Send the remainder of the order.

INFORMAL (COLLOQUIAL):

Send the balance of the order.

bases; basis

Bases is the plural of *basis*.

because of—See due to.

between—See among; between.

biannual; biennial; semiannual

Biannual means twice a year; *biennial*,
once in two years; *semiannual*, every
half year.

Bible; Bible references

See **Capitalization—Bible.** Write references as follows:

Proverbs 25:21
Acts 5:1-7
2 Kings 11:13-17

billion—See Numbers—Millions.

bimonthly; semimonthly

Semimonthly means every half month;
bimonthly means twice a month *or* every
two months. For clarity, use the proper
explanatory phrase for bimonthly.

blond; blonde

Blond is masculine; *blonde*, feminine.

brunet; brunette

Brunet is masculine; *brunette*, feminine.

but—See Punctuation—Comma, But.

but that; but what

But *that* is formal; *but what*, colloquial.

FORMAL:

We did not know but that they would
refuse.

INFORMAL:

We didn't know but what they would
refuse.

can; could; would

Could is the past tense of *can*. *Can* and
could imply ability. Use *could* if *would*
is in a related clause.

If you could come soon, we would decide
on the procedure.

See also **may, might.**

can; may

In formal writing use *can* for *ability*,
may for *permission*. To use *can* for
permission, especially in a question,
creates a friendly response. Compare
May we do this for you? with *Can we do
this for you?*

cannot; can not

Cannot is more generally used. Some feel *can not* is more emphatic.

cannot (or can't) help but

This phrase is not acceptable. Use instead:

FORMAL:
```
We can but advise you to . . . .
We cannot but advise you to . . . .
```

INFORMAL:
```
We can only advise you to . . . .
We cannot help advising you to . . . .
```

NOT:
```
We can't help but advise you to . . . .
We cannot help but advise you to . . . .
```

cannot (or can't) seem to

This phrase is informal; use *seem unable to* in formal writing.

FORMAL:
```
They seem unable to decide.
```

INFORMAL:
```
They can't seem to decide.
```

canvas; canvass

Canvas is a noun meaning cloth.
Canvass is a verb meaning to solicit.
```
The supplies were covered with canvas.
Mr. Williams will canvass all employees
    for the Community Drive.
```

capacity

The capacity *to* with a verb, as *the capacity to listen;* the capacity (volume) *of,* as *the capacity of the tank;* a capacity *for* (doing or receiving something), as *a capacity for making friends.*

capitol; capital

Capitol is always a building; capitalize it only when it is a part of a proper name. For all other meanings use *capital.*

cite; sight; site

Cite means to quote; *sight* means vision; and *site* means location.
```
He will cite the president's remarks in
    his editorial.
```
```
The accident resulted in injury to his
    sight.
The site for the new building has been
    selected.
```

claim

The verb *claim* has an antagonistic overtone. *Say* and *feel* are more tactful.

See **euphemisms.**

coincident

To be coincident *with* (occurring at the same time).
```
The change is to be coincident with the
    reorganization.
```

colloquial

A word or meaning marked *colloquial* in the dictionary is used in the conversation of educated people. Colloquialisms are acceptable in friendly business letters and informal writing.

comedian; comedienne

Comedian is masculine; *comedienne,* feminine.

comparable

To be comparable *with, to.*
```
Their product is comparable with (or to)
    ours in quality.
```

compare

1. To compare *to:* (a) unlike classes; (b) likenesses.
```
(a) He compared recreation to lost
    time.
(b) He compared her letters to those
    written by his former secretary.
```

2. To compare *with* (in like and unlike ways).
```
He compared traveling with education.
```

3. With *compared,* use either *to* or *with.*
```
I prefer traveling compared to (or
    with) studying.
```

compatible

To be compatible (in harmonious relationship) *with.*
```
The director is not compatible with his
    new assistant.
```

complected; complexioned

Always use *complexioned*, as *light complexioned*. *Complected* is a dialect word used only in certain localities.

complement; compliment

Complement means to complete, while *compliment* means to praise.

comply

To comply *with*, as *to comply with rules*.

concur

To concur (agree) *in*, *on*, or *with*.
> The directors concur with your decision on the subject in every detail.

conducive

To be conducive (contributive) *to*.
> Closing early yesterday was conducive to good morale.

confidant; confidante

Confidant is masculine; *confidante*, feminine.

confide

To confide *in* or *to* a person.
> He confided in (or <u>to</u>) her that he was resigning.

conform

To conform *to* or *in*.
> Your suggestion conforms to our general idea in one regard.

conformity

Conformity (agreement) *between* or *in;* in conformity *with*.
> There is little conformity between the two plans in content or in approach.
> This plan is in conformity with your first suggestion.

confront

To confront (face) *with;* to be confronted by.
> We dislike to confront you with this problem now, but we ourselves are confronted by an unusual problem.

Congress, Sessions of—See **Capitalization—Congress; Numbers—Congre** Sessions of.

connected with; in connection with

These phrases are wordy and usual can be shortened to *with* or *in,* omitted entirely.
> We are enclosing the bill for our serv ices in (not <u>in connection with</u>) the study of your five plants.

consensus of opinion

This phrase is objected to by purists redundant, but Webster says it ". . . now generally accepted as in good use

See **redundancy.**

considerable

Use of *considerable* as a noun is labele colloquial in the dictionaries.

INFORMAL:
> There is considerable to discuss.

consist

To consist *of* (parts, etc.); to consist (a description).
> The mixture consists of four herbs.
> Experience consists in doing things repeatedly.

consonant

To be consonant (in agreement) *to* with.
> It is consonant to good planning to start early.
> It seems consonant with good judgment to sell out.

consul; council; counsel

Consul means a foreign representative *council* means an assembly; *counse* means advice or to advise.

consult

To consult *about* or *with* (but usuall the *with* is redundant).
> The heir consulted (or <u>consulted with</u>) the lawyer about the will.

contact

Use of *contact* as a verb, meaning to communicate with a person or agency, is sometimes objected to. The dictionaries label it colloquial; the handbooks, a business usage.

contingent

To be contingent (dependent) *on* or *upon*.

Delivery is contingent upon the strike.

continual; continuous

Continual means constantly repeated with small breaks between. *Continuous* means constantly repeated without break.

There were continual interruptions.
The machine has been in continuous use
  since May.

Contractions—See **Punctuation—Apostrophe (3).**

contrary

To be contrary *to;* the contrary *of*.

To explain is contrary to my nature.
His description is the contrary of
  actual conditions.

contrast

To contrast one *with* another; in contrast *to*.

To contrast my work with hers is not
  fair.
The decision was in direct contrast to
  our hopes.

conversation—See **Punctuation—Quotation Marks, Conversation.**

Conversions

A conversion is using a word as an unconventional part of speech. Enclose the word in quotation marks only if the reader may think it a grammatical error or if you want to label it as clever usage.

1. A noun converted to an adjective—

The report draft is ready.

2. An adjective or adverb converted to a verb—

We nonstopped to Dallas.

3. An adjective converted to a verb—

He tried to pretty the picture with
  promises.

4. A noun converted to a verb—

The boy dogged his father's footsteps.

coordinate

To coordinate plans, records, etc.; to coordinate *with*.

They are coordinating the sales campaign
  with the buying habits of women.

correlate

To correlate (connect systematically) *one thing and another thing;* to correlate *with*.

The course correlates study and on-the-
  job training; it correlates learning
  with doing.

correspond

To correspond (agree) *with* or *to*.

The plan corresponds with (or to) ours.

could—See **can; could; would**

credible; creditable; credulous

Credible means believable; *creditable*, praiseworthy; *credulous*, ready to believe on weak evidence.

The reason is credible.
It is a creditable suggestion.
He is not so credulous as to accept
  that explanation.

data

Data is a plural noun defined as facts, figures, or information. *Data* takes plural forms when it refers to facts or figures. It takes singular forms when it refers to information or a group of facts as a unit.

The data are (or is) being prepared.
The data supporting our conclusion is
  enclosed.

date

To date *from*.

It dates from (not back to) 1962.

date (for engagement)

This meaning is variously termed *informal*, *slang*, *familiar*, *colloquial;* it is seldom suitable in business writing.

Degrees (Academic)—See **Capitalization —Degrees.**

descendant; descendent

To avoid a possible misspelling, use *descendant*, which is either a noun or an adjective. *Descendent* is an adjective only.

```
He is a descendant of John Adams.
He is descendent from John Adams.
```

deviate

To deviate (turn aside) *from*, as *to deviate from the rules*.

differ

One thing differs *from* another. Persons differ *with* each other.

```
The shipment differed from the order.
He differs with our conclusion.
```

different

Different from is always correct. *Different than* is sometimes used when followed by a clause.

```
The shipment was different from the
  order.
The circumstances were different than
  (or from those) he recalled.
```

digress

To digress (turn aside), to digress *from.*

```
I shall digress and define the terms
  before proceeding.
I shall digress from discussing the
  future to talk about today.
```

Dimensions—See **Abbreviations—Dimensions and Weights.**

discriminate

To discriminate *against* or *between.*

```
The casting director discriminates
  against blondes.
He discriminated between blondes and
  brunettes.
```

disillusion; dissolution

Disillusion means to see beneath the illusion (the deceptive appearance), or to destroy an illusion. *Dissolution* means a dissolving.

```
It was disillusioning to discover his
  true character.
All machinery is for sale because of the
  dissolution of the company.
```

disinterested; uninterested

Disinterested implies interest in the subject but with a lack of prejudice or selfish interest. *Uninterested* implies indifference to a subject.

```
Ethics requires a CPA to be disin-
  terested in a client's success.
He is uninterested in his future.
```

disparity

A disparity (inequality) *in.*

```
The disparity in their ages made them
  critical of each other.
```

dissolution—See **disillusion; dissolution.**

distinct

To be distinct (different) *in;* to be distinct (separate) *from.*

```
The belt is distinct in one respect.
This order should be kept distinct from
  the others.
```

distinguish

To distinguish *between* (even if more than *two*); to distinguish one *from* another; to be distinguished *for.*

```
It is difficult to distinguish between
  the three covers.
This cover can easily be distinguished
  from that one.
He is distinguished for his writing.
```

divert

To divert *from, to, with, by,* etc.

```
The speaker was diverted from the
  subject.
The camp funds were diverted to other
  uses.
The child was diverted by (or with)
  the clown's antics.
```

oubt

. To express doubt, use *if* or *whether* with the word *doubt*. When there is no oubt, use a negative before *doubt that* n formal writing.

WHEN THERE IS DOUBT:

```
I doubt if (or whether) there is time.
```

WHEN THERE IS NO DOUBT:

```
I do not doubt that there is time.
```

. To indicate doubt, see **Punctuation—Question Mark, Doubt.**

ue to

. The use of this phrase as a preposi-ion is controversial. Purists strenuously bject to it. *Owing to* and *because of* are ccepted substitutes for it.

CONTROVERSIAL:

```
Due to faulty brakes, we drove slowly.
```

FORMAL:

```
Owing to (or because of) faulty brakes,
   we drove slowly.
```

. In the example below *due* is a predi-ate adjective connected by the linking verb *was* to the noun *train*. *To arrive* is an infinitive phrase.

FORMAL:

```
The train was due to arrive at 9:05 a.m.
```

each

When used as a pronoun, *each* is singu-lar; as an adjective, *each* has no effect on the verb.

```
Each of them has its points.   (Pronoun)
They each have their points.   (Adj.)
```

eager—See **anxious; eager.**

effect—See **affect; effect.**

either; neither

These take singular verbs and pronouns.

```
Either day is convenient.
Neither has sent his photograph.
```

either . . . or; neither . . . nor

When these connectives join subject words, the word nearer the verb deter-mines the use of singular or plural verbs, and in some cases, the person of the verb. Usually the plural word is placed nearer to the verb.

```
Either Mr. Kane or his associates are
   planning to attend.
Neither the reports nor the book is
   here.
```

CORRECT BUT AWKWARD:

```
Either he or I am coming.
```

BETTER:

```
Either he is coming or I am.
```

else's—See **Possessives—"Else" Phrases.**

eminent; imminent

Eminent means high, lofty, distinguished; *imminent* means threatening or impend-ing.

```
Our guest is an eminent scientist.
Starvation is always imminent.
```

engage

To engage *in;* to engage the attention, the enemy, etc.; to be engaged *to, for, by,* etc.

```
She engaged him in conversation.
She engaged his attention while I . . . .
He was engaged by Mr. Kane for one year
   to direct the work.
```

enthused

This verb, formed from the noun *en-thusiasm*, is in fairly general use; but it offends purists. The dictionaries label it colloquial.

INFORMAL:

```
We are enthused about it.
```

FORMAL:

```
We are enthusiastic about it.
```

Enumerations—See **Punctuation—Enu-merations.**

equal

To be equal *in, to,* or *to that of;* the equal *of* or *in.*

```
They are equal in length.
It is equal to ten others.
It is equal to that of our competitor.
It is the equal of their device.
```

equivalent

To be equivalent *in* or *to;* the equivalent *of* or *in.*

> This position is equivalent in prestige to that of director.
> The contents are the equivalent of three quarts.
> The substituted merchandise is equivalent in value.

Errors (in quoted matter)—See **Punctuation—Brackets, Quoted Matter (A).**

Esq.—See **Abbreviations—Esq.**

essential

To be essential *to* or *in.*

> Health is essential to happiness.
> Accuracy is essential in this work.

etc.; and so forth; et cetera

The first two are common in business writing. If *et cetera* is dictated, the secretary usually transcribes it as *and so forth* or *etc.* To avoid them, substitute *and the like.* (See **Punctuation—Series, 5.**)

ethics

This word takes singular verbs and pronouns when it means a set of practices; plural forms when it means individual ones.

> Professional ethics prohibits our advertising.
> In several instances his ethics have been questionable.

euphemisms

This word means softened, tactful phrases for blunt or harsh facts. Some euphemisms are:

> laid to rest (for buried)
> left our employ (for discharged)
> the leisure class (for the rich)
> passed away (for died)
> say or feel (for claim)
> seems (for is)
> underprivileged; modest (for poor)

euphony

Euphony consists of pleasing speech sounds. It is achieved by:

1. Avoiding the harsh, ugly sounds: too many *f's, t's, ug's, og's.*

2. Repeating pleasant sounds.

3. Rhythm of accented syllables.

CHOPPY:
> We are glad indeed to be able to tell you that we . . . .

EUPHONIC:
> We are pleased that we . . . .

everybody; everyone

1. These take singular verbs and pronouns.

> Everyone is asked to wire his opinion.

2. For the distinction between *everyone* and *every one,* see **anyone; any one.**

except

To except against and *to except from* are correct but are very formal.

To object and *to excuse,* respectively, are better in business writing.

> See **accept; except.**

exception

To take exception *to* (*object to*).

> Perhaps you take exception to that point.

exclusive

To be exclusive *of* or *with.*

> The price is exclusive of tax.
> Eisenberg jewels are exclusive with us.

excuse—See **pardon; excuse.**

expatiate

To expatiate (enlarge) *on* or *upon* a subject.

> She bored everyone by expatiating on her son's accomplishments.

explicit; implicit

To be *explicit in* or *on* means to explain fully; to be *implicit in* or *on* means that something can be inferred or understood that is not actually stated.

    Catalogs are explicit in describing
      items.
    The letter is quite explicit on that
      point.
    His approval of that point was implicit
      in his approval of the full report.

expostulate

To expostulate (reason firmly) *about*, *for*, *on*, or *upon*, something; to expostulate *with* a person.

    I expostulated with him about (or for)
      misrepresenting the facts.

ex-President

The phrase *former President* is more dignified and preferred to *ex-President*.

    In his book former (not ex-) President
      Truman says . . . .

See **Capitalization—Titles of Persons (A).**

farther; further

In formal English, *farther* is used for distances (far away); *further*, for advancement, onwardness, or degree often with *into*.

    The airport is six miles farther.
    We can go into this further.
    Let's discuss it further.

At the informal level, *further* is used for all meanings.

favorable

To be favorable *to* or *for*.

    The weather is favorable to our cam-
      paign.
    The time is favorable for a decision.

federal—Capitalization—Federal.

female

This word is not acceptable in business or formal writing as a synonym for *woman*, *lady*, or *feminine*. *Female*, however, is used in records and statistics.

ferret

To ferret (search) *out* facts, data, etc.

    He ferreted out the data from the files.

few

As a subject, *few* is a plural pronoun and requires a plural predicate.

    A few are ready now.
    Only a few plan to come.

fewer; less

In strict usage, *fewer* refers to things that can be counted; *less*, to money and to things that can be measured. *Less* is beginning to be used for both meanings. (See **less; lesser.**)

    Fewer persons came this time.
    Less time is required.

fiancé; fiancée

Fiancé is the man to whom the girl is engaged; *fiancée*, the girl to whom the man is engaged.

flaunt; flout

Flaunt means to wave; to display boastfully, brazenly.
Flout means to treat with contempt or insult.

    She never misses an opportunity to
      flaunt her superior education.
    She flouts all rules and regulations.

follow-up; follow up

Follow-up is a noun or adjective; *follow up*, a verb.

    Make a follow-up on this bid.
    Send a follow-up letter next week.
    Follow up on this tomorrow.

Fractions—See **Numbers—Fractions.**

further—See **farther; further.**

Gerund

1. A gerund is the *ing* form of a verb used as a noun. It may be a

SUBJECT:

    You learn that editing takes time.

OBJECT:

    She learned editing from you.

SUBJECT AND PREDICATE NOUNS:

    Rewriting is not editing.

2. In formal writing a possessive is used with a gerund.

    His editing included Chapter 10.
    The team's winning made the players
    overconfident.

See also **Plurals and Possessives—Possessives, Gerunds, 6.**

EXCEPTION:

Do not use a possessive if the noun is modified.

    The No. 2 mill breaking down changes the
    situation.

OPTIONAL EXCEPTION:

If the noun is inanimate or abstract, a possessive may or may not be used.

    The mill('s) breaking down changes . . . .
    That is an example of a situation ('s)
    becoming overemphasized.

gobbledygook

This word was coined by a Texas senator after the gobbling of turkeys. It describes the involved, verbose English that officialdom and others sometimes use. It will be interesting to see if *gobbledygook* survives the newer coinage, *officialese.*

good; well

To *feel good* and to *feel well* are not synonymous. Both *good* and *well* are adjectives. *Feel* is a linking verb.

See **Linking Verbs.**

1. Use *well* when referring to health—when *in fine health* can be substituted for it.

    I feel well and energetic.

2. Use *good* when *pleasant* can be substituted for it. Do not use *good* when referring to health.

    I feel good about your promotion.

got; gotten

Either word may be used as the past participle of *got.*

government

This word takes singular verbs and pronouns.

    The government is setting up its budget.

See **Capitalization—Federal.**

graduated

Use either *graduated from* or *was graduated from.* In letters of application, use *was graduated from* in case the executive is a word purist.

FORMAL USAGE:

    He was graduated from Yale.

ACCEPTED GENERAL USAGE:

    He graduated from Yale.

Honorable

Use this title of respect during term of office. Use a first name, initials, or title between *Honorable* and the surname. See **Abbreviations—Honorable.**

    Hon. Alan Kane
    Honorable A. R. Kane
    the Honorable Mr. Kane

              NOT:

    the Honorable Kane

"hope" phrases

The phrases *in hopes of* and *no hopes of* should not be used for *in the hope of* and *no hope of.*

however

Avoid starting a sentence with *however* when the meaning is *nevertheless.*

CORRECT:

    However you advise him, he will do as he
    pleases.

INCORRECT:

    However, we at least completed the
    report.

identical

To be identical *with* or *to* something *in* some way.

    The original letter is identical with
    the copy in content.

identified with

To be *identified with* (associated with) is colloquial according to some dictionaries.

INFORMAL

He was formerly identified with one of our competitors.

idioms

1. An *idiom* is an expression or phrase that is peculiar—an arbitrary grouping of words that is often illogical in construction or meaning but is acceptable in usage; for example, *to make ends meet, laid up with a virus, to take pains, by and large, catch a cold.*

2. A prepositional idiom is the preposition peculiar to one word or one meaning of a word, such as *conducive to,* to *live at, live by, live down, live for, live off, live within,* etc. Numerous prepositional idioms are in this Reference Guide.

"if" Clauses—See **Subjunctive Mood, 1 and 2.**

illusion; allusion

Illusion means a deceptive appearance, as an *illusion of success. Allusion,* from *allude,* means something referred to, as *the allusion to our policy.*

in; into; in to

In implies a set location; *into,* movement to a location; *in to,* the adverb *in* and the preposition *to.*

He is in his office.
He walked into his office.
He went in to find it.

in connection with—connected with.
in person—See **personally; in person.**

inappropriate

To be inappropriate *to* or *for.*

Satin dresses are inappropriate to office wear.
His use of slang was inappropriate for the occasion.

Inc.—See **Punctuation—Comma, Inc., Ltd.**

incidence

The incidence (occurrence) *of.*

The incidence of polio varies in different localities.

incident

To be incident *to* (naturally pertaining to).

The satisfactions incident to teaching outweigh the dissatisfactions.

incidental

To be incidental *to* (likely to happen).

There are also intangible advantages incidental to a partnership like ours.

incite; insight

Incite means to arouse; *insight* means understanding.

His speech was designed to incite the crowd.
The article provides a new insight into the problem.

incompatible

To be incompatible (out of harmony) *with.*

His constant bickering made him incompatible with everyone.

incongruous

To be incongruous (out of keeping) *with.*

The casual style of the letter is incongruous with the seriousness of the subject.

inconsiderate

To be inconsiderate *of.*

We know that it is inconsiderate of us to ask you to give up your holiday.

inconsistent

To be inconsistent *in* or *with.*

He is inconsistent in his arguments.
The statements were inconsistent with those he made earlier.

increase
For business usage of this word, see **raise; increase; increment.**

incredible; incredulous
A situation is *incredible* (unbelievable); a person is *incredulous* (unbelieving).
> It is incredible that he failed.
> I cannot help being incredulous about that story.

indifferent
To be indifferent *to.*
> He is quite indifferent to my reasoning.

Infinitives
1. An infinitive is the simple form of the verb, such as *go, see, do.* *To* before the verb marks it as an infinitive (although the *to* is dropped when the infinitive follows a few verbs, such as *make, help, need, may,* etc.).
> He will need to rest soon.
> Make him rest, if you can.

2. Use an infinitive phrase as follows:
NOUN (AS A SUBJECT):
> To go will be a privilege.

NOUN (AS AN OBJECT):
> He wants to talk with you.
> Please ask him to write the letter.

ADJECTIVE:
> The place to go is Spain.

ADVERB:
> He saved to go to Spain.

ABSOLUTE:
> To exaggerate a bit, the trip was great!

3. A split infinitive occurs when a word or words separate *to* and the *verb.* Use a split infinitive only when clarity or emphasis demands.
CLARITY:
> We asked him to at least write us.

EMPHASIS:
> We want to fully understand it before signing.

ingenious; ingenuous
Ingenious means inventive; *ingenuous* means (1) candid; (2) artless.
> It is an ingenious (inventive) solution.
> His ingenuous (candid) answers have helped me to understand it.
> Her ingenuous (artless) look misleads us.

inimical
To be inimical (hostile) *to.*
> This situation is inimical to harmony.

insensible
1. When *insensible* means to be indifferent, use *of.*
> The customer was insensible of our tolerance and patience.

2. When *insensible* means to be unconscious of, use *to.*
> He was insensible to time when he was working on a design.

inside of a; within
In statements referring to time, the phrase *inside of a* is colloquial for *within.*
FORMAL:
> We will know within a week.

INFORMAL:
> We will know inside of a week.

instinct
To be instinct (infused) *with;* an instinct (natural inclination) *of* or *for.*
> a plan instinct with efficiency
> the bargain instinct of women
> a woman's instinct for a bargain

interfere
To interfere *with* or *in.*
> He was reluctant to interfere with the established routine.
> He did interfere in the dispute.

interpose
To interpose (put) *in* or (come) *between.*
> Now and then he interposed a comment in the proceedings.
> He interposed between the two who disagreed.

intolerant
To be intolerant *of* or *in* (not forbearing).
> The senator was intolerant of any other concept of politics.
> He was intolerant in politics but not in religion.

Intransitive Verbs—See **Transitive and Intransitive Verbs.**

irregardless

There is no such word as *irregardless*. Use *regardless*.

Irony

To indicate the ironic use of a word or phrase, use one of these three methods (listed in increasing order of emphasis):

1. Precede it with *so-called*, as *his so-called helpful efforts*.

2. Follow it with a question mark in parentheses, as *his helpful* (?) *efforts*.

3. Follow it with an exclamation point in parentheses, as *his helpful* (!) *efforts*.

italics—See **Punctuation—Underlining, Italics.**

its; it's

Use *its* as a possessive; *it's* for *it is*.

```
Its concept is new.
It's a new concept.
```

job; position

Both of these words mean a post of employment, but there is a distinction between them. A laborer who uses physical effort has a *job* and is paid *wages* at an hourly rate. An employee who has special training or ability has a *position* and is paid a *salary* at a weekly or monthly rate. In personnel terminology *job* is used for both because it is short; for example, *a typing job*.

Junior; Senior (Jr.; Sr.)

Junior is usually dropped after the death of the father of the same name. *Senior* (or its abbreviation *Sr.*) is not needed and is almost never used after a man's name unless the two identical names are closely associated.

For usage forms, see **Abbreviations— Jr.; Sr.**

For use of commas, see **Punctuation— Comma, Jr., Sr., II, III.**

kind; kinds

Use singular verbs and pronouns with *kind*, plural with *kinds*. This guide applies to similar words like *type, types; class, classes;* etc.

kind of a; kind of

Many authors use *kind of a*, but in business writing *kind of* is preferred.

```
He is the kind of (a) person who wins.
```

later; latter

Later means after a time; *latter* means the second of two things.

```
I will reply later.
I prefer the latter.
```

latest; last

1. These words can be synonomous. A common distinction, however, is to use *last* to mean at the end in time or place; *latest*, to mean following all others in time only, but not necessarily at the end.

```
This is the latest edition of the book.
It is not the last edition because we
   are preparing for the next edition.
```

2. Last can also mean the next before the present.

```
Our latest model is gray.
Our last model was white.
```

lay; lie

1. The transitive verb *lay* means to put in place. Its principal parts are *lay, laid, laid.*

```
Lay the mail down.
He laid the mail down.
He has laid the mail down.
```

2. The intransitive verb *lie* means to recline. Its principal parts are *lie, lay, lain.*

```
The mail lies on the table.
The mail lay there yesterday.
It has lain there for two days.
```

See **Transitive and Intransitive Verbs.**

lead; led

The past tense of *lead* is *led*.

```
He led the opposition.
```

leave; let

Leave means to go away from; *let* means to permit or allow.

```
Leave the sample here.
Let our sample speak for itself.
```

lend—See **loan; lend.**

less; lesser

Less implies that which is smaller in extent but is not countable: *less haste, less confusion. Lesser* implies a difference in extent between two: *a lesser evil, a lesser work.* See **fewer; less.**

let—See **leave; let.**

lie—See **lay; lie.**

like

1. All reference books agree on the use of *like* as:

AN ADJECTIVE: in a like situation

A NOUN: paper, pencils, and the like

A PREPOSITION: type like an expert

2. Usage is divided on *like* as a *conjunction.* It is used for *as* and *as if* at informal and colloquial levels, a usage not yet accepted in formal writing.

INFORMAL: The report reads like he took pains with it.

FORMAL: The report reads as if . . . .

See **as.**

Linking Verbs

A linking verb has little meaning of its own but connects a subject with a predicate noun or adjective. A few linking verbs are:

am, is, was, etc.	feel	seem
act	get	sound
appear	grow	taste
become	look	turn

loan; lend

According to the dictionaries both *loan* and *lend* are verbs. (Some writers use *loan* as a noun only.) The principal parts are *loan, loaned, loaned; lend, lent, lent.*

look

When *look* means to see with the eyes, use adverbs with it; when it is a linking verb, use adjectives with it.

```
We shall look at it carefully.
We shall look tired by night.
```

loose; lose

Loose means not tight; *lose,* to suffer a loss.

```
It is easy to lose a loose button.
```

lot of; lots of

These phrases are colloquial and are hardly ever used in business writing. Use instead: *many, much, a great many, a great deal, a considerable number.*

Ltd.—See **Punctuation—Comma, Inc.**

mathematics

Use plural forms unless you mean the *science* of mathematics.

may—See **can; may.**

maybe; may be

Maybe means perhaps; *may be* is a verb construction.

```
Maybe (Perhaps) we can finish it.
It may be finished by noon.
```

may; might

Might is the past tense of *may. May* and *might* imply permission, possibility, or opportunity; *can* implies ability.

```
The letter says that he may sell.
They might have sold it.
The letter says that he can sell it.
```

See **can; could; would.**

militate; mitigate; militant

Militate means to have an effect for or against; *mitigate* means to moderate or soften; *militant* means to be aggressively active in.

His age will militate against him.
A kind judge will tend to mitigate the
  punishment.
He was militant in his efforts to defeat
  the bond issue.

million—See **Numbers—Millions.**

monopoly

A monopoly *of;* a monopoly *to* (with a verb).

Their monopoly of supply permits them
  to charge any price.
They have a monopoly to process it.

more nearly; most nearly

These phrases are used in formal writing to express comparative and superlative degrees for adjectives that cannot be compared, as *a more nearly perfect circle* and *the more nearly square design.*

more than one

Even though this phrase is plural in meaning, the subject which follows it takes a singular verb.

More than one rule was ignored.

most—See **almost all; most.**

national—See **Capitalization—Federal.**

necessity

Use *necessity of* or *for* with the *ing* form of a verb.

the necessity of (or for) checking
        NOT:
the necessity to check

need

A need *for* or *of;* a need *to* (with verb); a need *to be* (with a verb).

a need for (or of) checking
a need to check
a need to be checked

neither—See **either; neither.**

neither . . . nor—See **either . . . or; neither . . . nor.**

news

This word takes singular verbs and pronouns.

no—See **yes; no.**

nobody

This word takes singular verbs and pronouns.

none; no one; not one

None is more commonly used with plural verbs and pronouns; *no one* and *not one* take singular forms. When in doubt, use *no one* or *not one.*

None of the officers were present.
Not one of the officers was present.
No one wants to discuss it.

not; and not

When either of these joins two subject words, the first word determines whether the verb is to be singular or plural.

Results, not wishful thinking, count.
Your record, and not your promises,
  counts.

nothing but; nothing else but

Use *nothing but; nothing else but* is uneducated usage.

We can add nothing but our thanks.

not only . . . but also . . .

In this construction the noun closer to the verb governs whether singular or plural forms are used.

Not only the orders but also his report
  was late.
Not only the report but also his orders
  were late.

notorious

This word means well known for unfavorable reasons. Use *noted, famed, celebrated,* etc., for favorable reasons.

not so . . . as—See **as . . . as; not so . . . as.**

number—See **amount; number.**

number of

The number of takes singular forms; *a number of,* plural forms.

The number of replies is gratifying.
A number of replies are gratifying.

O; Oh—See **Punctuation—Exclamation Point, O, Oh.**

oblivious

To be oblivious (unmindful) *of* or *to*.

    She was oblivious of those working
      around her.
    She was oblivious to his frowns.

observant

To be observant (attentive) *of*.

    She was observant of the details of
      form and usage.

of—See **Punctuation—Comma, Of.**

off; off of

Use *off;* not *off of*.

    It fell off the machine.

OK; O.K.; okay

Use *okay* in formal writing.

    FORMAL:
      okay, okays, okayed, okaying
    INFORMAL:
      OK, O.K., OK'd, O.K.'d, etc.

one—See **we; they; one; you.**

one of the (people) who; one of the (things) that

These constructions take plural verbs and pronouns in formal writing, but singular forms are commonly used in spoken English.

    FORMAL:
      He is one of the directors who agree.
    INFORMAL:
      He is one of the directors who agrees.

oneself

Oneself is preferred to *one's self*.

    One has only oneself to blame.

only

Use *only* near the word it limits according to the meaning of the sentence.

1. As an adjective or an adverb:

    Only the typists write form letters,
      not the secretaries.
    The only typist who writes form letters
      is Miss Kaye.
    She only types; she does not take
      dictation.
    The typist writes only form letters
      that the sales department requests.
    The typist writes form letters only
      when there is time.

2. As a conjunction:

Only means *but for one exception*. Grammarians, but not dictionaries, label it colloquial.

    DIVIDED USAGE:
      The plan is completed, only it has to
        be approved before we can start.

3. As a preposition:

Only should not be used as a preposition for *except* or *but*.

    INCORRECT:
      No one is interested only Mr. Kane.

on; onto; on to—See **in; into; in to**

opposite

To be opposite *to;* the opposite *of*.

    It is exactly opposite to my thinking.
    Your opinion is the opposite of mine.

or

When two subject words are joined by *or*, the verb agrees with the nearer word.

    Only one or two are needed.
    No pencils or paper was furnished.

oral; verbal

According to the dictionaries, *oral* means spoken; *verbal* refers to words, spoken or written. In usage both *oral* and *verbal* mean spoken. Retain the dictionary distinction in formal writing.

    FORMAL:
      His oral agreement is tantamount to
        a written contract.
    INFORMAL:
      His verbal agreement is . . . .

ordinance; ordnance

Ordinance means a decree; *ordnance* means military supplies.

    The city council passed an ordinance.
    The troops outpaced their ordnance.

out of date; up to date, etc.

Hyphenate *out of date, out of doors, up to date*, etc., before nouns.

    He is an out-of-doors man.
    He works out of doors.

See **Words—Compound, Adjective Modifiers.**

wing to—See **due to.**

pair; pairs

The plural of *pair* is *pair* or *pairs*.

Only ten pair(s) of gloves were sent.

See **Two-Part Objects (scissors, etc.).**

pardon; excuse

Pardon is used for things of considerable importance, *excuse* for things of lesser importance.

Please pardon us for billing you when
    you had already settled your account.
Please excuse the slight delay in
    answering your inquiry.

Participles (Dangling)

. A participial construction should modify a related, logical word, except when the construction is absolute.

DANGLING:

Leaving the office, the letter was dropped.

RELATED:

Leaving the office, I dropped the letter.

. An absolute construction is one that is independent of the rest of the sentence and modifies no word in it.

ABSOLUTE:

The situation having developed, let's
    accept the change it necessitates.

peeve

The noun *peeve* is not given in all dictionaries. The verb *peeve* is labeled *colloquial*.

NOUN:

A goldbrick is his pet peeve.

VERB (INFORMAL):

It peeves Mr. B. when anyone goldbricks.

people

This word takes plural verbs and pronouns.

His people are Scotch, but their
    ancestral home is in Ireland.

percent; percentage

Dictionaries give *per cent*, *percent*, and *per cent.* (with period). The first two are in common use.

Percentage is always one word and is never used with a number; *proportion* is often better in formal writing.

See **Numbers—Percent.**

permit

To permit *of* means to be possible.

It permits of several interpretations.

person; individual; personage; party; people

A *person* is a human being; an *individual* is one apart from a group; a *personage* is a person of importance; a *party* is a legal term or slang for *person* and as such is rarely used in business writing. Use *people* for large masses; *persons* for small numbers.

personal; personnel

Personal means private; *personnel* means a body of persons.

The letter was personal.
The office personnel will. . . .

personally; in person

These terms intensify meaning. They are used at business and colloquial levels but avoided at the formal level.

We personally guarantee each one.
Mr. Kane made the award in person.

pertinent

To be pertinent (relative) *to.*

The comment was pertinent to the
    problem.

place; "place" Compounds

Place is a noun and cannot be used for the adverb *where*. There are no one-word compounds such as *anyplace, everyplace, noplace, someplace*. Use instead *anywhere, everywhere, nowhere, somewhere*.

See **"where" Compounds.**

politics

This word is commonly used with singular verbs and pronouns.

His politics varies (or vary).

position—See job; position.

practical; practicable

Practical means *sensible* when applied to persons, *efficient* and *useful* when applied to things. *Practicable* implies something that can be put into practice.

My practical secretary has suggested
a practicable method for handling
follow-ups.

precedence

The precedence *of* people by rank; to have precedence *over* other persons or things.

Guests were seated according to
precedence of diplomatic positions.
Today dictation must have precedence
over everything else.

predominant; predominate

Predominant, an adjective, means prevailing; *predominate*, a verb, means to tower over, to exert controlling power over, to surpass in authority.

The predominant feature is its flexibility.
His very size makes it easy for him to
predominate over others.

prefer

To prefer something or somebody *to* other things or persons; to prefer *against*.

He prefers gray to black.
He preferred charges against the man
for failing to stop.

Prepositions

1. Only when necessary to avoid awkward phrasing should a preposition be used to end a construction.

Dr. Aurner says that a collective noun
takes a singular verb when the group
is thought of.

2. For prepositional idioms, see **Idioms, 2.**

presume

To presume (encroach) *upon* or *on* to presume *to* with a verb (to take liberties).

He presumed upon our generosity.
He presumed to advise me.

prerequisite

A prerequisite *for;* to be prerequisite *to*

Understanding the process is a prerequi
site for producing good results.
The ability to remember is prerequisite
to learning.

principal; principle

1. *Principal*, as an adjective, means main; as a noun, it means the main person; or in business, a capital sum.

ADJECTIVE:

The principal actor handled his part
skillfully.

NOUN:

The principal acted his part skillfully
The principal has been placed in a trust
fund.

2. *Principle* is a noun meaning rule truth, guide, etc. It never refers to a person.

He follows the principle of "least
said, soonest mended."

privilege

To be privileged *to* (with a verb); to be privileged (exempt) *from;* the privilege *of.*

You are privileged to hear Toscanini.
You are privileged from taking the
examination.
Thank you for the privilege of presenting my suggestion.

proficient

To be proficient (expert) *in.*

He is proficient in mathematics.

profit

To profit *by;* the profit *on, from,* etc

The company has profited by its fair
dealing.
The profit on (or from) the sale was
high.

roof

proof *of*, *to*, or *against*.

I shall send a proof of the advertisement to you.
He is proof against flattery.

roved, proven

ither word may be used as the past
articiple of *prove*, but *proved* is pre-
rred.

You have proved (or proven) your point.

roposition

The verb *proposition* is not used in
usiness writing; its connotation is dis-
putable.

OT USED:
He propositioned us to join him.

The noun *proposition* depending up-
n context, means:

N ASSERTION:
. . . the proposition that all men are
created equal.

DIGNIFIED PROPOSAL:
Our proposition has been carefully
worked out.

SELFISH, SHREWD PROPOSAL:
The proposition needs scrutiny.

oximity

he proximity (nearness) *of* or *to*.

You will find the proximity of the hotel
to the meeting hall to be convenient.

ublic

his word is commonly used with singu-
r verbs and pronouns.

The public quickly tires of its
favorites.

antities—See **amounts; quantities.**

ise; increase; increment

usiness uses all three words for a
gher wage or salary. *Raise* is the
mmon word, *increase* the more digni-
d, and *increment* a personnel word.

rely; rarely ever

me writers consider *rarely ever* to be
lloquial.

real; really

Use *real* only as an adjective, *really* as
an adverb.

It really concerns us that the real
facts are so obscure.

reason is

The *reason is* takes a predicate-noun
construction. Do not use the *reason is
because*.

The reason is that my secretary has
been ill.

recourse

To have recourse (to resort) *to* a person
or agency *for* help *for* or *because of*
something.

You have recourse to the courts for
financial relief because of their
failure to deliver the bricks on time.

Redundancy

Redundancy is the needless use of
words. Each of the phrases below is
redundant. The underlined word is
sufficient to make the meaning clear.

both <u>alike</u>	<u>depreciate</u> in value
close <u>proximity</u>	month of <u>April</u>
<u>continue</u> on	<u>repeat</u> again
customary <u>practice</u>	sum <u>total</u>

See **consensus of opinion.**

relevant

To be relevant (pertinent) *to*.

Your timesaving suggestion is relevant
to our efficiency program.

remainder—See **balance; remainder.**

replete

To be replete (filled) *with*.

His writing is replete with metaphors.

requisite

A requisite *for;* to be requisite *to*.

Typing is a requisite for the position
that is open.
Concern for others is requisite to
happiness.

resolve

To resolve (settle) something; to resolve (determine) *that*, *on*, or *upon;* to resolve (separate) *into;* to resolve *to* (with a verb).

```
He resolved the problem.
We resolve that it won't recur.
We resolved on three trials.
The problem resolved itself into three
   issues.
He resolved to improve.
```

resolved—See Capitalization—Whereas; Resolved.

responsible

To be responsible *to* someone; *for* action or a dependent.

```
You are responsible to the court for
   the handling of these funds and for
   the rearing of the child.
```

restrain

To restrain *from;* to be restrained *by*, *from*, or *in*.

```
He restrained himself from answering
   bluntly.
You can be restrained by law.
```

Restrictive Clause—See that; which; who.

result

To result *from* or *in;* the result *of*.

```
Bigger savings have resulted from
   increased production.
The contest resulted in ten new
   accounts.
It is the result of much work.
```

retroactive

To be retroactive *to*.

```
The law is retroactive to last May.
```

Reverend

Use a first name, initials, or title between *Reverend* and the surname.

```
Rev. Maxfield Dowell
the Reverend M. A. Dowell
the Reverend Dr. Dowell
```

See also Abbreviations—Reverend.

salary, wages

For the difference in meaning betwee *salary* and *wages*, see job; position.

II; 2d; 2nd

For usage forms, see Abbreviations-II, 2d, or 2nd.

For use of commas, see Punctuation-Comma, Jr., Sr., II, III.

"self" Pronouns—See Punctuation-Myself, Himself, Yourself, Etc.

Series; Lists

For introductory words and prope punctuation, see Punctuation—Series.

set—See sit; set.

shall; will

Will is commonly used for first, secon and third person in future tense. I formal writing, to express future tens use *shall* in the first person, *will* in th second and third persons. To expres the emphatic future, reverse the posi tions of *shall* and *will*.

should; would

1. *Should* is used in uncertain situation *would* in requests.

```
He should be ready to go soon.
Would you mail it today?
```

2. In the first person both *should* an *would* are commonly used.

```
I should (or would) like to go.
```

sic—See Punctuation—Brackets, Quote Matter (A).

similar

To be similar *to* or *in*.
```
It is similar in appearance to mine.
```

sit; set

1. *Sit* is intransitive; a person or objec *sits*. The principal parts are *sit, sat, sa*

. *Set* is usually transitive; a thing is set or placed. The principal parts are *set, set, set.*

See **Transitive and Intransitive Verbs.**

low, slowly

Both words are adverbs. Both *drive low* and *drive slowly* are correct.

so-called—See **Irony, 1; Punctuation— Quotation Marks, Words Different in Tone (B).**

solicitous

To be solicitous *about, for,* or *over* something; to be solicitous (anxiously desirous) *of.*

```
He is solicitous about her health, for
  her future, and over her failure to
  improve.
He is solicitous of Mr. King's respect.
```

sparing

To be sparing (saving) *in* the use of supplies; to be sparing (cautious, chary) *of* the exchange of gossip.

species

This word is both singular and plural.

```
That species is extinct.
These species were grouped for study.
```

Split Infinitives—See **Infinitives, 3.**

Sr.—See **Punctuation—Comma, Jr.**

State—See **Capitalization—Federal.**

stationary; stationery

Stationary means stable, fixed; *stationery* means writing paper.

statistics

Use plural verbs and pronouns except when you mean the *science* of statistics.

Street Addresses—See **Abbreviations— Street Addresses.**

Subjunctive Mood

In formal writing the subjunctive mood is commonly used in:

1. Contrary-to-fact clauses
2. Clauses expressing doubt
3. Clauses expressing wishes or regrets
4. *That* clauses expressing demands, motions, recommendations, etc.

```
If time were available, I would come.
If that be true, we must act.
I wish I were confident of the outcome.
We recommend that it be tried.
```

Professor Porter G. Perrin in his book *Writer's Guide and Index to English* says that, actually, subjunctives are a trait of style rather than a matter of grammar.

submit

To submit *to* or *with;* to submit (urge courteously) *that.*

```
We submit to your wishes with pleasure.
We submit that the whole report be made
  available to us before presentation.
```

succeed

To succeed *to* a position; to succeed *in, with,* etc.

```
He succeeded to the presidency upon
  Mr. John's retirement.
He succeeded in improving the plan.
```

such as—See **Punctuation—Comma, Such As.**

suitable

To be suitable *for* or *to.*

```
The dress was not suitable to (or for)
  the occasion.
```

superior

To be superior *to* a person *in* rank; to be the superior *of.*

```
His new position makes him superior
  to the director.
He is the superior of the director.
```

sympathetic

To be sympathetic (favorable) *to* or *toward* is colloquial; it is often used in business writing, as *We are sympathetic to the idea.*

sympathize

To sympathize (share concern) *with*.

> He sympathizes with us but has no
> solution to offer.

tactics

Use plural verbs and pronouns except when you mean a military *science*.

tantamount

To be tantamount (equivalent) *to*.

> His criticism of the layout is
> tantamount to rejection.

tempt

To tempt *by* or *with;* to be tempted *to* (with a verb) or *by*.

> We tempted him by promising him profits.
> We tempted him with promises.
> He was tempted to try.
> He was tempted by the promises.

tendency

A tendency *to, toward*, or *of*.

> There is a tendency toward (or to)
> conservatism.

that; which; who

1. *That* and *which* are not always interchangeable. *That* is preferred when it introduces a clause that cannot be omitted (a restrictive clause).

> The phrasing that you suggest is good.

2. *Which* is preferred to introduce a clause that can be omitted (nonrestrictive clause).

> The second phrasing, which seems
> clearer, is better.

3. *Who* refers to persons, personified objects, and sometimes to animals.

> the members who; Lady Luck who;
> Native Dancer who

they—See **we; they; one; you.**

till; until

Until is preferred at the beginning of a sentence.

Titles of Books, Articles, Etc.

1. A title used as a noun takes singular forms.

> Executives Report says in its last
> issue . . . .

2. For forms of typewritten titles, see **Punctuation—Titles of Published Matter.**

Titles of Persons

For the correct use and form of titles, see **Abbreviations—Titles; Capitalization—Degrees** and **Titles of Persons.**

together with—See **as well as; together with.**

Trademarks—See Capitalization— Trademarks.

Transitive and Intransitive Verbs

1. Dictionaries label verbs *transitive* or *intransitive; transitive* verbs take objects, *intransitive* verbs do not.

> TRANSITIVE: Send the letter today.
> INTRANSITIVE: She fainted this morning.

2. Some verbs are both transitive and intransitive.

> TRANSITIVE: I wrote a full report.
> INTRANSITIVE: I wrote yesterday.

try

To try *to* (with a verb).

> We shall try to (not and) arrange it.

Two-Part Objects (scissors, etc.)

Words like *scissors*, while singular in meaning, take plural verbs and pronouns. Preceded by *pair of*, they take singular forms.

> His gloves are new.
> His pair of gloves is new.

type of

Use *type of*, not *type*.

> RIGHT: This type of process is new.
> WRONG: This type process is new.

uninterested—See **disinterested; uninterested.**

United States

1. Always use *the* before *United States* in formal writing.

2. Since it is awkward to use *the* before an adjectival construction, rephrase the sentence to retain *the*, or, if possible, use *American* as the adjective.

WRONG:

According to United States laws

RIGHT:

According to laws of the United States

until—See **till; until.**

useful

To be useful *for, in,* or *to.*

You will find the book useful to you in many ways, especially for reference.

value

To be valued *at* or *for;* the value *of.*

It is valued at more than a dollar.
We value it for sentimental reasons.
What is the value of the land?

verbal—See **oral; verbal.**

vest

To vest *with* authority; to vest authority *in* a person or agency.

The guardian was vested with the power to administer the inheritance.
Administration of the estate was vested in the court.

vice-president; vice-presidency—See **Capitalization—Titles of Persons (B, C).**

view

To view *with;* in view *of;* with a view *to.*

We view it with indifference.
In view of the time, we will adjourn.
With a view to prompt action, we . . . .

vital

To be vital *to.*

Good morale is vital to good production.

void

To be void *of.*

She is void of any spark of enthusiasm.

vouch

To vouch *for.*

We vouch for his good character.

vulnerable

To be vulnerable (sensitive) *to* something *in* some way or place.

He is vulnerable to criticism in business.

wages, salary—See **job; position.**

want

To want *for;* for want *of;* to want *something.*

He wants for nothing.
For want of a better word, thanks!

weights—See **Abbreviations—Dimensions and Weights; Numbers—Weights.**

well—See **good; well.**

we; they; one; you

These words are used as indefinite pronouns in business writing and refer to the group the writer represents, the reader's group, or to people in general. Maintain consistency and agreement within sentences and usually within paragraphs.

We wired our reply.
If one considers it, he (or <u>one</u>) becomes annoyed.
If you like, you may wire your reply.
If they reject it, please write me.

Whereas—See **Capitalization—Whereas; Resolved.**

"where" Compounds

Anywhere, everywhere, nowhere, and *somewhere* are adverbs. One-word *place* compounds *anyplace, everyplace, noplace,* and *someplace)* are incorrect.

RIGHT:

He lives somewhere in Ohio.
He wants some place that's quiet.

WRONG:

He lives someplace in Ohio.

whether; whether . . . or; whether or not

1. Use *whether* in indirect questions.

We wondered whether you planned to go.

2. Use *whether . . . or* and *whether or not* for alternatives.

State whether you will go or stay.
State whether or not you will go.

which; who

For the correct usage of *which* and *who* see **that; which; who.**

who; whom

Use *who* as the subject of a verb; *whom* as the object of a verb, a preposition, or the subject of an infinitive.

```
Send it only to those who asked for it.
Who do you think will be made chairman?
Everyone upon whom I called accepted.
Whom shall I test first?
They asked whom to be chairman?
```

will

For correct usage of *will*, see **shall; will.**

within

Within is used in formal writing. See **inside of a; within.**

wonder

To wonder *about, what, why,* or *that;* the wonder *of.*

```
I wonder that he answered.
The wonder of it is that he answered.
```

worthwhile; worth while

Write this as one word or two; hyphenate the two-word form before a noun.

```
It is worthwhile (or worth while).
It is a worthwhile (or worth-while)
   project.
```

would—See **can; could; would should; would**

yes; no

Type these words in any of these ways:

```
He will probably say "Yes."
He will probably say "yes."
He will probably say Yes.
He will probably say yes.
He will probably say Yes.
```

See also **Punctuation—Comma, Words that Answer.**

yield

To yield *to* a person *with* a feeling; to yield *to* reasoning; a yield *of* grain.

you—See **we; they; one; you.**

zealous

To be zealous (arduous) *in* doing things, *for* causes.

yet—See **Punctuation — Comma, Yet.**

COINED WORDS

Coined and picturesque words do not need quotation marks or underlining if they are hyphenated or if they are appropriate to the context. Set such words off only if the reader may misinterpret them or if you want to label them as clever usage.

```
Her shrug-of-the-shoulders attitude
   annoys everyone.
The regulations are written in
   officialese style.
```

See also **Usage—conversion.**

Observe these practices when coining words with prefixes and suffixes.

Hyphens

Use a hyphen before the suffix if the solid word would be hard to read.

```
He is an uh-er and an ah-er.  (not
   uher and aher)
```

Prefixes

For the handling of prefixes, follow the practices given under **Compound Words.**

Suffixes

-able and -ible. Use the suffix *-able*, not *-ible;* join it to the word, as *electable.*

-er and -ee. Join *-er* to a verb to indicate the person acting, *-ee* to indicate the person receiving the action, as *maintainer, maintainee.* When the verb ends in *e*, drop one *e*, as *raver, ravee.*

-ize. Add the *-ize* to a noun or adjective to form a verb, as *winterize.* Use a hyphen if desired if the base word ends in a vowel, as *Sohio-ize.*

-like. Join the suffix *-like* to the word; use a hyphen if the word ends in *l*, as a judgelike manner; a wall-like effect.

-proof. To imply imperviousness, add *-proof* to the base word, as *fearproof.* If the base word is long, use a hyphen, as *suggestion-proof.*

Other Suffixes. To use any other suffix in a coined word, look up the suffix in the dictionary and follow the form of the examples given.

COMPOUND WORDS

A *compound* is written solid, joined with hyphens, or written as individual words. Consult a dictionary first for the proper form of the compound. If the word is not given, see **Punctuation— Hyphen.** See also **Coined Words; Usage —place, "where" Compounds.**

DIVISION

1. Do *not* divide:

   A. Words of one syllable

      freight   through

   B. Words of four letters and, if avoidable, those of five or six letters.

   C. Names of persons, dates, abbreviations, and numbers. Do not separate titles, initials, and professional and scholastic degrees from the name.

   D. At a beginning or ending syllable of one or two letters in a word.

2. Avoid dividing the last word:

   A. In over two successive lines.

   B. On a page or in a paragraph.

3. Divide hyphenated words only at the hyphen.

   half-sister   profit-sharing

4. Divide words:

   A. After a single-vowel syllable.

      criti-cism   tele-vision

   EXCEPTIONS: Do not divide *able, ible,* or *ical.*

   B. Between two vowels separately pronounced.

      radi-ator; sci-ence; cli-ents

   C. Preferably at a prefix or suffix.

      semi-   -ing
      mis-   -tion

   D. Between double consonants unless they come at the end of the simple form of the word.

      neces-sary   tell-ing

FOREIGN WORDS

1. In typewritten text underline words labeled *foreign* in the dictionary. If not labeled *foreign,* they are considered to be Anglicized. Do not underline Anglicized words.

FOREIGN:

   It can always be done mañana.

ANGLICIZED:

   You are an ex officio delegate.

2. Diacritical marks are retained on many foreign and Anglicized words. The trend is to omit them in typewritten text except when needed for clarity or pronunciation. Put them in with pencil or black ink, whichever matches the typing better.

   résumé   visé

> **WORDS—COINED; COMPOUND; DIVISION; FOREIGN—Page 752**

3. Do not hyphenate foreign or Anglicized compounds used as modifiers.

   a Sturm und Drang session
   a bona fide sale
   our per diem rate

THE C. J. KREHBIEL COMPANY
PRINTERS AND BOOK MANUFACTURERS
ESTABLISHED 1871
3962 VIRGINIA AVE. (FAIRFAX)   CINCINNATI, OHIO 45227   AREA CODE 513 271-6036

December 10, 19--

Mr. Edward Caldwell
Akron Chamber of Commerce
74 South Main Street
Akron, Ohio 44308

Dear Mr. Caldwell

This letter is typed in block style with open punctuation.
Every line begins at the left margin. Only essential punctuation marks are used in the opening and closing lines.

The distinctive feature of this letter style is that the
date, the inside address, the salutation, the attention line
(when used), all lines in the body, the complimentary close,
and all signature lines begin at the left margin. No tabulator stops are necessary.

Typing time is accordingly reduced. First, time required
to set tabulator stops and to use the tabulator is saved.
Second, by omitting all except the essential punctuation
marks, the number of typing strokes is decreased.

The use of "open" punctuation is appropriate with this letter
style.

Cordially yours

James Harvey

James Harvey, Consultant

ao

AMERICAN TELEPHONE AND TELEGRAPH COMPANY

195 BROADWAY, NEW YORK, N.Y. 10007

AREA CODE 212   393-9800

December 10, 19--

Mr. Thomas James
Caswell-Higgins Associates
Suite 385, Maumee Tower
Toledo, Ohio 43604

Dear Mr. James

SUBJECT: The Modified Block Letter Style

This letter is typed in modified block style with blocked
paragraphs. Open punctuation is used in the opening and
closing lines.

Contrast this style with the block style, and you will notice that the date line has been moved to begin at horizontal
center (although it would be appropriate also to end at the
right margin) and that the closing lines have been blocked
at the horizontal center of the letterhead. All other lines
begin at the left margin. These modifications of the block
style give the style its name--modified block.

When an attention line is used in this style of letter, it
is begun at the left margin. If a subject line is used, it
is begun at the left margin or centered over the body of
the letter a double space below the salutation.

Although open punctuation is used in this letter, it is
equally appropriate to use mixed punctuation.

Sincerely yours

David M. Balz

David M. Balz, Director

mac

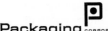

Packaging CORPORATION OF AMERICA
2029-30 CAREW TOWER • CINCINNATI, OHIO 45202 • AREA 513 621-9248
A Major Component of Tenneco Inc.

December 10, 19--

Mr. William Summers
The Electromagnetic Corp.
One Erieview Plaza
Cleveland, Ohio 44114

Dear Mr. Summers:

This letter is typed in modified block style with indented paragraphs. Mixed punctuation is used in the opening
and closing lines. This punctuation style calls for a colon
after the salutation and a comma after the complimentary
close. All other end-of-line punctuation is omitted in the
opening and closing lines, unless a line ends in an abbreviation that requires the usual abbreviation period.

Note that the date line is centered (although it could
have been typed to begin at center or to end at the right
margin); the subject line is centered; the first line of
each paragraph is indented 5 spaces (although 10- or 15-space
indentions are also commonly used); the closing lines are
blocked at the horizontal center of the letterhead. All
other lines begin at the left margin.

Although mixed punctuation is used in this letter, it
would be equally acceptable to use open punctuation.

Sincerely yours

George R. Sanders

George R. Sanders

ok

ADMINISTRATIVE MANAGEMENT SOCIETY
Cincinnati Chapter
Formerly NOMA

Dated Today

Ms. Office Secretary
Better Business Letters, Inc.
1 Main Street
Busytown, U. S. A.

SIMPLIFIED LETTER

There's a new movement under way to take some of the monotony out of
letters given you to type, Ms. Secretary. The movement is symbolized
by the Simplified Letter being sponsored by AMS.

What is it? You're reading a sample.

Notice the left block format and the general positioning of the letter.
We didn't write "Dear Miss -----," nor will we write "Yours truly" or
"Sincerely yours." Are they really important? We feel just as friendly
toward you without them.

Notice the following points:

1. Date location
2. The address
3. The subject
4. The name of the writer

Now take a look at the Suggestions prepared for you. Talk them over
with your boss. But don't form a final opinion until you've really
tried out The Letter. That's what our secretary did. As a matter of
fact, she finally wrote most of the Suggestions herself.

She says she's sold--and hopes you'll have good luck with better (Simplified) letters.

Arthur E. Every

ARTHUR E. EVERY - STAFF DIRECTOR, TECHNICAL DIVISION

cc: R. P. Brecht, W. H. Evans, H. F. Grebe

**Four Basic Letter Styles. (1) Block style, open punctuation, (2) Modified block style
with blocked paragraphs, open punctuation, (3) Modified block style with indented
paragraphs, mixed punctuation, (4) AMS Simplified style**

William Allen

Charlton Apartments
Charlton Bay, Massachusetts 01507

December 10, 19--

Dear Henry,

The inside address typed at the end of a letter removes the business touch and tone from the letter and makes it more personal.

This letter form is used also for very formal letters, such as letters to public officials and honored persons. In addition, letters of appreciation or sympathy or congratulations are typed in this form.

The reference initials are omitted. If the person receiving the letter knows the writer well, it is not necessary that his name be typed as part of the signature.

Cordially,

Bill

Mr. Henry D. Ransom
302 Peachtree Street
Atlanta, Georgia 30308

Packaging CORPORATION OF AMERICA Form 11-0001-1

INTEROFFICE MEMORANDUM

TO : New Members of the
        Stenographic Pool

FROM: Judith L. Rees
        Correspondence Supervisor

DATE : December 10, 19--

SUBJECT: Interoffice Correspondence

The interoffice or interdepartment letterhead is used, as the name implies, for correspondence between offices or departments within the company. One advantage of this form is that it can be set up quickly. For instance, this letter requires settings for only the margins and one tabulator stop. Titles (<u>Mr.</u>, <u>Mrs.</u>, <u>Dr.</u>, etc.), the salutation, the complimentary close, and the formal signature are usually omitted.

Triple-space between the last line of the heading and the first line of the message. Short messages of no more than five lines may be double-spaced; longer messages should be single-spaced.

Reference initials should be included. When enclosures are sent, the enclosure notation should appear below the reference initials.

sva

Interoffice Memorandum

**Personal and Formal
Style Typed on
Personal Letterhead**

J. L. Bell
245 Compton Road
Cincinnati, OH 45215

CONFIDENTIAL

↑
2"
↓

SPECIAL DELIVERY ←

←2½"→

Mr. Robert L. Simpson
219 Kenway Drive, Apt. 3
Des Moines, IA 50310

↑
2½"
↓

←4"→

Continental Products
Attention Mr. Robert L. Simpson
320 Euclid Avenue
Des Moines, IA 50313

FORM AND PLACEMENT OF ENVELOPE ADDRESS PARTS FOR OPTICAL CHARACTER READERS

Notations to Post Office

Begin at least three line spaces above the address, below the stamp. Type in all capital letters. Underline if desired. Such notations include:

AIRMAIL
SPECIAL DELIVERY
REGISTERED
HAND STAMP

On-Receipt   Notations

Type (in all capitals) a triple space below the return address and 3 spaces from the left edge of the envelope. Such notations include:

HOLD FOR ARRIVAL
PLEASE FORWARD
CONFIDENTIAL

Type an *attention line* immediately below the company name in the envelope address.

Requirements for Optical Character Readers

Post office optical character readers are programmed to scan a specific area on all envelopes; so the address must be completely within this read-zone, *blocked in style, single-spaced.* The state abbreviations shown on page 769 (typed in upper case) must be used. An apartment or room number should follow the street address *on the same line.* Acceptable placements for a No. 10 and a No. 6¾ envelope are specified in the illustration above.

COMMUNICATIONS GUIDE—Page 755

PROOFREADER'S MARKS

INSERT MARKS FOR PUNCTUATION

᠄ Apostrophe

[/] Brackets

: ⊙ Colon

♢ ⅋/ Comma

ˣˣˣ/ Ellipsis

!/ Exclamation point

-/ Hyphen

♢ ⌃ Inferior figure

···/ Leaders

(/) Parentheses

⊙ Period

?/ Question mark

ᶜ⅋ ⅋ᶜ Quotation mark

; ⑤ Semicolon

ᵛ ᵛ Superior figure

OTHER MARKS

‖ Align type; set flush

ℓᶠ Boldface type

× ⊗ Broken letter

≡ Cᵃₚ Capitalize

C+ₛc Capitals and small capitals

ℓ Delete

ℬ Delete and close up

∧ Insert (caret)

ital Italic, change to

Bf ital Italic boldface

stet Let type stand

ℓc Lower case type

⊔ Move down; lower

⌐ Move up; raise

⊏ Move to left

⊐ Move to right

¶ Paragraph

no ¶ ⊏ No new paragraph

out s.c. Out; omit; see copy

ⓖ Reverse; upside down

rom Roman, change to

⟿ Run in material

run in Run in material, on same line

Space, add (horizontal)

> Space, add (vertical)

◡ Space, close up (horizontal)

< Space, close up (vertical)

ⓢₚ Spell out

tr ⌒ Transpose

(?) ⊘ Verify or supply information

wf Wrong font

same ℬ/c All marks should be made in the margin on the line in which the error occurs; if more than one correction occurs in one line, they should appear in their order separated by a slanting line.

ℓc >

Errors should not be blotted out.

756

author ⟶ [1]Erwin M. Keithley, <u>A Manual of Style for the Preparation of Papers and Reports</u> (Cincinnati: South-Western Publishing Co., 1959), p. 7.

authors (editor) ⟶ [2]E. Jerome McCarthy and J. A. McCarthy, <u>Integrated Data Processing Systems</u>, ed. Durward Humes (New York: John Wiley & Sons, Inc., 1966), p. 74.

Ibid. ⟶ [3]<u>Ibid.</u>, pp. 111-113.

authors ⟶ [4]A. B. Carson, Arthur E. Carlson, and Clem Boling, <u>Secretarial Accounting</u> (8th ed.; Cincinnati: South-Western Publishing Co., 1967), p. 59.

or more authors ⟶ [5]M. E. Jansson et al., <u>Handbook of Applied Mathematics</u> (4th ed.; New York: D. Van Nostrand Co., Inc., 1967), p. 42.

published material ⟶ [6]Paul S. Greenlaw, <u>The In-Basket as a Training Instrument</u> (Mimeographed report, Dayton Rubber Company, 1959), p. 8.

Op. cit. ⟶ [7]Carson, <u>op. cit.</u>, p. 63.

government agency ⟶ [8]U.S. Treasury Department, Internal Revenue Service, <u>Your Federal Income Tax</u>, Publication No. 17 (Washington: U.S. Government Printing Office. 1964), p. 87.

magazine article ⟶ [9]"Why Whirlybirds Are Taking Off," <u>Business Week</u> (April 20, 1968), pp. 100-120.

cle from bound volume ⟶ [10]John T. Dunlop, "New Forces in the Economy," <u>Harvard Business Review</u> (Boston: Graduate School of Business Administration, Harvard University, 1968), Vol. 46, No. 2 (March-April, 1968), p. 121.

newspaper article ⟶ [11]"Factory Orders Surged by 3.4% During March," <u>Wall Street Journal</u> (May 6, 1968), p. 5, col. 1.

Loc. cit. ⟶ [12]Keithley, <u>loc. cit.</u>

FOOTNOTE CONSTRUCTION: Indent to paragraph point; single-space; double-space between items. Use quotation marks with titles of publication *parts*; underline titles of *complete* publications. *Ibid.* refers to the immediately preceding source; *loc. cit.* refers to the same location of a previous citation with intervening footnotes; *op. cit.*, to a different page of a previous citation.

---

authors ⟶ Carson, A. B., Arthur E. Carlson, and Clem Boling. <u>Secretarial Accounting</u>, 8th ed. Cincinnati: South-Western Publishing Co., 1967.

cle from bound volume ⟶ Dunlop, John T. "New Forces in the Economy," <u>Harvard Business Review</u>. (Boston: Graduate School of Business Administration, Harvard University, 1968), Vol. 46, No. 2 (March-April, 1968), p. 121.

newspaper article ⟶ "Factory Orders Surged by 3.4% During March," <u>Wall Street Journal</u>. (May 6, 1968), p. 5, col. 1.

published material ⟶ Greenlaw, Paul S. <u>The In-Basket as a Training Instrument</u>, a mimeographed report by the Dayton Rubber Company, 1959.

or more authors ⟶ Jansson, M. E., et al. <u>Handbook of Applied Mathematics</u>, 4th ed. New York: D. Van Nostrand Co., Inc., 1967.

author ⟶ Keithley, Erwin M. <u>A Manual of Style for the Preparation of Papers and Reports</u>. Cincinnati: South-Western Publishing Co., 1959.

authors (editor) ⟶ McCarthy, E. Jerome, and J. A. McCarthy. <u>Integrated Data Processing Systems</u>, edited by Durward Humes. New York: John Wiley & Sons, Inc., 1966.

government agency ⟶ U.S. Treasury Department, Internal Revenue Service. <u>Your Federal Income Tax</u>, Publication No. 17. Washington: U.S. Government Printing Office, 1964.

magazine article ⟶ "Why Whirlybirds Are Taking Off," <u>Business Week</u>. (April 20, 1968), pp. 100-120.

BIBLIOGRAPHY CONSTRUCTION: Present the items alphabetically by the first word of an item that is not an article. Start each item at the left margin; indent subsequent lines 5 spaces. Invert the order of only the first author's name. Give page references only for citations of *parts* of publications. Omit parentheses around publication facts except for periodicals.

FORM AND ARRANGEMENT OF BUSINESS LETTER PARTS

Letter Part	Line Position	Horizontal Placement	Points to Be Observed	Acceptable Forms
DATE	If a floating date line is used, the date is typed from 12 to 20 lines from the top of the letterhead or plain sheet, depending upon letter length. A fixed date line is usually typed a double space below the last line of the letterhead.	*Block, AMS Simplified Styles:* Even with left margin. *Modified Block Style:* Begun at center of the sheet; to end flush with right margin; or according to the letterhead.	1. Do not abbreviate names of months. 2. Unusual 2- and 3-line arrangements are not commonly used. 3. Do not use *d, nd, rd, st,* or *th* following the day of the month.	December 14, 19-- 2 May 19-- (Used primarily in government and military correspondence.)
ADDRESS	*With Floating Date Line:* Typed on 4th line below the date. *With Fixed Date Line:* Typed from 3 to 9 lines below the date, depending on letter length. *Government Letter:* Typed on the 14th line. *Personal Style:* Placed at the left margin 5 or 6 lines below the last closing line.	Single-spaced with all lines even at left margin. Use at least three lines for address. Place business title at end of first line or beginning of second line, whichever gives better balance. For a long company name indent the second line 2 or 3 spaces.	1. Follow addressee's letterhead style. 2. Do not abbreviate *Street* or *Avenue* unless it improves appearance. 3. For the name of a town or city, do not use *City.* 4. Use postal zip codes in addresses. 5. Do not use *%* for *In Care Of.* (This follows the name line.)	Miss Rose Bannaian Manager, Rupp Steel Co. 2913 Drexmore Avenue Dallas, Texas 75210 Mr. Russell H. Rupp 68 Devoe Avenue Dallas, Texas 75206 (Refer to the Reference Guide for specific comments.)
ATTENTION LINE	*Preferred:* Typed a double space below address and a double space above salutation.	Typed even with left margin or begun at the paragraph point.	1. Do not abbreviate *Attention.* 2. Unnecessary to use *of* as in *Attention of Mr. R. H. Rupp.*	Attention Mr. R. H. Rupp Attention Purchasing Agent Attention Mr. L. Cox, Agent
SALUTATION	Typed a double space below last line of address or a double space below attention line. (Note: Omitted in the AMS Simplified style and in interoffice correspondence.)	Typed even with left margin. 1. Use *Gentlemen* for a company, a committee, a numbered post-office box, a collective organization made up entirely of men (or of men and women). 2. In addressing women, substitute *Ladies* or *Mesdames* for *Gentlemen; Madam* for *Sir; Miss* or *Mrs.* for *Mr.;* use *Ms.* when the marital status of a woman is unknown.		Dear Mr. Rupp Gentlemen Dear Sir: Dear Russell: Dear Ms. Willis My dear Mrs. Cox

SUBJECT (or REFERENCE) LINE	Typed a double space below salutation. Some printed letterheads indicate position for subject or file number (usually at the top of the letterhead).	1. *Subject* may be typed in all capitals or with only first letter capitalized. *Subject* may be omitted; if it is used, it should be followed by a colon. (In the AMS style, the word "Subject" is omitted and the line is typed in all capitals a triple space below last line of address.) *Modified Block Style:* Typed even with left margin, at paragraph point, or centered. 2. Do not abbreviate *Subject*; capitalize important words in the subject line.	Subject: Pension Plan SUBJECT: Pension Plan Pension Plan Pension Plan PENSION PLAN Your File 987 Reference: File #586 Re: File 586
BODY	Typed a double space below salutation or subject (reference) line. *AMS Simplified Style:* Typed a triple space below subject line.	*Block Style:* First line of each paragraph typed even with left margin. *Modified Block Style: First* line of each paragraph typed even with left margin or indented 5 or 10 spaces.	1. Keep right margin as even as possible, avoiding hyphens at ends of lines where possible. 2. For enumerated material, indent 5 spaces from both margins and double-space after each item. (In the AMS style, indent listed items 5 spaces except when numbered.)	Single-space lines of paragraphs; double-space between paragraphs. A short one-paragraph letter may be double-spaced with indented paragraphs.
SECOND-PAGE HEADING and BODY	*Heading:* Begin approximately 1" (6 blank lines) below the top edge of the sheet. *Body:* Begin on the 3d line from the heading, using the same margins as for the preceding page. Do not begin with the last part of a divided word. Include at least two lines of a paragraph.	Type the second and succeeding pages on plain paper. The heading is typed even with the left margin in block form or in a one-line arrangement (illustrated below). Use the one-line arrangement if a page might be crowded. Mr. Jerry W. Robinson Page 2 (Current Date) Mr. Jerry W. Robinson 2 (Current Date)		
COMPLIMENTARY CLOSE	Typed a double space below the last line of letter body. Omitted in the AMS Simplified letter style and in interoffice correspondence.	Begin at the center except in block style where the complimentary close is typed even with the left margin.	1. Do not extend the longest of closing lines noticeably beyond right margin. 2. Capitalize first word only. 3. Avoid contractions.	Very truly yours,* Sincerely yours,* Cordially, or Cordially yours,* Respectfully yours,* *Also written with *Yours* as the first word
COMPANY NAME	If used, typed a double space below the complimentary close.	Typed even with the beginning of the complimentary close.	1. Capitalize all letters. 2. Type name exactly as it appears on letterhead.	TRIMOUNT CLOTHING COMPANY JOHNSON & RAND SHOE CO.

FORM AND ARRANGEMENT OF BUSINESS LETTER PARTS (Continued)

Letter Part	Line Position	Horizontal Placement	Points to Be Observed	Acceptable Forms
SIGNATURE (Name and Title of Signer)	Typed 3 blank lines below complimentary close (or company name, if used). *AMS Style:* All capital letters at least 4 lines below last line of body. NOTE: If both the name and title are used, they may be typed on the same line or the title may be typed on the next line below the typed name. The style giving the best balance should be used.	Typed even with first letter of complimentary close (or company name, if used). *AMS Style:* Even with left margin.	1. Capitalize important words in title. 2. When dictator's name appears in letterhead, use the title only. 3. Do not use *Mr.* in typing a man's name. (See pages 197–198 for secretarial signatures.)	Harold A. Wenchstern Director of Personnel Bruce Ryan, Manager Purchasing Department *AMS Style:* LOUIS K. COX - AGENT
IDENTIFICATION NOTATION	Typed a double space below or on the same line with the last of closing lines.	Typed even with the left margin. (For a complete discussion on the use of reference initials, see page 193.)	Omit dictator's initials when his name is typed as part of closing lines.	jc JWR/jc jwr/jc JWR:jc JWRobinson/jc
ENCLOSURE	Typed a double space below the identification notation.	Typed even with the left margin.	While *Enc.* and *Encl.* are not preferred forms, they are in common use because they save time.	Enclosure Enc. Encl. Enclosures Enclosures 3 Catalog #23 Encs. 2 Price List #8 Enclosures: Check Contract
POSTSCRIPT	Typed a double space below the identification notation or the last typed line.	Indent or block the postscript according to the style used in other paragraphs of the letter.	Initials of the writer may be typed below the postscript in place of a second signature.	P.S. Or omit the P.S. and write in the same form as a paragraph in the letter.
CARBON COPY NOTATION	Typed a double space below the identification notation or the last typed line. (If notation not to appear on original, type at top of carbon copies.)	Typed even with the left margin. (When typed at the top of carbon copies, may be centered or placed at the left margin.)	1. *cc* or *Copy to* are generally used to indicate "Carbon Copy to." 2. Use *BC* for "blind copy" if notation is typed on carbon copies only.	cc: BC cc: Mr. H. R. King Miss K. Neilen Copy to Mr. H. R. King, Cashier BC to HRKing
MAILING NOTATION	Typed midway between date and first line of address; may be typed two lines below the last typed line.	Typed even with the left margin.	1. Typed in all capital letters. 2. May be typed on carbon copies only.	AIRMAIL SPECIAL DELIVERY REGISTERED MAIL CERTIFIED MAIL
SEPARATE-COVER NOTATION	Typed a double space below last typed line.	Typed even with the left margin.	Indicates method of transportation and number of envelopes or packages.	Separate Cover - Express Separate Cover - Mail 2

CORRECT FORMS OF ADDRESS AND REFERENCE

Person and Address (Envelope and Letter)	Salutation	Complimentary Close	In Referring to the Person; Informal Introduction	In Speaking to the Person
U.S. PRESIDENT The President The White House Washington, D. C. 20500	Sir Mr. President Dear Mr. President My dear Mr. President	Respectfully yours Very truly yours	The President Mr. (Name)	Mr. President Sir (in prolonged conversation)
WIFE, U.S. PRESIDENT Mrs. (Last Name Only) The White House Washington, D. C. 20500	Dear Mrs. (Last Name Only) My dear Mrs. (Last Name Only)	Respectfully yours Sincerely yours	Mrs. (Last Name Only)	Mrs. (Last Name Only)
U.S. VICE PRESIDENT The Vice President United States Senate Washington, D. C. 20510	Sir My dear Mr. Vice President Mr. Vice President	Respectfully yours Very truly yours Sincerely yours	The Vice President Mr. (Name)	Mr. Vice President Mr. (Name)
U.S. CHIEF JUSTICE The Chief Justice The Supreme Court Washington, D. C. 20543	Sir Mr. Chief Justice Dear Mr. Chief Justice	Respectfully yours Very truly yours Sincerely yours	The Chief Justice	Mr. Chief Justice
U.S. ASSOCIATE JUSTICE Mr. Justice (Name) The Supreme Court Washington, D. C. 20543	Sir Mr. Justice My dear Mr. Justice Dear Justice (Name)	Very truly yours Sincerely yours	Mr. Justice (Name)	Mr. Justice Mr. Justice (Name)
CABINET OFFICER The Honorable (Name) Secretary of (Office) Washington, D. C. 20520 The Secretary of (Office) Washington, D. C. 20520	Sir My dear Mr. Secretary Dear Mr. Secretary Madam My dear Madam Secretary Dear Madam Secretary	Very truly yours Sincerely yours	The Secretary of...., Mr. (Name) The Secretary Mr. (Name) The Secretary of....; Mrs. or Miss (Name) The Secretary Mrs. or Miss (Name)	Mr. Secretary Mr. (Name) Madam Secretary Mrs. or Miss (Name)
SPEAKER OF THE HOUSE OF REPRESENTATIVES The Honorable (Name) Speaker of the House of Representatives Washington, D. C. 20515	Sir Dear Mr. (Name) My dear Mr. Speaker Mr. Speaker	Very truly yours Sincerely yours	The Speaker, Mr. (Name) Mr. (Name) The Speaker	Mr. Speaker Mr. (Name)

CORRECT FORMS OF ADDRESS AND REFERENCE (Continued)

Person and Address (Envelope and Letter)	Salutation	Complimentary Close	In Referring to the Person; Informal Introduction	In Speaking to the Person
U. S. SENATOR, SENATOR-ELECT The Honorable (Name) The United States Senate Washington, D. C. 20510 or The Honorable (Name), Senator-Elect	Sir Dear Senator (Name) My dear Senator (Name) Madam My dear Senator (Name) My dear Mrs. or Miss (Name)	Very truly yours Sincerely yours	Senator (Name)	Senator (Name) Mr. (Name) Senator (Name) Mrs. or Miss (Name)
U. S. REPRESENTATIVE The Honorable (Name) The House of Representatives Washington, D. C. 20515 Representative (Name) The House of Representatives Washington, D. C. 20515	Sir My dear Representative (Name) My dear Sir Madam Dear Representative (Name) My dear Mrs. or Miss (Name)	Very truly yours Sincerely yours	Representative (Name) Mr. (Name) Representative (Name) Mrs. or Miss (Name)	Mr. (Name) Mrs. or Miss (Name)
U. S. GOVERNMENT OFFICIAL The Honorable (Name) Director of Bureau of the Budget Washington, D. C. 20503 Librarian of Congress Washington, D. C. 20540	Sir Dear Mr. (Name) My dear Mr. (Name) Madam Dear Mrs. or Miss (Name) My dear Mrs. or Miss (Name)	Very truly yours Sincerely yours	Mr. (Name) Mrs. or Miss (Name)	Mr. (Name) Mrs. or Miss (Name)
AMERICAN AMBASSADOR The Honorable (Name) American Ambassador Paris, France	Sir My dear Mr. Ambassador Madam My dear Madam Ambassador	Very truly yours Sincerely yours	The American Ambassador[1] The Ambassador Mr. (Name) Madam Ambassador Mrs. or Miss (Name)	Mr. Ambassador Mr. (Name) Madam Ambassador Mrs. or Miss (Name)
AMERICAN MINISTER The Honorable (Name) American Minister Ottawa, Canada	Sir My dear Mr. Minister Madam My dear Mrs. or Miss (Name) My dear Madam Minister	Very truly yours Sincerely yours	The American Minister, Mr. (Name)[1] The Minister; Mr. (Name) The American Minister, Mrs. or Miss (Name) The Minister Mrs. or Miss (Name)	Mr. Minister Mr. (Name) Madam Minister Mrs. or Miss (Name)

Person and Address (Envelope and Letter)	Salutation	Complimentary Close	In Referring to the Person; Informal Introduction	In Speaking to the Person
U.S. REPRESENTATIVE TO THE UNITED NATIONS The Honorable (Name) The United States Representative to the United Nations New York, New York 10017	Sir Dear Mr. (Name) My dear Mr. (Name) *With Ambassadorial Rank:* My dear Mr. Ambassador (Name)	Very truly yours Sincerely yours	Mr. (Name)	Mr. (Name)
FOREIGN AMBASSADOR IN U.S. His Excellency (Name) The Ambassador of France Washington, D. C.	Sir Excellency My dear Mr. Ambassador	Respectfully yours Sincerely yours Very truly yours	The Ambassador of....., Mr. (Name) The Ambassador Mr. (Name)	Mr. Ambassador Mr. Ambassador Mr. (Name)
FOREIGN MINISTER IN U.S. The Honorable (Name) Minister of Italy Washington, D. C.	Sir My dear Mr. Minister	Respectfully yours Sincerely yours Very truly yours	The Minister of....., Mr. (Name) The Minister Mr. (Name)	Mr. Minister Mr. (Name)
AMERICAN CONSUL (Name), Esq. The American Consul United States Embassy (Foreign City, Country)	Sir Dear Mr. (Name) My dear Mr. (Name)	Very truly yours Sincerely yours	Mr. (Name)	Mr. (Name)
FOREIGN CONSUL (Name), Esq. The French Consul (American City, State)	Sir Dear Mr. (Name) My dear Mr. (Name)	Very truly yours Sincerely yours	Mr. (Name)	Mr. (Name)
GOVERNOR OF A STATE His Excellency the Governor of (State) or The Honorable (Name), Governor of (State) (Capital City, State)	Sir Dear Governor My dear Governor (Name)	Respectfully yours Very truly yours Sincerely yours	Governor (Name) The Governor The Governor of (State)	Governor (Name) Governor
MEMBER, STATE LEGISLATURE The Honorable (Name) The State Senate or The House of Representatives (Capital City, State)	Sir Dear Senator or Representative (Name) My dear Mr. (Name)	Very truly yours Sincerely yours	Mr. (Name) Senator (Name) Representative (Name)	Mr. (Name) Senator (Name) Representative (Name)
MAYOR OF A CITY The Honorable (Name) Mayor of the City of..... (City, State)	Sir Dear Mayor (Name) My dear Mayor (Name)	Very truly yours Sincerely yours	Mayor (Blank) The Mayor	Mayor (Name) Mr. Mayor

CORRECT FORMS OF ADDRESS AND REFERENCE (Continued)

Person and Address (Envelope and Letter)	Salutation	Complimentary Close	In Referring to the Person; Informal Introduction	In Speaking to the Person
JUDGE OF A COURT The Honorable (Name) Judge of the ....Court (Local Address)	Sir Dear Judge (Name) My dear Judge (Name)	Very truly yours Sincerely yours	Judge (Name)	Judge (Name)
MILITARY PERSONNEL (Rank) (Name) Post or Name of Ship City, State	Sir Dear (Rank) (Name) My dear (Rank) (Name)	Very truly yours Sincerely yours	(Rank) (Name)	(Rank) (Name)
CLERGYMEN (PROTESTANT) The Reverend (Name), D.D. or The Reverend (Name) Parsonage Address City, State	Reverend Sir Dear Dr. (Name) My dear Sir My dear Mr. (Name)	Respectfully yours Sincerely yours Yours faithfully	The Reverend Doctor (Name) Doctor (Name) The Reverend (Name) Mr. (Name)	Dr. (Name) Sir Mr. (Name)
RABBI (JEWISH FAITH) The Rabbi of Congregation (Name) Local Address	Sir My dear Rabbi (Name) My dear Rabbi	Respectfully yours Sincerely yours Yours faithfully	Dr. (Name) Rabbi (Name)	Dr. (Name) Rabbi (Name)
PRIEST (ROMAN CATHOLIC) The Reverend (Name), (Degree) Local Address	Reverend Father Dear Father (Name) Reverend and dear Sir	Sincerely yours Respectfully yours Yours faithfully	Dr. (Name) Father (Name)	Dr. (Name) Father (Name)
SISTER (ROMAN CATHOLIC) Sister (Name) Local Address	Dear Sister Dear Sister (Name)	Sincerely yours Respectfully yours Yours faithfully	Sister (Name) Sister	Sister (Name) Sister
PRESIDENT (COLLEGE OR UNIVERSITY) Dr. (Name) or President (Name), (Degree) Name of University City, State	Dear Sir Dear President (Name) Dear Dr. (Name)	Very truly yours Sincerely yours	Dr. (Name)	Dr. (Name)

POSTAL RATES, FEES, AND INFORMATION

(As of June, 1968—Consult Postmaster or *Postal Manual* for current information)

FIRST-CLASS MAIL[1]

Kind of Material	Descriptive Information	Postage Rate
All first-class mail, except postal and post cards weighing 13 ounces or less (Over 13 ounces air parcel postal rates apply.)	Includes: 1. Matter wholly or partially in writing or typewriting, except authorized additions to second-, third-, and fourth-class mail 2. Matter closed against postal inspection 3. Bills and statements of account	6¢ per ounce or fraction of an ounce (A rate per ounce means 6¢ an ounce or fraction thereof—a fraction of a unit being treated as a whole unit in the computation of charges.) This rate applies to the U.S., Canada, and Mexico.
Single postal cards and post cards	Single postal cards—government cards with imprinted stamps. Post cards—private mailing cards; stamps must be affixed.	5¢ each
Double postal cards and post cards	Reply portion of a double post card does not have to bear postage when originally mailed.	10¢ (5¢ each portion)
Business reply cards	The senders return these free.	7¢ each
Mail enclosed in business-reply envelopes	Weight not over 2 ounces	6¢ per ounce or fraction plus 2¢ per piece
	Weight over 13 ounces	Air parcel post plus 5¢ per piece
	A business must first obtain a permit to distribute business reply envelopes from the post office where they are to be returned. The senders return these free.	
Airmail Postal or post cards	Use airmail cards, or write AIRMAIL conspicuously above the address.	8¢ each
Letters and packages	7 ounces or less—Over 7 oz. Air Parcel Post rates apply.	10¢ an ounce
Business reply cards		10¢ each
Airmail other than cards	Weight not over 2 ounces	10¢ an ounce plus 2¢ a piece
	Weight over 7 ounces	Air parcel post rate plus 5¢ a piece
	EXCEPTIONS (Nonmailable) a. Letters, cards, and self-mailers less than 3 inches in width or 4¼ inches in length b. Pieces having shapes other than rectangular c. Cards having a thickness of less than 0.006 of an inch	

[1]First-class mail is discussed on page 231. Weight limit, 70 pounds. Size limit, 100 inches in length and girth.

765

SECOND-CLASS MAIL[2]

Kind of Material	Descriptive Information	Postage Rate
Newspapers and periodicals	Must have second-class mail privileges Special rates for bulk mailing by authorized nonprofit organizations	Single-Piece Rate: 5¢ for first 2 ounces, 1¢ each additional ounce or fraction, or fourth-class rate, whichever is lower Bulk Rate: If there are as many as 6 pieces bundled for delivery to one five-digit ZIP Code. See postmaster for rate.

THIRD-CLASS MAIL[3]

Kind of Material	Descriptive Information	Postage Rate
Circulars, books, catalogs of 24 pages or more and other printed matter, merchandise, seeds, cuttings, bulbs, and plants	Weight less than 16 ounces Special rates for bulk mailing by authorized nonprofit organizations	Single Rate: 6¢ for first 2 ounces, 2¢ each additional ounce or fraction Bulk Rate: If there are as many as 10 pieces bundled for delivery to the same 5-digit ZIP Code
Keys and identification devices (cards, tags, etc.)		6¢ each 2 ounces or fraction of 2 ounces

FOURTH-CLASS MAIL[4]

Kind of Material	Descriptive Information	Postage Rate
Special fourth-class rate for certain books, films, museum materials, playscripts, and manuscripts, etc.	Package must be marked *Special Fourth-Class Rate* and title of contents shown. See local postmaster.	12¢ for first pound or fraction of a pound. 6¢ for each additional pound or fraction
Library books and educational materials sent between educational, religious, and philanthropic institutions	Package must be marked *Library Rate*. See local postmaster. Postage is not differentiated by zone.	5¢ for first pound or fraction of a pound 2¢ for each additional pound or fraction

[2]Second-class mail is discussed on page 232.
[3]Third-class mail is discussed on page 232.
[4]Special fourth-class mail is discussed on page 234

POSTAL CARDS
ENVELOPES AVAILABLE

Kind	Denomination	Less than 500
	Cents	Cents (each)
Regular........	6	8
Airmail........	10	12

POSTAL CARDS AVAILABLE

Kind	Selling price each
Single............................	5¢
Airmail single (use for airmail only)...	8¢
Reply (5¢ each half).............	10¢

ADHESIVE STAMPS AVAILABLE

Purpose	Form	Denomination and Prices
Ordinary postage	Single or sheet	1, 2, 3, 4, 5, 6, 8, 10, 11, 12, 15, 20, 25, 30, 40, and 50 cents; $1 and $5.
	Book	32 6-cent and 8 1-cent: $2.00.
	Coil of 100*	6 and 25 cents.
	Coils of 500 & 3,000	1, 4, 5, and 6 cents.
	Coils of 3,000	25 cents.
Airmail postage (for use on airmail only)	Single or sheet	8, 10, 13, 15, 20, and 25 cents.
	Book	40 10-cent: $4.00.
	Coils of 100,* 500 & 3,000	10 cents.

*Dispenser to hold coils of 100 stamps may be purchased for 5¢ additional.

(Up to ½ oz.)

Aerogramme................................	13¢
Canada and Mexico— Domestic Rates Apply.	
Asian and African Countries..............	25¢
European Countries.......................	20¢
South American and Caribbean Countries	15¢

SPECIAL HANDLING
Third- and Fourth-Class Only
SPECIAL HANDLING FEES
(Fees in addition to postage)

Weight	Fee
Not more than 2 pounds.............	25¢
More than 2 pounds but not more than 10 pounds......................	35¢
More than 10 pounds................	50¢

SPECIAL DELIVERY
SPECIAL DELIVERY FEES
(Fees in addition to postage)

Class of Mail	Weight		
	Not more than 2 pounds	More than 2 pounds but not more than 10 pounds	More than 10 pounds
First class and air-mail (including air parcel post)..	30¢	45¢	60¢
All other classes..	55¢	65¢	80¢

MONEY ORDERS
MONEY ORDER FEES

Amount of Money Order	Amount of Fee Domestic
$0.01 to $10................	$0.25
$10.01 to $50...............	.35
$50.01 to $100..............	.40

FEES (IN ADDITION TO POSTAGE)

LIABILITY	FEE
$0.01 to $15..................	$0.20
$15.01 to $50.................	.30
$50.01 to $100................	.40
$100.01 to $150..............	.50
$150.01 to $200..............	.60

Liability for insured mail is limited to $200.
Restricted delivery. (Not available for mail insured for $15 or less)............. 50¢
Return receipts. (Not available for mail insured for $15 or less):

COD MAIL
Consult Postmaster for fees and conditions of mailing.

CERTIFIED MAIL
Fee (in addition to postage).............	30¢
Restricted delivery.....................	50¢

REGISTRY
REGISTRY FEES
(IN ADDITION TO POSTAGE)

Declared actual value (No limit)	Fees If mailer does not have commercial or other insurance	Postal Liability
$0.00 to $100...	$0.75	Without commercial or other insurance—declared value. With commercial or other insurance—declared value or prorated
$100.01 to $200...	1.00	
$200.01 to $400...	1.25	
$400.01 to $600...	1.50	
$600.01 to $800...	1.75	
$800.01 to $1,000...	2.00	
HIGHER VALUES	Consult Postmaster for fees.	
Maximum postal insurance for shipments NOT commercially insured.		$10,000
Maximum postal insurance for shipments commercially insured.		$1,000

Restricted delivery (additional fee)............. 50¢

RETURN RECEIPTS
Certified Mail—Numbered Insured—Registered

Requested at time of mailing:
Showing to whom and when delivered............... 10¢
Showing to whom, when, and address where delivered.............. 35¢
Requested after mailing:
Showing to whom and when delivered.............25¢

AIR PARCEL POST ZONE RATES[5]

Weight over 7 ounces and not exceeding: (Lbs.)	RATE					
	Local Zones 1, 2, and 3	Zone 4	Zone 5	Zone 6	Zone 7	Zone 8
1	$0.80	$0.80	$0.80	$0.80	$0.80	$0.80
1½	.98	1.02	1.07	1.14	1.18	1.24
2	1.16	1.23	1.34	1.47	1.55	1.68
2½	1.40	1.48	1.62	1.79	1.91	2.08
3	1.64	1.73	1.90	2.11	2.27	2.48
3½	1.88	1.98	2.18	2.43	2.63	2.88
4	2.12	2.23	2.46	2.75	2.99	3.28
4½	2.36	2.48	2.74	3.07	3.35	3.68
5	2.60	2.73	3.02	3.39	3.71	4.08
6	3.08	3.23	3.58	4.03	4.43	4.88
7	3.56	3.73	4.14	4.67	5.15	5.68
8	4.04	4.23	4.70	5.31	5.87	6.48
9	4.52	4.73	5.26	5.95	6.59	7.28
10	5.00	5.23	5.82	6.59	7.31	8.08

FOURTH-CLASS (PARCEL POST) ZONE RATES[5]

Pounds	Local	Zones						
		1 and 2 — Up to 150 miles	3 — 150 to 300 miles	4 — 300 to 600 miles	5 — 600 to 1,000 miles	6 — 1,000 to 1,400 miles	7 — 1,400 to 1,800 miles	8 — Over 1,800 miles
2	$0.40	$0.50	$0.50	$0.55	$0.60	$0.70	$0.75	$0.80
3	.40	.55	.60	.65	.75	.85	.95	1.05
4	.45	.60	.65	.75	.85	1.00	1.10	1.25
5	.45	.65	.70	.80	.95	1.10	1.30	1.45
6	.45	.70	.80	.90	1.05	1.25	1.45	1.65
7	.50	.80	.85	1.00	1.15	1.40	1.60	1.85
8	.50	.85	.90	1.05	1.30	1.50	1.75	2.00
9	.55	.90	.95	1.15	1.40	1.65	1.90	2.20
10	.55	.95	1.05	1.20	1.50	1.75	2.10	2.40

[5]Parcel post is discussed on pages 232-3. Space permits publication of rates up to 10 pounds only although weights up to 70 pounds may be sent by either surface or air parcel post. Charts are available from the local post office. The charts above will enable the reader to compare costs of sending parcel post by surface and by air.

TWO-LETTER STATE ABBREVIATIONS*
Approved for Use with ZIP Code *Only*

Alaska...................	AK	Montana.................	MT
Alabama.................	AL	Nebraska................	NB
Arizona.................	AZ	Nevada..................	NV
Arkansas................	AR	New Hampshire..........	NH
California...............	CA	New Jersey..............	NJ
Canal Zone..............	CZ	New Mexico.............	NM
Colorado................	CO	New York................	NY
Connecticut.............	CT	North Carolina...........	NC
Delaware................	DE	North Dakota............	ND
District of Columbia.......	DC	Ohio.....................	OH
Florida..................	FL	Oklahoma................	OK
Georgia.................	GA	Oregon..................	OR
Hawaii..................	HI	Pennsylvania.............	PA
Idaho...................	ID	Puerto Rico.............	PR
Illinois..................	IL	Rhode Island............	RI
Indiana.................	IN	South Carolina...........	SC
Iowa....................	IA	South Dakota............	SD
Kansas..................	KS	Tennessee...............	TN
Kentucky................	KY	Texas....................	TX
Louisiana...............	LA	Utah....................	UT
Maine...................	ME	Vermont.................	VT
Maryland................	MD	Virginia.................	VA
Massachusetts............	MA	Virgin Islands............	VI
Michigan................	MI	Washington.............	WA
Minnesota...............	MN	West Virginia............	WV
Mississippi..............	MS	Wisconsin................	WI
Missouri................	MO	Wyoming................	WY

*Canal Zone, District of Columbia, Puerto Rico, and Virgin Islands also included.

Index

A

A.D., B.C., 711
a.m., p.m., 383, 701
Abbreviations, 701–703; of state names for optical scanning, 769
Abstracting services, 457
accept, except, 726
Acceptances or regrets, formal, 218
Account numbers, ABA bank, 532; social security, 581
Acknowledgment letter, 214
Addresses, alphabetic filing, 352; cable, 305; envelope parts, 755; inside, 754, 755; street, 702, 706, 707
Addressing machines, 120, 401
adhere, adherent, 727
Administrative role of secretary, 680–694
affect, effect, 727
Affidavit, 606, 607
Air express, 252
Air freight, 253
Air travel, 368–375; See Travel, air; Travel arrangements
Airmail, 234, 235; envelope notation, 755; postal information, 765; priority in transcribing, 186
Altrusa International, 674
American Association of University Women, 674
among, between, 728
Amounts, expression of, 728
Ampersand, 701, 728
A.D., B.C., 711
a.m., p.m., 383, 701
Appendix to a report, 507
Application blank, 652; for employment, 645–651; letter and résumé, illustrated, 646
Appointment calendar, illustrated, 52, 53
Appointments, canceling, 57; scheduling, 51, 56
Appositives, commas with, 714; dash with, 717; possessives with, 712
Apostrophe, alphabetic filing, 352; compound words, 712; contractions, 713; plurals of abbreviations, 702; plurals of numbers, 711
Arabic numerals, 506
Attention line, 754
Automation, See Banking services, Data processing
Automobile travel, 377
Averages in statistical presentations, 476
Ayer's Directory of Newspapers and Periodicals, 461
Azograph (direct process) copying, 118

B

Babson's Business Service, 458
Babson's Reports, 561
Back-feeding envelopes, 101
Backing sheet, cushion sheet, 124; legal papers with, 612
Bank accounts, for executive, 575; See Banking services
Banking services, 526–553; account numbers, 531, 532; American Ex-

press money orders, 552; bank draft, 546; cable money order, 552; canceled checks, 539, 540; checking account, 526–542, with magnetic ink characters, 533; See Checks; collateral note, 550; commercial drafts, 550, 551; credit and collection instruments, 549–553; credit-card statements, 544; deposit slips, 530, 555; deposits, 527–533, See Deposits; discounting notes and drafts, 552; filing bank forms, 54; foreign bank draft, 553; foreign remittances, 552, 553; indorsements, 528–530; locating errors, 540, 541; magnetic-ink system, 532; making deposit in checking account, 527; making out deposit slip, 530, 555; microfilming deposits, 109; money order, 546; negotiable instruments, 549; night depository, 533; passbook, 527; paying bills, 542–547; petty cash fund, 547; preparing checks for deposit, 528; preparing coins and bills for deposit, 527; promissory note, 549; reconciling bank balance, 539–541, 555; safe-deposit boxes, 541; service charge, 540; sight and time drafts, 551; signature card, 526; special services, 541, 542; stop-payment procedures, 538; trade acceptances, 551; voucher check, 537; withdrawals from checking accounts, 534–538; writing checks, 535–538; writing checks for cash, 537; writing check stubs, 534, 541
Bartlett's Familiar Quotations, 167, 466
B.C., A.D., 711
BC, blind copy notation, 196, 760
Bellboy telephone service, 306
Bible references, 703, 725, 730
Bibliography, 498, 507, 757; cards, 468
Billions, expressing, 709
Bills, paying, 542–544
Bills (currency), preparing for deposit, 527
Bills, verifying, 543
Bills of lading, 254
Blind copies, 196; notation, 196, 760
Block letter style, 754, 758–760
Body of letter, 754, 759
Body of report, 495–507
Bond paper, 71; letterheads, 73
Bonds, 558, 559; fidelity, 574; interest on, 591; registered, 599
Brackets, 713
Bus express, 252
Business information, abstracting services, 457; atlases, 464; city directories, 463; dictionaries, 464; government publications, 461; handbooks, 465; periodicals, 460, 461; library sources, 466–469; secretary's reference shelf, 465, 466; special directories, 463; year-books, 465; See Reports
Business letter styles, 754, 755
Business letters, courtesy, 217
Business reports, See Reports

C

COD mail, 239, 767
Cable addresses, 305
Cablegrams, 302
Calendar, appointment, 52, 53; follow-up after meeting, 411; itinerary serving as a, 390; secretary's desk, 52, 53
Callers, register of, 45
Calls, telephone, See Telephone services
Capitalization, 701–707; abbreviations, 701; after a colon, 714; enumerations, 718
Carbon copies, 190; blind, 196; erasing on, 91, 92; identifying, 195, 196; keeping transcripts confidential, 192; printed-form dictation, 175; publicity and news releases, 220–222; readying for filing, 198; rough draft, 501; second sheets for, 72, 73; telegrams, 281; typing fractions on, 709; See Carbon packs, Carbon paper, Reports
Carbon packs, 88; corrections with, 90–92; desk method, 88; machine method, 90; typing without removing another carbon pack, 283
Carbon paper, 73–78; guides to, 75, 76, 77; handling, 86; plastic-base, 76; specialty, 78; topcoated, 73
Carbon ribbon, 70, 71; erasing, 92
Card Dialer telephone, 307
Cards, addressing by front-feeding, 102; bibliography, 468; cross-reference, 325; edge-punched, 433; filing on, 322; government postal, 102; insurance index, 574; library catalog, 467; punched for data processing, 436–440; real estate, 569; social security, 581; stamped, 242; stock-transaction, 564
Case problems, 60, 61; 140, 141; 226, 227; 311–313; 362, 363; 424, 425; 522, 523; 618, 619; 696, 697
COD mail, 239, 767
Cents, expressing, 709
Certificates of deposit, 551, 552
Certificates of mailing, 240
Certified mail, 241
Certified Professional Secretary (CPS), 673
Charts, 481–490; circle, 484; flow, 488, 489; organization, 488, 490; pictorial, 485, 486
Checking accounts, 526–542; See Banking services
Checks, writing, 534–538; See Banking services
Circle graphs or charts, 484
Cities and states, 715, 755
Civil service, federal and state, 634
Civil service, foreign, 634, 635
Code, area, 276; binary (electronic), 440; data processing, 431, 440; telegraphic, 283, 303
Coined words, 701, 753
Coins, preparing for deposit, 527
Colon, 714; in time expressions, 711
Comma, adjacent numbers, 708; business-letter style, 754; dimensions, 715; four-digit numbers, 708; general usage, 714–717; nonrestric-